The War in the West

www.transworldbooks.co.uk

The War in
the West

A New History

Volume I: Germany Ascendant
1939–1941

James Holland

BANTAM PRESS

LONDON • TORONTO • SYDNEY • AUCKLAND • JOHANNESBURG

TRANSWORLD PUBLISHERS
61–63 Uxbridge Road, London W5 5SA
www.transworldbooks.co.uk

Transworld is part of the Penguin Random House group of companies
whose addresses can be found at global.penguinrandomhouse.com

Penguin
Random House
UK

First published in Great Britain in 2015 by Bantam Press
an imprint of Transworld Publishers

A CIP catalogue record for this book
is available from the British Library.

ISBNs 9780593071656 (cased)
9780593071663 (tpb)

Typeset in 11.25/14pt Minion Pro by Falcon Oast Graphic Art Ltd.
Printed and bound by Clays Ltd, Bungay, Suffolk.

Penguin Random House is committed to a sustainable
future for our business, our readers and our planet. This book
is made from Forest Stewardship Council® certified paper.

MIX
Paper from
responsible sources
FSC® C018179

1 3 5 7 9 10 8 6 4 2

For Rachel

Contents

List of Maps

EUROPE, THE ATLANTIC AND NORTH & SOUTH AMERICA, July 1939

CANADA

UNITED STATES OF AMERICA

M E X I C O

BAHAMAS

CUBA

JAMAICA HAITI

DOMINICAN REPUBLIC

BELIZE

GUATEMALA HONDURAS

EL SALVADOR NICARAGUA

COSTA RICA

PANAMA

VENEZUELA

GUYANA

COLOMBIA

SURINAME

ECUADOR

PACIFIC OCEAN

PERU

BOLIVIA

PARAGUAY

CHILE

ARGENTINA

URUG

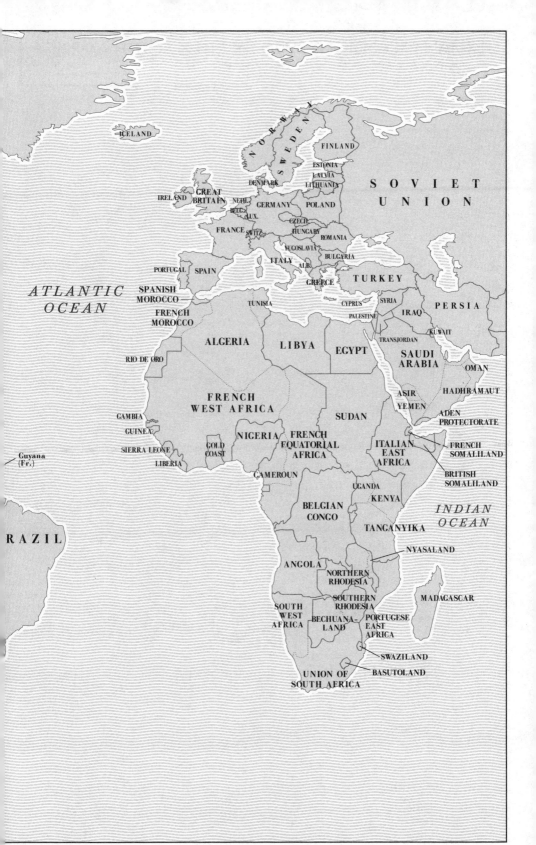

GERMAN EXPANSION, 1936–39

Baltic Sea

Danzig
Free State

Memel
Territory

LITHUANIA

March 1939

Danzig

EAST
PRUSSIA

SOVIET
UNION

Bydgoszcz

Bialystock

Vistula

Poznan

Warsaw

Brest-Litovsk

Warta

September 1939

Lodz

POLAND

Lublin

Breslau

Oder

Vistula

Lvov

Dniester

Moravia

Slovakia

Ruthenia

Bratislava

Tisza

Debrecen

Budapest

HUNGARY

YUGOSLAVIA

KEY

- Germany after 1919
- troops into demilitarized Rhineland March 1936
- Anschluss (union with Austria) March 1938
- occupation of Sudetenland October 1938
- original Czechoslovakian border
- formerly Czechoslovakia, occupied March 1939
- Moravian territory to Poland October 1938
- Memel Territory to Germany March 1939
- Protectorate of Slovakia territory to Hungary Nov 1938
- Czechoslovakian territory to Hungary March 1939
- conquest of western Poland September 1939

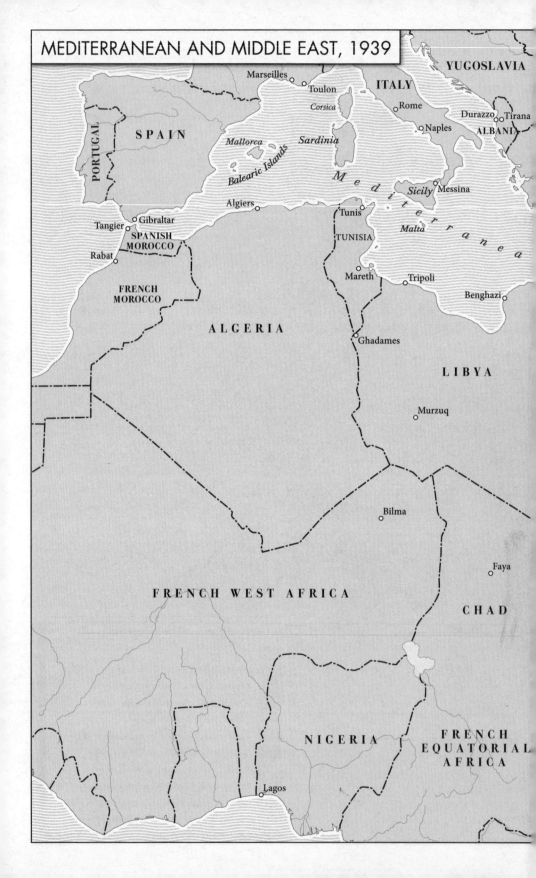

MEDITERRANEAN AND MIDDLE EAST, 1939

YUGOSLAVIA

ITALY

Marseilles
Toulon
Rome

Corsica

PORTUGAL

SPAIN

Mallorca

Sardinia

Balearic Islands

Naples

Durazzo Tirana
ALBANI

Mediterranea

Sicily Messina

Algiers

Tangier Gibraltar

SPANISH
MOROCCO

Rabat

Tunis

TUNISIA

Malta

FRENCH
MOROCCO

ALGERIA

Mareth

Ghadames

Tripoli

Benghazi

LIBYA

Murzuq

Bilma

Faya

FRENCH WEST AFRICA

CHAD

NIGERIA

FRENCH
EQUATORIAL
AFRICA

Lagos

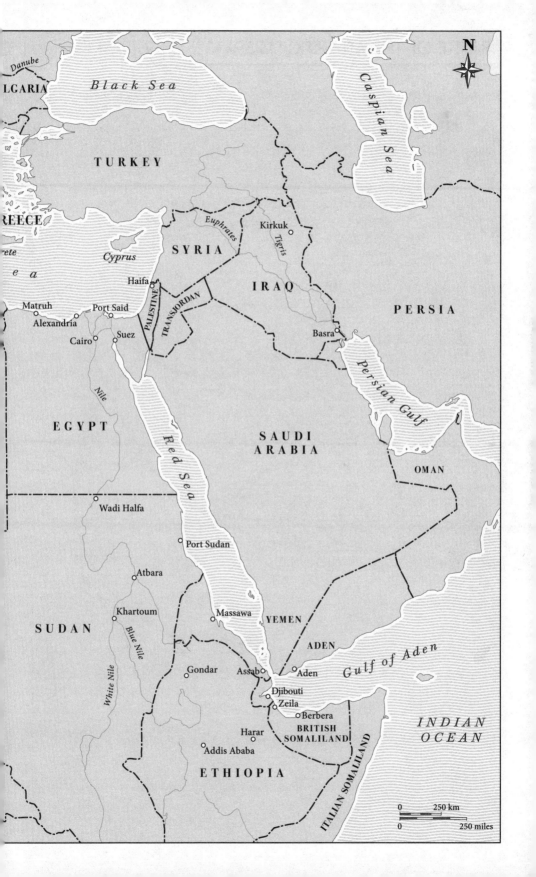

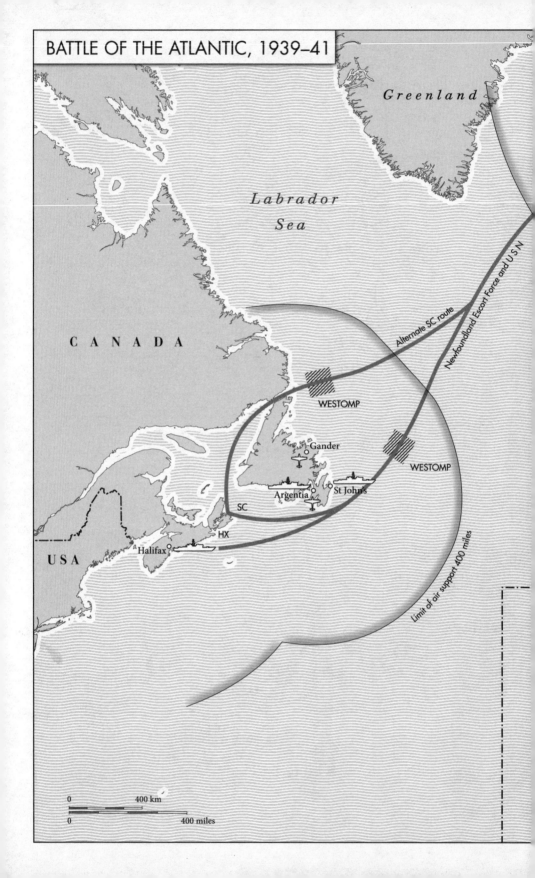

BATTLE OF THE ATLANTIC, 1939–41

Greenland

Labrador
Sea

CANADA

Alternate SC route

Newfoundland Escort Force and U S N

WESTOMP

Gander

WESTOMP

Argentia   St John's

SC

HX

Halifax

USA

Limit of air support 400 miles

0   400 km

0   400 miles

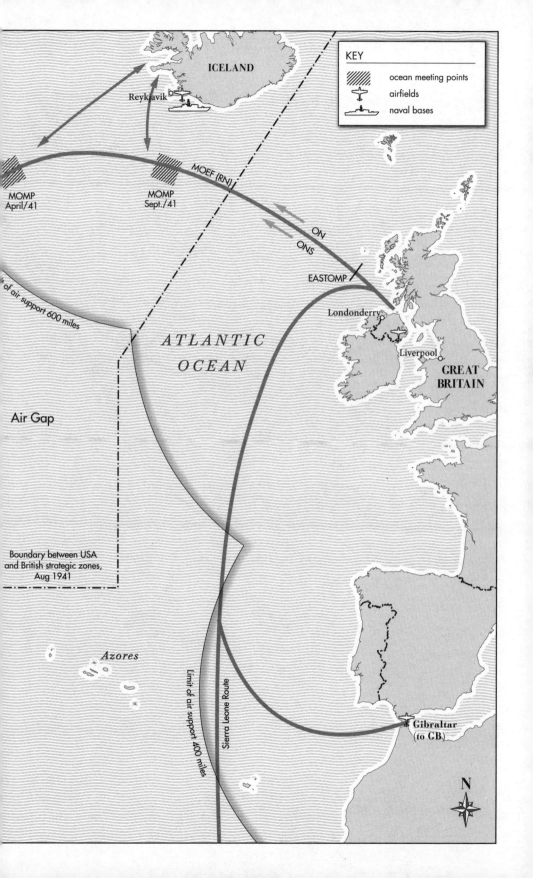

ICELAND

Reykjavik

KEY

//// ocean meeting points

airfields

naval bases

MOMP
April/41

MOMP
Sept./41

MOEF (RN)

ON

ONS

EASTOMP

Londonderry

Liverpool

GREAT
BRITAIN

of air support 600 miles

ATLANTIC
OCEAN

Air Gap

Boundary between USA
and British strategic zones,
Aug 1941

Azores

Limit of air support 400 miles

Sierra Leone Route

Gibraltar
(to GB)

N

LIST OF PRINCIPAL
CHARACTERS FEATURED

(Ranks at September 1941)

General Sir Harold Alexander
– *British*
Commander of 1st Division in
France, last man to leave Dunkirk,
later commander, Southern Division,
then British Forces in Burma, before
becoming C-in-C Middle East in
August 1942. Appointed com-
mander, 18th Army Group, in
February 1943.

Sergeant Cyril 'Bam' Bamberger
– *British*
An NCO fighter pilot in 610 and 41
Squadrons during the Battle of
Britain, he was later commissioned
and flew with 261 Squadron on
Malta and then 93 Squadron in
Tunisia.

Capitaine Daniel Barlone – *French*
Reserve officer commanding 92/20th
Horse Transport Company in 2nd
North African Division.

Capitaine André Beaufre – *French*
Staff officer at General Headquarters.

Jean-Mathieu Boris – *French*
Officer in the Free French Army.

Pfc Henry 'Dee' Bowles – *American*
Served in 18th Infantry Regiment,
1st Infantry Division, in North
Africa.

Pfc Tom Bowles – *American*
Served in 18th Infantry Regiment,
1st Infantry Division, in North
Africa.

Air Commodore Sydney Bufton
– *British*
Commander, 10 and 76 Squadrons,
RAF Bomber Command, then
became Station Commander at RAF
Pocklington before being made
Deputy Director of Bomber
Operations at the Air Ministry.

Gino Cappozzo – *Italian*
Gunner in 17th Battery, 3rd Alpine
Artillery Regiment.

Capitaine René de Chambrun
– *French*
Reserve officer in 162e Régiment
d'Infanterie de Forteresse,
Reynaud's personal emissary to the
United States.

Count Galeazzo Ciano – *Italian*
Italian Foreign Secretary and
son-in-law of Mussolini.

Lieutenant-Colonel Mark Clark
– *American*
G3 Staff Officer at General
Headquarters, US Army.

Jock Colville – *British*
One of the secretaries to the Prime Minister, first Neville Chamberlain and then Winston Churchill.

Gwladys Cox – *British*
Civilian living in London.

William Cremonini – *Italian*
Soldier in the Giovani Fascisti division.

Admiral Sir Andrew Browne Cunningham – *British*
Commander of the Mediterranean Fleet until 1942, then posted to Washington.

Pilot Officer Roald Dahl – *British*
Hurricane pilot with 80 Squadron in Greece.

Général Charles de Gaulle – *French*
Army officer then leader of the Free French.

Admiral Karl Dönitz – *German*
Commander of the Kriegsmarine's U-boat fleet.

Margarete Dos – *German*
Teenage girl living in Berlin at the beginning of the war, and a member of the Bund Deutscher Mädel, the girls' wing of the Nazi Youth Movement.

Captain Norman Field – *British*
Officer in the Royal Fusiliers in France and Belgium, then an officer in the Auxiliary Units in the UK, before joining the airborne forces.

Andrée Griotteray – *French*
French civilian and member of the Resistance.

Ted Hardy – *Australian*
Sapper in 2/3rd Field Company, 9th Australian Division, serving in North Africa and the Middle East.

Major Hajo Herrmann – *German*
Flew Heinkel 111s in Poland and Norway with KG4 before becoming a *Staffel* commander and switching to Ju88s. He later served in the Mediterranean before transferring to Norway to command III/KG30. In July 1942, he joined the Luftwaffe General Staff.

Harry Hopkins – *American*
President Roosevelt's closest friend and advisor, and unofficial emissary to Winston Churchill.

Henry Kaiser – *American*
Construction tycoon and director of Todd California Shipbuilding Corporation.

Feldmarschall Albert Kesselring – *German*
Commanded Luftflotte I in Poland, then Luftflotte II in France and during the Battle of Britain. Later transferred to the Mediterranean.

Major Siegfried Knappe – *German*
An artillery officer, he took part in the invasion of France and then served on the Eastern Front.

Heinz Knocke – *German*
Trainee fighter pilot in the Luftwaffe.

Bill Knudsen – *American*
Chairman of General Motors and then Chairman of the Office of Production Management, and later, in 1942, Director of Production at the Office of the Under-Secretary of War.

Private Joseph 'Lofty' Kynoch – *British*
Served in 2/5th Leicestershire Regiment in Norway.

Oberst Helmut Lent – *German*
A Luftwaffe nightfighter ace, who served in Norway then in Holland with NJGI and later NJGII.

Corinne Luchaire – *French*
French film star and daughter of Vichyist Jean Luchaire, and married to a Frenchman serving with the Luftwaffe.

Hauptmann Hans von Luck – *German*
Served with Rommel during the invasion of France and then throughout most of the North African campaign. He later commanded a panzer battalion in 21. Panzerdivision in Normandy and north-west Europe.

Oliver Lyttelton – *British*
Appointed Controller of Non-Ferrous Metals at the outbreak of war, became President of the Board of Trade in 1940, was elected MP for Aldershot and later joined the War Cabinet as Minister of State, Middle East. He returned to the UK in 1942 as Minister of Production.

Commander Donald Macintyre – *British*
Served as a convoy escort commander on destroyers, firstly on HMS *Hesperus* and then on HMS *Walker*.

Maggiore Publio Magini – *Italian*
Pilot and staff officer in the Regia Aeronautica.

Hauptmann Helmut Mahlke – *German*
Stuka pilot serving in France then the Balkans and Mediterranean.

General George C. Marshall – *American*
Chief of Staff of the United States Army.

Walter Mazzucato – *Italian*
Sailor in the Regia Marina, serving first on the battleship *Vittorio Veneto* and then on escort destroyers in the Mediterranean.

Flight Lieutenant Jean Offenberg
– *Belgian*
A fighter pilot who flew with 4ᵉ
Escadrille, 2ᵉ Groupe, 2ᵉ Régiment
Aéronautique I, of the Belgian Air
Force, then later joined 145 and 609
Squadrons of the RAF.

Martin Pöppel – *German*
Served as a *Fallschirmjäger* –
paratrooper – over Holland and
Norway in 1940, in Crete and Russia
the following year, and later in Sicily,
Italy, Normandy and the Lower
Rhine.

**Air Chief Marshal Sir Charles
Portal** – *British*
Commander-in-Chief of Bomber
Command from April 1940, then
became Chief of the Air Staff in
October the same year.

Ernie Pyle – *American*
A journalist and war correspon-
dent for Scripps Howard
Newspapers.

Paul Reynaud – *French*
French politician and Finance
Minister, then Prime Minister from
March to June 1940, and was later
imprisoned first by the Vichy
Government and then the Germans.

Generalmajor Erwin Rommel
– *German*
Commanded 7. Panzerdivision in
France in 1940, then took command

of the Deutsche Panzerkorps in
North Africa in February 1942, and
later became commander of the
Italo-German Panzerarmee Afrika.
Promoted to Feldmarschall in July
1942.

Leutnant Günther Sack – *German*
In the RAD – Reichsarbeitsdienst
– at the start of the war, Sack became
a *Fahnenjunker* with a heavy flak
unit, then switched to light flak in
March 1940. After serving in the
invasion of France and the Low
Countries, he served in the Balkans
and Greece, then returned to France.
After briefly serving at Leningrad, he
returned to the Western Front.

Giuseppe Santaniello – *Italian*
Soldier in 48th Artillery Regiment,
Bari Division.

Generalmajor Adolf von Schell
– *German*
General Plenipotentiary of Motor
Vehicles within the War Economics
and Armaments Office.

Hans Schlange-Schöningen
– *German*
First World War veteran and former
politician, during the war he
continued his family duties as owner
of a large estate in Pomerania.

Eric Sevareid – *American*
War correspondent and broadcaster
for CBS.

Flight Lieutenant Tony Smyth
– *British*
Bomber pilot with RAF Bomber
Command then later RAF Middle
East.

Gunnar Sonsteby – *Norwegian*
Fought in the Norwegian Army in
1940, then joined the Resistance
Movement. He later joined the
British SOE and went to Britain
for saboteur training, and became
chief of operations in the
Resistance.

**Lieutenant-General Sir Edward
Spears** – *British*
Member of Parliament and
Chairman of the Anglo-French
Committee, and then Churchill's
Personal Representative to the
French Prime Minister. Later became
the PM's Personal Representative to
the Free French.

Reichsminister Albert Speer
– *German*
Hitler's chief architect, and from
November 1942 Minister of
Armaments and War Production.

**Hauptmann Johannes 'Macky'
Steinhoff** – *German*
Fighter pilot and commander with
JG2 and JG52.

Henry L. Stimson – *American*
US Secretary of State for War.

Arthur 'A. G.' Street – *British*
Wiltshire farmer, writer and
broadcaster for the Ministry of
Information.

**Korvettenkapitän Reinhard 'Teddy'
Suhren** – *German*
First Watch Officer on *U-48*, then
took command of *U-564*, before
leaving the service in October 1942
to become an instructor.

Air Marshal Sir Arthur Tedder
– *British*
Director of Research at the Ministry
of Aircraft Production then posted
to the Middle East to become Air
Officer Commanding. Later, in
February 1943, he became C-in-C
Mediterranean Air Command.

Generalleutnant Georg Thomas
– *German*
Head of the War Economics and
Armaments Office and chief
economic advisor to the Army from
1939 to 1942.

Robert Cyril Thompson – *British*
Ship designer at Joseph L. Thompson
in Sunderland.

Oberleutnant zur See Erich Topp
– *German*
1WO on *U-46* and then commander
of *U-57* and *U-552*.

Lieutenant Hedley Verity – *British*
Officer in 1st Green Howards.

Pilot Officer Adrian Warburton
– *British*
RAF reconnaissance pilot.

General Walter Warlimont – *German*
Served as Deputy Chief of the
Operations Staff to the
Oberkommando der Wehrmacht
(OKW).

Else Wendel – *German*
Civilian living in Berlin and working
at Kraft durch Freude.

**Lieutenant-Commander Vere
Wight-Boycott** – *British*
First Lieutenant on the destroyer
HMS *Delight* and served in the
Norwegian campaign until he took
command of his own destroyers,
HMS *Roxborough* and then HMS
Ilex, carrying out convoy escort work
in the Atlantic and Mediterranean.

Note on the Text

I AM VERY CONSCIOUS that the narrative in this book repeatedly switches from one perspective to another: from British to German, and from French to Italian and then to American and even Dutch and Norwegian. In an effort to help distinguish who is who, I have written ranks in the language of the respective nationality. Thus it is Captain Field, but Capitaine Barlone, and Major-General Kennedy, but Generalmajor Rommel. The aim is not to be pretentious but rather just to help with the flow of the narrative.

I have applied this rule somewhat inconsistently to military units too. As a rough rule of thumb, any unit of corps or above in size has been written in the vernacular, but there are also a few other examples, especially German, where I have used the original words. Luftwaffe squadrons are *Staffeln* because actually, a German *Staffel* was not quite the same as a British squadron. German paratroopers and mountain troops are written as *Fallschirmjäger* and *Gebirgsjäger*. This will certainly help lessen any confusion by the time I reach Volume III and D-Day, for example, where there were German, American, Polish, Canadian and French airborne troops all operating, and in the case of Americans, Poles and Germans, often with similar sounding surnames.

I should also explain how some military units were written. A corps is numbered in Roman numerals and a military operation in upper case. Luftwaffe *gruppen* were written in Roman numerals, but *staffeln* in Arabic numbering. There were three *staffeln* per *gruppe*, so 5/JG2, for example, would be in II/JG2, but 7/JG2 would be in III/JG2.

Introduction

THE SECOND WORLD WAR witnessed the deaths of more than sixty million people from over sixty different countries. Entire cities were laid waste, national borders were redrawn and many millions more people found themselves displaced. Over the past couple of decades, many of those living in the Middle East or parts of Africa, the Balkans, Afghanistan and even the United States may feel, justifiably, that these troubled times have already proved the most traumatic in their recent past. Yet, globally, the Second World War was, and remains, the single biggest catastrophe of modern history. In terms of human drama, it is unrivalled; no other war has affected so many lives in such a large number of countries.

Yet much of what we think we know about the Second World War is steeped in perceptions and myth rather than fact. For the past sixty-odd years, we have looked at this cataclysmic conflict in much the same way, particularly when it comes to examining the War in the West – that is, the conflict between the Axis, led by Nazi Germany, and the Western Allies.

Seventy years on, the generation that fought through the war is slipping away fast. At the time of writing, the vast majority still living are into their nineties; there has been an urgency about the way in which veterans have been interviewed before it is too late, and there is no doubt that it is the human experience of war that has been the focus of much of the recent mainstream books on the subject.

The human drama of the war is what first drew me to the subject. It still seems incredible that just a short time ago we in Europe were embroiled in such a bitter and destructive conflict. I have often wondered what I would have done had I been a young man back then; would I have joined the Air Force, the Navy or the Army? How would I have coped with the loss of friends and family? How would I have dealt with the fear, or with the often brutal conditions? Or with being away from home for up to years on end?

The questions are still fascinating, and the immensity of the drama is still compelling, but as my knowledge and understanding have grown, so have I realized how many questions still remain and how vast a subject the war really is.

It is, however, easier to unearth new material and learn fresh perspectives than it once was. The comparative cheapness of travel, the opening up of many archives, and, especially, the advent of digital photography have all played important parts; I should know, for in the past decade I have travelled to Germany, Austria, Norway, France, Italy, America, Canada, New Zealand, India, Egypt, Tunisia, Libya, South Africa and Australia, visiting archives, interviewing veterans, and walking the ground. When I began, a visit to the archives meant taking hugely time-consuming notes in pencil; now, what once took a week can be achieved in a fraction of that time. When I was at the Citadel, the Military College of the South in Charleston, South Carolina, I photographed most of General Mark Clark's entire papers in a day. Back home, these papers can then be examined more thoroughly, and at leisure; it means greater detail can be absorbed and analysed.

Despite the continued appetite for the subject, and despite a steady stream of books, documentaries, magazines and even movies about the war, it is amazing how often they still conform to the traditional, and in many regards mythical, view of the conflict. That general perception goes something like this: that at the start of the war Nazi Germany had the best-trained army in the world with the best equipment and weapons. In 1940, Britain, now stranded and alone, managed to hold out and keep going until the United States entered the war. Thereafter, American economic might overwhelmed German military prowess, which in any case was fatally weakened by the much more significant, and large-scale, war on the Eastern Front. These basic presumptions have dominated thinking for the best part of sixty years.

There has, however, been something of a quiet revolution going on in academic circles, and, just occasionally, this work has managed to burst out into the mainstream, which is all to the good. My own views began to change dramatically when I started writing a series of wartime novels. Although fiction, they needed to be rooted in detailed research, but while writing them I suddenly realized I needed to know a great deal more about the minutiae of war – that is, the uniforms and weapons that were used, and, more importantly, how they were used, and why particular tactics were developed.

This level of study was revelatory, because suddenly a very different picture was emerging. The narrative focus has been very land-centric – as it was, incidentally, in Hitler's own mind – and we have often been rather too seduced by the action at the front. Yes, tactical flair is important, but it's not going to win a war unless other facets are carried out with equal ability.

In the early narrative, the focus was on the high level of war – the decisions by generals, for example. Personal memoirs followed: first the generals and decorated war heroes, then the 'ordinary' men – and women. Over the past thirty years, much work has also been done on the human experience of the war, but what has been conspicuously lacking is the context to go with these personal accounts. After all, it is all very well having the testimony of an American soldier, cowering in his fox-hole as he came under mortar fire, but why was he there and why were the mortars being fired? Just how did armies, air forces and navies operate? And what were the differences in their approaches? All too often, accounts of men in the war revert to old myths and stereotypes: British troops were slow and spent too much time 'brewing up' tea; Americans were scruffy and lacked discipline; German machine guns were manifestly the best on either side; the Tiger tank was similarly the best tank of the war, and so on.

But on what basis have those judgements been made? And are they fair? Very often not. Talk to a GI or Tommy who had to confront a German Tiger tank, to pick one example, and he'll most likely tell you it was a terrifying beast and vastly superior to anything in the Allied arsenal. It was huge. It had a big gun. It had lots of armour. The Allied soldier's view is entirely valid. But the Tiger was also incredibly complicated, mechanically unreliable, very difficult to sustain in combat, unusable for anything other than short distances, and could only be moved any distance by rail, for which it needed a change of tracks because otherwise it would not fit on the continental railway loading gauge; it was ludicrously thirsty in terms of fuel – of which the Germans had precious little by 1942 when the Tiger first appeared – and was too heavy to use most of the bridging facilities available at that time of the war, so would have been useless for any force operating on the offensive. The GI confronting such a terrifying weapon is not concerned about any of these issues – it's big and scary and he's literally staring down the barrel of death. But the historian does need to consider such things. Believing a particular weapon was more deadly than others just on the word of someone who confronted it in battle isn't good enough. There's a more nuanced picture to consider, and in analysing these things and questioning some of these long-held views, quite different pictures emerge.

In warfare, there are understood to be three important levels: the strategic, the operational and the tactical. Strategy refers to the big picture – the overall aims; the tactical level is the fighting on the front line and how that is conducted; and the operational refers to the means of making both the strategic and the tactical happen – in other words, the nuts and bolts: the kit, the ammunition, logistics, resources – the economics of war – getting men and machines from A to B. Sustaining the battle.

Talk to a British veteran of the Battle of Britain, for example, and he might describe how he could be shot down one day but be flying again the following morning. So where did he get his new plane and in such quick order? I once put this to Tom Neil, who flew Hurricanes with 249 Squadron in the summer of 1940. 'Where they came from and how they got there, I have no idea,' he said. 'But every morning, as if by a miracle, we had a full complement of aircraft again.'

And talk to an Allied tank man who fought in Normandy in 1944 and he will almost certainly say much the same thing: his Sherman was knocked out one afternoon, but the following morning he was in a new one and back in action. Where did it come from? 'We just went back to Echelon and picked up another,' one British squadron commander in the Sherwood Rangers told me. When I pushed him, he confessed that he lost three tanks between landing in Normandy and the end of the war the following May, but he never went a single day without a tank.

It is this operational level that has been most neglected in the historiography of the Second World War. But don't be put off – it's also one of the most interesting, because when one starts to understand this more complex level, all kinds of new perspectives appear, which cast our understanding of the war in a different light. And that is very exciting.

*

I have been researching these three volumes for years, but as I began writing, it occurred to me that I should, from the outset, set down my aim and the parameters I have given myself. Above all, this is meant to be a compelling narrative history – one that can be easily read and digested, and hopefully enjoyed, yet which brings together not only my own research but also much of the recent academic thinking on the subject. The aim is not to write only a military history, but a social, political and economic history too. One of the things I have come to learn is that when studying the Second World War, none of these themes should be separated. Or, rather, a much clearer picture of what was going on emerges when these different facets are interwoven.

This is not intended to be a detailed account of the fates and fortunes of every single country that took part in the War in the West. Rather, I am focusing on the principal participants: Germany and Italy on the Axis side, Britain and the United States on the Allied (although in fact they were in a coalition, not a formal alliance). In between them is France – one of the Allies to begin with, then on the Axis side (albeit with elements fighting for the Allies), and then back with the Allies towards the end. Other countries – such as Norway, Holland, Greece and Belgium – will also be examined, but not in as much detail. Nor will the wider war be ignored. What was happening in the Soviet Union and the Far East had an enormous impact on events in the West; it is impossible to entirely separate east from west.

The spine that I hope will hold the narrative together will be provided by a cast of individuals – from politicians, generals and industrialists to captains, privates and civilians. Their stories will be illustrative of the experience of war and the conduits to explaining the bigger picture. The narrative of the Second World War in the West is a wide and sweeping one: in the air, on the land and out at sea; from the mountains and fjords of Norway to the heat of the African desert, and from the sparkling Mediterranean to the briny grey of the Atlantic. It's an epic story and still, after all this time, one about which there is much to learn.

PART I

WAR BEGINS

CHAPTER 1

Countdown

Tuesday, 4 July 1939, and a hot, humid Independence Day in New York City. Far away, across the Atlantic, Europe appeared once more to be cantering towards all-out war for the second time in a generation, but here in America, the land of the free, the growing crisis seemed remote. Most in the United States had quite enough worries of their own after ten long years of bitter depression. True, there were signs of recovery, but there had been similar signs three years earlier and then there had been another dip. The first concern of Americans was to have a job and put bread on the table, not to get embroiled in what was happening back in the old countries. In any case, while many in the US might only have been first- or second-generation Americans, they had made the trip across the Atlantic for a reason, and for the majority that was to escape to a better life. America promised to be a land of opportunity, and a land of peace, and even with the pain of depression it stood unrivalled as the most modern and forward-thinking country in the world. Europe, with its history of despots and wars, famine and plague, was a world away . . .

And so now there was another round of bickering on the other side of the Atlantic. Let them fight it out for themselves; there were other things to think about than a madman, with a dodgy moustache, called Adolf Hitler.

Things to think about like baseball, and, on that sticky summer day in New York, one ball player in particular. The game was the country's national sport, an obsession for many millions, and Lou Gehrig was not only one of the greatest hitters ever to have played the game, but a house-hold name across the United States – as famous as any man alive in America. In a career with the New York Yankees that had spanned seven-teen seasons, he had hit more than forty home runs six times, had dipped below thirty only once since 1927, was one of the highest run-producers in history and consistently had one of the highest batting averages. His record of a staggering 2,130 consecutive games was one that would stand for over fifty years, which was why, when his form had so dramatically collapsed at the start of the 1939 season, it had seemed unfathomable. Clearly, there was something wrong. He'd noticed himself that he had begun feeling tired midway through the previous season, but during spring training he appeared to have lost all his strength, such a feature of the Iron Horse's game. At one point, he had even collapsed on the field. He struggled badly on the opening day, then benched himself. His career was over.

Sent to the famous Mayo Clinic in Rochester, Minnesota, he was diagnosed with a rare degenerative disease, amyotrophic lateral sclerosis, on his thirty-sixth birthday, 19 June. This was a terminal wasting disease that would lead to paralysis, difficulty in speaking and, in due course, death. Life expectancy was around three years, if he was lucky.

The Yankees and the baseball world were in shock. Lou Gehrig was not so colourful a character as his former team-mate Babe Ruth, but he was respected for his quiet humility and for his amazing strength and agility. He had always let his batting do the talking, but on this 4 July, 1939, 'Lou Gehrig Appreciation Day', he was to make one of the most famous speeches in sporting history. Nearly 62,000 fans had crammed into the Yankee Stadium to see a double-header against the Washington Senators, and between the games the great slugger would make his final appear-ance on the plate in a ceremony attended by Babe Ruth and New York's mayor, Fiorello H. La Guardia.

Among those watching was John E. Skinner, a fourteen-year-old from New Brunswick, across the Hudson in New Jersey. A keen and promising young ball player himself, he was a Yankees fan and had been taken to see Gehrig for the last time by a friend of his father's. What had shocked him most was the change in the great slugger's appearance. Gehrig had been a big man, but he looked shrunken now, his famous Number 4 jersey hanging off his shoulders and his pants bunched badly at his waist. 'Before the ceremonies began,' says Skinner, 'you'd picture Gehrig belting a ball out of the park, but then, when you have to see him pull himself up by his hands to get out of the dugout, it was a very sad thing.'

As speeches were made and gifts handed over, Gehrig stood, twisting his cap in his hand and looking awkward. Eventually, it was time for the quiet man to say a few words. The crowd was chanting and applauding as he stepped up to the microphone. As he cleared his throat, he stopped, hands awkwardly planted on his sides and head stooped. 'For the past two weeks,' he said, 'you've been reading about a bad break.' He paused, then added, 'Today, I consider myself the luckiest man on the face of the earth.' The times he'd had, the players he'd played with, the family he had. 'Sure I'm lucky,' he said.

Behind John Skinner, two huge men were bawling like babies. 'They were . . . really moved,' says Skinner. 'It was a moving experience.' It was a speech of humility and bravery, from a sporting hero who was demonstrating astonishing courage in the face of cruel adversity. Before the coming war was out, John Skinner would need some of that courage himself. So would millions of other Americans, not that they could know it that hot summer afternoon in New York.

A few hundred miles south of New York, just a day later, the President, Franklin Delano Roosevelt, was floating down the Patuxent River in Maryland on the presidential yacht, the USS *Potomac*, a vessel he liked to call the 'floating White House'. He had come to visit his close friend and advisor, Harry Hopkins, who was laid low and convalescing at Delabroke, a beautiful pre-Revolution house on the river loaned to him for the summer. Hopkins had organized, overseen and run many of the key projects of Roosevelt's New Deal – relief agencies in which the government invested heavily in an attempt to provide jobs and public works projects and help the country crawl out of depression. The biggest of these jobs programmes, the Works Progress Administration, or WPA, had been the centrepiece of the New Deal from 1935 and had been run by Hopkins until the previous summer, when he'd been recovering from a vicious bout of cancer that had seen two-thirds of his stomach removed. Now, eighteen months after his treatment, he could no longer ingest properly. Like Lou Gehrig, it seemed that Hopkins was dying.

His death would be a huge blow to the President, who had developed a close bond with this thin, sickly man with the rapier wit, dynamic organizational skills and shrewd judgement. More recently, FDR – as the

President was widely known – had started using Hopkins in a different role. The imminent war in Europe may not have been foremost on the mind of most Americans but it certainly was now centre stage in the President's thoughts, and had been for some time, the more so because of the events in Munich the previous autumn. Back then, war had threatened to engulf Europe, but both France and Britain had stepped back from the brink; they had allowed Hitler, the German Chancellor, to annex the German-speaking Sudetenland from the rest of Czechoslovakia unopposed. The Czechs had had their country sliced up, and war had been averted, but then in March that year, just six months after the Munich agreement, Hitler's troops had marched into the rest of Czechoslovakia, and in so doing the German leader had flagrantly gone back on his promise. Now he wanted part of Poland too. A pattern was clearly emerging: bully, threaten, watch the rest of the world step aside, and then walk in. Land grabs had never been so easy. The issue, as Britain, France and Roosevelt were all too aware, was that Hitler was unlikely to stop unless made to by military force. And that meant war.

Thus a European conflict seemed to the President to be increasingly likely, but while many in Washington assumed that a future European conflict had little to do with them, FDR was not so sure. He had also begun to realize that the Atlantic was no longer the barrier it had once been. Air power was growing rapidly, as was naval power. Charles Lindbergh, an American, had famously flown across the Atlantic in a single flight back in 1927; it was only a matter of time before fleets of bombers could do the same. And, in any case, there were now aircraft carriers, floating airstrips that could deliver air power to all corners of the globe. Technology was advancing rapidly. The world was becoming a smaller place.

Be that as it may, it was not a view that was widely shared within the United States. Americans were quite aware of the emergence of Hitler and the Nazis, the suppression of civil rights in Germany, and the rising persecution of Jews and other minorities, and yet the overwhelming view was that these were problems for Europe to resolve not the United States. Americans had reluctantly become drawn into the last war and had been given, in the eyes of many in the US, precious little thanks for it.

Yet they had entered the war in 1917 on the back of idealism – an idealism that had long since been exposed for its naivety and resentfully cast aside. It had been Woodrow Wilson, the US president at the time, who had been the architect of this American world-view, outlining his vision for a future world peace early in 1918 with his 'Fourteen Points' speech. He had attended the subsequent Paris Peace Conference with lofty ideals for global free trade and a future League of Nations, in which he saw the United States playing a central and progressive role – the New World showing the Old Order how to create a better, fairer globe. The subsequent Treaty of Versailles, however, had fallen some way short of such ideals; the peace terms revealed no utopian future but rather exposed deep-rooted national mistrust and hatred, made worse by four years of slaughter – much of it on French soil and in the heart of Europe.

One of those who had observed the Paris Peace Conference first hand had been Roosevelt, then Assistant Secretary of the Navy, although perhaps his most significant conversation was not at the conference itself, but with Woodrow Wilson on the return crossing afterwards, when the President was still fired with enthusiasm for his proposed League of Nations. 'The United States must go in,' he told FDR, 'or it will break the heart of the world, for she is the only nation that all feel is disinterested and all trust.'

It was not to be, however. When Wilson returned to the United States, he was unable to persuade the Senate to ratify the treaty and with it American membership of the President's proposed League of Nations. The appetite for playing a leading role in world affairs had gone. Few wanted a large military either; after all, what was the point? What's more, it appeared to many that the Old Order had prevailed in Europe after all, with Britain and France the major beneficiaries. The New World had tried to help but had had that offer thrown back in its face. Well, if that was the way they wanted it, then fine.

None the less, this new isolationist stance had short-term consequences. Four million men in uniform had to be demobilized and sent home, while the booming wartime armaments industry was to be equally rapidly reduced. It was inevitable that the economy consequently took a dip.

It was hardly any surprise, then, that at the next elections the Democrats were out and the Republicans came to power with the promise of a return to a more inward-looking future. Far from promoting free trade, they increased import tariffs, reduced taxes and encouraged spending. A more laissez-faire approach ensued, in which central government was reduced. The brief dip turned swiftly to boom. Americans were free to enjoy the time of plenty in this young, vibrant and liberal country. The Roaring Twenties and the Jazz Age had arrived.

But while the US had turned its back on leading the world into a progressive modern age, this did not mean America was keeping out of European affairs altogether. Far from it, and throughout much of the 1920s it was the United States which played the most significant part in getting Germany back on to its feet. When the severity of the reparations led to hyperinflation and wheelbarrows of printed money, it was the Dawes Committee that oversaw a dramatic reduction in the payments. Led by General Charles G. Dawes, a Chicago banker and industrialist, and with another American industrialist, Owen Young, the chairman of General Electric, driving the scheme, they also brought in increased foreign investment, re-established the Reichsmark on gold at its pre-war level against the dollar, and helped stabilize the German economy. The New York bankers J. P. Morgan then backed these changes with a massive loan of $100 million.

A further measure was the establishment of a Reparations Agent – in this case a rising Wall Street financier, Parker Gilbert – who had the power to halt any reparations payments if they looked set to endanger the stability of the German economy. Suddenly, the flow of foreign capital – and particularly dollars – was enough to not only get the Reichsmark back on its feet, but also for Germany to easily pay its reparations to Britain and France without default. This money was then ploughed back into the US, which was insisting France and Britain honour their wartime debts. Thus, the money was effectively going round and round, but in the process Germany was climbing back out of the abyss and emerging once more as the modern, industrial economy at the centre of Europe that it had been before the war.

This was all very well until suddenly America, and then the rest of the first world, was mired by the Wall Street Crash of October 1929. The loans to Germany dramatically dried up, while in the US the days of boom were for the time being over. By the time FDR became the thirty-second President of the United States and brought the Democrats back to power for the first time in twelve years, America was in the grip of the worst depression in its history, with unemployment soaring to 25 per cent and the economy in a nosedive. Roosevelt had got into power on the back of greater isolationism and on the promise of relief, recovery and reform: relief for the poor and unemployed, recovery of the economy, and reform of many of the US's financial institutions. These pledges were almost entirely domestic and continued America's inward-looking progress. There was now little room for Germany.

Another central tenet shared by both sides of the American political divide had been the need to reduce the military. It had been Roosevelt, for example, who, as Assistant Secretary of the Navy, had overseen much of the demobilization of that part of the services. A strong military, the theory went, did not act as a deterrent but as a provocation. And for America, now pursuing an isolationist stance, there was simply no need to spend billions on large armed forces.

It was a very different world now, however. The democratic Weimar Republic had gone, the German policy of the 1920s had been cast aside, and in its place there ruled an absolute dictator in Adolf Hitler, and a Nazi party that let no opportunity to rattle sabres and display its martial strength slip by.

Roosevelt had not forgotten that conversation with Wilson on the ship back to America after the Paris Peace Conference, however, and no matter how inward-looking he had pledged to be on taking office in 1933, he had become convinced that Hitler was a madman bent on world domination, and that should Germany crush France and Britain, then it would most likely turn on the USA. He still hoped to prevent war, but believed the best way of doing that was to discard the policy of the past two decades and rapidly rearm, and particularly in terms of aircraft. The Germans were known to have more aircraft than Britain and France, and, in the summer of 1939, greater ability to maintain that advantage.

Late in 1938, FDR had sent his friend Hopkins on an undisclosed mission to the West Coast of America to assess the capacity there to build aircraft and how to increase production urgently. Hopkins had reported back favourably. FDR had hoped to sell aircraft, especially, to France and Britain. Perhaps if Germany knew this, it would think twice about taking on the two biggest powers in Europe; he viewed Britain and France as America's front line, where the critical struggle would take place in the air. American aircraft might make all the difference.

There were two stumbling blocks, however. The first was that this represented a major political volte-face and would require some incredibly deft public relations to pull off, even though there were signs in the polls that increasing numbers of Americans accepted rearmament as a policy. The second was legal – namely, the Neutrality Act of 1937, which placed an embargo on the sale and shipment of arms to any belligerent, whether aggressive dictatorships or friendly democracies. Britain, for example, could get round this by using existing funds in the USA and shipping arms in its own vessels from Canada, but there was no doubt a repeal of the act would show intent and represent a warning shot to Nazi Germany.

A bill to repeal the Neutrality Act had gone before the House of Representatives the previous month, and a fudged, half-baked, amended version of this had been passed on 30 June, 1939. Now, as Harry Hopkins and his daughter, Diana, and sons, Robert and Stephen, joined the President on his yacht, they were awaiting the verdict of the Senate.

Its answer came a few days later on 11 July. The embargo would remain, but the cash-and-carry provisions were removed. From now on, American ships could trade freely if it came to war. As for full repeal of the Act, well, that was deferred until the next session – in 1940. It was what one commentator called 'a negative compromise between isolationism, collective security, Washington heat, and partisan politics'.

What was certainly true, however, was that the United States, for all its isolationism, had played a major part in the rise of Hitler and the Nazis. There is no question at all that it was the harshness of the Treaty of Versailles that had fired Hitler and his sympathizers. Nevertheless, until 1929, his Nazi party had been largely insignificant. Germany, until then, had been pursuing a democratic course, in which a policy of international co-operation and growing industrial strength was perceived to be the quickest and most effective way of restoring the French-occupied Rhineland and returning the country to the premier stage. Only once Germany began to collapse again following the Great Depression did Hitler and the Nazis start clawing their way into mainstream politics.

In other words, it was Versailles that caused the emergence of the Nazis, but it was the Wall Street Crash that helped get the Nazis into power.

Far across the sea, in Rome, the Italian Minister of Foreign Affairs, Galeazzo Ciano, Count of Cortellazzo and Buccari, was struggling to come to terms with the fact that one of those closest to him was dead. His father, Amiragglio Costanzo Ciano, a highly decorated First World War hero, had died on 26 June, somewhat unexpectedly and at only sixty-three years old. His son was desolate. The news, he wrote in the single longest entry in his diary, shocked him deeply. 'It was a great blow to me, physically and mentally,' he scribbled. 'I felt that something was torn away from my physical being. Only at that moment, after thirty-six years of life, did I come to realize how real and deep and indestructible are the ties of blood.'

Ciano's father had also been at the forefront of the rise of Fascism, which had been more directly attributable to the effects of the last war than had the emergence of Nazism. Italy may have ended up on the winning side, but it had been a pyrrhic victory. Like Germany, Italy was a new country, and was still, for all its rich history, music and arts, a fragmented nation, underdeveloped and struggling to emerge into the modern age. War had exposed one of its greatest weaknesses: a lack of the kind of natural resources needed to drive development and modernity. Italy may have been one of the big five – along with Britain, France, the USA and Japan – to have thrashed out the Treaty of Versailles, but its influence had been minimal, its ambitions unfulfilled, and the country had been left broke. In 1920, the lira crashed and inflation rocketed. Weak governments tumbled one after another.

It was into this maelstrom that Benito Mussolini, a journalist with a fiery and bombastic charisma, emerged. Copying much of the liturgy of the right-wing poet-prince, Count Gabriele d'Annunzio, Mussolini developed a new political movement. Fascism was a belief in the bond of nationhood – the *Patria* – encapsulated in the spirit and personality of a common leader. Fractious, weak and democratic politics were replaced with strong leadership and plenty of theatre to help unite that sense of a common bond. Thus, in came blackshirts, Roman salutes, banners, slogans – and militarism.

And Amiraglio Ciano, known as 'Ganascia' – 'the Jaw' – the famous war hero and celebrated in poetry by d'Annunzio, was quick to declare himself for Fascism. The admiral was also there beside Mussolini in October 1922 when the Fascist leader and some 30,000 of his paramilitary squads left their northern strongholds in Milan and the Po Valley and began marching on Rome. Fearing civil war, the King, Vittorio Emanuele III, handed power to Mussolini and his National Fascist Party. Mussolini declared it a revolution, and the March on Rome became part of the mythologizing of Fascism. At any rate, his dictatorship had begun.

The admiral continued to play a major role in Mussolini's ministry, eventually taking over as President of the Italian Chamber of Deputies in 1934. Being an ennobled war hero in the heart of the new regime brought plenty of riches; the admiral was nothing if not corrupt. At any rate, it was into this world of power and new-found wealth that his son, Galeazzo, emerged. Clever and ambitious, he married Mussolini's daughter, Edda, in 1930 and swiftly rose through the political ranks. After a posting as Consul in Shanghai, he returned to Italy in 1935 to become Minister of Press and Propaganda. This put him at the heart of Mussolini's government, although he left Rome to command a squadron of the Regia Aeronautica – the Royal Air Force – during the Italian invasion of Abyssinia. On his triumphant return he was appointed Foreign Minister. Young, suave, handsome and an *aviatore*, as well as a known womanizer, he was the very embodiment of Mussolini's new Italy.

A few days after his father's death, however, the new and second Count Ciano was trying to immerse himself in work – as good an antidote as any for grief. His office, the Palazzo Chigi in the heart of Rome, was suitably grand and luxurious, but these were difficult times for the Foreign Minister. Just a couple of months earlier, Mussolini – *Il Duce* – had concluded a formal alliance with Nazi Germany, known as the 'Pact of Steel'. Together, Italy and Germany were now collectively known as the 'Axis'. The pact had been drawn up almost entirely in Berlin and bound Italy to support Germany in any foreign affairs, including war. During the negotiations, in which Ciano had played a leading part, there had been much discussion about buying time for Italy to properly rearm, but he had been reassured that Germany was planning nothing soon – and certainly not an imminent attack on Poland. Ciano had been reassured and had returned to Berlin on 21 May to sign the following day. He had thought Hitler looked well, although he heard from Frau Goebbels, wife of the Führer's propaganda chief, that she was tiring of their leader's monologues. 'He can be Führer as much as he likes,' Ciano had written in his diary, 'but he always repeats himself and bores his guests.'

At the signing ceremony, senior Nazis had crowded around Ciano and the Italian delegation. Joachim von Ribbentrop, the Foreign Minister, had been given a special Collar of the Annunziata; Göring, Hitler's deputy and head of the Luftwaffe as well as the leading industrialist in Germany, had looked on enviously. Heinrich Himmler, head of the SS, was also there to witness the removal of any threat to Germany's ambition from the south. The following day, Ciano had arrived back in Rome to be greeted by a considerable crowd. 'However, it is clear to me,' he noted later, 'that the pact is more popular in Germany than in Italy.'

Seven weeks on, however, it seemed their German allies were not showing them the kind of respect the Italians had expected. Rather, Germany was flagrantly keeping them in the dark; in fact, the Germans had lied to Italy about their intentions towards Poland. Ciano was greatly disturbed.

Openly, the main bone of contention was the Danzig Corridor, a narrow passageway to around seventy miles of the Baltic coastline and including the port of Danzig. Beyond this to the east lay East Prussia, separated from the rest of Germany. The creation of the Second Republic of Poland had been part of the Versailles Treaty and proposed by President Wilson in one of his Fourteen Points. Poland had been an independent country once before but by the end of the eighteenth century had been partitioned three ways by Prussia, Russia and Austria. In other words, it had been part of these countries and with German and Russian peoples living there for almost as long as the United States had been an independent country.

When these lands had been handed back to the Poles in 1919, there had been further war with the Soviet Union, which they had won, but it was unsurprising that both Russia and Nazi Germany wanted these lands back. The Poles felt they had won a historic new independence, free from the yoke of their neighbours; Russia and Germany felt part of their respective countries had been unfairly carved up.

In the intervening years, Poland had managed to fuse these territories into a nation state, but, politically, it had become increasingly authoritarian. A military coup in 1926 was followed by the gradual erosion of parliamentary politics. By 1935, Poland was, to all intents and purposes, a dictatorship. None the less, so long as they toed the political line, most Poles lived freely enough, and while many would have preferred a return to democracy, at least they were independent. The Poles were nothing if not a proud people.

Meanwhile, although non-aggression pacts had been signed with both Germany and the Soviet Union, it was clear Poland was extremely vulnerable to attack from its antipathetic neighbours. Little, however, was done to build up much by way of defences; defence plans were based on the assumption that its armed forces would not be called upon to fight before 1942. The Army was small and poorly trained. It did have a tank that was superior to both the German Panzer Mk I and II, but had only 140 of these 7TPs and in all just two armoured brigades – that is, around one division. Its Air Force had only about six hundred aircraft of all types and most were inferior to those in the Luftwaffe. It wasn't remotely strong enough to take on Germany; and certainly not the Soviet Union as well.

Germany's claims, while not justified, were certainly understandable; much of Poland had been German in living memory, and there were plenty of Germans still living in Poland who twenty years earlier had been living in territory that had been Prussian, then German, for more than 125 years. Prior to 1919, Poland had not been an independent country since the eighteenth century – in other words, well beyond living memory. Hitler was well aware, however, that the Poles had no intention of handing over any of this new-found independence. Therefore the only alternative was to take it by force.

Neither Britain nor France was particularly bothered about what happened to Poland, but they were concerned that Hitler should not be allowed to keep land-grabbing. After all, where would it stop? All of Europe? The entire world? After they had backed down at Munich the previous October over the Sudetenland, it was clear that the buck now had to stop. They had to stand up to the ambitions of Hitler and his Nazis.

Equally uninterested in the fate of the Poles was Count Ciano. He didn't give a fig about Danzig, but he did care about being drawn into a war for which Italy was clearly not ready. It had not been ready in 1914, and, although it had backed the winning side, the war had been a catastrophe for Italy. Mussolini had since claimed he would create a new Italian empire and one that rivalled Ancient Rome, but the wars of conquest in East Africa had not solved the resources problem. What's more, it was one thing taking on native Africans, as they had done in Abyssinia – and that had been harder than might have been imagined – and another storming into a backward and crumbling Albania, as the Italians had done in April that year; but it was quite a different matter altogether ending up in a full-blown European war against Britain and France. Industrially, economically and materially, Italy could not compete – not unless it had a very huge amount of help from its newest ally.

CHAPTER 2

Diplomacy

Paris, France, on the evening of Monday, 31 July 1939. It had been a particularly fine summer in Paris. The street cafés and parks had been as busy as ever, and the usual Bastille Day military parade just a fortnight earlier had been especially splendid. Mounted cavalry, breast-plates shining in the sun, troops from Africa, infantry in their finest bright uniforms, and huge new tanks and artillery pieces had all marched down the Champs-Élysées in a display of military might and confidence as befitted one of the leading and most powerful nations in the world.

At the austere Château de Vincennes in south-east Paris, the head-quarters of the General Staff of the French Armed Forces, instructions for the forthcoming military talks with the Soviet Union had just arrived from their British counterparts. A printed document around an inch thick, it was a dossier that well reflected the unease both Britain and France were feeling about dealing with the Russians and, in particular, their Communist dictator, Joseph Stalin.

Talks with the Soviet Union had begun that April, with both Britain and France expressing their willingness for some kind of pact based on the old entente that had encircled Imperial Germany back in 1914. The trouble was, Russia was very different now. For Western democracies, Communism was as bad as Nazism, while Stalin's purges of the past few years hardly encouraged trust. Foreign observers were stunned to learn, in the summer of 1937, that a large number of senior Red Army officers had been arrested and immediately executed, including Marshal Mikhail Tukhachevsky, a brilliant man who had impressed the British during a visit in 1936. But Tukhachevsky was hardly alone. Three out of five marshals were executed, thirteen out of fifteen Army commanders, fifty out of fifty-seven corps commanders, and 154 out of 186 division commanders. In other words, much of the Red Army leadership had been wiped out, and one of the key figures behind the purge was Vyacheslav Molotov, who, from the beginning of May 1939, was the new Soviet Foreign Minister. While neither the British nor French knew the precise figures of the Red Army purge, they knew enough. These were hardly the kind of people to do business with, and it was one of the reasons why they had chosen to isolate the Soviet Union in recent years.

On the other hand, would Germany be foolish enough to invade Poland if it meant going to war with the Western powers *and* the Soviet Union? If war could be averted, surely, the British and French persuaded themselves, it would be worth dealing with the Russians?

Yet there had been mutual mistrust from the outset. The Russians were uncertain how honest were Western intentions. Precisely because of the purge, which had left the Red Army greatly weakened, Stalin was concerned about being left alone to face a hostile Nazi Germany on the Soviet borders – the inevitable outcome should Germany invade Poland. On the other hand, Britain and France, democracies both, were politically far removed from Communist Russia. Furthermore, Britain was still a monarchy. The Russians had executed their own royal family only twenty years earlier. In fact, Stalin seemed to execute rather a lot of people. In France, concerns were not only about the unsavoury nature of Stalin and his henchmen, but also about encouraging the growing support for Communism and fears of Soviet encroachment.

Then there were the Soviet demands. Both Britain and France had agreed to honour Poland's sovereignty, but now Stalin wanted the two Western powers to honour the sovereignty of the Baltic States as well. Another thorny issue as yet unresolved was the Soviet insistence that the Red Army be allowed passage across Poland should the need arise, something the French had repeatedly tried in vain to persuade the Poles to accept.

Back and forth the negotiations went. Britain's heart was not in it – the Prime Minister, Neville Chamberlain, especially, had only been persuaded to enter talks at all by the weight of support to do so from his Cabinet. The French had been more anxious to come to some kind of agreement, but both sides were unable to find the form of terms on which they could agree.

Then suddenly, out of the diplomatic blue on 17 July, Soviet negotiators had demanded military talks, inviting a British and French military mission to Moscow. Such discussions face to face, the Soviets claimed, were essential before a political agreement could be agreed. So now, at the beginning of August, it appeared there was still a chance of striking a deal after all.

The British had swiftly drawn up their own proposed set of instructions for the talks in Moscow, and it was this weighty printed document that had now reached the Château de Vincennes. Among those in the French mission now wading through the British instructions was Capitaine André Beaufre, a thirty-seven-year-old staff officer recently posted to the General Staff from French North Africa. What struck him about the British dossier was its caution. The British were insisting there should be absolutely no passing on of any secret information, and that the Western allies should bear in mind constantly that German–Soviet collusion was possible. In other words, the Russians were not to be trusted under any circumstances.

In fact, it was all too clear to Beaufre that the prime objective of the British was not signing a treaty with the Soviet Union, but, rather, to spin out negotiations for as long as possible. Nevertheless, he still believed the mission offered a breath of hope; the Russians must, he thought, be serious about coming to some kind of accord. And that was something.

The President of the United States had always loved the sea and had a fascination both with the Navy and with sailing of any kind. Thus it was that he would take himself off on the presidential yacht whenever time allowed, and why, just a month earlier, he had taken his friend Harry Hopkins for a trip down the Patuxent River.

Another man who liked messing about in boats was Feldmarschall Hermann Göring, and that first weekend of August found him cruising around the Baltic islands in *Carin II*, his luxury yacht, named after his adored first wife, who had died eight years earlier.

No other leading Nazi enjoyed the opportunities for riches and extravagances as much as he. While Hitler liked things to be big – warships, offices, buildings, guns and so on – there was something of the puritan about him; his clothes were drab, he did not smoke or eat meat and nor did he drink. The same could not be said for Göring, who had had made for him a large array of flamboyant uniforms, had become fat on the excesses of food and fine wine, smoked the best cigars, and not only had a luxury yacht but also a fleet of luxury cars, and houses and estates filled with great works of art, games rooms and even, at Carinhall, his mansion to the north of Berlin, a large model railway over which mechanical aircraft moved on wires. Göring loved luxury.

Although often portrayed as an overweight figure of ridicule, Göring was, rather, a highly intelligent and politically astute operator. Charismatic, he was also an arch-Machiavel and had cleverly used a combination of guile, charm and ruthlessness to attain a position of power and authority within the Nazi party that was second only to Hitler himself.

During the First World War, Göring had transferred from the trenches to the Air Force and had risen to command Jagdgeschwader 1, formerly led by Manfred von Richthofen, the Red Baron. After the war, he had continued flying, barnstorming at air shows and then for a Swedish airline. Making something of a name for himself in Swedish society, he had met the explorer Eric von Rosen, who had in turn introduced Göring to Carin von Kantzow, who became Göring's first wife. It was also while staying at von Rosen's country estate that Göring had spotted the swastika symbol; supposedly it was after seeing this Nordic rune in Sweden that Göring suggested to Hitler it be adopted as the symbol of the Nazis.

At the time that Göring met Carin von Kantzow and von Rosen, he had already begun to develop political ambitions, and back in Germany he met Hitler and was instantly captivated by this man and his fledgling political movement. Göring was by Hitler's side at the Beer Hall Putsch in 1923, when the Nazis attempted to seize power, and was shot in the groin for his trouble. His subsequent long and painful recuperation was aided by copious amounts of morphine, to which he became addicted. It was a habit he had never kicked; among the drug's side-effects are the creation of a sense of euphoria, but it also plays havoc with glands and hormones, prompts outbursts of increased energy and vanity and also delusions, as well as monumental lows. Göring displayed all these symptoms. It did not stop him, however, from sticking loyally by Hitler's side, or, during his moments of energy, demonstrating a razor-sharp political grasp and vision.

Throughout much of the 1920s and into the 1930s, the Nazis, or the National Socialists as they more formally called themselves, were at best a political irrelevance and at worst a joke. Only after the Crash of 1929 did Hitler and his Nazis start to gain ground, and even then it was slowly.

In 1928, the Nazis had gained just 2.5 per cent of the vote; sales of Hitler's memoir-cum-manifesto, *Mein Kampf*, had fallen so badly his publishers decided to hold back the second volume. In 1931, however, in the wake of the Crash, Britain dropped out of the gold standard, the anchor around which sterling, the world's leading trading currency, had been based. This move turned a bad recession in the international community into a deep depression. Eleven other countries followed Britain in floating their currencies, but France, Germany and others stayed fixed on gold at their old parity. As sterling and other currencies devalued, so German exporters struggled; and it was on economic growth – industrial exports – that Germany's peaceful and democratic growth and strategy for return to the forefront of world powers had been based.

Germany might well have devalued the Reichsmark, but such a move had its own risks and in any case had too many painful associations with the post-war hyperinflation of 1922–3. The USA also warned against such a move, telling the government it wanted to see Germany not only service its long-term loans but also protect its balance of payments by maintaining existing exchange controls. Thus, Germany found itself stuck to the gold standard but facing the devaluation of many of the currencies in which it gained most of its burgeoning foreign exchange.

The net result was rapidly rising unemployment and a surge in nationalism. Hitler and his Nazis had been unequivocal: the struggle – the '*Kampf*' – was one for food, resources and living space, or *Lebensraum*. That, Hitler argued, could not be achieved by mutual international economic interdependence. It could be achieved only by military conquest. In other words, liberalism did not work.

With the policy of the 1920s now in ruins and the hard times returning, Hitler's vision of nationalism started to gain ground. In the summer election of 1932, the Nazis won 37.2 per cent of the vote, and although there was no clear majority for any party, General Hindenburg, the German President, resisted the chance to make Hitler Chancellor. The Nazi leader refused any lesser post. This disappointed his supporters, and Hitler's National Socialists actually lost ground in the second election that year, in November, when they got 33 per cent of the vote.

By the start of 1933, there were also just the beginnings of economic recovery, but with politics now fractious and the current Chancellor, General Kurt von Schleicher, holding on to power in a weak coalition, a small group of disaffected right-wing conservatives – including the former Chancellor, Franz von Papen, ousted the previous summer – had then conspired to force Hindenburg to form yet another government, and one that included the Nazis. This meant offering Hitler the Chancellorship, even though the National Socialists' popular vote was down. It was a post Hitler accepted.

In no way, however, was he brought to power by an overwhelming desire by the German people to adopt the Nazis' policies of aggressive rearmament, military conquest, anti-Semitism and anti-Bolshevism. Rather, Hitler's elevation came about as a result of Germany meeting a series of unpredicted forks in the roads and repeatedly taking the turn that led towards the emergence and then rise of the Nazis.

And, once Chancellor, Hitler had wasted no time in dismantling parliamentary democracy. A further election was called in March 1933, and by using strong-arm tactics and bullying the Catholic Centre Party, Hitler got the two-thirds majority he needed, and which then led him to pass the Enabling Law. This allowed his government to rule by decree and so ended parliamentary democracy in Germany. Other parties were banned, and a restriction was placed on the press. Jews and other non-Aryans were excluded first from the arts and then from owning land. The timing had been perfect: in the US, Roosevelt had just taken office and America was suffering a second dip in the depression, while France was equally preoccupied with its own political turmoil. The rest of the modern world was thus distracted. By the summer of 1934, when Hindenburg died, Hitler became the sole leader of the Third Reich, as Germany had become. He was now not only the Führer of the Nazis but of all Germans.

All through Hitler's early struggles and the Nazi party's long and troubled journey to power, Göring had never wavered in his loyalty to Hitler and in his dedication to the cause. Furthermore, while Hitler supplied the vision and rhetoric, Göring had been responsible for much of the apparatus. It was he who created the Schutzstaffel, or SS, initially Hitler's personal bodyguard. Göring also created the Sicherheitsdienst, the SD, of which the Gestapo, the secret police, was a part. He was also responsible for establishing the concentration camps, initially detention centres for political prisoners. He became Speaker of the German Parliament, President of the Reichstag, Prime Minister of Prussia, President of the Prussian State Council, Reich Master of Forestry and Game, and the creator of the new German Air Force, which, under his command in 1935, became the Luftwaffe.

That same year, Hitler had given him control of Germany's synthetic oil and rubber production – a vital role given the Reich's lack of oil – and then, in 1936, he became Special Commissioner for the Four-Year Plan, over and above the Economics Minister, Hjalmar Schacht. His brief was to completely overhaul the German economy, to continue rearmament, oversee the stockpiling of resources, reduce unemployment, improve agricultural production, develop public works and stimulate other areas of production and industry.

This was a gargantuan undertaking and yet by surrounding himself with leading industrialists and bankers and by using his abundant charm, he concluded a number of bilateral deals in Yugoslavia, Sweden, Romania, Turkey, Spain and Finland, enabling Germany to build up resources of vital minerals such as tungsten, oil, nickel and iron ore, all of which were vital for war production. The German economy had been already on the rise before Hitler came to power, but by 1936 it was stable enough to begin a much larger rearmament programme. Early works projects had driven up employment figures, and although Germany remained dependent on imports, by continuing to drive down consumer spending the Nazis had been able to limit consumer imports, which enabled them to continue to buy in the raw materials needed for rearmament. Hitler had also harnessed German business to his plans for military conquest by banning trade unions and promising a bright future; this meant big companies like Krupp, IG Farben and Siemens were prepared to accept IOUs guaranteed by the Reichsbank, which enabled the process to get started almost as soon as Hitler took power.

Göring took these measures a stage further with the Four-Year Plan, revolutionizing the German economy even more and running much of the process through his own private cabal of advisors and specialists brought in from his own Prussian Ministry.

There were also plenty of bribes, secret deals and favours granted, but in the process he created a vast industrial empire. Realizing iron and steel production was under-performing, he set up his own iron and steel works, absorbing many smaller companies in the Ruhr Valley, Germany's industrial heartland, as well as in Austria. His Hermann-Göring-Werke, or HGW, became one of the biggest conglomerations in Europe; what's more, HGW was never state- or Nazi-owned – rather, it remained Göring's own private concern. Furthermore, as the master of the Nazi economy, he controlled Germany's entire foreign exchange reserves, while no independent corporation could purchase any imports without his say-so.

Göring's achievements should not be belittled, even though the Führer's backing made his task unquestionably easier. That Hitler could even contemplate risking war by the summer of 1939 was, to a large extent, thanks to his right-hand man. On the other hand, making a luxury-loving morphine addict and former barnstormer overlord of the Reich's economy was a high-risk strategy to say the very least. But, then again, Hitler was an arch gambler, as the world was about to discover.

Göring was hardly risk-averse either, although he understood, perhaps better than the Führer, that Germany was still far from ready for all-out war against the world's superpowers. Taking on Poland was one thing; taking on Britain, France and the Soviet Union as well, with the USA hovering in the background, was quite another. If Poland were to be attacked and the Danzig Corridor forcibly reclaimed, then it had to be done without the risk of drawing those other nations into the conflict.

During that first weekend in August, as he cruised on *Carin II*, he repeatedly asked his intelligence chief, Beppo Schmid, 'What will the British do?' A few days later, on 7 August, he clandestinely met seven British businessmen at a remote farmhouse on the west coast of Schleswig-Holstein. His friend, Birger Dahlerus, a Swedish businessman who had persuaded Göring he could mediate with the British on behalf of Germany, had set this up. At the meeting, Göring warned the British businessmen that Germany might well still negotiate with Russia. Over lunch, he then proposed a toast to peace. The businessmen, sent with the British Foreign Office's backing, returned with an offer for Göring to meet with Chamberlain. In the days that followed, Göring and Dahlerus waited for a response. On 12 August, Göring telephoned his friend to tell him he had ordered Goebbels to go easy on the British in the press.

From the British, however, there remained only stony silence.

In Britain, as July had made way for August, the long, hot summer continued. Tuesday, 1 August 1939, was a fine, sunny day in southern England, and, in Kent, Edward Spears was visiting his old friend Winston Churchill, at Chartwell, the latter's house near Westerham. Churchill was now a parliamentary colleague on the back benches, but Spears had come to know him during the last war. At the time, in 1915, Spears had been British liaison officer to the French 10ᵉ Armée and had accompanied

Churchill, the First Lord of the Admiralty, on a tour of inspection; a friendship had been forged. Later in the war, Spears had been promoted and had become a liaison officer between the French Ministry of War and the War Office in London; although his parents were British, he had been born and brought up in Paris and not only spoke faultless French but was unsurprisingly an ardent Francophile – as was Churchill.

After lunch, Churchill took Spears upstairs to the long, bright and sunny room where he worked. From there could be seen sweeping views across the rolling and peaceful Kent countryside. Spears had asked Churchill to read through his new book about the last war, which his friend had done with a few comments, passing on his condolences at Spears having just finished a book on one war when another looked likely to be about to begin.

Churchill was worried about Britain's weakness in the air. Britain had put air power at the centre of its rearmament drive and yet, Churchill thought, the RAF was not strong enough. As it happened, Britain and Germany were virtually neck and neck in terms of aircraft production, at around 8,000 per annum, but Germany had been producing those kinds of figures for longer. At any rate, the Luftwaffe had some 2,000 front-line aircraft ready for action; the RAF had half that. Nor, he added, was the Air Force of the French strong enough – not compared with the German Luftwaffe. Materially, this was not the case; together, Britain and France could muster more planes than the Luftwaffe; operationally and tactically, however, Churchill was nearer the mark.

But both men had great faith in the French Army. Spears, especially, having spent so much time with the French in the last war, was 'very fond' of their army and shared in the martial pride of the officers he had known and worked alongside. He felt sure the current crop of young officers and men were worthy of their fathers. In a couple of weeks' time, the two men were due to meet again, but this time in Paris as guests of Général Alphonse Georges, Deputy Commander-in-Chief of the French General Staff. Georges had promised them a tour of the Maginot Line and of French defences, something Churchill had been very keen to see for himself.

The conversation moved on to the forthcoming Anglo-French military mission to Russia, about which neither felt confident. Churchill, especially, had no doubt that the Russians would willingly turn the tables on Britain and France should they consider it to their advantage to do so.

In the meantime, they could only hope that a miracle might happen in Moscow. If so, then perhaps, even now, war might be averted.

One person who did not share Churchill's and Spears's unequivocal faith in the French Army was Capitaine André Beaufre. This bright and perceptive staff officer had been too young to take part in the last war, but had seen action in Morocco in the Rif campaign, where he had been badly wounded and almost died. Recovering, he been sent to the École de Guerre, and then had taken staff jobs at General Staff headquarters as well as posts back in French North Africa. Beaufre was a dynamic young officer and deep thinker – about all military and political matters – and it bothered him greatly that the French armed services, and the Army especially, seemed to be so instinctively defensive, so bereft of ideas.

Beaufre was among those in the French mission heading for talks in Moscow. The plan was to go to London first, meet the British team, then together sail to Leningrad. None of this suggested a huge amount of urgency. It was diplomacy, and it was all part of their efforts to avert war, but no one in either party appeared to have his heart in the process.

While Feldmarschall Göring had been cruising in his yacht, Beaufre and the French team under Général Aimé Doumenc (a senior, but not very senior, commander of the French 1st Military Region) arrived in London on the boat train on 4 August. The following day, they travelled to Tilbury Docks on the River Thames and boarded the *City of Exeter*, an ageing Ellerman Lines ship used for the South Africa run but chartered by the Royal Navy especially for the trip to Leningrad. Crewed entirely by turbaned Indians, the ship was, thought Beaufre, 'a silent witness to the Empire'. With comforts Beaufre thought a little 'passé', the ship had a whiff of faded grandeur that could equally be applied to the joint mission.

Doumenc was the youngest general in the French Army but still sixty. Heading the British team was the fabulously named Admiral The Hon. Sir Reginald Aylmer Ranfurly Plunkett-Ernle-Erle-Drax, aged nearly sixty. Like Doumenc, he was a senior officer but by no means top-drawer. The senior British airman was the ruddy-faced, bushy-eyebrowed Air Vice-Marshal Sir Charles Burnett, who regaled Beaufre with tales from the Boer War. Capable and experienced though the mission undoubtedly was, it was hardly the line-up to dazzle the Russians.

As they steamed up towards the Baltic, there was the chance for the two missions to meet twice daily in what had been the children's play-room and talk shop, and work out an agreed combined text that might be put to the Russians. The rest of the time they continued their leisurely cruise east, and bonded over copious meals of curry and deck tennis tournaments.

Eventually, on 9 August, they reached Leningrad. It was eleven o'clock at night, but the sky was still light with a milky brightness. On the quay, a few scruffy bystanders and some soldiers wearing green caps looked up to the bridge of the *City of Exeter* to see twenty-six officers in full Mess kit while the Indian crew, equally spick and span, brought the ship in. 'It would be difficult,' noted Beaufre, 'to find a neater picture to sum up the difference between the two worlds which were now to confront one another.'

By the second week of August, the Italians were becoming increasingly worried, and none more so than Count Ciano. With mounting frustration and anger, he had realized they were being duped by their Axis partner over Poland. A few days earlier, Ciano had suggested to Mussolini that he meet *mano a mano* with von Ribbentrop and try to discover just what on earth was going on. He planned also to pursue Mussolini's latest idea of holding a world peace conference. The last thing Ciano wanted was for Italy to become embroiled in a war at this time. Gold reserves were already reduced to nothing after catastrophically expensive campaigns in Abyssinia, misadventures in the Spanish Civil War, and limited rearmament. Stocks of metals were low, and the military was far from ready. 'If the crisis comes,' noted Ciano, 'we shall fight if only to save our "honour". But we must avoid war.'

And so the Italian Foreign Minister had flown to Salzburg in Austria the previous evening, and from there driven up to the Obersalzberg over-looking Berchtesgaden, where Hitler and so many of the Nazi elite had mountain villas.

The talks proved deeply unsatisfactory. With the Alps looming all around them, Ciano found his German counterpart evasive and the conversation tense. It was clear, though, that Hitler and Germany were set on war. They were, thought Ciano, 'implacable'; von Ribbentrop rejected all Ciano's suggestions for compromise. 'I am certain,' he scribbled later, 'that even if the Germans were given more than they ask for they would attack just the same, because they are possessed by the demon of destruction.' He was becoming horribly aware of how little their German allies valued Italian opinions.

The following day, after a dinner at which an icy chill of distrust had descended, Ciano met Hitler, whom he found every bit as determined to wage war as von Ribbentrop. 'France and England will certainly make extremely theatrical anti-German gestures,' Hitler told him, 'but will not go to war.' The Führer spoke highly of *Il Duce* but then glazed over and stopped listening the moment Ciano started telling him about the disastrous effect war would have on the Italian people.

Incensed, Ciano flew back to Rome, where he immediately reported to Mussolini at the Palazzo Venezia, recounting what had happened and admitting his disgust with Germany, its leaders and its way of doing things. 'They have betrayed and lied to us,' he said. 'Now they are dragging us into an adventure which we have not wanted and which might compromise the regime and the country as a whole. The Italian people will shudder in horror.' He urged Mussolini to declare that Italy would not fight against Poland and to simply step away from that obligation of the Pact of Steel. At first Mussolini agreed, then changed his mind and said that honour compelled Italy to march with Germany. Ciano left him, aware that he would have to work hard over the ensuing days to turn *Il Duce*'s mind and 'arouse in him every possible anti-German reaction in any way I can'. War alongside Germany, Ciano was convinced, would spell doom for Italy. Somehow, some way, it had to be averted.

CHAPTER 3

Running Out of Time

MONDAY, 14 AUGUST 1939. In a shady corner of a restaurant in the Bois de Boulogne on the edge of Paris, Edward Spears and Winston Churchill were having lunch with the French Deputy Commander-in-Chief, Général Alphonse Georges, and his Aide-de-Camp. It being August, with much of the beau monde having deserted the capital for the holidays, the place was almost empty. It would be Georges's birthday the following day – his sixty-fourth – but despite his advancing years and now almost white and thinning hair, he seemed, Spears thought, as full of energy as ever.

Spears had been in France a week, having driven over with his wife before meeting up with Churchill, conscious this might well be his last chance for a holiday for some time. They had stayed with old friends but Spears had been disturbed by their resentment towards Britain. The shadow of war hung heavy, just as it did in England, but it was clear they felt the British were not pulling their weight and were using France as a shield in the inevitable forthcoming conflict with Germany.

It was a relief, then, to find Général Georges on such good form, apparently ready to shoulder the burden of responsibility that would inevitably fall upon him should there be war. As they ate wood strawberries soaked in white wine, Churchill grilled the general about the French defences and, in particular, the Maginot Line, the series of fortifications that ran along the eastern edge of France, where there was a shared border with Germany. What concerned him was the shoulder of the line, facing the forests and valleys of the Ardennes. Churchill pursed his mouth and gazed at the fruit on the table with a distant expression in his eye, before warning Georges it would be unwise to think the Ardennes was impassable to a modern army. 'Remember,' he said, 'that we are faced with a new weapon, armour in strength, on which the Germans are no doubt concentrating, and that forests will be particularly tempting to such forces since they will offer concealment from the air.'

Capitaine André Beaufre had reached the Polish capital on the evening of 19 August, and now, the following morning, he was hurrying to the head-quarters of the Polish General Staff and was struck by the apparent lack of concern of the Poles he saw out and about. No sandbags, no trenches being dug – rather, people just ambling about enjoying the August sunshine.

That he was there at all was because talks in Moscow had not gone well. In fact, they could hardly have got off to a worse start when they had met for first discussions on 12 August. The Russian delegation was led by Marshal Kliment Voroshilov, the Commissar for Defence and a more senior commander than either Doumenc or Drax; that he was meeting British and French delegates junior in rank and status felt like a snub.

As they had sat at a round table in the banquet room of the Spiridonovka Palace, Voroshilov had asked whether the French and British missions had written authority to negotiate on all military matters. Doumenc announced that he did, but Drax, shifting awkwardly and breaking out into uncontrollable coughing, was forced to admit that he did not; whether it was embarrassment or the thick cigarette smoke that caused the spluttering was not clear. At any rate, Voroshilov was far from amused. Matters plunged further downhill when Drax confessed the British only had a mere four infantry divisions – around 60,000 men – to contribute to any future military alliance. For the Soviets, who were well aware that the Germans had nigh on a hundred divisions, this was a risibly small contribution.

A further and bigger stumbling block, however, had been over the passage of Soviet troops through Poland. On 14 August, Voroshilov had asked point-blank whether they had secured permission from the Poles on this matter before beginning these talks; Doumenc and Drax had been forced to admit they had not. It was for this reason that Beaufre had been put on a train and urgently sent to Warsaw, reaching the Polish capital on the evening of the 18th. His mission was to find out whether there were any circumstances in which Russian forces would be allowed to pass through Poland.

Reaching the Polish General Staff headquarters, he was ushered in to see General Stachiewicz. 'I understand your point of view perfectly,' the Polish general told him. 'But I ask you also to understand ours. We know the Russians better than you do; they are a dishonest people whose word is not to be relied upon by us or anyone else, and it is quite useless to ask us to even contemplate a proposition of this nature.' Beaufre hung around another day, but, despite the best efforts of the French embassy staff, the answer remained steadfastly the same: 'With the Germans we risk the loss of our liberty, but with the Russians we lose our soul.'

The next day, Monday, 21 August, Beaufre took a train to Riga, from where he planned to catch a flight to Moscow. It was another beautiful sunny day. On the train were families heading on holiday. From the window he watched bathers splashing in the rivers. All looked so happy, so carefree; Beaufre could feel nothing but deep sadness.

He reached Moscow later that evening, just as a telegram from Édouard Daladier, the Prime Minister, reached the French mission instructing them to lie about the Poles' resolute stance. But, by then, it was too late in any case, because that night the British and French mission received a bombshell. The Russians, it was reported in *Pravda*, the Soviet news-paper, were about to sign an altogether different agreement – a non-aggression pact with Nazi Germany.

That very same evening, Monday, 21 August, the German Führer, Adolf Hitler, was holding court at the Berghof, his mountain retreat on the Obersalzberg, in the Bavarian Alps. During supper, the 34-year-old Albert Speer watched as the Führer was handed a note. Reading it swiftly, Hitler stared momentarily into space, flushed, then banged a fist on the table so hard that the glasses shook. Then, with a voice tremulous with excitement, said, 'I have them! I have them!' A few moments later, having regained his control, he continued eating. No one else dared say a word, least of all Speer. A trusted member of Hitler's inner circle, Speer was the Führer's chief architect, responsible for the enormous parade grounds at Nuremberg and also the vast new 146-metre-long Reich Chancellery in the heart of Berlin. He had also drawn up plans to rebuild Berlin which included a three-mile-long grand boulevard and a huge 'Great Hall' over 200 metres high and capable of holding 180,000. Speer, like Hitler, preferred to think big.

This was one of the Führer's chief attractions as far as Speer was concerned. He assumed that the Führer's ultimate goal was world domination, and Speer could think of nothing better; it was the whole point of his buildings, which, to his mind, would have looked grotesque if Hitler were not to spread the wings of Nazi Germany. 'All I wanted,' he said, 'was for this great man to dominate the globe.'

The next stage in Hitler's planned expansion of territory was finally revealed after supper, when the Führer called his guests together and announced the non-aggression pact with Russia was about to be concluded. Speer was stunned. 'To see the names of Hitler and Stalin linked in friendship,' he noted, 'was the most staggering, the most exciting, turn of events I could have imagined.'

Having left Churchill and Général Georges, Edward Spears and his wife continued their holiday, staying with friends in a chateau in south-west France. Once again, he had found the atmosphere in France heavy with apprehension. His friends felt the world had gone mad. What on earth was that lunatic house-painter Hitler thinking of? And why, if Britain and France were intending to challenge him over Poland, had they not rearmed in line with Germany? That Britain and France together had more tanks, men and artillery pieces, many more ships and only fractionally fewer aircraft would have stunned most of Spears's French friends. These well-educated and intelligent *amis* were also incredulous that both France and Britain should risk war over Poland. After all, they pointed out, it had been bad enough trying to defend France last time around, so why do so for Poland? That seemed crazy!

Spears's own special prayer was that nothing would happen to spoil his holiday, which he had been looking forward to all year. His prayers, however, were in vain. That morning, 22 August, news of the impending Soviet–German pact was announced around the world. 'This is very bad news, isn't it?' Spears's host had asked. He could only agree that it was. Later that day, word reached him that Parliament had been recalled for a special session two days later. The Spearses would have to abandon their holiday and head back to England just as fast as they could.

Edward Spears and his wife were not the only two people forced to interrupt their holiday. That same day, men throughout Britain and France found themselves being mobilized into service. Bill Cheall, three days shy of his twenty-second birthday and on a camping holiday near

Crediton in Devon, heard the news in an announcement on the wireless. All those in the Territorial Army were to report to their headquarters without delay. He had joined the 6th Battalion, The Green Howards, its Territorial battalion, back in April when it had been announced there would be a doubling of the TA force. At the time, Cheall had been working in the family grocery business in Middlesbrough, but realizing war was most likely just around the corner and that he would be called up at some point, he decided to join up right away, telling himself it was better to enlist on his own terms rather than waiting to be ordered to do so.

Life in the Territorials meant weekly sessions in the drill hall at Lytton Street in Middlesbrough and annual camp near Morecambe Bay earlier in August. Drill, route marches, rifle practice – that made up the bulk of his training. The rest of the time, he continued as before, working in the family business.

The holiday to Devon, however, had been a big adventure. Bill had never been so far south, and he and his mates had driven the long journey down in his cherished Morris Ten. That morning, the sun had shone, larks had sung vibrantly above them and, having been out for a quick dip in the river at the bottom of the field, Bill had called in at the farm to collect eggs and milk. He'd been lying back on the grass, thinking all was well in the world, when the call to arms had been announced.

Immediately, they set to, taking down the tent, loading the car, and, soon after, speeding on their way back north to Yorkshire.

In Paris, that Tuesday, René de Chambrun had gone to work as normal, to the law office he had set up four years earlier. It being August, the city seemed empty, and that evening, on his way home, he had looked up at the cloudless sky and had felt somehow that the entire city belonged to him.

At his apartment on the Place du Palais Bourbon his wife was waiting for him. His birthday was the following day, and he immediately went into a family council to decide what they should all do to celebrate it. After a short discussion, they agreed he would take the day off and they would all motor to Deauville and have a day by the sea.

Unaware of news of the proposed Soviet–German pact, he had gone to bed happily looking forward to his birthday. Early the following morning, however, there was a knocking at the door. Chambrun hurried down to find two policemen waiting for him.

'Monsieur René de Chambrun?' asked the first, and on receiving a nod in reply drew out a summons from his leather bag informing him that, as a reserve officer, he was to report to his unit immediately.

'This time it means business,' said the second policeman.

A couple of hours later, having dusted down his uniform, packed his bag and bade farewell to his wife and all whom he loved, he was heading for the Gare de l'Est. His birthday trip would have to wait.

Tuesday, 22 August 1939. Hitler invited all his senior generals to a 'tea party' at the Berghof. They were to come in civilian clothes. While everyone wore sombre suits, Göring took the opportunity to don grey stockings, knickerbockers, white blouse and green leather jerkin, with a heavy gold dagger hanging from his side; he looked as though he'd come to a fancy dress party as Robin Hood. This comical appearance rather belied the fact that Göring had been at the heart of the diplomatic manoeuvres. With continued silence from Britain to his overtures – despite repeated and thinly veiled hints of German collusion with the Soviet Union – it had been he who had encouraged von Ribbentrop to contact Stalin; it was a move Hitler had been considering since the spring. Göring had greeted the news of the subsequent pact as triumphantly as the Führer. He was convinced, like Hitler, that Britain and France would not now interfere.

With his generals before him, Hitler outlined his plans for war with Poland. It was, he told them, better to test German arms now. The situation with the Danzig Corridor had become intolerable; German prestige was at stake, and it was almost certain that the West would not uphold its pledge of war. Of course there was a risk, but it was one he was prepared to take, and with iron resolve. 'We are faced,' he told them, with his usual black or white world-view, 'with the harsh alternatives of striking or of certain annihilation sooner or later.' The only choice remaining was to invade and to crush Poland. 'Act brutally,' he told them. 'The wholesale destruction of Poland is the military objective.'

Hitler was never one to use one word when ten would do, and this speech lasted more than two hours. As one of the senior officers summoned to the Berghof, Oberst Walter Warlimont was among those listening with a sinking heart. Warlimont was Acting Chief of Operations at the Oberkommando der Wehrmacht, or OKW, the Combined Staff of the Army, Navy and Air Force, and since the spring had been trying to counter Hitler's plans, which he was convinced would plunge Germany into a war that ultimately they could not win. The 44-year-old Warlimont was bright, well-educated and with an incisive intellect, and, unlike most of the German senior staff, had not only studied English in Britain, but had also been to the United States before the Crash to study American methods of industrial mobilization, an experience that had impressed him deeply. Then, in 1936, he had been sent to Spain as military attaché to General Franco. Combined with his experience as a gunner in the First World War, he was in a unique position at the OKW in having both active military experience and a realistic world-view.

Needless to say, his attempts, and those of the Operations Staff, to dissuade Hitler from the course on which he was set had failed dismally. His immediate boss was General Wilhelm Keitel, who was rarely prepared to stand up to Hitler, which was precisely why he'd been appointed. Back in January 1938, Keitel had been described to the Führer as little more than an office manager. 'That's exactly the man I'm looking for,' Hitler had replied. A month later, Hitler had scrapped the War Office, made himself Commander-in-Chief of the Wehrmacht and created the Oberkommando der Wehrmacht instead. This new establishment was the world's first ever combined services operations organization and, on the face of it, a good idea. But Hitler liked to rule by creating rival and parallel organizations; the OKW had never been given any executive power and where it stood in relation to the Army's Oberkommando des Heeres (OKH), for example, was not clear.

Warlimont, as Acting Chief of Operations, had early in the summer drawn up plans demonstrating that Germany could not hope to keep pace with the armaments potential of the Western democracies – which he had witnessed first hand – but Keitel had flatly refused to put this to Hitler. Next, Warlimont and his staff had suggested a series of summer war games in preparation for possible conflict not only with Poland, but also Britain and France. Again, Keitel had demurred. As the summer months had passed, with no word reaching the OKW on just how, when and if an attack on Poland might be launched, Warlimont and his staff found themselves existing in Berlin in a rather uneasy vacuum. Only as July gave way to August had it become clear that a possible advance into Poland was imminent and plans stepped up accordingly.

Now, at last, the waiting game appeared to be over. It was clear to Warlimont that the main purpose of Hitler's speech was to convince his generals of the rightness of his decision, and assure them Britain and France would keep out. The Führer's confidence was based on a number of factors, not least his experiences back in March when German troops had marched into Czechoslovakia unopposed. He had been braced then for a more dramatic response from the Western democracies, and yet he had got away with it. He had been getting away with it for years; not a shot fired as his troops had reclaimed one chunk of territory after another: first the Rhineland, then Austria, then the Sudetenland of Czechoslovakia and then the remainder of the country. The rest of the world had stood by and watched; it stood to reason an attack on Poland would be treated in the same way despite the threats, and even more so now a pact had been signed with Stalin.

Because of his staggering lack of geo-political understanding, because he had a rampant ego, and because such was the adulation in which most Germans held him, and the sycophancy of his inner circle, Hitler had begun to believe his 'will' alone made him invincible. And, like most megalomaniacs, he could rarely, if ever, see any point of view other than his own. To his mind, it made no sense that France and Britain would risk war over Poland. Therefore they would not.

Also listening had been the 33-year-old Hauptmann Gerhard Engel, who was Hitler's Army Adjutant. Engel thought the Führer had seemed calm and objective, but it was clear to him that the generals had not been convinced. 'Grave' was what Engel thought them. 'Not just over Poland,' he scrawled in his diary, 'but what will follow. They are expecting definite consequences with France and Britain.'

The next day, Hitler told his commanders the invasion of Poland would begin on 26 August, in just three days' time. For Warlimont, and all the other service staffs, this was ridiculous – three days! It was no time at all and flew in the face of all accepted military practice. It was one of the many problems thrown up by having a Commander-in-Chief who had promoted himself to the top job from the rank of corporal, and with no military experience or staff training in between.

Later that evening, Wednesday, 23 August 1939, Albert Speer joined the Führer out on the terrace that led from the main drawing room at the Berghof. From the veranda, the view out across the Untersberg was stunning. Curiously, that night the aurora borealis, the Northern Lights, was showing over the Alps. The sky was alive with a dazzling array of shimmering lights while a shroud of deep red was now cast across the

Untersberg and the valley between. Hitler marvelled at the sight, but Speer noticed the same red light bathed their hands and faces, and, as if all minds were now filled with the same thought, the small gathering suddenly became pensive.

Hitler turned to one of his military adjutants. 'Looks like a great deal of blood. This time we won't bring it off without violence.'

He could not have been more right. For all his talk of Britain and France bluffing, the one who was really doing so was Hitler. The carefully orchestrated parades, the even more carefully managed showreels of German troops and tanks and skies thick with aircraft, were, to a very large extent, a projection of military might rather than representative of the reality. Germany was by no means ready for all-out war. It did not have enough tanks, vehicles or trained soldiers, and certainly not enough natural resources, to carry out anything more than a short, sharp campaign against a massively inferior enemy: Germany possessed little iron ore, no oil, no copper, tungsten, bauxite or rubber, and, crucially, did not have enough land, sufficiently farmed, to fulfil the food requirements of both the population and a massive military. Few, if any, nations had access to all the resources needed for war-making, but, unlike Britain and France, Germany's merchant fleet was small and access to global resources was limited.

Meanwhile, for all the concerns of men like Churchill or Général Georges, the disparity in air power was not as great as they feared. In Britain, aircraft production was almost on a par with that of Germany; monthly British output was 662 aircraft, compared with 691 in Germany. France was one of the leading powers in the world and had a sizeable standing army, with the administration and infrastructure in place to mobilize more than a hundred divisions in a matter of days should it come to war.

It was true Britain's army was small by comparison, but it was growing rapidly. Within the Royal Navy and Air Force, rearmament had been going on since 1935, and Britain now had the world's first fully co-ordinated air defence system. It also had the world's largest Navy by some margin and stood at the centre of the biggest global trading network the world had ever seen. It was rich – the richest country in Europe, even after the depression – had the kind of access to resources Germany could only dream of, and it was, and had been for some time, the world's largest armaments exporter. With its Empire and Dominions, it also had access to an unprecedented amount of manpower. In almost every way, Britain was better equipped for a major conflict than Germany.

The gloomy mood in Britain and France that last summer before war was because most knew they were not bluffing Hitler. If Germany invaded Poland, that would mean war; there was to be no more acquiescing to a megalomaniacal despot, who had repeatedly shown he could not be trusted in any way. That was profoundly and deeply depressing. No wonder the mood had been sombre, yet although they would go to war reluctantly, Britain, especially, could do so with a fair degree of confidence.

As Hitler stood on his balcony that night of 23 August, his hands bathed in red, his mind was more determined than ever. Poland would be invaded.

It was to be one of the most catastrophic decisions ever made.

CHAPTER 4

The Point of No Return

'THE DAY IS charged with electricity and full of threats,' noted Count Ciano on 23 August. Since his return from Salzburg, the Duce had been vacillating badly. One minute he was bellicose and all for entering the fray alongside Hitler, the next he appeared persuaded that war would be disastrous for Italy. In truth, much depended on whom the dictator spoke to. If it was Generale Alberto Pariani, the Under-Secretary for War, he was all for fighting; if it was Ciano, or Maresciallo – Marshal – Pietro Badoglio, the Chief of the General Staff, he became more cautious.

That evening, as Hitler had stood on the balcony at the Berghof, Mussolini had had one of his talks with Pariani. The upshot was predictable.

'This evening the Duce is favourable to war,' wrote Ciano. 'He talks of armies and attacks. He received Pariani who gave him good news of the condition of the army. Pariani is a traitor and a liar.'

It was a curious feature of Mussolini's dictatorship that he was never quite as powerful as he would have liked, and certainly with none of the absolute power of his Axis colleague, Hitler. Despite seventeen years of Fascism, Italy was still a monarchy, and ultimate authority belonged to the King, Vittorio Emanuele III, and to the senior generals of the Regio Esercito, the Royal Army. Collectively, these men were quite powerful enough to have thrown out both Mussolini and Fascism at any time should they have chosen to do so.

So it was fortunate for Ciano that the following day, 24 August, he had the opportunity to speak with the King, who, he knew, was both hostile to the Germans and vehemently opposed to war. The King was staying at Sant'Anna di Valdieri, an Alpine resort in Piedmont on the French border, so yet again Ciano left Rome and headed north for this latest audience.

The diminutive King Vittorio Emanuele, who had acceded to his throne in 1900 and presided over Italy's disastrous involvement in the last war, could not have been more withering about the state of the armed forces, and the Army in particular. The officers, he told Ciano, were not fit for purpose, their weapons old and obsolete, and during his thirty-two recent inspections of various units and border defences he was appalled by the sad state of preparedness. If the French chose to march into Italy, he was convinced they could at any time. What's more, the Italian 'peasants' all curse the 'damn Germans'. 'We must, therefore, in his opinion,' noted Ciano, 'await events and do nothing.'

Meanwhile Neville Henderson, the British Ambassador, had visited Hitler at the Berghof and handed him a letter from Neville Chamberlain. 'No greater mistake could be made,' Chamberlain warned, if Germany believed the German–Soviet pact made any difference to Britain's obligation to Poland. But he also stated that in his mind, 'war between our two peoples would be the greatest calamity that could occur'. It was not too late, he wrote, to resolve the issues between Germany and Poland by negotiation, not force.

But of course it was too late. Hitler had made up his mind. The die had been cast, his Rubicon crossed.

The Führer was in a highly charged mood – a dangerous blend of high excitement, nerves and resolve. He was, he had told his generals, now fifty. An assassin might claim him at any time. Only he had the strength of will to lead Germany to victory. The attack on Poland had to be now, while he was fit and alive and well. He was convincing himself of the rightness of his course as much as the generals.

No letter from Chamberlain was going to make him change his mind, but Britain's continued pressure and insistence on honouring its pledge to Poland was making him seethe. He berated Henderson, partly because of his own heightened mood and partly because giving verbal tongue-lashings had always been a tried-and-tested means of getting what he wanted. His aim was to browbeat Henderson and the British into backing down. Britain's aggressive stance, he told the Ambassador, was making negotiation impossible. Germany had continually offered friendship and that offer had been thrown back in Germany's face – forcing it to seek an alliance with Russia. The British Government, he told him, preferred anything to co-operation with Germany; if war came, it would be a life-and-death struggle, and Britain would have more to lose.

What Hitler simply could not understand was that both Britain and France found him and his regime utterly repellent. The vast majority of British people viewed totalitarianism as repugnant, and while the British Union of Fascists had gained a certain amount of ground during the 1930s, it had remained a minority movement. Certainly, the instruments of the Nazis – the SS, the secret police, the sinister storm troopers and swastikas – chilled most British people to the core. Then there was Nazi anti-Semitism. Many in Britain and even more in France had a wariness of Judaism, but persecuting a particular religious group was not considered the action of civilized people. Furthermore, the violence towards and ostracization of Jews in the Third Reich had truly shocked many British citizens. 'Kristallnacht', as the pogrom of the night of 9–10 November 1938 had come to be known, had appalled people throughout the free world. 'No foreign propagandist bent upon blackening Germany before the world,' noted *The Times* of London on 11 November 1938, 'could outdo the tale of burnings and beatings, of blackguardly assaults on defenceless and innocent people, which disgraced that country yesterday.'

All these factors combined to make it very hard for Britain – and France – to cosy up to Germany in any way. Nevertheless, however, Britain was not standing up to Hitler now to defend the Jews; rather, it was doing so because it feared that Hitler had designs not just on the German-speaking corners of Europe, but the entire world. Where would his ambitions end if not checked now? Defending Poland was about maintaining the balance of power.

By the 24th, Hitler and his entourage were back in Berlin, at the Reich Chancellery built by Speer the previous year. Also there, returned from Moscow, was von Ribbentrop, who now revealed that a secret part of the pact had been that the Red Army invade Poland from the east a short time after Germany's attack from the west. Poland was to be divided. This news stunned Göring. He was beginning to feel increasingly on edge. It was essential, he firmly believed, to keep Britain categorically out of the war and he had finally by now made direct contact with the British Secret Service; it seemed a meeting with Chamberlain might happen after all. At this point, however, Hitler refused to let him go. Later that day, he saw his Swedish friend, Birger Dahlerus, who was now talking about arranging a four-power conference between Britain, France, Germany and Italy. Göring asked Dahlerus to let Chamberlain know about this latest revelation concerning the German–Soviet pact.

On the 25th, Hitler made an offer to Britain, repeated by Göring through Dahlerus. If Britain kept out of Germany's squabble with Poland, then the Reich would be prepared to enter an agreement in which it would safeguard the British Empire and even guarantee German assistance should it be required. This Hitler told Henderson in person at the Reich Chancellery at 1.30 p.m. At 3.02 p.m., he ordered Case WHITE, the invasion of Poland, to begin at dawn the following morning.

The 'offer' was clearly no more than a simple bribe, a carrot dangled to encourage Britain to take a step back. Hitler remained convinced, outwardly at any rate, that Britain was still bluffing. This was where his lack of geo-political understanding, his myopic world-view, skewed his judgement. The point had been reached where neither Britain nor France could possibly stand by if Germany invaded Poland; to do so would be to abandon all political and moral authority, not just in Europe but in the world. They could not allow such a loss of influence and prestige.

That same day, Friday, 25 August, almost as soon as the order for Case WHITE had been issued, Göring received intelligence that suggested the attempt to cow the British had failed. As well as his many state offices, command of the Luftwaffe and control of the HG Works, Göring also had his own private intelligence service, the Forschungsamt. This was an extensive and highly efficient monitoring service of radio, wireless and telephone communications, involving deciphering as well as phone-tapping. Among those regularly being deciphered and tapped were Dahlerus, Neville Henderson, Monsieur Coulondre, the French Ambassador, and Attolico, the Italian Ambassador. Traffic from Ciano's Palazzo Chigi was also regularly being intercepted.

Incredibly, Hitler both was aware of its existence and did nothing to make Göring hand over control to the SS or the Abwehr, the Wehrmacht's secret intelligence service, or any other Nazi apparatus. As a consequence, Göring was not only able to keep one step ahead of many of his rivals within the party, but also to control vital intelligence that he could then pass on to the Führer. Thus it was that his Forschungsamt heard Neville

Henderson telephone London saying the German offer was nothing more than an attempt to drive a wedge between Britain and Poland, when earlier, to Hitler, he had told the Führer he thought it would be worth him flying personally to London to present the proposal to the British government. In other words, to Hitler, Henderson had hinted there might be some ground for manoeuvre, whereas on the telephone he had made it clear he thought the opposite.

Then, at 5 p.m., the Forschungsamt detected Count Ciano dictating a formal note warning that Italy would not fight. Half an hour later, the French Ambassador delivered a message to Hitler insisting on France's determination to fight for Poland. Half an hour after that, at 6 p.m., the British announced they had ratified their alliance with Poland.

At this, even Hitler briefly lost his nerve. The invasion was still due to begin the following morning, but the Führer now telephoned Keitel and ordered him to stop everything.

'Is this just temporary?' Göring asked Hitler.

'Yes,' he replied. 'Just for four or five days until we can eliminate British intervention.'

'Do you think four or five days will make any difference?' Göring responded.

Friday, 25 August, had been a fraught day for Ciano. In the morning, he had been warned that *Il Duce* was still in a furiously warlike mood and indeed this was how he found him on his arrival at the Palazzo Venezia. With the King's opinions to help him, Ciano gradually talked Mussolini out of his latest belligerent stance and suggested he send Hitler a communiqué announcing Italian non-intervention until Italy was better prepared for war.

With this agreed, Ciano left happy that he had at last got his way. However, no sooner had he reached his office at the Palazzo Chigi, some six hundred metres away down the Via Corso, than Mussolini called him back, having yet again changed his mind. 'He fears the bitter judgement of the Germans,' Ciano scrawled wearily, 'and wants to intervene at once. It is useless to struggle.'

At 2 p.m., a message for Mussolini from Hitler arrived, hinting at imminent action against Poland and asking for Italian 'understanding'. Ciano then used this latter phrase as a pretext to persuade Mussolini to reply stating categorically that Italy was not ready for war. It was this that was picked up as it had been written by the Forschungsamt.

This news and the subsequent formal communiqué from Mussolini had taken some of the puff out of Hitler's sails, and Hauptmann Engel thought the Führer seemed suddenly totally downcast and at a loss as to what to do, even though this did nothing to divert him from the course on which he was set. He did not blame Mussolini, but rather what he believed to be the Anglophile Italian aristocracy, and not least upper-crust playboys like Ciano. The implication was clear, though, and Mussolini would have wept with shame to hear it: a proper dictator would have thrown out the King and silenced any dissenting voices.

Hitler's response was to ask Italy for a shopping list of what they needed in order to come into the war. This reached Rome by 9.30 p.m.

The Germans were given this list the following day, and it included more than 18,000 tons of coal, steel, oil, nickel, tungsten and other raw materials, all of which were vital ingredients of modern war and none of which Italy could produce itself. As Ciano admitted with thinly disguised glee, this gargantuan figure would require no fewer than 17,000 train carriages to ship them.

The ploy worked exactly as Ciano had hoped. The Germans, in reply, offered a fraction of the material asked. They understood the Italian position and released them from their obligation to fight by their side. For the time being, at any rate, Italy could keep out of the war that was about to erupt. It was a blow for Mussolini's damaged pride, but as far as Ciano was concerned, Italy had been saved from tragedy.

In some ways it is odd that Hitler should have been so alarmed by Italy's stance. Italy was clearly not ready for war and unquestionably would have been more of a hindrance than a help. Perhaps, though, he liked the idea of standing shoulder to shoulder rather than Germany going it alone; perhaps, too, the sheer scale of the Italian demands both shocked and alarmed him. The German High Command had known Italy was militarily weak, but perhaps not quite as weak as was the reality. On the other hand, the Germans had hardly behaved like allies in recent months; rather, they had played a game of smoke and mirrors, flagrantly lying and pulling the wool over Italy's eyes, and showing scant regard or respect for their Axis partner. It hardly augured well for the future.

Oberst Warlimont had been hugely relieved to learn that Case WHITE had been called off, although on being summoned by Keitel to the Reich Chancellery the following day, 26 August, he was told not to start celebrating; the invasion had not been cancelled, just delayed. Although this meant there would still be war, at least it gave the Wehrmacht a bit more time to mobilize.

Two days later, Henderson returned to Berlin with Britain's formal response to Hitler's offer, which he handed to the Führer at 10.30 p.m. that night, Monday, 28 August. The letter expressed the desire to 'make friendship' and a 'lasting understanding' with Germany, although it insisted a settlement be reached with Poland first. The Poles, wrote the British, had expressed a willingness to open negotiations. In turn, on the 29th, Hitler accepted the suggestion and proposed that a Polish negotiator be sent the next day, 30 August.

No Polish emissary arrived that day, however. Instead, German proposals for these possible talks grew increasingly demanding, while von Ribbentrop in his conversations with Henderson became more heated. The Poles, meanwhile, promised a reply by noon on the 31st.

By this time, it was too late; in fact, Hitler had never intended anything other than a delay. He had always been a gambler and had made his mind up days before. His course had been set; there could be no deviation. Invading Poland was a gamble he was going to take, whether Britain and France declared war or not.

At 12.40 p.m. on Thursday, 31 August, Hitler issued his 'Directive No. 1 for the Conduct of War'. Case WHITE, the German plan for the invasion of Poland, was to begin at dawn the following day, Friday, 1 September 1939.

Propaganda had been a key component of Nazi politics from the outset, and while there were some who had not been persuaded, it had unquestionably been hugely effective, not just within the Reich but around the world too. To a large degree, this was due to Dr Josef Goebbels, the Reich Minister for Popular Enlightenment and Propaganda, and Gauleiter – administrative leader, an old Frankish term that had been resurrected by the Nazis – of Berlin. A former failed journalist and one of the first Nazis, he was utterly devoted to Hitler, so much so he had even given up an affair with a Czech film star with whom he was deeply in love because the Führer asked him to. The son of a shop assistant, Goebbels was highly intelligent and despite those humble beginnings had attended several universities and gained a doctorate. Marriage to Magda Quant, a society divorcee, gave him the kind of money and status he needed to help him climb up the Nazi ladder. He had become Propaganda Minister in 1933, the year Hitler became Chancellor, and had immediately announced that his prime goal was to achieve the 'mobilisation of mind and spirit' of the German people. 'We did not lose the war because our artillery gave out,' he said of defeat in 1918, 'but because the weapons of our minds did not fire.'

In many ways, Goebbels was as responsible for Hitler's position as Hitler was himself. It was Goebbels who had largely shaped the Nazis' public image. It was he who had insisted on draping swastikas – the bigger the better – from as many places as possible; it was he who taught Hitler how to whip a crowd into a frenzy; it was also Goebbels who had elevated Hitler into a demigod in the eyes of many. He knew all about manipulation theories and orchestrated heavy-handed mob violence, and in the 1933 election created the 'Hitler over Germany' campaign; it was the first time aircraft had been used to take a candidate around a country in an effort to reach more people. It worked spectacularly well.

With the Nazis in power, Goebbels had also done much to whip up the virulent anti-Semitism that lay at the heart of Nazi ideology and had helped turn Nazism into a form of surrogate religion, in which harking back to a 'purer' Aryan past worked to bind the people both together and behind the party and, more importantly, the leader. Goebbels's influence – his genius – should never be underestimated.

Yet despite his position, and despite the job title, Goebbels did not have complete control over propaganda. Hitler's divide-and-rule style of leadership was to encourage jealousy and back-stabbing among his acolytes, so von Ribbentrop's office was given foreign propaganda and the OKW any military reporting. Further muddying the waters was Otto Dietrich, the Reich Press Chief, and although on paper subordinate to Goebbels, he was still part of Hitler's inner circle.

Even so, Goebbels was the top dog despite these checks on his power and had masterminded a cunning way of getting the prescribed message across. Key to this was repetition and radio. There were many innovations of the 1930s in which Germany lagged behind other leading countries in the world, but the embracing of radio sets was not one of them. Goebbels had realized that radio was the ideal way to get his message across and so was instrumental in making sure radio sets were both cheap and accessible. First up into the mass market was the *Volksempfänger* – the 'People's Receiver'. Using the word 'Volk' was another Nazi trick, which suggested togetherness rather than exclusivity. This was later followed by the *DKE*, or *Deutsche Kleinempfänger*, the 'German Little Receiver', which, as its name implied, was both pioneeringly small and also affordable. The net result was that by 1939 almost 70 per cent of the population owned radios. For those remaining 30 per cent still without one, however, there were communal listening points: in cafés, bars, restaurants, the stairwells of blocks of flats, the corners of town squares with accompanying loud speakers. Radio coverage in Germany was more dense than anywhere else in the world. Finally, to really ram home the message, there were radio wardens to coax people into listening to key speeches and programmes, all of which were mixed in between unceasing light music, martial marches, Wagner and popular entertainment. 'Radio must reach all,' claimed Hans Fritzsche, the Nazis' chief radio commentator, 'or it will reach none.'

Alongside radio, there were news films shown at every cinema and movies that equally promoted Nazi ideology: Jews were played as villainous, duplicitous and money-grabbing, the heroes were tall, broad, blond and fulfilling the Aryan ideal. There were documentaries too, like Leni Riefenstahl's *Triumph of the Will*, about the 1934 Nazi rally at Nuremberg. Cinema goers had grown massively through the 1930s, from 250,000 in 1933 to three times that number by 1939.

Finally, there were state-controlled newspapers. Every city had one and there were national ones too, not least the principal party mouthpiece, the *Völkischer Beobachter*, the 'People's Observer'. One of Goebbels's key instructions to journalists was to make the writing more readable, more conversational and less dry. Again, it was a policy that worked a treat: the *Völkischer Beobachter* had climbed from a circulation of 116,000 in 1932, to almost a million by 1939. In little more than a year's time it would become the first newspaper in Germany to pass a daily circulation of over a million.

The result was that very few in Nazi Germany could avoid hearing the oft-repeated propaganda put about by Goebbels and his carefully orchestrated team at the Propaganda Ministry.

In the run-up to the launch of Case WHITE, this was broadly very effective. Most people believed what was being put across both on radio and in the state-controlled press, namely that the Poles were committing all kinds of atrocities on former Prussians living in Poland, that they were war-mongering and using threatening language, and that not only was the Danzig Corridor rightfully part of Germany, but it was the duty of the Reich to defend those subjects living there.

Heinz Knocke, eighteen years old, was from Hameln in central Germany and typical of many of his age. He had absolute faith in the Führer and the rightness of the German cause. Wanting to join the Luftwaffe as a pilot, he had had his preliminary examinations and was eager that with war imminent his call-up would be accelerated. 'The Polish atrocities against the German minority make horrible reading today,' he scribbled in his diary on 31 August. 'Thousands are being massacred daily in territory which had once been part of Germany.' It was absolute nonsense.

Oberleutnant Hajo Herrmann, a 24-year-old pilot with the bomber group III/KG4, also thought the Poles had brought war upon themselves. As far as he was concerned, the Danzig issue was one of principle. It had been German before 1919, was still inhabited mostly by Germans, and since the Poles had rejected any peaceful solution, what did they expect? 'The anger that I felt inside at their unreasonableness,' he noted, 'matched my sacred conviction: that of German rightness.' Others, like another eighteen-year-old, Martin Pöppel, a young *Gefreiter* in 1. Fallschirmjägerregiment, were simply hugely excited at the sudden turn of events. A paratrooper in the Luftwaffe, he was less worried about the rights of Germans in Danzig and more concerned about seeing some action before it was all over.

Such was the callowness of youth, but there were many who did not share this bravado. 'September 1, 1939, was no day of jubilation for us,' said Oberleutnant zur See Erich Topp, then a 26-year-old First Watch Officer (1WO) on the U-boat *U-46*. 'We were aware of our weaknesses from the beginning, notably in the Navy. Everyone knew it would be a long war.'

For Oberleutnant Hans von Luck, an officer in 7. Armoured Reconnaissance Regiment, the escalating situation had brought a sudden recall from leave just a few days earlier. He had found everyone at the garrison in Bad Kissingen near Schweinfurt in high spirits. Neither he nor his friends believed a word of Goebbels's propaganda about the Poles, but they did believe Danzig and the corridor should be part of Germany once more. 'We were not hungry for war,' von Luck noted, 'but we did not believe the British and French would come to Poland's defence.' How wrong he was.

CHAPTER 5

War Declared

IN ENGLAND, it had been a gloriously hot last week of August, and the first day of September had been every bit as lovely. At Hove, on the south coast, it was the Friday of the Brighton and Hove cricket week, and the Sussex team were playing host to Yorkshire, already crowned county champions for a record-breaking seventh time that decade.

The match was also a benefit game for Jim Parks, a stalwart of the Sussex side and an England player too, and while other games around the country had already been cancelled because of the imminent out-break of war, the fact that it was a cricket festival week and a benefit match encouraged both sides to keep playing and finish off the three-day game. The tension in the air that day was palpable. Some felt they shouldn't really be playing sport at a time like this, and yet alongside that was a very keen sense that this could be the last match for a very long time. Sussex reached 387 in their first innings, and Yorkshire 393, when, after lunch on that Friday, the hosts began batting again. There had been a thunder-storm on the Wednesday night, but now the sun was blazing hot, baking the wicket in what were ideal conditions for spin bowling.

Hedley Verity had proved the finest spin bowler of the past decade, playing for both Yorkshire and England and taking vast numbers of wickets. He'd twice achieved the feat of claiming all ten wickets in an innings and had taken nine seven times – an unequalled record. Still only thirty-four, he could have had a long career yet ahead of him. For the time being, however, it seemed as though it would most likely be put on hold. Not, though, before he had bowled out Sussex in their second innings.

That afternoon, as German soldiers pushed into Poland and the Luftwaffe screamed overhead, amidst the genteel calm of the Sussex county ground at Hove, Verity took seven wickets for nine runs as the hosts were bowled out for just thirty-three. Not long after, Yorkshire cantered home to an emphatic victory. If it was to be Verity's last match for a while, those were exceptional bowling figures on which to end.

Straight after the match, the Yorkshire players headed back north in the team coach, no one much mentioning the cricket, even though it had been a fine match. Outside London, they saw streams of vehicles filled with people and possessions evacuating the capital. A blackout was now in force, and so they halted for the night at Leicester. If it was war – and with the news of the invasion of Poland, it would be any moment – most of the country's cricketers would be expected to play their part; sporting heroes would not be exempt. Verity knew this but had decided to enlist anyway; he'd been thinking about it for almost a year ever since the Munich crisis and had not only spoken to Lieutenant-Colonel Arnold Shaw of The Green Howards, a local Yorkshire infantry regiment, but had also spent considerable time reading military textbooks. For Verity, it was simple. Hitler and Nazism were evil, Britain was under threat, and it was his duty to play his part.

In France that same day, mobilization continued. By law, every Frenchman, or naturalized Frenchman, was obliged to serve in the Army, Navy or Air Force unless he was unfit to do so, and that included those living in French colonies. Originally after the last war, Frenchmen were required to do their 'Colour Service' for just one year. This was the annual conscript class, normally called up in October, for all 21-year-olds. Back in 1935, as the effects on childbirth of the First World War started to take effect, this was raised to eighteen months. The following year, 1936, it had been raised to two years, and still numbers were down.

Once a conscript had seen out his Colour Service, he was then considered *en disponibilité* for a further three years. The idea was that in peacetime, all units, regiments and divisions would operate at around a third of their strength. If hostilities broke out the numbers *en disponibilité* would then be immediately called up and would bring the active armed services up to war strength. After this period of service, a Frenchman would be in the 1st Reserve for a further sixteen years. Finally, there would be a final period of seven years when they would be on the 2nd

Reserve. In theory, most people would only expect to do their service in the Colours. Provided peace held, those *en disponibilité* or in the 1st and 2nd Reserves would not expect to have to put on their uniforms again, and even in a time of crisis it might well be the case that only those reserves who had most recently served would be called up.

These were not ordinary times, however, and now all reserve officers and those *en disponibilité* had been called up, which was why men like René de Chambrun had been hastily brought back into active service with immediate effect and not even the chance to enjoy a birthday outing. By 1 September, Chambrun was a captain once more and a company commander in 162ᵉ Régiment d'Infanterie based at Amanvillers, near the border city of Metz in Lorraine and right on the Maginot Line. When he had reached the village, large groups of men had been arriving, mostly in civilian clothes, some on bicycles, others on foot. On arrival, each had been issued with a uniform and no fewer than 142 items, from ammunition pouches to steel helmets. Chambrun had seen one man, newly equipped and dressed, leaning sadly on a farmhouse door. In a voice choking with grief, he had explained that his wife of five years had been killed the day before in a threshing machine accident and that, now called up, he'd had to leave his three-year-old daughter with friends in his village – which was worryingly close to the German border. The French General Mobilization, however, made no exceptions; this man would have to do his duty, grief-stricken or not.

At Amanvillers the following day, René de Chambrun had attended Mass in a field next to the small village church. The priest, now wearing the uniform of a corporal, told the assembled officers and men, 'Remember – many things are more painful to bear than war. Slavery is one of them, and, with the help of God, let us fight so this soil will remain French forever.' Chambrun had followed his eyes to the horizon, where the menacing turrets of the Maginot Line thrust upwards out of the ground.

Barely had German troops crossed into Poland than embassies in Warsaw and Berlin began furiously transmitting communiqués to their respective governments. In Britain, the Prime Minister, Neville Chamberlain, called his cabinet together at 11.30 a.m. The previous day, the Italians had made one more final attempt to resolve the situation by calling for a world peace conference, but it was too late, and the British rejected the overture.

So, what had been threatened all summer had finally occurred;

attempts to deter Hitler had failed. 'The events against which we had fought so long and so earnestly have come upon us,' Chamberlain told his colleagues, 'but our consciences are clear and there should be no possible question now where our duty lies.' Had Chamberlain looked deep into his heart, perhaps his conscience about British abandonment of the Czechs might have been a little less clear. However, be that as it may, he was right on one point: Britain had to declare war on Germany. It was agreed a final warning would be issued to Germany to withdraw immediately, and they would also have to work out procedural details with the French, but Chamberlain's mind was clear.

The House of Commons met at 6 p.m. that evening. The moral agony of the Prime Minister was all too evident; there was no doubting he had, for the past year, acted in the hope of avoiding war, regardless of whether his judgement had been correct. But he insisted there could be no peace in Europe while Hitler and the Nazis remained in power, and in this he was unquestionably correct.

There was still no announcement, however, about just *when* Britain would declare war. Since the warning to Germany to withdraw immediately was sent that evening, it would presumably be the following day on the assumption that Germany would ignore the threat. It became clear that evening, however, that France was wobbling. The French had not rejected the Italians' offer of a peace conference outright, and Georges Bonnet, the French Foreign Minister, now called Lord Halifax, his British counterpart, to say that constitutionally they could not declare war until Parliament had met and that would not be until the evening of Saturday the 2nd, although general mobilization had been ordered. It was Général Maurice Gamelin, Chief of the General Staff, who was most nervous; he worried that German bombing might hamper mobilization and that France needed a little longer to get ready.

While the French were playing for time rather than dodging their commitments, Chamberlain and Halifax faced revolt from both the Cabinet and the House of Commons when it met late the following day, Saturday, 2 September. The Prime Minister and Foreign Secretary had been delaying only to keep a united front with the French and to give Germany a chance to withdraw – any chance of peace, however slim, was, to their mind, worth pursuing. But their colleagues did not see it that way. Edward Spears was far from alone in feeling increasingly incensed by the delay.

'Speak for England!' shouted the Conservative Leo Amery. And the Labour MP Arthur Greenwood did so, urging the Prime Minister to be decisive, to save Britain's honour. 'The moment we look like weakening,' he said, 'the dictators would know we were beaten.' Chamberlain, horrified by the hostility he had met, feared the Government might fall. The Cabinet met again at 11.30 p.m. that night. Outside, a violent thunderstorm raged. A shaken Prime Minister now accepted that, as Greenwood had urged, decisive action was needed, regardless of the French stance. It was agreed that an ultimatum would be presented to Berlin at 9 a.m. the following morning, which would expire two hours later.

Later that evening, Gwladys Cox, her husband, Ralph, and their cat, Bobby, arrived back at their flat on the top floor of Lymington Mansions in West Hampstead. For a couple of days, they had gone to Guildford to stay with Gwladys's sister, Ruth. Like many others in London, they had decided to evacuate, fearing gas attacks and other horrors. It was the threat of gas attacks that particularly troubled Gwladys – Ralph suffered badly from asthma and during the numerous Air Raid Precaution trials in August, he had been unable to cope with wearing their newly issued gas masks.

After two days in Guildford, however, they decided to return; they had been wracked by indecision ever since they had left – or, rather, abandoned – their home. They had only moved into their flat a year before and had been delighted with it. On the top floor, it had come equipped with electric plugs, a shower in the bathroom and an Ascot heater in the kitchen, so that hot water was both constant and plentiful. It had a south-facing view that caught the sun and had lovely views of London, so that they could easily see St Paul's Cathedral, Big Ben and other landmarks. In Guildford they were miserable; no matter what lay ahead, it was better to face the future from their own home with their own things.

Almost 1.5 million were leaving Britain's cities – a massed evacuation that had begun on 1 September. Although most taxis and cars were being used, the Coxes managed to find a car and driver, and reached West Hampstead at sunset. 'I shall never forget my first sight of the barrage balloons,' scribbled Gwladys in her diary. 'Hundreds of them dotted the sky and glittered silvery pink in the setting sun.'

That night, as darkness fell and once more back in Lymington

Mansions, they put up the blackout curtains for real for the first time; then, before going to bed, she switched off the light and looked over London. 'The sky was heavy with dark clouds,' she noted, 'and countless searchlights combed the heavens.' As though anticipating what was to come, the weather had then dramatically turned. Gwladys was woken in the morning to the sound of thunder. Sheet lightning flashed across the sky. She noticed all the barrage balloons, suspended high above London to prevent low-flying enemy aircraft, had gone.

Sunday, 3 September, dawned, warm and sunny. At 9 a.m., the ultimatum was issued. Two hours later there had been no response from Berlin, and Chamberlain wearily announced to the nation, after a quarter of an hour, that Britain was at war with Germany. Those at church were told by priests at the conclusion of the morning service. Later that afternoon, the French finally followed suit. Around the world, the governments of Canada, Australia and New Zealand, all British Dominions, also declared war. Two days later, so too would South Africa.

It had come to pass.

That morning, Edward Spears had joined a meeting of the Eden Group, an informal gathering of Conservative anti-appeasers led by the former Foreign Secretary, Anthony Eden. They met at a house in Queen Anne's Gate, near St James's Park. Sunlight poured in through the drawing room windows. Spears looked out at the blue sky and the trees of St James's Park, wishing not to miss a moment of sunshine or colour.

The assembled group had not only been discussing the inevitable out- break of war, but also the news that Churchill was to be brought back into the Cabinet. Spears was relieved, as they all were; Churchill would be resolute in his determination to stand up to Germany, and it was essential he was in the Cabinet. Spears, for one, believed he might well become Prime Minister. If he were to lead the country through this war, he needed to be at the centre of the Government now.

Not far away, Churchill and his wife, Clementine, had listened to Chamberlain's broadcast then heard the wail of an air raid siren droning out over London. Hurrying up to the flat roof of the house, they looked out to see what was going on. Slowly rising above the roofs and spires of London were as many as forty silvery barrage balloons. There was no sign of the enemy, but aware of the prescribed air raid drill, the

Churchills grabbed a bottle of brandy then hurried to the nearest shelter.

In an empty lecture hall of the London School of Economics, the 24-year-old Jock Colville heard the news with a sense of numbness, from which he was only awakened when he heard the same air raid drone. Colville was a young member of the Foreign Office who, that morning, had discovered he had been reassigned to the brand-new Ministry of Economic Warfare, which was being established in empty rooms at the LSE. A Cambridge graduate, he had travelled widely through Russia, Asia, Turkey and Europe after leaving university, learning German and French in the process. After attempting a career in the City, he decided it wasn't for him and so had sat exams for the Foreign Office. To his surprise and delight, he got in. He had not looked back.

Now, though, with the siren blaring, it seemed likely that aerial apocalypse was about to arrive, so he hurried to the nearest shelter with several of his colleagues and played bridge until the all-clear sounded. They were back at their desks by lunchtime, but with nothing to do and with no bombs falling after all, he decided to head home, reflecting that Britain seemed hardly ready for Armageddon.

Churchill, meanwhile, had hurried to the House of Commons, where MPs were due to meet at noon. Listening to Chamberlain's statement on the declaration of war, Churchill suddenly felt a serenity of mind descend over him, then a sense of uplifted excitement that Britain was at last standing firm. Afterwards, the Prime Minister asked to see him. Not only did he want to offer him a place in the War Cabinet, but also the post of First Lord of the Admiralty. It was the position Churchill had held twenty-five years earlier when Britain had last gone to war.

In Britain, uncertainty filled the air. Mobilization was in full swing, over 1.5 million children were still being evacuated from Britain's cities, and yet, despite the air raid siren sounding only twenty minutes after the declaration of war, the aerial onslaught that many had predicted and feared had not yet materialized; on the face of it, peacetime and wartime Britain did not seem so very different. Reaching home, Jock Colville met his brother, Philip, who was awaiting his call-up to the Grenadier Guards, and together they drove up to Trent Park in north London, owned by a friend. 'It had an excellent private twelve-hole golf course,' noted Colville, 'on which my brother and I peacefully spent the first afternoon of war.'

In France the mood was more palpably tense. Britain was – had its population stopped to think about it – still a long way from German airfields and so unlikely to be receiving massed bomber formations that first day of war. In any case, the Luftwaffe was busy destroying the Polish Air Force; fears of its size and strength had been greatly exaggerated. Moreover, France and Germany shared a border, and the French had experienced, first hand, just a generation before, the agony of being invaded and the country carved up.

In Paris, many were devastated, including Andrée Griotteray, nineteen years old, who worked in the passport and ID department at the police headquarters. 'That's it,' she wrote starkly in her diary. 'War has been declared.' She had enjoyed a happy and carefree childhood with her French father, Edmond, and her Belgian mother, Yvonne, and three siblings – an older sister and brother and one younger brother, Alain. In 1930, they had left Paris for Cannes and then Nice, where her father had opened an antiques and interior-decorating business. They had returned to Paris six years later, and Andrée had been sent to England for a year, where she had made friends, become an Anglophile, and learned English. Life for her had been good – as a family, they had not wanted for much – but now suddenly it seemed as though her world had come to an end. Bright, vivacious and pretty, Andrée instinctively knew the advent of war would change all their lives. A few days after the declaration, she noted, 'We are now at war and we will have to live with it. Hitler has to be stopped. We must believe in France's victory and shout from the rooftops of Paris, "Vive la France."' The doubt, however, was unmistakable; it was as though she wanted to believe in French victory but feared the worst. Her brother, Alain, she scribbled, kept repeating, 'what bastards they all are.' 'As for me,' she added, 'I am totally heartbroken.'

Now back in Paris along with the rest of the French mission to Moscow was André Beaufre, although it had been no easy task getting home and had involved a long, circuitous journey through Finland, Sweden and Holland; during the flight from Sweden to Amsterdam, their aircraft had even been buzzed by a German fighter plane. In Holland, the Dutch Army was also mobilizing, so the airfield at Schiphol was teeming with troops. Finally back in Paris on 29 August, the situation was equally frenetic as mobilization got underway.

Beaufre had discovered a city full of grim resignation. At Army HQ in the Boulevard Saint-Germain, he found most of his friends already gone to set up General Headquarters, so he took an empty office and settled back into staff work. Around him, Parisians carried gas masks over their shoulders, blackout curtains went up over windows, and after dark the city's lights remained switched off, cloaking Paris in darkness. But, as yet, there was no sign of any bombers coming to terrorize them.

Along the front, however, Order X had been enacted. This called for the complete evacuation within three hours of all the villages in front of or next to the Maginot Line. Lieutenant René de Chambrun had been given the agonizing task of clearing the hamlet of Gomelange, home to some 318 inhabitants. A piercing bugle call had signalled the start of the task shortly after midnight on that Sunday, 3 September. Men, women and children were woken and told they had an hour to clear out; they could take only what they could carry. Vehicles, animals, carts – all had to stay behind. A bridge over the river was blown, as was a dam so that the fields might be flooded – an extra line of defence. Chambrun saw a small child of about five point towards one of the soldiers in the half-dark. '*C'est Papa!*' he cried out then ran to the soldier's arms. 'Well, as long as the fields are flooded,' a farmer said philosophically, 'what else can we do but go away?' Chambrun was deeply moved by the stoic fortitude of the people of Gomelange.

André Beaufre might have escaped Moscow in time, but others were finding themselves trapped on the wrong side of the fence now that war had been declared. Among them was Eric Brown, a twenty-year-old Scot who was something of a Germanophile – an attitude that was not uncommon in Britain. After all, many British considered themselves Anglo-Saxons; the Royal Family was of German origin; and until the turn of the century Germany had been a firm ally, albeit never a formal one. The vast majority of British people instinctively disliked the Nazis and all they stood for, but not all – famously, two of the Mitford sisters, noted society beauties, had courted Hitler and his entourage, while the British Union of Fascists had also formed links.

Eric Brown had first visited Germany during the 1936 Olympics – his father, a former balloon observer and pilot in the Royal Flying Corps, had been invited along with other ex-pilots to the opening ceremonies by Göring and other former First World War pilots. While there, he had met Ernst Udet, a fighter ace and stunt pilot but by then in charge of the

Luftwaffe's technical department, the T-Amt. Udet had been delighted one of his old adversaries had brought his son and, learning of young Eric's interest in aircraft, had offered to take him for a flight from Halle in his Bücker Jungmann biplane.

Udet, who was probably the finest aerobatic pilot in the world, put the plane – and Eric – through their paces. After twirling and pirouetting around the sky, Udet finally took the plane in to land, Brown still clutching his stomach and relieved he had not disgraced himself. Suddenly, Udet flipped the plane over. Brown watched upside down as they continued to approach the airfield. 'In fact,' says Brown, 'we were coming in so low I thought the silly old fool's had a heart attack!' Thinking it was the end, Brown braced himself, but then, when there was only just enough space, Udet rolled the plane back again and made a perfect landing, looked at his ashen passenger and burst out laughing. 'He was young at heart, really, Udet,' says Brown.

As they walked clear of the plane, Udet had slapped him on the back and told him he would make a good fighter pilot but had to do two things – learn to fly and learn to speak German.

Brown took Udet at his word and did both, studying modern languages at Edinburgh University and joining the University Air Squadron. In the summer of 1938, he returned to Germany, renewing his acquaintance with Udet, and was back again the following summer. This time, however, it was courtesy of the Foreign Office, which had been recruiting at Edinburgh and had suggested Brown spend the next year in Europe before returning to Edinburgh to complete his degree.

On 3 September, he had only recently reached Salem on Lake Constance and was staying in a small *Gasthaus* when he was rudely awoken by three members of the SS. 'I'm afraid you'll have to come with us,' he was told, 'because our countries are now at war.'

Gathering together all his belongings, and also taking his MG Magnette, they took him to Munich and put him in a cell. It was the first day of the war, and, as far as Brown was concerned, it seemed likely he would be a prisoner of the Germans for the duration.

Other people were trying to leave not just Germany, but Europe. On board the SS *Athenia* was the eighteen-year-old James Goodson, heading back home to Toronto. Goodson had been born in the USA to British parents but had been brought up in Canada and had recently been in

France studying at the Sorbonne; with all the talk of war, it had seemed it was time to head home.

Chamberlain's announcement had been broadcast by radio throughout the ship, and Goodson, along with a number of other passengers, had listened to it in the Third Class lounge.

For a moment after the Prime Minister had finished speaking there was silence, then Goodson said, 'This is the way the world ends: not with a bang but a whimper!', quoting T. S. Eliot.

'Well, we're well out of it,' said another. Most seemed to agree. The ship was heading for Montreal and crammed with over 1,100 passengers, including more than three hundred Americans, a large number of Canadians, a few English, Scottish and Irish, and a number of European refugees. There were also over three hundred crew.

By evening, they were off the Hebrides. There was a cold, strong westerly wind, and the ship was pitching and rolling. Goodson had just climbed the staircase and was making for the dining room when he felt the ship lurch violently and heard a huge explosion followed by a loud crack. A moment later, the lights went out and people began to scream. Slewing to a halt, the *Athenia* began to list. Around Goodson, people were running in all directions, shouting, calling out to one another. Suddenly the emergency lights went on and Goodson hurried back to the companionway from which he'd come. Looking down, he saw a large gaping hole filled with surging water and broken bits of wooden stairway, flooring and furniture. A number of people were clinging to this flotsam, so Goodson clambered down and tried to pull as many women as he could to safety. Some were screaming that they couldn't swim. Throwing off his jacket and kicking off his shoes, he plunged into the water and helped those unable to swim out onto the broken companionway, carrying children and others one by one out of harm's way. When Goodson asked the crew for some help, they all shook their heads sadly and confessed they could not swim.

Despite working alone, Goodson finally managed to clear the corridor and join some of the crew, who asked him to help search the upper corridors. By now the ship was listing much further and Goodson found himself wading and then swimming once more. He found no one, just the dead body of a young man who earlier had sung Scottish ballads in the lounge.

Clambering back up, cold and soaking wet, Goodson was helped up onto the deck and then he and some surviving crew headed towards one of the lifeboats. It was packed and suddenly one of the ropes on the davits slipped, the front of the boat dropped and the passengers were tipped, screaming, into the water. There was nothing Goodson could do, so he hurried to the other side of the ship and saw the very last lifeboat about to be lowered.

There was no room for him, but from the deck he saw a lifeboat out at sea just a hundred yards away. Using one of the davit ropes, he began climbing down then dropped into the water and, after eventually coming back to the surface, swam as hard as he could towards the lifeboat he had seen, although it now looked horribly far away.

Eventually, he reached it, although several of the passengers tried to push him away, banging his knuckles as he gripped the side of the boat. A seaman yelled at them and then a young woman came to his rescue, pushing his assailants aside and helping to pull him up. As he collapsed, exhausted, into the boat, a blanket was wrapped around him. Looking up, he saw the girl who had rescued him. She was about his age, pretty and dressed only in bra and underclothes. It seemed she had been dressing for dinner when the boat was struck. The girl was American and had been touring Europe that summer with several of her friends. They began telling jokes and singing songs, then, when they had rowed far enough from the ship not to be pulled down with it when it finally sank, they stopped, huddling together to keep warm and praying they would be rescued.

It was well after midnight when the *Athenia* went down. Slowly, the stern disappeared and then the bow began to rise, water surging off her as she rose vertically, towering above them. For a moment, she seemed to pause there before plunging downwards until, with a final surge of water erupting into the air, she disappeared from view.

Little did Goodson or his fellow passengers on the lifeboat know it at the time, but the SS *Athenia* had been hit by a torpedo fired from *U-30*, one of Germany's U-boats already patrolling the Atlantic.

On the first day of hostilities, it was at sea, and against civilians, that Germany had first struck at Britain.

CHAPTER 6

All at Sea

JAMES GOODSON WAS RESCUED along with all those in his lifeboat at around 4.30 a.m. on the morning of 4 September by an empty Norwegian tanker called the *Knute Nelson*. Recovering soon after below deck, rough blanket around him, Goodson fell into a deep sleep. By the time he awoke, they were slipping into Galway Bay in the neutral Republic of Ireland. Huge crowds were there to greet them, and as Goodson stepped on to dry land once more, other survivors, picked up by British destroyers, rushed towards him and the others from the tanker asking about missing friends and relations. A brother and sister, both about twelve, asked him whether he had seen their parents.

At this, Goodson felt an overwhelming fury sweep over him. No one, he thought, had the right to cause such suffering to innocent people. There and then, Goodson decided he would do something about it; he knew what he had to do. He would get back to the United States, then head to Canada and join the Royal Canadian Air Force.

Winston Churchill had chaired his first meeting of the Admiralty Board on the evening of Sunday, 3 September, just a few hours before the *Athenia* had been struck. These rooms at the Admiralty were rich in history. It was here that the naval campaign to defeat Napoleon had been plotted; it was here that Wellington and Nelson had met one another for the only time, albeit briefly. And it was here that Churchill and Lord Fisher had quarrelled back in 1915 over the Dardanelles campaign; it had ended badly for both men.

Now he was back, sitting at the same desk and with the same familiar high-backed dark leather and mahogany chair. Watching him was a portrait of Nelson, Britain's great naval hero. The last time he had been in that room, Churchill reflected, Britain had been fighting Germany. A quarter of a century later, they were doing so again. 'Once again we must fight for life and honour,' he noted. 'Once again. So be it!'

On his first night back, Churchill worked late, brimming with energy and excitement at the prospect of being at the heart of Britain's war strategy. The First Sea Lord, the most senior naval officer in the land, was Admiral Sir Dudley Pound, a straightforward and uncomplicated fellow who lacked imagination and flair but who was a good foil to Churchill and happy to play second fiddle.

The Royal Navy was known as Britain's Senior Service for a reason. It was comfortably the world's largest, with 15 battleships, 7 aircraft carriers, 15 heavy cruisers, 49 light cruisers, 192 destroyers, 73 escort vessels, 9 patrol vessels, 52 minesweepers, 2 gun monitors and 62 submarines. Only the USA, which was not in the war, had anything like this number of vessels. And there was a lot more shipping on the way; in shipyards from Belfast to Glasgow to Tyneside, more ships were already being built as Britain entered the war: 19 more cruisers, 52 destroyers, 6 battleships, 6 aircraft carriers and 11 more submarines, to list just some of this building programme. There has been considerable criticism thrown at the Royal Navy of 1939, not least by those who argue it was ageing and stuck in the past. It is true that its two newest battleships, the *Nelson* and *Rodney*, were completed back in 1927, but battleships were meant to last. They took four years to build from scratch and were unbelievably complex pieces of engineering, and fantastically expensive. Even so, each of Britain's fifteen battleships had either undergone a major refit or been largely reconstructed, especially with regard to firepower and fire control gear. During the inter-war years, Britain had out-built all the other navies of the world in almost all classes except for submarines.

It also made sense to build up this large fleet of capital ships – battleships, aircraft carriers and cruisers – during peacetime. Such vessels took years to build and were not something that could be brought to being in a hurry. The Navy was well aware of the battleships and cruisers entering the service of the Kriegsmarine, the German Navy; the response was to have an even greater force to check any thoughts of German naval dominance. Once war came, it was much easier and quicker to build destroyers, armed merchant vessels and smaller escorts like corvettes and sloops.

There were, however, other reasons why Britain had maintained such a large navy. It was an island nation with the largest empire the world had ever known. This kind of vast global reach meant, even in this emerging age of aviation, linking the sea lanes around the world. The Navy was needed to protect not only its foreign territories but also the country's trade. Nor was Britain's reach around the world purely linked to its empire – rather, most of its trade was extra-imperial: with Europe, and especially Scandinavia, and with countries in both North and South America, where British companies had huge interests. Entire railways in Argentina, for example, had been built with British money and were run by British companies, even though the country was not within the Empire.

Britain was also a major exporter: the leading supplier of armaments in the 1930s and also of coal, to name but two trades. And for all this she needed a sizeable number of merchant vessels; so as well as having the world's largest Navy, she also had the world's largest merchant fleet, amounting to some 33 per cent of global merchant shipping. On top of that, Britain had access to around another 50 per cent of the rest of the world's merchant navies, such as those of Norway, Greece, Holland and other major players in world maritime shipping.

Strategically, then, Churchill had inherited a fairly comfortable position. In terms of threats to Britain, it was only really Germany in that September of 1939. Imperial Japan had been increasingly threatening over the past decade and with Britain's large interests in the Far East, this was a worry. However, at present, Japan was more than busy in China and with fighting the Soviet Union, so it posed no immediate threat. Italy, too, had shown that it was not ready to fight just yet if at all. Italy's Navy was perhaps the most up to date of its armed services, but while it had the most submarines in the world (106), it had no aircraft carriers and only four battleships. Britain and France together would have made short work of it.

What this meant was that Britain could keep the Mediterranean Fleet firmly in the Mediterranean, maintain a significant presence on the China Station, and have the Home Fleet at Scapa Flow in the Orkneys north of Scotland, as well as deploying further forces all around the United Kingdom. It also meant that they could immediately implement an economic blockade of Germany. Britain's naval power should not be underestimated.

The news of the sinking of the *Athenia*, however, had still been a terrific shock, not least because it was a civilian liner and thus supposed to be exempt from attack under the Prize Rules conditions of the Hague Convention, to which Germany had signed up. These not only forbade the sinking of passenger ships but decreed that merchant vessels could only be sunk once their crews had been safely rescued. Churchill had barely finished meeting his new team when the news reached them. The very next day, he sent his first minute on his return as First Lord, to the Director of Naval Intelligence, demanding a statement on the German U-boat force, both 'actual and prospective'. The answer was sixty now and ninety-nine expected by early 1940. This wasn't far off the mark. In fact, the Kriegsmarine had fifty-seven submarines available, although for those in the U-boat service this didn't seem like very much.

Commanding Germany's U-boat force was Admiral Karl Dönitz, a post he had held since 1935. The previous four years had been frustrating for him, because he strongly believed that the U-boats had come very close to winning the last war and felt certain they held the key to this renewed conflict, and particularly in the war against Britain. Submarines had come a long way since 1918. They were more rugged, could dive quicker, were faster and larger, with more numerous and more powerful torpedoes, which were battery-powered and wakeless (making them harder to detect), and had greater range. Radio and radar equipment had also advanced considerably, so that now U-boats could communicate not only with their base, but also with each other. In fact, U-boats, traditionally lone hunters, could now operate in packs. Conversely, anti-submarine weapons had also improved, but not, Dönitz believed, enough to pose a significant threat.

Britain was utterly dependent on seaborne trade, so clearly it was the task of the Kriegsmarine to sever those sea lanes. Frustratingly for Dönitz, however, it seemed that no one else in Germany believed as he did that U-boats were the weapon to deliver that victory. Rather, Admiral Raeder, who as Commander-in-Chief at the Oberkommando der Marine (OKM), or Naval High Command, was commander of the Kriegsmarine, preferred to build a predominantly surface fleet. After Munich, Göring had begun a renewed rearmament programme in Germany that was to dwarf the earlier, yet still considerable, military growth. The Luftwaffe, for example, was to increase fivefold to some 21,750 aircraft, while the Kriegsmarine was to begin a major fleet-building programme, called

the 'Z Plan', which had been prepared over the summer of 1938, principally by Commander Heye of the operations department of the Naval
War Staff under Raeder's instructions. Heye made the entirely valid
assumption that should Germany go to war with Britain, the latter would
not be able to overcome an economic blockade for any significant length
of time, so disrupting British overseas trade had to be the prime objective.
Heye believed that primarily this should be achieved by a cruiser war –
that is, long-range, powerfully armed cruisers and 'pocket' battleships;
submarines had an important part to play but not the lead role. This
appealed to Hitler, who had already enthusiastically backed an earlier
battleship programme, not because of any particular military logic, but
because battleships were enormous and gave a fabulous physical
impression of power.

The flaw in Heye's plan was how to support this cruiser force in far-off
seas without a series of strategically based foreign ports and bases, as
were available to the British, and also to the French for that matter;
Germany's access to the world's oceans via the narrow Baltic Sea wasn't
really going to cut it. Realistically, German ships could not safely pass
through the English Channel because of mines, proximity to Britain and
its defences, which meant going around the north of Scotland to reach
the wide oceans – and this could be easily hampered by the Royal Navy's
blockade. Admiral Carls, the Commander-in-Chief of the Fleet, made
this exact point, arguing that the only way to get these overseas colonies
and secure sea routes was by conquest. 'A war against Britain,' he commented, 'means a war against the Empire, against France, probably also
against Russia and a number of countries overseas, in other words against
one half or two-thirds of the whole world.' He was absolutely spot on,
although far from baulking at this apocalyptic vision, Carls instead called
for large-scale land conquests and the rapid development of a huge fleet
that would be able to achieve his dream of global naval domination.
Coming from a senior military commander, it betrayed a level of self-
delusion that was astonishing.

How much Carls's views were taken into account is not clear, but the Z
Plan, announced in mid-October 1938, called for 10 battleships, 15
pocket battleships, 5 heavy, 24 light and 36 small cruisers, 8 aircraft carriers and 249 U-boats. It was nothing more than pure fantasy; realizable
perhaps on some far-off day once the rest of the world had been taken
over, but not in the medium to short term. Germany did not have the

industrial capacity or the raw materials required, nor the cash. And even if a fraction of this force had been built, the country would not have had the fuel to power it.

A far more sensible approach would have been to have done precisely what Dönitz was urging and concentrate largely on submarines. These were quite expensive enough, but would have been easier and cheaper to build than large numbers of surface vessels – and they used less fuel. During the summer, he had again pressed his point, more convinced than ever that war with Britain was looming now rather than to be expected in 1942, when the planned 249 U-boats in the Z Plan were due to be completed. In July, he had urged Raeder to tell Hitler his continuing concerns about the paltry size of the U-boat fleet – at the time he had just twenty-seven ocean-going submarines, of which only nineteen were ready for war. In his memo to Hitler he made it clear that to make a substantial contribution against Allied Atlantic shipping, at least one hundred boats always needed to be operational. This was based on the 'third' principle: a third on active duty, a third heading to or returning from active duty, and a third undergoing repair, re-equipping and refitting. Soon after, Raeder conveyed the Führer's reply. 'He would ensure that in no circumstances would war with Britain come about,' noted Dönitz. 'For that would mean *finis Germaniae.*'

Well, now they were at war, and Hitler immediately tore up the Z Plan and promised to make U-boat building the priority for the Kriegsmarine – and so much so that it took precedence over even key projects such as the new Junkers 88 long-range bomber. It was, Dönitz believed, too little too late. 'Seldom indeed,' he noted, 'has any branch of the armed forces of any country gone to war so poorly equipped.'

For the time being, the U-boat arm would have to do what it could with the few submarines it did have. Most seaworthy U-boats had actually been sent out to the Atlantic at the end of August, which was why *U-30* had been able to intercept the *Athenia* on the first day of war against Britain. The commander, Oberleutnant Lemp, had spotted her zig-zagging and off the normal shipping course and so had assumed it was a troopship and therefore fair game. It was a mistake, and the Germans tried to hush it up, but it still prompted huge outrage on both sides of the Atlantic – the sinking brought back memories of the torpedoed *Lusitania* in 1915.

One U-boat playing more closely by the rules was *U-48*, under the command of Kapitänleutnant 'Vati' Schultze. The *U-48* had left Kiel and slowly made its way around the north of Scotland, just as the crew had done on numerous practice patrols over the past year. First Watch Officer was the 23-year-old Reinhard 'Teddy' Suhren, who despite joining the Navy back in 1935 had moved to the U-boat arm just the previous year.

Suhren had always loved the sea and as a boy had become hooked on sailing, first with the Hanseatic Yachting School and then on school trips to the Frisian Islands. His time under training had seen him repeatedly in trouble; even his nickname, 'Teddy', had come about when one of his comrades had suggested he marched so badly he looked like a teddy bear. The name stuck.

After time as a midshipman on destroyers, and believing he would never make *Leutnant*, Suhren thought of resigning from the Kriegsmarine altogether. It was his brother, Gerd, already a *Leutnant* himself, who talked him into staying put and simply changing his attitude. From then on, Teddy was determined to try harder, play by the rules, and keep his sheet clean. It very quickly paid off. Within a few months, in April 1938, he was promoted to *Leutnant* and soon after transferred to submarines, and to *U-48*. So far, Suhren had had no cause to regret the transfer. He particularly liked the camaraderie and the understanding and even warmth of his fellow crew. They were a band of brothers, and no longer did Suhren feel like the junior, constantly pushed around. 'Now I came back to life,' he noted, 'and felt myself more at home in the Navy by the day.'

On 4 September, they spotted a lone Swedish freighter and, surfacing, flashed the signal for the merchantman to stop at once and not use its radio. The Swedish ship ignored them, so, to show they meant business, Schultze ordered men on to the 88mm gun on the foredeck. Climbing up on to the bridge was Suhren, but to his horror he saw there was no one manning the gun – the men had been swept overboard in the swell. Fortunately, they had remembered to clip on the safety harnesses and so were hauled back on board, and before they had need to open fire, the freighter hove to.

They let the Swedish captain continue on his way, but the following day they spotted another freighter on the horizon. Diving swiftly they then emerged just in front of what they now saw was a British 5,000-ton merchantman, *Royal Sceptre*. 'Stop at once and show papers!' they signalled. Schultze gave the British crew ten minutes to get into the safety of their lifeboats. 'We couldn't hang around for long in this area,' noted Suhren, 'without getting ants in our pants.' They were still nerve-wrackingly close to Scotland.

They watched the men clambering into the boats, then from 600 metres fired a pair of torpedoes that hit square amidships. When they heard radio signals being sent off, they fired a few shots with the gun and watched the *Royal Sceptre* sink beneath the waves.

'Pity about the nice ship,' said Suhren.

'Well, this war is none of my choosing,' Schultze replied.

The *Royal Sceptre* had barely slipped out of sight when a further freighter was spotted. Once again, they intercepted the vessel; it too was British, the *Browning*, and this time the ship sent boats to meet them. Suhren, once more up on the bridge, was astonished to see the boats full of black women and children. As they drew alongside the German U-boat with tears running down their faces, they held up their screaming babies and pleaded with their captors to save them. Suhren saw Schultze look at him helplessly. 'Good God,' he said, 'what do we do now?'

'No way am I prepared to torpedo it,' declared Suhren.

'No more am I,' his captain replied.

There was a pause while Schultze thought for a moment, then he said, 'We'll send them back to their ship. They can pick up the survivors from the *Royal Sceptre* and carry on with their voyage.'

Communicating this, however, was no easy matter. The women were in a state of shock and needed some convincing that they would be safe if they returned to the *Browning*. Eventually, though, having warned them not to use their radio, Schultze ordered *U-48* to draw away from the boats. Seeing them leave, the women and crew hurried back to the ship as instructed. 'It all went according to plan,' noted Suhren. 'They didn't radio, continued on their course, and made it into port three weeks later in South America.'

On 8 September, they sank another British freighter, the *Winkleigh*, then a further ship, the *Firby*, both after following the Prize Rules and sparing the crews. The captain of the *Firby* had been distraught and close to tears. It appeared he had taken his son with him on the trip and now pleaded with Schultze to take the boy. That, however, was not possible, so instead Schultze ordered a plain text signal to be sent: '*To Mr Churchill – We just sank the British steamer* Firby. *Please save the crew! Posit 59°40'N 13°50'W.*' Schultze's action meant that the *Firby*'s captain and all thirty-three crew were soon rescued by a British destroyer. The U-boat was then ordered home, its first wartime patrol drawing to an end. With three ships to their name and some 15,000 tons of Allied shipping now at the bottom of the ocean, it had been a good start.

U-48 had been ordered home along with nine others of the eighteen U-boats that had been in the Atlantic during the opening week of the war. Dönitz wanted a good number of ocean-going U-boats back for rest and refitting ready for a renewed hunt in October – and a hunt in which his flotillas would not be operating singly, but together. This was a new idea Dönitz was keen to test. This new group of U-boats, he had decided, would be called a wolfpack.

Despite Churchill's urgent demand to know the true strength of the U-boat force, the Admiralty was certainly not particularly worried by the threat as hostilities began. Perhaps some of the Royal Navy's ships were a little old and creaking, but their giant fleet was certainly well served by a first-class infrastructure. During the last war, the British had created a global organization called Naval Control of Shipping (NCS) and intricate naval intelligence systems. Since the end of the war, it had been repeatedly improved and upgraded, and had been further enhanced by the setting up of an Operational Intelligence Centre (OIC) at the Admiralty just two years before in 1937.

Naval intelligence was not only served by the Government Code and Cypher School at Bletchley Park, where civilian mathematicians and scientists had been recruited in an attempt to break enemy signal codes, but also by a network of Radio Intercept Stations and reports from ports around the world sent via secure underwater telegraph cables – an intelligence exchange known as the VESCA system – and, of course, aerial reconnaissance carried out by both RAF Coastal Command and the Navy's own Fleet Air Arm. All merchant shipping was brought under the control of NCS, which tracked the movements, cargoes and destinations of almost all Allied shipping. This meant that, in theory at any rate, it was possible to know exactly where any ship was at any moment of any given day. The key objective was, as far as was possible, to keep Allied shipping away from danger.

Another means of securing the safe passage of ships was by putting them into convoy, and no sooner had the *Athenia* been sunk than the Admiralty ordered NCS to reintroduce the convoy system. This was nothing new and had operated well in the final year of the last war, working on the principle that a tight formation escorted by armed vessels was considerably less vulnerable than a lone and unescorted freighter. A mass of ships with the protection of destroyers, corvettes and other escorts was no easy proposition for a lone U-boat.

In any case, although U-boats like the *U-48* had picked off several lone freighters in the opening days of the war, the Royal Navy was pretty well placed to deal with the threat the Kriegsmarine posed. The Home Fleet alone was considerably larger than anything the Germans could put to sea, while the U-boat force was simply not large enough to do more than inconvenience Allied shipping. Of course, it was to be expected that Germany would build more submarines, but there was every sign that British shipyards were building more escorts than German shipyards were building U-boats. There was, then, quiet reason for confidence as far as the war at sea was concerned. And since war was as much about logistics and supply of materials as anything, it seemed that Britain and its ally France were, for the time being at any rate, well placed.

Before the year was out, there would, however, be some shocks in store.

CHAPTER 7

Offensive Reconnaissance

O N THE FIRST DAY of the war, the RAF's Bomber Command had carried out its first operation, when twenty-seven bombers had been sent to search for the German Fleet.

Among those heading out over the North Sea had been six Handley Page Hampdens of 83 Squadron, based at Scampton, just to the north of Lincoln. Among the pilots was Guy Gibson, a 21-year-old flying officer fresh back from leave on the last day of August. The squadron's Hampdens were twin-engine bombers like those of the Luftwaffe. The Hampden was nimble, could carry a decent bomb-load and was faster than most bombers of the day, with a cruising speed of over 250 mph. Gibson, however, was not a great fan of the model and thought his own personal mount, *C-Charlie*, was 'lousy'. 'On take-off, she swung like hell to the right,' he noted, 'and flew in the air with her left wing low. Sometimes an engine died out, but that was nothing.'

Gibson had been told he would be flying soon after Chamberlain's announcement, with take-off scheduled for 3.30 p.m. that same afternoon. He had been quite terrified at the prospect; just a few days earlier he had been sunbathing, carefree and having the time of his life. Now he was flying off to war, and, he was convinced, never to return. He had been so nervous, he had had to run to the toilet four times, and as he'd been about to take off had discovered his hands shaking like a leaf. One of the ground crew said to him, 'Good luck, sir, give those bastards a real hiding.' Gibson had given him a sickly smile.

He found, though, that once the engines were running and he was at last rumbling down the grass runway he became calmer, even though this was the first time he had ever flown *C-Charlie* with live bombs strapped underneath. As he got airborne and flew over Lincolnshire, he struggled to believe he could possibly be flying towards Germany in an act of war. He desperately wished he could turn back. Passing over Skegness in the sunshine he thought how just a couple of months ago he had gone there with some of the boys. It seemed surreal. And then he was out over the North Sea.

As they approached the north German coast, he remembered what he had read about the aces of the last war and began to constantly swivel his head, scanning the skies. He spotted a German Dornier seaplane but flew on until, as they were within forty miles or so of Wilhelmshaven, the cloud dramatically descended. Suddenly, they were flying through driving rain, and the sea below looked wild. They ploughed on until around ten miles from target they saw the faint flash of enemy guns. Far from being alarmed, Gibson now realized the anti-aircraft guns were providing a wonderful target marker, but, to his surprise, the formation leader banked away. Duly following, Gibson slowly realized they were, in fact, turning back. All would make it safely home again, but Bomber Command's first operation had been something of a damp squib.

The following day, Bomber Command returned to Germany, and although most once again struggled to find the German Fleet, a handful of Blenheims did manage to hit the pocket battleship *Admiral Scheer* and the cruiser *Emden*; unfortunately for the attackers, however, the bombs failed to explode on the *Scheer* and caused only some damage, although more was caused by one of the Blenheim bombers crashing on to it. Four other Blenheims were shot down.

That was Bomber Command's last aggressive operation for a while; for the next few months it carried out leaflet dropping only. How that was going to help the Poles was anyone's guess.

When President Roosevelt had appealed to all belligerents on 1 September to refrain from unrestricted warfare, both France and Britain had agreed. Attacking the German Fleet was all right because warships were a purely military target; the same could not be said for land targets, where there were civilians and non-military buildings and infrastructure. From France's perspective, there was considerable anxiety over possible retaliation on French cities, and, as far as Britain was concerned, there was good sense in conserving its bomber force and building strength for when it was really needed. Leaflet dropping, on the other hand, was still dangerous and potentially costly in terms of aircraft and lives, but achieved absolutely nothing. It is hard to think of a greater waste of resources than sending bombers to drop paper on one's enemy.

Perhaps the air forces would have had a bit more gumption if there had been more determination on the ground. The onus for such a move was clearly on France, since the British Army was still very small and only just starting to arrive on the Continent. Back in May, Général Gamelin had assured the Poles that on the outbreak of hostilities with Germany, France would take the offensive, and that after fifteen days of mobilization at the latest would throw its full weight behind a campaign. This was another reason why the Poles had been prepared to dig their heels in with Germany.

Now that push came to shove, however, Gamelin was making comments about not wanting to begin the war with another Battle of Verdun and, far from putting the full weight of the Army into a decisive invasion of western Germany, ordered just nine divisions to make an 'offensive reconnaissance' along a sixteen-mile front into the Saar region.

Among those taking part was Capitaine Daniel Barlone, another reserve officer recently called up and sent to take command of the 92nd/20th Horse Transport Company of the headquarters of 2nd North African Division. Having been in a civilian job in Paris just the week before, he was armed with a hefty copy of *Journal de Mobilisation*, which outlined what he was expected to do and what stores he should draw. After a long journey east, they had been based at the tiny village of Pillon, north-west of Metz and not far from Verdun. 2nd North African Division was a mobile division, but Barlone was surprised to find it so short of weapons, munitions and vehicles, and yet the situation was much improved since the previous year, when he'd last been on exercise. 'How should we come off if we had to start the fray now?' he wondered in his diary. 'We should manage somehow, I suppose.'

A few days later, they were on the march, after dark for fear of German planes. It took a long time: a long column of horses and wagons, plodding forward in the dark and what seemed like incessant rain. After several days they were south of Luxembourg and south of the Saar, and then reached the Maginot Line. 'We skirt some huge earthworks,' wrote Barlone, 'but I am amazed to see that nothing, absolutely nothing, has been prepared in depth.' The Maginot Line, he discovered, was a single thread 100–150 yards wide with webs of wire. He wondered what would happen if any part of it were breached. How would the men behind the line be able to stem the flood which would pour through and outflank the forts? He was later assured that a more elastic system of defence did exist. 'Not in this sector at any rate!' he noted.

Eventually, the division headquarters reached the village of Holling, which, like all other border villages, had been evacuated. For several days they remained where they were; Barlone had established his company headquarters in a now-empty café. The German border was just two and a half miles away, and each night Barlone could hear unending streams of artillery, equipment and supplies heading up to the border. Everyone was keenly aware that an attack was about to be launched; news from the front filtered back that the Germans had abandoned their border villages too but had left them riddled with booby traps – a combination of artillery and engineers was now clearing them. 'The attack is on the point of being launched,' Barlone scribbled, 'that is as clear as day. The Polish front will be eased.'

In fact, it was a bit late in the day for easing the Polish front. The Poles had already lost their freedom of action after just a few days, and by 11 September, German forces were sweeping in a wide swathe across a third of the country. Warsaw looked set to fall within a matter of days. As it stood, the result was no longer in doubt, although if the French attacked as wholeheartedly as Gamelin had promised back in May, there was a golden opportunity to drive straight on to Berlin without much to stop them. And that would have been a major game-changer.

Barlone and his men certainly felt ready and prepared. 'We are all burning with desire,' he noted, 'and jumping for joy at the idea of entering the fray.' He was especially confident in French firepower; having served in the last war, he knew their artillery had been something to be reckoned with back then and was even more so now.

But a further week passed and still the attack had not been ordered. Then, on 18 September, Barlone heard whispers from division HQ that it would be launched the following morning. By this time, Barlone was wondering whether it was now going to be too late – news had arrived that Warsaw was surrounded. Still, his men remained confident and raring to go, but then, the following day arrived and still there was no order to attack. Instead, news reached them that the Russians had invaded

Poland from the east. Barlone was dumbstruck by this devastating piece of news, as were most people in the West. 'Poland is done for,' he admitted in his diary. 'Since yesterday activity has slowed down, no more artillery, no fresh troops. The Staff give me to understand that the offensive will not take place. What a pity that nearly a fortnight has been wasted before being able to attack.'

In fact, there *had* been an offensive – albeit a very limited one. The French had pushed just five miles, reached the outposts of the extremely thinly held Siegfried Line, and then gone no further. Casualties had been extremely light and were mostly caused by mines. As one regiment diary noted, 'X Platoon tried to continue its advance; it was halted by the fire of an automatic weapon.' A generation earlier, French *poilus* had advanced over ground torn up by shellfire into withering storms of machine-gun and rifle fire; now entire advances were being held up by a single weapon.

Along the Maginot Line, René de Chambrun and his regiment had disappeared into the depths of the Fort of Rotherberg, from where no enemy could be seen at all. As if to show solidarity in the effort, the Hochwald Bastion further along the line fired the odd shell, although its 75mm gun, the only artillery piece that could actually reach Germany, fired only a few shots and then jammed.

At Army headquarters in Paris, André Beaufre was bristling with shame. 'The Germans did not react,' he noted. 'Gamelin decided to pull back. So much for our help to Poland.' Before the war, Gamelin had calculated that Poland would be able to hold out until the spring. In fact, the Poles, despite showing unquestioned bravery and determination to fight, had been overwhelmed by a two-pronged assault from west and east and capitulated after just twenty days. It was slightly worrying for the Allies that Gamelin and his generals seemed to be operating on a much slower timescale than the Germans in this war.

All French troops were back behind the Maginot Line by 4 October, and Gamelin, for one, was only too relieved that the pledge of honour to the Poles had been, to his mind, satisfied. Now, the Allies could do what they had always planned to do: sit and wait and build up strength, and hope that Germany would not attack them before they were ready to meet the challenge.

Unquestionably, fear of military inferiority played a large part in French thinking. On one level, this was misplaced, because the French were pretty well equipped for war with Germany. There were already the best part of a million men before mobilization, and that figure grew rapidly: over six million men were mobilized in September. The Army was also equipped with the most heavily armed and heavily armoured tanks in the world and had good numbers too. The Somuas were well protected and had 47mm guns, while the Char Bs mounted both 75mm and 47mm guns. The only German tank – or panzer as they were known – to mount a 75mm gun was the Panzer Mk IV, the tank model of fewest numbers. The French were very well equipped with artillery pieces, and their small arms – such as rifles and machine guns – were perfectly good. The Châtellerault light machine gun, to give just one example, was solid and reliable, had a rate of fire of some 500–600 rounds per minute, and its muzzle velocity was more powerful than any other model in the world.

In the air, the French had some 1,735 front-line aircraft and a further 1,600 reserves, and when these were combined with the RAF's, the Allied total actually exceeded the number of aircraft available to the Luftwaffe. The Farman 222, while not the fastest, could carry more bombs than any aircraft flying at that time – more than four tons. Its fighter aircraft, though not as fast as the Messerschmitt 109, were not far off the pace; the Dewoitine D520, for example, was also well-armed, with machine guns and a 20mm cannon, and had exceptional range for a fighter. And then there was the French Navy, which was the second largest in Europe, behind Britain's.

There were also signs of a resurgent economy, which helped the huge rearmament drive. France in the 1930s had been riven by political factions, failing governments and even civil unrest. Édouard Daladier had been Prime Minister twice earlier in the decade – and once for only a few days – but, after the failure of Léon Blum's Popular Front, had taken the premiership again the previous year, in April 1938, and eighteen months on was still there. He had brought a grim authoritarianism, running the country almost entirely without Parliament and hurriedly increasing rearmament. The speed of French mobilization was impressive and backing it up were factories that were outproducing Germany in terms of tanks, guns and aircraft.

After long years of depression and political fractiousness in France, the message now was one of unity – of the nation pulling together in this hour of need as, once again, they faced a resurgent enemy. In a speech on national radio on 10 September, the Minister of Finance, Paul Reynaud, had made a rallying call to arms. Housewives, even the elderly, were called upon to do their bit. Anyone capable of helping the production effort but evading this duty deserved, he said, to be called deserters. France was also better off, he told them, than it had been in 1914. 'We shall prevail,' he said, as he finished, 'because we are stronger.'

A former lawyer from Verdun, Reynaud was a month shy of sixty-one, and small and dark, with narrow eyes and a trim moustache. Known as something of a maverick, he had none the less proved a hugely successful Finance Minister, going against the wishes of many of his political colleagues and implementing a tough austerity programme combined with large amounts of deregulation – such as scrapping the forty-hour working week. It was these reforms as much as anything that were responsible for the economic recovery in France, which saw a rise in the nation's coffers from 37 billion francs at the time of Munich to 48 billion by the outbreak of war. It was this that was funding France's massive rearmament programme.

Despite all this, there remained, however, a curious degree of both complacency and military insecurity at the heart of France's military leadership, most of whom had not only served in the last war, but had worn the burden of higher command. Général Gamelin, for example, had been a divisional commander, while Général Georges had served on the General Staff at Army headquarters. And the previous war pervaded the thinking of this crop of senior French commanders, who believed any fighting against Nazi Germany would follow a similar pattern to that of the last war: it would be long-drawn-out, attritional and, above all, largely static. Speed of manoeuvre did not really come into it.

Compounding French thinking was a systematic belief that no matter how many guns or tanks or forts were built, the Germans had more, and German propaganda about their incredible military might was swallowed hook, line and sinker. A classic piece of German cunning had been to invite Général Vuillemin, the head of the Armée de l'Air, to some Luftwaffe manoeuvres. The Germans switched aircraft from one base to another, changing registration numbers as they did so and thus giving the impression they had many more aircraft than was the reality. When Vuillemin returned to France, he told Daladier that when it came to war, the French Air Force would be annihilated in a matter of days.

And yet when, in October, Edward Spears as the new Chairman of the Anglo-French Committee brought a delegation of British politicians over to France, he was once again reassured by the good spirits of those he saw. At a meeting with Daladier, Spears was told about a visit to the front. After talking to some troops, a soldier had said to the Prime Minister, 'We are glad to observe that the morale of Monsieur le Président du Conseil is good.' Daladier had laughed as he recounted this to Spears. 'There was I investigating the morale of the troops and it was they who were looking into mine!'

En route to the Suez Canal and the Mediterranean was the British destroyer HMS *Delight*, making its long way back from the China Station. For the ship's First Lieutenant, Vere Wight-Boycott, it was all rather frustrating as they were not sure whether they were to be joining the Mediterranean Fleet or heading on back to Britain. The news had been patchy to say the least, and what they heard had been learned via the captain's private wireless set, and that had been decidedly intermittent. 'We have heard of the sinking of the Donaldson ship with Americans,' he wrote to his mother on 19 September, 'the Kiel air raid, the dropping of leaflets, and the fact that British troops are in France, but that is as far as we have got.'

Wight-Boycott was more up to date than he had imagined, not least in that more and more troops of the British Expeditionary Force were being shipped to France. One of those escorting the soldiers was Lieutenant-Commander Donald Macintyre, skipper of the ageing destroyer HMS *Venomous*. Now thirty-five and a career officer in the Royal Navy, Macintyre was a ruddy, round-faced man with a twinkle in his eye and a phlegmatic determination that had served him well. Having joined as a midshipman back in 1922, he had been commissioned three years later and served in the Mediterranean before transferring to the Fleet Air Arm and learning to fly. He served on the aircraft carriers *Hermes* on the China Station and *Courageous* with the Home Fleet and loved every minute, although frustrated by the Navy's perceived reluctance to see the real potential of air power. As Macintyre saw it, the time and money spent on improving and building further battleships would have been better spent on larger aircraft carriers. He may well have had a point . . .

His flying came to an end when he became seriously ill in 1935 and, although he recovered, was declared unfit for further flying. He was not unfit, however, for service back on sea, and his disappointment at ending his flying career was largely made up for by his delight at being promoted and given command of his first ship. This was a new kind of anti-submarine vessel, the *Kingfisher*, and it was during this time that he began to take an overriding interest in submarine hunting, not least because his ship became the experimental vessel at the Anti-Submarine School in Portland and so was trialling every new gadget and piece of equipment that was devised.

After a further stint commanding a destroyer back out in the Far East, he returned home in the spring of 1939 and, when the Reserve Fleet began to be mobilized in the summer, was given command of *Venomous*. Laid down back in May 1918, it was one of a number of old vessels that had been given a quick once-over and brought back into service. His new crew was largely drawn from the various reserves now hastily being called up. First among them were the Royal Fleet Reserves – men who had served their time but were being brought out of retirement. Then there were the Royal Naval Reserves – officers and seamen drawn from the merchant navy and fishing fleet and with a fair amount of seafaring behind them. Finally, there were the Royal Naval Volunteer Reserves – or RNVR – who were mostly weekend amateurs: keen sailors but with little military training or experience. They were eager, but still had a lot to learn.

Macintyre had been disappointed to have been given *Venomous*, and regarded her as something of a dubious proposition. Her 4-inch guns were obsolete and she had none of the latest anti-shipping equipment he had so enjoyed testing down at Portland; he had imagined that no sooner had war been declared than he would have been off on the hunt for U-boats, but for the time being at any rate it was not to be. There were other forces to deal with the paltry U-boat presence; Macintyre's job was to escort the ships carrying the renamed British Expeditionary Force across the Channel to France.

Almost nightly, at around midnight, and along with two or three other escorts, *Venomous* would rendezvous at the mouth of Portsmouth Harbour and then lead the cross-Channel packets requisitioned for the task across to Cherbourg or Le Havre. They would have an hour or two in the French port while the packets unloaded, and then would steam back again. Sometimes they could get ashore and buy French scent for their wives and girlfriends and also wine. 'The former,' noted Macintyre, 'made us very popular ashore on our return and the latter soon gave *Venomous* a remarkably fine cellar for a modest price.'

＊

Among those British troops being ferried over to France was Lieutenant Norman Field of the Royal Fusiliers, aged twenty-two and hastily married on the outbreak of war. It was quite irregular for anyone in the regiment to be wed so young; the rules were that officers had to be at least twenty-six before taking the plunge, but he and another friend in the battalion, Harley Archer, had both married on the same day. If he was honest, it hadn't really occurred to Field to get married quite so swiftly, but, as he was discovering, unexpected things happen in a time of war.

It had come about because the battalion had been posted to Grand Shaft Barracks in Dover. His then girlfriend was great friends with Harley Archer's girlfriend, but they now lived a long way away in Gloucestershire, so together he and Archer had arranged for the two girls to move down to Kent to be near them. Just after the news that Germany had invaded Poland, their company had been on a route march when the girls had pulled up in a car and told them they had been to the Archbishop's office in Canterbury and got special marriage licences; soon their boyfriends would be off to war and the girls wanted to be married right away. That meant that very afternoon.

But how to get permission from the new commanding officer? It was noon by the time they were back at the barracks and, knowing the colonel was partial to some port, Field and Archer stayed behind after lunch, pushed a bottle in his direction and then asked him whether he might possibly agree to them getting married later that day.

Much to their surprise, the CO said, 'Of course. What can I do about it?'

And so they were married at five o'clock that same afternoon, Friday, 1 September. 'Someone found a crate of champagne,' says Field, 'and we were allowed out of barracks that night, but we were back on duty the following morning.'

A week later they left, their new brides waving them off. Field couldn't tell his wife where they were headed – he had no idea in any case – but the train took them to Southampton, where they boarded a boat to Cherbourg and from there went on to a village just outside Le Mans. Field was sorry to say goodbye to his new wife, but, at the same time, heading overseas to France seemed like something of an adventure.

Norman Field was a Regular soldier, having joined after leaving school four years earlier. Sent straight to the Royal Military College Sandhurst for officer training, he only joined the 2nd Battalion, Royal Fusiliers, after he was commissioned. The Regular British Army had been small then, at just 192,325 in 1936, a figure that actually fell slightly the following year. In addition, there were 141,000 members of the Territorial Army, for whom there was occasional weekend training and an annual two-week camp, and a further 57,500 British troops in the Indian Army. All of these men were, like Norman Field, volunteers.

By 1936, when Field joined the Army, there had been much discussion in Britain about rearmament and strategic military policy, but this did not mean there was not already a considerable armaments industry in Britain – because there most certainly was. It was true that the Army had been much reduced since the end of the First World War, but in terms of building warships, aeroplanes, guns and even tanks, Britain was leading the way. Firms like Vickers Armstrong and its subsidiary, Vickers Aviation, Hawker Siddeley, Rolls-Royce and de Havilland employed thousands and invested huge sums in research and development.

Neville Chamberlain, Chancellor of the Exchequer in 1935, had been a leading advocate of rearmament and particularly of further development of the Air Force. It was in no small part thanks to him that the RAF now had two modern fighter planes in the Hawker Hurricane and Supermarine Spitfire. As Prime Minister, he had continued to oversee Britain's further investment in the arms industry; just because he had favoured appeasement at Munich the previous year, it should not be assumed he was in any way slow to build up Britain's military strength. The scale of aircraft construction, of the Royal Navy's latest warship-building programme, and of the construction of new ordnance factories was immense, and most areas of military production were, by the outbreak of war, greater than those of Germany.

History, however, has all too often suggested otherwise, not least because of the size of the Army. It has to be remembered, though, that Britain was in a very different position to either France or Germany or even Italy. Britain was an island at the heart of a huge global trading empire. Its military strategy was not an aggressive land-grabbing one – it was, in the first instance, to defend the nation's sovereignty, regardless of its commitment to Poland. To do this, a powerful navy and a strong Air Force were more important than troops on the ground, something that Chamberlain never failed to argue throughout the rearmament discussions right up to the outbreak of war.

Moreover, there were important logistical considerations militating against a large army. If Germany or France needed to move their armies, they simply walked or put them on to trains or into vehicles. If Britain wanted to do the same, the Army had to get into a vast armada of ships. Gradually transporting the ten divisions of the BEF to France was one thing; moving a force of millions in quick order was quite another. What's more, once overseas, a large army needed ever-larger amounts of material support. Maintaining such a force in peacetime was clearly non-sensical, and should it come to war and a larger army be required, then it could be built up rather as it had been in the last war. The hope, however, was that such a force would not be necessary – not with France as an ally and with greater emphasis on sea and air power.

Furthermore, history had repeatedly shown that nations with strong navies tended to come out on top, and this was a theory that had certainly worked for Britain. A series of successful wars and the world's largest empire, with an invincible navy at its core, were testimony to that. While books such as the American Captain Alfred Mahan's *The Influence of Sea Power Upon History* had become standard reading across the board, air power was a less well-known quantity. An Italian general, Giulio Douhet, had written about it and been widely read, but in truth no one was quite sure how air power would manifest itself in the next war, despite its use in recent conflicts such as the civil war in Spain; air power and aeroplane technology were changing fast, and twenty years on from the last great war machines were very different. However, it was a safe bet that air power would prove very important; clearly, whoever controlled air space would have a crucial advantage.

With this in mind, no matter how hard the Army chiefs argued the point, the Prime Minister was determined that Britain should forget about a million-man army and stick with just five Regular home divisions, while focusing on air power and naval dominance instead.

There was, however, another reason for this stance. Britain may have been a warfare state in the late 1930s, but it was not a militaristic state like Germany. It was also a democracy, and it was inconceivable that British society would have accepted conscription – and that would have been the only way to raise an army of the size that could compete with the likes of France, Germany and Italy. In any case, the kind of colonial police work that dominated much of Britain's military operations on the ground – such as in Palestine and along the Northwest Frontier – was far better suited to Regular troops than conscripts. Should war become increasingly likely, then Britain could think again, but, until that point, it made more sense to Chamberlain and others to build up Britain's strength through mechanization and technology rather than manpower. And there was unquestionably a sound logic to this, because in these areas Britain was second only to the USA. This is not to say that Britain and France had been necessarily right to adopt a policy of appeasement the previous autumn, no matter how compelling the reasons seemed at the time; but appeasement did not mean in any way that Britain was delaying rearming. It was not.

Chamberlain's stance on the size of the Army changed following the German march into Czechoslovakia that March, although the Chiefs of Staff, Britain's senior service chiefs, had received intelligence of a supposed German invasion of Holland in January, which had focused their minds on possible war. There had been no joint staff talks with the French since 1936 and none at all during the Munich Crisis the previous autumn, so finally an approach for such discussions had been made, to which the French agreed. These took place at the end of March. First, though, the Chiefs of Staff drew up their own 'European Appreciation, 1939–40', which, although in some ways it became outdated almost immediately, set Britain on the strategic course that it would take in the forthcoming war with Germany.

Among the assumptions were that Britain would have the support of its Dominions – Australia, New Zealand, Canada and South Africa – but also the Republic of Ireland. The USA would be friendly, but unlikely to intervene. Portugal would remain neutral, and Egypt would fulfil its treaty obligations of allowing British troops to maintain a sizeable presence.

A lack of resources was considered the major Achilles heel of both Germany and Italy. For Germany, most of its industrial capacity was concentrated in the Ruhr, while for Italy – as far as it went – it was in the north, around Turin, Milan and Genoa. The other threat was from Imperial Japan, but Britain and France together had greater economic resources than their three potential enemies combined.

While Britain and France's naval forces were greatly superior, it was recognized that these would be considerably stretched should it come to war. Initially, the combined armies of both countries would be smaller than Germany's, but not for long. The Luftwaffe was known to be superior, and while British aircraft production was increasing greatly, France's was not doing so at the same pace.

With these factors in mind, the policy was to play for time as long as possible and then initially to go on to the defensive. The Axis economic limitations suggested they would opt for a rapid and decisive victory within a matter of months. British staff conclusions were that Britain and France must withstand this initial Axis strike, then continue the build-up of military strength and then, when this had been achieved, strike back. No timescale was put on this, but it was considered that when Britain had achieved the full fighting strength of the Empire it could confront the war from a position of some strength and, thanks to its naval power, strike at a place of its choosing.

In the subsequent talks, France had broadly agreed with this appreciation, although if Italy entered the war, there was agreement that it was both militarily and economically weak and should be dealt with decisively. Should it come to war with Germany, the RAF would be expected to make a major commitment, as would the Royal Navy, but the French also demanded more effort from Britain in terms of men on the ground; even Chamberlain was finally having to give way on this. In January, he had already called for more volunteers to join the armed services and finally, in April, with the Cabinet confident public opinion had sufficiently shifted, limited conscription was announced. And, as the government had hoped, the announcement had been accepted by the British public.

The result of British conscription, French mobilization and continued and increased rearmament in all areas was that by the autumn of 1939 Britain and France together had more men in uniform than Germany, considerably greater naval power, and air forces that were only fractionally weaker in numbers.

Man-for-man, Britain and France looked stronger, not weaker, than Germany. Furthermore, they would be initially on the defensive, and, as the Germans were well aware, accepted military thinking was that any attacker needed at least a 3:1 advantage in manpower to achieve a decisive breakthrough. On paper, at least, the Allies could face the German threat with confidence.

CHAPTER 8

Vehicle Shortages

W HEN THE YOUNG Scotsman Eric Brown had been picked up by the Gestapo in Bavaria, he had assumed that for him the war was over before it had even started. But, to his intense relief, after three days he was freed and told he would be taken to the Swiss border. Bundled into a large Mercedes, he was driven out of Munich. Following behind was another SS officer driving his MG.

Once at the border, he was told he could have his car back. Brown was perplexed.

'You've taken my books, my money, my clothes. Why are you giving me my car?' he asked.

'Because we have no spares,' came the reply. It was a curiously prophetic comment.

Brown's troubles were not over, however. The Swiss border guard then detained him until his presence was cleared with the Swiss government at Bern. Eventually, he was escorted to the British Embassy, where he was interviewed by the Ambassador. 'You've got to go back home,' he told Brown, 'because I've got your call-up papers here.' The Ambassador then gave him enough petrol coupons to get him to England and sent him on his way.

This small episode said much about Britain's and Germany's separate situations regarding resources, and particularly with regard to motor vehicles. Brown was solidly middle class but not especially well-off, yet he already had a car of his own; it was a luxury very few Germans of his age enjoyed. In 1935, there was one vehicle for every 65 people in

Germany, and four years later, despite building autobahns, that figure was still only one vehicle for every 47 people. In Britain in 1935, the figure had been one vehicle for every 23 people and had risen to one for every 14 by the outbreak of war. In France, the leading user of motor vehicles in Europe, the figure had been one vehicle for every 19 people in 1935. In the United States, it had been one vehicle for every 5 people back in 1935 and had risen to almost one for every 3 by 1939. In contrast, in Italy in 1936, there had been just one car for every 104 people. Italy and Germany may have had already well-known – and Grand Prix-winning – names such as Mercedes, Audi and Alfa Romeo, but this only underlined just what an elite sport it was; it was no reflection on the wider German or Italian society.

For a nation like Germany that had entered into war against two of the leading and richest nations in the world, this was a major problem, because the lack of motor vehicles in the country had all kind of knock-on effects that went beyond a simple shortage of vehicles on the front line. The fewer vehicles there were meant there were also fewer factories than in say, France or Britain, making them. The fewer factories there were, the fewer people there were with the know-how to make vehicles, and the fewer mechanics there were to repair them; it meant there were also fewer people who knew how to drive them, and fewer petrol pumps to fill them. This shortfall in expertise could not be magicked out of thin air. It took time to build up.

Nazi propaganda had worked hard to give the impression that the Wehrmacht of 1939 was the most modern, most mechanized in the world. Nothing could have been further from the truth, as those trying to manage the Polish campaign and its aftermath had been struggling to come to terms with. Rather, just fifteen divisions out of the fifty-four used had been mechanized in any way; the rest had been dependent on vast numbers of horses and the men marching on their own two feet – just as Prussian and then German armies had moved for hundreds of years. Nor was there any 'Blitzkrieg' strategy – certainly it was not a phrase anyone would have been familiar with in Germany; rather, it was coined later, by *Time* magazine in the US on 25 September. Furthermore, because Hitler had ordered Case WHITE very suddenly, the planned war games in which air forces and ground troops would put theories to the test had to be cancelled. The time to test their Army and Air Force became the invasion itself, and although the campaign was effectively over in just eighteen days, the Poles were hardly much of a yardstick by which to judge the efficacy of their war machine. The planning had been good, but plenty of difficulties had arisen, not least with the limited amount of motor transport employed.

One of the men trying to deal with this really rather massive problem within the Wehrmacht was Oberst Adolf von Schell, who was General Plenipotentiary for Motor Vehicles under General Georg Thomas, head of the War Economics and Armaments Office (WiRüAmt) at the OKW. Now forty-six years old, von Schell had been a career soldier who had fought throughout the First World War from its opening manoeuvres in Belgium, through some of the major battles on the Western Front and across to the Eastern Front and the Carpathians. He had been wounded four times and awarded the Iron Cross First Class twice, and, having emerged still in one piece at the end, had remained in the Reichswehr, the much-reduced German Army.

By 1930, he was a captain, had served both in infantry regiments and as a staff officer at the RWM, the Reich Ministry for Economic Affairs, and had then been sent to Fort Benning in the United States as an instructor at the Infantry School. The Americans had been impressed by this hugely experienced infantry officer, and the US Army had even published a book based on his lectures there, called *Battle Leadership*. For his part, the genial and inquisitive von Schell had made the most of the opportunity of being in the United States to study the American motor industry, including spending time at the Ford motor plants in Detroit. When he returned to Germany the following year, he did so with his mind full of ideas about just how the Army could become more mechanized and what was needed from the German motor industry.

As he discovered, staff appointments at the Ministry of War as well as a stint as tactics instructor at the Institute of War gave him the opportunity to speak out about his views and what he had learned in the USA, the most automotive society in the world. By 1937, he was Chief of Staff of the Inspectorate of Mechanized Troops; a year later, he had been appointed Under-Secretary in the Ministry of Transport and had begun to be noticed by both Hitler and Göring. First came an appointment as the Automotive Engineering Delegate for the Four-Year Plan. Finally, in November 1938, as Göring had announced his plans to massively increase the rate of rearmament, he was given the key role of General Plenipotentiary of Motor Vehicles. This meant he was the man who was to co-ordinate and oversee the mechanization of the Wehrmacht. For so long he had striven to influence the Wehrmacht and help make the Army, especially, more mechanized. Now, at last, he had that position of influence. Little did he realize at the time, however, just what a poisoned chalice this would be.

Even by the spring of 1939, some of the problems that would plague Germany's drive for a more mechanized Wehrmacht were becoming all too apparent to von Schell. He recognized that only a motorized economy could produce motorized armed forces; it was not enough to simply demand greater mechanization – as both Hitler and Göring did – and expect it to happen out of thin air. Eventually, in the long term, maybe; but in 1939 there was a huge discrepancy between what was being demanded and what was actually achievable in the short term. The building of fortifications, for example, such as those along the Westwall, or Siegfried Line, required more trucks than had been anticipated; so too did the new divisions that were being raised. There was, however, no mass production as there was in the United States, and no co-ordination of effort, rather just a lot of innovative models being produced in low numbers. There was also a conflict between commercial and military requirements. The disparate and largely small-scale German motor industry was made up from individual companies that continued to produce their own, different types of trucks, cars and other vehicles. When von Schell had taken over as General Plenipotentiary of Motor Vehicles, there had been no fewer than 131 different types of truck and 1,367 different types of trailer, all of which required different parts, different repair knowledge and, all too often, different tools too.

The second big problem was that of raw materials. On the one hand, the Nazis were demanding more mechanization for the Wehrmacht, but on the other had reduced the iron ore quota, for example, as priority was switched elsewhere. Because of this, von Schell warned Göring in a long memo back in March, only 50 per cent of truck orders could realistically be delivered by the beginning of 1940. For the already inefficient factories, this was a disaster, because it meant there would be a lag of time when there was not enough work, and owners would have no choice but to lay people off. 'Once this has happened,' von Schell told him, 'then an increase in production is unimaginable for several years. This would damage the motorization of the Wehrmacht, the Reich and commerce, from which it would hardly be able to recover.'

Amidst these conflicting demands and the deeply entrenched privatized motor industry, von Schell had spent the best part of a year valiantly trying to make improvements with a series of measures that became known as the 'Schell Plan'. He knew that the still-privatized motor industry needed greater state interference, but the Nazis were curiously reluctant to do this, not least because it went against Hitler's – and Göring's – penchant for divide and rule.

None the less, von Schell would have to impose himself on the motor industry if he was to have any chance at all of making it more efficient, and top of his list of measures was to reduce the number of vehicle types – in the case of trucks, from 131 to twenty-three. The aim was for the old types to be discontinued through 1939. Because of the shortage of fuel, he also planned to increase the number of vehicles operating not with petrol but with gas generators of solid fuels, aiming for nearly 160,000 such trucks by 1941. Also encouraged was the production of the militarized version of Hitler's planned car for the masses, the Volkswagen. Both the civilian and military version, which became known as the *Kübelwagen*, or 'bucket car', were designed by Ferdinand Porsche. However, even though Porsche's first designs for the *Kübelwagen* were drawn up in 1938, it was still not in production by the invasion of Poland; instead, a handful only were field tested in the campaign. Full production was still a few months off, as the design was repeatedly refined and tweaked. Meanwhile, time was ticking away.

Another of von Schell's plans was to improve maintenance, so he came up with the Home Motor Pool Organization, in which repair shops and garages would remain independent and in private hands but would be under the Wehrmacht's control. This meant the military would take priority over civilian requirements, and there would at least be some form of pooling of maintenance resources. Finally, there was compulsory requisitioning. Some 50 per cent of all civilian trucks were taken for military use, on the basis that half could be taken without crippling the economy too severely.

Since his appointment as controller of all motor vehicles, von Schell had been aiming to fulfil all his plans by 1942, and by the beginning of September 1939 there was an awful lot of work yet to be done. Getting the various companies to toe the line had been no easy task and still there were too many variations and production was too low.

Film crews were careful to focus on the units that did have trucks and panzers, and stopped the cameras rolling whenever things started to go wrong. However, even before troops crossed over into Poland, it was clear there were nowhere near enough maintenance facilities. This was because that part of Prussia was an area of especially few motor vehicles, which had meant there were fewer civilian repair shops to incorporate into the Home Motor Pool Organization. And once they were in Poland, the roads had proved particularly bad, putting a greater strain on the vehicles themselves, all too many of which were originally civilian and never designed for robust military use. Inexperienced drivers were also too rough with them. The grinding of gears, numerous potholes, pressure of battle and a host of other factors all conspired to make mechanical breakdown a major issue. Once kaput, the problem was further exacerbated by the still large range of vehicles. Getting the right spares to the right broken-down vehicle, deep inside Poland, was no easy task. Von Schell was relieved it had been all over bar the shouting within a couple weeks. A much longer campaign, and the mechanized arm of the Wehrmacht would have ground to a halt.

It wasn't only the outside world that had thought of the emerging Wehrmacht as a giant, modern, mechanized force. Most Germans believed it too, including Siegfried Knappe, who, as a nineteen-year-old back in October 1936, had joined the artillery with visions of becoming part of an elite force of modern motorized guns. His father had been a naval gunnery officer in the last war and during Siegfried's childhood had told him many thrilling tales of his wartime exploits. During his final years at the *Gymnasium*, his secondary school, and his six months' conscription in the Reich Labour Service, Knappe had read much in the newspapers and magazines about the new self-propelled artillery weapons that were coming into service so, on joining the Army, signing up for the artillery had been an easy choice.

As he had arrived at the barracks in Jena, however, Knappe had been in for a shock. Far from being kitted out with shiny modern equipment, there were instead vast rows of stable blocks.

'You mean they still pull the artillery with horses?' he asked his companion, desperately hoping it was not true.

'Yes, I am afraid so,' came the reply.

The following morning, before dawn and in the cold darkness, the new recruits were taken straight to the stables and each man was given a horse stall to clean. A deflated Knappe began what would now become a daily routine – mucking out. 'I still could not believe,' he noted, 'I was actually in the horse-drawn artillery. It all seemed so backward in this modern age.'

Almost three years later, Knappe, now a lieutenant and battery commander, had come to terms with his earlier disappointment. He had become a keen horseman and was proud of his battery, his regiment and their high standard of training. They knew their task so well that operating and firing had become instinctive; they had trained with the infantry too, and while their guns were still horse-drawn, they were high-quality pieces all the same: 24. Artillerieregiment began the war with justifiable confidence.

Not all the regiment had headed into Poland, however. Twenty per cent had been left behind to form a new regiment. This was because only a comparatively small part of the German Army was fully trained. Fully trained Regular troops had amounted to around 684,000, while there were a further 410,000 fully trained reservists. Some 709,000 reservists had received only very rudimentary training, and on top of that there were nearly 1.7 million older reservists and First World War veterans. The Field Army was 2.5 million strong, while the Replacement Army numbered 1.2 million.

The Field Army was made up from a mixture of fully trained Regular troops and reservists, while a fifth of the personnel of Regular Army divisions were pulled out of the Field Army and put into the Replacement Army. Siegfried Knappe was among the 20 per cent taken from 24. Artillery Battalion and sent to form the cadre of a new formation. Generally speaking, replacement divisions were spread around the country and drew on locally mobilized men, largely because they then had less distance to travel – and with the chronic shortage of vehicles and an already over-burdened railway network, this made good sense.

In 1939, the unit by which the scale of a fighting force was judged tended to be the division. Numbers varied, but as a rule of thumb, most were between 14,000 and 17,000 men strong, and this was the case for British and French – and even American and Italian – divisions too. Two or more divisions made up a corps, while two or more corps made up an army and two or more armies made an army group. Divisions were described by the make-up of their core regiments, either panzer (armoured), panzer grenadier (motorized) or infantry. In an infantry division, for example, there would be three regiments consisting of three battalions each, as well as pioneers (engineers), artillery and support troops. Each regiment would be 3,250 strong with a number of ancillary companies and battalions of around 800 troops. The British had regiments, but while these were divided into battalions, the equivalent formation to a German regiment was known as a brigade, i.e. made up of three battalions, but usually from different regiments.

At any rate, the German Army of September 1939 was made up of 106 divisions, which included the Field and Replacement Armies. Only half of those divisions, however, were what were called 'First Wave' troops, i.e. those sent into Poland.

Knappe and the 24. Artillery Battalion had been based at Plauen, in south-east Germany, near the Czech border. With much of the regiment gone, the remainder stayed behind at the barracks waiting for new replacements to arrive. For Knappe, it meant a lot of new faces, including a new battery commander, who was over forty and a reservist, as well as 150 others and the same number of horses. At least, however, he was able to keep his own horse, his beloved Schwabenprinz.

Within a few days, this newly formed artillery regiment moved out and headed west, taking up positions near the Luxembourg border. There they immediately began a vigorous training programme in order to accustom the horses and men to working together and to get them ready as soon as possible to face a potential attack by the Allies. Still no attack came, so that by the end of September, and with confidence rising, Knappe heard the troops starting to make jokes about it. A few days later, they pulled back a short distance out of their bunkers to more comfortable surroundings. It seemed that the French were not going to attack after all. 'Even though we were technically at war with England and France,' noted Knappe, 'everyone assumed that the war was really over with the defeat of Poland.'

Siegfried Knappe wasn't the only German soldier thinking such thoughts. Hans von Luck, who had fought in Poland and survived unscathed along with most of his colleagues, had also heard much talk that the war was now over, both from soldiers and from German civilians as they returned to Bad Kissingen. But von Luck wasn't so sure; he'd noticed the propaganda machine was once again cranking up against Britain and France. Hitler, he knew, held a deep-rooted loathing of France ever since the last war. The names 'Alsace' and 'Lorraine', taken in the

Franco-Prussian War in 1871 but handed back to France in 1919, were also cropping up repeatedly.

Von Luck was quite right not to be seduced by premature thoughts of peace, although many of those at the very top of the Wehrmacht, horrified by the declaration of war by Britain and France, had hoped the war could be brought to an end by political means now that the campaign in Poland was over. Even the more pessimistic, like General Walter Warlimont at the OKW, hoped that by adopting a firm defensive approach and building up military strength further, they might eventually draw the Allies to the negotiating table.

They were, however, about to be stunned by a bombshell. Warlimont had been visiting Hitler's forward headquarters, temporarily set up in the Casino Hotel in Zoppot, in Poland, on 20 September, when he saw an ashen General Keitel. The Chief of the OKW then told him that Hitler intended to launch an offensive on the West almost immediately. It was, he told Warlimont, top secret and he was not to breathe a word; Keitel confessed he had only heard through one of Hitler's aides.

Warlimont was dumbstruck. At no point had Hitler ever discussed the matter with any of his senior generals – not Keitel, not General Walther von Brauchitsch, the head of the Army, not even Göring. The Polish campaign was all but over by then, but, even so, it had shown up some worrying deficiencies, not least shortages of just about everything, from vehicles and vehicle spare parts to ammunition. The fighting in Poland was also demonstrating the lack of training in many of the divisions. Taking on Poland was one thing, but going on the offensive against the two powerhouses of Europe was quite another. Hitler had decided to strike quickly before Britain and France could build up a sufficient advantage in terms of men, machines and equipment. What he singularly failed to realize was the Wehrmacht needed time to build up strength too, because Germany was simply not ready for all-out war in the autumn of 1939. Furthermore, winter was coming, which massively affected the efficiency and operational capability of forces on the ground and in the air; using the Luftwaffe in tandem with the Army on the ground was a key part of Germany's war plan, but in the shortening days and worsening weather this was much harder to put into action. Yet again, Hitler's lack of understanding of the operational art of war was becoming all too apparent; he was envisioning attacking the West within a matter of weeks. That would lead to a plan that was insufficiently prepared and inadequately thought through. It was madness.

Warlimont was so horrified he decided to try to take things into his own hands. Recognizing that neither Keitel nor General Alfred Jodl, the Chief of Staff of the OKW, would act, he decided to ignore Keitel's warning of secrecy and let the Army General Staff know what the Führer was planning. Despite this tip-off, the Army did nothing.

A week later, on 27 September, Hitler assembled his Commanders-in-Chief at the Reich Chancellery in Berlin, along with Keitel and Warlimont, and announced they would be attacking in the West as soon as possible. Warlimont noticed he had been holding a small piece of paper with some notes on it; having said his piece, he tossed the paper into the fire. No one said a word in protest.

CHAPTER 9

The Modern Army

OBERST ADOLF VON SCHELL was in no doubt whatsoever that a fully mechanized army was the way forward. It was true that horses did not require petrol, but they did require fuel and lots of it. Fodder had to be transported, and in any case its production used ground that could otherwise be utilized for the production of food for both the armed forces and the general population. In fact, von Schell had calculated that a fully mechanized army would be 80 per cent more efficient in terms of the supply of men and materiel.

It was with these sorts of calculations in mind that Britain had decided its entire field force should be fully mechanized. Back in March the Territorial Army had been doubled from thirteen divisions to twenty-six and since then mobilized – Bill Cheall, the young Yorkshireman from The Green Howards whose Devon holiday had been interrupted at the end of August, was part of this call to arms. On the outbreak of war, the National Service (Armed Forces) Act had been immediately passed, introducing full conscription. On 8 September, it was agreed that the aim should be to equip fifty-five divisions by the end of the second year of war, i.e. 1941, which would include fourteen from the Dominions of Canada, South Africa, Australia and New Zealand, and a further four from India. At least twenty divisions were to be equipped within the first twelve months. Priority was to go to the Field Force being sent to France, soon named the British Expeditionary Force in a nod to the army sent overseas back in 1914.

By the end of September, almost 160,000 Army personnel and 22,000 vehicles, along with nearly 10,000 men of the RAF, some 36,000 tons of ammunition and 25,000 tons of fuel had safely been shipped to France, and it was planned that this fighting force would grow significantly over the ensuing months. Because of this rapid growth in the Army, especially, there were now worrying shortages of equipment, particularly guns and tanks, but output was growing on a weekly basis.

Despite these shortages, the British Army was still the best equipped and most modern in the world, not least because its Field Force was entirely mechanized. There were no horse-drawn artillery units, and all infantry were ferried from A to B in trucks. The 15 cwt and 30 cwt lorries equipping much of the BEF were rugged and robust – the motor firms Bedford and Morris producing most of them. British artillery was also of good quality, and most guns were now equipped with pneumatic tyres, which meant they could easily be towed by trucks and gun tractors, unlike most of the German equivalents, which were largely towed by horse. There was also a tracked troop carrier simply called the Universal Carrier. Infantry had never been so well served by machines.

In fact, the British Army was going through something of a revolution. Hand in hand with rearmament had come the recognition that attitudes had to change, that a modern war required modern equipment, and that Britain needed to use its global reach to full effect. Ironically, the impression from German propaganda of a Reich that was creating a modern, mechanized military Moloch had done much to kick-start this new outlook.

Much had changed in the past three years, right down to the uniforms. With the scent of war in the air, Britain had, in 1938, designed the Battledress, a highly innovative concept and the most modern and practical combat uniform adopted by any European power. Made of hard-wearing khaki wool serge, it consisted of a short jacket that came down to its wearer's midriff. This was very sensible given the high-waisted trousers of the day; the battle blouse, as the jacket was called, therefore only covered the waistband of the trousers, and in so doing saved a significant amount of fabric on earlier designs and on those worn by almost every other army the world over. It was generously cut under the arms, allowing easy movement, and considerable thought had been given to the pockets – two large ones on the inside of the jacket, two large breast pockets, side pockets on the trousers and a further generous pocket on the thigh, big enough for a map or documents. The old knee-high puttees had also gone, relics of a former era, replaced by durable canvas ankle gaiters. This new soldier's uniform had no frills, wasted no material, and was exceptionally cheap and easy to mass-produce, while at the same time allowing its wearer easy manoeuvrability and warmth.

Also recently introduced was the new Bren light machine gun, capable of firing at a theoretical rate of 500 rounds per minute, which, as had been shown by the phenomenally effective German Maxim gun of the previous war, was around the optimum rate of fire; much faster firing rates created problems of overheating and, obviously, used more ammunition, and in any case there was an argument for having a weapon that could kill twenty enemies with one bullet each rather than one soldier with twenty. Fed by thirty-round magazines, the Bren was rarely allowed to overheat and, in any case, had a thick barrel and wooden grip that made barrel-changing very straightforward. It was also what was considered a light machine gun, and could be operated by just one man. Designed in Brno, Czechoslovakia, and adapted and modified by Enfield in England – hence Br–en – it was versatile, robust and accurate, and had a barrel designed to fire 220,000 rounds. It was a fine piece of kit.

Now out in France with the Royal Fusiliers, Lieutenant Norman Field's platoon of thirty-six men had three sections of ten men plus a six-man platoon headquarters, and each section was now equipped with one Bren and nine Short Magazine Lee Enfield rifles, the latter capable of firing two five-round clips without a change of magazine. No other rifle at the time could fire as many, and, because the firing bolt came back only a short way, whoever was firing it could pull the bolt back without altering his aim. As this capacity was not something shared by other bolt-action rifles at the time, a reasonably trained rifleman in the British Army could expect to fire around thirty rounds per minute, while the French and German infantrymen could manage only half that.

British webbing – the soldier's pouches, packs and belts – had also changed with the advent of the Bren and the Battledress. Back in 1914, the British Army had realized that leather, which had been used for centuries to make ammunition pouches, was not so effective in sustained and continuous combat. It was also expensive – very expensive – and if it got wet could become brittle when it dried out again. Far more effective was canvas, which was both cheap and durable. Ever since then, British webbing had been made of this cotton-based material, and the new 1937 pattern included two pouches large enough to carry three Bren magazines each.

Certainly, there were no complaints from Norman Field and his men about the new uniforms. 'It was a vast improvement,' he says. 'In the old service dress, one always felt rather stiff and buttoned up. It was much easier to slither around on the ground in Battledress.'

The British infantry, at any rate, were now well-equipped for war. They had plenty of firepower, trucks and tracked Carriers to move them around rapidly, and new, modern-design uniforms.

None the less, it was, of course, easier to equip a smaller army than a large one. Rearmament since 1935 had focused so heavily on the Navy and RAF, and these decisions by men like Neville Chamberlain, first as Chancellor of the Exchequer and then as Prime Minister, not only largely dictated Britain's actions in the build up to war, but the approach it would also take as the conflict unfolded. The First World War had underlined to Britain's war leaders the futility of labour-intensive campaigns, in which huge numbers of men were thrown at increasingly powerful weapons, and which had produced long years of attritional stalemate. The British intention was to invest in machinery and technology to help create a strategy that was less wasteful of men's lives and, hopefully, would bring about victory sooner. Quite intentionally, the number of men at the coal face of fighting was to be kept as low as possible. In this new war, man-power would be used not just as soldiers on the ground and on ships, but in many more aircraft and, most of all, in factories and shipyards. And considering Britain's global reach and already heavy investment in research and technology, it was an entirely sensible approach.

With this in mind, Britain was preparing for a massive increase in the size of its Army, but still had no intention of going beyond fifty-five divisions, even though Germany had over a hundred by the outbreak of war, and France, after rapid mobilization, now also had close to a hundred. The men behind these decisions were not only the Prime Minister, peacetime Cabinet and now War Cabinet, but also the Chiefs of Staff, which consisted of the three service chiefs and the man at the top of the pile, the Chief of the Imperial General Staff (CIGS). This had been General Lord Gort, who had won a Victoria Cross, Britain's highest award for valour, in the last war. He had now taken command of the BEF, so General 'Tiny' Ironside had become CIGS in his place. Assisting them were the Vice-Chiefs of Staff, the Joint Planning Staff and the Joint

Intelligence Committee, or JIC, both of the latter, as their names implied, representing all three services working both separately and together.

Collectively, the planning teams, Vice-Chiefs and Chiefs of Staff and Government had had the vision and wherewithal to create a modern and well-equipped army, but while training now taught soldiers how to operate with all this mechanization and with radio sets and Bren light machine guns, much of the Regular Army had spent the years since 1918 carrying out its more traditional role: policing the Empire. And containing angry Arabs or troublesome Pashtuns on the Northwest Frontier was no real preparation for coming into combat against the combined forces of Nazi Germany.

Intellectually, the British Army was also stymied by a somewhat insouciant and deeply entrenched regimental system, which laid great emphasis on both loyalty to the cap badge and tradition, and which encouraged a culture that frowned on too much talking shop. In the Mess, one discussed cricket, polo or pig-sticking, not how to effectively co-ordinate tanks and infantry. In any case, the cavalry had largely remained cavalry throughout much of the 1920s and 1930s, even though Britain had invented the tank, and its regiments were among the most influential within the British Army. Tanks were the preserve of the Royal Tank Corps and rather looked down upon by the cavalry as a bunch of low-grade Johnny-come-latelys. When the cavalry regiments did finally begin to mechanize, most of their number were appalled. Certain members of The Royal Scots Greys, for example, were so disgusted at the idea of mechanization that in 1938 they lobbied Parliament against such a move and wrote angry letters to *The Times*.

Yet, by the summer of 1939, most had succumbed to the inevitable and modernized. As Britain began this new war, the thinking was that tanks would perform a variety of roles, which required different types of tank. Cavalry regiments tended to be equipped with light, fast tanks, for use in a forward screening and reconnaissance capacity, such as they had performed in the last war and beyond, while the newly formed Royal Armoured Corps, which contained the new regiments of the Royal Tank Corps, used slower, more heavily armoured tanks in direct support of the infantry.

British tanks were, for the most part, on a par with, if not better than, German versions. The Matilda had the thickest armour of any tank in the world and was virtually immune to most of the guns in the German arsenal, while the Mk II variant had a high-velocity 2-pounder gun that was more than a match for all German panzers apart from the Panzer IV. Early British cruiser tanks were not so good, with complicated suspension systems, and they suffered from being jacks of all trades and masters of none. None the less, the A10 had armour as thick as a Panzer IV's and was also equipped with a 2-pounder, while the next version, the A13, was fast, was soon upgraded to 30mm of armour and was similarly equipped with the 2-pounder. When this anti-tank gun had first appeared in 1938, it was probably the best of its kind in the world and could fire a 37mm shell at some 2,700 feet per second; by the outbreak of war, this was still a velocity that ranked favourably with most German guns, and could penetrate 50 millimetres of armour at a thousand yards, that is two-thirds of a mile. The thickest armour on any panzer was 30 millimetres. Early British tanks have taken a large amount of criticism over the years, but by the standards of the first year of war they were really not bad at all. What's more, production was rising rapidly.

By August 1939, the only units where horses and vast amounts of leather were still used were those in the Yeomanry regiments. The Yeomanry had first been raised during the Napoleonic Wars, volunteer units whose members had to own or have access to a horse. By the summer of 1939, this recruitment policy still held, which was why most of its members were landowners, countrymen, mad-keen huntsmen and steeplechasers.

One of those regiments still equipped with its chargers was the Nottingham Sherwood Rangers Yeomanry. One of the TA units to have been mobilized on the outbreak of war, it had had a fine record in the last war, where it had served in the Middle East, but since then had been confined to weekend training and the obligatory summer camp each August. Its last camp had been at Welbeck, the estate of the Duke of Portland, and was, in many ways, rather like a grown-up Scout camp on horseback.

Already, though, its ranks were being swelled by an influx of new officers and other ranks, drawn from a much wider pool. One of those was Stanley Christopherson, who was twenty-seven and had already seen something of the world, having been brought up partly in South Africa and having worked there in the gold-mining business after leaving Winchester College. He had since returned and gone into stockbroking in the City, living the life of a highly sociable and extremely charming young bachelor about town. A few years back, he had also joined the Inns of Court, a TA cavalry regiment for barristers, solicitors, stockbrokers and former public schoolboys like himself.

The Inns of Court had not been mobilized at the outbreak of war, but all its members had. Christopherson and two of his old Inns of Court pals had been sent to join the Sherwood Rangers. Having been to see the regimental tailor and boot-maker in London, a week or so later they boarded the train to Malton in Yorkshire, where the Rangers were based, proudly wearing their one pip of a second-lieutenant and sporting riding breeches, boots, spurs and tunics. 'We were slightly apprehensive,' Christopherson noted in his diary, 'as we had heard the Regiment boasted three Masters of Fox Hounds and the pre-war officers were extremely wealthy and very insular.' To his delight, however, he not only found old City chums like Micky Gold and Mike Parrish were already in the Sherwood Rangers, but so too were Peter and Michael Laycock, with whom he had been at prep school.

At Malton, the Rangers would carry out intense training and complete the business of switching from peacetime TA unit to full-time soldiers. For the time being they would be keeping their chargers; the Sherwood Rangers would not be heading to France, however, but to Palestine. There was no immediate sign of war breaking out in the Middle East, but the problems of the Empire did not stop now that Britain was at war with Germany; on the contrary, in many cases they were exacerbated. The area had been stable enough in the 1920s, but by the late 1930s threatened to break out in violence at any moment. Arab nationalism was an easy way for the Axis to make life difficult for the British, and while Italy had kept out of the war, Italian agents were still agitating in the region. British strategy was therefore not only to make sure there was no uprising but also to ensure there were enough troops out there should Italy enter the war and make a move against British possessions there.

There was, it was true, something about the Sherwood Rangers Yeomanry that harked back to an earlier age, but they were by no means representative of the rest of the rapidly enlarging British Army. In any case, these few outmoded Yeomanry and Regular cavalry units affected only one level of warfare – and, in Britain's case, only one of its three armed services. War, it was widely understood, was to be fought on three levels: the strategic, the operational and the tactical. Tactically, in the Army at any rate, Britain had some growing up to do, but operationally and strategically, she was on much firmer footing. The biggest issue during this first winter of war, was size. Britain was mobilizing fast, but the Army's growth to fifty-five divisions would take several years, not months. There was no panic yet, however, because France's Army was huge.

And so with the Nazi swastika now fluttering over Warsaw, the plan as agreed between Britain and France back in the spring still held true: so long as they could hold any German offensive at bay, all would be well. They would sit tight, build up strength and then strike back. There had never been much question of storming into Germany within moments of war being declared; the deal with Poland was to enter the war on its behalf. No one mentioned actually trying to save the beleaguered Poles. Not right away, at any rate.

Certainly, thanks to its existing Air Force, Navy and access to vast resources of merchant shipping, Britain's own sovereignty was in no way under threat. New, modern factories were already making arms with increased vigour. Sixteen new ordnance factories had been authorized in March, and a further twenty-nine were given the green light in December. Planned spending on arms for 1939/40 was £580 million, half of all government expenditure. More guns, more aircraft, more ships – more war materiel – and with no sign of there being any let-up until Germany was beaten. And this was the point: Britain's – and France's – war aims were not for the war to fizzle out in some negotiated peace with Germany. Rather, it was to take on the Third Reich and rid the world of Hitler and Nazism, and beat Germany once and for all. This, however, would take time, so as far as Britain's war leaders were concerned, the longer Germany delayed the better.

Britain's appreciation of the situation was precisely what Hitler feared and was why he was demanding his generals prepare for an immediate assault on the West. Hitler's geo-political understanding was often very suspect indeed. But on the need to crush Britain and France swiftly and decisively, he was absolutely right.

CHAPTER 10

Leading the Nation

IN THE WEEKS that had followed the outbreak of war, the American journalist Eric Sevareid had been providing broadcasts almost every day, responding to a seemingly insatiable appetite for war news from the other side of the Atlantic. And during that time he had managed to get out of Paris and have a look at what was going on along the front lines. He'd seen the arrival of British troops at Cherbourg, and then he and several others, including the New Zealander Geoffrey Cox, who was writing for the British *Daily Express*, had even managed to get to the Maginot Line. There was an understanding that no journalists were to go there, but no written prohibition, so, leaving early in the morning, they drove out of the city and on reaching one checkpoint after another sweet-talked their way through, until they reached the city of Metz and drove on right up to the front-line forts.

It was damp and cold, and twilight had settled on the land as they reached a village near the border. Increasingly as they had approached the front, they had seen long lines of Parisian buses, painted in camouflage and teeming with troops, and plodding horses pulling soup kitchens. The men wore the same oval helmets they had in the last war, and even their uniforms looked much the same too: they wore overcoats, or *capote*, with the skirts buttoned back off the front of the legs, just as they had in 1914 – this was a purely nineteenth-century design and, if anything, harked back even to Napoleon's day. Around their legs, they still wore puttees that wrapped all the way to the knee. Much of the uniform was now, at long last, khaki, rather than blue, although some troops still wore

blue trousers. A new golf-style baggy set of plus-fours had been introduced but these were not widespread yet; in any case, they made the
French soldiers look even more like they were in the nineteenth century.
Webbing was a combination of canvas and leather, but it was curious that
the *poilus* should look so old-fashioned when in a few other areas great
advances had been made; while the standard uniform was bulky, heavy
and utterly ill-suited to modern fighting, mountain troops, for example,
a small elite within the French Army, had superb kit: modern cotton and
serge short jackets, woollen pullovers, excellent boots and practical short
gaiters. If only the entire French Army had been equipped in such a way,
because the cost was certainly not the issue; a long, bulky, standard-issue
greatcoat used much more material than the shorter, more comfortable
cotton and serge jacket, for example. Uniforms were very, very important, and not only from a pragmatic point of view. Put on a modern,
comfortable, radical design of uniform and the wearer will feel he is part
of something equally forward-thinking. Conversely, wear a uniform that
looks at least forty years out of date, and the opposite is likely to be the
case. This certainly struck Eric Sevareid. 'It was all the same,' he noted.
'The projector had stopped in 1918 and now was turning again.' After
seeing a large number of Moroccan troops and hearing just one lone gun
fire a single shell, he and his colleagues turned back to Paris.

   Not long after, Sevareid and his increasingly good friend, Geoffrey
Cox, had driven north to Belgium, Holland and tiny Luxembourg,
conscious that, as yet, no broadcasts had been sent from this trio of neutral countries. Britain and France had hoped they could set up a defensive
line along the Belgian border with Germany, but as in 1914 Belgium had
refused; not until such time that Germany abused its neutrality would
Belgium allow Allied troops to cross its borders. Effectively, these
countries were now no-man's-land, caught in the middle and clearly
hoping that somehow they could avoid becoming embroiled in a conflict
in which they wanted no involvement whatsoever. The reality, which was
abundantly clear to any outside observer – and not least Eric Sevareid
and Geoffrey Cox – was that this was wishful thinking of the highest
order. It did not take a master strategist to realize the Germans were
unlikely to attempt an assault across the Maginot Line or that Hitler was
going to sit back and wait for the Allies to attack. It was therefore a
reasonable bet that Belgium – at the very least – would be fought over.
Had these countries allowed Allied troops in earlier, then it would have

been possible to create a much stronger and unified line while there was still time. This was not to be, however. Both King Leopold of Belgium and his Government and Queen Wilhelmina of the Netherlands and her Government stolidly stuck to their neutral stance, accepting Hitler's assurances that their neutrality would be respected. Why they should have thought these promises were more likely to be kept than others that had flagrantly been broken is not clear. Maybe it was wishful thinking. Or maybe they hoped that by remaining neutral they would be dealt with more leniently should the war reach them.

Certainly, their own defences were as nothing compared with what they might have been had the French, in particular, been allowed in. A united Europe that stood up to Nazi ideas of territorial expansion would have added up to more than the sum of its individual parts. This was already horribly clear after the rolling over of Czechoslovakia. Most of the Czechs' considerable defences had been in the Sudetenland, which had then been ceded without a fight after Munich. Had they remained intact, and had France and Britain persuaded the Low Countries, and the states of Scandinavia, that together, through mutual aid and alliances, they could build an impregnable ring around Nazi Germany, there is every chance the war would never have started. Had that been the case, there is also every reason to suppose the Pact of Steel may never have been signed. Even Hitler understood the importance of not fighting on more than one front at any time; it was widely accepted that this was what had led to defeat in the last war, as the Germans had battled to fight Russia in the east and the Allies in the west, and it was this fundamental weakness of geography that made Germany both so vulnerable and an unlikely military superpower; avoiding fighting on multiple fronts was deeply ingrained into every one of his senior commanders.

But this ring of iron around Germany had not been achieved, and already Hitler had been able to start rendering its constituent parts harmless, first the Sudetenland, then the rest of Czechoslovakia and now Poland; this was the failure of appeasement, not the mythical late entry into rearming. The threat from the East had been neutralized. The worry for the West was that Germany would be able to undermine it further by strikes north and west into the Low Countries.

As Sevareid and Cox drove around, they were depressed by what they saw. It was true the Ardennes, that area of densely wooded hills and narrow valleys, was widely considered a natural barrier impassable by modern mechanized armies, but, even so, the few log barriers they saw were going to stop nothing, let alone the full weight of the Nazi war machine. At one point, as they drove deep into the Ardennes, they came across a Belgian patrol, who stopped them and asked them whether they had any liquor, then asked for a joyride in their car. As Sevareid and Cox made to drive on, one of the Belgian soldiers said in a slurring voice, 'Post's jush down nex' turn. Don't tell the captain we're already drunk.' A Belgian colonel they met and spoke to told them at least 50 per cent of his regiment were absent without leave in Antwerp.

When they reached Holland and Sevareid explained to the American consul that he wanted to make a broadcast about the military situation in the country, he was met with incredulity; the consul had assumed Sevareid would want to tell his listeners about canals, tulips and winter skating. Everywhere they went, they saw normal life continuing – the mobilization André Beaufre had seen as he had travelled back through Amsterdam had, as far as Sevareid was concerned, melted away.

Across the Atlantic, Americans continued to be fascinated by the war, and not least Harry Hopkins, who was still weak and confined to bed but had miraculously survived what had looked like an early end to his life just a couple of months earlier. 'The only interest here,' wrote Harry Hopkins in a letter to his brother, 'is the war,' although he hoped and believed America could still keep out of it. 'Fortunately there is no great sentiment in this country for getting into it, although I think almost everyone wants to see England and France win.'

This, in a neat nutshell, was the terrible dilemma facing the President, Franklin D. Roosevelt, who most definitely wanted France and Britain to win but knew that his fellow countrymen had no appetite to help them achieve that victory. The first wartime poll in the United States in September showed that only 2.5 per cent of the population believed America should enter the war on the side of the Allies. The largest proportion – 37.5 per cent – believed the US should take no sides and stay out of the war entirely, but offer goods to anyone on a cash-and-carry basis. A further 29.9 per cent felt America should have nothing to do with the war whatsoever.

Roosevelt's motives were based on both morality and self-interest. As far as he was concerned, it was imperative a free and democratic Western world prevailed, and that meant the defeat of Nazism. Nor did he believe the United States was immune from the current European war. 'We in the Americas,' he had said in a speech in Canada the year before, 'are no longer a far-away continent to which the eddies of controversies beyond the seas could bring no interest or no harm . . . The vast amount of our resources, the vigor of our commerce and the strength of our men have made us vital factors in world peace whether we choose it or not.' His worst-case scenario went something like this: Britain and France would be defeated, and then Nazi Germany would turn west, probably first towards Latin America, then to the USA. Meanwhile, an emboldened Japan would strike in the Pacific.

The dilemma facing Roosevelt was that while he deeply believed America could not stand idle, he would face political suicide if he pushed against the tide of public opinion too heavily. Furthermore, the following autumn, in November 1940, there would be a presidential election. To stand for a third term would be unprecedented, yet to allow an isolationist into the White House could, to his mind, spell disaster. If he were to stand again, he would have to tread even more carefully. He was walking on glass, as he well understood.

Roosevelt had not given up on amending the Neutrality law, however, and with the outbreak of war had made immediate and renewed moves to get it changed. In a speech to Congress on 21 September, he told them it was not a question of being interventionist or isolationists – they were all united in wishing to avoid war. Neutrality revision, he argued, was essential to ensure peace at home. Personally, he favoured a complete repeal but instead proposed a sales of arms and goods on a cash-and-carry basis. In other words, any country would be able to buy arms, so long as it was for cash and they collected and shipped them themselves. This would almost exclusively benefit France and Britain, because Germany had neither the cash nor the shipping to do so. Roosevelt would then further be able to help the Allies by assisting Anglo-French purchasing teams as far as possible and co-operating with the British blockade of Germany, which had been put into effect immediately war broke out. Because Germany's access to the world's oceans was through the North Sea, the Royal Navy was able to block that access fairly easily. Immediately on that opening day of war, British submarine patrols began on the approaches to Wilhelmshaven and the Kiel Canal that linked the Baltic to the mouth of the River Elbe. Air patrols were stepped up, the Humber force of two cruisers and eight destroyers began cruising off the Norwegian coast, and the main body of the Home Fleet was put to sea some 400 miles west of the Hebrides in north-west Scotland. This screen was substantial enough to ensure there was little chance that any German vessel would be able to get through.

Throughout the debates in both the Senate and the House of Representatives, the President was careful not to mention either Britain or France by name and to stress the importance of the reforms for America's chances of continued peace. 'Our acts must be guided by one single hard-headed thought,' he told Congress, 'keeping America out of this war.'

His cause was helped by the vivid images of the destruction of Poland and by careful lobbying, so that by the beginning of November both houses had voted comfortably to repeal the arms embargo. For FDR, it was an important stepping stone – a move in the right direction at the very least.

America was still only slowly emerging from the Depression, but it had size, manpower and natural resources in abundance – the three components needed, above all, to create a large and successful armaments industry. That Britain and France could now, albeit in a limited fashion, draw on that resource was very much to their advantage and to the detriment of Nazi Germany.

It was also one of the principal reasons why Hitler was so anxious to strike west and knock Britain and France swiftly out of his way, and it made sense that it should be the OKW that would draw up plans for such an attack. After all, they were the combined operations staff and so were, on the face of it, best placed to plan and co-ordinate not only future operations that involved the Army, Luftwaffe and Navy, but also to draw up appreciations of possible future scenarios and to put in place plans should those ever be realized. Among their staff there were the men perfectly capable of doing this – men such as Oberst Warlimont, for example. In fact, as Deputy Chief of the Operations Staff, this was precisely what the job title suggested, but instead he and his department in Section L, as the Operations Staff were known, acted more as Hitler's personal military office. Their task was to distribute the Führer's directives and orders, and try and ensure the Wehrmacht was as efficiently equipped as possible – which was why, for example, Oberst von Schell's military vehicle office was within the OKW. In other words, the OKW were facilitators of Hitler's military will, not architects of military strategy and operations.

Warlimont and the operations staff could therefore offer little more than opinions, and the OKW as a whole was generally despised by the staffs of the other services, who considered them little more than Hitler's puppets. Keitel, for example, was known as 'Lakeitel' – lackey – a pun on his name. For Warlimont it was not only frustrating, but made no military sense whatsoever. 'Such lack of foresight,' he noted, 'seems almost incomprehensible.' The already fraught relationship between the OKW and the Army was made worse by the strong public support given to Hitler's decision to strike west without delay by those at the top of the OKW – Keitel, its chief, and Jodl, as Chief of Staff. As it happened, Keitel had suggested to Hitler that it was, perhaps, not such a great idea and even offered his resignation; this, however, had been waved aside. Instead, Keitel's public support for what was palpably military suicide merely lost him – and the OKW – even more respect among the Army command. And in the absence of any planning by the OKW, it was the Army, and, specifically, General Franz Halder, the Army Chief of Staff, that was given the task of preparing the attack in the West. The idea of launching an offensive within a matter of weeks and with winter approaching appalled Halder every bit as much as it did Warlimont.

Halder, who was fifty-five, crop-haired and bespectacled, came from a long line of military duty. He had spent most of his career in staff posts and, although he had served during the last war, had never seen front-line action or commanded men in battle. But he did have a fastidious eye for detail and was known as an expert on training, and since joining the OKH as von Brauchitsch's Chief of Staff had done well, helping to gel a highly competent team. No great admirer of either Hitler or the National Socialists, he had none the less produced an exemplary plan of attack for Poland and now had to produce another for the West.

To aid him, the Führer had issued some rather woolly thoughts in a memorandum on 9 October, forwarded dutifully as 'Directive No. 6' by the OKW. The aim, Hitler announced, was to defeat the French Army and any forces fighting on their side, and at the same time to win as much territory as possible in Holland, Belgium and northern France, 'to serve as a base for the successful prosecution of the air and sea war against England'. Just what form this air and sea war was going to take was not mentioned.

Halder's approach was to make the plan so self-evidently bad that even Hitler would be forced to demur. His first effort was much the same as the German plan of 1914, with a thrust through Belgium to the coast. Hitler, however, saw through this and ordered him to think again. At the same time, Halder became embroiled in a plan to assassinate the Führer, hatched at Zossen, the headquarters of the OKH to the south-east of Berlin, and which also involved General Wilhelm Ritter von Leeb, commander of Armeegruppe C, one of three army groups likely to be used in any future offensive in the West, General Carl-Heinrich von Stülpnagel, Halder's deputy at the OKH, and Generaloberst Ludwig Beck, Halder's predecessor, who had resigned in opposition to Hitler in August the previous year. This was a deeply fraught time for Halder because he believed the only way to save Germany from catastrophe was to get rid of Hitler, but to do so the plotters needed support; however, securing that support was risky, to put it mildly. He took to carrying a loaded pistol in his pocket in case he had the chance to pull the trigger on the Führer himself.

With increasingly frayed nerves he continued drawing up plans for action in the West. His second plan, produced at the end of October, was much the same as the first but included a second and simultaneous thrust further south. This brought a furious response from Hitler when von Brauchitsch, with the support of all his senior commanders now on the Western Front, presented it on 5 November. His field armies, von Brauchitsch tried to explain, were simply not ready for a major offensive. The torrent of invective from Hitler left the Army C-in-C quite stupefied; he later confessed to Halder that he had been unable to stand up to Hitler's iron and maniacal will. Like Keitel, von Brauchitsch immediately offered his resignation, although it was similarly refused. Hitler wanted men like his Army chief in charge – men he could boss about and reduce to a quivering wreck. The Führer despised the traditional Prussian military elite; they were necessary to him, but he took every opportunity possible to growl and make them feel intimidated. Von Brauchitsch was head of the OKH for the same reason Keitel was the top man at the OKW: because Hitler knew they would not stand up to him.

It was after von Brauchitsch's ordeal in front of Hitler that Halder cut his ties with the resistance. Von Brauchitsch had also told him how Hitler had raged against the 'spirit of Zossen', and with mounting panic Halder had assumed the Führer had somehow learned of the plot. This was not the case, but Halder realized he was not the assassinating revolutionary kind, so, having ensured all incriminating documents were destroyed, decided instead to embrace the coming offensive. If he could not prevent it – and clearly he could not – then the best chance was to try and produce a plan that might just, somehow, some way, work – or at least might avoid total defeat once more for Germany. Just what this new plan might be, however, was not, in the last weeks of 1939, at all apparent to him or any of his planning team at Zossen.

CHAPTER 11

Attention to Detail

IT IS TEMPTING still to assume Nazi Germany in those first months of war had the finest Army the world has ever seen, in terms of both training and equipment, and especially when compared with other armies at that time. Propaganda certainly shielded both most Germans and the wider world from the truth of its levels of mechanization. As regards its tanks, again the reality was rather different from the perceived wisdom. The vast majority were Mk I and Mk IIs and Czech T35s and T38s, all of which were small, under-gunned and under-armoured. The Panzer Mk I, for example, stood about six feet off the ground and carried nothing more than a brace of machine guns. This accounted for around a third of all German tanks.

The artillery – both field howitzers and higher-velocity anti-aircraft and anti-tank guns – were good, but the majority were designed to be coupled with horsepower, as Siegfried Knappe had discovered to his horror. The German soldier was well equipped with personal weapons. The rifle, the K98, was accurate and reliable, even if it could only fire a maximum of five bullets before reloading. Also starting to come into wider use was the MP38 *Machinenpistole*, or sub-machine gun. This was ideal for close combat and house-clearing, with its ability to lay down considerable fire in a short, sharp burst. Its practical range was little more than 30–40 yards, but it was beautifully balanced and engineered, and no other side had anything like it.

The basic infantry light machine gun was the MG34, which had been developed in the early 1930s by the firm Rheinmetall and was designed to be used in a number of different roles, including as an infantry weapon, as an anti-aircraft gun, and also on vehicles. It was originally even designed to go in aircraft. As it happened, it was rejected by the Luftwaffe as an aircraft-mounted weapon, but thanks to a series of different mountings could be used in either a mobile or a 'light' role with just a bipod, or in a static or 'heavy' role with a more elaborate and sturdy mount. It had been quite deliberately designed to have these different functions, which had first been suggested in the previous war, and which, on one level, certainly made sense.

To be any use as an anti-aircraft gun, for example, it needed a high rate of fire. Military advisors also wanted their machine gun to pack a big punch in any initial engagement, and so, unlike the Maxim, the MG34 fairly ripped out the bullets, with a rate of fire of around 900 per minute. Like the MP38, it was beautifully made with rolled steel and a number of attractive touches, such as wooden, metal or Bakelite grip, a detachable stock and with an assortment of accoutrements, such as detachable sights, the bipod, whose two legs could be clipped together and tidied away entirely, and an array of impressive maintenance equipment, all delivered in leather-lined wooden boxes and with no small detail overlooked. There was a heavy mount, an additional optical sight and a lightweight tripod too. In fact, the MG34 was the most elaborate machine gun ever built, with more than a hundred individual parts on the main weapon itself. Unquestionably, its incredible finish was designed to impress any onlooker, and no doubt it did.

It was a fine weapon and its rate of fire had a debilitating and demoralizing effect on the enemy – at least, certainly at first, as the Poles found out. The MG34 was one of the weapons that seemed to demonstrate Germany's highly advanced weapons technology and superiority on the battlefield.

There were, however, drawbacks to the MG34, regardless of its sophisticated lethality. To start with, it was expensive, which was understandable with the level of fine engineering devoted to each and every one. For example, nearly 50 kilograms of iron was needed to make the weapon, which weighed just 11 kilograms when it was finished; this was a pretty wasteful use of precious metal. The end product was also on the heavy side for a 'light' machine gun. It cost 312 Reichsmarks, which amounted to around $1,300 in 1938 prices. This was no small sum, but perhaps is not so surprising considering the amount of iron, the number of parts and the fact that it took around 150 man-hours to make. The Bren, by contrast, took just fifty. In other words, Britain could, in theory, produce three times as many Brens as MG34s in the same time, or could use the saving in time to make something else, such as more aircraft or ships.

The other problem was that while there was an unquestioned advantage in being able to lay down an incredible amount of bullets in any initial exchange, there was a pay-off for being able to spit out lead at such a rate. The MG34 was air-cooled, but with some fifteen bullets per second detonating their charge in the breech and down the barrel, it soon got very, very hot. In fact, it quickly became so hot that the barrel began to melt. The way round this was twofold. First, its users had to maintain a very resolute fire discipline and employ it in short, sharp bursts of a few seconds' length, and second, they had to frequently change the barrel. Each MG34 had to be accompanied by no fewer than six spare barrels, all of which had to be carried with the weapon itself, which on its own weighed around 20 pounds. Unlike the Bren, there was no wooden handle attached to the perforated sheath of the barrel, but experienced handlers none the less quickly got the hang of the rapid barrel change – a clip was flicked open, the breech unlocked and the over-hot barrel tipped out, usually extremely close to the user's face. Crews were given a giant padded mitt to help, but in practice these were rarely used.

Training manuals were quite firm about not getting carried away when firing. 'Shooting more than 250 shots in one continuous burst from one barrel,' noted one instruction manual, 'is forbidden.' That meant absolutely the longest continuous burst of fire was around sixteen seconds. In practice, however, the barrel would have started to lose accuracy well before that, while the amount of smoke from so many bullets being fired at that rate caused further problems. A well-trained machine-gunner would expect to fire around only 120 rounds per minute, which, coincidentally, was about the same as for a Bren, even though the Bren's theoretical rate of fire was only a little over half that of the MG34.

The final problem was that if users were not sparing with the trigger, they tended to get through an awful lot of ammunition very quickly. The MG34 could use twin 34-round drums, but more commonly was belt-fed and these were usually 250 rounds in length and weighed no small amount. The Bren was absolutely a light machine gun and could easily be operated by just one man; the MG34 was a hybrid, and really needed two men to operate it – one to fire and one to feed the belt, and to get the best from it the weapon needed a highly trained crew. In practice, the entire ten-man *Gruppe* – the German equivalent of the British section – tended to be used to service this one weapon. This wasn't necessarily a bad thing, as the heavy rate of fire did, certainly, have advantages. But like almost every weapon in war, for all the plus points, there were invariably minuses too.

There were, in some ways, a number of curious paradoxes to the German Army. It may have had innovative sub-machine guns and other finely engineered weaponry, for example, but despite the impression of vast military might, there was also something rather old school about the German Army in other areas. Certain forward-thinking officers, such as General Heinz Guderian, may have spent time writing treatises on the future of armoured warfare, but for the most part the Army was still dominated by a traditional Prussian military aristocracy that cited an inheritance which stretched back to Frederick the Great and the Seven Years' War in the middle of the eighteenth century. Men like von Clausewitz, von Moltke, von Schlieffen, von Hindenburg, von Ludendorff were all household names in Germany – and now the Army was commanded by von Brauchitsch. Even in Nazi Germany, it was hard to climb to the top of the pole without a 'von' before your name.

It still had a rather nineteenth-century look to it too. The *Pickelhaube*, the old pointed helmet, had gone, but the large amounts of leather, the high jackboots, the baggy-thigh breeches and the traditional high-collared tunics all harked back to an earlier era when looking the part – looking militaristic – was very much the brief. They looked smart, they looked efficient. They looked like they meant business, which was precisely the effect they were supposed to achieve.

This more traditional military look was eagerly adopted by the Nazis, not least because a powerful military tradition was what set the German character apart; Germany had been forged in 1871 with the Prussian states at its heart, and they, during the 1860s, had drawn upon militarism as being at the very core of their existence. There is no question that the German nation which emerged from the collection of kingdoms, duchies and principalities less than seventy years earlier was a militaristic society, but the idea that the Prussian – and later German – military was manifestly superior to any other in the world was a dubious claim. Prussia – the largest German kingdom prior to unification – had fought only a handful of small wars in the century that separated the end of the

Napoleonic Wars and the conflict in 1914. When it had gone to war alongside Austria against Denmark in 1864, it had barely fought since Waterloo fifty years earlier and most certainly did not out-perform Austria militarily. Two years later, Prussia was at war with its former ally, but Austrian mistakes were every bit as important to Prussia's subsequent victory as any military genius. Four years after that Prussia was at war again, this time against the mighty France, and it was on this stunning success that much of its military swagger, which would be sustained and would grow further within the newly formed Germany, was based. Interestingly, however, all three wars, and indeed German unification in 1871, were orchestrated not by a military leader but by a political one, namely Otto von Bismarck.

Following unification, the military was elevated in society, with veterans venerated and uniforms and military bearing considered the aspiration of every self-respecting young German male. No one was more fond of standing ramrod straight and wearing military garb than the Kaiser, Wilhelm II, who was always to be seen in a variety of uniforms, shiny breastplates and *Pickelhaube*, but had never actually seen any combat himself or, frankly, been much of a soldier.

Also woven into the military heritage was von Clausewitz's widely read and acclaimed work *On War*, but this was based on analysis of Napoleon, who was French, and was, in any case, interpreted to suit Nazi ideology. The other iconic figure was the Prussian king, Frederick the Great, who belonged to the eighteenth century, and who, despite continued veneration by a stream of Germans from Admiral Tirpitz through to Hitler, had won just eight of his sixteen battles and even one of those, the Battle of Zorndorf in 1758, might more accurately be considered a stalemate. None the less, von Clausewitz's military theories and Frederick's victories certainly added to the belief in Germany's military inheritance. Somehow, the Prussians, and then Germany, had created not only a militaristic society in which soldiers were greatly venerated, but also a reputation for military brilliance, which was based on not a huge amount if they were really honest. At the turn of the twentieth century, when Britain had threatened Imperial Germany with economic blockade and the destruction of its Navy if it became involved in the Boer War, the Kaiser backed down and kept out of it. This humiliation – and his obsession with ships – contributed to the vast building programme of capital vessels, and resulted in a giant fleet that ventured out once, at

Jutland in 1916, then retreated, and was scuttled at the end of the war.

Germany's great military tradition was thus based on a somewhat spurious reputation and had, in any case, taken a massive blow with the catastrophic defeat of 1918. The Nazis were emerging at a time when morale within Germany was low, but they cleverly appealed to this suspect military tradition and to German pride in that sense of martial inheritance. By strutting around with straight backs and chests out, wearing snappy brown or black uniforms, and with starkly striking insignia that harked back to ancient Aryan runes, the Nazis were inviting people to come and join an exciting new club. The message was simple: be a National Socialist, and wear a smart-looking uniform and be reinvigorated with a renewed sense of national pride, identity and purpose. It was hardly an original ruse, but the cut and design of the uniforms were very deliberately intended to look both smart and debonair while also nodding to the military past. Nazi uniforms were as beautifully tailored as an MG34 was engineered, and when it came to dressing the rapidly growing Army, these principles were rigorously maintained.

The field tunics of the ordinary German soldier were not quite so sartorially elegant as the SS outfits, but they were smart enough and certainly supremely well made. A private was not paid much, but he was given very decent kit. The jacket, the *Feldbluse*, was lined in soft cotton or rayon, was thigh length with two generously large and pleated pockets on the chest and two on the waist; it was also pleated at the back, while the cuffs had buttons that could be undone and the waist four lots of eyelets through which metal belt clips could be threaded. The buttons were all aluminium, rounded at the edges for easy use and with a dotted pattern, and quite deliberately designed as opposed to simply mass-stamped. The collar of the *Feldbluse* was well stitched and around the inside was another row of buttons on to which a smart and comfortable collar liner could be attached. It was warm, comfortable and produced with the kind of attention to detail that would make a bespoke tailor smile with pleasure. In 1939, each soldier was given no fewer than seven uniforms: field, service, watch, parade, report, walking out and sport. The numbers of cloth suppliers and tailors involved with making all these uniforms was immense, but like most German war production there was no adherence to the principles of mass production. There were, for example, no fewer than 323 different companies producing just one particular type of military linen. This was a trend repeated across the board.

Most of the soldier's webbing was made of black leather: the ammunition pouches, holsters, belts, straps and even the case that held the stout short-handle entrenching tool. Boots came up almost to the knee rather than the ankle. Field packs, although made of canvas, came with leather straps and a fur-covered outer flap. One particularly well-engineered piece of personal kit was the gas mask case, a steel cylinder with grooves down the side to give it added strength. It was quite large and even bulky, but the attention to detail on it was impressive, with a spring metal catch and inside, within the lid, a further little compartment in which spare lenses for the mask were stored and held in place by a delicate spring-loaded catch. The intricacy with which these millions of tins were manufactured – each some 25 centimetres tall – was impressive; and they even came with a leather carrying strap. It became an instantly iconic piece of the soldier's equipment.

Young officers, such as Hans von Luck and Siegfried Knappe, for example, had even more elaborate uniforms. Their field dress was made of the same wool as those of their men, but their service dress was gabardine with silk or rayon lining and with a cuff that doubled back almost halfway to their elbows, which was almost eighteenth century in its design. Officers were given wool greatcoats or full-length leather versions. There were different uniforms for mountain troops, different uniforms for paratroopers, yet more uniforms for the panzer arm, and even more for the Luftwaffe. Pilots like Hajo Herrmann could choose from a staggering array of breeches, woollen trousers, leather trousers, cotton, wool and leather jackets of differing shades of brown and black, some fur lined, others not.

This attention to detail and to producing a sartorially unbeatable armed services was all well and good and had certainly, in the early years of the Nazis at any rate, served a valid purpose. Unlike Britain, however, Germany had few sheep farms and no Dominions on the far side of the world from where it could easily purchase what it lacked at home. In fact, Germany had very few natural resources of its own at all – no oil, very little iron ore, no tungsten, no bauxite, no copper; a coal industry was about all it did have and even that was as nothing compared with Britain's, for example. And because so much of the economy was now devoted to war production, Germany had little to export in return. Yet rather than watching the pfennigs in areas where costs could easily have been kept down, there was, in 1939, no army that was more expensively turned out. The cost of German uniforms, however, was, from the Nazi perspective, a small price to pay to make soldiers believe they were part of a modern and technologically advanced militaristic society.

The standard of training was, by and large pretty good, particularly among the Regular Army divisions, and helped by a rigid adherence to discipline. Good training could paste over many deficiencies elsewhere. Young soldiers began the process of militarization and indoctrination to the values of National Socialism with the Hitler Youth, which boys would join at fourteen, and then followed this with a stint in the Reichsarbeitsdienst, or RAD, in which young men fresh from school were further indoctrinated, given a harsh daily routine of early rises, extensive drill and then back-breaking manual labour, such as building roads or defences. By the time they were recruited into the military proper, at eighteen, they were already halfway to being soldiers, having been taught rigid discipline and imbued with powerful national ideals. Divisions tended to have a strong regional base, with recruits largely drawn locally. They would then be taught as part of a training battalion within the division. This helped morale but also saved on transport. It did mean, however, that the quality of the division tended to depend on the quality of the command.

However, now, after Poland, over half the Army's divisions had the added advantage of having tasted combat, the greatest trainer of all. Throughout the 1930s, as the Army expanded and also searched for answers to the failure of 1918, much thought was given to the form that future warfare would take. Unlike in the British Army, where it was considered infra dig to discuss military matters out of hours, within the German Army it was positively encouraged. Hans von Luck eagerly absorbed all the latest military thinking. He had been particularly impressed by General Heinz Guderian, who was emerging as something of a pioneer of mobile tactics, as opposed to the largely static warfare that had been experienced during the previous war. Guderian, who had written articles and a book on his theories, had visited every single company in von Luck's 8. Panzer Reconnaissance Battalion, and discussed his ideas with all officers and NCOs, which had gone down very well; junior officers and NCOs were not usually spoken to by generals, and von Luck, for one, found it inspiring. He also thought his training right up to the outbreak of war was consistently intensive, and was concentrated primarily on two aspects. 'On the one hand we were made familiar with the technology and armaments,' he noted, 'on the other, we practised mobile engagements in the field.'

Martin Pöppel was also training every bit as intensively. The *Fallschirmjäger* had been on standby for an airborne drop, but in the event had been surplus to requirements. Pöppel and his comrades had been deeply frustrated not to see action in Poland, but, with hostilities over, training continued as hard as ever: more drops and, crucially, more radio exercises at both regimental and divisional level.

Along the Western Front, Siegfried Knappe was now training alongside the infantry, and as a junior officer was incredibly well drilled in all facets of artillery tactics and deployment. At the very least, this gave him and his men a huge amount of confidence. Knappe may have been startled to discover horses rather than a tracked self-propelled gun when he had first joined the Army, but any doubts had long been swept aside. And self-belief and discipline were crucial elements of any fighting power. It was true that the Wehrmacht was not nearly so well equipped as the propaganda suggested, but at the ground level, at any rate, the men believed they were ready for war with the West. Time would tell soon enough whether their confidence was well placed.

CHAPTER 12

Case YELLOW

I N THE WAR at sea, the Royal Navy had scored some valuable points but had received a number of bloody noses too; it was nothing that Britain couldn't take on the chin, but two attacks in particular had been more than just a little humiliating for the country that prided itself on and set great store by its naval supremacy. The first had occurred in September when the aircraft carrier *Courageous* had been sunk by a U-boat off Ireland. At the time, *Courageous* had been U-boat hunting with only a small screen of destroyers. The sinking of such a valuable asset showed that U-boat hunting was not the right role for such large and important capital ships – it was a lesson learned the hard way.

The second setback had been a carefully planned attack on the British Home Fleet at Scapa Flow, their base on the Orkney Islands north of Scotland. The Fleet had already been out on several aggressive sweeps across the North Sea, hunting German surface vessels, but it was German submarines that once again were to prove the thorn in their side. Scapa Flow, while providing a good anchorage, had been neglected in terms of defences, and Admiral Forbes, commander of the Home Fleet, had been ordered to move to a safer base at Loch Ewe on the west coast of Scotland. However, in early October, the German battle cruiser *Gneisenau*, and several other Kriegsmarine surface ships, had been reported as venturing into the North Sea, so Forbes's main force was sent to intercept them north-east of the Shetlands. The German ships beat a hasty retreat, but on the night of 13–14 October, several capital ships from the Home Fleet were still back at Scapa, and with the Northern Lights flickering across the sky, a single U-boat, *U-47*, captained by the imperturbable Günther Prien, managed to slip into the narrow passage and successfully sink the battleship *Royal Oak*, with the loss of 833 men. It was a severe shock not just to the Navy, but to Britain as a whole.

It was also a PR coup Germany milked for all it was worth. Prien became an overnight pin-up in Germany; if there was one area in which Germans felt a palpable inferiority complex it was over their Navy. That Prien had shown such daring, cunning and skill by successfully slipping into the lion's den and slaying one of the beasts showed what could be done. No one was more pleased than Admiral Dönitz, for while there was no immediate increase in U-boat production as a result, the sinking of the *Royal Oak* showed Hitler that a single, relatively inexpensive, vessel manned by fewer than fifty men could destroy a huge battleship crewed by 1,200. It demonstrated what might be achieved with a U-boat fleet of the kind of numbers Dönitz had been suggesting.

The British were, naturally enough, defiant and no one more so than the First Lord, Winston Churchill. On 8 November, he gave a speech to the House of Commons on the loss of the *Royal Oak*. Listening from the gallery was Jock Colville, who, since the outbreak of war, had left the Foreign Office after being asked if he would like to join No. 10 as one of the Prime Minister's secretaries. He'd been assured of very long hours and plenty of tedium too, but the chance to be close to the centre of things was an opportunity he was unwilling to let slip. Now, at the House of Commons, he thought Churchill was acquitting himself well, particularly when it came to rubbishing German bragging. 'When I recall the absurd claims which they are accustomed to shout around the world,' Churchill told the House, 'I cannot resist saying we should be quite content to engage the entire German Navy, using only the vessels which at one time or another they have declared they have destroyed.' That, Colville thought, was his best point. 'The latest German claim,' Colville noted later, 'is to have sunk HMS *Kestrel*, which turns out to be a naval sea-plane base some miles inland.'

Bragging aside, the Kriegsmarine had not had it all its own way in any case. Three U-boats from the tiny total force were sunk in October, and in December the pocket battleship *Graf Spee* had been chased to the River Plate in Argentina. Before this, the *Graf Spee* had been cruising British trade routes on the hunt for merchant shipping. It had sunk three merchantmen before being tracked down by a British hunting group of two heavy and two light cruisers. Having been blockaded in the mouth of the River Plate, the ship's captain had been ordered by Berlin to scuttle her rather than let her fall into British hands. Just as the Germans had milked the sinking of the *Courageous* and the *Royal Oak* especially, so the British made much of the so-called Battle of the River Plate. A month later, in January, the *Graf Spee*'s supply ship, the *Altmark*, was caught near Trondheim in Norway on its return from the South Atlantic. The ship was boarded by sailors from the destroyer HMS *Cossack*, and found to be armed and holding 299 prisoners, who were released.

This was, in fact, an infringement of Norwegian waters and neutrality. 'The wireless has just given the first news of the boarding of the *Altmark*,' wrote Vere Wight-Boycott, whose ship had recently returned to Britain and was now part of the Home Fleet. '*Cossack* seems to have done some fine work.' He did wonder, though, what the American reaction might be to this violation of neutrality. As it happened, not a lot; the US was already showing double standards on such matters. At any rate, already Admiral Carls's emphasis on attacking Allied shipping with a fast cruiser force was beginning to look a little misjudged. It is impossible to know what would have happened had the U-boat force been some 200 or even 300 strong in the opening months of the war, but there is no question that with that number, with well-trained crews, and before the Royal Navy had really organized its measures for anti-submarine warfare (ASW), Germany's chances of bringing Britain swiftly to heel would have been far higher. The sea lanes were Britain's lifeline. Without them, it would have been paralysed. And since much of Britain's overseas shipping passed through the Atlantic, whether it was coming from the Americas or the Far East, the Atlantic battleground should have been Germany's top priority in the war against Britain. Hitler, and the Wehrmacht command, however, were continentalists. The entreaties of enlightened men like Admiral Dönitz were given scant regard.

As it was, nine of the small number of U-boats had been lost by the end of 1939. *U-48*, however, was not one of them. Rather, under Kapitänleutnant Schultze, the submarine had continued to sink Allied ships, so that by the New Year the crew had no fewer than twelve to their name, and the 1WO, Teddy Suhren, had been promoted to Oberleutnant zur See. But as January gave way to February, Suhren and his comrades noticed the war was becoming harder; the Allies had started arming merchant vessels, and shot at anything that looked like a sub. The convoy system, too, was harder to penetrate, and the escorts more numerous. The weather was a factor as well. That first winter of war was terrible, and Suhren wondered whether, somehow, war and catastrophe could influence weather patterns. The Kiel Canal froze over, while out at sea their oilskins would become caked in ice while they were on the bridge. Drops of water froze and remained hanging from eyelids and beards, while inside the *U-48*, everything remained continually damp, with condensation glistening on the bulkheads, breath hanging in the air like fog, and food moulding.

As if the weather weren't enough, the U-boat crews had to contend with the enormous risks of their wartime profession. For merchant vessels, the word U-boat conjured up images of a dark, sleek and stealthy killer – and as a ship destroyer it was certainly highly effective. Yet for the crews, bottled up in a damp, stinking, foetid tin can, it was an unbelievably tough and threatening existence, in which hunter could become hunted at any moment. If hit, the crew faced drowning or suffocation, which was a long, lingering and awful death. They knew the chances were they would never be found, that wives, lovers and family would be left wondering what had happened to them. Such matters did not bear thinking about, and yet sometimes it was hard not to. Oberleutnant Suhren had lost a good friend when *U-41* was sunk on 5 February by a British destroyer off the coast of Ireland. The two U-boats had been alongside one another at Heligoland before that patrol, and Suhren had seen his old friend Jürgen, an officer on *U-41*. Jürgen had seemed downcast – his brother, a pilot in the Luftwaffe, had been killed, and now he was convinced he was for the chop too. 'He was absolutely right,' noted Suhren. 'There were no survivors . . .'

Suhren was lucky not to end up permanently at the bottom of the sea himself. For a submariner, there can have been few things more unsettling than being repeatedly depth-charged. These were explosive devices that were set to sink to a certain level and then explode. For those under attack, there was the constant fear of knowing that at any moment an explosion might come that could seal the fate of the sub and all within it.

On 14 February, they were positioned off the south-west coast of Ireland, over towards St George's and the Bristol Channel. It was early morning, with a heavy fog, when suddenly out of the mist loomed the outlines of ships. A large convoy was heading straight for them.

'Kapitän, on the bridge! Alarm! Crew to action stations,' came the cry, and with Schultze hurrying back down the conning tower, they hastily dived with a roar and sank to periscope depth. Everyone on board now had a specific role to play. Zurn, the LI, or Chief Engineering Officer, set the trim of the U-boat, i.e. tried to keep it steady on an even keel and depth. Schultze himself was still in the conning tower at his station on the periscope, which he lowered, then lifted up again, put the right pedal down and swung it a full 360 degrees. Directly below, in the control room, Suhren waited, listening, ready to pass on Schultze's orders. In an attack, it was the captain who made every decision about when to fire, when to dive, what depth, what speed. At the bow of the U-boat, the caps of the torpedo tubes were opened. At the TDC, the torpedo-attack computer, the No. 1 sat and waited, listening carefully to what Schultze told him. This device fed information into the torpedo tubes – it worked through adjustors that were air-drive gyros; as the torpedo was fired, the gyros started up and steered the missile in the right direction.

Quiet descended through the boat. All that could be heard was the low hum of the electric motors as the submarine travelled slow-ahead.

'OK, Chief?' asked Suhren, sticking his head up through the open hatch.

Schultze nodded. 'We're standing well off to port. In five minutes I'll be ready to shoot.'

'Much in the way of escorts?'

Schultze nodded again. 'Enough.'

Five minutes passed, with everyone on board concentrating on their station. No one spoke. Then Schultze raised the periscope once more and looked around. Instructions were passed down, trim and course adjusted, then he called out, 'Tubes one to four, stand by!' followed by, 'Tube one – fire! Tube two – fire! Three – fire! Four – fire!'

After that, what felt like a long wait. The target was 1,800 metres away, and the torpedoes travelled at thirty knots. That meant around 120 seconds – two whole minutes. The stopwatch ticked. The LI was struggling to keep the U-boat at periscope depth and asked for more speed.

'Eighty seconds,' called out the *Obersteuermann*. Then 90, 100, 110.

Schultze ordered the boat be turned to starboard, then a dull thud – a hit! They had just struck the SS *Sultan Star*, a large 11,300-ton British freighter filled with meat from the Argentine.

'Quick, go deep!' ordered the captain.

'What's up?' asked Suhren.

'An escort's spotted us. She's coming straight for us!'

Everything now happened at once. Two more explosions – their torpedoes had hit the ship twice more – but, even then, the submarine was rapidly diving, creaking and groaning as it did so as the pressure around it increased. At 120 metres down, a fusilade of eight depth charges erupted, and in frightening proximity. *U-48* lurched and rolled. Above them, they could clearly hear the enemy ASDIC, the ship's onboard sonar, *ping-ping-ping*, and the low whirr of the propellers. The submarine was now effectively pinned down, and there was damage already.

'Exhaust valves making water!' came a report from the engine room.

'Zurn,' said Schultze, 'make sure the valves are closed down as far as they'll go.'

Zurn did so, but they were still taking on a small amount of water.

Above, the convoy continued on its way – Suhren, who had taken the hydrophones from the radio operator, could hear the engines, but then the sound of the escorts' propellers drowned it out – it sounded like a nail being scraped across a plate. It was 0700. More depth charges, bubbling down towards them. He handed back the headphones and braced himself. An explosion, the boat rocked, then five more in quick succession. But they were still in one piece. Calmly, Schultze ordered a change of course west.

That was not the end of the attacks, however. The U-boat dropped to 120 metres. The explosions seemed to be getting closer. They dived further, the hull creaking and grinding until, with a bump, they stopped at 135 metres – the charts put them at the Cockburn Bank. It was as deep as they could go. Above them, a destroyer was raking over them once more, the ping of the ASDIC still quite audible. The whirr of the propeller, followed by gurgling bubbles as the depth charges fell, then *peng-wham! Peng-wham! Peng-wham!* Once more *U-48* rolled and shook and was tossed off the seabed and thumped back down again. 'We can scarcely stay on our feet,' noted Suhren. 'We look for a handhold and hang on wherever we can.'

Inside, no one dared speak; they barely dared breathe. A bit of metal fell on the deckplate, prompting angry glares towards the man responsible. Another hour passed, then another, each marked by a further attack. By noon, they had been pummelled with depth charges no fewer than eleven times. Suhren had made some calculations – the hydro-phones had picked up the smack of the depth charges as they hit the water; they sank at 4 metres per second and the explosions occurred after twenty-eight seconds – that meant they were detonating at between 110 and 120 metres; just 15 metres above them.

'What do you think?' Schultze asked Suhren. 'Should we leak out a bit of oil? Then they'd be sure to think they'd hit us.'

'No,' replied Suhren, shaking his head. 'No movement at all. Just play dead. Once it gets dark, they'll knock it off.'

They all looked tense, strained and drawn. Only Schultze appeared to be as calm and imperturbable as ever; imperturbability was one of the key attributes for any submarine captain.

Down in the U-boat, it was neither daylight nor night, but up above, on the ocean's surface, darkness had fallen. But every half-hour, more depth charges burst around them; there was no let-up. The hissing sound of the ventilator began to grate on the crew's nerves, but there was nothing they could do about it. 'We wonder,' noted Suhren, 'whether we would have had so much patience, or whether we'd already have reported "enemy destroyed". Gradually my doubts return. How long can an execution take?'

Hours passed, slowly, painfully, the tension never lessening for those inside the U-boat. Then at 2200, a flurry of eight depth charges, not five. Was that significant? Maybe – yes.

'Listening Room, what can you hear?' asked Suhren.

'Herr Oberleutnant, I can hear the two destroyers getting further away!'

But Schultze was not moving just yet. Another half-hour – just to be safe.

The half-hour passed – and still no sound from above, so Schultze ordered the pumps to start, which they did with high-pitched humming Suhren found hard to bear as they battled against 13.5 atmospheres of pressure. Slowly, slowly, the vessel lost weight and gradually, gingerly, lifted off the seabed. They were now going forward, climbing gently until finally, at long last, they broke the surface. Suhren followed Schultze up on to the bridge. As they opened the hatch and clambered out, Suhren could feel his eardrums throb with the equalizing of pressure. To their horror, they saw bright lights all around them – they were encircled by about twenty fishing boats at anchor on the Cockburn Bank. But it was night and nothing was stirring, so half submerging and relying on their electric motors, they quietly slipped away, undetected.

They were barely clear of the fishing boats when new shadows loomed up ahead as they closed in on more merchant shipping. Once more, Schultze ordered them to attack, aiming for a large freighter. Torpedoes were fired and after a hundred seconds came an explosion – another ship gone, added to *U-48*'s mounting tally.

'There you are, Suhren,' said Schultze. 'Attacking again and getting a hit are the best medicine.'

That February, there were never more than ten operational U-boats at sea, but fifty-six Allied merchant ships were sunk, along with three U-boats. There could be no doubting that the war at sea was now well underway. In contrast, nothing much was stirring on the ground – nor in the air for that matter. The appalling weather put paid to that.

This did not mean there was a lack of activity, however. Rather, factories from England to German-occupied Poland and Czechoslovakia continued to build more tanks, aircraft, munitions and other instruments of war. At parade grounds and training camps, men drilled and learned the rudiments of soldiering, while along the Western Front the opposing sides readied themselves, prepared defences, drilled for the clash that suddenly seemed as though it might never happen at all.

At Zossen, the OKH continued to do their level best to prevent any imminent assault in the West while at the same time putting together a plan of attack that might have some chance of success, however slim. But in the ten weeks between von Brauchitsch's dressing-down by Hitler at the beginning of November and the first couple of weeks of the New Year, General Halder was not making a huge amount of progress.

There were, however, a couple of senior commanders within the Army who thought they might have found a way. One was General Erich von Manstein, who was Chief of Staff of Armeegruppe A, one of three groups of armies already assembled, and who, during that time, had produced and sent to Halder no fewer than seven drafts of a daring plan in which the main thrust was a surprise attack through the Ardennes. The idea was that a sizeable thrust would be made in the north, through Holland and into Belgium. The Allies would assume this was the main attack and would then move their troops forward, through Belgium, to meet this thrust. At the same time, however, the real main attack would go through the thick forest and rolling hills of the Ardennes in south-west Belgium. The invading force would emerge and cross the River Meuse, the main French line of defence, and then drive straight towards the Channel coast. The vast bulk of the French, Belgian and British armies would then be caught in a massive encirclement. That was the plan: a two-pronged attack, one a feint in the north, where the Allies most expected it, and the other the main attack, or *Schwerpunkt*, where it was least expected.

The Ardennes was an area of thick forest, rolling hills and steep river valleys that ran across the south-west part of Belgium, which, as in 1914, was firmly neutral. In truth, each draft was much the same and was based on the premise that if the Germans could reach the mighty River Meuse and cross it in a surprise operation, a rapid thrust using what mechanized troops they did have could blaze through France before the slow, more methodical enemy army had a chance to react.

Halder, however, had dismissed von Manstein's suggestions, for while his basic idea was certainly bold and daring, it was, to his mind, dependent on far too many variables for comfort: that the extremely complicated logistic operation through the Ardennes – an area widely considered impassable to large-scale mechanized troop movements – would go to plan; that Allied air forces would not detect it; that the French would be surprised; that the French would not be able to recover sufficiently; that untested panzer units could cut such a swathe across France. After all, by the spring – the most obvious time in which to launch an offensive – there would be just ten panzer divisions and six mechanized divisions in the entire Army. Could those few *really* be expected to sweep through France in the way that von Manstein was envisioning? Halder wasn't convinced by any stretch of the imagination, but he was also keenly aware that it was precisely the kind of daring and outrageous plan that Hitler would immediately latch on to. Furthermore, Hitler had even suggested a thrust across the Meuse at Sedan on the edge of the Ardennes himself, not through any genius of military thinking, but rather because it was there that the Prussians had successfully crossed in 1870. With this in mind, Halder therefore put von Manstein's memos to one side.

In the New Year, however, two events happened that made Halder think again and dramatically reconsider the possible merits of von Manstein's plan. The first took place on 10 January, when a German aircraft made a forced landing near Mechelen in Belgium. On board was a

Luftwaffe operations officer with copies of the latest German offensive plans, which still held that a thrust through the Low Countries was to be the main point of attack. Realizing how important the documents were, the German officers hastily tried to burn them. They were captured, however, before the plans had been destroyed. What had been a terrible security leak had suddenly become a stunning opportunity for deception, despite Hitler's ire, because the incident prompted a rapid response from the Allies, who began extensive troop movements, going on to the alert all along the front and moving reserves forward, all of which was watched and noted by Luftwaffe reconnaissance planes. It showed that the Allies had been expecting a German attack exactly as outlined in Halder's current plans.

The second event happened a few weeks later. At the end of January, von Manstein had been sidelined and given command of a corps that existed in name only. Frustrated by this, Generals Günther Blumentritt and Henning von Tresckow, two admirers of von Manstein, took it upon themselves to give von Manstein's plans to General Schmundt, Hitler's military aide. They were then shown to Hitler, who, of course, embraced them immediately.

The situation by mid-February, however, was very different to the one back in October. It was true the Allies were by then out-producing Germany in terms of aircraft and tanks, but the months of uneasy calm along the Western Front had been of considerable help to the Wehrmacht too. In that time, ammunition stocks, which had fallen so drastically low during the Polish campaign, had been replenished and increased, and, more importantly, valuable lessons had been learned and incorporated into training. Poland had been a crucial test-run. While France and Britain had been holding the line and building defences, the German Army had been preparing for offensive operations, now with experience to throw into the mix. Numbers of new aircraft were certainly well below what Göring and the Luftwaffe wanted, and only a few new U-boats were entering the war on shipping, but the Army was in immeasurably better shape than it had been just a few months earlier.

Another factor that helped change Halder's stance had been the slow French response to recent German regrouping movements along the front: intelligence suggested they had taken as much as two weeks to realize there had been a change in German troop dispositions. Thus if it should prove possible to move enough forces through the Ardennes forest of Luxembourg and Belgium and reach the main French defences in less time than that, it would, theoretically, be possible to catch them out. 'Surprise may now be regarded as assured,' he noted with confidence in his diary after a February Führer conference. What's more, any thrust through the Ardennes would have a far better chance of success if it was done in good weather and when the days were long, with plenty of sunlight. Fortunately for Halder, bad weather had meant continual postponements of Hitler's proposed assault. This too was playing into Halder's plans to ensure the Army was sufficiently ready for an operation of this magnitude before being committed.

Furthermore, Hitler was now beginning to think of striking at Denmark and Norway first, before an assault on France and the Low Countries. The winter's armaments drive had shown just how much iron ore was needed by Germany. The trouble was, most of it came from Sweden via Norway, so securing its safe passage away from the British Navy was essential. Invasion and occupation were the only way to guarantee this. Moreover, Norway would provide important bases for future attacks on British shipping. All in all, such an attack offered a number of benefits, and especially before any strike in the West.

So now, in February 1940, Halder was faced with better conditions for an offensive, the chance to make the most of an unintentional deception plan, and the opportunity to secure a northern flank and crucial iron ore first. Finally, war games at the beginning of February had also shown this daring plan of attack might just – *just* – work after all. What Halder had gradually realized through the first two months of 1940 was that they faced a stark choice: a more cautious plan that would avoid any quick defeat, or a go-for-broke gamble that risked everything but which also offered the only realistic chance of decisive victory.

Thus by the end of February, when Halder submitted his latest plans, he had completed his dramatic volte-face: Armeegruppe B would noisily thrust into Holland and northern Belgium with the support of the majority of the Luftwaffe, while the panzers of Armeegruppe A would hurry through the Ardennes and attack the French across the Meuse. With luck, the Allies would be coaxed into a trap, rushing forward to meet the northern thrust, while the main German attack burst through the back door around Sedan, ensnaring the bulk of the Allies' northern front in a huge encirclement before they had time to effectively respond. The operation was to be codenamed *Fall Gelb* – Case YELLOW: a codename, like Case WHITE, that was neutral and deliberately bland.

The trouble was, though, that while Halder and even von Brauchitsch were now convinced their plan was the right one, it was all too clear that most of the senior commanders in the Wehrmacht did not agree. And even for Halder there was no doubt that Case YELLOW was a massive, massive gamble. There was still much that could go wrong.

CHAPTER 13

Home Front

IN GERMANY, the war had descended on the Third Reich like a shroud. The campaign in Poland had been brought to a swift and decisive conclusion but by Christmas any hopes that the West could be brought to the peace table seemed to have evaporated. For the fifteen-year-old Margarete Dos, war had already changed her life irrevocably. A keen athlete, she had dreamed of representing Germany in the 1940 Olympiad, but that would never happen; there could be no Olympic Games now that war had broken out.

Margarete lived in Charlottenburg in Berlin with her mother, younger brother, Dieter, and her stepfather, Karl Spaeth, a veteran of the last war and now a staff officer at Kriegsmarine headquarters. Despite his position, one of the first direct effects of the war was the requisitioning of their family car – Oberst Adolf von Schell needed it for the war effort. Some men from the SS came to collect it, and while they offered compensation, the men pointed out that since the family would no longer be able to purchase fuel, there was no point in keeping it in any case.

A blackout had been imposed immediately and everywhere were posters saying 'THE ENEMY SEES YOU. PUT OUT YOUR LIGHT.' In their home, Margarete and her family put up blackout curtains and blinds across all the windows. Even along Unter den Linden, the most famous thoroughfare in Berlin, camouflage netting was now spread from one side of the street to the other, so that they seemed to be walking the length of a huge tent.

Margarete did not mind so much about the car – she had her bicycle and there were the U-Bahn and S-Bahn in any case – and nor was she so bothered about the blackout. She did mind, however, about the rationing, which was severe and had begun in August. They were allowed margarine but not butter, meat was rationed and so too was bread, that most basic staple. All cereals, fats, cheese, milk, sugar and eggs were rationed. Thin tasteless broth became a staple. Ration cards with tear-off coupons called *Essensmarken* were not just for meat and bread, but also for soap and clothing. They were colour-coded – such as red for bread – and valid for twenty-eight days, which meant the authorities could alter the rations from month to month. Rationing of clothes, with further different-coloured cards, was also quite stringent – Germany produced no cotton, while wool was scarce and there were still incredibly elaborate military uniforms to make. For a beautiful young girl like Margarete, just emerging into young womanhood, clothes rationing was depressing. 'Our clothes were always too small or too large, or very ragged,' she noted, 'and our shoes never fit . . . my toes grew crooked, my feet always hurt.' And almost everything was brown – her pullovers, her skirts, her shoes.

Margarete found it all unsettling, not just because food and other items were rationed, but rather because it was often inconsistent. Sometimes there was almost nothing even with the ration coupons, then there would suddenly be plenty of a particular type of fruit. Bread changed too – other ingredients were added. Sometimes there would be no bread either. Coffee also vanished and was replaced by *Ersatzkaffee*, made from chicory and burnt wheat grains. '*Muckefuck*' was the name it was given. Margarete hated it.

In fact, the Nazis had tried to prepare for the twin problems of fighting a war and still feeding the nation adequately. State agriculture was run by the Department of Food and Agriculture – the Reichsnährstand, or RNS – and led by Walther Darré, an early Nazi and friend of Hitler's. In many ways, the origins of the Nazi fantasy of a 'master race' came from Darré, who was obsessed not only with agriculture but also with selective breeding. Heinrich Himmler, the head of the SS, was particularly taken with Darré's philosophy of 'blood and soil' and looking after the German farmer, whom he viewed as being the essence of the Nordic race; Himmler himself had dabbled at being a chicken farmer after taking a degree in agriculture.

The Nazis had realized they needed to deal with agriculture and the potential problems of feeding both the nation and armed services from the outset, although this was just another of the economic headaches facing them. The big problem was that balance of payments continually plagued them. To rearm, they had to import raw materials because they lacked their own. However, because those arms were for their own use they could not then be exported, which would have provided them with much-needed foreign cash. In other words, lots of German money was going out, but not much was coming in. One way of keeping the amount of overseas spending down was to import less food and depend more heavily on home production. Consequently, to the Nazis, the German farmer had a critical role to play in aiding rearmament.

The Germans liked to give many of their state projects martial overtones. In the nineteenth and early twentieth centuries, there had been the 'war on nature' in which Germany had battled to straighten untidy rivers like the Rhine or improve the flow of water to growing industrial conurbations with huge dam projects. In November 1934, Herbert Backe, a Nazi agrarian technocrat, launched the 'Battle of Production' (*Erzeugungsschlacht*). While there was never any question of becoming entirely self-sufficient, the Battle of Production was designed to maximize domestic output and certainly greatly improve what was being achieved at the time.

The big areas for improvement were not in cereals, in which Germany was already self-sufficient, but in animal feedstuffs and fats, as well as some raw materials, which led to an increase in fibre-bearing plants. The Battle of Production was launched with a massive PR campaign – German farmers were to be persuaded not compelled; Darré was convinced that appealing to German honour and national pride was the way to go. Unfortunately for Darré and Backe, however, the Battle of Production could hardly have got off to a worse start. Two bad harvests in a row meant an increase not a decrease in food imports, while other measures mismanaged by the RNS compounded the problems. One was asking farmers to surrender 70 per cent of their rye harvest, which would normally be used for animal feed, in return for imported barley. Most farmers understandably thought it was a whole load of unnecessary hassle to give up one crop in return for another that was meant for the same purpose. The net result was a bad shortage of domestic fodder. The Battle of Production had not gained very much ground.

Supervision of farmers became tighter again with the start of the Four-Year Plan in 1936. From then on, every farmer with a farm of 12.5 acres or more had to have a record card. Recording and issuing these was an exhausting process because there were more than two million farm holdings that fell into this category, accounting for 90 per cent of all farmland in Germany. In other words, there were way too many farms to ever make German agriculture truly efficient. The size of these small farms made the introduction of mechanization quite difficult – although another problem was the decidedly small motor industry in Germany. By 1939, Germany had just one tractor for every 1,000 acres; in Britain, that figure was just over 300 acres. In truth, there wasn't much the Nazis could do without investing heavily in farm machinery – which was out of the question – or without radically altering the nature of German farming from lots of small-scale holdings to much larger enterprises. This would have gone against Nazi ideology, and in any case would have taken too long to implement, so it was equally a non-starter. So food production was going to continue to be a problem, with no obvious major solution in sight other than creating *Lebensraum* – living space. Another term for it was colonization, or territorial expansion.

In fact, rather than gaining extra farmland, rural Germany lost some one million acres due to the construction of the Siegfried Line along the country's western border, and further land was lost to the autobahn project that involved the construction of dual-lane roadways linking the major cities; by 1939, there were 3,500 kilometres of autobahns, most of which passed through agricultural land. Since the Germans had very few cars and most military traffic travelled by rail, they were rather pointless, although they had been designed originally with the idea of transporting some 300,000 troops from east to west Germany in forty-eight hours. Nor were they particularly an answer to unemployment since rearmament ' had taken care of that already. They were opened, however, with another major PR drive and certainly made Germany appear very modern and forward-thinking.

Yet more farmland was taken away by state requisition for both military training areas and for the growth of industry. This loss of land, of course, had an effect on production. It was one of the ironies of Nazi Germany that the Battle of Production on the land was, above all, designed to help rearmament, and yet rearmament was now hindering the farmers' ability to provide that help.

The only real way, then, to improve production within Germany itself was to use more fertilizers. This the RNS managed to implement fairly successfully, largely by making prices cheaper; between 1933 and 1939, fertilizer use rose by a third and home production did rise, albeit not substantially. As it happened, Germany was already 81 per cent self-sufficient by 1936, and this rose to 83 per cent by 1939. However, imports had also grown in that time, by about a quarter, which meant that overall, since the Nazis had come to power in 1933, self-sufficiency had risen by only 3 per cent, which was clearly not a huge amount. The other big problem that had not been addressed was fodder for animals. Germany ate proportionally more pork than any other country, but the problem with pigs was that they competed with humans for foodstuffs, in contrast to sheep, which ate grass.

The solution was to reduce the number of pigs, but that then meant less fat was available, which in turn meant people ate more sugar beet and potatoes; this in turn led to less fodder for what pigs there were. British people, on the other hand, ate a higher proportion of mutton, which was a more practical meat source because sheep only required grass and their wool could be made into uniforms. In fact, the figures for pigs and sheep were almost mirror opposites of those in Britain: Germany had 4 million sheep in 1937; Britain had 4 million pigs; Germany had 23 million pigs, Britain 24.5 million sheep. But national eating characteristics cannot be easily changed.

With the outbreak of war and the immediate imposition of a blockade by Britain and France, maximizing the home production of food was now even more essential. Even so, there were some reasonable grain reserves, ration cards had already been printed back in 1937, yields were on the up, and the country was virtually self-sufficient in grain, potatoes and sugar. Margarete Dos may have found the onset of rationing discomforting, and may have spent days at a time feeling hungry, but no one in Germany was starving yet, despite these hardships.

However, even though the current food situation was reasonably satisfactory, it didn't take much to realize that ahead lay trouble, as Walter Darré was all too aware. Wartime conscription and rearmament were taking men from the land, while fuel would be in shorter supply, as would the chemicals to make fertilizers – chemicals that were also used in military production. Back in February, Darré told a group of troop commanders that food was the most urgent problem facing Germany. He had a point.

Food, then – that essential component of war – was just one more of the many factors informing Hitler's war plans, and, as with everything else, it pointed to one thing: the need for a short, sharp and decisive battle with the Western powers. There really was no alternative with Hitler and the Nazis in power. The West would never trust them and nor would the USSR, mutually beneficial pacts notwithstanding. Yet nor could Nazi Germany solve those shortages of resources – those barriers to rising German strength – without military conquest. Clearly, wars of plunder could, in theory, kill two birds with one stone: by taking land by force, the Reich could grab the resources it needed while at the same time neutralizing the threat from its neighbours. It was, of course, a high-risk strategy, but one that slotted in neatly with Hitler's mindset as the arch-gambler. If it worked, and the German nation rose to the challenge, then there would be a Thousand-Year Reich. If it failed, then Germany did not deserve to rise again.

Just when Hitler realized a European war was inevitable is not clear, although he had certainly begun to shape his plans several years earlier. Back in November 1937, at a meeting called to discuss Raeder's complaints that the Kriegsmarine was not getting a large enough share of steel and other raw-material allocations, the Führer had decided instead to outline his expansionist policies to Raeder, Göring, General Werner von Fritsch and Baron Konstantin von Neurath, the last two being chief of the Army and the Foreign Minister at the time. He pointed out that Germany had neither enough food nor a strong enough economy as things stood, and that therefore they would have to plunder what they lacked by force – and sooner rather than later before France and Britain became too strong militarily. 'German policy,' noted Oberst Friedrich Hossbach, writing the minutes of the meeting, 'had to reckon with two hate-inspired antagonists, Britain and France, to whom a German colossus in the centre of Europe was a thorn in the flesh.'

It was with this in mind that Hitler had marched into Austria and then Czechoslovakia, overrunning potential enemies and absorbing both territory and resources into the Greater Reich. Poland had been part of the same plan. Britain and France had declared war, but that was fine by Hitler: soon would come the moment of truth. He would turn his armies on both and defeat them both, and then his hand would be free to build up Germany's strength further, enriched as the Reich would be by European space and plunder. And then, with the West subdued and Germany's neighbours vanquished, he could turn East.

That was all very well, but in the meantime Berliners like Margarete

Dos and her family were hoping – and believing – the war would be over soon. Christmas had lacked its normal magic as dancing halls had been shut down, bars and restaurants were no longer allowed to stay open late, and while shop windows were still twinkling with an array of tantalizing goods, most of it was just for show rather than for sale.

Coal, too, was rationed – needed for industrial processes and for running the trains rather than people's homes, and it was a particularly cold winter – the coldest in decades right across Europe. Margarete had heard that a man had been found frozen to death in the street. On New Year's Eve, her mother had sent her to see Herr Strichler, who owned a restaurant with a *Biergarten* across the street. Wrapping up as warmly as she could, she headed out into the snow. She liked Herr Strichler, who always seemed cheery and liked to talk. He pointed out one of the many placards that had been put up around the city: 'NO ONE SHALL BE HUNGRY. NO ONE SHALL FREEZE.' 'Now we're not even allowed to be hungry any more!' he told her.

In France, despite the cold, they were not going hungry, even though farming was as troubled in France as elsewhere in Europe. The tradition of the French peasant farmer was, as in Germany, deeply rooted, but agriculture and its farming community had taken a battering during the 1930s. Thanks to Napoleonic inheritance laws, the majority of farms were small family affairs that had embraced neither investment nor modern technology. France as a whole may have been highly automotive, but farmers tended not to be. There were exceptions, however. Around the Paris basin and the wide, open arable land of the north, large, modern and vibrant farms produced large amounts of wheat. The battlefields of the last war, for example, had received massive reinvestment and had become more productive than ever. The problem was that throughout the 1930s wheat prices tumbled, partly because of the wider global depression and partly because as other foods became more accessible, so the French were eating less bread. The harvests of 1932 and 1933 were the best ever, yet rather than being good news for farmers, this was a disaster, even with a protected home market. France simply had too much grain. It was drowning in it. Farm spokesmen – and farmers were always volubly represented – reckoned that wheat should be sold at no less than 300 francs per quintal (100 kilograms). By 1930, they were getting just 147 francs, and by 1935 it had plummeted to 70 francs.

Most other farm products suffered similarly. Wine sales dropped drastically. It was both economically and emotionally a key product, yet American prohibition, cheap Algerian wine and an earlier *Phylloxera* epidemic had hit the industry very hard indeed, so that wine producers could not even benefit from one of the most perfect ever grape harvests in 1933. The meat market also suffered thanks to cheaper refrigerated imports and an outbreak of bovine TB, which prompted the lucrative British market to stop all French imports. Milk prices also collapsed. Seventy-eight per cent of French milk came from small producers, but consumption by the mid-thirties was 75 per cent lower than it had been before the last war.

Many farmers believed their way of life was dying out. Successive governments – and there were a staggering thirteen between 1930 and 1934 alone – tried to help ameliorate this agrarian collapse but if anything made the situation worse. Another factor in the malaise was that proportionally more young French farmers had been killed in the last war than any other part of the population.

Thus by the outbreak of war French farming appeared to be in terminal decline. War, however, promised to change that. Food imports were reduced and both the nation as a whole and its armed services needed feeding. In times of war, an abundance of grain and milk – which also provided fats – was just what was needed. Henri Queuille, the Minister for Agriculture, made considerable play of not introducing rationing – unlike both Britain and Germany. In this, Queuille had Daladier's backing, but there were plenty in the government who disagreed with the policy, and not least the Finance Minister, Paul Reynaud, who thought it a highly dangerous policy. In a long war, he argued, stocks needed to be preserved, not frittered on peacetime levels of consumption; he had a point.

None the less, few of the population were complaining. In the freezing cold of winter, most were grateful there was at least food on the table.

On the Normandy coast at Deauville, the beautiful French film star Corinne Luchaire had been sitting out the autumn and onset of winter. Still only eighteen, she was one of the most famous women in France, but after making two films earlier in the year she had been invited by her father to join him in the fashionable Normandy resort. Throughout much of August, she had partied hard, making friendships with English peers, having an affair with the Aga Khan's son, Ali Khan, and living the gay, carefree life of the rich. Even with the declaration of war, it seemed initially as though not much would change. 'War was just an accident,' she wrote. 'Everybody thought it was going to be very short.' Restaurants, dancing clubs and the casinos all stayed open. The biggest change was the requisitioning of her hotel, the Normandy, to become a hospital. Corinne and her father moved into an empty villa with some friends and spent the next few weeks smoking, drinking and playing cards. There was no mobilization for them.

Corinne had been born to artistic, socially well-connected parents. Her mother was a painter, while her father, Jean Luchaire, was a successful political journalist and editor of a weekly newspaper, *Notre Temps*, and her grandfather was an acclaimed playwright. But although her first years were spent in bohemian Parisian society, she had also spent time in Germany as a young girl when her mother began an affair with a German politician, Gustav Stresemann. There were also visits to Florence, where her grandfather had a house, and throughout her childhood she constantly met a large number of artists, politicians and writers – men like Kurt Freiherr von Schröder, the German financier, and Otto Abetz, the German Ambassador to France and later secretary to von Ribbentrop. She was also well acquainted with Paul Reynaud and the right-wing Pierre Laval. Otto Abetz had married her father's secretary, but to Corinne they were just friends of her parents – friends that gave her dolls or puppets. She was particularly close to her father (who had only been seventeen himself when she had been born), and he liked to take her with him whenever he could. Once he had taken her along to a conference with President Poincaré. When the President arrived earlier than expected, Corinne's father hid her under the conference table. All had been well until Corinne had become bored and grasped the President's leg, thinking it was her father's. Poincaré had not been amused.

Beautiful and precocious, and given excessive freedom by her parents, she had left school at fourteen and enrolled in Raymond Rouleau's School of Dramatic Art, and although she was not much good as an actress to begin with, she persevered and after doing well in a stage performance of one of her grandfather's plays, she was cast in her first film at just fifteen. It was the movie *Prison sans barreaux*, filmed a year later, that made her a star, however. 'At that time,' she noted, 'I didn't question the easy life I had thanks to money and fame. I was fully confident in my future. Nothing could happen to me but happiness.'

A couple of years later, a string of failed affairs behind her and with war grinding the French movie industry to a temporary halt, life wasn't quite so blissful as it had been. By Christmas, she was finally back in Paris, doing her bit for the war by holding parties for British and French pilots and taking them out to nightclubs; in the French capital, there may have been a blackout, but the champagne still flowed, cars still ran, and there was no sign yet of any rationing.

In Britain, food production was an equally pressing problem, not least because British agriculture was in apparently terminal decline and because more than 70 per cent of all food was imported, whether it be for human or animal consumption. In effect, an industrial nation that had neglected its countryside had to be saved from possible famine. Britain was not preparing for a short, sharp war but, rather, a long battle of attrition and in that scenario shipping was going to be at a premium and needed for transporting crucial war materiel rather than food. Somehow, some way, British farmers needed to pull their collective fingers out and create a very dramatic farming revolution – one which meant that much food for consumption became home-reared rather than imported from overseas. A figure of between 80 and 90 per cent home-produced food – like Germany – was needed and in swift order. It was a massive challenge.

'So once again in a time of national danger,' scribbled Arthur 'A. G.' Street, on 8 September 1940, 'our industry of farming is to be transformed from Cinderella, not into a fairy queen, but into Britain's fourth line of defence.' He was aware that the BBC had started referring to the Air Raid Precautions, or ARP, as Britain's fourth line of defence after the Army, Navy and Air Force, but A. G. was insistent that it was farming which deserved that moniker. 'After all,' he added, 'what is the good of starving to death in an air raid shelter? Better to die outside with a full belly.'

British farming had been in the doldrums since the 1870s as Britain's global reach extended further with the advent of free trade; the policy had been to export high-end goods in return for cheap food and raw materials. Suddenly, wheat was flooding into Britain, grown more cheaply in the wide expanses of North America, while refrigeration meant meat could be sailed from the Argentine and even New Zealand on the far side of the world. Since the 1890s, the worst of the decline was past, but there had been only a temporary recovery during the last war when, as food imports had fallen, so agricultural prices at home had risen. A poor harvest in 1916 and the German policy of unrestricted submarine warfare meant the new Lloyd George government had needed to act swiftly. County Agricultural Executive Committees had been established to oversee the ploughing up of grassland and take possession of poorly run farms. Guaranteed prices had been set for cereals and potatoes.

It did not last, however, and by 1921 guaranteed fixed prices were dropped and farmers were once again left to fend for themselves. With livestock sold, cereal prices falling, losses in the workforce and the break-up of many country estates, farming declined once more. By the late 1930s, British farming had reached its nadir. Hedgerows had grown wild, large parts of the landscape lay fallow and had reverted to scrub, decrepit barns dotted farmsteads, and yards were filled with abandoned carts and agricultural equipment. Large numbers of estates had been sold during the twenties and thirties, tenant farmers were disappearing, and owner-occupiers were going bust on an almost weekly basis. Those that remained were feeling besieged, unwanted and increasingly bitter. By 1939, the amount of land under the plough had been reduced to two-thirds of what it had been in 1801 and there were 25 per cent fewer farm workers.

Most farms were less than a hundred acres and were livestock rather than arable. Nor was there much sign of modernization. Despite the advent of tractors and other modern machinery, fewer than one in six farms had a single tractor by 1939. While this was a far higher figure than that of Germany, it was none the less considerably below Britain's potential levels of agricultural mechanization. Crop yields were much the same as they had been fifty years earlier. This meant that by 1939 just 12 per cent of wheat and flour was home-grown, while just 16 per cent of sugar, oils and fats, and 9 per cent of butter came from British farms. Admittedly, 50 per cent of meat was home-reared, but 8.75 million tons of feedstuffs were imported to feed British livestock. In all, around a third of all imports were food. And that was way too high a figure now that Britain was at war.

Of course, it wasn't doom and gloom for all British farmers, and some regions had done better than others. The biggest single agricultural product consumed at home was milk – some 94 per cent was home-produced – so the dairy farmers of the south-west were doing better than most. A. G. Street, who had a farm at Wilton in south-west Wiltshire, was a progressive farmer always on the look-out for new schemes and farming methods, and had adopted the Hosier milking system. This was a mobile milking unit that enabled seventy cows to be milked at once out in the open air. It was a great success, but rather depended on the better southern climate. Even so, A. G. supplemented his income not only by writing books, but also by running his own milk-round in Salisbury throughout much of the 1930s. Like most farmers, he worked nearly all day, every day of the week.

And Street was a success, the more so after his first book, *Farmer's Glory*, published in 1932, had become an overnight hit. More tomes had followed, and with them came demands to lecture and speak and even advise on rural matters. Despite all this, the Streets were never more than comfortable; his daughter, Pamela, went to a local private school, but it was a struggle to pay the fees. Ditchampton Farm was a lovely spot, but the farmhouse was hardly a mansion and there were few luxuries. Farming was tough, even when you were doing well.

Admiral Dönitz was fully aware of how dependent Britain was on imported food, and had assessed that his U-boats needed to sink around half a million tonnes of shipping per month. If they were successful, within a year, he reckoned, Britain would be brought to the point of starvation. 'No weapon ever invented,' wrote the author and poet Laurie Lee, 'is more deadly than hunger.' It was all very well Britain rearming and having access to resources from all around the globe, but if the British people could not be fed, it was all for naught, as farmers like A. G. Street were all too aware.

But so too was the government, and despite the rural decline, considerable thought had been given to this potential problem should war erupt once more. In 1935, the then Minister of Agriculture, Walter Elliott, had set up a committee to investigate how farming might be organized in the event of war. Among its recommendations were the reconstitution of the County Agricultural Committees. These had worked well in the last war, and were based on the principle that local farmers were best placed to implement state directives in their regions as they not only knew the soils and best local farming practices, but invariably knew the other farmers in the region too. The following year, a provisional list of chairmen, executive officers and secretaries was agreed should the War Executive Agricultural Committees – as they were to be called – need to be enacted.

Further steps were taken. A new Agricultural Act was passed in 1937, offering grants to farmers to buy crucial fertilizers such as lime and basic slag and to invest in land drainage; it was part of an effort to increase the badly neglected fertility of the land. By the spring of 1939, the new Minister for Agriculture, Sir Reginald Dorman-Smith, was buying large stockpiles of phosphates, oil seeds, cereal feeds and even tractors. Stocks of other foodstuffs were also built up, and Dorman-Smith instigated a renewed ploughing-up campaign with an incentive of £2 for every acre of permanent pasture turned over to arable, a sum in 1939 that was not to be sniffed at. There were also financial incentives for growing barley and oats to replace imported animal feed. Manpower was also protected as farming was considered a reserve occupation.

In addition to these measures, at the end of August 1939, the Minister of Agriculture was given full powers to control and direct food pro-duction, including, most controversially, the authority to requisition any farm or terminate any tenancy where land was being neglected or farming practices were unnecessarily poor. The Ministry was also attempting to dramatically increase mechanization on farms, not least with a big rise in the number of tractors. The American company Ford had opened a 66-acre site in Dagenham in Essex back in 1932. Six years later, Ford offered to increase production to eighty tractors a day within three months with the help of government financing. This was initially turned down, but as other measures were being put in place a deal was struck, with Ford agreeing to increase production and to keep 3,000 in reserve should war break out. The Fordson Model N was not the best tractor around, but it was the only one being mass-produced, and in the govern-ment's new drive to increase food production that was what mattered.

The War Agricultural Executive Committees were also enabled and could begin their work immediately, as those on each of the county committees had already been appointed and begun work in readiness. Wiltshire's War Ag – as they immediately became known – was made up of highly respectable farmers, squires and yeomen. A. G. Street broadly approved of the choice and certainly the principle – he thought it made perfect sense that those who knew the local conditions and capabilities of the land were best placed to prepare Wiltshire for the 1940 harvest. 'In this instance,' he noted, 'decentralisation has already scored a notable triumph.'

With the outbreak of war, Britain did at least, then, have measures in place to attempt the dramatic increase in home food production that was urgently needed. Now that war had come, farmers were asked to plough up a further million acres of grassland. It had to be this way. During peacetime, people wanted fresh meat, fresh milk, fresh eggs, fresh vegetables and fresh fruit. Now, however, what was needed above all was grain and potatoes – after all, it was possible to feed a great deal more on bread than on the eggs produced by feeding that same grain to hens.

Britain was fortunate to have so much grassland that could be ploughed up. None the less, A. G. Street was conscious that this was asking a lot of many farmers, who would now have to alter farming systems and reduce livestock, which would add a significant layer of work and worry. Many still did not have the mechanical equipment, horses or labour to tackle this sudden demand for more acreage. Street himself had lost his foreman, Charlie Noble, who, as a territorial, had answered the call to arms, while at the same time his family was suddenly inundated with evacuees. All across Britain, between the end of June and the first week of September, some 3.5 million had left the cities for the countryside, most of whom were children and young mothers; the Streets were now looking after three girls from Portsmouth, which required quite some adjusting, not least because none of them had ever seen plumbing and running water before let alone had any experience of country life. Soon after, the mother of one of the girls also arrived, carrying a baby. Most hosts had little choice in taking on evacuees, although who was sent where tended to be a little less haphazard; billeting officers were always local figures who knew the potential bedroom space their neighbours had. Needless to say, this enormous evacuation put a huge strain on many families, schools and local facilities.

A. G. was, however, philosophical. A passionate champion of British farming but also a patriot, he believed that whatever hardships stood at his door or lay before him in the future would prove a small sacrifice. It was essential, he believed, that the countryside, collectively, show the towns and cities that without their farms they could not hope to survive the war. But more than that, it was a matter of conscience. 'Whenever I see an aeroplane performing its dangerous evolutions above my farm,' he noted late one evening at his desk, 'I realise that youth is taking the dangerous share, and that middle-aged countryfolk should be only too glad to toil in safety on the fields below.'

Despite the seriousness of the potential food production crisis in Britain, there was, however, no panic yet as the country entered the first winter of war. For sailors like Vere Wight-Boycott, out on the North Sea, the weather was an enemy more savage than any German. In London, Jock Colville was getting fed up with walking through endless snow and slush, while in her flat in West Hampstead, Gwladys Cox was finding the cold quite debilitating. 'Colder than ever!' she noted on 20 January. '24 degrees of frost on Hampstead Heath. Pipes in bathroom frozen, milk solid in larder.' When the milk boy came he looked so numb with cold she sat him down by the kitchen fire and plied him with hot coffee.

But for farmers like A. G. Street, who always liked to look on the bright side, there were benefits; cold it may have been, but it was at least dry, and that meant he could get on with threshing the previous summer's harvest. He had also made silage for the first time the previous autumn – high-moisture, fermented and stored hay – so was feeding his dairy cows with that rather than hay, as he had done all his previous farming years. He had become an immediate convert: silage could be fed to his cows out of doors even if it was raining and didn't blow about in the wind either.

He had also converted his tractor to pneumatic tyres, which made beetling about the farm in the snow much easier and had enabled him to lay up his farm van for the time being. Also put away in one of the sheds was his big car, leaving just an old Austin Seven for him and his wife. In the big scheme of things, however, Street, like many farmers, was finding it easier to get around than most in Europe at this time. Petrol rationing had been introduced from the outset of war, with non-essential users limited to 1,800 miles per year and essential users given an annual allowance of 9,000 miles. Farmers with mechanical machinery were also given concessions against the petrol ration.

Food rationing, however, had been repeatedly postponed. The Government had been worried about public opinion and so, although it had been preparing for it, did not actually bring it in until the New Year. Gwladys Cox in north London had been issued her ration books in November and had promptly left them with 'the butcher, Atkinson, grocer Dimmer, and milkman, Limited Dairies'. On 8 January, she jotted in her diary, 'Today, butter, sugar and bacon rationing starts. ¼ lb butter, ¾ lb sugar per head.' In March all meat was rationed. Gwladys Cox was not grumbling and, although there were plenty who were, it was not especially severe – not to begin with at any rate – and in addition people were encouraged to produce their own food, whether it be growing vegetables or rearing rabbits. Early in the New Year, this scheme had been given a catchy name, coined by one of the national newspapers: 'Dig for Victory'. Flower beds gave way to vegetable patches, while public parks, railway embankments, school playing fields and recreation grounds were dug up for new allotments. The Prime Minister let it be known he was growing potatoes, and King George VI that potatoes, cabbages and other vegetables were replacing the flower beds around the Queen Victoria Memorial opposite Buckingham Palace. The Dig for Victory campaign successfully killed two birds with one stone: it would provide a not insignificant amount of extra food and also gave Britons a useful sense of unity of purpose.

But while British people of all ages and classes were now united in growing vegetables, that same unity of purpose was not shared by the War Cabinet, the Chiefs of Staff or even their French allies. At the end of November, the Soviet Union had invaded Finland. This followed on from their invasion of east Poland in September, as agreed in the German–Soviet Pact, and then by the absorption of the Baltic States through a series of 'mutual-assistance pacts'. It then tried to secure the Gulf of Finland, demanding the Finns hand over a number of ports, including those to the north touching the Barents Sea. When the Finns refused, the Red Army attacked.

This prompted a crisis of future strategy in London and Paris. The long, hard winter may have provided Allied factories with an essential chance to increase armaments, but the inactivity on the ground had caused problems. At a crucial moment, prevarication was replacing decisiveness . . .

CHAPTER 14

Iron in the Soul

IN FEBRUARY 1940, President Roosevelt sent a special envoy to Europe on a personal fact-finding mission. Sumner Welles was a refined and high-born Under-Secretary of State and FDR's main diplomatic advisor. Reserved, impeccably groomed, fastidious and imperturbable, Welles was a man of high intellect and little humour. On his trip to Europe, he would visit Rome, Berlin, Paris and London; his task: merely to talk with leaders of all four countries, gauge the temperature and report back. It was a mission that reflected Roosevelt's very personal approach to diplomacy. It certainly went against the grain to send such envoys – after all, the United States had ambassadors and embassies in all these places; but FDR mistrusted the State Department – the foreign ministry – disliked a number of his ambassadors, and, because his own poor health limited his movement, had always relied on a few, close and, most importantly, trusted friends and aides to be his extra eyes and ears.

Welles reached Naples by ship on 25 February and then took a special train ride straight to Rome. The following day, after a brief meeting with the King, he visited Count Ciano at the Palazzo Chigi. Welles found Ciano frank and intelligent and more sympathetic to the Allies than he had perhaps expected. Next up was a visit to see Mussolini himself in the Duce's huge office in the Palazzo Venezia, known as the Sala del Mappamondo. He thought Mussolini looked older than his fifty-six years and was surprised by how laboured his movement was. However, the Duce was cordial and assured Welles he still thought a real and lasting peace was possible between Germany and the Allies.

All in all, Welles left for Berlin the following day feeling the trip had been a success and that the Italians were less hostile and more desirous of peace than he had supposed. Whatever optimism he may have had leaving Italy, however, was dashed in Berlin, where during a series of meetings with leading Nazis, including von Ribbentrop, Göring and even Hitler, the message was crystal clear: there was no chance of any peace until Britain and France had been crushed into submission. Of any compromise there was not even a whiff. Unlike Rome, which had seemed bright and light and opulent, Welles found Berlin rather sinister with its swastikas, SS guards and endless uniforms. Later, after driving back to Berlin from Carinhall, Göring's house, he noticed long lines of Berliners queuing for food and, whether it was his imagination or not, recorded that he did not see one smiling face. He was glad to leave Germany behind.

And so on to France and to Paris, a city he had been to before and which struck him as much changed. Key monuments were now sandbagged and there was, he thought, a feeling of sullen apathy. The Prime Minister, Daladier, confided to Welles that he would not rule out a deal with the Nazis, but it was his meeting with Léon Blum, the Jewish, socialist leader of the Popular Front and former Prime Minister, that left a more lasting impression. There was a profound sadness in Blum's remarks. Welles had the impression Blum thought that for France 'the hours were numbered'.

Finally, Welles went to London, where he met most of the leading British politicians, usually accompanied by the US Ambassador, Joe Kennedy, a man who was deeply anti-Communist and who had more than a passing admiration for the Germans. His most important meetings were two separate interviews with Neville Chamberlain and the Foreign Secretary, Lord Halifax. Although it was not part of his remit, Welles did try to outline a compromise that might lead to peace, including disarmament of all the major belligerents. Both the PM and Halifax made it clear there could be no negotiations with Hitler unless the Führer agreed to give up 'most of what Nazidom stands for'. It was an honourable effort by the urbane American, but he was clutching at straws. Chamberlain, particularly, rather took to Welles. 'I felt that I had established a personal relation with him that may be useful,' the Prime Minister wrote in a letter to his sister, 'and it was evident that he attached much importance to what I said to him.'

*

Before he sailed home, Welles returned to Rome for one more round of talks with Ciano and Mussolini, and in a final effort to bridge the gap between Allies and Axis suggested there was far more room for manoeuvre on the part of Britain and France than was the case. It all came to naught. This time, a reinvigorated Mussolini warned Welles that the German offensive in the West was very, very close. 'The minute hand,' he told Welles with sinister gravity, 'is pointing to one minute before midnight.' Later, Welles did telephone the White House, asking whether he had permission to begin a vague attempt at a negotiated peace through Mussolini. Roosevelt refused him this. In fact, the very same day, the President gave a speech making his own stance as crystal clear as Hitler had made his, ruling out peace while there was oppression and cruelty and while small nations lived in fear of powerful neighbours. 'It cannot be a moral peace,' he said, 'if freedom from invasion is sold for tribute.'

Mussolini had not been at all impressed with Welles, although Ciano, for his part, had liked him. 'I have had too many dealings with the pack of conceited vulgarians that make up the German leadership,' he noted, 'not to appreciate the fact that Sumner Welles is a gentleman.' In his views of Welles, Ciano was neatly reflecting the increasing divergence in opinion between himself and his father-in-law, *Il Duce*.

Not much had changed between Italy and Germany: they were still allies, still part of the Axis, but Germany was at war with Britain and France, and Italy was not. None the less, Mussolini had been hurt and angered by Germany's deal with Russia, although by January he was thawing. At the time, there had been no chance of a meeting with the Führer and so instead he had written a long letter to Hitler, warning him about any further close ties with the Soviets. 'I feel that you cannot simply abandon the antisemitic and anti-Bolshevist banner which you have flown in the wind for twenty years and for which so many of your comrades have died,' he wrote. 'You cannot foreswear your gospel, in which the German people have blindly believed.' Russia was Germany's *Lebensraum*; Italy, he assured him, was accelerating military preparations and should be seen as Germany's reserve. The letter was intended to reinforce Italy's position as Germany's number one ally.

Mussolini was now more determined than ever to enter the war, although he was keenly aware how badly unprepared for conflict Italy was. For all the grandstanding, military parades, uniforms and chest-puffing, any impression of military strength was an utter charade. Italy was simply not wealthy enough nor blessed with enough raw materials to even remotely compete with the major belligerents. That was a big enough disadvantage, but was compounded by the inexorable bureaucracy and, frankly, low calibre of the senior leadership. In August and September, hundreds of thousands of reservists had been called up and had duly turned up to barracks and depots throughout the country only to find severe shortages of just about everything and infrastructure that was on the point of collapse.

That was just mustering the Army, before anyone began training or even fighting. Generale Pariani, the Under-Secretary for War, oversaw a Regio Esercito – Royal Army – that was deficient in artillery, tanks, vehicles, rifles, most equipment and even uniforms.

The Regia Aeronautica – Royal Air Force – was hardly any better, and its commander, Generale Valle, was every bit as incompetent as Pariani. Valle continually told Mussolini the Air Force had around 2,200 aircraft when, in fact, only a third of that number were what could be considered relatively modern, and of those some 240 were grounded for repair. Both men were subsequently sacked, but even bringing in new blood did not alter the fundamental problems facing Italy now that Germany, Britain and France were at war.

In a nutshell, they were twofold. The first was that Italy had almost no raw materials of its own, and not much to speak of from its limited overseas possessions. The second problem was that most materials were transported around the globe by sea, but Italy had no access to the oceans – or rather, it did, but both those access points – the Straits of Gibraltar and the Suez Canal – were controlled by the British. In fact, between them, the Allies controlled 80 per cent of Italy's raw materials and food imports transported by sea. This meant Britain had control of all oil, rubber, copper and tin, materials without which war would be impossible. In addition to this was the direct supply of 15 per cent of Italy's coal. As much as 70 per cent of its coal came from Germany, but two-thirds of this was shipped to Italy from Bremen, and, with the outbreak of war, from Rotterdam in neutral Holland. Only a fraction came by train through the Brenner Pass in the Alps. The situation was made worse when, on 21 November, Britain announced it was including all German exports as well as imports in the blockade, which closed the Rotterdam supply route as well. This meant that Italy's coal shipments from Germany were now cut off, although Ciano did then manage to negotiate an exemption for Italy's precious coal via Rotterdam. This, however, was clearly merely a short-term reprieve; the moment Italy began making bellicose overtures, Britain would turn off the tap.

In an effort to placate any Italian war-talk, however, Britain then offered to supply Italy with 70 per cent of its coal requirement for all of 1940 in return for arms and other goods, but, despite Ciano's careful diplomacy, Mussolini baulked at the idea and put a stop to it. 'I have the pleasure,' Mussolini told Ricardo Ricci, the Minister of Corporations, 'and let me emphasize, *the pleasure*, to inform you that English coal can no longer come into Italy.' As far as the Duce was concerned, it was a good lash of the whip for Italians to learn to depend on their now reduced resources. The shortfall in coal would be made up from Italian lignite, or low-grade 'brown coal' as it was known. This, however, was no real solution as not only was lignite less efficient, but the Italians did not have the machinery to extract it in any case. Mussolini was operating in a world in which he believed his will was enough; in this, he was tragically mistaken.

For Ciano, this was calamitous. Since the outbreak of war, he had been working to keep Italy out of the fighting, gathering around him key supporters of this policy and chipping away at Mussolini's resolve whenever he had the chance. Ciano ensured he kept a dialogue going with both Sir Percy Loraine and André François-Poncet, the British and French ambassadors, and made ill-concealed digs at his German allies whenever he had the chance. In December he made a widely reported speech to the Chamber criticizing the Russian invasion of Finland and by inference, and nothing else, Germany. Italian public opinion was also for the Finns and outraged at German perfidy; at the time, Mussolini had been full of outrage too. With glee, Ciano had scribbled in his diary how the Italians would never now march with the Germans. 'Everybody,' he wrote, 'knows and understands that Germany has betrayed us twice.'

In this, however, he was wrong. It seemed all too obvious to him and many others, leading industrialists included, that Italy would be ruined if it went to war; after all, where would all the raw materials needed for the fight come from? And how on earth could they fight with such an ill-prepared and obsolescent army? 'The Duce must be aware,' Percy Loraine told Ciano, 'that the Britain of today is no longer the Britain of a year ago.' 'It is hard for me to argue with him,' Ciano noted, 'because I share his opinion and he knows it.'

But Mussolini thought otherwise. While Ciano was convinced the Allies would win in the long term, the Duce believed Germany would crush the feeble-minded Allies. In any case, it was a question of honour. It was humiliating and degrading to have to dance to the tune of the British over their blockade, and he hated a situation in which he believed Italy stood between a rock and a hard place: needing to keep the Allies sweet but not compromising the alliance with Germany.

On 1 March, Britain announced its temporary reprieve on Italy's coal shipments from Rotterdam was now over, and four days later thirteen coal ships bound for Italy were seized by the Royal Navy. Mussolini was incandescent. 'It is not possible that of all people I should become the laughing stock of Europe,' he ranted to Ciano. 'I have to stand for one humiliation after another. As soon as I am ready I shall make the English regret this. My intervention in the war will bring about their defeat!'

Just how Italy was going to do this was not clear; it was as though verbal outrage would be enough to send Britain packing. At any rate, whatever slim chance Ciano thought he had of turning Mussolini away from the charge towards war, it was ruined by the announcement that his number one least favourite German, von Ribbentrop, was coming to Rome. 'A *coup de théâtre*,' jotted Ciano, 'dear to the low-class tastes of the Germans.' He dreaded Mussolini having any contact with von Ribbentrop. 'Under the circumstances,' he added, 'Ribbentrop will need no great oratorical power to urge the Duce on a course which he, the Duce, desires with all his soul.'

Just as Ciano had feared, von Ribbentrop whipped up Mussolini even further, assuring him the Allies would be crushed, and then proposed a meeting with Hitler. This took place at the Brenner Pass on 18 March, the day after Ciano's and Mussolini's second meeting with Sumner Welles. He had, however, already told von Ribbentrop a week earlier that his mind was made up: at the appropriate moment, Italy would enter the war on the side of its ally. The die, it seemed, had been cast.

The British, with their global fleets and world trade, had always been wedded to the idea that war was really a battle of supplies. All manner of raw materials were needed to fight a war, and not one country in the world had an abundance of all, not even America and the USSR, despite their vast size and geographical range.

Among those raw materials were metals, and in Britain few people understood the myriad and truly international world of metals better than Oliver Lyttelton. Having survived four years of the last war fighting with the Grenadier Guards and winning a Distinguished Service Order and Military Cross in the process, he had made it home and gone on to forge a highly successful business career. By 1939, he was chairman of the British Metal Corporation, who were, in essence, metal merchants and under his leadership had become the biggest metal company in the UK. They had further consolidated their position by striking a number of affiliations with Continental partners, which had enabled Lyttelton to become a director of the German metals firms Metallgesellschaft and Norddeutsche Raffinerie. This had given him an invaluable picture of the German metal trade and the importance of non-ferrous metals in any future war. He had learned, for example, that back in 1914, just a few months into the war, the directors of Metallgesellschaft had been approached by the German General Staff because they were already running out of copper and needed help in finding more. Copper, tin, lead and zinc were all needed – copper and zinc especially – in times of war.

It was with this in mind that in the spring of 1939 Lyttelton had begun a plan to buy up as much of these all-important metals as possible. As he was well aware, many of the leading mining companies around the world would be worrying about the uncertainty war might bring – would they still be able to ship their metals? Would existing buyers continue to purchase them? He had already been approached by the Ministry of Supply to become the Controller of Non-Ferrous Metals should it come to war, and so back in March, with the Germans walking into Czechoslovakia, he had approached Noranda in Canada, Broken Hill in Australia and others, and begun negotiating. What he was proposing was assured purchases, no matter whether they had the shipping or not, in return for guaranteed quantities at a low price.

Much to his immense frustration, he was unable to galvanize the Ministry of Supply into buying these metals right away, even though he knew Germany had been stockpiling copper, so although Lyttelton had personally secured small stocks of nickel, it was not until the outbreak of war that he was finally made Controller of Non-Ferrous Metals and given carte blanche to start purchasing. He hoped it would not already be too late. Lyttelton, like most others in Britain, was expecting a German offensive almost immediately, but was hoping the enemy would delay any action for as long as possible.

In the autumn of 1939, Lyttelton was forty-six and the epitome of the debonair and cultivated Englishman, with his lean features, slicked-back hair and trim moustache. From an aristocratic background, he had been educated at Eton and Trinity College, Cambridge, and had an exemplary war record. Indeed, the war had taught him much: the extremes under which the human body and mind can be placed, the awfulness of the slaughter, the importance of never, ever, giving in. He had been temporarily blinded by gas, had been nearly broken, but somehow had kept going so that when peace finally came he was among an elite of his generation who had fought for almost the entire war and was still standing.

During the war, he had also got to know and befriended a number of key people, from Winston Churchill and Anthony Eden to soldiers now generals in the Army. In the intervening years, he had travelled widely, learned everything he could about both modern business and the world of metals, and developed an outstanding and international web of contacts, as well as finding time to get married and raise a family. Intelligent, worldly and imbued with a razor-sharp business acumen, he was one of the key civilians from the business world from which Britain would greatly benefit now that war had come.

And with war declared, and Lyttelton now Controller of Non-Ferrous Metals, the British Metal Corporation was taken over by the Government and sent to new offices out of London in Rugby in the Midlands. With his own home inundated by young evacuees, he was almost relieved to get away. 'I had little dreamt,' he noted, 'that English children could be so completely ignorant of the simplest rules of hygiene, and that they would regard the floors and carpets as suitable places upon which to relieve themselves.' Already, the war was forcing differing classes in Britain, traditionally so separated, to confront one another.

Once installed at Rugby, Lyttelton and his hundred or so staff worked at 'white heat' and six weeks later, despite frustrating and unnecessary amounts of red tape from the Treasury, they had secured Britain's projected requirements. This had been done in precisely the manner Lyttelton had envisaged. The total sum was a staggering £250 million but had come at a fraction of the price per ton for which these metals had been purchased in the previous war.

But while non-ferrous metals were essential and urgently needed for the acceleration of armaments production, there was no question that, above all, the two raw materials needed for the successful prosecution of modern war were oil and iron ore. Not one of Britain, France or Germany had enough of either, although in the case of Britain and France this was not too much of an issue due to a combination of overseas trade and the resources of their respective empires. France, for example, gained most of its iron ore from its possessions in North Africa. With their large navies and merchant navies and with the U-boats sinking less than 1 per cent of all Allied merchant shipping, securing supplies of metals, ferrous or non-ferrous, was not – as Oliver Lyttelton had discovered – proving too problematic.

The same could not be said for Germany, whose geographical isolation from the rest of the wider world was one of its major Achilles heels. Because the Kriegsmarine was still so comparatively small, Germany had no means of breaking the Allied naval blockade that had been imposed the moment Britain had declared war, and so, by December, British intelligence deduced that of the 22 million tons of iron ore imported in 1938, the equivalent of 9.5 million tons of that supply had come from sources now closed to it. Details of current stocks were unclear, but they were believed to be low. In order to maintain its war effort and avoid industrial meltdown, it was reckoned that Germany needed to import 750,000 tons of iron ore per month from its one major supplier still available: Sweden. In fact, if anything, these figures were on the conservative side, as the Swedes had assured Germany of some 10 million tons of ore in 1940 and a further supply of lower-quality ore of between 1 million and 2 million tons. Certainly, back in April the previous year, the OKW had accepted that maintaining Swedish ore deliveries was a 'basic demand of the Wehrmacht'.

The biggest Swedish iron field was in the far north of the country in the Kiruna–Gällivare district. From here, ore was shipped either through the Norwegian port of Narvik, just a short rail link away, or through the Swedish port of Luleå in the Gulf of Bothnia, the narrow stretch of sea between Sweden and Finland. This second route, however, was frozen and impassable during winter months. The problem for the Allies was that although the Narvik route was the prime means of transporting the greater proportion of Germany's essential iron ore requirements, Norway was neutral and any infringement of its neutrality would be illegal. In effect, it would be an act of war. Running roughshod over the rights of neutrals wasn't really what freedom-loving democracies were supposed to do.

Be that as it may, it was the First Lord of the Admiralty, Winston Churchill, who first suggested back in September that if diplomacy could not persuade the Norwegians to help the Allied cause, then brazenly violating its neutrality and mining its coastal waters was vital. This way, German ships faced either the risk of hitting a mine or venturing out to sea, where they could be picked off by the Navy. The concern for Churchill, however, was not so much the violation of neutrality, but rather the possibility of retaliation, for Britain, too, received a fair amount of Swedish iron ore through Narvik.

Churchill had considerable sympathy for the Finns, as did most in Britain and France; but while he was all for taking the initiative in the war, mining the Norwegian Leads – the waters around Narvik – rather than sending half-cocked aid to the Finns, seemed to him a simple and bloodless operation that could achieve much. It would, he suggested in a widely circulated memo, be a blow struck at Germany's war-making capacity 'equal to a first-class victory in the field'. Yes, it would mean violating Norwegian neutrality, but the Allies were fighting to protect small countries like Norway. This was true to a point, but there was no doubt Norway would take a very dim view, to put it mildly, should Britain and France make such a move. Did that matter? Well, yes, because while militarily Norway was weak, it did have a sizeable merchant fleet that Britain had been negotiating to charter. Furthermore, it could cut off the supply of Swedish ore to Britain. Even more pertinent was the reaction of Sweden, which would understandably take it equally badly should an important trade be forcibly severed.

So, on the one hand, cutting off Germany's major iron ore supply during this crucial first winter of war would undoubtedly hurt the Nazis, but on the other, there would be a price to pay in terms of shipping, Britain's own supply of ore, and also the loss of the moral high ground, which was not to be underestimated.

While there were arguments for both mining and leaving well alone, one thing was not in doubt: taking the risk of mining the Leads would only be worth it if the British did so right away, during the winter months when passage through Narvik was the only practical supply route for Germany. Come the spring, the Gulf of Bothnia would be open to shipping once more.

Despite Churchill's convincing rhetoric, the Cabinet and Chiefs of Staff did a great deal of teeth-sucking about the matter, squirming with indecision. Churchill, as a member of the War Cabinet but nothing more than that, could not influence them into decisive action. When they decided to test the water, the response from the Norwegian and Swedish governments was unsurprisingly severe. Thus for the time being, it was decided, they would drop the plan of mining the Leads, but continue to apply diplomatic pressure to get both Sweden and Norway to go along with the proposed plan. By that time, of course, it would be too late. The whole point, as Churchill, with mounting frustration kept stressing, was acting decisively, now!

But while Churchill's mining plans had been firmly parked, the Cabinet did continue, albeit with no real enthusiasm, to support French plans to help the Finns – even though that would mean passing the aid through the Norwegian port of Narvik and Sweden, against those countries' wishes, and thus would also be a violation of their neutrality.

Championing this idea in Britain was the most senior military man in the country, General 'Tiny' Ironside, the Chief of the Imperial General Staff, who proposed using the cover of helping the Finns to invade both the north of Norway and Sweden and secure the principal Swedish iron mines. To Churchill, this seemed ludicrous. If mining the Leads – a far safer and more effective option – had already been rejected, why was this second plan even being considered? It was not an unreasonable question.

It was with the Scandinavian conundrum still rumbling away that Jock Colville had trudged through the snow and slush to No. 10 on the morning of Monday, 29 January. The day before had been his twenty-fifth birthday, and he'd spent the day with a friend who had evacuated with her children near the Epsom Downs. The return trip to London should have been a breezy forty-minute train ride but because of the chaos caused by the snow took three and a half hours.

'The French are becoming excited about Finland and Scandinavia,' he jotted in his diary. 'They claim to have alarming evidence of energetic Russo-German collusion to force the issue in Finland.' It was to much of the rest of the world's surprise that the Finns were still battling on against the Red Army; a quick Russian walkover had been expected. As far as the Allies were concerned, there were some obvious likely consequences of the war in Finland. It seemed to the French, especially, that should Russia take control of Finland, the path would be open for a German strike into Sweden and Norway, which certainly made strategic sense – not only would the Germans then secure control of all Swedish iron ore for themselves but in doing so would also deny it to Britain. Anticipating such a move, the French were therefore proposing to send a naval force to Petsamo in the extreme north of Finland and mountain troops to take the iron ore fields.

In the days that followed, the prospect of war with Russia appeared increasingly likely. However, with German forces breathing down the necks of the Allies along the Western Front, getting embroiled in a war with Russia seemed a high-risk strategy to say the least. None the less, from the French perspective, anything that might draw German troops and resources away from France and into an entirely different sphere of conflict was to be encouraged in a big way. Fear of a return to the horror of fighting on French soil was ever-present in the minds of the French war chiefs. Thus Britain and France were both considering involvement in Scandinavia, but for different reasons. These differences were undermining the Western Allies' ability to act decisively.

Despite Ironside's initial enthusiasm, Chamberlain and the War Cabinet continued to prevaricate, seemingly crippled into indecisiveness by conflicting military and diplomatic arguments they were unable to square. Discussions rumbled on through February – about the scale of the operation, the risk to Scandinavian neutrality, where to find the men and shipping. The Cabinet was presented with a joint report from the Chiefs of Staff and the Foreign Office on 18 February. This was a day after Captain Philip Vian on the destroyer *Cossack* had boarded the German ship *Altmark* and in so doing had indeed violated Norwegian neutrality. The Norwegians protested, and the British replied that Norway should never have allowed such a vessel to use its waters. The Norwegians left it at that.

The French and British then agreed in principle a plan that involved sending a brigade of French *chasseurs alpins* and one British brigade, which would include three companies of skiers, who were promptly packed off to the Alps for training. The operation would involve the seizure of the main Swedish iron mines as well as military support for the Finns. Three divisions and a large part of a further division were to be withdrawn from France and sent to occupy southern Norwegian ports; their role was to support the Swedes if Germany invaded. Just the British part in the operation would involve some 100,000 troops and 11,000 vehicles; this represented a considerable amount of men and effort, but was still likely to be insufficient to do what was required. How these men were supposed to move about and fight in snow and ice was also not really given too much thought. At any rate, a handful of skis was certainly not going to cut it.

It was towards the end of February that Brigadier John Kennedy was invited to become Chief of Staff to Major-General Pierse Macksey, who had been appointed to command the British part of the proposed Scandinavian operation. Kennedy, a career soldier and veteran of the last war, had been recovering from being knocked down and nearly killed by a car outside the Cabinet Offices in the blackout and had just been given the all-clear to return to duty. Keen to get back to work once more, and equally pleased not to return to the War Office, where he had been Deputy Director, Military Plans, the 46-year-old Kennedy accepted.

Even so, after being fully put in the picture, Kennedy thought the plan seemed both rather ambitious and fraught with potential problems. The intention, Kennedy was told, was to land at Narvik on 16 March. 'I could hardly believe that the scheme was going to come off,' he noted, 'but we had to work on the assumption that it would.' So Kennedy set to it, and put in a fortnight's work trying to implement a plan that would successfully get enough men to Norway in the very short time left. On 11 March, with the operation just a few days away, he attended a Chiefs of Staff meeting where it became clear as it broke up that, despite Ironside's enthusiasm, not everyone agreed it was worth doing. Cyril Newall, the Chief of the Air Staff, turned to Kennedy and said, 'I think the whole thing is hare-brained.' General Ismay agreed. So did Kennedy, for that matter.

The following day, Kennedy was summoned to Downing Street for a further meeting with the War Cabinet, Chiefs of Staff and with Major-General Macksey. It became abundantly clear that there was no real enthusiasm at all from the PM and his War Cabinet unless the operation could be achieved without any major opposition from the Norwegians or Swedes. This, of course, could not be guaranteed. Even so, no final decision was made on whether it would go ahead or not.

On the 13th, Kennedy had to put the final touches to the troops' orders, right down to the minutest detail; they were due to sail in two days' time, but were already in Scotland ready and ships were being loaded. Then news arrived of the impending armistice between Finland and Russia, and orders reached Kennedy that further troop movements were to be stopped. Then they were reduced to forty-eight hours' notice; finally, the operation was cancelled altogether. On the morning of the 15th, rather than slipping down the River Clyde, Kennedy was instead having breakfast with Ironside at the Carlton Club. 'You know it wasn't my fault we took so long to make up our minds,' Ironside told him. 'We need more drive at the top.'

Later that day, Kennedy went home and spent the afternoon digging his garden. The whole episode had been interesting, he realized, because it had taught him some valuable lessons. 'I learned how futile the waging of war becomes when the higher command refuses to grasp the nettle and delegate command to chosen subordinates,' he wrote. 'I learned afresh the dangers of hesitation when embarking on a course whose only hope of success is to be bold.'

Kennedy was quite right. Churchill had been urging swift action since the autumn. Time and again he had underlined the importance of decisiveness. The whole point had been to deny Germany its iron ore during the crucial winter months when other routes were closed. The Finns suing for peace had saved the Allies from what would have almost certainly been a complete fiasco. As a sign of British and French intent, the whole Scandinavian scheme had hardly augured well.

CHAPTER 15

All Alone

HITLER AND von RIBBENTROP may have done a good job convincing Mussolini they would sweep Britain and France from the board, but that kind of gung-ho rhetoric wasn't persuading many within the Wehrmacht, who felt nothing but a sense of impending doom – and, frankly, with good reason. If any country stood alone in 1940 then it was Germany in the spring of that year. There was the pact with the Soviet Union, but neither Hitler nor anyone else in Germany were kidding themselves that it had any long-term future. Economically, Germany was isolated. Part of the deal with Russia had been a trade agreement and although the raw materials now coming in from the east were much needed, they did not make up for the sudden and dramatic loss of overseas trade as a result of the Allied blockade. Because of Germany's geographical position, the blockade was relatively easy to enforce – even with half of Poland now morphed into the Reich, there was still only a comparatively short coastline facing the North Sea and a further stretch tucked away in the Baltic. The opportunities for reaching the world's oceans were limited, to say the least. This had been a problem for the Kaiser's imperial plans back at the turn of the century and had crippled the German effort in the last war. It was every bit as much of a problem for Hitler now. Great powers of the modern age needed either plentiful natural resources or easy access to the global sea lanes, or, even better, both. Germany had neither.

The truth of the matter was that, despite the Four-Year Plan, Germany had begun the war still heavily dependent on overseas imports – imports

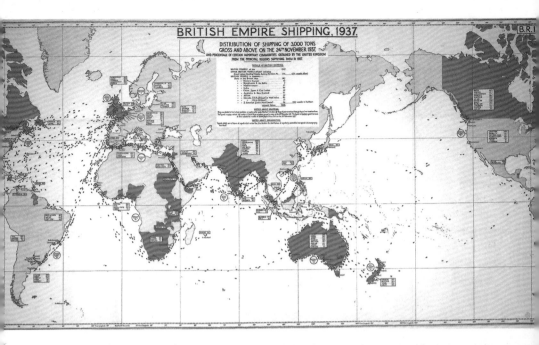

Above: Britain's vast global reach and access to resources, much of which went beyond both its Empire and Europe.

Right: The Führer at the Berghof. A man of iron will but also a gambler without geo-political understanding – a fatal shortcoming.

Below: Count Galeazzo Ciano, the Italian foreign minister, who in the summer of 1939 was both appalled by the machinations of Italy's German allies and desperately trying to keep his country out of war.

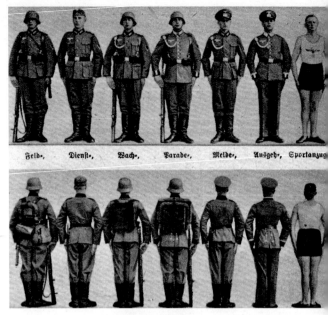

Above left: The point of no return. Two days later, on Sunday, 3 September 1939, Britain and France honoured their threat and declared war against Germany.

Above right: The seven uniforms of the German infantryman: elaborately designed, beautifully made – and expensive.

Above: German soldiers fire the much-vaunted MG34. A fine weapon but over-engineered, costly and with serious drawbacks that were often overlooked.

Left: German infantrymen, wearing the standard *Feldbluse*. Both the cut and the leather webbing were, in many ways, rather old-fashioned.

Right: A British soldier wearing modern battle-dress with canvas webbing: sartorially questionable, but certainly practical and inexpensive to produce.

Above left: One of England's finest-ever cricketers, Hedley Verity played his last match for Yorkshire on 1 September and volunteered three days later.

Above right: French troops. Some units had superb modern kit, but most, as this lot, looked like relics from the last century.

Left: The British Home Fleet at Scapa Flow. In 1939, Britain had comfortably the world's largest navy.

Below left/right: The Stuka (*left*), and the Heinkel 112. The latter was discarded, despite being a superb fighter plane and a far better partner for the Me109 than the Me110.

Left: German troops in Gudbrandsdal Valley in central Norway, April 1940.

Right/below: Helmut Lent and his broken Me110 at Fornebu, where he crash-landed and captured the airfield.

Sunken German ships at Narvik, 10 April 1940. On land, Germany held all the aces, but at sea, the Kriegsmarine suffered terribly.

British and French troops share cigarettes at Narvik, their only — and brief — success on land.

A German armoured column. This was the image projected to the rest of the world, but in truth Germany was one of the least automotive nations in the West.

Above left/right and right: No army in the world has ever been as dependent on horses as the Wehrmacht. There is a centuries-old feel to these pictures but they are, in fact, of a German artillery unit on the move in France in 1940. The field gun does not need modern pneumatic tyres when pulled by horses.

Left: General Maurice Gamelin (*second left*), with General Lord Gort.

Below: Belgian refugees. The Allied commanders had not considered how to move troops or deliver urgent messages along roads clogged with civilians. It was a terrible oversight.

Below: Dead French soldiers lie where they fell.

Below: Knocked out Char Bs. The French had the most numerous and best-armed and -armoured tanks, but lacked modern radios to put in them – another bad oversight.

A German armoured column. This was the image projected to the rest of the world, but in truth Germany was one of the least automotive nations in the West.

Above left/right and right: No army in the world has ever been as dependent on horses as the Wehrmacht. There is a centuries-old feel to these pictures but they are, in fact, of a German artillery unit on the move in France in 1940. The field gun does not need modern pneumatic tyres when pulled by horses.

Left: General Maurice Gamelin (*second left*), with General Lord Gort.

Below: Belgian refugees. The Allied commanders had not considered how to move troops or deliver urgent messages along roads clogged with civilians. It was a terrible oversight.

Below: Dead French soldiers lie where they fell.

Below: Knocked out Char Bs. The French had the most numerous and best-armed and -armoured tanks, but lacked modern radios to put in them – another bad oversight.

Left: The BEF retreating towards the Channel coast, late May 1940. Many were ordered to fall back before they had even fired a shot.

Below: A downed German Ju52. The Luftwaffe lost a staggering 353 aircraft on 10 May 1940, the opening day of the campaign.

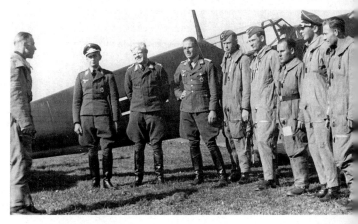

Above: Norman Field was one of those desperately trying to defend the perimeter around Dunkirk.

Right: Siegfried Bethke (*fourth left*), with his fellow fighter pilots in JG2.

Left: The image of the German soldier fighting in France: tough, well-armed and highly trained. In fact, these Waffen-SS troops were poorly trained and few in number.

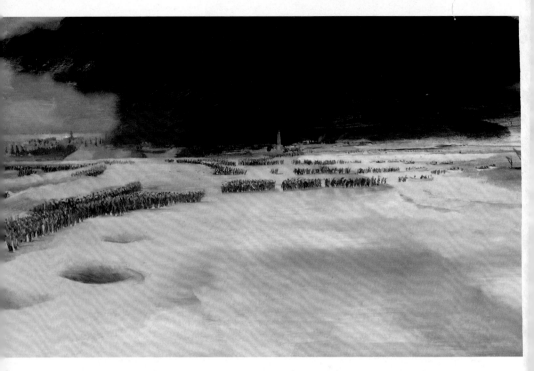

Above: The evacuation of Dunkirk. Smoke from burning oil depots and low cloud shroud the beaches.

Below: French troops en route to Britain. After the armistice, the vast majority chose to return to France rather than stay and fight under the banner of de Gaulle's Free French.

that were now largely cut off by the blockade. Even without British mining of the Leads, little iron ore was getting through that first winter of war, and oil and copper imports fell to almost nothing. So critical was the shortage of copper that Germany had been forced to ask Italy for crucial supplies, exchanging coal for this much-needed metal. Since Italy did not have the 3,500 tons demanded, Mussolini extorted it from the people – effectively stealing housewives' copper pans and chalices from the Church. Ciano warned him the Church would take a poor view of such an action, but the Duce ignored him.

By March, Germany had suffered an 80 per cent reduction in its pre-war imports; this meant it was bringing into the Reich less than a third of the raw materials it had consumed in 1932, the nadir of the Depression and a time when more than half its industrial capacity had ceased to function. It was almost as though the Hindenburg Programme of 1916–17 were happening all over again; back then, increasing industrial output had been achieved only by taking from agricultural production. The result had been food shortages and increased prices, leading to a nation, by 1918, that was on the verge of starvation. It was knowing all this that had so horrified many of the leading figures within the Wehrmacht when Britain and France had declared war. The Führer had told them the Western Powers had been bluffing and he had been wrong; it had shaken their faith in his judgement. Those who remembered the blockade of the last war, the terrible deprivations, and the bitter defeat and consequences after being economically crushed, feared history would repeat itself.

For men like General Georg Thomas, head of the military-economic staff at the OKW, and Walther Funk, the Minister for Economic Affairs, the only small sliver of hope lay in hardening the economy and trying to sustain a long, drawn-out war in which eventually all sides concluded a negotiated peace. It would mean absolutely no offensive action whatsoever. Thomas reckoned Germany could spin out resources in this way for about three years at the most.

This was so far from Hitler's view that it is no wonder he felt both contempt for and deep frustration with men like Thomas. For Hitler, it was always all or nothing. There was no grey area in any aspect of his thinking. The Third Reich would last a thousand years or it would crumble into dust. He had gambled on Britain and France not declaring war and had lost; this time, he would gamble again in a go-for-broke, all-or-nothing strike for a decisive victory. Even Hitler, with his tenuous grasp on reality, correctly recognized that he had but one choice: to hurl everything on one throw of the dice. There would be no stockpiling of resources; there would be no succour for the civilian population – the Volk of the Reich would have to stomach rationing, coal shortages, commandeered cars and other privations in the interest of bringing all German resources to bear on a rapid and crushing victory over the West.

Drastic measures were ordered. The Z Plan for the Kriegsmarine was scrapped – there would be no more battleships, cruisers or, most importantly, aircraft carriers, even though they were already emerging as the pre-eminent modern warship. Smaller, cheaper U-boat building increased. Instead of the scrapped Z Plan came the *Führerforderung* – the 'Führer Challenge' – to raise the production of ammunition by three and a half times in 1940 and by five times by 1941, and to dramatically increase Luftwaffe production, particularly of the Ju88 bomber. At the same time, armaments were also to be increased – more small arms, more mortars, more guns. Hitler's first demands for such an increase came at the end of the Polish campaign. Of course, results took time to kick in – which was too late for Funk, who was summarily axed in December – and were not helped by a crisis on the Reichsbahn, the state railway. Thanks to the massive amount of troop movements and a lack of investment in rolling stock or motor vehicles, bottlenecks occurred with immense railway traffic jams the consequence. In February, Göring had warned that transport issues were Germany's biggest problem affecting the war economy. In the short term, however, the Reichsbahn traffic problems were eased in the nick of time as the front settled once more.

In March, Fritz Todt, a 48-year-old construction engineer, was made Minister for Ammunition. Todt had worked his way up the Nazi pole, catching the eye of Hitler with his work on the autobahns and then the Siegfried Line, or Westwall as it was known. To do this he had drawn together government organizations like the Reichsarbeitsdienst – the Reich Labour Service – with private enterprise and created a manual labour force, the Organisation Todt. Within a week of taking charge of ammunition production, he had instigated a number of measures, including a loosening of price controls, decentralization and the cutting of debilitating red tape.

Ammunition figures rose rapidly after his appointment, even though the groundwork had been laid in the autumn of the previous year. At any rate, with Thomas now toeing the line and with the Russian raw materials finally making their way through the system, ammunition levels were starting to soar, and the Ju88 – slower, heavier than had been conceived, but with dive-bombing capabilities – was finally in full production. War against the West the previous autumn would have been suicide, but while it was true British and French rearmament had been stepped up in the same period, at least now Germany had the shells and bombs with which to launch an offensive.

Hitler's demands had, by April, largely been met. The price had been severe hardship at home and the neglect of other areas of the Nazi war machine. But if Hitler could smash the Western Allies in his do-or-die all-out strike, then these sacrifices would have been worth it.

In France, Capitaine Barlone and his Horse Transport Company were now stationed near Valenciennes, along with the rest of 2nd North African Division, on the North-East Front near the Belgian border. Barlone was billeted at a large, warm and comfortable house, which also doubled up as the Mess, but for most of the men the freezing temperatures were appalling. At the end of January, the temperature dropped to well below freezing, with the snow turning to ice. By day the men were now detailed to help the engineers build block houses along an anti-tank ditch that ran along the border. Barlone was not impressed – the anti-tank ditch was retained by light wattle and he rather suspected that after a brief bombardment the earth would crumble and the ditch would become easily passable once more.

In between digging and pouring concrete, Barlone and his fellow officers did what they could to keep up the spirits of the troops. Films were shown once a week and plenty of football was organized. 'Fine,' he noted, 'but the best thing would be to carry on with training and work the men hard instead of letting them rust.' These, however, were the orders from GHQ, so had to be obeyed.

Along the Maginot Line in Lorraine, Lieutenant René de Chambrun was equally concerned about the lack of activity. Life on the front had become more and more monotonous as the weeks and months had gone by. The debilitating freeze had given way to the thaw of spring, but he and his men in 162ᵉ Régiment d'Infanterie were still doing little more than the odd patrol. He had felt that in September 1939 his men – most of whom were farmers and peasants – had been ready to fight. 'He was not so ready,' he noted, 'to remain inactive in trenches or billets for eight long months with the feeling that his fields were abandoned and neglected.'

Chambrun also felt the division should have been working harder; it was all just a bit slack. Across the Rhine, he had the impression there were large numbers of highly motivated and incentivized German troops, ferociously building defences and readying for the fight. Chambrun, who was, by instinct, to the right of the political spectrum, worried that the rise of the Socialists and Communists in France in recent years had done much to discourage the concept of hard work. Both the Government and the Army had been so worried about these left-wing influences they had not stood up to them. 'During four years,' he noted, 'the word "travail" had been banned in the public utterance of politicians. There was also a stigma attached to the word.'

At Army headquarters in Paris, André Beaufre was also feeling increasingly frustrated. He understood the corrosive effect of inaction and had a pragmatic solution. While France's war chiefs stuttered over unworkable plans to help the Finns and seize iron mines, and talked of bombing the USSR's chief oil hub at Baku, or considered raising a Caucasian Legion, Beaufre believed the solution lay on their doorsteps. Italy was palpably weak both militarily and in resources, but threatened French possessions in Tunisia and British control of Egypt and the Suez Canal. Striking hard against Italy – and before Germany struck against the Allies – could well have upset the Axis balance of power decisively. After all, Germany was hardly going to sit back and accept a hostile southern flank. For Beaufre, knocking Italy out immediately killed more than one bird with a single stone. It secured the Mediterranean and the Middle East, freed up Allied naval power and resources, gave the French Army some fighting to do, and showed Germany the Allies were not afraid to take the initiative. He reckoned at least thirty divisions could have been drawn from the Maginot Line, which already had a 3:1 manpower advantage over the enemy along that stretch of the front, and there were a further ten French and three British divisions in the Middle East that could have been called upon.

There was something in Beaufre's logic, and a strike against Italy did not lack supporters. 'But nothing was done,' noted Beaufre, 'because such a decision required a firmness which was quite foreign to the nature of our leaders.' Gamelin preferred to wait, as did the British, and Général Georges had concerns about crossing the Alps and weakening his North-East Front. Instead, France continued to make diplomatic overtures to Italy, responding to Ciano's encouragement. By the time Mussolini had resolved to go to war, it was too late.

Like Beaufre, Edward Spears was of the opinion that the French leadership was flawed. His friend and colleague Winston Churchill had asked him to head back to France in February. The First Lord had had an idea to mine the River Rhine and disrupt German river freight – which was considerable – opposite the Maginot Line. It was to be a Royal Navy operation but required authority and co-operation from the French.

Spears's trip included meetings with both Georges and Gamelin as well as Daladier and Reynaud. Georges he knew of old, but the general had, he thought, lost much of his lustre since being severely wounded a few years before in Marseilles, when King Alexander I of Yugoslavia had been assassinated. Another problem was that Georges was commander of the North-East Armies and the senior French battlefield commander, yet was strongly disliked by Général Gamelin, the head of the Army, not least because Georges was heir-designate as Commander-in-Chief. It did not make for a smooth chain of command. Gamelin had further put distance between himself and Georges by reorganizing General Headquarters, which had been run by a major-general at Gamelin's HQ at Vincennes. As of January, however, 'General Headquarters' was moved halfway between Vincennes and Georges's HQ under the command of Général Aimé Doumenc, and would control all fronts, including Georges's North-East. It was a cumbersome and unnecessary extra level of staff. Georges also warned Spears that Daladier and the Government would be unlikely to support the mining of the Rhine. The Government was doing everything it could to divert the war away from its own frontiers. This had remained the principle reason for its interest in Finland, but it was also actively pursuing opportunities in the Balkans, as well as considering Beaufre's plan for a pre-emptive strike on Italy. The British operation on the Rhine risked German retaliation on the French.

'But the Germans are blowing up our ships all round our coast,' Spears pointed out. 'The mines are our answer.'

'The politicians and maybe the public won't see it that way,' Georges replied. 'They will connect your attack on enemy rivers with the probable German retort against ours. I am all for Churchill's plan and will give him every facility. But I am telling you.' Spears answered curtly that those who shunned striking blows for fear of being hit back were better off not engaging in war in the first place.

A trip to the front hardly assuaged Spears's increasingly nagging doubts about his beloved France. The much-vaunted tank-trap looked, much as it had to Capitaine Barlone, rather feeble, while the pillboxes were mostly incomplete. Spears heard there had been both a shortage of concrete and arguments about design.

In Paris, he met Gamelin and had dinner with Paul Reynaud. Time and again, Reynaud returned to the same theme: the lack of drive in the prosecution of the war, and the absence of any will to take the offensive from either the French or the British Government. 'Neither,' Reynaud told him, 'have begun to realise what it is all about.' He also told Spears about an inspiring and dynamic cavalry officer – a certain Colonel de Gaulle – for whom he had much esteem. De Gaulle had both studied armoured tactics and written a book about them. Despite getting some attention, however, his tactics of using armour as a highly mobile spearhead rather than purely as infantry support, which was the current French thinking, had not gained wide approval. Another concern was the state of the aircraft industry, which had been nationalized. Rather than streamlining production, however, the effect had been dire. Indiscipline and, again, a lack of drive, Reynaud told him, were stifling efficiency. 'It sounded ominous,' noted Spears.

A few weeks later, on 21 March, the Government fell. The lack of action in Finland and the subsequent surrender of the Finns on 12 March prompted a public outcry. Regardless of the inherent risks of military involvement in Scandinavia, the public had demanded action; in a democracy, and one so politically diverse as France, public opinion counted for a great deal, whether that opinion was right or wrong. There was also palpable disenchantment at the front and in the cities, and an increasing perception that the Daladier Government was weak and indecisive. In Parliament, a vote of confidence was called and while the Daladier administration got 239 votes, 300 deputies abstained. The Government no longer had the confidence of the House, and Daladier had no choice but to resign.

In his place came Paul Reynaud, chosen by a majority of just one vote. One of the difficulties for Daladier had been the divergence of politics in France. At the outbreak of war, the Prime Minister had created a *Union Sacrée* – an all-party coalition as had been established back in 1914. The trouble was, the extremes of political views made it hard for the coalition to gel in any shape or form, despite the wartime need for political co-operation. Paul Reynaud and Georges Mandel were determined to galvanize the country, streamline production, and instil patriotic fervour and chutzpah into the French war effort, but on the other side of the spectrum were 'softs' like Georges Bonnet, Anatole de Monzie and Camille Chautemps, whose view was far less hawkish and whose main aim was to restore peace as soon and as bloodlessly as possible.

So while Reynaud had the kind of steely resolve and dynamism to drive the French war effort, he was horribly stymied by the need to continue the *Union Sacrée* and a lack of emphatic support. He would have liked to have included in his Cabinet the highly capable and more hawkish former Prime Minister Léon Blum, but such was the anti-Semitism manifested towards him in political circles that it would never have been accepted. Other 'hards' – or hawks – suggested by Reynaud were also blocked. The result was another Cabinet destined to achieve little, containing six Socialists, five Radical Socialists, six members of the Democratic Right, three of the Union of Socialists and Republicans, five of the Democratic Alliance, five Independents, two of the Democratic Union and one deputy who was unattached to any political group. In other words, a potent mixture of the far right and far left, Communists, conservatives worried about revolution, defeatists and pro-Fascists. The chances of these men ever agreeing on anything seemed rather unlikely.

'The stake in total warfare is the whole stake,' Reynaud told the Chamber on 23 March. 'To conquer is to save everything. To succumb is to lose everything.' Despite this rallying cry, the session descended into a slanging match between the various parties, all of whom felt the composition of the Cabinet was unfair. All Reynaud wanted to do was find enough commonality to stem the tide and breathe new life and vigour into France. He was facing an uphill battle.

On 4 March, just as Admiral Dönitz was preparing to send his U-boats in wolfpacks out into the Atlantic, his headquarters received orders to stop any further sailings. Instead, they were to be redirected to Norwegian waters as a prelude to invasion and to help ensure the Allies did not try a similar move first. Dönitz was against the move, and he was not alone. Most of the U-boat crews thought it a mad idea, and not least Oberleutnant Erich Topp. 'A submarine is designed to be a commerce raider,' he wrote, 'and requires vast areas of sea space to be effective . . . Deploying U-boats in Norway's narrow fjords, however, went against all experience and common sense.'

Topp was twenty-five and taller than many submariners, with pale-blue eyes and a resolute chin. He often wore a somewhat wistful expression but, like most in the German Navy, greatly enjoyed the camaraderie and somewhat special, exclusive, status of the U-boat force. He had first volunteered for the sea back in 1934, even though there was no naval tradition in his family; rather, he had been brought up inland in Hanover, where his father was an engineer, but after starting medical studies he decided to join the Navy instead, following the lure of the sea and the promise of adventure. And his training and first years in the service, not least aboard the cruiser *Karlsruhe*, did allow him to see something of the world: there was a voyage, for example, that took them to South America, around Cape Horn, and then up to California, under the command of Admiral Günther Lütjens. A couple of years later, in 1937, Topp joined the U-boat arm along with Engelbert Endrass, who had joined the Navy at the same time and was on the same officers' course. They both passed out at the beginning of June 1938, Endrass to join *U-47* under Günther Prien, Topp to take over as 1WO, the commander's No. 1, aboard *U-46*.

He had been in that post ever since, although since the outbreak of war he and the crew of *U-46* had proved one of the least successful in operation with just two sinkings to their name. They were not going to add to that score skulking in the Norwegian fjords. At the beginning of April, they were still at their station, watching, waiting, but otherwise doing little. Topp found it exhausting. 'You have to have been with us to know what a seemingly endless waiting period can do to you,' he wrote in his journal. 'While on earlier patrols one surprise followed another in close succession, now we are practically devoured by the monotony of our daily routine.'

This, clearly, was a waste of a very valuable asset, one that needed to be made the most of if Germany was to have any chance of effectively severing Britain's supply lines. Dönitz was the one senior commander who properly understood the potential of the U-boat arm and yet already those above his head, but with less understanding of naval power, were interfering with his handling of this vital weapon.

Everyone, it seemed, was getting drawn into Scandinavia.

At the beginning of April, it was remarkable how disunited most of the major countries were. In Italy, much of the leadership was fervently against war but was nevertheless unable – or unwilling – to challenge the will of the Duce. Similarly in Germany, while Hitler was set on gambling not only Nazism but Germany itself with one of the most audacious and unlikely campaigns ever launched, the vast majority of commanders in the Wehrmacht were harbouring massive doubts and reservations, while the civilian population was praying war would be over with all speed. Even the Berlin teenager Margarete Dos was beginning to wonder whether Hitler was pulling the wool over their eyes; she and her friends had started listening to the BBC's German broadcasts and were horrified by the different picture being painted; that it was every bit as much propaganda as that which Goebbels was peddling was neither here nor there – Margarete was doubting both Hitler and the point of the war, and she was far from alone. In France, political in-fighting and a pronounced disenchantment with war also threatened to undermine fighting morale and confidence.

Only in Britain was there anything like a unity of purpose. It was, of course, different for Britain; the last war had not been fought on its soil, and the Germans were far away, not just the other side of a river. It had the security of wealth, of global reach, even of past victories. Its politics, too, reflected that and were more stable, with just three main parties covering a far narrower political spectrum. Morale surveys showed the vast majority of people not only accepted the necessity of the war, but also believed it was Britain's right and moral duty, as the world's leading global power and democracy, to rid the world of Nazism. Back in January, Gwladys Cox had listened to two speeches on the radio, one by the Foreign Secretary, Lord Halifax, and the other by Winston Churchill. 'Lord Halifax does indeed seem to be imbued with a profound sense of the rightness of our cause,' she jotted afterwards. 'He declared he would a hundred times sooner be dead than live in a world under Nazi domination.' Churchill's speech on the other hand was 'vigorous, pugnacious, and confident'. It was precisely this belief in the rightness of cause that had prompted the England cricketer Hedley Verity to join up; the Empire may have been on the wain, but the belief that Britain had to take the moral lead in the world was accepted by the majority of British people.

And there was confidence too. Jock Colville, a young man at the heart of Britain's war machine, recognized the war might 'wreck our economy and ruin our prosperity in the process' but never doubted they would win in the end. The 'assurance of victory' was an oft-repeated line in newspapers and on the radio, and most in Britain believed that victory was indeed assured. The path to that victory might well be rocky, and it might well be long, but the defeat of Germany *would* be the outcome.

Events, however, were about to take place that would shake that confidence.

PART II

GERMANY TRIUMPHANT

CHAPTER 16

Operation WESERÜBUNG

Sunday, 7 April 1940, and a fine spring day. Leutnant Helmut Lent and the rest of his *Staffel*, 1/ZG 76, were flying over the Baltic sea in their twin-engine Messerschmitt 110 Zerstörers. Below, Lent could see a large formation of German ships, including two battleships, the mighty *Scharnhorst* and *Gneisenau*, heading north, a sight that made him feel proud and one that he would not readily forget. The task of the Luftwaffe was to protect this fleet from any aerial attack, but why the Kriegsmarine was steaming north was anyone's guess. 'One could speculate,' noted Lent, 'but one couldn't come up with any answers.'

Not until the following day did Lent and his comrades discover the truth. Called together that morning, Monday, 8 April, they were told they were being posted north from their base at Jever to Westerland on the island of Sylt, just off the western side of the German–Danish border. The reason for the move was that at dawn the following day Germany was going to invade both Denmark and Norway. The task of the Zerstörers was to protect the airborne drop planned for the airfield at Fornebu near Oslo in Norway and then to land there themselves. 'It was,' scribbled Lent, 'to be the most daring operation ever in German history.'

Lent may well have been right, but Hitler had felt compelled to act, terrified that the Allies would snatch control of the all-important Swedish iron ore so crucial to his war aims. General Thomas and the economists at the OKW pointed out that a shortfall would be disastrous should the war continue for longer than around six months. In other words, not only was the Narvik route still of vital importance, but so was ensuring all other shipping routes remained open too, which rather gave weight to Churchill's original strategy for Norway.

But it wasn't just about supplies of iron ore. Throughout the autumn of 1939, Admiral Raeder, Commander-in-Chief of the Kriegsmarine, had repeatedly stressed to Hitler the value of having bases along the Norwegian coast, both to deny them to the Allies and for use by U-boats. As Raeder pointed out, British naval and air bases in Norway would be a serious problem for Germany, not least because it would mean a significant tightening of the economic blockade. Of course, the converse was also true: a Norway in German hands would unquestionably work against the Allies and Britain especially.

With his mind focused on an assault in the West, Hitler had initially favoured a policy of ensuring both Sweden and Norway remained neutral. But Raeder continued to chip away, even introducing the Führer to Vidkun Quisling, leader of the admittedly small Norwegian Fascist party, the Nasjonal Samling.

Whether it was Quisling who prompted Hitler into action is not clear, but certainly the Führer was listening to the repeated argument about the danger of a British occupation of Norway. He still favoured keeping Norway neutral but was becoming open to the idea of striking there swiftly should there be any sign the British were to make a move in that direction.

To be ready for this eventuality, preparations needed to be made. Initially, the OKW was asked to draw up a feasibility study, then at the beginning of February a new *Sonderstab* – or 'special staff' – was formed within the OKW especially to prepare operational plans for an attack on Norway. These were drawn from Jodl's and Warlimont's staffs and were ordered to do their work in utmost secrecy.

Everything about these plans had the mark of Hitler's direct involvement and they were hurriedly accelerated following the *Altmark* incident, when the British boarded the German ship inside Norwegian waters. Hitler summoned General von Falkenhorst, an Army commander who back in 1918 had once served in Finland, for consultation about fighting in the north. Apparently liking the cut of von Falkenhorst's jib, he there and then appointed him as the commander of Operation WESERÜBUNG, as it was to be called, without any further consultation with either the OKW or the OKH whatsoever. Von Falkenhorst had then hurried out, still in a state of shock, and had hastily bought a Baedeker travel guide and begun making his own plans.

Neither Halder and von Brauchitsch nor Göring and the Luftwaffe staff were consulted on any aspect of the plans. Both parties were furious about it when they were finally briefed at the beginning of March, not just because they had been kept in the dark, but also because they felt they were massively pushing their luck with the plans for the Western offensive as it was; attacking Norway and Denmark seemed a highly unnecessary diversion of resources at a critical moment. At the conference at the Reich Chancellery in Berlin on 5 March, Göring pronounced the plans unworkable and refused to subordinate the Luftwaffe to von Falkenhorst as Hitler had proposed. Instead, he appointed his deputy, General Erhard Milch as commander for WESERÜBUNG. Hitler responded by shutting Göring, second only to himself in the Nazi hierarchy, out of any further planning discussions. It was an unconventional way to prepare a major military operation, to say the least. As Warlimont later noted, sensible military practice was to consult fully with senior commanders and staffs, co-ordinate those requirements and appreciations, and carefully weigh up the pros and cons. Such an approach did not wash with Hitler, however.

As far as Warlimont was concerned, the end of war in Finland should have put an end to the plans. The attack in the West would be launched soon and would tie down British and French troops. If they were successful in the West, Warlimont reasoned, they could tackle Norway far more easily later. What was the point of undertaking an operation that would unquestionably draw on important resources? It was an entirely unnecessary risk. There was much in what Warlimont said.

But Hitler now had his mind irrevocably set on the Scandinavian venture. When Göring's private listening service, the Forschungsamt, picked up a Finnish diplomatic telegram in March revealing Allied plans for Norway, the Führer decided to act. On 2 April, he announced that Operation WESERÜBUNG was on. The attack would begin on 9 April at 5.15 a.m., and would be, he pronounced, one of the 'rashest undertakings in the history of modern warfare'. High-risk military gambles with minimal consultation or co-ordinated planning were very much Hitler's style.

The final plan that had been outlined to Helmut Lent and his comrades on 7 April was astonishingly bold, and involved six naval task forces – or *Marinegruppen* – for Norway and five for Denmark. This required pretty much the entire Kriegsmarine, including thirty-one U-boats – the entire operational submarine force, which had thus given Allied Atlantic trade a welcome respite from attack. The invasion force also included Luftflotte X, an entire air corps of over 1,200 aircraft, and some eight Army divisions plus reserves and other units amounting to around 120,000 men; more than 30,000 troops would be part of the first wave. Simultaneously, this force intended to occupy Denmark and key cities in Norway, from the capital, Oslo, in the south to Narvik in the north and including Trondheim, Bergen, Egersund and Kristiansand. Rash it may have been, but there was certainly nothing half-cocked about the plan. The Germans meant to occupy both countries in their entirety.

The Allied intervention in Scandinavia had appeared to be dead in the water following the end of the fighting in Finland and the subsequent resignation of Daladier. But the new French Prime Minister, Paul Reynaud, had been determined to show a bit more grip and offensive spirit and had quickly proposed a series of actions that included mining the Leads, submarine attacks in the Black Sea and air strikes on the oil fields of the Caucasus; the French were prepared to go to war with Russia if it meant disrupting the flow of all-important oil to Germany. In fact, anything was fair game so long as it meant distracting the Germans away from France's back door.

In the meantime, the British Chiefs of Staff had decided to opt for a continuation of the waiting strategy; they wanted to further rearm before taking the offensive, yet they appreciated the need to work in tandem with the French. At yet another meeting of the Supreme War Council on 28 March, they managed to dissuade the French from any attack on the Soviet Union and to get Reynaud to agree to mine the River Rhine, an operation the British had been urging for months. In return, they agreed to the mining operation of the Leads. It was also subsequently agreed, at the urging of both Churchill and his French counterpart, Amiral François Darlan, to put an Allied expeditionary force on standby for Norway because they both thought it likely that mining the Leads would prompt the Germans into an attempt to seize the iron ore mines.

All this having been agreed, Daladier, who had remained Minister of National Defence and War, and the French Comité de Guerre then refused to authorize the mining of the Rhine. For a while, the Narvik operation was once again off. On 4 April, Churchill, with Edward Spears in tow, hurried once more to Paris to try and change Daladier's mind, flying in an ageing de Havilland. Spears felt as buffeted about as if they were a 'salad in a colander manipulated by a particularly energetic cook', but they none the less made it in one piece.

It was soon clear that Daladier's refusal to play ball over the mining of the Rhine was as much to do with his personal animosity towards Reynaud as it was about any military considerations; certainly Edward Spears was in no doubt. 'The two men detested each other,' he noted, 'and Daladier was determined to exert his utmost power to humiliate Reynaud in every way possible.'

In Paris, Churchill tried but failed to persuade Daladier to reconsider the Rhine mining project. The French, Daladier told him, did not have the air force to retaliate should the Germans bomb France's cities in response to the mining of the Rhine. In fact, Daladier was mistaken. The Armée de l'Air had almost the same number of aircraft as the Luftwaffe, that is around 3,500. Nor would Daladier agree to have dinner with both Churchill and Reynaud, which the former had hoped to use to bring about some unity of purpose. 'What will centuries to come say if we lose this war through lack of understanding?' Churchill asked him. Churchill, determined that Britain should not be drawn into the same personal conflict, advised the War Cabinet and British Chiefs to go ahead with the Norwegian mining operation in the interest of maintaining good relations with their French ally. This was agreed, as was a further plan, known simply as 'R.4', to land troops in Narvik should the Germans either set foot on Norwegian soil or show clear signs that they intended to do so. These troops would be ready and waiting to be shipped out as soon as the minelaying operations began.

'The PM for his part is not over-enthusiastic,' noted Jock Colville on Saturday, 6 April, 'but feels that after the expectations aroused by the meeting of the Supreme War Council the other day, some effective action must be taken.' It was hardly a ringing endorsement from Britain's war leader, but finally, some seven months after Churchill had first suggested the operation, and after much heartache, general teeth-sucking, negotiations and prevarication, Norwegian neutrality was to be cast aside. 'The laying of the minefield in Norwegian waters,' added Colville, 'is timed for dawn on Monday.'

As the German invasion forces steamed north through Sunday, 7 April, RAF reconnaissance aircraft picked them up and later more than thirty British bombers attacked the naval groups heading for Trondheim and

Narvik, but their bombs missed. Meanwhile, that afternoon, the Commander-in-Chief of the British Home Fleet, Admiral Sir Charles Forbes, finally received more precise details of the numerous German forces, and by just after nine that evening, after some hastily changed plans, his ships had put to sea. There were already a number of British destroyers and minelayers stationed at the mouth of the Vestfjord, the gateway to Narvik, and further south near Ålesund for the planned mine-laying operations, so a clash was inevitable.

It was incredible that after so much Allied vacillation over Norway, both sides should have been beginning their offensives at the same moment and both be ignorant of the other's plans. Just a few days earlier, the Prime Minister, a very reluctant war leader, had declared in a speech on 4 April that he now felt ten times more confident of victory than he had at the outbreak of war. He was not so very surprised that Hitler had not launched the offensive that had been promised; applying the calm methodical approach to war that had dictated his own strategic views, he assumed Hitler had decided such an attack was not worth the do-or-die risk it would inevitably prove to be. Chamberlain clearly still hoped the war would fizzle out into a negotiated peace. He was, of course, making the fatal error of judging Hitler by his own standards. The British Prime Minister and the German Führer could not have been more different. Chamberlain would never have recklessly gambled all; Hitler was instinctively compelled to do so. At any rate, one thing was certain, Chamberlain assured his audience: Hitler had missed the bus. How those words would come back to haunt him.

Now, on the evening of 7 April, frantic recalculations had to be made. Clearly, a sizeable German naval operation was underway; just precisely what its intention was, though, was not so clear. Both Admiral Forbes and the Admiralty believed what was now important was to bring their superior naval forces to bear to deal a crucial blow to the Kriegsmarine. Forbes ordered his Home Fleet to try and bring the German capital ships to battle, while in London Churchill, without consulting either Chamberlain or Forbes, ordered the four cruisers at Rosyth, jam-packed with troops for Narvik, to disembark the soldiers and then head with all speed to seek battle. This was to prove a bad mistake.

The first major clash happened around 8 a.m. the following morning when HMS *Glowworm* intercepted the German heavy cruiser *Admiral Hipper* and four destroyers. *Glowworm* had been part of the minelaying force in the Vestfjord but had been left behind to look for a sailor who had fallen overboard. Initially, the British destroyer had tried to run, having sent crucial signals as to the size and location of the German force, but was soon obliged to fight. Badly crippled, the ship continued firing in return and then, with its decks on fire and beginning to sink, her skipper gave the order to ram the *Admiral Hipper*, sheering off forty metres of armour and torpedo tubes from the German warship in the process. It was the end of *Glowworm*, which rolled and blew up, killing all but thirty-eight of her crew.

Meanwhile, the British battlecruiser HMS *Renown* and nine destroyers had been ordered to prevent any German force reaching Narvik. Throughout the day, the weather deteriorated with gales and a heavy swell, so it was not until dawn the following morning, 9 April, that the British force finally spotted the two German battleships, *Gneisenau* and *Scharnhorst*, and their accompanying destroyer force. Both sides quickly went into action, the big ships slugging it out with their heavy guns despite the still rough seas. The British destroyer force was struggling to keep up with *Renown*, but the weight of their fire convinced the Germans they were facing stronger opposition than was the reality, and with *Gneisenau*'s main fire support system destroyed, the Germans turned away.

By that time, the invasion of Denmark and Norway was already well underway.

At the Royal Palace in Oslo, King Haakon VII of Norway had been woken at 1.30 a.m. on the morning of Tuesday, 9 April. Several unknown ships had been spotted moving into the Oslofjord. Soon after, further reports of ships had been reported at Bergen and Stavanger, and a little while later they were confirmed as German.

'Majesty,' the King's aide told him, 'we are at war!'

'With whom?' replied the King.

Both the King and the Government had learned about the arrival of British ships off Narvik the previous day, and since then their focus had been on Britain and the minelaying operation; the sudden appearance of the Germans had caught them off guard. An immediate mobilization had been ordered, but no one in the Government, it was quickly realized, knew how the mobilization should proceed. A few hours later, the Germans formally requested the Norwegians to capitulate and offer no resistance; the aim of the operation, the Germans claimed, was to protect

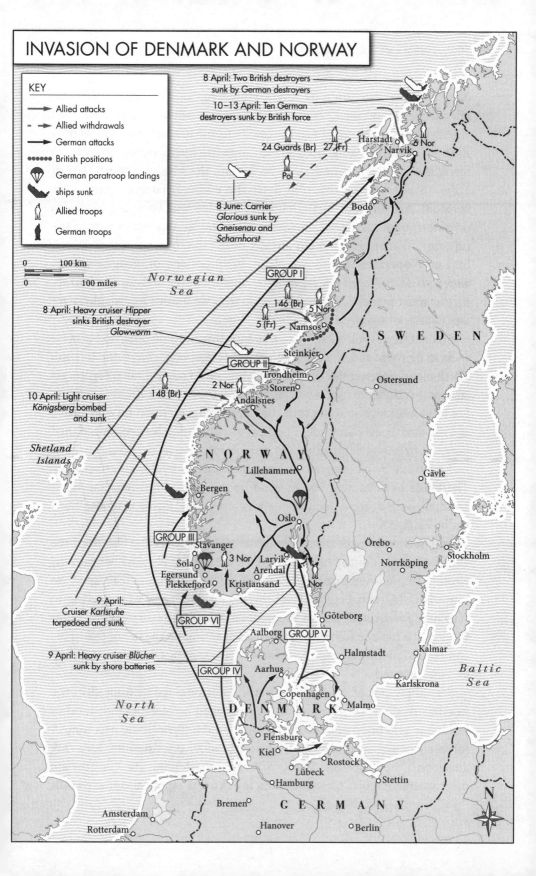

INVASION OF DENMARK AND NORWAY

KEY

→ Allied attacks
⇢ Allied withdrawals
→ German attacks
•••• British positions
🪂 German paratroop landings
⬛ ships sunk
👤 Allied troops
👤 German troops

0 _____ 100 km
0 _____ 100 miles

8 April: Two British destroyers sunk by German destroyers

10–13 April: Ten German destroyers sunk by British force

24 Guards (Br)   27 (Fr)

Harstadt
Narvik
6 Nor
Pol

8 June: Carrier *Glorious* sunk by *Gneisenau* and *Scharnhorst*

Bodö

GROUP I

8 April: Heavy cruiser *Hipper* sinks British destroyer *Glowworm*

Norwegian Sea

146 (Br)   5 Nor
5 (Fr)   Namsos

S W E D E N

Steinkjer
Trondheim
Storen
Ostersund

10 April: Light cruiser *Königsberg* bombed and sunk

GROUP II

148 (Br)   2 Nor
Andalsnes

Shetland Islands

N O R W A Y

Lillehammer

Gävle

Bergen

Oslo

Örebo
Stockholm
Norrköping

GROUP III

Stavanger
Sola
Egersund
Flekkefjord   3 Nor   Larvik
Kristiansand   Arendal
Nor

9 April: Cruiser *Karlsruhe* torpedoed and sunk

GROUP VI

Göteborg

9 April: Heavy cruiser *Blücher* sunk by shore batteries

GROUP IV

GROUP V

Aalborg

Halmstadt
Kalmar

Aarhus

Baltic Sea

Copenhagen
Malmo
Karlskrona

North Sea

D E N M A R K

Flensburg
Kiel

Rostock
Stettin

Lübeck
Hamburg

Amsterdam
Rotterdam
Bremen
Hanover
Berlin

G E R M A N Y

N

Norway from occupation by Anglo-French forces. The Norwegians dismissed this out of hand.

While the Government was frantically trying to react as swiftly as possible but faltering badly, the German invasion forces were beginning to reach their objectives and land. At 7 a.m., the Messerschmitt 110s of 1/ZG 76 were taking off from Sylt. The entire Zerstörer *Gruppe* was involved that day, but 1. Staffel, including Helmut Lent and his radio operator/gunner, Walter Kubisch, were to play an important part in the capture of Fornebu, the main airfield near Oslo. In what was to be the first ever operational airborne drop, paratroopers, or *Fallschirmjäger*, were to land, followed twenty minutes later by waves of troops in Junkers 52 transport planes. Lent and his comrades were both to provide cover and to attack targets on the ground.

Eight of them took off at 7 a.m. that morning heading north to Fornebu so as to be there at 8.45 a.m. when the *Fallschirmjäger* were due to land. Thick cloud covered the sky, so they climbed to some 13,000 feet to get clear of it and an hour and a half later were at the entrance to the Oslofjord. Lent did not know it at the time, but already the German invasion force at Oslo had been badly hit. The heavy cruiser *Blücher*, commissioned only the previous September and one of only five in the Kriegsmarine, had been hit by Norwegian shore batteries and at 7.23 a.m. had sunk. There had been some 1,600 men on board, of whom more than three hundred were dead. A second heavy cruiser, the *Lützow*, had also been badly damaged.

Lent saw nothing of this, although as they flew over the Oslofjord the clouds cleared. 'For the first time we see the land of Norway beneath us,' wrote Lent, 'a wonderful sight!' Opening the throttles, they sped on towards Oslo, then Lent realized the rest of the *Staffel* were veering to starboard towards the sun. A moment later, he saw a Norwegian Gloster Gladiator, a biplane fighter, away to his left sitting on the tail of one of his comrades. Banking sharply, Lent opened fire and the Gladiator peeled off and disappeared.

Seemingly out of nowhere, however, Lent now found himself in the middle of a swirling dogfight. He managed to get behind another Gladiator, and briefly opened fire only to find bullets arcing past him. A further Norwegian plane was now on his tail. 'I dive, pull up, turn. My attack fails,' he scribbled. 'We Zerstörers are faster, but the Glosters are more manoeuvrable.' Moments later, the sky was empty and the Me110s were regrouping, only for two more Gladiators to appear out of the clouds and attack. One plunged downwards, trailing smoke, the other disappeared once more.

Now they were over Fornebu and there was no sign of the airborne troops. Desperately looking around, all Lent could see was a Ju52 attempting to land but under heavy fire. Lent glanced at his fuel gauges – there was just fifteen minutes' worth left. The plan was to land at Fornebu themselves once it had been secured, but if they weren't on the ground soon, they would fall out of the sky for lack of fuel. Lent and his *Rotte* of three further Zerstörers dived down over the airfield and began shooting up the defences themselves. As he swooped over, a machine-gun nest he had not spotted opened up, riddling the plane. Lent pulled up past the end of the airfield, only to hear Kubisch call out, 'Starboard engine on fire!'

'Calm down, Kubisch! We'll land!' Lent replied.

Quickly shutting down the smoking engine, Lent thought quickly. Apart from the Ju52, no other plane had landed, but he decided he might as well be the first. Lowering the undercarriage, then the flaps, he banked and turned in towards the runway but realized he was too high – and the airfield looked horribly short. Would he get away with it? More bullets were spitting towards him from the right. The ground rose towards him and then – touchdown. Brakes, then Lent felt himself lurch forward and suddenly he was at the end of the runway with no more time for thought, only the hedge at the end of the field rushing towards him. Bracing himself, he felt the Zerstörer tear through the bushes then collapse as the undercarriage was wrenched off. Now they were sliding, tearing across the grass on the aircraft's belly until finally they came to a halt just yards short of a fence by a country house.

Lent hurriedly opened the canopy, saw Kubisch was as alive and well as he was, then spotted an airman striding towards him. 'Heil Hitler,' called out the man and seeing the pistol in Lent's hand asked him whether he was going to fire.

'If you don't fire, I won't,' Lent replied. The two men quickly agreed an armistice, by which time Lent saw that other Zerstörers had landed. Fornebu, it seemed, was now in German hands. Soon after, the transport planes arrived, filled with troops: one Ju52 after another was landing in quick succession, until no fewer than fifty-three had touched down, soldiers pouring out of every one.

*

In his parents' flat in Oslo, Gunnar Sonsteby, twenty-one years old, was woken early by the sound of an air raid siren. Every radio in the building suddenly appeared to be on, blaring the astonishing news that the Germans had invaded and instructing people to make for the nearest air raid shelters. Hurrying out of bed, his first reaction was one of defiance. He was both appalled and indignant, so much so that while everyone else in the building trooped downstairs, Sonsteby remained where he was. So with his parents now living in Rjukan, a hundred miles west of Oslo, he made his breakfast and calmly ate his egg.

Although he had registered to study economics at the university, he made ends meet with a job at a nearby motorcycle shop, and, still bristling with anger and thoughts of rebellion, he soon after headed out to work. Walking through the city, he repeatedly had to take cover in doorways as planes hurtled over and machine guns barked out. Having made it to work in one piece, he discovered his colleagues gathered there chattering about what was happening, and so Sonsteby headed back out again to have a look around. To his horror, the city already appeared to be occupied by German troops. A column of them were marching down Karl Johan, the main street in the city, while machine guns had been set up in the park behind the Royal Palace. Other Norwegians passed on the news and rumours: Oslo had fallen and the King and Government had escaped and were now 'somewhere in Norway'. 'Everyone I met,' noted Sonsteby, 'was as stupefied as me.'

In fact, the resistance of the shore gunners, small warships in Oslofjord and the tiny Norwegian Air Force had proved crucial. The German invasion of the capital, swift though it unquestionably was, had been held up just long enough to allow King Haakon and the Government to escape, to Hamar, seventy miles to the north. Incredibly, the nation's gold reserves had also been smuggled out almost from under the noses of the Germans now swarming over the city. However, with more troops landing at Fornebu and with German merchant ships cunningly already in port stacked with arms, ammunition and other supplies previously hidden on board, the capital and the surrounding area were now in German hands. Operation WESERÜBUNG may have been an incredibly rash undertaking, but once again Hitler's penchant for extreme risk-taking appeared to be paying off.

CHAPTER 17

The Battle for Norway

Across the Baltic, Denmark had capitulated fully. At the same time that the Norwegian government had been given the chance to accept German occupation, a similar offer was made to King Christian X, who accepted. Fighting still broke out, but the entire country was in German hands in a matter of hours, surely the fastest conquest of a country in history, and which included an airborne drop by German *Fallschirmjäger* and no fewer than five simultaneous naval landings. Swift, ruthless and utterly efficient, it was hard to fault German execution of the plan, no matter how unorthodox the planning might have been. And now the Germans had bases and airfields even closer to Norway.

Even so, the two countries, and Denmark especially, were militarily weak, and these swift conquests flattered to deceive. In any invasion, so long as it has been kept secret right up to the final moment, the attacker holds a number of aces: surprise and choice of where to strike, and the benefit of the confusion caused among the enemy as a result. Invasion day, 9 April, had gone pretty well, despite a few significant losses, and by nightfall the port of Stavanger and the nearby Sola airfield had been captured by the *Fallschirmjäger* in a further successful airborne drop. Kristiansand had been taken as well, Bergen and Trondheim were in German hands, and General Dietl's mountain troops, the *Gebirgsjäger*, had successfully landed at Narvik, having evaded the Royal Navy. It was clear that the only ones who had missed any bus were the British, whose Navy had been completely wrong-footed by German intentions and who initially had assumed the Kriegsmarine had been attempting a massed breakout into the Atlantic.

Yet as General Walter Warlimont at the OKW was all too aware, planning had been done by von Falkenhorst's staff, seconded from direct control of the Army, and the special team devised at the OKW. Halder and von Brauchitsch had been completely sidelined despite their preparations for Case YELLOW, so that entire divisions already planned to take part in the all-or-nothing strike in the West were taken away from them despite their objections. Göring, having thrown his toys out of the pram when he had discovered what was being planned behind his back, had then been given completely free rein with the Luftwaffe. The Navy, too, had refused to keep warships in Norwegian ports after the landings, to which Hitler had curiously acquiesced, even after his operational order had been issued. Warlimont had been appalled. Hitler's micromanagement of WESERÜBUNG, he noted, 'broke all the rules'. Somehow, these disparate services had all come together beautifully for the all-crucial launch of the operation, but there was no doubt that Allied failures and the military weakness of Denmark and Norway helped mask some serious flaws.

Nor did Germany have it all its own way in the days that followed. In fact, early the following morning, 10 April, the German naval force now at Narvik was surprised by the arrival of a British destroyer flotilla. At around 5.30 a.m., HMS *Hardy* unleashed torpedoes and blew up the German flagship, the *Wilhelm Heidkamp*, killing eighty-one, including the force commander. Another ship was repeatedly hit and set on fire, then, as more British destroyers joined the fray, a second ship was sunk. The action continued down the Vestfjord, and, although *Hardy* was sunk in turn and another destroyer badly damaged, all of General Dietl's guns were sent to the bottom when a German supply ship was destroyed.

Over the next couple of days, the Royal Navy continued to get the better of the Kriegsmarine. At Narvik, the five remaining German destroyers were trapped and three days later, with the arrival of the British battleship HMS *Warspite* and a force of nine destroyers, were annihilated.

It should not have been so one-sided that day at Narvik. Lurking in the mouth of the fjord were both *U-46* and *U-48*, part of the entire available U-boat fleet still operating around Norway. On board *U-46*, Erich Topp had been as alarmed as all the crew to find themselves trapped at Narvik with far too many British destroyers lurking and not enough room for their boat to manoeuvre. On the night of the 11th, they had taken up their position offshore from the town, when suddenly air raid sirens were blaring and then aircraft were overhead and bombing them. Everyone ran for cover apart from Topp and a couple of others who manned their machine gun. 'Despite tremendous anti-aircraft fire we do not hit a single enemy plane,' jotted Topp. He saw a bomb destroy a shed just fifty yards away on the shore. 'Only 20 yards away one of our crew is instantly killed by another bomb, while another man is simply laid flat by the blast.'

Meanwhile, during its entire time in Norwegian waters, *U-48* had been unable to hit a single ship, even though there had been no shortage of targets. Nor was it alone. Time and again, U-boats had fired their torpedoes only to discover they then failed to explode. *U-47*, which had sunk the *Royal Oak* at Scapa Flow back in October, should have made it two, when she fired two torpedoes at *Warspite*, only for them to miss and for her to be nearly sunk in turn by vengeful destroyers. In fact, *Warspite* was attacked no fewer than four times, British cruisers were fired at fourteen times, and ten destroyers and ten transport vessels were also attacked without success. The problem, it seemed, was with the torpedoes' detonation devices. German torpedoes used magnetic pistols, which enabled a torpedo to detect its target by its magnetic field. This then triggered the fuse for explosion. The trouble was that in such northern waters the magnetic pistols were not working properly. Other torpedoes, equipped with contact pistols, which detonated on impact, had been insufficiently tested beforehand and were also failing. The net result was that golden opportunities to sink significant numbers of British warships had been let slip, and normally fearless U-boat captains lost confidence – possibly the single most important attribute needed for the successful submarine skipper.

U-46, on the other hand, did not even have a chance to try and attack. After being repeatedly bombed and depth-charged, running aground, and then finally slipping out of Narvik, it had finally reached the open sea on the 18th having somehow escaped what Erich Topp could only describe as a 'witches' cauldron'. When the U-boat eventually made it back to Kiel, its flotilla commander had looked very grave. 'Was it the sight of our pale, hollow faces that got to him?' Topp wondered. 'Or sympathy for our exhausting, unsuccessful mission?'

While impotent U-boats failed to make much of a mark, the Royal Navy and RAF were able to take their toll on Germany's surface fleet. The cruiser *Königsberg* was sunk, as was the *Karlsruhe*. *Lützow* had also been hit on 11 April and had to be towed back to Kiel, so badly damaged there was no chance of her being used in the Atlantic any time soon.

While the British Navy had swiftly recovered its composure, the Allies' own invasion plans never really recovered, even though, with the fleeing Norwegian Government now only too happy for their help, they at least had the opportunity to proceed without any further moral conundrum.

For most of the troops earmarked for the previously planned landing at Narvik, these were confusing and frustrating days. Most were Territorials – the regulars were all in France. British infantry regiments were broken down into battalions; the 1st and 2nd were usually the Regular battalions, while the 5th and even the 7th – if needed – tended to be made up with Territorials; this was the case with the Leicestershire Regiment, and it included local men like the 21-year-old Joseph 'Lofty' Kynoch, who had been brought up in the village of Thorpe Acre near Leicester and had joined the TA a couple of years earlier. His call-up papers had arrived the day he had returned from annual summer camp; he had reported to the TA centre in Leicester the day the Germans had marched into Poland.

After training throughout the winter near Durham in the north of the country, and despite rumours that they would be heading to Finland, it was not until the beginning of April that suddenly and dramatically they were on the move. Late on 6 April, Kynoch and his pals of 2/5th Leicesters boarded a train, and after an interminable journey of numerous and lengthy halts they finally reached Scotland on Sunday the 7th. In Edinburgh, the battalion was split up. Kynoch, the Bren carrier platoon and the rest of Headquarters Company disembarked at Leith, Edinburgh's port, while the rest went on to Rosyth. Waiting for them was the merchant vessel *Cedarbank*, while drawn up in a line along the quay were brand-new lorries and tracked carriers. The men drove them on to nets and then watched them hoisted on board.

Even once the troops were aboard, Kynoch and his mates were still none the wiser as to what was going on.

'It's just an exercise, Lofty,' one assured him. 'After all, the war in Finland is over.'

Later that day, they were told to disembark and were sent on lighters across the Forth to the liner *Orion*. At this point, Kynoch and many others parted company with their kit bags. They were never to see them again.

Since the German invasion had completely wrong-footed the Allies, the confusion was perhaps understandable. The truth was, the Allies had anticipated a completely different order of events: they would mine the Leads, then Germany would react, which would take them time, and then British and French troops would land, with Norwegian blessing, and secure key ports, not least Narvik. There was an astonishing naivety to this, as though no variation of this scenario were remotely possible. In part, this was because the war leaders of both Britain and France were still feeling their way as partners, and while the broad strategy was agreed, geo-politically they were in different positions and so had different agendas. It was the British who were leading the Norwegian operations, and yet there was no overall Allied commander as there was in France. The British Chiefs of Staff were also still settling slowly into their wartime modus operandi, and tending to put their own service interests first rather than thinking and acting as the integrated team that was necessary. With French politicians bickering, British Chiefs of Staff jockeying for position, and national sensitivities also playing their part, the net result was a joint decision-making process that was a little cumbersome, to put it mildly.

The response to the German invasion was a case in point, as plans were discarded, then changed, then changed again, all of which was costing precious time – time in which the German position in Norway, on land if not out at sea, was getting stronger by the day.

The revised plan, as agreed by both the British and the French, was that a force of British troops and French *chasseurs alpins* – mountain troops – would be sent to Narvik, and a further British component to Namsos, north of Trondheim, and Åndalsnes to the south. The idea was that these latter two forces would advance on Trondheim, in between Namsos and Åndalsnes, in a pincer movement. The whole of the north of Norway would then be in Allied hands.

A further problem was that these troops had been originally only lightly equipped – it had been expected that the Norwegians would help with guns and vehicles. There was also little air support, as it had been also supposed that around Narvik, especially, the fighting would be too far north for either side. So more guns, trucks and even troops had had to be hurriedly found. The French had bolstered their contribution, for example, by sending an entire light division to Narvik, although these would not arrive there until a week after the British. Not much could be done about the lack of air support, so that although in terms of men on the ground the Germans did not have an overwhelming advantage, in guns and aircraft they most certainly did. All in all, prospects for the Allies in Norway, despite successes at sea, did not look promising.

Even so, as far as Britain was concerned, it was not a lost cause just yet. The RAF may not have been able to send much in the way of fighters, but it was willing to use its bomber force. Among those flying on 11 April was Pilot Officer Tony Smyth, who had recently been transferred from flying Blenheims to the bigger, heavier Wellingtons. Smyth was twenty-four and had joined the RAF Volunteer Reserve back in 1937; having realized it was the perfect way to avoid working for the family paint firm, Manders, he had applied and was accepted for a permanent commission a year later. An intrepid cyclist and mountaineer, he had travelled throughout Europe – and Nazi Germany – and climbed many of its highest peaks. Flying had been treated as yet another adventure and, as he was discovering, it was already more than living up to the billing he had given it.

Small, wiry and with quick, sharp eyes and a sweep of strawberry blond hair, Smyth was a man able to think on his feet and apply his highly practical brain to most given situations. This had been very useful when his Wellington had lost an engine soon after take-off back in March. New to the squadron, he was only the second pilot, but after the plane had crash-landed in flames, he had escaped miraculously unhurt only to then go back into the burning wreckage and pull out the wireless operator, navigator and centre gunner, and then, despite blistering to his face from the heat, with the captain, 'Darkey' Powell, rescued the rear gunner as well.

With all their crew now in hospital, Smyth and Powell and the rest of the sub-flight had been hurriedly posted temporarily from 101 Squadron to 115 Squadron, based at Kinloss in Scotland. Attached to A Flight, they had been sent to bomb a reported German cruiser in Kristiansand, only to be recalled, but now, on the evening of the 11th, they were approaching the Norwegian coast and Stavanger, along with five other Wellingtons, in what was to be the first intentional bombing raid of the European mainland by Bomber Command since the start of the war.

Flying low, and in formation, they overshot, so Powell, at the controls, banked and went around for another run. This time, streams of tracer and puffs of flak lit up the fading light. Smyth saw an aircraft on fire on the ground, but again their line was too far awry and so they went around again, for a third attempt. By now, every gun and small arm on the ground was firing at them and Powell was forced off his run yet again, this time by having to dodge radio masts that suddenly loomed towards them. Smyth saw one of their fellow Wellingtons hit and burst into flames, then a moment later there was a deafening and blinding explosion in the cockpit of their own plane. They had been hit by several cannon shells, one piece of shrapnel hitting Powell in the side, another hitting a buckle on Smyth's shoulder and a third, very small piece hitting his cheek.

'I've had enough, I'm going home,' Powell told Smyth, climbing and then safely jettisoning their still undropped bomb load. Meanwhile, Smyth went back to see what other damage there was. It seemed the Wellington had been hit along the fuselage too. The rear gunner had been badly injured and had to be hastily bandaged and given morphine, while the hydraulics had been shot away so that both the flaps and the under-carriage were now inoperable. This was bad luck for Powell, who, already wounded, now had to fly all the way back to Scotland – unable to trim the plane as he was, there was no real way of swapping places with Smyth.

The main compass had also been smashed, but they not only managed to make it back to Kinloss, but Powell was able to safely belly-land the Wellington. 'I went to bed,' noted Smyth, 'troubled only by the thought that in three weeks, of the eighteen aircrew in the sub-flight, twelve were dead, five were in hospital, and I alone was on my feet.'

Also flying that day had been Guy Gibson and seven other Hampden crews from 83 Squadron. He had found his first operation back in September a terrifying proposition, but after months of very little activity he and the rest of the squadron were now chomping at the bit. 'To say that we were all keen,' he noted, 'would be a masterpiece of understatement.' They took off around 11 p.m., with 1,500lb magnetic 'M' mines strapped in the bomb bays and instructions to reconnoitre Danish towns and ports to hide the real purpose of the trip. Gibson thought the plan seemed sen-sible enough – from Kiel to Norway, German ships had to pass through one of three fairly narrow channels, so mining these was a good idea. 'Everyone,' he noted, 'was very optimistic.'

The trip was remarkably uneventful. They crossed the North Sea, stooged around Denmark, then found the right spot and dropped the mine, clearly seeing it, in the pale night light, gurgle into the dark water. It was a long trip, however. Having flown all night, Gibson and his crew did not land back down again until breakfast the following morning – they had been airborne about eight hours and Gibson himself clambered out feeling pretty cramped.

Three nights later, on the 14th, Gibson and his crew were minelaying again, but this time the weather was atrocious and really they should never have been sent out. Despite high winds, rain and a low cloud base, they somehow managed to find their target, which was a narrow strip of water at Middelfart in the Baltic off the Danish mainland. Flying so low they were almost touching the water, Gibson suddenly spotted Middelfart Bridge directly up ahead; it was too late to fly over it, so Gibson went underneath it instead. Immediately, the bomb bay was opened, and the two mines were dropped, and then suddenly a flak ship was firing at them. 'We were only about one hundred feet,' noted Gibson, 'but we soon pulled up in to cloud.'

They headed for home, the Hampden buffeted and bucked about and crackling with static electricity. After more than seven hours in the air, they touched down not at Scampton, but at Manston, on the tip of Kent. Gibson was exhausted, but while he and his crew had safely made it, another from 83 Squadron had been unable to find Manston and had disappeared, presumably into the sea. Nothing was ever heard of them again.

They were not alone. Losses were being suffered on most operations – one here, two there – but because Bomber Command was still so small, every one was felt. In fact, there is no question that the comparative lack of activity up to the invasion of Norway had been a godsend to the command, as it had allowed crews the chance to train in relative peace. However, Air Marshal Edgar Ludlow-Hewitt, the commander of Bomber Command, had also recognized that as the command expanded, so more instructors would be urgently needed to train recruits and work up reserves – and these could only realistically be drawn from existing squadrons. And so he took the drastic, but entirely necessary, measure of reducing the front line of Bomber Command in order to help the rapid expansion that was planned. Soon after the outbreak of war, no fewer than seventeen squadrons had been withdrawn and converted to Operational Training Units instead. It had caused consternation at the time, but had been a shrewd policy; and it was one of the reasons why Bomber Command had been so quick to agree to refrain from unrestricted air warfare and to spend time carrying out reconnaissance and leaflet dropping instead. It had given the command a chance to cut its teeth and for the old hands to train up new blood.

Despite British naval successes at sea, the Norwegian venture was unravelling fast for the Allies. Even if they were now able to secure Narvik and the north of the country, the truth was that German forces were swallowing up much of the southern half. Just how Allied troops were going to keep this planned northern redoubt while the Germans with their much shorter lines of supply held the south was something no one back in London appeared prepared to consider, although there was no denying that securing the northern – and frankly pretty remote – part of Norway made more sense than any venture further south, where the advancing Germans clearly now held all the aces.

What was certainly true was that the only hope of successfully taking and keeping hold of Narvik was by putting as many forces there as possible, something Churchill repeatedly stressed. As he pointed out, at least careful plans had been made for Narvik; Trondheim was altogether a much more speculative proposition. However, the French were urging that troops be sent to Trondheim to take both the port and the railway that went right across the peninsula. Both Halifax and Chamberlain agreed to this plan. Troops would still land at Narvik, but Trondheim would be the main effort.

British troops were thus steaming towards this land of mountains and fjords, with the situation highly fluid and with plans still being changed even as the men were being shipped over the North Sea. While Brigadier D. R. Morgan and the first few battalions of 148th Brigade were making the crossing, he was given yet another set of orders. 'Your role to land Åndalsnes,' the signal told him brusquely, 'then operate northwards and take offensive action against the Germans in the Trondheim area.'

It made it sound so simple. But Morgan had just one lightly equipped brigade, some of whom, like Lofty Kynoch, were still in Scotland, and had no air cover and no tanks or vehicles. With these Territorials, he was expected to defeat the German forces now surging up the Gudbrandsdal Valley in central Norway, then, having seen them off, turn on Trondheim. It was ludicrously over-optimistic.

This latest change of plan had come at the behest of the Norwegians, whom the Allies were now keen to oblige, even though fire-fighting and dissipating forces was never an ideal military policy. The Norwegian

Army had few Regulars and so, like France, was dependent on a mass mobilization. However, such had been the surprise of the attack that these plans had also been thrown into confusion and many of those who might have answered the call found themselves occupied before they had the chance. As it was, the entire Army was infantry with neither tanks nor anti-tank guns. One of the last acts of the Government as it had fled Oslo had been to sack the Commander-in-Chief and replace him with Oberst – hastily promoted to General – Otto Ruge, who was younger, more vigorous and determined to fight on. His men had been battling their way through the centre of the country, delaying the German advance but little more. It was his appeal to the British military attaché that had brought about the latest change of plan; 148th Brigade was to help the Norwegians block the German advance north. The reason for focusing on the town of Dombås was that German paratroopers had landed there on 14 April. The Norwegians were battling hard against these isolated German troops, but Ruge wanted British help and as quickly as possible.

One of those trying to resist the Germans was Gunnar Sonsteby, who with a friend had decided that even though Nazi swastikas were fluttering over Oslo, they would head out of the city and join the fight. On Friday the 11th, they had taken a train – which amazingly was still running – and, armed with their skis, had headed to Grua, some thirty miles to the north of Oslo. There they met up with Lieutenant Philip Hansteen, a reservist, at his mountain hut. The following day, Friday, 12 April, with more than a dozen now gathered with Hansteen, they pushed north again, to Brandbu, on the edge of Lake Randsfjord, where there was a depot acting as a mustering station. By the evening of the next day, Saturday, there were more than a thousand men, who were hastily organized into makeshift military units.

Sonsteby was told to remain with Lieutenant Hansteen, his men now formed into a special ski company of four platoons of thirty men each; Sonsteby was put into 4 Platoon under Hansteen's brother, Axel. So began for Sonsteby and these men a long, desperate retreat. 'We continually saw burned farms and blown bridges,' noted Sonsteby, 'the latter the act of our withdrawing forces, the former the vengeful work of the Germans.'

Meanwhile, the rest of 148th Brigade was making its way across the North Sea. Late on 20 April, Lofty Kynoch and the second half of the 2/5th Leicesters finally set sail, on yet another ship, not from Rosyth or even Leith, but Aberdeen in the north-west of Scotland. The following afternoon, as the ship rolled in a rising swell, Kynoch was awoken from a fitful sleep to learn that the *Cedarbank*, with all their equipment stored aboard, had just been torpedoed. Clambering to his feet, he looked across the water to see the vessel slip beneath the waves amid a swirl of foam. Moments later there was a huge explosion that shook every timber and rivet on their own ship and caused a hum of consternation from the men. It was a depth charge from one of the destroyers escorting them; on this occasion, the U-boat's firing pistols had obviously worked. 'Whatever else had been on the *Cedarbank*,' wrote Kynoch, 'we now had only our rifles, a few anti-tank rifles and Bren guns to face the enemy with, also the clothes we stood up in.' He had about a hundred rounds for his rifle, and that was it.

They finally reached Åndalsnes at around 8 a.m. on the morning of 22 April. Little did they realize that the situation in Norway was now even worse.

CHAPTER 18

The Go-for-Broke Gamble

THE GERMAN ARMY command may have been sidelined over Norway and Denmark, but they most certainly were not over Case YELLOW. At OKH headquarters in Zossen, the Chief of Staff and chief planner, General Franz Halder, had been tirelessly making preparations. After his somewhat Damascene volte-face in February, he had continued to prepare for von Manstein's two-fisted assault.

Speed was unquestionably going to be of the essence if Case YELLOW was to have any prospect of success at all, yet although Halder only belatedly woke up to this realization, the concept of using speed to wrong-foot the enemy was absolutely nothing new at all, and was, if anything, deeply embedded in the Prussian military psyche. Indeed, for all its air of being bold and radical, von Manstein's plan was nothing of the sort. Making a lightning strike in an effort to knock the enemy off balance and force a rapid result was what the Prussians and Germans always did. It was what they did against Denmark in 1864 (and it worked), what they did against Austria in 1866 (it worked again, just), what they did against France in 1870 (worked initially then ran out of steam), and what they did in August 1914 (failed, but only just). It was also what they had done in Poland (very successfully), Denmark (ditto) and Norway (which was looking good so far), and what they planned to do now against France and the Low Countries. The Prussians had coined a term for this rapid operational level of war: *Bewegungskrieg*. And the goal of *Bewegungskrieg* was *Kesselschlacht*, which translated literally as 'cauldron battle', but which really meant a battle of encirclement, in which the enemy would be trapped.

Frederick the Great, the Prussian king whom Hitler so admired, once pointed out that Prussia's wars needed to be short and decisive because in a long drawn-out conflict discipline would falter and their resources would quickly be exhausted. He was spot on, and not much had changed in the intervening years, although under the Nazis there was every chance discipline would not falter quite so readily. But certainly Germany had extremely limited resources, and its location – in the heart of Europe and with a comparatively narrow coastline – meant it had not only few means of securing the necessary shortfall but was also vulnerable to attack from more than one quarter. That other great Prussian military thinker, von Clausewitz, also pointed out that in war there are two means of achieving victory: through a war of exhaustion or a war of annihilation.

Both geographical insecurity and a shortage of natural resources meant German strategy was the same as it had always been: to strike swift and hard and win the day in quick order, which was why the only real option for Prussia/Germany had always been and remained to follow the principles of *Bewegungskrieg* and *Kesselschlacht* – and to aim for annihilation of the enemy.

The trouble was, this was easier said than done, not least because their enemies tended to have around the same resources as them, if not more, in terms of men and firepower – and this was certainly the case for the attack in the West about to be unleashed. The key was to make sure the Allies had their forces spread so the Wehrmacht could focus its attack at one point and ensure it concentrated far more forces at that single point than the enemy. This was known as the *Schwerpunkt* principle.

In essence, then, von Manstein's basic plan was not in the least original, because it rigidly adhered to the principles Prussians had been following for ever; and, in truth, they had no alternative, which is why the Allies, if they had studied their history more carefully and applied their knowledge of Germany's geo-economic situation to a military appreciation, should have been able to anticipate the likely approach their enemy would make. After all, an assault on the Maginot Line made little sense, advancing purely through the Low Countries was very obvious, while a passage through the Ardennes not only had been used in 1870, but was the only real chance the Germans had of achieving tactical surprise. Merely stating that the Ardennes were unpassable, as Gamelin had declared, without ever really working this claim through, was more reckless than the plan itself.

Where Case YELLOW *was* highly original, however, was in the means by which the spearhead was going to reach the *Schwerpunkt* – the main point of attack – and then engage the enemy, and for that, the man responsible above all others was not really von Manstein, but rather General Heinz Guderian – the panzer general who had so impressed Leutnant Hans von Luck two years earlier.

The 51-year-old Guderian was not only a dynamic soldier, but also a deep thinker on military matters and a couple of years earlier had published *Achtung Panzer!*, a treatise on the use of tanks in modern warfare. Von Manstein had since been sidelined but Guderian had not, and was proving instrumental in breathing new, modern life into the old Prussian principles of *Bewegungskrieg*. Accepted doctrine in the German Army was that tanks could not advance without infantry support. What Guderian was suggesting was that his panzer divisions would carry the motorized infantry with them as part of the division, enabling them to operate entirely independently of the infantry divisions, who, reliant on their feet or horse-drawn carts, would slow them down. Guderian and his staff were therefore working on how to move mechanized divisions of tanks, trucks and other motorized vehicles both swiftly and in such a way that surprise was maintained until the last minute. Then, once they reached the Meuse, armour, infantry and artillery would work together and in harmony with aerial artillery in the form of the Luftwaffe, and controlled and commanded primarily by radio communication. No other side had thought to construct an armoured division in such a way.

In other words, it was the plans they were developing to achieve this breakthrough that were radical and new, not the concept per se.

On 17 March, Guderian and the senior commanders of Armeegruppe A had attended a conference with Hitler at the Reich Chancellery. Guderian was the last of the Army and corps commanders to brief Hitler on his plan. He told the Führer and his Army Group superiors that on the fourth day after the advance began, he would reach the Meuse. By the end of the fifth, he would have established a bridgehead across it.

'And then what are you going to do?' Hitler asked.

'Unless I receive orders to the contrary, I intend on the next day to continue my advance westwards.' He added that in his opinion he should drive straight to the Channel coast.

General Busch, who commanded 16. Armee, which consisted almost entirely of infantry divisions, said, 'Well, I don't think you'll cross the river in the first place!' In saying this, he was speaking for almost all Armeegruppe A's senior officers, including its commander, Feldmarschall Gerd von Rundstedt.

Hitler, visibly tense, turned to Guderian, waiting for his response.

'There's no need for *you* to do so in any case,' Guderian replied. The last thing he wanted was slow, cumbersome infantry divisions lacking almost any mechanized transportation getting in his way.

Not only was most of Armeegruppe A against the plan, but so too was much of Armeegruppe B. Its commander, Generaloberst von Bock, called in on Halder in his Berlin apartment and pleaded with him to abandon it entirely. 'You will be creeping by ten miles from the Maginot Line with the flank of your breakthrough,' he told Halder, 'and hope the French will watch inertly! You are cramming the mass of the tank units together into the sparse roads of the Ardennes mountain country, as if there were no such thing as air power! And you then hope to be able to lead an operation as far as the coast with an open southern flank two hundred miles long, where stands the mass of the French Army!' This, he added, transcended the 'frontiers of reason'.

Von Bock was talking a lot of sense. On paper, it looked hopelessly optimistic. And von Bock knew, as Halder knew, that of the 135 divisions earmarked for the offensive, large numbers were far from being the elite, crack units the rest of the world seemed to think they were. In the entire Army, there were only ten panzer and six fully mechanized divisions. These mere sixteen divisions were the modern, fully equipped units of the German Army. In the spearhead that would thrust through the Ardennes, there were only ten such modernized divisions, divided into three corps, of which Guderian's had three panzer divisions. Since there were not enough roads through the Ardennes for all three corps to advance at once, the movement would have to be done in stages.

And yes, the panzer divisions were modern and well equipped, but the majority of their panzers were hardly the latest in cutting-edge tank design. Only Panzer IIIs and IVs had decent-sized guns, and there were only 627 of them. The remaining 1,812 were Mk Is, with only their machine guns, Mk IIs, which had a rather feeble 20mm gun, and Czech T35s and T38s, which also had below-par firepower. In contrast, the Allies could call on some 4,204 tanks, almost double the number in the German Army. Of these, a significant number were bigger, better armed and better armoured than anything the Germans had.

Of the rest of the German Army, only a quarter were active-duty troops that could be used in the first wave of the offensive – that is, Regular peacetime units reinforced with reservists, such as Siegfried Knappe's 87. Division. The second wave consisted of mostly younger fully trained reservists. After that were those reservists who had only been cursorily trained. Then there were the Landwehr units – Territorials – who were mostly older, veterans of the Great War and barely trained at all since 1918.

This meant that only half of all German soldiers had had more than a few weeks' training, while more than a quarter were over forty. Nazi propaganda had kept this rather startling reality close to its chest.

In Italy, Mussolini had now put down on paper a 'secret report' summarizing the situation and outlining future military strategy. In effect, it was a kind of war directive, because he had now convinced himself utterly that Italy had no choice but to intervene. To act like *puttane* – whores – with the West was not an option; neutrality would simply downgrade Italy for a century; it was absurd to think they could simply sit by and watch. The only conceivable course was a war parallel to that of Germany and which would unshackle them from their Mediterranean prison.

This report was issued to his senior commanders at the beginning of April, but although Maresciallo Badoglio showed a small inkling of offensive spirit, there was hardly much enthusiasm from anyone else, which came spectacularly to the fore at a meeting of service chiefs held in Rome on 9 April – the same day the Germans were invading Denmark and Norway. Maresciallo Rodolfo Graziani, the grizzled Chief of Staff of the Army, was appalled, particularly when it became clear that there was no suggestion of any joint operations with Germany. 'But we won't be able to do anything in that case,' he complained to Badoglio, 'even if France collapses.' Amiragglio Domenico Cavagnari, the Chief of Staff of the Navy, was equally despairing. The enemy, he said, would place one fleet at Gibraltar and another at Suez, 'and we shall all asphyxiate inside'. Generale Pricolo of the Air Force, no less unenthusiastic, warned that too many illusions were being entertained about what might be achievable. All agreed that an offensive against the British from Libya was impossible, while even in Abyssinia the current situation was precarious – and that was just dealing with current unrest from native Africans.

The only person slightly thawing about Mussolini's bellicose rhetoric was Count Ciano. Contemptuous about the Allied response in Norway, he was also scenting a whiff of desperation in the escalating diplomatic efforts from France and Britain. On 24 April, a personal letter for Mussolini from Reynaud was presented to Ciano by François-Poncet, the Ambassador, inviting the Duce to meet the French Prime Minister. 'Mussolini read the letter with pleasure and scorn,' noted Ciano, adding, 'it is a strange message, a little melancholy and a little bragging.' Mussolini refused the invitation with a reply that was, Ciano recorded with ill-concealed glee, 'cold, cutting and contemptuous'.

Yet however contemptuous he may have been feeling towards the French as a whole, Ciano was certainly quite content to shower attention on one particular French woman. The film star Corinne Luchaire was making a new film in Rome called *L'Intruse* and was thoroughly enjoying being made a fuss of by Roman society, and not least Ciano, who took her to dinner and gave her the full broadside of Italian aristocratic charm. Luchaire, for her part, was flattered but refused to give in to him, knowing his reputation as a philanderer. None the less, she thought him handsome and good company. 'I was proud to go everywhere arm in arm with the Italian Foreign Minister,' she noted. 'Our friendship got me prestigious invitations.'

But although she never once talked politics or was particularly aware of the increasingly strained relationship between her country and Italy, she was none the less playing a dangerous game for one quite so beautiful and famous and, as a result, so often photographed and written about. One day, she was taken to a show-jumping competition, which was eventually won by the German team. Conscious that many eyes were looking at her to see how she would react, she decided that since it was only a sporting event, it would be acceptable to applaud. But then a swastika was raised, the German national anthem began to be played and the entire crowd stood and gave the Nazi salute. Suddenly, she was aware how compromised she had become. 'I, only, remained sitting among thousands of people standing up,' she recorded. 'My behaviour was noticed.'

And after that, the invitations dramatically dried up. Ciano no longer came calling or sent her flowers. The press turned on her, and she was strongly advised to return to France. The film, however, was not yet finished, so she remained in Italy. It would prove a bad mistake.

Back in Paris, the political and military leadership was as fractious as ever. Reynaud had been desperately trying to instil some resolve and fighting spirit and, more importantly as far as he was concerned, a sense of urgency. Back on 30 March, Amiral Darlan had warned Gamelin to get ready for swift action in Norway, quite sensibly pointing out that Germany was unlikely to stand idly by once British mining operations began. A few days later, Reynaud had also asked him to be ready to move at a moment's notice; three days later, on 8 April, the Prime Minister had rung him to tell him of German shipping movements towards Norway.

Yet, as far as Reynaud could make out, Gamelin had done absolutely nothing, and at an emergency meeting of the War Cabinet on 12 April he tried desperately to secure both a greater and swifter reinforcement of Norway. The trouble was, the operation was largely a British one, and such was the structure of the French military machine, it was simply incapable of acting quickly. The petty squabbles, the poisonous personality clashes, the fact that Reynaud was stymied by the cabal of Radicals controlled by Daladier, and the inherently backward-thinking French military machine all worked directly against quick-fire military action. It wasn't so much that Général Gamelin was not willing to act, but that he was simply unable to do so with the urgency Reynaud was demanding. As it happened, after the emergency meeting, he offered his resignation to Daladier – not Reynaud, who would have accepted it – but it was refused.

So the meeting got them no further. A frustrated Reynaud had to sit back and listen to reports showing that in this contest of speed between Germany and the Allies, Hitler was winning hands down.

On 22 April, the British war leaders arrived in Paris for a further meeting of the Supreme War Council. That day, at the Quai d'Orsay, the mood was fairly buoyant. The first troops had landed near Narvik a few days earlier, although not in a direct assault on the town as Churchill had requested, but spread out so as to cover the main landing area and approaches to the town, and from where a firm base could be established first. The capture of both Narvik and Trondheim was enthusiastically supported, despite the footholds the Germans already had and despite the gobbling up of the southern half of Norway. Even Churchill had warmed to the Trondheim enterprise, although he pushed for, and got, the promise of further *chasseurs alpins* for Narvik. After Narvik had been taken, air forces were to fly in to establish a firm base. Denying Swedish iron ore to the Germans, it was agreed, was still to be a top priority, which could be achieved by capturing the port through which it passed. For about the first time since discussions had begun about their involvement in Scandinavia, the Supreme War Council appeared to be finally singing pretty much from the same hymn sheet.

The following day, discussion focused on the Western Front and an agreement that the moment the Germans made a move in the West, Allied forces would advance into Belgium, whether the Belgian government agreed to it or not. Reynaud, however, gave a sombre appreciation. The Germans, he told them, now had 190 divisions, of which 150 could be used in the West. Germany, he said, had an advantage in manpower, in artillery and in stocks of ammunition. None of this was true; once again, German projection of military might was clouding judgement, and there is no doubt that it was putting the Allied war leaders into a defensive – not to say demoralized – mindset. Had Hitler, Goebbels or even generals like Halder been flies on the wall, they would have been delighted.

Meanwhile, in Norway, the German troops appeared to be backing up the image so carefully presented by the Nazis, although the opposition in central Norway was weaker than anything they had experienced in Poland. It was hardly the fault of the hapless British 148th Brigade, which was appallingly badly equipped, having no mechanized or tank support, almost no guns and no air support. Taking on the advancing Germans with only their rifles, a few Brens and some grenades but with nowhere near enough ammunition even for those meagre weapons, and with ill-trained and equally ill-equipped Norwegians fighting alongside them, was only ever going to end one way.

In truth, the situation was quite hopeless by the time they had finally reached Åndalsnes. Splitting the force originally intended for Narvik and then splitting it again between Namsos and Åndalsnes had merely made an already bad situation much worse. At the same time, to the north, a further brigade, the 146th, had landed at Namsos, but so too had a French *demi-brigade* of *chasseurs alpins*. Since the French were also without transport, they remained at Namsos while 146th Brigade then began the march south towards Trondheim. These depleted and poorly equipped troops were made short work of by German *Gebirgsjäger*, whose own position was strengthened by a landing of reinforcements. The road to Trondheim was now blocked. An evacuation was the only option.

Meanwhile, to the south, the first half of 148th Brigade had managed to reach Dombås, where the *Fallschirmjäger* had unexpectedly been defeated by the Norwegians, and then head on further south, almost to Lillehammer. This was the largest town in central Norway and by the evening of 21 April, when the first British troops reached the front, it had already fallen. The men were tired, hungry and very badly armed. It was also bitterly cold, with thick snow all around. The men had greatcoats but nothing more.

Lofty Kynoch and the missing halves of the two British battalions reached the small village of Tretten to the north of Lillehammer the following day, 22 April, where the British and Norwegians had hastily retreated to make their next stand. A German bomber circled overhead as they clambered out of the train, then swooped so low that Kynoch could see the pilot as it flew off. Soon after, Messerschmitt 109 fighters appeared, hurtling low over them, strafing them with machine-gun fire. Kynoch found the experience petrifying.

'Geddown and lie flat!' yelled the Company Sergeant Major, as bullets whistled past, snicking through the pine trees around them and kicking up gouges of snow and dirt. Moments later, the fighters were gone.

Of course, this tiny force of British and Norwegian infantry had no chance. More aircraft arrived, this time Stukas. The explosions of the bombs was deafening in the narrow confines of the valley, with smoke and debris fizzing and swirling into the air. Kynoch, totally unprepared from his training for such an eruption of violence, watched the scene with mesmerized terror. He felt barely able to move a muscle. The following morning, 23 April, the Luftwaffe was back.

Around 10.30 a.m., German troops reached the British and Norwegian defenders, blasting their way forward with artillery and mortars and then tanks and infantry, and they were quickly forced back, around a sharp bend in the narrow valley to Tretten itself. Lofty Kynoch, earlier sent on a patrol up into the mountains, had watched with dismay as Norwegian troops valiantly began firing an ancient artillery piece that looked to him more like something from the Napoleonic era.

Later that afternoon, it was all over and the stragglers were falling back. Kynoch and the rest of his patrol had managed to work their way back down to the valley and get a lift on a civilian lorry along with a number of other men, leaving the carnage temporarily behind. What had become of most of their mates, they had no idea. Hungry and freezing cold, Kynoch, for one, felt utterly demoralized and miserable.

*

Back in London on the evening of 23 April, after the end of the Supreme War Council meeting in Paris, the British contingency learned that while landings at Namsos and Åndalsnes had been unopposed, the attempt to take Trondheim in a pincer movement had failed and that news from central Norway was hardly any better. Jock Colville found the Prime Minister somewhat depressed by the meetings in Paris, less because of the unfolding situation in Norway than by Churchill's evident frustration and accompanying rampages.

'I have an uneasy feeling that all is not being as competently handled as it might be,' scribbled Colville in his diary the following day. It worried him that troops had been sent to the snowy north of Norway without skis or snowshoes, that the judgement of the Chiefs of Staff appeared to be wanting, and that there was an absence of clear, well-thought-through clockwork efficiency. 'Of one thing I am convinced,' he added, 'we make our minds up lamentably slowly and we do not ensure against every eventuality like the Germans do.' A young man he may have been, but Colville was perceptive with regard to Allied failings. Singleness of purpose, decisiveness, clear-headed military thinking and efficiency had been strikingly lacking in the Allied adventure in Norway. It was no wonder it was all going so badly wrong.

By the end of April, it was only Narvik, the original objective, which was still within Allied grasp. The *Gebirgsjäger* there were effectively surrounded by a combination of British, Norwegian and, with the arrival of the *chasseurs alpins* on 28 April, French troops. However, because the British and French had been landed at various points around that web of headlands, fjords and inlets, any concerted Allied assault would be difficult, and these problems were compounded by the terrain, heavy snow and freezing conditions. Three thousand men of the French Légion étrangère (Foreign Legion) arrived on 6 May, followed three days later by a brigade of Poles. Here, at least, the Allies had some kind of manpower and material advantage even if they still had no air support – Narvik was well beyond the range of Allied aircraft.

In central Norway, however, British intervention had been disastrous, and the fighting there was all over by the time the French Foreign Legion had arrived at Narvik; it was as though two quite different campaigns were being fought, albeit in different parts of the same country. Lofty Kynoch and the remnants of 148th Brigade had managed to fall back to

Åndalsnes, in part thanks to 15th Brigade being thrown into the fray and briefly holding up the German advance. A squadron of British biplanes had been posted to Norway and had landed on a frozen lake, only to be wiped out within two days – one of them was shot down by Helmut Lent in his Me110 Zerstörer. At Åndalsnes, the remaining British troops began to be evacuated on the night of 30 April, but not before the Luftwaffe had pounded the largely wooden town so that it was left burning and with dark smoke pluming thousands of feet into the sky. Lofty Kynoch was one of around 150 men from 148th Brigade to reach the wreck of the town early on the 30th after a long, fraught and repeatedly disrupted forced march and then train journey. They spent two terrible days waiting to be lifted off, hungry and exhausted, watching the town burning and the repeated air attacks, several of which were too close for comfort.

Among the ships steaming to Åndalsnes for the evacuation was HMS *Delight*, which as part of the screen around the cruiser HMS *Manchester* was cutting through the glassy-calm waters at some 25 knots. As they entered the fjord, First Lieutenant Vere Wight-Boycott looked in awe at the snow-capped mountains rising sheer from the water's edge. 'Their height, combined with the narrowness of the fjord,' he noted, 'gave one the impression of steaming down a corridor so narrow that there was no room to turn out of it.' They soon came under air attack, but the cruisers and destroyers swiftly responded. *Delight*'s own 3-inch gun opened fire and with the first shot hit a leading plane, which burst into three flaming pieces. The rest of the aircraft then melted away.

Reaching the town, Vere-Boycott was shocked to see the burning remains and the still smouldering pier. Through his binoculars, he wondered how long it was going to take to lift 4,000 men and rather gloomily guessed it would not be done before daylight. However, one ship pulled alongside the pier, then another next to her, and then *Delight*, and much to his surprise the operation was a lot quicker and smoother than he had imagined. *Delight* cast off around 1 a.m. and skimmed through the water at 29 knots on the way out.

Delight was not carrying Lofty Kynoch, who managed to board HMS *Sheffield* and get away. 'I turned and took one last look at the place where we had landed just a few days ago,' wrote Kynoch. 'No pretty houses now, only smouldering black chimney stacks standing erect like ghostly fingers. Over all a black pall of smoke that rose in the air and spilled outwards and upwards over the fjord.' By 2 a.m., it was in German hands.

*

Only at Narvik, nearly eight hundred miles north of Åndalsnes, was there any hope left for the Allies. This small – but crucial – port was finally within their grasp, although how they would hold on to it once it was captured was another matter.

None the less, German successes elsewhere in Norway had not stopped Hitler from becoming increasingly agitated about Narvik. On 17 April, as it became clear British landings around Narvik had been made successfully, he had urged the Army to evacuate the town; by the following day, he had calmed down, but with the further Allied landings, his anxiety rose to fever pitch once more.

Placated by continued good reports from central Norway, he had been told on 30 April that the campaign had now all but been won. As Warlimont noted, success had been achieved 'in spite of his amateurish interventions'.

Hitler was now ready to launch his assault in the West. After months of planning, after all the delays, soul-searching and long winter months of stockpiling, the moment had at last arrived. The days had lengthened, the weather was good, and the men involved in this huge undertaking were as ready and confident as they were ever going to be.

Yet despite the victories in Poland, Denmark and over much of Norway, Hitler's forces were not as strong as Nazi propaganda liked to make out. There were 157 divisions in the German Army, not 190 as Reynaud had claimed, and 135 divisions available for Case YELLOW. As soon as they crossed into Holland and Belgium, those two neutrals would join the Allies, who together would then have no fewer than 151 divisions. Germany would be attacking with 7,378 artillery pieces, but the French alone had 10,700 and the Allies collectively more than 14,000 – that is, almost double those of the Germans. France alone had a third more tanks than Germany. Even in terms of aircraft, the Allies could call on more planes than the Luftwaffe. It was one thing thundering into militarily weak nations like Poland and Norway, or even defeating poorly equipped and disorganized British infantry operating in snow-covered and mountainous terrain, but quite another to take on such massed forces in their own back yard.

But there was now no other choice. Hitler's invasion of Poland had got Germany into a war it was ill-equipped to fight. A go-for-broke, all-or-nothing gamble was the only chance Germany had of victory.

CHAPTER 19

Attack in the West

AT HALF PAST FOUR in the morning of Friday, 10 May, Hitler's private train, curiously named *Amerika*, pulled into the tiny station of Euskirchen between Bonn and Aachen and near to the Belgian border. Heading out into the still dark, crisp air, the Führer of Germany and his entourage climbed into a six-wheeled Mercedes limousine and sped off, climbing up to a hilly, wooded region and came to a halt at the mouth of a bunker dug into the rock. This complex, known as Felsennest, was to be Hitler's command post. Some 1,200 feet up, the entrance was hidden but none the less commanded views towards the Belgian border, only twenty miles to the west.

Hitler, at least, was in a buoyant and confident mood. The hour was finally upon him and upon his people. There was now no turning back. Key to the German chances of success would be the speed with which the panzer and motorized divisions in Armeegruppe A could reach the Meuse, around a hundred miles from the German border, get across it, and smash the French line before they had a chance to properly counter-attack.

As one of the principal architects of this plan, General Heinz Guderian was every bit as confident as Hitler that this could be achieved. The key was speed. Guderian had reckoned that to catch the French out, they would have to reach the Meuse in three days and get across it in four. The only way this could be achieved was through intricate planning and sticking rigidly to a very tight timetable, but this was no small challenge and dependent on all too many factors playing out like clockwork.

In fact, there was much that could derail the entire plan. The ten mechanized divisions of Armeegruppe A equated to 39,373 vehicles, 1,222 panzers and a further 545 other tracked vehicles, which, bumper-to-bumper, meant a theoretical march length of around nine hundred miles. These ten divisions had been divided into four different corps groupings. A new and untested group of three panzer corps had been formed for the main spearhead under the command of General von Kleist, of which Guderian's three-division corps was leading the way. The first potential problem was one of generalship. Commanding Armeegruppe A was Feldmarschall Gerd von Rundstedt, who, as Guderian had discovered in planning meetings, had little understanding of panzer tactics and their capabilities. General von Kleist, also above Guderian in the chain of command, had a similar lack of understanding and repeatedly failed to grasp the essence of the plan at all. Both were conspicuously more cautious than Guderian, who had done all he could to prepare his own corps with as little interference as possible.

The second potential hazard was that the four corps had different objectives but had to pass through the dense Ardennes forest using just a handful of roads. The possibility of immense gridlock was only too obvious.

A further problem was that before any of these spearheads reached the Meuse, they had to overcome a number of obstacles. Panzerkorps Guderian had to cross the Luxembourg border barriers, then the Belgian fortification line, and after that the second line of Belgian defences. Then there was the River Semois to cross, which was bound to be defended, and finally they had to face the French border fortifications, which stood some six miles from the Meuse. None of these were expected to offer too much resistance but it only needed one of them to hold up the advance for any period of time, and the whole timetable would be shot to pieces.

The scepticism of men like von Kleist and others was entirely understandable.

Further to the north, the men of Armeegruppe B were also preparing to attack. The plan was that they would thrust into Holland and Belgium and draw the Allies forward, hopefully hoodwinking them into thinking this was the main attack. At 5 a.m., having already roused the men of 24. Artillery Battalion, Leutnant Siegfried Knappe was astride his horse, Schwabenprinz, and reporting to his CO, Major Raake, that all the batteries were ready. Based in the Eifel region, they would be supporting 87. Infanteriedivision as it advanced into Belgium. Also ready to move out were the men of Flakregiment 22, who had been ordered to advance into Luxembourg having first crossed the River Mosel. Among the men was Günther Sack, an eighteen-year-old *Kanonier* of the lowest rank, who had only joined 2. Battalion on 1 April. A young man full of ardent zeal, he had been initially placed on to an officer-training programme but attached to a heavy flak regiment. This, he felt, did not have the right caché for someone of his ambitions; flak artillery pieces were defensive weapons and he desperately wanted to prove himself in action. With this in mind, he had applied to leave the Luftwaffe – which was responsible for all anti-aircraft units – and join the Waffen-SS Leibstandarte Adolf Hitler instead. Much to his great disappointment, however, this had been refused. Piqued, he had abandoned his officer training and insisted on transferring to light flak; at least that way there was a chance of getting closer to the front, or so he hoped. Since joining 2. Battalion, however, he had been bored witless. There had been no aircraft to shoot and monotonous daily duties: practising changing overheated barrels, moving the guns into position and other routine exercises. Now, on the morning of 10 May, however, there was at long last the promise of action.

Leading the way was the Luftwaffe, which was concentrated in the northern area both to help maintain the deception plan and also to hit as many Allied airfields as possible in the hope that a large proportion of enemy aircraft could be destroyed before they got airborne. Furthermore, giving the impression of concentrated might would also help to cow the enemy. Newsreels had been pumping out footage of massed bomber and Stuka strikes, and it was essential to maintain this impression.

Among the Stuka units was I.St/186, which had not taken part in the Norwegian campaign. Commanding the second *Staffel* was Hauptmann Helmut Mahlke, twenty-six years old, and their target was the hangars and ground installations of the French air base at Metz-Frescaty. They were due to hit them early, at 6 a.m. It was Mahlke's first combat sortie, and the night before he had struggled to sleep, worried about how he would perform and whether he had done all that was possible to prepare his squadron.

They had been up at 4 a.m. and just under an hour later were walking to their machines. The ground crew helped the pilots and gunners into their harnesses, pulling the straps tight, and then went to stand by the starting handles. As they turned them the engines began to whine, slowly at first, then faster until the mechanic yelled and Mahlke switched on the ignition and the engine erupted into life with a roar. Around him, nearly thirty others burst into life as well.

Mahlke taxied out, and soon after they were airborne and the entire formation was crossing the River Moselle and flying on, the countryside beneath them growing with the light of dawn. At last, Mahlke spotted the target and called out on his radio, 'Anton 2 to Anton: target on the port beam below!'

The *Gruppenkommandeur* now led them into line astern for the attack formation and on a wide left-hand turn so they could dive on the target against the wind, as prescribed. Metz's flak guns now opened fire – a few grey puffs staining the sky. Mahlke, his tension rising, watched the first Stukas make their dives.

Then it was the turn of his own *Staffel*. Bomb switches on, radiator flaps closed, dive brakes extended, close throttle, drop the left wing, and then he was putting the machine into an eighty-degree dive and the ground began hurtling towards him. He could see his target and kept it in the cross-hairs. The airship hangar – his own target – now came rushing towards him at a terrifying rate. Two thousand metres, one thousand five hundred, one thousand, then at five hundred metres he pressed the bomb button – a slight jolt – and next he was pulling out of the dive and into a climbing left-hand turn. His bomb had hit almost dead centre, but nothing seemed to happen, until suddenly he could see the sides of the hangar bulge as though the whole building was being inflated. A moment later the entire hangar collapsed in on itself. All around, the depot was now engulfed in swirling smoke.

They touched back down at their new forward base at Ferschweiler at 6.40 a.m. only to discover the ground crew had yet to catch up. Even so, this first mission, over which Mahlke had so agonized, had been a complete success. 'The general feeling,' he wrote, 'was that we had given them a very nasty wake-up call.'

Hajo Herrmann and his fellow crews in KG4 were also busy from the outset, but so too were the transport planes as they ferried *Fallschirmjäger* to drop on key bridges, airfields and the Belgian fort at Eben-Emael. Among them was Gefreiter Martin Pöppel, part of 1. Battalion, 1. Fallschirmjägerregiment, whose task was to capture intact an important bridge at Dordrecht, to the south-east of Rotterdam.

Glancing out of the window of the 'Tante Ju', as the transports were known, Pöppel thought the large number of aircraft looked like flocks of birds gathering in the autumn. Stuka dive-bombers flew below them, fighters above. A few jolts as bursts of anti-aircraft fire peppered the sky, and then, at 5.10 a.m., it was time to jump. Suddenly, Pöppel was out, floating down peacefully, not a line of tracer in sight, and landing safely away from the many ditches that criss-crossed the flat landscape. Unfastening his 'chute, he ran towards the containers to help gather weapons and radio equipment, and together he and the rest of his company quickly set up HQ in a hastily abandoned farmhouse where there was still-warm tea and buttered bread on the table.

On the banks of the River Dordtsche Kil at 's-Gravendeel south-east of Rotterdam, Korporaal Gerrit den Hartog and the rest of 28th Infantry Regiment, part of Group Kil, hurriedly scrambled out of their cots and, still dazed from sleep, dressed and grabbed their rifles. They had heard the sound of aircraft but had initially assumed they were heading to attack Britain, so it was a shock when they began dropping hordes of para-troopers and dive-bombing.

The Dutch Army was ill-equipped for battle. Holland had not fought a war in nearly 150 years and had determinedly held fast to its neutrality in the last war. It had no tanks and little artillery, and most of what it did have was horribly out of date. Gerrit den Hartog had been a reservist, and at thirty-one had left his wife, four young children and market-gardening business at the outbreak of war, even though Holland remained neutral and refused all offers of alliances or aid. Now, eight months on, the country's neutrality counted for nothing.

The Army, commanded by General Henri Winkelman, had recognized that, in the event of a German invasion, there was no point in trying to defend the whole country. Instead, and with French help, it would protect the western group of islands on which were the largest of the Dutch cities. It was hoped that the wide rivers separating them from the rest of the Netherlands would provide a natural defensive barrier; these sea rivers and canals had traditionally been the key to Dutch defence. No one in the Dutch command had counted on airborne forces swooping down on them, however.

Den Hartog was a quiet man, devoted to his wife and children, and although a qualified marksman was not, by nature, remotely martial.

Most of his fellows were similarly older reservists and in no way equipped to take on highly motivated and well-trained young *Fallschirmjäger*. In fact, none of them had even been issued with ammunition, and within a very short time the Zwijndrecht bridges between Dordrecht and Rotterdam, just to the north of their positions, had been captured and communications with the garrison in Dordrecht cut.

Den Hartog's commander, Major Ravelli, was promised reinforcements but they hadn't appeared. In the afternoon, the 28th crossed the River Kil and formed a bridgehead at Wieldrecht, and in the evening the promised support finally arrived in the form of two sections of heavy machine guns. Later, as dusk fell, they pressed forward towards Amstelwijk, hoping to link up with other Dutch forces. Instead, they found a deserted command post littered with dead Dutch troops. So far, den Hartog had heard a lot of bombing and shooting, and had seen a mass of enemy troops dropping from the sky, but he had yet to engage the enemy at all. What exactly was going on was hard to tell, but it was clear the battle was not going well for the Dutch.

Meanwhile, the Allied air forces were desperately trying to meet this threat from the air. At Nivelles airfield in Belgium, the pilots of the country's Air Force had been woken in the very early hours. It was around 1 a.m. that Jean Offenberg, a 23-year-old pilot in 4ᵉ Escadrille of 2ᵉ Régiment de l'Air, had been roused. 'Go to hell,' Offenberg told his friend, Alexis Jottard, the man shaking him awake. 'If you can't find a better joke than that, go back to bed.'

'No, it's not a joke,' Jottard insisted. 'Get up. It's the real thing.' Reluctantly, and sensing a ring of truth in Jottard's words, Offenberg got out of bed and put on his sweater and flying suit. Outside, in the shadows, Siraut, the duty officer, confirmed the worst. 'It's war,' he said. They were to be ready to fly at first light and to evacuate the airfield, as rehearsed, in case the enemy, as expected, bombed it. They were to move to an emergency airstrip at Brusthem near Saint-Trond.

At 4.30 a.m., flying in their open-cockpit Italian Fiat CR.42 biplanes, they were at 3,000 feet over Gossoncourt, looking down at the even more antiquated Fairey Foxes dispersed around the perimeter, and then they were landing at Brusthem as planned. Nivelles, they soon discovered, had already been bombed. 'Don't worry,' Offenberg told Jottard. 'They're bound to bomb this too. We've only got to wait like children. I should like to go and have a good bash at those bastards!'

Soon after, he got his wish. Taking Jottard and another pilot, Maes, with him, the three took off. As they slowly climbed, Offenberg wondered how he would feel when he finally met a German aircraft for the first time. He did not have to wait long, for suddenly, off to port, he could see a twin-engine bomber – a Dornier, he recognized – with its distinct black cross and swastika. His heart suddenly beating quicker, he waved to his two comrades only to see Maes already diving away without waiting for orders as instructed. Then Jottard was pointing furiously and there, up ahead, Offenberg saw a formation of aircraft stacked up. *Messerschmitts.* In what seemed like moments, they were among them and Offenberg was diving between them, bullets from the rear gunner of the Me110 arcing towards him as he fired his own machine guns. Then his starboard machine gun jammed, he pulled out of his dive and found the sky miraculously empty once more, with no sight of Maes, Jottard or even any Messerschmitts . . .

It was now 6.45 a.m., and Offenberg was at 5,000 feet over the town of Diest when suddenly he spotted another Dornier – or was it the same one? – below him. Quickly checking the skies were clear, he sped down towards it in a shallow dive as the rear gunner from the bomber opened fire, bright sparks rushing towards him like sunlight on a diamond. Offenberg opened fire in turn but the Dornier was escaping, so giving up the chase he headed for home only to run into yet another Dornier approaching him and getting bigger by the second. A dive and a turn and Offenberg was right above him and opening fire with a long burst of his now-cooled machine gun. 'The old Fiat vibrated and bucked from the recoil of that machine-gun,' he noted. 'Spirals of black smoke began to pour from his port engine.' Pulling on the stick to avoid a stream of German tracers, he saw the Dornier bank and dive away, rapidly losing height. At 7.45 a.m., Offenberg landed back at Brusthem, happy to have made it back alive, to have scored his first kill, to see Maes and Jottard in one piece too, and to find the airfield had still not been attacked.

Further to the south-east, at Vassincourt, near Rheims, 1 Squadron of the RAF's Advanced Air Striking Force (AASF), had been woken at 3.30 a.m. and told to make straight for their airfield. Among the pilots was Billy Drake, a 22-year-old career pilot who had joined the RAF four years earlier having seen an advert in a copy of *Aeroplane* magazine. He'd been rather taken with flying ever since enjoying a brief flight with Alan

Cobham's Flying Circus as a boy. Having finished school in Switzerland and determined not to follow his parents' preferred choice of career as a doctor or diplomat, he applied and was accepted.

At 5 a.m., as they sat around the dispersal tent at the airfield, the 1 Squadron pilots were scrambled and ordered to patrol Metz at 20,000 feet. They ran to their Hurricanes and took off in flights, climbing up through the haze until, at around 5,000 feet, they emerged into bright sunshine. The trouble was, the haze below was still sufficiently thick for them to be able to see very little. Eventually, though, B Flight did spot a formation of Dorniers, which they attacked, managing to shoot one down. Drake, however, soon became separated, having been watching some Me109s in the distance. Two of the German fighters attacked him, but he managed to dodge their fire and get on the tail of one of them, which then dived. Following him down, they sped towards Germany and, having crossed the border, the German pilot flew under some power cables, presumably hoping this might shake off his pursuer. Drake followed him, however, opened fire with his eight Browning machine guns and to his satisfaction watched the 109 crash into a wood and explode.

Both France and Britain had been expecting a German offensive in the West for some time. Even though theirs was a modern world, the obvious campaigning season was spring and summer, so since the particularly harsh winter had ebbed away, they had been increasingly aware that Hitler could strike at any moment. Even so, Hitler's offensive could not have come at a worse moment for the Allies, as both Paris and London were gripped by political crisis. In London, matters had begun to boil over on 7 May, when a debate had begun in the House of Commons about the campaign in Norway. In a subsequent vote of confidence the Prime Minister had suffered a crippling moral defeat, which had cut the Government's majority to a mere eighty-one. In peacetime, this would have quickly blown over, but now, in wartime, it looked like a fatal blow. The results had prompted, first, a gasp around the packed House, then pandemonium.

An ashen and rather shell-shocked Chamberlain had walked stiffly from the Commons just after 11 p.m. on 8 May amid jeers and taunts of 'Missed the bus!', 'Get out!' and 'Go, in the name of God, go!' A more sensitive man than his sometimes austere persona suggested, Chamberlain had been profoundly humiliated by events.

In the corridors of Westminster the general opinion was that Chamberlain would now have to go; he had always been unpopular with the British left, including an increasingly powerful trade union movement. Nor had he made any effort to woo leading Labour members of Parliament; there had certainly been no effort to create a wartime coalition. Thus there were many now only too happy to seize the chance to oust him. Despite this, the 71-year-old Prime Minister had woken early on Thursday morning, 9 May, determined to fight his corner. As the day wore on, however, it became increasingly clear to him that his premiership was over. The damage was too great, and the mood for change had swung too far against him. But who would take over?

Most felt that Lord Halifax was the obvious choice. A former Viceroy of India, a hugely experienced politician and a man widely respected for his sound judgement, Halifax was certainly top of Chamberlain's list as successor. The other leading Tories were either too young, lacking a sufficient following, too unpopular or too inexperienced, but Halifax, it was widely felt, would be safe, dependable and a voice of calm reason in the traumatic days that seemed likely to lie ahead.

However, Halifax was not quite as suitable as at first he appeared. He was not much interested in military matters and although, unlike Chamberlain, he had served in the First World War, he had spent most of his army career in a staff position. It was certainly fair to say he lacked the modern soldier's perspective. Moreover, he was a peer, which meant he could not sit in the House of Commons; someone else would have to run that side of things. In fact, the very thought of becoming PM at this difficult time had brought on a psychosomatic bout of nausea, and he told Chamberlain that morning that he would be very reluctant to take over the reins.

There was one other possible candidate for the post. Winston Churchill, back in the Cabinet since the outbreak of war, had all the military credentials Halifax lacked, as well as a stack of political experience. He was fascinated and energized by war. He had fought at the Battle of Omdurman, had taken part in the Boer War, had served in India and had commanded a battalion in France in the last war. Yet while this rich experience was undoubtedly to his credit, there were many who viewed him as a maverick, inconsistent and hot-headed; he drank too much; smoked too much. His methods were unorthodox. And there was mud on him he had been unable to shake off: he had been the architect of the disastrous Dardanelles campaign of 1915, and Chancellor during the General Strike of 1926. In more recent times, he had fought hard against the Government over Indian independence and against Chamberlain's appeasement policy with Germany; he had sided with Edward VIII during the abdication crisis of 1936, which had further distanced him from the establishment. And although he had largely avoided censure during the two-day debate, there were many – Jock Colville included – who felt he was more to blame for the failure of the land campaign in Norway than Chamberlain. For all his enormous energy, drive and undoubted oratorical skills, he was widely regarded as a man lacking sound judgement. A man unsuited to the highest office. At the very least, making Churchill Prime Minister would be a big risk.

Later that afternoon, at another meeting, this time with Churchill included as well as Halifax, Chamberlain told them his mind was made up; he would resign but would be happy to serve under Halifax or Churchill. Halifax, whose stomach ache now started anew, repeated his reluctance to take over, citing the impotence he felt he would have as a peer while Churchill ran defence and, effectively, the Commons.

And this was the crux of the issue. Halifax, rather than holding no ambition for office, believed he would merely be a lame-duck Prime Minister while Churchill took effective control. Far better for the country, he believed, if Churchill was PM while he, as Foreign Secretary, acted as a restraining influence from within the Cabinet. Chamberlain acquiesced; so long as the Labour contingent agreed to serve under Churchill, the transfer of power would be made. But as the Germans launched their assault in the West, confirmation had still not been received; on that day of days, Britain's political leadership remained in turmoil. Not until the evening would Churchill finally be confirmed as the new Prime Minister of Great Britain.

Across the Channel, Paul Reynaud had also offered his resignation the previous day, just seven weeks into his premiership. The cause, once again, had been the ever-widening split between him and former PM but still Minister of National Defence and War, Édouard Daladier. Reynaud had been determined to put some life into Général Gamelin, whom he blamed for the painfully slow response to the Norwegian campaign. Failure in Norway was bad enough, but the speed with which the Germans had moved did not augur well. What if Germany should attack France? Would

Gamelin's forces also be too slow to respond to that? It was this slow, methodical approach to war that Reynaud was desperate to change. In identifying this as a malaise of the French Army, he was quite right, as Capitaine André Beaufre had been increasingly aware ever since being part of the Anglo-French mission to Moscow the previous August. The trouble was, it was rather too late to do anything about it. Sacking Gamelin might only make matters worse, not better.

At any rate, after long difficult weeks banging his head against a brick wall and finding himself almost powerless to do anything, Reynaud had decided he needed to force the issue. The previous day, he had called the Cabinet together to demand Gamelin's resignation. As expected, Daladier had refused to accept the move, so Reynaud had decided to enact his plan. He would resign his Government in the hope that President Lebrun would ask him to re-form another one, this time with the Prime Minister as Minister of National Defence and War, not Daladier. Then he could sack Gamelin without further ado.

Reynaud had been expecting to see Lebrun the following day but then, in the early hours of the morning, 10 May, had come the news that his move had, like the French and British in Norway, been too late. His own resignation and the sacking of Gamelin were now out of the question.

'General,' wrote Reynaud to Gamelin that morning. 'The battle has begun. One thing only counts: to win the victory. We shall all work in unison to this end.' Gamelin wrote in reply in full agreement: 'France alone is of importance.'

Capitaine André Beaufre was awoken that morning, 10 May, by the sound of bombs. In fact, the German attack had not come as a complete surprise as there had been intelligence reports from Belgium that suggested something was afoot the previous evening and an order to stand to had been issued to all French troops. Beaufre had spent the last few months working with Général Aimé Doumenc, who had been part of the Moscow mission the previous summer and was now the commander of GHQ Land Forces, based in a Rothschild chateau at Montry on the River Marne. This lay roughly halfway between Georges's North-East Front HQ and Gamelin's headquarters at Vincennes in Paris. The creation of this third major headquarters was another layer of totally unnecessary bureaucracy, drawing on key members of Georges's staff and breaking up teams who had been working perfectly well. GHQ Land Forces was designed to prepare elaborate orders – and also to place a check on Georges. At the same time, both Army intelligence and the operations staff were also split up between Georges's HQ and this new one under Doumenc. Transport and supply were taken completely from Georges's HQ and placed under Doumenc. None of this made any sense whatsoever, especially for an army that relied so heavily on telephone and telegraph – and not radio – for communication.

With the sound of bombs falling, Beaufre was sent to report to Gamelin at Vincennes and arrived there at 6.30 a.m. By this time, the Commander-in-Chief had already put the great plan of attack into action and ordered his forces to start advancing into Belgium to meet the enemy. The move into Belgium had not been made lightly. There were certainly advantages, as his troops would be swelled further by the thirty divisions of the Dutch and Belgian armies. It also meant fighting clear of France and its northern industrial area. On the other hand, if they stayed in France, they would get the benefit of well-prepared defences.

Furthermore, Gamelin had had to decide where the attack was most likely to fall. It was true he had millions of men, but the Germans, in attacking, could concentrate their forces and the trick was to be able to meet any attack with similar strength. He had discounted an enemy assault on the Maginot Line, but also believed a thrust through the Ardennes, with its deep valleys, limited roads and thick forests, unlikely. The Ardennes, Gamelin had declared, was 'Europe's best tank obstacle'. This left an advance through the Low Countries, which is what the Germans had done in 1914, and it was on this assumption that Gamelin had made his plans. One version, known as 'Plan E', was to advance a short way, to the River Escaut. A second version, 'Plan D', was to see his troops advance to the River Dyle – around eighty miles. It would mean a bit of a logistical headache but could be done. In March, an addition to the plan had been made, known as the Breda Variant. This would see French troops thrust further north to Antwerp to link up with the Dutch. On paper, this seemed like a small addition, but logistically it was a major change. Breda was twice as far from the French border as it was from the German, and so it was a race Gamelin could not hope to win. It also required a lot more manpower. In the basic Plan D, ten French and five British divisions would advance to the Dyle. The Breda Variant required a further fifteen and the movement of the entire French 7e Armée – a force Général Georges had intended to keep in reserve.

Be that as it may, it was the Breda version of Plan D that was now being put into effect. And as Beaufre reached Vincennes, he found Gamelin striding up and down, humming, with a pleased look on his face. The signs were that the Germans were advancing through the Low Countries, just as Gamelin had predicted.

The newly promoted Capitaine René de Chambrun had also been awoken that morning by the sound of battle, although in his case it was a nearby battery of anti-aircraft guns. He had recently been promoted to captain and posted as a British liaison officer, first to British headquarters near Arras and then had almost immediately been told to report to 151st Brigade, part of 50th Division, for a few days pending the arrival of a further British division, at which point he would join this new staff instead. On the morning of 10 May, he was based in a family home in the village of Don, some ten miles south of Lille and in among the coalfield villages rebuilt since the end of the last war. Around about were old German bunkers, now mostly reclaimed by grass and weeds.

The firing of the guns made him sit up with a jolt. He could hear the tiles on the roof rattling from the vibration, then, as he quickly dressed, he heard the drone of bombers followed by the lighter roar of fighter aircraft and the rat-a-tat of machine guns. Downstairs, the family he was billeted with were gathered around their wireless set, still in pyjamas and nightgowns, listening to Belgian radio. Moments later, a deafening explosion could be heard nearby, shattering the window panes. Chambrun rushed outside and saw in a field a few hundred yards away the burning remains of a German Heinkel 111 and three airmen floating down in their parachutes. Clutching his revolver, he ran towards the nearest and, along with some British and French troops, captured the man, a young, blond pilot.

All three men were then taken to brigade HQ in the village and there Chambrun questioned them. 'The Nazi lieutenant told me that Germany had no grievance against France,' noted Chambrun. 'He stated that Germany's real enemy was Great Britain, the power of which had to be destroyed.' Soon after, as Plan D was put into effect, Chambrun was told the brigade would be moving into Belgium – although not until sunset and then to an area around eight miles south-west of Brussels. Chambrun was to go ahead and help arrange billeting.

The journey was a long and tortuous one. Accompanied by his British driver, Chambrun experienced at first hand the troubles that were to dog the Allies in the days to come as hordes of Belgian civilians tried to flee the cities, towns and villages. This would become known as the '*exode*', prompted by a combination of panic, memories of German atrocities during their advance in 1914, and a desire to escape the violence of war and bombing that many believed must surely follow.

Just outside Tournai, only just across the border, Chambrun's car was forced to a traffic-induced standstill. Suddenly, Stuka dive-bombers screeched overhead, then dived down and bombs fell around them. Fortunately, most fell in the fields either side, but one did land on a Belgian family in their car, blowing them to smithereens; it was a chilling real-life demonstration of this terror weapon, already familiar from news-reels of Poland. As they eventually crawled past the wreckage, an old man stopped by Chambrun's car and said, '*Il faut qu'on gagne car c'est pire qu'en quatorze!*' We must win because this is worse than fourteen!

They were not the last Stukas Chambrun saw that day, and by the time he reached the village south of Brussels he was already eight hours behind schedule. Having found the burgomaster and seen to the billeting, and pausing for an omelette and beer in an inn, he and his exhausted driver began the tedious journey back. Far from experiencing an ordered and efficient advance, Chambrun had witnessed chaos, confusion and a civilian population in panic. In the preparations for Plan D, for the Breda Variant, and during all the appreciations of what might happen should the Germans attack, little, if any, thought had been given to what might happen if fleeing civilians were to clog the roads. It was already looking like quite a bad oversight.

CHAPTER 20

Race to the Meuse

THE FIRST British troops had moved forward into Belgium at around 10.20 a.m., nearly four hours after the first orders had been issued. Two British corps were to be in the advance, from which three divisions would hold a six-mile stretch of the River Dyle, sandwiched between the French and the Belgians. Commanding II Corps was the bespectacled and rather hawkish General Alan Brooke, fifty-six years old, a fiercely intelligent career soldier who, as a gunner, had survived the last war and built up a reputation for being a first-class planner. He was also something of a Francophile, having been brought up and educated mostly in France, and as a result speaking with the overly pronounced and crisp English accent of a man raised speaking a different tongue.

Like Gamelin, Brooke rather felt they had plenty of time to reach the Dyle and dig in before the Germans might arrive and so spent the morning ensuring everything was fixed and ready before his infantry got going. All seemed well. There had been plenty of enemy aircraft going over, but they were clearly aiming for targets other than the BEF. In the afternoon, II Corps finally set off, the sun high and bright in the sky. 'It was hard to believe,' scribbled Brooke in his diary, 'on a most glorious spring day, with all nature looking quite its best, that we were taking the first steps towards what must become one of the greatest battles in history!'

Meanwhile, the German invasion was going to plan, with the Luftwaffe destroying much of the Dutch Air Force on the ground and almost all the key objectives for the airborne troops being taken as well. At Dordrecht, Martin Pöppel and his comrades had come into contact with Dutch troops, who had begun firing at them from buildings some 500 metres away. When Oberleutnant Schuller asked for volunteers, Pöppel answered the call, and moments later nine men, led by Schuller, began crawling along the ditches and hedgerows until they were near the buildings from where the Dutch were firing. Crawling under a window, Pöppel could see and hear Dutch soldiers shooting wildly from inside, then suddenly a German machine gun opened up, the enemy took cover, and Pöppel, clutching a Luger pistol in one hand and a grenade in the other, ducked down and hurled the grenade through the window, then moved on to the next. With the explosions and screams from inside, Pöppel's comrades charged the building and soon after a white cloth was shown and the entire Dutch position surrendered. 'Sixty-three Dutchmen came out,' noted Pöppel, 'and there were only twelve of us.' None the less, the para-troopers lost several men in the attack – including Schuller, who was mortally wounded. 'We have seen our first men killed,' wrote Pöppel, 'and stand before them in silence.'

Small and large battles had been taking place all across the front, both in the air and on the ground. The Luftwaffe, who had spared the Belgian 4ᵉ Escadrille earlier in the day, caught up with them at their new airfield at around 3 p.m. that afternoon, the Stukas with screaming sirens diving down on the men and machines below. Jean Offenberg and his friend Jottard dived for the nearest ditch while bombs fell all around, the ground trembled and the sound of diving bombers and bombs detonating filled their ears. When their attackers had finally gone, there was not a single airworthy aircraft in 3 Squadron left, although their own, in 4ᵉ Escadrille, miraculously appeared to be in one piece. It was hardly much cause for joy. News that key bridges had been captured, airfields destroyed and the important fort at Eben-Emael captured was made worse by the news that one of their comrades had been killed. 'Night,' wrote Offenberg, 'fell mercifully on our grief . . .'

The RAF's 1 Squadron had also been kept busy. They had been pounced on by Me109s as they'd attacked some Dorniers, losing one of their Hurricanes in the process. Back on the ground, the survivors were ordered to move to another airfield at Berry-au-Bac. B Flight took off and Billy Drake managed to help shoot down a Heinkel 111. Landing again, they were attacked once more, although most of the bombs fell wide. Soon after, they took off on yet another patrol. By now the haze had gone and they could clearly see smoke rising from the towns and villages below. Other airfields had also been hit. They finally went to bed, exhausted, as darkness fell. 'There was a feeling that total chaos was reigning,' says Drake. 'Germans were everywhere and we were constantly being bombed.'

René de Chambrun would have no doubt agreed with Drake. It took him all night to travel back to Don, pausing en route to take some wounded children to hospital in Tournai. He finally reached the village only to find the brigade was already on the move and that he was now to report to Alost, the main supply base for the British division due to arrive. The endless congestion of the roads, the frequent air attacks, and the appalling rumours that were circulating and sending the civilian population into a flat spin meant he and his driver did not reach Alost until nightfall on the 11th.

Finally, at long last, he found the divisional camp, spread out around a race course. Setting himself down in the grandstand along with a large number of snoring Tommies, he quickly fell asleep. An hour later, with dawn already spreading, he was awoken again by an air raid on the Brussels suburbs and counted a number of bombers plummeting from the sky.

One of the civilian refugees now clogging the roads was the nineteen-year-old Freddie Knoller, a Viennese Jew who had fled Austria eighteen months earlier following *Kristallnacht* in November 1938. Austrian Jews had had less time to adjust to the Nazis' draconian anti-Semitic laws than those in Germany; before the *Anschluss*, Knoller had not personally noticed much evidence of anti-Semitism in Austria. That night, however, he and his family had seen one of their Jewish neighbours thrown out of his flat, down into the courtyard below and killed. From that moment, Knoller's parents had been determined that he and his two older brothers should escape the country. Otto, the oldest, managed to get to Holland then England through a friend with good connections; Eric, the second son, found sponsorship to go to America through the cousins of one of their neighbours; and Freddie had been told he would find help from another cousin of his neighbour who lived in Antwerp, and so it was to Holland that he made his way via an illegal entry across the Dutch border at Aachen.

Despite urging his parents to leave too, they had repeatedly assured him and his brothers that it was the young who were in danger – and so they had remained. Freddie had been the first to leave – still only seventeen at the time, he had been severed from his family and all that he knew and loved. His feelings had been mixed. 'On the one hand,' he wrote, 'I had no idea how I would cope without my parents' guidance or my brothers' comradeship. On the other the prospect of having nobody to tell me what to do was intoxicating.' Leaving his family had been heart-wrenching. They all came to see him off on the train. He was weeping and so was his mother. 'We clung to each other for a long time,' he noted. 'I felt only the utter, incomprehensible desolation of parting.'

He had survived, however; the Apte family in Antwerp had helped him; he had made friends, then realized they were leading him astray and so had discarded them; some summer work had been found in a hotel in a Dutch resort; the Jewish Aid Committee had helped too – Knoller had been far from the only Jewish refugee. His parents had even managed to send him his beloved cello – music had been an important part of his family life.

By the summer of 1939, Holland and Belgium were flooded with Jewish refugees and Knoller had been sent to a refugee camp at Merksplas on the Dutch–Belgian border. At the same time, he had heard from his parents that their application for an American visa had been lost. Soon after, another letter told him they were being forced to return to Poland. Unable to help them, Knoller was miserable with worry about them.

However, he did have his cello, and in February he moved to a new camp at Eksaarde and joined a small orchestra that performed for a refugee audience every weekend.

The German attack brought this existence to an immediate end. Told to head to either Ostend or France and to take nothing but essentials, Knoller had been forced to abandon his cello – it felt as though he were leaving a part of himself and his old family life in Vienna for good. He began heading to the French border, along with the mass of other refugees. Knoller was glad he was on foot and not encumbered with vehicles, wagons and older family members to look after. A German plane flew over, strafing them. Knoller managed to quickly dive out of the way, but others were not so lucky.

Eventually, he reached Tournai and, along with many others, squeezed himself on to a platform at the station, desperately hoping to board a train for France. He had not been there long when the town was attacked by Stukas. Knoller managed to take cover in a piece of concrete piping. He was so terrified, he realized he had wet himself. An entire section of the station was engulfed in flames, and as the bombers departed and the all-clear was sounded, Knoller crawled out and looked around through the smoke and dust at the devastation. The moans of the injured, the screams of others, were terrible to hear. 'As the air cleared,' he recalled, 'we saw bodies, whole and dismembered, lying in pools of blood. I vomited what little food I had in me.'

It was certainly the strength of German air power that dominated on that opening day of the battle. Integrating air power into the initial operation on the ground was a key component of the German assault. Although air power was still comparatively new, the principles developed by the Luftwaffe slotted neatly into the age-old Prussian theories of *Bewegungskrieg* – the lightning war of movement. Feldmarschall Göring had, like Hitler, arrived near the front by personal train. His one was called *Asia* and was even more elaborate and ornate. On paper, his air forces had amounted to 5,446 aircraft that morning, but strength on paper was not the same thing as actual strength, and actual strength could be quite different again from operational strength. Hajo Herrmann's III/KG4, for example, now equipped with the heavier and slower but sort-of-dive-bombing-capable Ju88s had an actual strength of thirty-five bombers, but eight were out of action, so the operational strength was twenty-seven. This was quite normal. Almost no unit was fully operational. Furthermore, there were still a large number operating in Norway and yet more held back for home defence. This meant the Luftwaffe had begun its assault in the West with around 1,500 bombers and 1,000 fighters – or, in other words, less than half its strength on paper.

Göring was personally unaware of this – Luftwaffe staff and intelligence officers had learned that it paid to tell the chief what he wanted to hear rather than tedious and unwelcome truths – but the shortfall did not affect the general plan, which was to destroy as much of the enemy air forces as possible and as quickly as possible too. They were confident of doing so too, not least because their intelligence had underestimated the true enemy strength, reckoning the French had under a thousand bombers and fighters and that the RAF, which they calculated had around double that amount, was unlikely to commit all its aircraft to the fighting in France.

In fact, the Allies' strength on paper was much the same as that of the Germans, and while it was true that the French had just under 900 combat aircraft at the front, they did have a further 1,700 combat-ready which could, in theory, be thrown into the fray quite easily. That they were not was a deliberate policy to avoid being attacked on the ground should the Germans launch a surprise attack. On the face of it, this was quite sensible.

German assessment of the RAF was closer to the mark, however. The RAF was divided into three home commands: Coastal, Bomber and Fighter. Aircraft for France had to be drawn from those commands and then placed in a new set-up, known as British Air Forces in France, which was then further split into thirteen squadrons of the BEF Air Component, and the Advanced Air Striking Force (AASF). The former was answerable to General Lord Gort and to the French, while the AASF was not, command and control instead coming under the auspices of Bomber Command. It was a complicated set-up, but in all, that morning, 10 May, the RAF had around 500 combat-ready aircraft. Add to that the combined Dutch and Belgian air forces, and the Allies had good numbers with which to take on the Luftwaffe.

The big advantage the attackers had, however, was not so much their numbers, but the huge benefit of both surprise and choosing when and where to attack. The Dutch and Belgians certainly had no co-ordinated air defence system, but then nor did the French. With almost no radar and no ground controllers, Allied aircraft did not have the means of anticipating where Luftwaffe aircraft might attack and so were left to patrol the skies, often aimlessly, on the off-chance that they might spy an enemy formation. For those on the ground, such as René de Chambrun, it might have appeared as though the skies were black with German planes, but at 15,000 feet up the sky seemed a much bigger place. The furthest a human eye could see an aircraft at was only around three miles. The invasion front covered thousands of square miles. In fact, command and control of the Armée de l'Air was pretty hopeless. Most of its aircraft were modern types and more or less a match for those in the Luftwaffe, but these were divided into *Zones d'Opérations*, each with its own aircraft and independent command structure. The net result was that it was unable to bring to bear any concentration of force in the way that the

Luftwaffe could. In short, the Allies were not best prepared. Having half-decent aircraft wasn't enough.

One person witnessing this at first hand was Squadron Leader Horace 'George' Darley, who had recently been posted to help run the Operations Room at Merville near Lille. Darley had joined the RAF from school back in 1932 and now, aged twenty-six, was an experienced pilot and officer whose career had developed with that of the Air Force. Stints of operational flying in Aden and East Africa as well as time as an instructor and ground controller made him a very rounded and highly experienced officer.

At Merville, however, Darley's task was an uphill one. Based in a small house beside the airfield, he was supposed to field calls from the ground forces and then send up fighters in response. 'But all the communications were by field telephones,' he said, 'and I had about twenty.' One of them would ring and it would take him precious time just to work out which one it was. Needless to say, more often than not, the Hurricanes were scrambled too late to have much effect.

In fact, such was the dispersion of Allied air forces and so disjointed command and control that the comparative parity in numbers became less important. The Luftwaffe could pick them off a bit at a time – bombing airfields, catching them on the ground or pouncing on them when they ventured into the air.

For the most part, the signs were encouraging for the Germans. Eben-Emael had been taken, the airborne landings around Rotterdam had been a success, key bridges had been captured, the Dutch Air Force had been all but destroyed. The RAF had seventy-five aircraft lost or damaged, the French seventy-four. Airfields had been bombed. Chaos had reigned.

Yet the Luftwaffe had suffered horrendously that opening day, with 192 bombers and fighters lost and damaged and a staggering 244 transport planes. In all, 353 German aircraft and 904 pilots and crew would never fly again. After one day of battle. These were substantial losses.

Across the Atlantic, the President of the United States had heard the news of the German attack at around 11 p.m., Eastern Standard Time, on the night of 9 May. Sitting in the presidential study in the White House in Washington DC, he called together several of his key people, including the Secretary of the Treasury, Henry Morgenthau Jr, and gave the order to freeze all Low Countries assets immediately.

The dilemma facing Roosevelt was how to make the majority of the American people see the rapidly worsening crisis in Europe as one that threatened the security of the United States as well – especially when he had been so firmly isolationist himself throughout much of the 1930s. FDR still hoped that America might keep out of the war, but clearly they had to be ready. His approach was twofold: to help the Allies, Britain and France especially, who would be, in effect, the USA's first line of defence, and to build up America's own defences, which had, during the 1920s and 1930s, dwindled to almost nothing, partly due to cost and partly because of a deliberate policy based on the belief that maintaining large armed forces during peacetime was unnecessarily provocative. As a result, much of its Navy had been mothballed, the Air Corps had been reduced to just 20,000 men, and the Army had shrunk to just 119,913 in 1932, and on 1 July 1939 had increased only to 188,565 – just 10 per cent of the German troops marching into Poland. In 1939, the US Army was the nineteenth largest in the world, smaller than that of tiny Portugal.

Small amounts of growth had been instigated. A new shipbuilding programme had been launched back in 1938, and warships had been brought back into eastern ports for the first time since the last war. A small increase in the Army had also been authorized, but only to 227,000 men. The United States in May 1940 could hardly have been less ready to go to war.

This needed to change, but FDR's problem was that most Americans simply did not believe the threat. Poll after poll revealed that around 95 per cent of all Americans believed the US should not be drawn into the war, and while an increasing number thought America should strengthen its own defences, this was not a voice loud enough to convince Congress, where the isolationist lobby still shouted the loudest. And no matter how sound his reasons, the truth remained that Roosevelt was making a major political u-turn.

Compounding matters was the upcoming presidential election in November 1940. A precedent had been set by George Washington that no president should hold office for more than two terms; FDR had served two, but he was pretty certain he was the only leading political figure who could both win the next election and lead the US in the direction it needed to go. But could he really stand for a third term? It was something being muttered about, something FDR had clearly been thinking over, but for the time being he was keeping his thoughts and plans to himself. It was, however, the elephant in the room and would have to be confronted soon.

The biggest immediate challenge was how to build up US defences quickly and efficiently and organize the economy in such a way as to get this done without challenging the basics of democracy or unduly rousing the isolationist lobby, among whose number were some powerful and very vocal names, including the celebrated aviator Charles Lindbergh and the Ambassador to Britain, Joe Kennedy. Mistrust seethed through Washington. Isolationists and interventionists traded blows, and so did New Dealers with the big businessmen; there was, it seemed, no middle ground: capitalism or social revolution, war or isolationism. Roosevelt had a very tricky line to walk, and well he knew it.

None the less, the German assault in the West unquestionably acted as a spur. Roosevelt had been careful to play his hand very lightly; now he would have to take risks and push forward his plans both for rearmament and for educating the American public. And to do this, he would need a new team of men around him.

One person who was there to help the President was Harry Hopkins, who had not, as widely expected, died the previous autumn. Rather, Hopkins had made a very slow but steady recovery. The problems had not gone away – they never would with two-thirds of his stomach gone – and he was thin, anaemic and physically weak, but his mind, it seemed, was as sharp as ever. The son of an Iowa harness-maker, Hopkins had a very different background to Roosevelt, with his privileged East Coast upbringing, yet they shared a razor-sharp sense of humour and equally razor-sharp political instincts. 'He knows instinctively when to ask, when to keep still, when to press, when to hold back; when to approach Roosevelt direct, when to go at him roundabout,' wrote one columnist about Hopkins. 'Quick, alert, shrewd, bold and carrying it off with a bright Hell's bells air, Hopkins is in all respects the inevitable Roosevelt favourite.' Both men had also fought life-threatening illness – in Roosevelt's case, it was the polio that had crippled a once tall and athletic man in his prime and confined him to a wheelchair for the rest of his life. Their mutual affection ran deep, and it was no surprise that on 10 May, the day the Germans had launched their offensive in the West, and the day of political turmoil in Britain and France, FDR should dine with his closest and most trusted friend, colleague and political advisor.

After dinner, Hopkins had started to make a move for home – back to the rented house in Georgetown – but the President instead insisted he stay. Hopkins acquiesced, and after being lent some pyjamas was given a bedroom on the second floor overlooking the South Lawn – the very room in which President Abraham Lincoln had signed the Emancipation Proclamation seventy-seven years earlier.

Hopkins not only stayed in the White House that night of 10 May, but the following night too, and the next after that as well. Roosevelt needed him close at hand, and, as ever, Hopkins was willing to do his master's bidding and embark on a new stage in his career. Throughout his political life, he had been concerned primarily with social reform. Military matters and foreign affairs had not interested him. That, however, was about to change.

Back across the Atlantic, the momentum in the battle now raging in the West was all with the Germans, despite the aircraft losses; everyone felt it: the civilians fleeing from their homes, the defenders, who seemed to be overawed by the combination of air power and the speed with which the Germans were operating, and the Germans themselves. Hans von Luck, for example, was now in the Reconnaissance Battalion of 7. Panzerdivision, commanded by the young and dynamic Generalmajor Erwin Rommel. They were part of Armeegruppe A, but in Panzerkorps Hoth, aiming to cross the Rhine further north than Guderian, at Dinant. Von Luck and his men were highly trained, believed in the new panzer tactics of speed, and were confident of success. When some of the older men had warned them it would not be a walkover like Poland, 'We younger ones replied that there could not, and must not, be any trench warfare as in 1914–18,' noted von Luck. 'Our tank force was too mobile, our attitude too positive.'

While von Luck and the rest of Panzerkorps Hoth were hurrying through the Ardennes, the Allies were lumbering into Belgium and Holland to meet the northern thrust, and in so doing had fallen for the German deception plan hook, line and sinker. By 12 May, the German 6. Armee, part of Armeegruppe B, had linked up with the airborne troops still holding Eben-Emael. The Albert Canal, a key obstacle that ran from Antwerp to Liège, had been crossed. The Dutch Army had fallen back to Rotterdam and appeared to be finished. Gerrit den Hartog and his fellows in 28th Regiment had stumbled from one confused encounter to another. On the 11th, they had headed north from Amstelwijk to the bridges at Zwijndrecht, linking the island of Dordrecht to Rotterdam, which had been taken the day before. By this time, den Hartog was exhausted, hungry and scared. Rather than wrest the bridges from the Germans, however, they had been met by unarmed Dutch soldiers warning them not to shoot. As they had approached, German troops had appeared and captured the lot, Gerrit den Hartog included.

Meanwhile, to the south, the French 7ᵉ Armée, fulfilling their role as part of the Breda Variant, had advanced only to be forced back towards Antwerp. By the 13th, German troops had reached the Dutch coast, while the Belgians were starting to fall back too, desperately trying to link up with the British and French now taking up positions along the Dyle. Not all were yet there, however. The French 1ᵉ Armée was still struggling to wade through the mass of refugees clogging the roads ever more densely. Bombing by the Luftwaffe continued; telephone lines were cut and roads blocked, and dispatch riders were heading into the morass on little more than a fool's errand. The Allied air forces, having proved themselves worthy opponents in the air, were being butchered on the ground instead.

And, all the while, the panzers in Armeegruppe A that were the main thrust were pushing through the Ardennes, forging their way past the long list of obstacles and potential time hazards so that miraculously, by 13 May, just as Guderian had predicted, they had reached the River Meuse.

CHAPTER 21

Smashing the Meuse Front

Freddie Knoller had made it to France, but his Austrian passport ensured he was immediately arrested and handcuffed, even though it was stamped with a large 'J' for Jew. Concern over Fifth Columnists outweighed any sympathy for Jewish refugees. At the police station, he was made to show his interrogator his circumcised penis. His story was believed, but this didn't stop him and other German speakers from being marched to the train station through the streets under armed guard. '*Sales Boches!*' people shouted at them. One woman emptied her pisspot over them.

Bundled on to a cattle truck along with a number of Germans who *were*, Knoller discovered, Fifth Columnists, he tried to ignore their taunts, wondering all the time where he was being sent. Eventually, after an interminably long two-day journey with nothing but straw and a wooden floor to sit on, his journey ended. They had reached a town called Saint-Cyprien, about six miles from Perpignan, a way to the south. This, Knoller learned, was an internment camp originally set up for refugees of the Spanish Civil War. Led off the trains and into a large assembly hall, they were then addressed by a French officer. 'All of you are enemies of France,' he told them. 'Any attempt to escape is punishable by death.'

Among the first troops reaching the Meuse were the recently promoted Hauptmann Hans von Luck and his comrades in the 7. Reconnaissance Battalion. Incredibly, they had reached the river just a few miles north of Dinant ahead of schedule on the night of 12 May. Their advance had been through difficult terrain, but they had not met much resistance. Ahead of them now, though, was a river a hundred metres wide and, beyond that, sharply rising craggy cliffs. The first crossing was made over a footbridge by a weir and lock system that was, astonishingly, not only unguarded, but also lay on the boundary between two French corps. It was a sloppy oversight, especially since it was the precise spot where Germans had crossed in 1914, but, even so, one footbridge was not going to be enough to get an entire German division across.

The main assault began the following morning around first light. Generalmajor Rommel arrived in his scout car and told von Luck and his men to stay put. Crossing the river, he said, was a job for the infantry. Paddling over in boats, they soon came under heavy fire, but eventually, through counter-fire and by setting houses ablaze to create smokescreens, they made it, with Rommel himself crossing that afternoon. The French had been badly caught out. Dinant was in Belgium and although the French 9ᵉ Armée had begun moving forward to the Meuse once the offensive began, Général André Corap, the Army commander, had not expected the Germans to reach the river there – if at all – in less than ten days and more likely two weeks. Some French troops had arrived but had not dug in. Even so, their commanding position should have enabled them to hold off such a wide river crossing and buy them time to bring up reinforcements. Key to stopping the Germans in their tracks was to defend these nodal points such as rivers, bridges and crossroads. They had failed at this first test.

It could still have been so different. Panzerkorps Hoth was separate from the rest of Panzergruppe Kleist, the main panzer formation in Armeegruppe A, and operating further north. Panzergruppe Kleist was made up of three panzer corps – those of Guderian, General Reinhardt and also General von Wietersheim. Guderian's three divisions had benefited from being the spearhead, but Panzerkorps Reinhardt, heading towards the Meuse further north of Sedan at Monthermé, soon ran into the world's biggest traffic jam as infantry units, supposed to be following behind, cut in across them. General Reinhardt's divisions became increasingly separated and split up – his leading division, for example, was shredded as no fewer than four infantry divisions tried to cut across its advance. By the morning of 13 May, there were queues some 170 miles long.

This meant the vast bulk of Armeegruppe A was a sitting duck for any

Allied aerial attack. On the night of 10 May and again the following morning, Allied reconnaissance aircraft had spotted German columns going through the Ardennes, but the reports were not taken seriously. On the night of 11–12 May, another recce pilot reported seeing long columns of Germans, but, again, it was ignored. On the afternoon of the 12th, yet another reconnaissance pilot reported the same, but although his claims were passed on to the intelligence section of the French 9ᵉ Armée, they were dismissed as absurd. Had they been taken seriously, and had a mass of Allied bombers been sent over, much of Armeegruppe A would have been stopped in its tracks and, with it, the key component in the German plan of attack.

But the opportunity had been missed: another big black mark against Corap and his staff and the French High Command.

The Germans had not anticipated these traffic jams, as strict traffic orders had been put in place, and it was only because the infantry divisions, separate from Panzergruppe Kleist and not so well trained, had not stuck to the plan that these difficulties had arisen. That the spearhead would get to the Meuse in three days if all went according to plan was always going to be a tall order, but that General Reinhardt's men reached Monthermé as well as Guderian's troops reaching the Meuse was an absolutely extraordinary achievement, and was due to a masterpiece example of the German *Bewegungskrieg*.

The men of Panzergruppe Kleist unquestionably conformed to the German stereotype of myth: they were well trained, motivated, decently equipped and confident, and knew exactly what they had to do. Yet speed had been the name of the game in reaching the Meuse. Fighting quality would not add up to a hill of beans if the three panzer corps of Guderian, von Hoth and Reinhardt did not get there in three days and cross it in four, because if they took much longer the French reserves would beat them to it and reinforce this weak spot in the French front line.

With time at a premium, the logistics of the operation needed to be flawless. Luckily for them, the Panzergruppe's Chief of Staff was the particularly able Oberst Kurt Zeitzler.

'If ever the success of an operation depended on supplies,' noted Zeitzler, 'that is the case with our operation.' With this in mind, he set about resolving one logistical headache after another. Logistics normally came under the logistics unit of the parent army command, but Zeitzler decided that because the Panzergruppe was to be operationally independent then it should be logistically independent too. Zeitzler called this the 'Rucksack Prinzip' – the 'Rucksack Principle'. 'To use an analogy relating to railway operations,' he wrote, 'you might say, the unit must no longer hand its supplies over to the next higher duty station for transportation. Instead, it must have its supplies with the train itself as a backpack or hand baggage.'

There were 41,400 vehicles in Panzergruppe Kleist, a very large number to cater for, and Zeitzler ensured that every single one was loaded to the maximum capacity with ammunition, rations and, most importantly, fuel. Very well-stocked fuel depots were set up from where the panzer groups formed up within Germany all the way to the Luxembourg border. Zeitzler insisted that every single vehicle – tank, truck or motorcycle – should be loaded full with fuel not only as it passed the Luxembourg border, but the Belgian border too. This was resolved by placing numerous fuel-carrying trucks into the spearhead. At key points, jerrycans were handed over to the crews as the vehicles drove past, and the vehicles were refuelled at the next rest or enforced stop. The empty jerrycans were left on the side of the road at designated points and then picked up and refilled at the next dump.

Another potential headache was the problem of repairs to this vast army of vehicles. All the more than 41,000 had to reach the Channel over 400 miles away, so they carried plenty of mechanics and spare parts, and there were planned air-drops of further supplies.

Leading the advance to the Meuse was 1. Panzerdivision, part of Guderian's panzer corps. The Divisional Chief of Staff was Hauptmann Johann Graf von Kielmansegg, who knew what they were up against. 'Every minute counts,' Guderian repeatedly told his men, and that meant relentlessly pushing forward all day and all night. Von Kielmansegg took this to heart, organizing relief panzer crews to be transported in trucks so that the advance never need stop. Guderian had warned his men they would be unlikely to get any sleep for three nights, and so it proved for a large number of them. Once again, von Kielmansegg had thought ahead, packing some 20,000 tablets of an amphetamine called Pervitin to be handed out to anyone consumed by fatigue.

The slick execution of this operational plan, combined with a big dose of good fortune, had ensured that both Reinhardt and Guderian were ready to cross the Meuse on the 13th, not the 14th – that is, a day earlier than anticipated. A curious feature of the German attack was the repeated

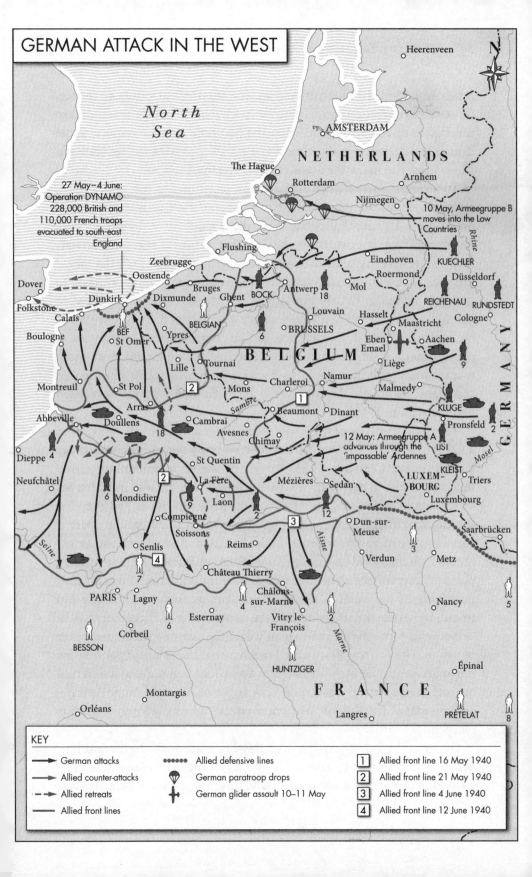

GERMAN ATTACK IN THE WEST

North Sea

NETHERLANDS

Heerenveen

AMSTERDAM

The Hague

Rotterdam

Arnhem

Nijmegen

Eindhoven

Roermond

Düsseldorf

KUECHLER

10 May, Armeegruppe B moves into the Low Countries

Mol

Antwerp 18

Hasselt

Maastricht

Cologne

REICHENAU

RUNDSTEDT

27 May–4 June: Operation DYNAMO 228,000 British and 110,000 French troops evacuated to south-east England

Flushing

Zeebrugge

Oostende

Bruges

Ghent

BOCK

Louvain

BRUSSELS

Eben Emael

Aachen

9

Dover

Folkstone

Calais

Dunkirk

Dixmunde

BELGIAN

6

Liège

Boulogne

BEF

St Omer

Ypres

BELGIUM

Tournai

Charleroi

Namur

Malmedy

KLUGE

Montreuil

St Pol

Lille

2

Mons

Sambre

Beaumont

Dinant

Pronsfeld

2

Abbeville

Arras

Doullens

18

Cambrai

Avesnes

Chimay

12 May: Armeegruppe A advances through the 'impassable' Ardennes

LIST

Dieppe 4

Neufchâtel

2

St Quentin

La Fère

9

Laon

Mézières

Sedan

12

LUXEM-BOURG

Triers

6 Mondidier

Compiègne

Soissons

2

3

Dun-sur-Meuse

Luxembourg

Saarbrücken

Senlis

4

7

Reims

Château Thierry

Aisne

Verdun

3

Metz

PARIS

Lagny

6

Esternay

Châlons-sur-Marne

4

Vitry le-François

2

Marne

Nancy

5

Corbeil

BESSON

HUNTZIGER

Épinal

Montargis

FRANCE

Orléans

Langres

PRÉTELAT

8

KEY

→ German attacks

→ Allied counter-attacks

⇢ Allied retreats

── Allied front lines

•••••• Allied defensive lines

🪂 German paratroop drops

✠ German glider assault 10–11 May

| 1 | Allied front line 16 May 1940 |

| 2 | Allied front line 21 May 1940 |

| 3 | Allied front line 4 June 1940 |

| 4 | Allied front line 12 June 1940 |

insubordination of senior commanders towards their superiors. Guderian, for one, was operating almost entirely in a bubble in which he was deaf to the wishes of von Kleist, for whom he had little time or respect. So he agreed to attack across the Meuse at 4 p.m. on 13 May but ignored von Kleist's order to make the assault further north of Sedan.

To a certain extent, Guderian's refusal to be tied to the orders of his superiors was nothing new. Rather like the plan itself, he was adhering to principles of command that had developed as a by-product of *Bewegungskrieg*. Because of the fast-moving nature of this form of warfare, a flexible system of command was essential, which meant lower-ranking commanders tended to be given a fair amount of leeway to use their initiative. Orders would focus on the objective, while those in the thick of it were left to their own devices as to how that objective could be best achieved. It was known as the 'independence of the lower commander', or, in German, *Selbständigkeit der Unterführer*. In more recent times, this has come to be called *Auftragstaktik*, or mission command, although this was not a term Germans would have been familiar with in 1940.

This independence of the lower commander applied to all ranks, from a lowly *Gruppe*, or section, commander, right up to a corps commander like Guderian. Certainly, Guderian felt he was in a far better position than von Kleist to decide both crossing points and the way in which his attack should be directed. He also knew the town well, for he had attended the German Staff College, which had been based there back in 1918; it was why he had opted for Sedan in the first place and why he was determined to use his local knowledge for what he considered the best crossing places. Guderian had also, quite independently, organized direct air support from the Luftwaffe, as not all his artillery had arrived. Calling an old friend, Generalleutnant Bruno Loerzer, commander of Fliegerkorps VIII, he had asked for a rolling barrage of wave after wave of Stukas and other bombers. The aim was to stun the French by near-constant attacks. To his horror, however, he then learned that von Kleist had ordered a different one-off massed attack from Loerzer's superior, General Hugo Sperrle, commander of Luftflotte 3. 'My whole attack,' noted Guderian, 'was thus placed in jeopardy.'

Guderian had clambered up a chalky hill a few miles to the south of Sedan from where he could see the attacks unfold. The Meuse was to be crossed in three places, one at precisely the same point as where German troops had attacked in 1870. It was with great anxiety that he peered through his binoculars waiting for the arrival of the Luftwaffe and for the attacks to start. Much to his enormous relief, however, when the first Stukas arrived, including those of Helmut Mahlke's 2.St/186, it was to attack in exactly the way he had discussed with Loerzer rather than had been dictated to him by von Kleist. He later discovered that Loerzer had similarly ignored instructions from Sperrle.

Hurrying back down the hill, he headed for his command car and then the central crossing point at the suburb of Gaulier. Like Rommel, Guderian was very much a commander who led from the front and liked to be both in the thick of it and seen by his men.

In the air, it appeared the Luftwaffe was still very much in control. The ability to choose when to attack and in what numbers was proving an enormous advantage.

Among those witnessing this superiority at first hand was Squadron Leader Sydney Bufton, a career RAF pilot with a stack of experience after having been stationed in various corners of the world from Iraq to North Africa. He had recently completed the RAF's Staff College course, and had then been posted to the Headquarters Staff of the Advanced Air Striking Force in France. However, within a few days of the German assault, months of careful co-ordination with both the French Army and the Armée de l'Air had been rapidly undone. At dawn on 14 May, for example, having been on duty all night at AASF's HQ at Chauny, he had witnessed a mass of German bombers fly over and hit the large French military camp nearby. In response to this there was neither anti-aircraft fire nor any fighters of their own. The following night, he attempted to go to bed to the sound of an ammunition dump at Laon exploding. Then at 11.30 p.m., they were suddenly ordered to move. 'All the work of the past nine months was undone,' he wrote in his diary. The air effort had become completely dislocated – severed at the head.

This was why those sent to bomb Sedan on 13 May had been able to do so without interference. Escorting the bombers were fighter pilots of 2/JG2, including 23-year-old Siegfried Bethke. The escort to Sedan had been his third sortie of the day, but they had still barely seen an enemy plane. 'We're almost disappointed,' he scribbled in his journal. Circling around and watching Stukas dive-bombing was not how he had imagined it would be.

One person who might have gladly swapped places was Billy Drake, who, along with the rest of 1 Squadron RAF, had had more than enough action. He now had four and a half confirmed kills – five would qualify him as an 'ace' – and was on yet another sortie when he began suffering oxygen supply problems and so told the others he was returning to base. Losing height to avoid the need for oxygen, he spotted a flight of Dorniers, flew up behind them and shot one out of the sky. He was watching it spiral down in flames when suddenly there was a loud crack and a brief moment later flames were engulfing his Hurricane. Desperately glancing around, he realized he had an Me110 Zerstörer on his tail and still firing.

Panicking, he frantically undid his radio leads and unclipped his harness but then couldn't remember how to open the canopy. Covered in petrol and glycol, he knew he had to get out and fast, and as he tugged on the canopy the Hurricane flipped over of its own accord so that the flames were suddenly drawn away from him. Finally, the canopy opened, and he dropped out. 'Still the 110 was shooting at me,' he noted, 'and then he was past and gone.' He pulled the ripcord on his parachute, it billowed open and he floated gently to earth. He was very, very lucky to be alive. The fuel tanks in the Hurricanes were in the wing roots and once the machine guns had been fired, air whistled through the gun ports. If the fuel tanks were hit, this would fan the flames straight into the cockpit. Pilots had a matter of seconds to escape. Drake had also been wounded in the leg and back. Only a short while before, 1 Squadron pilots had added armour plating behind the cockpit – at the insistence of the CO, 'Bull' Halahan. Unbeknown to Drake at the time, a bullet had hit the armour plating at head level. Without it, he would have been dead.

As it happened, he landed on friendly ground and, despite being fair and slightly Germanic in appearance, was able to persuade the French farmers who arrived on the scene that he was English. Taken to hospital in Chartres and later back to England, he was, for the time being at any rate, one less RAF pilot for the Germans to worry about.

As dusk fell on 13 May, at Dinant, at Monthermé and at Sedan, German troops had not only successfully crossed the mighty Meuse but had made firm bridgeheads. At Sedan, all three crossings had linked up, but it was the action of Oberstleutnant Hermann Balck and his exhausted men of 1. Rifle Regiment that sealed the day. Their objective for the day had been

Hill 301, a dominant position overlooking the entire town on which much of the French artillery was dug in. Balck had fought in the last war and remembered a time when they had failed to exploit a hard-won encounter at Mount Kemmel to their cost. 'What was easy today,' he urged his men, 'could cost a lot of blood tomorrow.' It was an inspired piece of leadership, as his men, exhausted but sensing victory, stormed the hill. By 10.30 p.m., it was in German hands. Below, Sedan was burning and, behind, the French troops were fleeing, panicked into believing the panzers were already across and running amok; in fact, the crossings had been achieved by the German infantry alone.

But the panzers would be there by the following morning. Overnight, ferries would carry over more men and materiel, bridges would be built, and then the panzers and trucks and armoured cars and artillery of those ten mechanized divisions of Armeegruppe A would stream across and in behind France's defences.

Very early the following morning, 14 May, at General Headquarters at the Château Montry, Capitaine André Beaufre had only just got to sleep when he was awoken by a telephone call from Général Georges.

'Ask Général Doumenc to come here at once,' Georges told him.

An hour later, at around 3 a.m., they arrived at Georges's HQ at Château Bondons, which was more like a large villa set on a hill. All was dark except the large drawing room, which was dimly lit but had been turned into a map room, with trestle tables around the edge at which staff officers were typing and fielding calls. The atmosphere, thought Beaufre, was that of a family in which there had been a death.

Immediately, Georges stood up and came over to Doumenc. 'Our front has been broken at Sedan! There has been a collapse . . .' He then flung himself into a chair and burst into tears. 'He was the first man I had seen weep in this campaign,' noted Beaufre. 'It made a terrible impression on me.'

Doumenc tried to reassure him, but Georges explained that the two divisions at Sedan were now fleeing. He then collapsed into more tears. The room was otherwise silent – all were shattered not only by the stunning news but by the sight of their commander in pieces. Doumenc tried to bring some calm. The gap, he said, had to be stopped. There were three armoured divisions, all of which could be redirected towards the Meuse. These three divisions, amounting to some 600 modern and powerful tanks, could be concentrated and drive the Germans back across the river. There was much in what he said. The German benefit of surprise had now gone, they would be exhausted, and they would have to rapidly enlarge their bridgeheads with men and weapons to ensure they hung on to them. The race wasn't over – in fact, a new one had just begun, and the French, now fully alerted, had a very good opportunity to win this time around. Georges agreed to all Doumenc's suggestions. Beaufre relit all the lamps, ordered coffee all round, and then they headed back. Even so, Beaufre couldn't help fearing the worst. 'All our doctrine was founded on faith in the value of defence,' he noted, 'and now, at the first blow, our position organized over nine months broke into little pieces. This revelation struck chill.'

Throughout that day, Beaufre's worst fears began to be realized. The counter-attack by 3rd Armoured Division, the unit closest to Sedan, was postponed – orders had been slow to reach them, as had the further orders within the division and its various units. They had simply not been ready. And all the while news kept arriving of further gains for the Germans. There had been other French armoured units in the Sedan area, but although they had had less distance to travel than the German panzers and were on the right side of the river, and even though the first panzers did not cross the Meuse at Sedan until 7.45 a.m. on the 14th, it was the Germans who were lying in wait for the French, not the other way round. The French Army had an operational speed that was slow and methodical. Nothing, not even the threat of complete collapse, it seemed, could alter that.

On the same day the Meuse was crossed, President Roosevelt had met Henry Morgenthau Jr, the Secretary of the Treasury, and General George C. Marshall, the Chief of Staff of the US Army, for a meeting at the White House. Marshall was fifty-nine, with the best part of forty years' military service under his belt. He had served in the American–Philippine War, and in the Great War, had been posted to France, first as a trainer and then later on had joined the planning staff of General Pershing, the Commander-in-Chief of US forces in France, where he made quite a name for himself during the important Meuse-Argonne offensive during the last months of the war.

Remaining in the US Army, Marshall had served in China, taught at the War College and had later been assigned to the War Plans Division in

Washington. By the summer of 1939, he had risen to Deputy Chief of Staff and was then promoted to the top job, being sworn in on the very day Germany invaded Poland. Intelligent, calm and soft-spoken, Marshall possessed both an inner steel and a clear, logical mind. As an administrator he had already proved himself to be exceptional, but, like Roosevelt, he was keenly aware how poor America's defences were. For several months he had been trying to persuade key figures in Congress and the Government of the need to increase defence spending. He had also put his case to Henry Morgenthau, but for men like the Secretary of the Treasury, who had been almost solely concerned with domestic issues, the world of dramatic rearmament was something new and involved dizzyingly high sums of money at a time when America had very little to spare. He was, however, supportive of Marshall, but knew the only option was to take the matter to the President. That the Germans had launched their attack a few days earlier was very much to Marshall's advantage.

Also attending were the isolationist Secretary of War, Harry Woodring, and the ineffective Secretary of the Navy, Charles Edison. The debate quickly became heated, and neither Morgenthau nor Marshall was getting through, until eventually Morgenthau asked FDR to listen to the Chief of Staff.

'I know exactly what he would say,' Roosevelt replied. 'There is no necessity for me to hear him at all.'

At this, Marshall got up, strode over to Roosevelt's chair and said with quiet authority, 'Mr President,' he said, 'can I have three minutes?'

Apparently disarmed, Roosevelt agreed, and Marshall then presented the President with some blunt truths. It was time, Marshall pointed out, for the President to make some tough decisions. The Army was in a woeful state. It really is hard not to overplay just how moribund the US armed forces were in May 1940. The Army's equipment was out of date, in terms of troop numbers it was tiny, and it was in no position whatsoever to confront the Germans. There were just a few hundred tanks, and no anti-tank guns whatsoever, and there was a shortage of mortars, machine guns and other essential weaponry. The Army Air Corps had just 160 fighters – or pursuit planes, as the Americans called them – and fifty-two heavy bombers. These were as good as nothing. The Navy was also in a bad way, with an antiquated structure and no central means of procurement. Roosevelt had increased naval shipbuilding since 1936, but it was not enough. If Japan decided to go to war against them too – and

Japan's imperial ambitions were becoming all too evident – then the US would be powerless to stop it. Fighting a war on a two-ocean front was unthinkable.

What Marshall urged Roosevelt to do was not only demand far greater spending on rearmament, but also to gather together a group of industrialists to help advise the government on how to achieve massive rearming as quickly as possible. Because, Marshall made clear, getting the cash was only half of it. Even more challenging was going to be mobilizing American industry for war. The US Army had only six working arsenals manufacturing weapons, and much of the machinery was both old and obsolete. The time for paying lip service to the isolationists was over; the US needed to act, and act fast. 'If you don't do something,' Marshall told him, 'and do it right away, I don't know what's going to happen to the country.'

Further warnings of doom had come from the new British Prime Minister, Winston Churchill. At the outbreak of war, Roosevelt had written to Churchill asking to keep informally in touch with him personally. The two had met – albeit only once before – back in July 1918, when Roosevelt, as Assistant Secretary to the Navy, had been in London on a fact-finding mission and had attended a dinner for the War Cabinet; Churchill had not impressed Roosevelt, while the Prime Minister had forgotten the encounter altogether. In other words, the two knew about each other, but that was all. On 15 May, the day after Marshall's entreaty, Churchill wrote his sixth letter to the President. 'The small countries,' he wrote, 'are simply smashed up, one by one, like matchwood.' He painted a darker picture than Churchill believed to be really the case, and warned of an imminent invasion of Britain. 'But I trust you realize, Mr President, that the voice and force of the United States may count for nothing if they are withheld too long.' He asked for more direct support in terms of arms and war materiel, and particularly the loan of forty or fifty old destroyers to bridge the gap while British shipyards made up the shortfall. He also pointed out the need to purchase steel from the US now that Britain's traditional markets in North Africa and Sweden were threatened. Roosevelt, who accepted that US security was directly linked to Britain's survival, responded the next day with as much encouragement as he dared.

And on that same day, 16 May, and bucked further by polls suggesting the public was warming to the idea that the US needed to adequately rearm, the President addressed Congress and asked not for the $24 million increase to the Army budget that had been originally put forward, but a staggering $1.2 billion, and to increase both the Army's and the Navy's air forces to some 50,000 aeroplanes. US aircraft manufacturers had produced just 2,100 military aircraft in 1939. 'These are ominous days,' he told a joint session of Congress. 'The American people must recast their thinking about national protection.' The generally isolationist Congress, shocked by what was happening in Europe, not only applauded the speech, but approved the President's request. It was a start – a step closer towards all-out rearmament.

Meanwhile, in France, the Germans had been enlarging their bridgehead west of the River Meuse. Guderian had once again ignored orders from von Kleist to wait to build up forces before advancing, although on this occasion it had been 1. Panzerdivision's Chief of Staff, Major Wenck, who helped make up his mind by reminding him of one of his favourite sayings: 'Boot them, don't slap them!' 'That really answered my question,' he admitted. Ordering 10. Panzerdivision to protect the bridgehead, he ordered 1. and 2. Panzer to head west – towards the Channel coast.

At any rate, there was no French counter-attack of any note along the Sedan front on 14 May, allowing the Germans the breathing space to get more forces across the river without much hindrance. An Allied bomber attack on Sedan was massacred, while, at Dinant, Panzerkorps Hoth continued to press forward. Hans von Luck was amazed to keep seeing Rommel among them and in the thick of the fighting, but his divisional commander had told them repeatedly, 'Keep going, don't look to left or right, only forward. I'll cover your flanks if necessary. The enemy is confused; we must take advantage of it.'

Even so, they would not have had such an easy time of it had the French 1st Armoured Division, on standby near Charleroi, got moving sooner. Again, the French were proving they simply could not operate with speed. In fact, the division was not even ordered forward until 2 p.m. on the 14th and then found itself battling against roads crammed with fleeing civilians. It managed twenty miles then leaguered for the night. Unbeknown to them, Rommel's lead panzers were also corralled for the night just a few miles away. By morning, the Luftwaffe had attacked and destroyed several French fuel convoys, and the French tanks were laboriously refuelling one tank after the other. The German refuelling method was completely different. Rather than using fuel bowsers, trucks would motor from tank to tank, with men dishing out large numbers of jerry-cans so that the panzers could be refuelled at the same time. At any rate, the lead tanks of the French 1st Armoured were caught out while still refuelling. After knocking out a number, Rommel ordered his lead units to push on, leaving 5. Panzerdivision to take on the French.

The French 1st Armoured had better tanks with better guns, but they were still destroyed that day. At dawn they had had 170 tanks; by evening just thirty-six. The following morning, that figure had dwindled to just sixteen. What had done for them was not the German panzers but the panzers' radios and German anti-tank guns. Some French tanks – but not all – had radios, but most of them had broken down because they were equipped with weak batteries. In contrast, all panzers had modern radio equipment and were able to communicate with each other and their anti-tank artillery units. In a nutshell, the panzers acted either in packs, beetling about and hammering their flanks all at once, or as bait, luring the French heavy tanks into a waiting anti-tank screen.

That same day, Panzerkorps Reinhardt also broke out of its bridgehead at Monthermé and charged thirty miles west, an astonishing achievement considering only 6. Panzerdivision had actually made it across the Meuse – the rest of the corps were still languishing in the traffic mayhem of the Ardennes. The next morning, 16 May, 6th Panzer met up with Guderian and 1st Panzer at Montcornet, some fifty miles west of Sedan. The audacious plan could not have gone better. The entire Meuse Front had completely collapsed, and the stunning German victory had been achieved by just six panzer divisions – three at Sedan, one at Monthermé and two at Dinant.

Now they had to complete the encirclement.

CHAPTER 22

Encirclement

'THE SUDDEN REVELATION of modern warfare,' wrote the French Prime Minister, Paul Reynaud, 'was a frightful surprise.' Yet much of the German equipment was no more modern and a lot of it much less so than the French. What was different – and modern – was Guderian's use of operational speed and of mechanized and infantry divisions operating independently. Even more ironic was the fact that most within the Wehrmacht expressed great scepticism about this 'modern' approach; it was only Guderian, and the corps and divisional commanders within the panzer arm, who had remotely bought into such ideas. Furthermore, until the attack in the West, it had not really been tested before. The US and now British press had caught on to the term Blitzkrieg – German for 'lightning war' – but the doctrine established within the Wehrmacht, and the methods used by Guderian et al. in the race to the Meuse and which were being unleashed now as they continued their dash west, were new to this campaign and had not been adopted in Poland or in Norway. The 'revelation' was that a war of manoeuvre could be fought at speeds the French had not anticipated.

The other shock was the effect of concentrated air power. The Luftwaffe was losing large numbers of aircraft – 353 on 10 May, 68 on the 11th, 54 on the 12th, 35 on the 13th and 59 on the 14th – so it wasn't as though it was having it all its own way. Helmut Mahlke's Stuka *Gruppe* lost eight machines and crews on the 14th, for example, including two from his own *Staffel*. 'This 14 May,' he noted, 'had been a black day indeed for our Gruppe.' In the air, the Allies were more than a match; Billy Drake was not the only pilot becoming an ace. The difference was the Luftwaffe's ability to attack at a time and in numbers of its own choosing; it was the *Schwerpunkt* principle applied to air warfare. More Allied aircraft were lost on the ground than in the air, which was why after a few days' fighting the Luftwaffe had lost many more pilots and aircrew than the Allies. The lack of any effective Allied early-warning system was proving a terrible oversight.

The Dutch Air Force had been almost entirely destroyed on the first day, and on the 14th Rotterdam was bombed with devastating results. In fact, it had been a mistake. The Luftwaffe had been asked to support the German 18. Armee's attack to help break Dutch resistance. The Germans had also threatened to bomb the city and, on hearing this, Dutch authorities had begun negotiating their surrender. Just after midday, the orders for KG54 to bomb Rotterdam were cancelled, but it was too late to tell the bomber crews. Red flares were fired, but fifty-seven Heinkel 111s never saw them and dropped their loads. In the catastrophe that followed, 2.8 miles of the historic heart of the city was destroyed and some 850 people were killed.

The attack had been watched by Gerrit den Hartog's wife, Cor, from their home in Leidschendam, on the edge of The Hague. Huge clouds of smoke rose above the ruined city, where she had a number of relatives living and working. Chaos ensued as survivors tried to flee the carnage. The bombing of Rotterdam rather put the earlier bombing of Guernica in Spain and then Warsaw into the shade. The frightfulness of war, and the Armageddon brought by massed bomber formations, forecast repeatedly through the 1930s, suddenly appeared to be a reality. However unintentional, there is no doubt that it did much to add to the view that the German military machine was unstoppable – a view that was gathering considerable momentum as marauding panzers were reported impossibly far distances west and Stukas and 109s continued to bomb and strafe columns of fleeing refugees.

Paul Reynaud could scarcely believe the scale of the disaster that was unfolding as a result of the collapse of the Sedan front. He had been urging the armed forces to show some vim and verve, had done all he could to get some consensus on the protraction of the French war effort, had time and again warned of complacency and a defensive mindset, and yet it had been repeatedly thrown back in his face. Now his worst fears were being realized. Everything had been staked upon the continuous front – if it was broken, there was no Plan B. As it stood, the best of the French forces had moved up into Belgium and Holland and were confronting the German Armeegruppe B there along the Dyle. But to the south, German forces were now pouring through a major hole in the line. He could see exactly what was likely to happen if something wasn't done very quickly: the bulk of the French, British and Belgian forces would become encircled, with no means of being resupplied. Millions of men would be caught in a massive trap. That had been the German plan all along, and they had fallen for it: completely, utterly, totally.

The only way of stopping it, he believed, was by the use of aircraft stemming the advance of the panzers and combating the power of the Stukas. At 5.45 p.m. on the 14th, he called Churchill and asked for urgent reinforcements of RAF fighter planes. Churchill replied that they would give the matter full consideration. The next morning, at 7.30 a.m., Reynaud telephoned him again for his response. When Churchill expressed surprise at the severity of the picture the French Prime Minister was painting, Reynaud said, 'We are beaten. We have lost the battle.'

One of those seemingly flying at will was Leutnant Siegfried Bethke, a fighter pilot with I/JG2 'Richthofen'. Born in Stralsund, on the northern Baltic coast, he had joined the fledgling Luftwaffe from school and by May 1940 had well over 300 hours' solo flying under his belt. Most pilots, whether French, British or German, tended to have around 150 hours by the time they were fully trained and joining their operational units, which meant that pre-war Regulars tended to have a huge advantage; they no longer had to think about flying, as that had become second nature. Rather, they could concentrate on combat flying, which was an altogether different matter. Even so, while Bethke knew how to throw his Messerschmitt around the sky, he was keenly aware that he had almost no gunnery training whatsoever. Consequently, he was unsure how he would be once in combat.

Bethke had been posted to Bassenheim near Koblenz ready for the offensive towards the end of April and had arrived with mixed feelings. On the one hand, he had been longing to get into action ever since he had first joined the Luftwaffe, but on the other he was apprehensive too, as well he might be. Three days into the offensive, however, and Bethke was beginning to feel a bit frustrated; flying over Sedan on 13 May had been so far the closest to action he had been. As they were supporting

Armeegruppe A, they had been operating further south; the main thrust of the air effort had been in the north in support of Armeegruppe B.

Still, he had no real cause for any complaints. On 15 May, they moved to a new airfield in Belgium, and the following morning while waiting for orders he sat in a deckchair jotting in his leather-bound journal, a gift from his girlfriend. 'My dear Siegfried!' she had written at the front, 'In these momentous times, one must keep a diary. What will you put in it? Stuttgart, September 1939, Your Hedi.'

'On a green field on edge of forest, sunny weather,' he scribbled. 'Next to me a tent for tools and equipment. Around me, the squadron troops, the vehicles, the clothes . . . A small stray dog is sitting beside me. We milked "our" free-roaming cows yesterday. They don't seem bothered by the hectic bustle of the planes and the noise of the engines.' They had milk, wine, chickens, even a slaughtered ox. It would not be so comfortable for long.

In London, Jock Colville had been watching the extraordinary events of the past week unfold. The Government had fallen, Chamberlain was no longer PM and in his place was Winston Churchill, a man about whom Colville had severe reservations. A new coalition government had been formed and with it a new War Cabinet of five, as well as the wider cabinet of ministerial positions. Churchill had wasted no time in asking Chamberlain to be one of the five, which he had accepted; the two had not always got along, but Chamberlain had been deeply touched by Churchill's graciousness towards him; the new PM had even suggested that Chamberlain remain at No. 10 for the time being. The gesture was both part of Churchill's natural character and politically savvy: Chamberlain was still Conservative leader and continued to command much support from within the party; Churchill needed his backing. Halifax remained as Foreign Secretary, while the two other places were taken by Clement Attlee and Arthur Greenwood. Major-General Hastings 'Pug' Ismay became Churchill's Chief of Staff and Deputy Secretary (Military) to the War Cabinet. And Jock Colville remained as one of the Prime Minister's secretaries, flitting between No. 10 and Admiralty House where Churchill continued to work.

As if the political upheavals were not enough, there was the disaster that was evolving across France and the Low Countries. Those in London, perhaps understandably, were not quick to see catastrophe unfolding as they were in France. Certainly, no one was breaking down and blubbing. 'Apparently,' noted Colville on the 16th, 'the French are still not putting their best leg forward.'

The same day, and still in her family home in Leidschendam, Cor den Hartog listened to the radio her husband had insisted on buying several years earlier, trying to pick up every scrap of news. German announcements told the Dutch that their troops would be entering the cities en masse and that all civilian traffic would be halted between 5.45 a.m. and 12.30 p.m. German 'credit certificates' were now to be accepted as cash, and beer was to be reserved for German troops. Blackouts would be strictly maintained. An air of menace and fear had descended; even on the first day, thousands upon thousands of leaflets had been dropped telling the Dutch to lay down arms and warning that anyone caught in acts of sabotage would be executed.

Worried sick about the fate of her husband, she now decided to go and look for him, even though she was pregnant with their fourth child; she was a devout Calvinist, but even prayer had been unable to give her any kind of solace. Placing her children in the care of Gerrit's parents, she took out her bicycle and prepared to start her search. Someone had said that POWs would be returned to their original posts and, knowing that her husband had been based at Strijen, she headed there first – although how she would find him and what she would then do once she did she had no idea. Gerrit's parents tried to talk her out of it – how could she know where he was? And what if the roads were destroyed? 'Then I will find other roads,' she replied.

She headed off, reminding herself that everything was part of God's plan, but, even so, the scenes of devastation were shocking: buildings reduced to rubble, wrecked aircraft, blown-down trees, dead livestock and abandoned guns. At a roadblock, Germans stopped her as a column trundled by and then she pedalled on only to discover other women also out cycling and hunting for missing sons and husbands. When she reached the place where Gerrit had been billeted, however, there was no sign of him.

Also on the 16th, Churchill flew to Paris for meetings with Reynaud and Gamelin. It was a beautiful day in Paris, and from the large meeting room in the Quai D'Orsay they could see the palace gardens, where bonfires had been lit – state papers were being burned. It hardly inspired confidence, although Churchill did his best to stiffen French resolve. The minutes of that meeting survive and make for interesting reading, not least because of the huge discrepancy between what Churchill and his British delegation thought was, could be and should be happening and the appalling, yet calm, defeatism of Gamelin and Daladier. Repeatedly, Churchill pointed out that the dash of a handful of panzers should not be of too much concern as they would be unable to support themselves or refuel. Gamelin accepted that, so long as counter-attacks could be successfully made the following day against the mass of enemy forces now pouring through the breech in the line, but warned that the French armoured divisions had already suffered heavy losses. He did not mention why counter-attacks had not already been ordered.

'Where is the strategic reserve?' Churchill asked.

'There is none,' Gamelin replied.

Churchill was dumbstruck. Over and over, the French asked for more aircraft – only then, perhaps, could the battle be turned. Churchill promised to ask the Cabinet and duly did so. In his mind, he was convinced of the need to send ten fighter squadrons. The question was whether in doing so they were backing a busted flush and were risking weakening their own defences.

Since the start of the German attack, the American journalist Eric Sevareid had been beetling about, heading to Général Corap's HQ, then to the Belgian border, but getting little news of what was actually going on. At one point he had to dive for a ditch as a British fighter plane, followed by two Germans, in the middle of a dogfight, thundered over at treetop height. He watched one German plane come down as well as the Hurricane, the British pilot manoeuvring the falling aircraft away from the nearby village. Sevareid hurried to the wreckage. In the field, the cows were grazing peacefully, but there was a big, dark crater, which contained smoking parts of the plane and a single flying boot. Two Frenchmen with sacks were moving around picking up bits of red meat which they buried as villagers stood watching and weeping. 'We found the plane's serial number,' noted Sevareid, 'and returned to the press headquarters in Cambrai, a little sick, very sobered, wondering what was happening to France.'

He wasn't the only one. For many of those caught up in the fighting, these were confusing, dizzying days. By 17 May, Jean Offenberg was one of just six pilots in his entire fighter group that still had an aircraft. After the first day, their experience had been of one retreat after another, as they pulled back further and further until finally they were ordered to Chartres, then Tours, headquarters of one of the Armée de l'Air's Zone of Operations. Offenberg took off with his fellow pilots unsure where Tours was or how they were going to get there. Eventually, having spotted the River Loire, they found it and landed. 'Unfortunately they did not know what to do with us there,' noted Offenberg. 'The French were not expecting us . . .' At least, though, they had survived the first week of fighting. Much of their country, however, now lay in German hands.

René de Chambrun had eventually caught up with 50th Division, part of General Alan Brooke's II Corps. The division was in reserve and preparing new defences south-west of Brussels along the River Dendre. In his role as liaison officer, he had spent much of his time interrogating downed Luftwaffe crews and suspected Fifth Columnists – supposed enemy agents spreading panic and mayhem behind the lines, even though most of that was taking place without any need for agents. Mostly, however, what he saw was a never-ending stream of refugees, including a lawyer from Louvain who had come to see him in Paris before the war. The man had been carrying a baby and a small valise. Chambrun had given him what money he could spare and had wished him luck. 'These sights on the Belgian roads,' he confessed, 'made my heart ache and I must confess that an intense feeling of discouragement began to undermine my morale.'

It was hard not to feel discouraged if you were in the Allied armies. On the 16th, orders had been given for the northern front to fall back from the Dyle to the Escaut, some forty miles further to the west, which ran roughly due south from Ghent to Cambrai in France. Many had marched to the Dyle, seen no action whatsoever, or very little, and then been told to retreat back through roads clogged with refugees. The British part of the line fell into that camp, but the problems facing the Allied command were twofold: in the north, the German Armeegruppe B had pushed ahead. Holland had fallen and the German 18. Armee was pressing south around the top of the Dyle Line. To the south of the British line, French forces had also been pushed back. In order to keep the line intact, therefore, they all had to retreat together.

The second and more threatening development was that of the

southern German thrust. Only at Stonne, a village to the south of Sedan, had the French showed much mettle. Here, the village changed hands no fewer than seventeen times between 15 and 17 May. Elsewhere, the three German panzer spearheads had continued to cut a swathe towards the coast. The chance to sever the head of this particular beast had not been taken. French units had counter-attacked but there had been no concentrated effort; it simply had not materialized. What French attacks there were had been contained and blunted. Other units, so startled to see German armoured columns thundering into town, had simply put their hands in the air. Such an eventuality had not been part of the script they had trained for. With no idea what else to do, surrender had seemed the only option. As a consequence, infantry units and even the first two Waffen-SS divisions, ill-trained but brilliantly equipped and mechanized, were able to follow on behind, mopping up and creating a wedge through the heart of France. For men like Hans von Luck, steaming across France, these were thrilling days. By 18 May, they were rolling into Cambrai. 'With our reconnaissance battalion we covered the tank advance on the left flank,' he noted, 'and were thereby involved again and again with the flood of retreating French soldiers, who in their panic mingled to a large extent with the civilian population.' Two days later, they crossed the all-important Saint-Quentin Canal, and news arrived that, on their southern flank, Guderian's men had reached Abbeville on the River Somme and were just fifteen miles from the Channel coast. They had advanced more than 250 miles in just ten days. Not in their wildest dreams had they imagined such an achievement.

It was on the following day, 21 May, that the great Allied counter-attack was due to take place. It had been instigated by the British, and General 'Tiny' Ironside, the CIGS, in particular, who had been visiting the front, both to see what was going on and to put some vigour into the Allied response. He had conceived it as a major and combined Anglo-French thrust from north and south that would drive a huge wedge through the panzers, isolate the spearhead and open up the entire battle for France once more. But on visiting Général Billotte, commander of the French First Army Group in the north, he found him moribund with depression. 'No plan, no thought of a plan,' Ironside noted in his diary. 'Ready to be slaughtered.' Billotte and his immediate subordinate, Général Blanchard, commander of the First Army, promised to do what they could, but the French Army was largely dependent on telephone wire and dispatch riders to pass on orders. Commanders like Blanchard were struggling to communicate with their forces; a dispatch rider could head out first thing in the morning and run into roads clogged with refugees. It might take the best part of the day to reach a unit and then get back again. Sometimes, he might never be seen again. Even if orders did reach division or corps headquarters, these would then have to send out orders in turn. Once those were received, the men then had to move into position. On top of that, the French Army was not designed or trained to operate with speed. Some two million people had fled their homes in the Low Countries and northern France. The populations of Tourcoing and Lille dropped from around 400,000 to just 40,000, and Rheims from 250,000 to 5,000. Add all these factors together and the inability of the French to move even comparatively small distances becomes a little more understandable, if not excusable.

In the end, only two British columns, each consisting of an infantry and armoured battalion, a battery of field artillery and anti-tank guns, and a few recce motorcycles and a handful of French tanks were all that could be mustered in time for the planned counter-attack at Arras. Crucially, there was absolutely no air support, not from the RAF or from the Armée de l'Air. Squadron Leader Darley was discovering just how impossible it was to control his fighter aircraft when phone lines were repeatedly cut and the armies retreated. 'The army retreated,' he said, 'and the first thing they left behind were the field telephones, and so our information that was getting through was nil.' Rather than a strike that would slice through the southern German thrust, the British counter-attack was more of a demonstration south from Arras and nothing more. At any rate, it soon ran out of steam and Rommel's forces, together with the rookie SS-Totenkopf, were able to regain their balance, isolate this key town, and then push on north towards Béthune.

None the less, it had shocked the Germans. As Generalmajor Rommel wrote to his wife, Lucie, about 'very powerful armoured forces' thrusting out of Arras, 'The anti-tank guns which we quickly deployed showed themselves to be far too light to be effective against the heavily armoured British tanks.' He was not alone in being impressed by the attack. 'A critical moment in the drive came just as my forces had reached the Channel,' noted Feldmarschall von Rundstedt, commander of Armeegruppe A. 'It was caused by a British counter-stroke southward from Arras on May 21. For a short time it was feared that our armoured divisions would be cut off before the infantry divisions could come up to support them. None of the French counter-attacks carried any serious threat as this one did.'

The failure of this counter-attack signalled the last hope for the northern Allied armies. The Belgian and French armies and the tiny British BEF were being corralled into a pocket – a long, increasingly narrow wedge of Flanders, crammed not only with troops and trucks and tanks and artillery pieces, but also refugees. It was a corridor of military failure and civilian misery.

Paul Reynaud was like a man in a ship that had first sprung a small leak but now had many, and although he was frantically baling out water as quickly as possible, the boat was still sinking. But a man who is drowning does not want to give up on life. Reynaud kept baling.

Daladier was finally shifted sideways, and Reynaud appointed himself Minister of National Defence and War. At the same time, he also finally sacked his *bête noire*, Gamelin, and replaced him with Général Weygand, who was recalled from Beirut. Also brought back to France from Spain, where he was Ambassador, was Maréchal Philippe Pétain, one of the great heroes of France and known to every Frenchman alive for leading the resistance and victory at Verdun, the greatest and most traumatic French battle of the last war. 'He seemed to everyone,' wrote Reynaud, 'like a living symbol of victory and honour.' Reynaud hoped these two men, with their wealth of experience, authority and determination to never surrender, would add some much-needed resolve and backbone.

Weygand arrived at General HQ at Montry on the 19th and insisted on installing himself and his staff there. Despite his age, he was a whirl-wind of energy. André Beaufre was delighted and was astonished to see the new C-in-C descend the stairs four at a time after his first lengthy briefing and go for a 100-yard dash across the lawn to freshen himself up. 'The morning he took over,' noted Beaufre, 'the whole tone of orders changed. The High Command became a dynamo of energy.'

Yet however admirable were this septuagenarian's energy levels, it still took time for him to take over, get briefed, see the front (even though he risked a plane ride to do so more quickly), assemble the senior commanders and explain the new plan. One of his first orders was to clear the roads of refugees for all but six hours a day; incredibly, no one had thought to do this up until then. But it wasn't until 21 May, as the British were thrusting south from Arras, that he briefed the Belgians,

British and his own forces at Ypres Town Hall, rebuilt since the end of the last war but about to be in the firing line again. It was perfectly obvious what needed to be done: the German southern thrust had to be severed and isolated and a continuous front re-established. Sadly, this should have happened days earlier. Weygand's plan was for the Northern Armies and the British to strike south, but it would have meant the Belgians taking over more of the northern front and ceding lots of their own territory at the same time. In any case, it was simply all too late. Most of the divisions were now battling to hold a shaky front. The French had been too exhausted to join the British at Arras and were now in even worse shape. Orders were issued – the attack would take place on 26 May – and hope was briefly rekindled at the highest quarters, but it had no chance of success. As it was, the British main supply route through Le Havre had already been cut off by the panzers, which meant they were soon going to run out of both ammunition and rations. How they were going to join a major thrust on a scale that had any chance of success in such circumstances was not clear.

Far clearer was the sudden realization in Ironside and Gort's minds that it was all over in France and that they needed to get what they could of the BEF out of there and bring them home before they were completely encircled and cut off.

Among those now in France, supporting the panzers in Armeegruppe A and hurrying across France, was Leutnant Siegfried Knappe and his 24. Artillery Battalion. Part of the follow-up forces, it had had a long trek from Cologne, as it followed the route of battle, seeing more and more carnage and destruction the closer it got to the fighting. Knappe was disturbed by the endless numbers of shell holes, destroyed buildings and dead cattle, with their stinking, bloated carcasses. 'I learned that the smell of rotting flesh, dust, burned powder, smoke and petrol was the smell of combat,' he recorded. Like so many soldiers, he also found his first sight of dead men deeply shocking. These had been French colonial troops, with mouths open and eyes still wide, limbs askew. 'It was devastating to realize this was what we had to look forward to, every day, day after day, until the war was over,' he wrote. 'We had been trained for combat, however, and we had to learn to accept the ever-present nearness of death.'

Hans von Luck was still in the vanguard of Rommel's advance, although while skirting along the La Bassée Canal looking for a crossing point, he was sniped at and hit in the hand. His pistol whirled through the air, several of his fingertips had been hit and he was bleeding profusely. It looked worse than it was, however, and soon after, with his arm in a sling and hand heavily bandaged, he was back with his men.

Rommel's men may have been still actively engaged, but those panzer divisions that had reached the coast had been forced to halt as they awaited orders. They had finally been ordered to push northwards on 21 May, much to General Guderian's relief. Ahead lay the channel ports of Boulogne, Calais and Dunkirk. Beyond them was Armeegruppe B.

Three days later and the British garrisons in Boulogne and Calais were still holding out but only just. It was at this moment, at 12.45 p.m., that Guderian received an urgent order, from Hitler himself, to halt along a line running north-west of Arras to Gravelines, just south of Dunkirk. Guderian was speechless. Momentum was with them – another day and they could close the ring entirely.

So too was General Halder, who had already countermanded such an order from von Rundstedt, recognizing that it was, in the circumstances, the wrong decision. Von Rundstedt had then taken this to the OKW, who had referred it to Hitler, who had then supported the original decision to halt and overruled Halder and the authority of von Brauchitsch, the Army C-in-C.

In Berlin, General Walter Warlimont had heard about it through the Army and was equally flabbergasted. It seemed to him to be entirely incomprehensible. He immediately hurried to see Jodl and find out what on earth was going on and learned that Keitel and Hitler had agreed that the coastal region in Flanders was too marshy for tanks, while Göring had assured them his Luftwaffe could finish off the encirclement. 'This being the state of affairs,' noted Warlimont, 'it soon became clear that it was entirely useless for me to emphasize that I had spent many holidays on the Belgian coast in the years before the war and therefore had personal knowledge of the fact that the terrain in Flanders had altered considerably since 1918.' He also expressed his doubts about Göring's boast, but this had no impact either.

At any rate, British intelligence picked up the details of the order and it was passed on to Gort's headquarters. Gort, no intellectual, but a man unafraid of tough decisions, now made one of his toughest. It was time to try and get the BEF home.

CHAPTER 23

Britain's Darkest Hour

Back in April the previous year, President Roosevelt managed to get Congress to finally pass the Administrative Reorganization Act after two years of wrangling. Its name suggested it was little more than a dull piece of governmental bureaucracy, but actually it was something altogether more radical. Under this Act, lots of Government agencies and bureaus, previously under the oversight of Congress, were moved under the authority of a newly created Executive Office of the President. Among those shifted under White House control were the Army–Navy Munitions Board, the Joint Chiefs of Staff, the Bureau of the Budget and the National Resources Planning Board. Also included in the terms of the Act was the Office of Emergency Management (OEM), which gave provision for the President to set up a new and special agency to deal with defence or any other emergency under his direct authority.

The significance of this act was not felt immediately, but Congress had, in fact, given the President enormous new powers to lead the US without consulting with either his administration or Congress. In other words, he could choose specific men to do specific tasks for the nation without challenge. It was hardly democratic but it not only suited Roosevelt's leadership and management style, it also ensured a far more focused and less fractious way of managing the proposed rearming of America.

For more than a year after the Act was passed, Roosevelt had not called upon the Office of Emergency Management, but now, on 25 May, he did. He planned to use it as the hub for other organizations, not least the National Defense Advisory Commission (NDAC). His idea was to gather together a group of industrialists and businessmen, rather than politicians, just as General Marshall had suggested, to advise on how best to make a massive and rapid expansion of the US's armed forces and defences.

But who were the right people for this new advisory committee? Roosevelt had conferred with Bernard Baruch, a hugely successful financier and long-time political advisor of both President Wilson and FDR. During the last war, Baruch had chaired the War Industries Board and very successfully too. Aged seventy in 1940, he was happier playing the elder statesman and being a sounding board than taking on an active position, but as an ardent interventionist he was only too happy to suggest names to the President.

In fact, it had been just one name. 'First, Knudsen,' he had told FDR, 'second, Knudsen; third, Knudsen.'

Bill Knudsen was the President of General Motors and was quite simply a giant of the automobile industry. He was physically pretty big too, standing at six foot four inches, with broad shoulders, a mop of neatly combed silver hair and matching moustache. Gentle and kindly-looking, he was a highly moral and honourable man, but also an extremely tough, determined and brilliant businessman and a superb engineer.

Born in Denmark in 1879, he had emigrated, aged twenty, in 1900, and on arriving in New York had worked first in shipbuilding, then repairing railway locomotives, before landing a job building bicycles in Buffalo for John R. Keim. However, Keim was switching to making steam engines, so Knudsen began building those instead and in the process learned about the importance of machine tools and how to build them.

A machine tool was a name that could be applied to any machine that could cut metal into identical shapes. It could do this in a number of ways, whether by drilling holes and shapes, turning like a lathe, grinding or cutting, or shearing and pressing. It was machine tools that could drill lumps of metal into engine blocks or turn and stamp pistons, and could press sheets of metal to make car doors, for example. Machine tools, of course, had to be made in the first place and were both incredibly complicated and time-consuming to construct, and had to be custom-made, so they were incredibly expensive. But once done, as Bill Knudsen realized during his time with Keim, these bespoke, intricate tools then made mass production possible. They were, in fact, the backbone of mass production and in turn warfare. This meant the machine-tool-makers themselves were the key to the machine age. And they were a rare and very specialized breed.

While at Keim, Knudsen developed a new type of alloy and began an assembly line making steel axle housings for Henry Ford's burgeoning motor car business in Detroit. Ford later bought Keim outright, and Knudsen was given the task of speeding up production. He concluded that the key to mass production was not speed per se, but rather creating a continuous and linear sequence that ensured every part could be fitted precisely where and when it was needed. 'Everything,' he said, 'depends upon the sequence of an operation and the flow of material.' Costs could be kept down not by cutting corners on materials but by economies of scale and by reducing the number and complexity of parts. Simplicity of both parts and construction was key. The less complex the parts, the easier they were to make, and the easier they were to make, the less the cost. The less the cost, the greater the demand for the end product.

Just as crucial was accuracy – each different part had to be exactly the same. Knudsen banned all files and hammers – if a part didn't fit, it would be sent back. 'Accuracy,' he said, 'is the only straight line in production.'

These factors were what made the Model T the first mass-produced car of the machine age. Until then, automobiles had been a luxury item of the privileged few. The Model T put cars in reach of the common man. What Knudsen had achieved for Ford was the creation of a simple production line, and one that could be readily replicated. To make a Ford car did not require vast numbers of skilled workers – it required men to assemble the bits in a simple and efficient way. This meant it was easy to set up branch factories – one factory was just like another – which were based on the principle of laying out the machinery first, then working out the flow of material, and then building the factory around it. By 1916, Ford had no fewer than twenty-eight branch factories.

Where Knudsen and Henry Ford began to diverge was over the patriarch's continued insistence that one model of car was enough. Knudsen believed that the way to sell more cars was not to keep churning out exactly the same automobile but to make punters feel dissatisfied with their current car and want better. In 1921, he left Ford and moved to General Motors, a failing company that had bought up many smaller businesses such as Buick, Pontiac, Oakland and Chevrolet. It was Chevrolet, almost finished as a car manufacturer, that Knudsen was brought in to save. And save it he did. Using the principles of the assembly line, he developed what became known as 'flexible mass production' – that is, one that enabled easy modification and change. This he did by discarding single-purpose machine tools and bringing in new ones that could be adapted to making different shapes and designs. Model Ts had been outselling Chevys at thirteen to one, but the 1926 Chevrolet cut that advantage to two to one. The 1927 Chevy did even better, selling over a million cars and forcing Ford to finally abandon the Model T.

Bigger, better, faster, more comfortable Chevys continued to appear every year, so that by 1931 Chevrolet was finally outselling Ford. Knudsen had proved that it was possible to introduce new products swiftly in response to new technology or changing demands without interrupting the flow of production. By 1937, he was President of General Motors, the biggest car manufacturer in the world. The point was, the principles he had applied to the production of automobiles could just as easily be applied to tanks and aircraft, as Bernard Baruch was well aware. This was why he had recommended to Roosevelt that he call up Bill Knudsen without delay.

Sure enough, Roosevelt duly rang Knudsen at GM and personally invited him to come to Washington on Wednesday, 29 May. He was met at the White House by Harry Hopkins, who told him in a hushed and conspiratorial tone, 'Mr Knudsen, the President has asked me to tell you that we can't pay you anything, and he wants you to get a leave of absence from your company.'

'I don't expect a pay check,' Knudsen told him. As far as he was concerned, America had been good to him, he had enough money in the bank, and he was more than willing to step down from GM to do his bit for his adopted country.

At the subsequent meeting, Knudsen met the six other people Roosevelt had assembled, all of whom had a specific role to play. Among them were Edward R. Stettinius Jr, for example, the Chairman of the United States Steel Corporation, who was to oversee the steady flow of raw materials, and Sidney Hillman, President of the Amalgamated Clothing Workers of America, who was to head a division that would train apprentices for non-combat duties from airfield ground crews to camp cooks. Among the others were Chester C. Davis, the Defense Commissioner for Agriculture and a highly able administrator, brought in to help ensure there was no conflict between agricultural and defence policies, and Ralph Budd, Chair of the Chicago, Burlington & Quincy Railroad, to advise on all transportation problems and prevent bottlenecks. Knudsen's task was to manage and advise all industrial manufacture of tanks, aircraft, engines, uniforms and other key war materiel. Only he, Stettinius and Hillman would be working full time.

Roosevelt had formed the National Defense Advisory Commission to kick-start industrial mobilization without Congress, politics and red tape getting in the way, but it was clear during that first meeting that its workings had not yet been thought through. This was hardly surprising, though, as the President had only decided on its formation a few days earlier. When Knudsen asked who was in overall charge, the President replied with a laugh, 'I guess I am.' After vaguely outlining his thoughts, the meeting ended with the promise that they would reconvene in a fortnight. The term 'advisory' was, however, clearly something of a misnomer. FDR didn't want these men advising. He wanted them – and Knudsen, Stettinius and Hillman especially – heading their new divisions, or departments, within the committee. The trouble was, the authority for them to do so was rather vague.

Knudsen left the meeting and returned to Detroit for one last weekend at home thinking long and hard about just what it was he was being asked to do and how he was going to do it.

In France, René de Chambrun had returned to the headquarters of the Corps of Liaison Officers near Hazebrouck on the morning of 26 May, and reported to his boss, Colonel de Cardes. They were now completely surrounded.

'You are to try and get to Paris,' Cardes told him. 'I know it will not be an easy job, but these documents must not fall into enemy hands, and I want them to be at our headquarters as soon as possible.' The only way for him to get there, Cardes explained, was to take a ship to England from Dunkirk and then to fly to Paris. Having hastily scribbled a note for his wife, he gave the pile of documents to Chambrun and told him not to waste any time.

Hurrying to Général Blanchard's headquarters nearby, he found a staff chauffeur prepared to take him to Dunkirk and off they went, dodging marauding Stukas all the way.

Meanwhile, the 6th Green Howards were also making their way to Dunkirk. Private Bill Cheall was not happy. He was hungry, no one seemed to know what the hell was going on, and none of them had enough weapons or ammunition. In fact, he reckoned he and his pals had had a pretty rough ride since arriving in March. Having joined his TA battalion, the 6th Green Howards, just before the outbreak of war, they had been given, as TA rather than Regular Army, very basic training indeed, with no real weapons training or tactical instruction. It had been intended that this would come in the fullness of time once the Army began to grow. When they were sent to France, it was as a labour battalion, and Cheall had taken a very poor view of their first task, which had been building latrines. Relief had come from his company commander, Major Petch, who asked him to become his batman – his soldier-servant. 'I was a little browned off with unsoldierly work,' admitted Cheall, 'so I said yes.'

Then suddenly, with the German onslaught underway, they had been ordered forward and by 22 May were holding a stretch of the line along the River Scarpe to the east of Arras, still armed with only their rifles and now officially on active service, although the part where they were trained how to fight had never actually happened. They were not there long before being ordered north-west. Bombed on Vimy Ridge, where British, French and Canadians had fought the Germans a generation earlier, they then both marched and were later entrucked up to the coast, where they took up new positions along the River Aa, around Gravelines, on the morning of 23 May. They hadn't slept a wink for two days and now on half-rations were ferociously hungry too. They had soon found them-selves in the thick of the fighting, firing at German panzers with Boyes anti-tank rifles none of them had ever used before. Here they had lost 'some good boys' but, to their credit, had seen off their attackers.

Then came the order to evacuate their position around Gravelines and fall back to the town of Bergues, just a few miles from Dunkirk. This was soon countermanded and they were sent to Haeghe Meulen, a few miles to the east of Bergues. Here they were to protect the perimeter around Dunkirk as the rest of the BEF retreated to the port. Given better weapons and plenty of ammunition, Cheall and his mates were none the less keenly aware how undertrained they were. 'But we were determined to give as good as we got,' he noted, 'and show the Jerries that we were not going to be a walkover.'

Also retreating were Capitaine Barlone and his Horse Transport Company attached to 2nd North African Division. There was no news, there were no newspapers and there was no wireless radio, but there were plenty of rumours, one of which was now confirmed – that the Germans had reached the Channel coast. 'So we are encircled!' he scribbled in his diary. 'It's flabbergasting!' Two days later, he received orders to retreat to Dunkirk, moving 15–25 miles by night. Everyone was pulling back, it seemed, including Lieutenant Norman Field and the 2nd Royal Fusiliers. They had been in France since the previous autumn, but also part of III Corps, their division, the 4th Infantry, had been in reserve during the BEF's move to the Dyle Line, and they had been based in Mouvaux, between Lille and Tourcoing. Apart from taking potshots at aircraft, they had barely seen any action at all but were part of the northern British line holding the German 6. Armee at bay. He didn't have much idea what was going on. 'We would have a few skirmishes with the Germans until we were told to withdraw again,' he says. 'It was all very peculiar and frightening. We didn't know what the next day would bring.'

Nor did General Gort, although he had warned London that it was likely most of the BEF and its equipment would be left behind in France, despite the evacuation order. In fact, RAF squadrons had been returning to England for some days, replaced by squadrons flying from the UK, while the 'useless mouths' – the wounded, sick and all non-combat troops – had evacuated through the Channel ports as early as 19 May, the same day warning had been given to the Director of Military Operations and Plans at the War Office to start considering an evacuation. Three days later, more advanced preparations were underway at the Admiralty for what was to be called Operation DYNAMO.

Boulogne had been evacuated on 23 May. One of those heading back to England through the port was Squadron Leader George Darley; much of the Air Component were already heading home, and, unable to even remotely keep an Operations Room functioning, he had been recalled. Boulogne surrendered two days later; Calais was still holding out, but it clearly would not be long before the British-held port was forced to surrender too. That left just Dunkirk, and it was from here that the evacuation of the BEF, or whatever small proportion was lifted off, would take place. With the co-operation of Général Blanchard, the French First Army commander, who seems to have stoically accepted the inevitable, Gort worked out an agreed plan. On the night of 26–27 May, British I and II Corps would leave a rearguard then fall back into the main central corridor. Blanchard's men would extend the line. The following night, the mass of the BEF would fall back again, behind another river line – the idea was to fight by day and fall back by night. Meanwhile, a perimeter, five miles inland and following a canal that ran all the way to Nieuport, twelve miles to the east, would be prepared. This was where Bill Cheall and his mates were now getting ready. There were not enough men to man a continuous line along the southern flank, so instead troops would defend highpoints, villages and towns. The idea was that these would keep the Germans along the southern flank of the corridor busy for long enough to allow the bulk of the BEF, both men and machinery, to reach Dunkirk. No one, however, including Gort, was very optimistic that DYNAMO would be a success.

On Saturday, 25 May, Edward Spears flew by Blenheim to Paris, as Churchill's special emissary. He was to be liaison officer to Paul Reynaud, and as he flew over Normandy on that perfect early summer's morning, he thought it had never looked lovelier or more somnolent. Safely reaching Paris, he hurried to the Quai D'Orsay, met Reynaud and was then ushered into his study to meet other members of the Comité de Guerre, including the new C-in-C, Général Weygand, Amiral Darlan and the Maréchal of France himself, Pétain.

During their talks, at no point had Spears been given the impression all was lost; clearly, the Northern Armies were in grave peril but the idea that France was about to collapse entirely still seemed, to him at any rate, remote. And then they were interrupted by an officer from Blanchard's Army Group HQ. Spears listened with mounting shock as Commandant Fauvelle began to make his report. 'As I realized that his catastrophic defeatism seemed to some extent at least to be accepted as the reflection of the real position,' he noted, 'I felt cold fingers turning my heart to stone. I have in my time seen broken men, but never before one deliquescent, that is, in a state where he was fit only to be scraped up with a spoon or mopped up.'

Spears listened, appalled, as Weygand and Fauvelle continued discussing the situation until, with exasperation, Weygand lifted his hands and said, 'This war is sheer madness! We have gone to war with a 1918 army against a German army of 1939!'

The discussions continued. A new chain of command was agreed. It was also accepted there was now no chance of saving the Northern Armies from the south – they were doomed. But Weygand vowed to fight on, come what may. Before leaving, however, Spears asked why on earth nothing had been done to stop German armoured columns running

amok through France. Why, he asked, had roadblocks not been organized, with 75mm guns placed on lorries? A simple order to civilians to
telephone ahead the direction these columns were heading would have
made such preparations possible. Bridges could be blown. How hard
could it be?

'A very interesting idea,' Weygand replied. 'I will consider it.'

Monday, 27 May, was to prove to be one of Britain's most perilous days in
its entire history. The night before, following a day of National Prayer at
home called for by King George VI, Operation DYNAMO was put into
effect on Sunday evening, 26 May, under the control of Vice-Admiral
Bertram Ramsay from Dover. Naval and auxiliary naval vessels, channel
steamers and a host of 'little ships' – small, privately owned vessels – had
been called upon to carry out the hazardous evacuation. Because of
minefields, the route was also much longer than it might have normally
been.

Yet it was not the chances of the evacuation that were the concern that
day, but the development of a potentially catastrophic split in the War
Cabinet – one that could yet see Britain capitulate.

During the first Cabinet meeting the previous day, Lord Halifax, the
most respected politician in Britain, the country's Foreign Minister, a
man whose very name was a byword for good sense and pragmatism, had
not only accepted that the Nazis were now militarily unbeatable, but that
Britain should, via Italian intermediaries, explore the possibility of peace
talks.

Winston Churchill, the new Prime Minster, whose judgement was
widely held to be questionable, and who to many people was little more
than a romantic old soak, thought this was tantamount to suicide. He was
insisting Britain should never accept Nazi domination of Europe, that
Britain and its Empire and Dominions should never even think about
entering into talks because to do so would inevitably mean agreeing to
terms that would affect their complete liberty and independence, which,
to his mind, was utterly unacceptable.

The discussion was not resolved then, because there was the service of
National Prayer in Westminster Abbey followed by a visit from Paul
Reynaud. At the next Cabinet that Sunday, Halifax had been more bullish,
unable to understand what harm there was in putting out feelers. Churchill
replied that even to do that, to give the Germans a whiff of the possibility

of suing for terms, would be a catastrophic sign of weakness that would send a terrible message to the entire world. The discussion became heated between the two, while the other three listened but added little. Churchill was keenly aware that if they sided with Halifax, he would be obliged to go along with them or resign, which amounted to the same thing. 'Herr Hitler has the whip hand,' Churchill told them. 'The only thing to do is to show him that he cannot conquer this country.'

With no resolution in sight, Churchill ended the meeting that day with vague agreements that Halifax should pursue possible means of an approach to the Italians, but clearly had no intention of letting anything of the sort occur. But it was late, and they needed clearer heads. The following morning, however, it would have to be thrashed out once and for all. Later, after dining with Anthony Eden, his new Minister for War, he confessed to feeling physically sick with anxiety.

So Monday, 27 May, dawned. Ironically, the battle to decide Britain's future lay in Whitehall, not Flanders. Churchill understood that the key figure was Chamberlain. The two new Labour men, Attlee and Greenwood, did not have the influence to decide this issue, but the former PM most certainly did. Naturally, Chamberlain would be most likely to side with Halifax. He was, in fact, not at all well and was suffering from cancer, although it had not yet been diagnosed, but he had loyally and tirelessly served his replacement since his forced resignation.

Not until the afternoon Cabinet meeting did the question of sending peace feelers raise itself. Halifax had drafted a letter to Mussolini, which he read out. When Churchill again underlined the dangers of going down this route, Halifax, normally so calm and measured, lost his temper. He simply could not understand the harm in making overtures. The argument rambled on, with Halifax eventually threatening his resignation, an act that would very likely bring down the Government at the worst possible moment. He stormed out into the garden at No. 10, Churchill following, doing his best to calm him.

News later arrived that Belgium had surrendered – it had been inevitable, but their doing so left a huge hole in the line that threatened the withdrawal of the BEF. The last Cabinet meeting of the day dealt with the implications of this latest piece of bad news. And fewer than 8,000 troops of the BEF out of some half a million in France had been lifted off on the first day of the evacuation. Britain, too, now stood on the brink.

*

That night, Lieutenant Norman Field, as Battalion Adjutant, was heavily involved in moving his battalion back yet again, this time behind the River Lys. Vehicles arrived in the rain at around 11 p.m. and the move got underway. Meanwhile, 3rd Division, at the end of II Corps's line, had to move behind 4th and 5th Divisions and fill the hole left by the Belgians on the corps's left flank. It meant travelling the entire division some fifty miles, yet by morning, under the careful eye of their commander, Major-General Bernard Montgomery, they managed it. Operationally, it was a superb achievement which gave the BEF a small, but crucial, breathing space.

Back in London, Churchill and Chamberlain had talked man-to-man, each expressing his loyalty to the other. Churchill was conscious that at no point had Chamberlain spoken for Halifax's view and sensed he now had the crucial support he needed. Later, the PM addressed the wider Cabinet, telling them that despite the terrible news from France, and despite the fact that the Germans would undoubtedly soon turn their attentions to Britain and look to invade, such an operation would be very difficult for them and it was far better for Britain to fight it out. At this there was only approval and no dissent.

With Chamberlain behind him and also the wider Cabinet, at the next War Cabinet meeting, that evening, Churchill ruthlessly dismissed any further talk of peace talks. There would be none. Halifax, beaten, raised no further objection. The crisis was over, never to be mentioned again.

Britain would fight on.

CHAPTER 24

Getting Away

F ROM THE MOMENT Churchill won his personal battle with Halifax, Britain's fortunes took a perceptible turn for the better. There was no getting away from the scale of defeat in France, but although Hitler's halt order had been lifted on the afternoon of 26 May, the BEF's gradual retreat to the Dunkirk perimeter had worked and the perimeter itself was holding. The land round about was perfectly dry, but it was flat as a board, advancing panzers could be seen for miles, and the area was riddled with canals and dykes that were impassable to tanks. All the BEF was inside the perimeter by 30 May, and all bridges were blown. What the Germans discovered was that it was a slow and difficult business budging an enemy that was well dug in and determined not to be budged.

Among those trying hard not to budge were Bill Cheall and his comrades in the 6th Green Howards. Bill reckoned morale was good after their encouraging brush with the enemy at Gravelines, and he, for one, had faith in their officers. On the 29th, their positions were in the process of being taken over by the Welsh Guards when they were attacked and almost an entire platoon in D Company killed. However, the attack was successfully beaten off and the men were ordered to head for the beaches.

As they neared them, the degree of destruction increased. A huge pall of black smoke hung over the town from the oil depots which had been hit by bombs, but there were burning vehicles and thousands more abandoned, and bodies, both troops and civilians, were lying unburied. Dead livestock lay bloated, while packs of dogs, mad and feral, scavenged greedily. Above them, somewhere beyond the pall, the sound of aircraft could be heard, while all around them guns boomed and small arms chattered and rang out.

They reached the promenade at Bray-Dunes, then walked along until they were among the dunes and clambered down on to the beach. They had been told to congregate at the 23rd Division assembly point, but they couldn't find it and suddenly no one knew what to do for the best, so they stood about, waiting, hoping, until darkness came. The following morning, they were finally told to head to Dunkirk itself, a few miles along the beach. As they were trudging along, a German fighter swooped down low, machine-gunning. They fired their rifles, but without success.

Eventually, they reached the East Mole. This was a narrow wooden pier which had not been hit by the Germans and lay directly under the pall of smoke. It had initially been thought it would not be strong enough to take ships, but early on the 28th a destroyer had pulled alongside it successfully and since then it had been in constant use. As a result, the numbers of men lifted off had dramatically increased. One bomb had hit it but not exploded, going straight through and out the other side. Planks had been strung across the hole. It was another stroke of luck. At last, Cheall stepped aboard a ferry, called *The Lady of the Mann*. At around six o'clock on 31 May, the boat slipped its moorings and set sail for England.

Also getting away were thousands of French troops, including Capitaine Barlone. By 29 May, he had lost all contact with division headquarters but was still with some of the fighting units. The 13th Rifles had been fighting, but only had 500 men left and most of the officers had been killed. It was a similar story for the 22nd Rifles, but Barlone was impressed with the way the NCOs were holding the men together. Despite the immense congestion, despite artillery fire, and despite being knocked by a horse himself, they trudged on towards Dunkirk. 'At some distance we see a soldier who appears to be quietly sitting in the road leaning on a sack,' he noted. 'The unfortunate fellow has had half his head blown away – a body crowned with an awful mass of mangled flesh.'

They reached Bray-Dunes and carried out a head count: there were just 1,250 men. 'That is all that remains of our fine North African Division of 18,000 men,' he scribbled. 'The rest: killed, wounded, prisoners, missing.' They made their way to the town, took shelter in bombed-out buildings as more and more German shells came crashing over, then at around 9 p.m. received orders to head for the Mole. Smoke filled the air, above planes were still circling, then sticks of bombs began falling. They fell flat on the ground, then picked themselves up again and dusted themselves down, although four of Barlone's men were killed and others wounded. It seemed they weren't ready to embark just yet, so they took shelter in the dunes until finally they were called back and at three o'clock in the morning on the 31st they boarded two ships, the *Keremah* and the *Hebe*, Barlone getting on the latter. By noon that day, 165,000 men had been successfully lifted off. It was already many, many more than had been feared a few days earlier.

Norman Field and the 2nd Royal Fusiliers were among those still defending the perimeter. Their positions were on the eastern edge, just west of Nieuport. There was no sign of any enemy troops, but the shelling was getting worse and worse. At one point, one of the most popular men in the battalion, Captain Malcolm Blair, who had been missing, turned up along with some others, giving them all a much-needed morale boost. A few hours later, however, he was dead, killed instantly by a direct shell blast. 'Tears came to my eyes,' admitted Field. 'It was bloody awful.'

Meanwhile, René de Chambrun had successfully made it back to Paris after his long, round-about trip via boat from Dunkirk to England and then by plane back to France. Having hurried to Vincennes and safely delivered the papers for Général Weygand, he had hastened to his home in the Place du Palais Bourbon. Every time he had felt in any real danger during these past weeks, he had immediately thought of his wife and wondered whether he would ever see her again, so it was an enormous relief to discover she was there. She was every bit as relieved to see him; she'd not received one of his letters and had had no idea whether he was even still alive. 'I believe that my unexpected return to Paris,' he wrote, 'was the happiest moment in our lives.'

No sooner had he walked through the door, however, than his wife was rung by William Bullitt, the US Ambassador. When she explained her husband had just arrived, he asked to speak to him and invited him to the embassy for a talk. Chambrun duly did as he was asked, and after he had given an account of what had been going on as he had seen it, Bullitt suggested he might go to Washington to talk to the President.

Early the next morning, 2 June, Chambrun answered the telephone to discover one of Weygand's aides-de-camp on the line, ordering him to report to the general at seven o'clock that evening. He added that

Chambrun should be ready to take the first Clipper and fly to the United States.

Meanwhile, at Dunkirk, it was not until late on the 31st that the Royal Fusiliers had finally received orders to pull back to La Panne on the coast; their part of the perimeter was being abandoned. Only 150 men survived from the 800-strong battalion, and under cover of darkness, and having immobilized their remaining vehicles by wrecking the engines, they headed off. On reaching the beach, they saw the evacuation taking place directly off the sands, but they soon came under fire once more. Field took cover in a broken house but was hit by a piece of white-hot shrapnel in his hand. 'I realized I'd been clobbered,' he said, 'but I didn't feel a thing, not then.' The shelling halted the evacuation, but there were around 7,000 men from the 3rd and 4th Divisions on the beach at La Panne. The intense barrage eventually stopped, and the evacuation began once more. With his wounded hand, Field was lucky enough to be put on a canvas rowing boat and ferried on to a minesweeper, HMS *Speedwell*. He fell asleep almost immediately, to be woken by the violent zig-zagging of the ship and the sound of crashing bombs. 'We were being dive-bombed by eight Stukas,' he recalled. 'They missed us. All I could see out of the corner of my eye were the spikes of water going up as some bombs landed in the sea only ten or fifteen yards away. Very scary.'

A handful of British and French battalions continued to successfully hold the bulk of the perimeter against four German divisions. Again, they were showing what determined defence in a good position could achieve, and that these comparatively few men, so outnumbered, held out so long was proving just what could and should have been achieved at Sedan and Dinant and Monthermé.

All senior British officers had now left. Commanding the rearguard was Major-General Harold Alexander, late of the Irish Guards and for much of the campaign commander of I Corps. Surely one of the most phlegmatic, calm and measured men in the British Army, he also happened to be one of the most experienced. Alexander was forty-nine, debonair and a much-decorated hero of the last war. He also had the unique qualification of having commanded men in combat at every level of rank up to major-general, including Germans, when, following the end of the Great War, he had been asked to command the Baltic Landwehr in Latvia against the Russians. He was fluent in seven languages, including, naturally, French, was amusing and self-effacing, and was in every way the ideal man to guide the final stages of the evacuation. Working together with the French Amiral Jean-Marie Abrial, he decided to continue the evacuation through the night of 2–3 June and try and lift all the remaining men. By this time, the perimeter had shrunk and it was now only the French who were making a last-ditch stand as German troops finally crept within spitting distance of the town. By that last night, there were just 30,000 French and 5,000 Tommies remaining. Naval demolition parties blew what remained of the port during the day while by darkness Vice-Admiral Ramsay back in Dover had assembled a mixed ensemble of some twenty-four destroyers and personnel ships and a host of further minesweepers and other vessels. The first troops began embarking at 9 p.m., with the harbour already being shelled by German guns. Burning fires didn't help, but still the Mole had not been hit – or rather, had not been put out of action. At around 11.30 p.m., Alexander and his Senior Naval Officer boarded a motor launch and sped down the length of the beach calling out for any stragglers. Satisfied they had now got the lot, Alexander sent one last signal: 'BEF evacuated. Returning now', and set sail for home. Operation DYNAMO was over, and some 338,000 troops, including nearly 140,000 French, had been safely lifted and taken back to England to fight another day. It was almost as much a miracle as the scale of the German victory.

The Italian leadership in Rome had been watching the events in France and the Low Countries intently, and by the last week of May Mussolini had decided the time had at last come to intervene and enter the war on the side of their Axis partner. The decision had been prompted not only by the sweeping gains made by the Germans but also by the increasingly desperate diplomatic offers made by the French, whose ambassador, André François-Poncet, was reeling off names of French possessions in Africa they would be willing to barter in order for Italy to keep out of the war. Indeed, much of Reynaud's visit to London had been taken up with what Britain and France might jointly offer Italy. Very reluctantly, Churchill had even agreed to Reynaud's suggestion to ask President Roosevelt to contact Mussolini and suggest both Britain and France were ready to barter both possessions and economically in return for Italy staying out. Roosevelt did as he was asked, but his ambassador in Rome was given short shrift. It was too late, Ciano told him. Italy was now set on war.

Mussolini had rejected the last-ditch overtures safe in the knowledge that France believed itself to be finished – which meant, to all intents and purposes, she *was* finished. Britain was still talking tough, but its Army had been defeated and humiliated and over 85,000 vehicles and more than 2,500 artillery pieces had been left behind on the Continent. Many of its men had been rescued, but what would they fight with now? Surely, Mussolini gambled, Britain would follow France. Before long, both would be suing for peace. Even if Britain didn't, it would be so weakened that even Italy would be able to take it on and win.

Mussolini did not want to miss out. Egypt, he knew, was lightly defended. If he could take Cairo and the Suez Canal, the sea link with his East African possessions would be open once more. Libya could be joined at the hip to Egypt, Egypt to Sudan, Sudan to Abyssinia. He wanted a north-east African colonial empire. Furthermore, through the Canal, Italy could access the world's oceans.

On the other hand, if he left it until both Britain and France were beaten, then Germany, not Italy, would have claim to Egypt and the Suez Canal, and that was not worth thinking about. To earn his place at the peace table, and to have his chance to take Egypt, he needed to strike soon and delay no longer.

His generals were as unenthusiastic as ever, but he fobbed them off with talk of going on the defensive and using the opening stages of the war to attack British naval bases using naval and air power only. The importance of maintaining influence was the reason he gave them for declaring war – a line they appear to have swallowed. Certainly Badoglio, the Chief of Staff, did. The Duce also secured new authority over the armed services from a reluctant King Vittorio Emanuele.

Count Ciano had broadly come round to Mussolini's line of thinking, although he was concerned by the British stance. 'A painful conference with Sir Percy Loraine,' he noted on 28 May.

The British Ambassador was unequivocal: 'We shall answer war with war,' Loraine told him bluntly, 'but, notwithstanding this, my heart is filled with sadness to think that blood must flow between our countries.' Ciano replied that it was sad for him too, but he could see no other way out.

Ciano's comment revealed the dilemma Italy faced. Mussolini's ambition was both for Italy to be a great power but also for a reconstructed and peaceful Europe in which Fascism dominated. He wanted Italy to grow and develop, but the country was resource-poor, its industry under-developed compared with Germany, Britain and France, and agriculture was still the biggest employer, accounting for around 47 per cent of the workforce. At the same time, the population was growing; it was around forty-three million, a little larger than France and some four million smaller than Britain, but with much less living space. Overseas expansion was a means of solving this problem, as well as offering potentially vast economically exploitable territory. In any case, a country, and indeed regime, was simply not going to be taken seriously as a world power without imperial possessions. So for Mussolini there were a number of very good reasons to try and create a new Roman empire.

Mussolini had also enjoyed playing the role of arbitrator at Munich nearly two years earlier and had set himself up to play a similar role the previous summer. War had changed all that. The British blockade was hurting too. On the other hand, if Germany beat France and dominated all of Europe, not only would Italy's influence dwindle but the country would become an irrelevance and possibly even a vassal Nazi state, which would be disastrous for both him and the regime.

Therefore Mussolini felt he had no choice but to actively enter the war, and to do so before the fighting was over. His armed forces were not ready, it was true, but with France all but beaten, and Britain, he hoped, sure to sue for peace too, this would not matter. He viewed Hitler and the Nazis as allies, but his war would be a parallel one for dominance in the Mediterranean and African sphere. In other words, if Italy stayed out of the war, the regime would be finished; but if it entered the war, albeit without being remotely ready, there was a good chance it could gain much for not a huge amount. It was, however, a risk, as Ciano was all too well aware.

Events in the West had brought Mussolini's plans forward, and after negotiations with Hitler over the precise date, Monday, 10 June, was agreed upon as the day for Italy's entry into the war.

'The decision has been taken,' Ciano wrote on 30 May. 'The die is cast.'

In their appreciation of 29 May, Britain's Chiefs of Staff had warned that there was a good chance that the Germans would stabilize the front in France and concentrate right away on a major assault on Britain. This, of course, was a report tinged with panic and mostly drawn up during the dark early days of the Dunkirk evacuation. Clearer, calmer heads may well have realized that the logistics of bringing up air forces to the Channel coast, reorganizing a weary Army and gathering together enough shipping for an invasion would mean no such thing could happen in the short term, and to leave France, now on its knees and waiting for the executioner's axe to swing, with the chance to regroup, made no logical sense whatsoever. Be that as it may, the country was to be brought to a state of high alert.

Already, on 14 May, Anthony Eden, the Secretary of State for War, had called for men aged seventeen to sixty to form a new force of 'Local Defence Volunteers'. They would be organized and armed and expected to help defend the country in the event of a German invasion. Some quarter of a million volunteered within a week, including the Wiltshire farmer A. G. Street. Beaches, normally just readying themselves for a summer of holidaying, were mined and strewn with barbed wire, and signposts were taken down. Pillboxes were built along the coast, by rivers and at road junctions in huge numbers. New batteries of guns and searchlights were also put in place along the south coast.

From her flat in Hampstead, Gwladys Cox had been following events on the Continent. London, she thought, was now 'curiously calm', although the city seemed quieter. 'The theatres,' she noted, 'partly on account of the black-out, partly through fear of air-raids, are not booming as in the last war – that was a soldiers' war; this, we know, is a civilians' war as well.'

On 4 June, the Prime Minister addressed the House of Commons, warning them that while the evacuation of Dunkirk had been a 'miracle of deliverance', it was still a terrible defeat. Watching was Jock Colville, whose earlier grave concerns about Churchill's suitability to lead the country were rapidly melting away. So impressed was he by the speech, he even copied out a long extract for his diary. Later it was broadcast to the nation too and around the entire free world. 'Even though large tracts of Europe have fallen into the grip of the Gestapo, and all the odious apparatus of Nazi rule, we shall not flag or fail,' Churchill told them. 'We shall go on to the end. We shall fight in France. We shall fight on the seas and oceans. We shall fight with growing strength in the air. We shall defend our island, whatever the cost may be. We shall fight on the beaches. We shall fight on the landing grounds, we shall fight in the fields and in the streets, we shall fight in the hills; we shall never surrender.'

The speech sent out an important message of British intent and served as a rallying cry for the entire free world. Rhetoric like this was priceless. Even so, there was one place they would not be fighting the Germans for much longer, and that was Norway, where the decision had now been made, with the French, to evacuate Narvik, the last Allied bastion there. Narvik – the most important objective for the Allies – had been captured, with the German mountain troops there successfully pushed back. It was the one part of the land campaign that had actually witnessed an Allied victory. However, with disaster unfolding in France, sustaining Narvik was no longer a priority. The Allies were getting rather good at evacuating troops and a clean and swift operation to pick up the 24,500 troops from this northern Norwegian port was put in place and began on 4 June. Three days later, it was complete.

It was not, however, the end of the battle for Norway. Mirroring the opening of the campaign, German naval vessels were steaming towards the Leads at the same time, and unobserved. The idea had been Admiral Raeder's, who was given consent by Hitler to mount an attack on British shipping protecting the entrance to Narvik as a means of relieving the pressure on the mountain troops stranded there.

While Allied troops had been lifted from Narvik without the Germans knowing, so Raeder's force had slipped out of Kiel and into the North Sea without detection. All the Kriegsmarine's remaining heavy warships were now at sea: just two battle cruisers, one heavy cruiser, four destroyers and two torpedo boats. One of those battle cruisers, the *Scharnhorst*, was an enormous vessel not much smaller than the *Bismarck* and *Tirpitz* battleships. Capable of 31 knots and armed to the teeth with nine 11-inch guns and fifty-two further guns of smaller calibres, as well as six torpedo tubes, there was no doubting her firepower.

On board was Hans-Hellmuth Kirchner, just twenty years old and undergoing his officer training as a midshipman, or *Fähnrich zur See*. He had been born and brought up in Neubrandenburg; his father served as a U-boat commander in the last war and so, having completed school and then his stint with the Reichsarbeitsdienst, the Reich Labour Service, it was perhaps not surprising that Kirchner had chosen to follow in his father's footsteps and joined the Navy. After sailing training, including a lengthy journey around much of the world, he was given extensive naval artillery training, which was why, when posted to the *Scharnhorst*, he had been attached to the anti-aircraft guns. He was at his post when news quickly went around the ship that the British aircraft carrier *Glorious* had been spotted with an escort of two destroyers.

There was no question that *Glorious* had been caught napping. Since the Kriegsmarine had received its bloody nose at the start of the Norwegian campaign, naval engagements had all but ceased in the North Sea. *Glorious* was steaming back to Scapa at just 17 knots, and with none of her aircraft armed or ready. This was tragic complacency.

From his gun position, Kirchner could see the British aircraft carrier frantically signalling, flashing Morse signals, 'What ship? What ship?'

Moments later, *Scharnhorst*'s 11-inch heavy guns opened fire, striking the aircraft carrier and immediately wrecking the main flight deck. 'As we approached the enemy formation, getting closer and closer,' noted Kirchner, 'the *Glorious* sustained hit after hit and finally went up in flames.' The two British destroyers *Ardent* and *Acosta* were under fire too, but still surged forward through their own smokescreen. *Ardent* launched eight torpedoes before being pummelled and sunk, and then *Acosta* managed to get a torpedo into the side of the *Scharnhorst*. Kirchner felt the entire superstructure waver and shake. The blast killed forty-eight of the crew, knocked out two of the engine rooms and reduced her speed to just 20 knots. *Glorious*, ablaze and rapidly filling with water, sank soon after, as did *Acosta*, but the destroyers' fearless attacks had put yet another of Germany's battleships out of action. Only around forty men out of 1,559 from the three British ships survived.

Scharnhorst limped to Trondheim, as the crew desperately tried to contain the damage. Many of the dead men had to be left floating in the flooded sections. Meanwhile, the last of the Allied troops had been lifted, as was the Norwegian King Haakon and his government. The Germans had been hunting for them since the invasion, but the King had repeatedly eluded capture. Also taken to Britain were most of the Norwegian Government's gold reserves. From Britain, the Norwegian King-in-Exile would continue the fight.

While the *Scharnhorst* was at Trondheim, Royal Navy torpedo-bombers from another carrier, *Ark Royal*, attacked her unsuccessfully, but a week later, on 20 June, the *Scharnhorst*'s sister ship, the *Gneisenau*, was also hit by a torpedo from a British submarine. Both would be confined to dry docks for the rest of the year.

Losing any ship was a blow to the British, especially an aircraft carrier, but for the Kriegsmarine, the losses of the Norwegian campaign were disastrous. One of 2 heavy cruisers, 2 of 6 light cruisers, 10 of 20 destroyers, one torpedo boat and 6 U-boats had been sunk. A number had also been damaged and were undergoing costly and time-consuming repairs, which meant that by 20 June the Kriegsmarine had just one heavy cruiser, two light cruisers and a mere four destroyers ready for action. Britain was simply not going to be subdued with quite so small a naval force.

On one level, the Norwegian campaign had proved a great success – after all, it had achieved its main objective of creating naval bases and denying the Allies the chance to sever German iron supplies. However, the passage of such ore via Narvik still remained fraught with risk, and much of the Kriegsmarine's surface fleet – upon which it had based its prewar naval strategy – lay either at the bottom of the sea or in dockyards undergoing repairs that were using money and materials needed else-where. Luftwaffe losses amounted to 242 aircraft, which was also no small number.

It is hard not to agree with Warlimont that Hitler would have been better off knocking out France and the Low Countries first, in which case they would have been able to storm into Norway without much of a fight; Britain would have been in no position to contest it on land at all. And had the attack in the West failed, Norway would not have done them much good anyway.

When Hitler invaded Poland, and Britain and France declared war, the Führer was forced into a conflict that required absolute victory and nothing less. The run of victories had been impressive; to defeat France had been an astonishing achievement. But in the long run these victories would mean nothing if Germany did not defeat Britain too. And to do that, Britain's Air Force and Navy had to be defeated as well as its Army. How this was going to happen with a surface fleet that had been largely destroyed and just a handful of U-boats was something Hitler did not appear to have yet thought through.

CHAPTER 25

The End in France

IN EARLY JUNE 1940, Maggiore Publio Magini flew to Tripoli in Libya, where he was to collect a plane and fly back to Italy. Thirty years old and the son of a teacher from Livorno, he had been called up for military service in 1931 and had duly joined the Regia Aeronautica and trained as a pilot. He had been stationed in Rome, and these had been good times: he had met and married his wife, and had enjoyed both the flying and the camaraderie of his fellows. But two years later, with his statutory service over, he had left the Air Force and moved to Florence, finding work as a chemist.

The job was no compensation for the excitement of flying, however, and in any case he missed his Air Force friends, so he rejoined and was posted to Brindisi in the south, where he became something of an expert at both night flying and operating flying boats. By 1938, he had been given the job of setting up a special training school for bad-weather flying near Rome and was still based there on the eve of Italy's entry into the war.

Although most of his work was at the school, there were the occasional trips such as this one, and on reaching Tripoli he was invited to dinner by Maresciallo Italo Balbo, in the Libyan Governor's castle. Magini was delighted to accept but was surprised when the Marshal began speaking out quite openly about Mussolini's plans to enter the war, something he thought would be disastrous. 'He thought any war with Britain was a mad idea,' noted Magini. Balbo thought Mussolini showed a total lack of understanding of the world, and of the ties between Britain and America, and the United States' industrial might. 'I worried about what he had said for a long time,' added Magini.

A few days later, in Rome, on the evening of 10 June, Pace Misciatelli-Chigi, a young and beautiful Tuscan aristocrat, had gathered together a number of friends at her flat in the Piazza Venezia. At 6 p.m., they had been told, just across the way from them on the balcony of the Palazzo Venezia, Benito Mussolini would appear and announce his declaration of war. The speech would be broadcast all around the country, from speakers in piazzas in every town, but Pace Misciatelli-Chigi and her friends had a grandstand view of the live event.

That day was Pace's first wedding anniversary. There had been talk of war the previous June, but she put it out of mind – the sun had been shining, she was marrying the Marquese Flavio Misciatelli in the cathedral in Siena and her thoughts were on anything but politics. A year on, it was unavoidable. Her husband was not even with her that day – he had left to join his regiment, the Genoa Cavalry, leaving her with their baby daughter, Maria Aurora. With a restriction on lights in place already, she had embraced him in the dim light and watched him leave; she had been determined not to cry in front of him, but after he had gone, she worried her heart would break.

At 6 p.m., as promised, *Il Duce* appeared on the balcony. 'An hour appointed by destiny has struck in the heavens of our fatherland!' he told the Italian people. 'We go to battle against the plutocratic and reactionary democracies of the west who, at every moment, have hindered the advance and have often endangered the very existence of the Italian people.'

From her flat, Pace Misciatelli-Chigi looked down on the crowds below. There were a few Fascist rabble-rousers, but for the most part the people listened in silence. A gigantic struggle lay ahead, Mussolini told them, but he also assured the people they would win. 'People of Italy!' he ended with a flourish, 'Rush to arms and show your tenacity, your courage, your valour!'

Pace Misciatelli-Chigi watched the crowd slowly and quietly disperse and then spotted some Fascists carrying a German and an Italian war veteran, blind and with no hands. Suddenly overcome, she began crying and hurried to her room.

Later, she was awoken by the sound of air raid sirens wailing. 'I got up calmly,' she noted, 'but that sound made me shiver.' No enemy planes arrived, however, and after the all-clear sounded, she determined to pack there and then; the following day, she and her daughter would escape Rome and head back to Siena, just as she had promised her husband.

Millions heard Mussolini's declaration of war that evening. Hitler was appalled – not that Italy was now in the war, but by the manner of its announcement, which he thought vulgar. As far as the Führer was concerned, one didn't make a declaration of war, one just got on and fought it. For others, however, it made a powerful impression. Listening in the Piazza Maggiore in Bologna, for example, was Sergio Fabbri, a 22-year-old financial worker. 'The declaration of war filled my friend and me with joy,' he wrote. It was greeted with equal excitement by the seventeen-year-old William Cremonini, who was listening along with a large group of his friends in the very same place. 'We were full of enthusiasm,' he said, 'and in a jolly mood. Maybe some of the older people didn't see it that way, but we were all excited.'

Cremonini had been brought up in Bologna, one of Italy's largest and most industrialized cities, and had greatly enjoyed being part of the numerous Fascist youth organizations while growing up. As Hitler had done in Nazi Germany, so Mussolini had recognized that young minds could be easily manipulated and that by introducing militaristic organizations it would be possible to create new generations of young Italians who both bought into the Fascist ideal of honour and duty to the state and learned important lessons in obedience and discipline. Cremonini had joined the Children of the She-Wolf at five, then the Opera Nazionale Balilla, a Fascist youth organization, before progressing into the Balilla Musketeers, the Avanguardisti and finally the Giovani Fascisti, the Young Fascists. In other words, from the age of five, he had been steadily indoctrinated in Fascist ideology, not that he had realized it at the time. 'In those days,' he says, 'everything worked well, discipline was respected and one might say that we were better off despite being worse off.'

No sooner had Mussolini's declaration finished than recruiting began to sign up young men like Cremonini and his friends into the Giovani Fascisti battalions, even though there were nothing like enough uniforms, let alone rifles and weapons, to go around. Cremonini was unperturbed. Joining the Bologna Battalion, he was then sent off to begin his training in Liguria. His war had begun.

But for all the youthful excitement of boys like Cremonini, it was the reaction of Pace Misciatelli-Chigi that was more commonplace, as Ciano, for one, was well aware. 'The news of the war does not surprise anyone and does not arouse very much enthusiasm,' he wrote in his diary. 'I am sad, very sad. The adventure begins. May God help Italy.'

Despite the irrational fears of the British, Germany took the obvious course of action and prepared to finish the job in France before turning attention elsewhere. It was clearly not a matter of if France would capitulate, but when. Général Weygand had promised to fight on, and so had Reynaud, but the men on the ground knew their cause was a lost one. Trapped in the giant pincer, the cream of their armies had been annihilated; by 5 June, some 1.2 *million* French troops had been killed, wounded, or taken prisoner. After such a defeat there really was no way back, physically or psychologically.

The pause prompted by the German assault on Dunkirk had given Weygand a slight breathing space to reorganize his forces roughly east–west along the Somme and Aisne rivers, but he now had just sixty-four divisions and no reserves opposing 104 divisions flush with victory and brimful of confidence. Weygand's air forces were also in disarray, while in the skies the Luftwaffe continued to reign supreme.

Case RED, the German operation to conquer the rest of France, was launched on 5 June. Some regrouping had taken place, with Panzerkorps Hoth, for example, now attached to Armeegruppe B and part of the sweep south-west towards Le Havre and Normandy. Armeegruppe A, on the other hand, was to wheel south-east towards Switzerland and achieve another encirclement. The plan was to attack the Maginot Line around the back.

As it turned out, the French did put up far stiffer resistance and performed much better than they ever had in the first phase of the campaign. Nevertheless, the Germans overcame resistance swiftly enough, and among the first to break through the line was Generalmajor Rommel's 7. Panzerdivision. Once again, Hauptmann Hans von Luck's recce battalion was in the van, charging across country to avoid road congestion. He managed to take the Somme bridges intact, but then ran into the main French defences and immediately came under heavy fire. It was still early morning and von Luck and his men were taking cover from French artillery shelling when he heard one of his runners say, 'Captain, your breakfast.' Von Luck turned around. 'I couldn't believe my eyes,' he noted.

One of his runners had crawled through enemy fire to deliver a tray of sandwiches and was even clutching a napkin.

'Man, are you mad? I'm hungry all right, but at the moment I have other things to do than eat breakfast.'

'Yes, I know,' the runner replied, 'but a hungry commander gets nervous. I feel responsible for your welfare.' Then he was off again, while those around von Luck collapsed with laughter.

Soon after, they broke through, the combination of artillery, armour and the Luftwaffe proving unstoppable. Von Luck and his men advanced around sixty miles in just two days. By the 7th, they were approaching Rouen, huge clouds of smoke guiding them from where the Luftwaffe had already called.

They were preparing to cross the Seine when they were ordered due west to Le Havre. Here they came up against one of the last British units, 51st Highland Division. This had been on rotation in the Maginot Line when the battle had begun and had been posted west when Case RED started. Rommel's men reached the coast on 10 June and cut the road to Le Havre, so, together with the remnants of the French IX Corps, 51st Highland Division was forced back to Saint-Valéry. An attempt was made to lift its men off but rain and fog hampered efforts, so that only a few more than 2,000 got away. The rest were forced to surrender.

Meanwhile, it was Hauptmann von Luck who took the surrender in nearby Fécamp, from where a smaller number of British and French had been trying to evacuate. He accepted the surrender of the mayor, ordered occupation of the southern hills, switched off the local radio station and sent out patrols. He then signalled to Rommel.

'Bravo, von Luck,' Rommel replied. For 7. Panzerdivision, the battle was over.

Paris was emptying. The American broadcast journalist Edward Sevareid had been told by his NBS bosses to leave the capital when the French Government left; now it had, so it was time for him to go too. He had already sent his wife and their baby twins back to the US, managing to get them on a train to Italy and then the last American ship to leave Genoa, which, he had correctly guessed, meant Italy was about join the fight.

A few days later, bombs had fallen on Paris, and specifically on the Citroën works and the Air Ministry. In the days that followed, Sevareid watched thousands of cars emerge from the garages and, with mattresses and luggage strapped to the roofs, head south.

On 10 June, dark smoke over the city obscured the sun, and he drove down the Champs-Élysées and looked at the empty cafés. Later that night, he made his last broadcast from the capital and then made his way south in his own black Citroën, along with endless miles of others. 'Paris lay inert,' he wrote, 'her breathing scarcely audible, her limbs relaxed, and the blood flowed remorselessly from her manifold veins. Paris was dying, like a beautiful woman in coma.'

On 12 June, a young Parisienne, Andrée Griotteray, arrived at police headquarters to find the courtyard full of trucks as all the archives were being taken and moved elsewhere. 'The latest news is the Germans are still advancing,' she jotted in her diary the following day. 'Bastards.' That day, the 13th, the Chief of Police, Monsieur Langeron, who had given Andrée her job in the first place, called all the administrative staff together and told them that if the city were to be occupied, the police and Head of Police would all stay and carry on with their jobs. Later, Andrée packed a suitcase just in case, although she had decided she must obey orders and stay and continue her job as requested. Her mother, brothers and sister, however, had already gone, having taken a train to Nantes. From there, they planned to go to England, where her mother had friends. 'All my friends have gone,' she wrote. 'We are alone and it is very scary.'

The same day that von Luck was taking the surrender in Fécamp and Eric Sevareid was heading south from Paris, a British delegation including Winston Churchill, Anthony Eden, General Dill, the Deputy CIGS and Edward Spears was flying to France for urgent talks with Reynaud and the French war leaders. The French Government had already left Paris – the meeting was to take place at Weygand's new HQ at Briare on the Loire.

Increasingly desperate calls for reinforcements had been coming from Reynaud. More fighter squadrons immediately, more divisions, more bombers. He had also been bombarding President Roosevelt, and on 10 June signalled again. 'I beg you,' he wrote, 'to state publicly that the United States will give the Allies all the moral and material support within their means, short of sending an expeditionary force.'

Most of Churchill's Cabinet and Chiefs of Staff were against sending France anything more, but the PM, as well as being a Francophile, was conscious of the need to be seen to be helping the French as much as possible. Resentment was growing on both sides: the French felt the Brits had cut and run, the Brits believed French incompetence had led to this disaster in the first place; Churchill believed gestures needed to be made, and that the longer the French were kept in the fight, the better Britain's position would be.

The talks achieved little. There was discussion about a 'Breton redoubt' in Brittany, an idea with which Reynaud was particularly taken. General Sir Alan Brooke had already landed back in France, at Cherbourg in Normandy, with a newly reconstituted BEF consisting of one division and two more to follow. It was a gesture and nothing more, yet Weygand was demanding more divisions to enter the fray immediately. They simply didn't exist. Churchill's biggest concern was the French Fleet and what would happen to it if the worst happened and France sued for terms. He was not given a clear answer until the following day, when he collared Amiral Darlan. The French admiral assured him the Fleet would never be handed over to Germany. The British contingent set off for home again early the following morning in bad weather and en route spotted a couple of German fighter planes; fortunately, the Germans did not see them.

When they had gone, Reynaud had a short talk with Pétain and Weygand. Under the terms of the alliance with Britain, one nation could not make terms with the enemy without the permission of the other, and Reynaud intended to honour that. Moreover, he believed they should fight to the last – that they could establish a redoubt in Brittany and that their sea and air forces could continue the fight alongside Britain. And if not Brittany, then North Africa. They should never surrender.

'The country will not forgive you,' Weygand replied, 'if, in order to remain faithful to Britain, you reject any possibility of peace.' Reynaud was horrified; it was not about Britain but continuing the fight and never surrendering to Nazi tyranny. That Weygand and Pétain believed servitude was preferable was anathema to him.

The following day, 12 June, the Council of Ministers met at Tours, to where the government had now moved. Général Weygand urged them to ask for an armistice. The arguments for and against raged with no con-clusion, but Reynaud's authority, never strong, was being undermined by the two old warriors.

A request had been made by the Council of Ministers to see Churchill. Reynaud invited him back and he came, barely thirty-six hours after he had last left. They met at Tours, but, bizarrely, Reynaud spoke to Churchill without his colleagues. Furthermore, he admitted Weygand wanted to surrender but told Churchill he hoped he could dissuade the defeatists so long as the USA entered the war. This was a line that had not been put forward at the Council of Ministers the previous day; no such thing had been suggested. At any rate, it was the last time the two met.

Meanwhile, Eric Sevareid had finally reached Tours and found a bar full of British and American journalists who were sitting waiting for news and comparing notes. Suddenly, a small fat Jewish Parisian journalist burst into tears, bit his knuckles, then rapped them on the bar until they bled, crying, 'France is finished! France is finished!' As Sevareid was well aware, he also meant, 'I am finished.'

That same day, 13 June, Leutnant Siegfried Knappe and his gunners in 87. Division advanced thirty miles and by 3 p.m. were at the River Marne with the Eiffel Tower visible in the distance. As evening fell, they were ordered to take up new positions on the Ourcq Canal. Calling up their 105mm gun, they pushed it into position only to come under return fire immediately, and at that moment Knappe felt something strike his hand – a bullet had gone clean through. Blood was pumping from the wound, but he felt no pain – not then, at any rate. He later discovered another bullet hole through the side of his jacket and map case; he had been lucky, all things considered. Their 105 had done the job, however. Opposite them, resistance had ceased, and the following morning they were in Paris.

'A day I will remember for the rest of my life,' scribbled Andrée Griotteray in her diary, that Friday, 14 June. The first thing she had seen as she had walked up the rue Auber to catch the Métro was a truck full of German soldiers. It felt like a stab in the back. Then, at 10 a.m. sharp, Germans marched into the police headquarters through the gates of Notre-Dame. 'I looked out of my office window and there they were. When I left in the evening the yard was full of disarmed policemen and German soldiers,' she confided to her diary. 'But what a loss of face for France. What a tragedy. Paris occupied by a foreign power. I cried and cried and cried.'

Above the city that day was General Walter Warlimont, who had flown over in a small Fieseler Storch to observe the front from the air. He knew German troops were close to Paris but could clearly see large columns of infantry already there. Remembering how much they had striven to reach this goal in the last war, he felt overwhelmed by a sense of exultation and joy. On a whim, he tapped the pilot on the shoulder and asked him to land at the Place de la Concorde. After circling around for a short while, they landed at the end of the Champs-Élysées.

A couple of hours later, he was watching Leutnant Knappe's 87th Infantry marching past and saw a French girl push by to see the spectacle for herself. 'I for once forgot my gloomy feelings about the misery of the war,' he said, 'and, in particular, the sufferings connected between the French and our own people.'

That same day, 14 June, General Brooke reported it was time to evacuate the last British troops in France. He had spoken with Weygand and Général Georges and they told him plainly it was over. Churchill berated him, but Brooke was insistent. Eventually, the PM concurred. As a result, a further 200,000 troops were evacuated over the next few days, from Cherbourg, Brest and other ports. More than half a million men had been successfully brought back from France. Considering the small size of the British Army, this was a significant proportion.

Another of those arriving in Britain was the French Major-General Charles de Gaulle, one of the few men to have seen off the panzers during an armoured battle at Abbeville, but who was now a minister in Reynaud's reshuffled Cabinet. As such, he had attended the meeting of the Supreme War Council on 11 June and had made quite an impression, not least because of his physical appearance. At well over six foot, de Gaulle was tall, with a beaked nose, trim moustache and curiously very little chin. He was also clearly determined to fight on. Churchill even muttered to him, 'L'homme du destin.'

As German troops entered Paris, the French Government moved again, this time to Bordeaux and, once there, de Gaulle grilled Reynaud about the possibility of continuing the fight in North Africa. At this, Reynaud ordered him to fly to London to ask for British help in making such a move. In fact, there was no aeroplane available, so instead he hurried by car to see his dying mother in Brittany and then to say farewell to his wife and children. After giving them instructions should the worst come to the worst, he drove to Brest, boarded the destroyer *Milan* and set sail for Plymouth.

The following morning, 16 June, he was at the Hyde Park Hotel in London and was shaving when Jean Monnet, a French businessman, and

Charles Corbin, the Ambassador to Britain, came in and suggested a scheme being discussed with the British to create a union between France and Britain – the two countries would become one. It was a plan with many flaws and born of desperation, but de Gaulle, who was due to have lunch with Churchill, agreed to propose it to the Prime Minister. They met at the Carlton Club, and realizing it was the only way to keep France and therefore the French Fleet in the war, Churchill offered to put the proposal to his Cabinet.

Suddenly, everyone became terribly excited, and a Declaration of Union was drafted. Jock Colville, who was snatching snippets of these developments, was astonished. 'The Cabinet meeting turned into a sort of promenade,' he noted, 'and everyone has been slapping de Gaulle on the back and telling him he shall be Commander-in-Chief (Winston muttering "je l'arrangerai"). Is he to be the new Napoleon?'

De Gaulle then telephoned Reynaud, who personally took down the Declaration of Union. 'He was transfigured with joy,' noted Edward Spears, who as Reynaud's British liaison officer was still with the French premier, 'and my old friendship for him surged out in a wave of appreciation at his response.' For Reynaud, this was a lifeline – a chance for France to stay in the war. The following day, he planned to meet Churchill again and discuss the matter in greater detail, but first, after Spears had hurried away to get copies of the Declaration typed up, he promised to put the Declaration to the Council of Ministers. 'It did not occur to us,' wrote Spears, 'that it might not be accepted.'

When he read it out, however, not one man spoke out in favour; rather, it was met with silence. Somehow, news of this offer of union had already reached them. 'It was clear,' wrote Reynaud, 'that Pétain and Weygand had won the day.' Reynaud became convinced that his phone lines had been tapped by Pétain and the defeatists, but Spears believed it came through another source: Reynaud's mistress, Madame de Portes, who was a known Anglophobe. Roland de Margerie, First Secretary at the French Embassy in London, had told Spears, 'She is ugly, dirty, nasty and half-demented.' No one, it seemed, had a good word to say about her, and why Reynaud was so under her spell was a mystery to all. Whatever the truth, the Council had been forewarned by someone.

At any rate, with that ice-cold response, this last-ditch attempt to keep France fighting was over. Reynaud resigned and a few hours later Maréchal Pétain was asked to form a new government. He made his first broadcast the following day, 18 June. Watching him in Bordeaux were Eric Sevareid and a host of other journalists who had somehow made the long journey south. Stepping carefully into the studio wearing a belted raincoat, he announced to the French people that the war was over and that troops should lay down their arms. He was, he told them, making a 'gift' of himself. Sevareid was not impressed. 'He seemed to regard it as a fair bargain for the nation,' he noted. 'Defeat, shame, and torture to be made palatable by his precious "gift" – a vain, doddering old man.' Pétain, the saviour of Verdun in the last war, revered by almost every living Frenchman, had an authority no other in France could match, yet his order to troops to lay down their arms when no armistice had yet been signed only added to the confusion.

'We learn by wireless that Pétain and Weygand have asked for an armistice,' jotted Capitaine Barlone in his diary. He had sailed from Plymouth back to France two weeks earlier, and had then gone on a wild goose chase with other officers and troops trying to catch up with the front. Barlone decided there and then to try and get back to England and continue the fight, and first ten, then twenty of his fellows agreed to join him. Most troops, however, starved of information and confused by what was happening, had no idea what they should now do. Many had not even seen a German at this point. In the next few days, a further million French troops became prisoners of war. Had they known they would be sent to German prison camps for the next five years, they might not have acquiesced quite so readily.

As it happened, the Germans had not been expecting Pétain's announcement either; Hitler was having talks with Mussolini, so the German armies pushed on, and with increasing ease. In the meantime, it was left to General Warlimont and his staff to try and draw up terms for the French.

These were eventually put to the French a few days later on 21 June, the same day that, across the Atlantic, René de Chambrun reached the White House. There he met Roosevelt, Harry Hopkins and others of the President's inner circle. He had come to plead for arms and US support, but it was, of course, all too late.

Back in France, Paul Reynaud had, in the meantime, managed to speak to Pétain and urged him to tell Amiral Darlan to sail the Fleet to the United States. Pétain refused, arguing that the Germans would not hesitate to carry out fierce reprisals if the Fleet either sailed away or was scuttled. None the less, Reynaud followed up this conversation with a letter suggesting that Pétain could explain such an action to the Germans as being Darlan's personal insubordination. The long-term benefit to France of helping the Allies, he argued, and gaining credit points with the Americans, could not be overestimated.

Pétain, however, was having none of it, and the terms of the armistice were unequivocal. The French Fleet would assemble in ports to be named later, and would be demobilized and disarmed under German or Italian supervision. 'The German Government solemnly declares to the French Government that it has no intention of using the units of this Fleet in its own operations of war.' As the Nazis had repeatedly shown, however, their promises counted for absolutely nothing, and with much of their own fleet now sunk or back in dockyards, the opportunity to absorb the world's fourth-largest Navy at a stroke was an obvious temptation. Why on earth wouldn't they? Pétain must have been all too aware of this.

In Paris, Andrée Griotteray felt sick at heart. She now saw Germans on the streets of her city every day. 'They walk around as if they own the place,' she wrote. 'They are continually to be found in our cafés and our bars, where they sing and dance.' Above, German planes buzzed and flew so low she was convinced they would hit a building. Through the streets, German officers could be seen speeding around in smart captured cars. She was disgusted beyond belief. Late on the 22nd she was at home, writing her diary and looking out of the window. 'It is pouring,' she noted. 'Thunder and lightning are raging all over Paris and I am depressed. Why must I feel so broken-hearted every time I walk past a German soldier?'

The armistice was signed that same day in the same railway carriage in Compiègne in which the Germans had signed their surrender back in 1918. For Hitler, who was there to observe France's humiliation, there could have been no sweeter moment of victory. He had told his disbelieving generals that Germany could destroy France and be masters of Europe, and so far he had been proved right. Next it would be Britain's turn.

CHAPTER 26

Air Power: I

ON 30 MAY, Siegfried Bethke had carried out his fiftieth combat sortie, and it had been over Dunkirk and Ostend, escorting Stukas as they had 'pelted' British ships evacuating troops. 'An eerie sight from the air,' he noted. 'Both places look like firebrands. Many small and large ships on the beach to pick up the English soldiers. Bombs, fires, anti-aircraft firing, Stukas, smoke and fumes.'

The following day, during an attack on some French LeO 45 bombers, he was hit by one of their machine-gunners and suffered the terrifying experience of flames licking into the cockpit and having to bale out. Already flying quite low, he knew he had to act quickly but initially struggled to get the canopy open. Desperately trying to work through the bail-out procedure in his head, he somehow managed to get the canopy open at last, flip over the plane and pull the ripcord on his parachute.

Looking down, he realized he was heading straight for a trench strewn with dead soldiers and a war memorial nearby from the last war. With the ground rushing up towards him, he then landed badly, knocking himself unconscious in the process. When he came to, he could see his 109, 'No. 7', burning on the ground and German infantry were pulling him to safety. Just 200 metres away, they told him, were black French colonial troops, who, fortunately for him, had made no effort to either shoot him or snatch him once he had landed.

When he was taken back to his airfield, the rest of the *Staffel* were gratifyingly pleased to see him alive, but despite only light burns to his hands and throbbing head, he was put aboard a Ju52 and packed off to hospital in Cologne. By 6 June, he had heard about the renewed offensive and was itching to get back to his squadron. 'I'm extremely ambitious,' he jotted in his journal. 'I want to be successful. Who knows how long this war will last? If I don't get the Knight's Cross, then at least the Iron Cross First Class.' He had, by that time, shot down four planes but felt certain he could have had more than double that if his marksmanship had been a bit better. 'It was my own ineptness and nervousness,' he scribbled. 'It was all my own fault.'

Also shot down had been Hajo Herrmann, who had been flying daily since the opening of the offensive. Over Dunkirk, he had been dropping his bombs one at a time in the hope of gaining greater accuracy – he would fly over, drop one, adjust, then repeat the process until he struck – and this had worked, with one ship definitely sunk as a result. It was, however, a risky business and on 31 May, now flying in a new Junkers 88 from Schiphol in Amsterdam, he had just dived on a ship, missed and was climbing for a second attempt when he was hit by a Hurricane and forced to crash-land in the sea, albeit close enough to the shore to be able to get himself and his crew safely out and quickly back on to land. Unsure which side he'd landed on, he was relieved to see German infantrymen approaching. 'I'd made it,' he wrote. It had been his fortieth operational flight, and that did not include the sorties he'd flown in Spain.

Helmut Mahlke had been hit over Dunkirk too. The smoke and cloud over Dunkirk had been so bad, he had chosen to lead his *Staffel* low, underneath the cloudbase – it was the only way they could hit their targets, despite their being sitting ducks for any flak. Suddenly, they had come under intense anti-aircraft fire and moments later there was a bang from behind.

'What's happened back there? Are you wounded Fritzchen?' he asked his rear gunner.

'No, but the control cables in the rear fuselage have been cut by flak.'

With his elevators cut, it was extremely difficult to control the Stuka. They headed south, and back towards the airfield at Calais Guise. Flying was just about possible, but landing would be a different matter and so he told his gunner, Fritz Baudisch, to bale out. Baudisch opted to stay, however.

After circling the airfield, Mahlke came into land with everything perfectly lined up, only to be shaken by a strong thermal gust at the last moment. The nose dropped like a stone and the Stuka crash-landed – the undercarriage was ripped off, and so was a wing, but moments later they came to a halt and were amazed to discover they were in one piece. As they jumped out and ran clear, the Stuka erupted into a mass of flames. 'We'd had the devil's own luck in getting out of it alive,' noted Mahlke.

They were flying again the next day and the days after that. On 1 June, Mahlke was harried by several Spitfires over Dunkirk and only just managed to evade them. On a second flight over Dunkirk that day, they managed to hit one ship only to be attacked by several Spitfires once more. Again, he got away by the skin of his teeth. Others were not so lucky.

In all, the Luftwaffe lost 1,814 aircraft during the Battle of France – around half the number with which it had begun the attack on 10 May – and the experiences of Bethke, Herrmann and Mahlke say much about the intensity of the fighting and how hard they and their fellow pilots were pushed. For those coming up against the Luftwaffe in May and June 1940, it seemed their mastery of the skies was complete, yet although the German Air Force was, without question, the finest in the world at that time, there can be no question that it was still fundamentally inefficient and complacent, and that its leadership had passed over opportunities that could have made it considerably better than it already was.

The problems were there at almost every level, but most obviously with the leadership. Feldmarschall Göring had been a fighter pilot and had even commanded the famed Richthofen squadron in 1918, but he had never been to staff college and had leapt up the Air Force ranks thanks to his position as Number 2 in the Nazi party. He knew little about military command, and not much about modern air warfare, and was, in fact, a far better businessman and politician than Air Force commander.

The trouble was, his junior commanders all knew this. The beating heart of the operational Luftwaffe was the young men, still in their twenties, who had joined the Luftwaffe in its early days in the mid-1930s, fought in Poland and France and had a mass of vital operational experience. These men were now squadron and group commanders and, of course, were able to pass on their knowledge to the younger pilots and aircrew. Hajo Herrmann was one such figure; another was Johannes 'Macky' Steinhoff, a *Staffelkapitän* in 4/JG2. Steinhoff was twenty-six, smart and a naturally gifted pilot. He had originally hoped to become a teacher, but coming from a working-class background had been forced to give up university for lack of funds and had joined the Kriegsmarine as a naval flier instead. From there he had transferred to the Luftwaffe in 1935 and had been at fighter school with many of the pilots already making a name for themselves, such as Adolf Galland, Werner Mölders and Johannes Trautloft. Much to his chagrin, Steinhoff had not gone to Spain, but he made a name for himself back in December 1939, when he and his comrades in 4/JG2 had intercepted a formation of Wellington bombers off Wilhelmshaven and shot down twelve of the twenty-two. Steinhoff had accounted for two of them.

Goebbels's propaganda machine made much of this, and Steinhoff and a few others had been ordered to Berlin and had met Goebbels, von Ribbentrop and Göring. Steinhoff had not been much impressed with any of them. 'I looked at these men,' said Steinhoff, 'and wondered how such weak-looking creatures could be running such a great country.' The C-in-C peppered them with questions about air combat, like an over-enthusiastic kid wanting to hear of adventures in the skies; he showed no gravitas, no grasp of strategy. 'I found him annoying, exhausting, and intrusive,' said Steinhoff. 'He loved to grab you, almost hug a man and slap your back. I found this uncomfortable.' Steinhoff and his friends called him the 'Fat One'. Steinhoff was not alone in his views; far from it – they were commonplace. That Göring attracted so little respect did not augur well.

Nor did Göring demonstrate much leadership of the Reichsluftfahrt-ministerium, or RLM, the Luftwaffe General Staff. Like Hitler, he pursued a policy of divide and rule, keeping rivals on parallel commands and ensuring there was discord among his subordinates. The one person who managed to successfully weave through this jungle, and also had a bucket-load of good sense, was General Walther Wever, the Luftwaffe Chief of Staff. It was Wever who had been planning an independent strategic bomber force. He had recognized, quite rightly, that the biggest threat to Germany lay in the East, and so creating a large heavy bomber force that would be the mainstay of the Reich's air defence was not only a sensible idea but one Göring concurred with at the time. Sadly for the Luftwaffe, however, Wever was killed in an air crash before his bomber force went into production.

In his place came firstly Albert Kesselring, a former artillery officer, then General Hans-Jürgen Stumpff, and finally Oberst Hans Jeschonnek, still in his thirties when he took on the job. One of the problems was that

Jeschonnek did not get on with General Erhard Milch, formerly running the Lufthansa civil airline but from the birth of the Luftwaffe Göring's deputy. Milch had little military experience and was another who was promoted from almost nothing, but was an extremely able administrator and a man who was able to go straight to the nub of a problem and get things done. For Göring, however, Milch was just a little *too* competent, so he clipped his wings by bringing in Ernst Udet as Head of the Office of Air Armament in early 1939. Udet was a brilliant pilot and fighter ace, one of Göring's best pals and hugely gregarious; it was Udet who had encouraged the young Scotsman Eric Brown to fly back in 1936. He was, however, no businessman, knew little about procurement, and lacked the Machiavellian ruthlessness and deviousness required. Furthermore, although technically his post should have fallen under Milch's jurisdiction, he was made directly responsible to Göring. It was a terrible move, because Milch and Udet had actually always got on rather well, and under Milch's watchful and pragmatic guidance he might have overcome his shortcomings. Instead, mistrust grew between them, and Udet became increasingly insecure about his position and his judgement.

By May 1940, Wever's original four-engine bomber programme had long ago been kicked into touch. Instead, bombers would operate with fighters in an integrated Luftwaffe that would be made up with air fleets – *Luftflotten* – and air corps – *Fliegerkorps* – that were designed to directly support the land forces. There was no bomber force that could operate independently of the ground forces – no strategic bomber force.

The Luftwaffe had plenty of old mid-1930s bombers such as Heinkel 111s and Dornier 17s, but the focus of all new bombers had become dive-bombing. Udet had been seduced by dive-bombing when he had seen American Curtiss Helldivers during a visit to the USA a few years earlier. Out of this had come the Junkers 87, the *Sturzkampfflugzeug*, or 'Stuka'. The principle behind dive-bombing was sound enough: by dive-bombing, it was possible to get closer to the target, which meant greater accuracy, particularly since Germany did not possess an effective bombsight. The greater the accuracy, the less ordnance and aircraft required, and it was this, above all, that made the dive-bomber so attractive; Germany had neither the infrastructure nor raw materials required to build up a substantial heavy-bomber force.

During the Polish campaign, in Norway and again in France, the Stuka had repeatedly proved itself as a highly effective weapon, made all the better for the addition of a siren that screamed as it dived and quite intentionally put the fear of God into those on the receiving end. For Goebbels, it had become the most potent symbol of Nazi Germany's military might. Newsreels, complete with sound effects, were shown around the world with Stukas diving, screaming and devastating Germany's enemies with their shock and awe.

In truth, one type of dive-bomber was probably enough for one air force. Udet and Jeschonnek, however, did not agree, and so decided to give dive-bombing capabilities to their latest bomber, the twin-engine Junkers 88. This had been conceived as a high-speed, long-range medium bomber, and one of the early prototypes achieved records for flying two tons of bombs over 600 miles at an average speed of 310 mph. No other bomber in the world could carry so much so far so quickly. In short, it was a triumph. Also in the pipeline was a four-engine heavy bomber, the Heinkel 177, but both these aircraft suggested a more strategic role for the Luftwaffe, which was at odds with Jeschonnek's views on how best to use air power.

Both Udet and Jeschonnek decided that instead of developing the Ju88 and He177 as they had been originally conceived, it would be far better to give them dive-bombing capabilities. This prompted great teeth-sucking from Junkers and Heinkel and a staggering 25,000 changes to the original design of the Ju88. Production was delayed massively, which was why it was not until the spring of 1940 that Hajo Herrmann and the rest of KG4 were equipped with them. Most bombing units were still using the rather obsolete Heinkel 111s and Dornier 17s. And the Ju88 was no longer particularly fast or long-range. In fact, it now had a top speed of just 269 mph, which wasn't much better than the Heinkel and Dornier. As for the Heinkel 177, it was so behind schedule, it was not even yet in production.

The problem was that dive-bombers necessarily needed to be small, because of the weight and problems of gravitational pull. Heinkel were trying to solve the problem by putting two engines on top of each other and powering a single propeller in each wing. It wasn't working, and test pilots were dying unnecessarily as a result. There was a four-engine aircraft, the Focke-Wulf 200 'Condor', which was being earmarked for long-range reconnaissance and anti-shipping work, but this had originally been designed as a transport plane and not a heavy bomber. In any case, there were structural issues with it that had not been resolved, the payload was only around four tons, and Focke-Wulf was never able to build it in numbers – only twenty-eight, for example, were built during all of 1940.

Then there were the fighter planes. The Luftwaffe had two, both of which were designed by Professor Willi Messerschmitt at Bayerische Flugzeugwerke AG, which, in 1938, had been renamed Messerschmitt AG. The single-engine fighter, the Me109E, was the best fighter aircraft in the world in 1940, because it could climb faster than any other, packed a bigger punch than any other, with fifty-five seconds' worth of machine-gun fire and eighty rounds of 20mm cannon shells, and could dive quicker than its rivals. It was a little difficult to master and, because of the tremendous torque produced by the Daimler-Benz 601 engine, was easy to topple over when taking off unless the pilot was highly experienced. The only other flaw was the very limited visibility in the cockpit. In all other respects, however, it was unrivalled. Furthermore, because its undercarriage was attached to the fuselage it was quicker to both build and repair – the wings, for example, could be manufactured quite separately.

The second was the Messerschmitt 110, which was a twin-engine fighter and originally conceived as a long-range bomber escort. It was a particular favourite of Göring, and so no one dared tell him it had numerous deficiencies, not least a slow rate of climb and dive, and a lack of manoeuvrability, which meant that in a dogfight with a half-decent single-engine fighter it was likely to come out second best. So taken was he with the Me110 that he named it the 'Zerstörer' (Destroyer) and created special Zerstörer fighter wings, plucking many of the best fighter pilots from single-engine units to pilot them. And again, over Poland and in Norway, where they faced no modern opposition, the myth surrounding their potency only grew.

There was, however, another single-engine fighter that could have offered a more effective support act to the Me109E. This was the Heinkel 112, which had been put forward as a fighter plane at the same time as the 109 and had initially performed even better. The Luftwaffe had ordered further prototypes of both and by the time Messerschmitt had developed the 109E, Heinkel's 112E had speeds of more than 350 mph, was considered highly manoeuvrable, had a solid, inward-folding undercarriage and elliptical wings, and had an astonishing range of more than 715 miles, which was significantly better than that of the Me110. Its rate of climb was not quite as good as the Me109E's, but it could still reach 20,000 feet in ten minutes, which was as good as anything else out there. When Heinkel protested to Udet that his fighter should be given a contract, he was firmly told to drop the matter, which he did; after all, rumours of Jewish blood always dogged Heinkel, so it paid not to kick up too much of a fuss, and, in any case, Udet and Messerschmitt were particularly good friends as well as the professor being a good party man. None the less, that a plane as good and versatile as the Heinkel 112 was rejected, especially with its incredible range, was astonishing. Range would be critical in fighting over Britain. For the Luftwaffe, this was unfortunate because the failure to back the Heinkel meant a truly winning combination had been passed over.

Another cause for concern was the shortage of training schools. Following Munich, Hitler had realized that Britain, especially, was increasing the rearmament of its Air Force and told Göring he wanted a fivefold increase in the size of the Luftwaffe. This was only passed on to the rest of the air staff several months later and was never enacted, largely because they lacked the means to do so, and partly because Jeschonnek was also wedded to the concept of the quick war, in which everything would be thrown into a rapid and decisive battle. By June 1940, the training schools had been largely stripped of all the Ju52s, which were used for training purposes, and many of the instructors. Nor were there enough schools in the first place – there was just one for the training of fighter pilots.

Stripping the flying schools in this manner supported the principles of a rapid war in which everything was flung at the initial assault, and so did not matter at all – as long as the Luftwaffe was not embroiled in a long drawn-out war.

The trouble was, cracks were already appearing. The loss of so many aircraft on 10 May had set off warning bells, but it was the air battle over Dunkirk that had really got alarms ringing. Göring had promised Hitler his Luftwaffe would destroy the BEF and prevent a mass evacuation. Listening to the telephone conversation was Göring's personal Luftwaffe intelligence officer, Oberst 'Beppo' Schmid. 'He described this mission as being a speciality of the Luftwaffe,' said Schmid, 'and pointed out that the advance elements of the German Army, already battle weary, could hardly expect to succeed in preventing the British withdrawal.' This showed a spectacular lack of understanding of what was happening on the ground by both Göring and Hitler, who after the successes so far in the war had become seduced by the invincibility of the Luftwaffe.

Yet, over Dunkirk, Göring had been unable to keep his promise. Dive-bombing was all very well with almost complete command of the sky and on fixed targets, but was not so effective when attempting to hit a moving target from skies swarming with enemy fighter planes. Ships did not keep still and, in any case, even from a couple of thousand feet often looked like little more than pencils; it was one of the reasons why so many men escaped. What's more, as the dive-bomber emerged out of its dive, it was flying so slowly it became a sitting target for any enemy fighter plane waiting, hawk-like, to strike from above. Not only had the Luftwaffe failed to stop the British escaping, but its bomber force, and particularly its Stukas and new Ju88s, had suffered grievously.

A technological disconnect was also evident. Back in December, when Macky Steinhoff and JG2 had intercepted RAF Wellingtons, they had been directed to the bombers by highly sophisticated Kriegsmarine radar. Despite this, radar was not used in such a way in any Luftwaffe operations. And while against the French 1st Armoured Division it had been radio that had enabled the Germans to control the battle, once airborne, Luftwaffe aircraft were largely on their own; they could communicate with other planes in their *Staffel*, but that was as far as it went. There were no ground controllers guiding them to targets, there was no communication with bomber units or other fighter units. It was curious that these technologies, in which Germany was so advanced and which had so clearly already proved their worth, had not been integrated into the air arm.

Now, however, with France out of the way, Göring's Luftwaffe, so unstoppable thus far, would have to operate across the Channel, on its own and in a way in which it was neither trained nor prepared, and defeat the RAF.

If Göring and his commanders were worried, however, they did not show it. Rather, their intelligence picture suggested that the RAF had been badly weakened by recent fighting and that knocking them out of the sky should be a walk in the park. Göring assured Hitler it would take just four days to clear the British skies of the RAF.

PART III

WAR IN THE AIR AND ON THE SEA

CHAPTER 27

Air Power: II

IN HIS ASSUMPTION that the RAF had been weakened by the recent fighting, Göring had been quite correct. The RAF had lost 1,067 aircraft and 1,127 pilots and aircrew since 10 May. Throughout much of this time, it had learned some extremely hard lessons. Bomber crews had been killed in large numbers, either singly or in groups, picked off by marauding enemy fighters. One aircraft, the Fairey Battle, a single-engine light bomber, had been particularly shown up. On 11 May, six out of nine Belgian Battles had been shot down, while the same day only one of eight RAF Battles had survived a bombing operation. The following day, five Battles had been sent to attack a bridge. Four were shot down and the fifth crash-landed on its return. It had proved so completely ill-suited to the task that it had been, to all intents and purposes, withdrawn from further operations.

RAF Bomber and Coastal Commands unquestionably had a vital role to play in the forthcoming air battle against Germany, hitting targets within the Reich and also pummelling German airfields in northern France. In fact, between 15 May and 4 June, when France had lifted its objections about bombing targets within Germany, Bomber Command had flown 1,700 operational sorties over the Reich.

Among those regularly flying over Germany were the Hampdens of 83 Squadron. On the night of 17 May, for example, they were among forty-eight bombers to attack Hamburg, Germany's biggest port. The target had been the oil refinery near the docks. Guy Gibson and his crew had decided to take off later than most – partly because there had been a film they'd wanted to see in Lincoln, but mainly because he aimed to arrive just as the first hint of dawn was creeping over the city to take advantage of improved visibility. They had reached Hamburg without incident, and saw the great city sprawling for miles. Gibson spotted one oil tank on fire and decided to try and dive low, through the clumsy sweep of search-lights and intense flak. He saw one of their fellow crews falling out of the sky on fire, then headed for the target, flying in at 6,000 feet before diving. The first bombs were dropped but did not appear to detonate. Round they went again and this time the bombs looked like they hit their mark, but now they were flying over the centre of Hamburg, flak was hurtling towards them, and they hit the cable of a barrage balloon, which damaged the starboard wing. 'At last we were out of it all,' noted Gibson, 'and save for the usual exchange of fire between ourselves and the flak ships we reached the coast safely.' The raid caused thirty-six separate fires, the Merck'sche fertilizer factory was gutted, 160 buildings were damaged and thirty-four people were killed. It was hardly mass destruction, yet that didn't really matter at this point in time. All Britain had to do right now was keep in the fight. That these attacks were getting up the noses of the Nazi war leaders was important, because it was an affront to their aura of invincibility. Moreover, it prompted an increase in both home defences and those on airfields, all of which took both time and resources away from the all-out effort being planned for the attack against Britain.

There was no denying, however, that in safeguarding Britain's air space, it was Fighter Command that had the key role. Both Air Chief Marshal Sir Cyril Newall, the Chief of the Air Staff, and Air Chief Marshal Sir Hugh Dowding, the C-in-C of Fighter Command, had been repeatedly urging Churchill not to send more fighters to France, especially once it seemed clear France was doomed. As far as they were concerned, it was throwing good money after bad. In all, 396 Hurricanes had been shot down over France and sixty-seven Spitfires. The latter had come directly from Fighter Command and had only been used from south-east England during the air battle over Dunkirk, but the result of this contribution was that by the beginning of June Fighter Command had just 331 fighters left. Dowding had reckoned he needed fifty-eight squadrons to adequately defend Britain, and that had been based on an assumption that the Luftwaffe would be attacking from Germany, not France.

As it had stood, then, at the beginning of June, Dowding's forces would have been facing an uphill struggle, yet of course Germany had then spent three weeks seeing off France and then had to prepare for the all-out air attack on Britain. Even Hitler recognized that no invasion would be possible unless the Luftwaffe ruled the skies over the invasion front, so clearly the first task was to destroy the RAF. That could not happen at the snap of a finger, however. Unlike the Heinkel 112, the Me109 had a very small range, which meant the mass of German fighters needed to be as near to England as possible. That necessitated creating a mass of fighter airfields in Normandy and the Pas-de-Calais, which would take time: airstrips had to be prepared, anti-aircraft defences brought up and dug in, workshops established, protective pens against bomb blast for the aircraft built. In other words, Dowding's Fighter Command had a bit of time on its side, although it scarcely seemed like that at the time after such a rapid and astonishingly complete defeat on the Continent.

And every day, every week, made a massive difference. On becoming Prime Minister, Churchill had looked to an old friend of his to shake up aircraft production. Unlike Ernst Udet, Lord Beaverbrook was a hugely rich and successful Canadian newspaper baron and about as Machiavellian and ruthless as it was possible to be. He might not have known much about aircraft but he knew a lot about business.

The Ministry of Aircraft Production had been created on 17 May, and Beaverbrook wasted no time in getting down to business. He had been given something of a head start, because a number of so-called 'shadow' factories had already been set up, including, for example, the one at Castle Bromwich, built by Lord Nuffield, owner of Morris vehicles, and designed to mirror the work of parent plants and cope with mass production – rather like the branch factories Bill Knudsen had set up for Ford. And it was also the case that the Air Ministry had earlier established a Supply Committee that had been building up stocks of iron and steel, Perspex sheeting and other key materials. The Government had also authorized, back in April 1938, the building of 12,000 aircraft regardless of cost.

Even so, the impact of Beaverbrook was considerable. He brought in a team of experts and highly able and competent people he knew and trusted. Lord Nuffield was sacked and Morris booted out of the shadow factory at Castle Bromwich, for example, and Vickers Aviation brought in instead. Castle Bromwich would make Spitfires, originally designed and built by the tiny Supermarine company in Southampton, for the rest of the war. Other shadow factories producing Spitfires would soon appear – at Salisbury, at Trowbridge and elsewhere; there were others producing different models. He also immediately limited all future production to just five aircraft: two fighters – the Spitfire and Hurricane – the Blenheim medium bomber, and the Whitley and Hampden heavy bombers. Red tape was cut, workers were expected to work seven days a week, normal labour regulations were cast aside, and orders and instructions were issued by telephone not snail mail. If there were bottlenecks, he sent one of his staff to go directly to the cause and sort it out.

When Beaverbrook had taken over, some 130 new aircraft were being produced every week. By the end of June, this had risen to 300 per week and, in all, some 446 new fighter planes were built in the month. It was considerably more than double what the Luftwaffe was producing. By the beginning of July, fighter command had over 600 fighter aircraft and Dowding was beginning – just – to breathe a little more easily.

Beaverbrook also transformed the repair and salvage of aircraft. This was handled by the Civilian Repair Organization (CRO). New more efficient damage categorizations and indoctrination in the need for long hours paid dividends, as did his taking over of all aircraft storage units, previously handled by the Air Ministry; in fact, the Air Ministry was bypassed entirely. In addition to nearly 300 new aircraft a week, his CRO was adding a further 250 repaired aircraft. In just a few weeks, aircraft production had risen by 62 per cent, new engines by 33 per cent and repaired aircraft by an astonishing 186 per cent. Not everyone at the Air Ministry approved of his somewhat bullying methods or the way he ran roughshod over any potentially conflicting organization, but Dowding was delighted.

Furthermore, Fighter Command had prepared for a defensive air battle over Britain. Dowding had taken over as the first Commander-in-Chief of Fighter Command in 1938 having been at the Air Ministry as Air Member for Research and Development. The latter had exposed him to much new technology, while as C-in-C of Fighter Command he had carefully overseen the development of the world's first fully co-ordinated air defence system.

Key to this was radar, or RDF, as the British called it. Unlike the German Würzburg radar, British radar, developed quite independently, was static and comparatively unsophisticated. Chain Home had a range of around 120 miles and consisted of three 360-feet masts sending out radio pulses and three 240-feet masts for receiving the echo-like reflections. Then there was Chain Home Low, which did not have the same range but could detect possible aircraft at lower heights and with greater detail. Britain now had a continuous chain of these radar stations covering all the southern and eastern coasts of Britain. If any German aircraft came over, they would be detected.

Supplementing this was the Observer Corps, who were volunteer civilians and some 30,000 strong. They were better able to gauge height than radar and also to provide a more accurate visual description. All information from the radar chains and the numerous Observer Corps posts was fed into a central hub at RAF Bentley Priory, the HQ of Fighter Command. This was done by telephone, and huge numbers of new lines were laid, with further back-up lines, so that this information could seamlessly reach the Filter Room at Bentley Priory. In the Filter Room, it was collated and assessed, and a picture of activity created that was fed out to the groups and sectors in Fighter Command. The Command was divided into four groups: 11 Group covered the south-east, 10 Group central south and south-west England, 12 Group the centre of the country and 13 Group the north. Each group was then divided into sectors. Both group headquarters and each sector had not only an Operations Room but also a spare some miles away should the principal one be bombed out. All looked exactly the same and were based on a large map table, a 'tote' board listing the state of play of the squadrons, and a raised dais on which the controllers could see this mass of information at a glance. Everyone in the process knew exactly what they had to do and all specific jobs were interchangeable, so that someone working at the sector station of Biggin Hill, for example, could move to Fighter Command HQ and do the same job.

The squadrons were scrambled to meet incoming enemy formations and then directed, or 'vectored', to their targets by ground controllers operating from the sector Operations Rooms, who communicated by radio. Language was partially coded, but for clarity rather than security. Each aircraft was also equipped with High Frequency Direction Finding, or HF/DF, better known as 'Huff Duff'. This sent out transmissions which would be picked up in the Operations Rooms and enabled ground controllers to see what bearing aircraft were on and so to better direct them to their target. Finally, there was a further piece of equipment in each aircraft called 'IFF' or 'Identification Friend or Foe', which transmitted a distinctive blip if it flew near the coast and was picked up by British radar.

The genius of the system was its simplicity. Lots of clever technology and human efficiency had been brought together to create a defence network that added up to considerably more than the sum of its individual parts. In France, the Luftwaffe had always maintained the initiative because its enemy could only guess where the German planes would be. This would no longer be the case over Britain. Dowding's system could be used both to meet the enemy and to avoid it. The Luftwaffe's prime task was to destroy the RAF. Fighter Command's main requirement was to ensure this did not happen.

The fate of the democracies rested on the outcome of the aerial battle about to be unleashed.

CHAPTER 28

Not Alone

THE SHOCK and scale of defeat on the Continent had plunged many in Britain, particularly its leaders, into deep despair, and there is no doubt that those days at the end of May and beginning of June had been among the darkest hours in its history. For those living in Kent, for example, it must have seemed rather alarming to think that just twenty-odd miles away Nazi swastikas were now fluttering in the summer breeze, and that the entire coastline from the Arctic Circle down through Europe to the west coast of Africa was now under the control either of the Nazis or of those sympathetic to Germany. An image was beginning to emerge of Britain as David battling the mighty Nazi Goliath and valiantly determined to defy Hitler's unstoppable hordes. On 18 June, a cartoon was published in the *Evening Standard* of a Tommy shaking his fist at Nazi-occupied Europe and saying, 'Very well, alone.'

Britain, however, was most certainly not David and nor was it on its own – cut adrift from the rest of Europe, maybe; alone, definitely not. This was quite deliberately underlined in Churchill's 'Finest Hour' speech the same day as Low's cartoon, in which he painted the situation in terms of a clash of good against evil, and a battle for Britain, its Empire, the United States and the rest of the free world against Hitler's designs for world domination. However isolated Britain might have now been from the rest of Europe, there was still much of the world behind it. More importantly, so too was the vast bulk of the world's shipping.

The trouble is that many at the time, and subsequent historians, associated the defeat of Britain's very small land contribution in France with failure of its war effort per se. The cause of this defeat, it was believed, was because of technical, industrial and military failure. It wasn't. Britain was already out-producing Germany in terms of aircraft, tanks and ships, and its purchasing power around the world and access to resources remained second to none. So powerful was Britain globally that it could bully lesser states into giving it credit, which would ensure it continued to out-produce Germany. And while it was certainly true that its Army was much, much smaller than that of Germany, this was part of a deliberate policy to use air and naval power and modern technology rather than millions of front-line troops to fight the war. Steel not flesh was the mantra. As far as Britain was concerned, large-scale armies were an inefficient use of manpower because they inevitably led to higher casualties. This was something Churchill passionately believed in and was nothing new: after all, it had been Churchill, while First Lord of the Admiralty in 1915, who had pioneered the development of the tank – or 'landship' as it had initially been called – with exactly this principle in mind.

The reason for the defeat in France was in part the nature of the Anglo-French alliance, for while it was notable how well the Supreme War Council all got on personally, they were none the less uncomfortable bed-fellows. The chains of command were awkward, for much of the time the political leadership had been ill-suited to the task and there had been far too much faffing about. While this had been a contributory factor, however, France had been the senior partner in the ground war, and so blame for defeat has to be laid largely at its door.

The truth was its commanders were too old – too rooted in the past, and quickly too mentally and physically exhausted to deal with the unfolding disaster. Georges was sixty-four, Gamelin was sixty-eight, Weygand seventy-three, Pétain eighty-four. By contrast, those in the German and British armies – not to mention the Dutch and Belgian – were almost all in their forties and fifties. The French structure was mired in bureaucracy and was very top-heavy, which had stifled initiative. The French Army had been designed to fight a defensive war to a very strict plan. When that plan had unravelled, its men had not known what to do. Complacency had crept in – there was not one landmine, for example, laid at Sedan, where Guderian's troops had crossed the Meuse; there should have been, but it had been overlooked. Reports of German gridlock in the Ardennes had been dismissed and ignored.

Communications were poor: there were few radios and most messages were sent by either telephone – and lines were frequently cut – or by dispatch riders, who struggled to get through the clogged roads. This meant co-ordinated counter-attacks became impossible. State-of-the-art tanks and millions of soldiers counted for little if they could not actually be deployed.

Be that as it may, Britain's situation had dramatically altered as a result of the defeat in France in two major ways.

The first was with regard to its armed forces. Britain's war strategy had been based on the assumption that most of the ground fighting would be France's responsibility, but now its ally was gone. The BEF had always been small, but while so many men had been brought home, the considerable amounts of equipment that had made them the most mechanized Army in the world had been left behind. In effect, Britain's Army now had to start again from scratch. Like the USA, it was suddenly very poorly equipped and in need of finding ways to rapidly expand and get back on to something like an even footing. Long term, the strategy remained the same. The Army would be built up to fifty-five divisions, although not more, and the priority would remain with air and sea power. Britain would enforce an ever-tighter blockade against Germany, hit back deep into the Reich with its air forces and also strike clandestinely through the occupied territories; Churchill, especially, was taken with the idea of fuelling resistance. Even greater effort and investment would be placed in intelligence. More factories were being built, more ships, more aircraft, more everything – but the fruits of this, aircraft production aside, would not be felt in the next few months. Right now, with Nazi Germany breathing down British necks from across the Channel, there were worrying shortfalls. The country did not have enough anti-aircraft guns, for example. British shipyards were building large numbers of destroyers and smaller corvettes, but it would not be until the following year that the benefit of these would be felt, which was why Churchill had asked Roosevelt for fifty destroyers now.

A far lesser problem was how to arm the Local Defence Volunteers, soon to be renamed the Home Guard. Since 14 May, some 600,000 had volunteered. This force had not even been considered prior to 10 May, and so arming and equipping this huge number of men had not been part of the War Office's considerations before then. The solution was to turn to the USA. The impression often given is one of Britain having sunk so low following Dunkirk that it did not even have enough of that most simple weapon, the rifle. But this is a massively misleading view. Rather, buying 1.7 million rifles for cash from the USA, which Britain did, showed that the UK could swiftly resolve a problem that had unexpectedly arisen. If anything, it demonstrated Britain's strength.

Anyway, a more important point is that before the Army and Home Guard could ever be called upon to fight off an invasion, the Germans would have to defeat the RAF and Royal Navy, so unsurprisingly it was these two services that were causing the biggest concern for Churchill and Britain's war leaders. One of the thorniest issues was what to do about the French Fleet. The Royal Navy had done a good job of crippling the Kriegsmarine's surface fleet, but now the Italians were in the war and if the French Navy were to get into Axis hands too, then combined they could prove a truly serious threat. The Germans had promised solemnly not to commandeer the French Fleet, but Britain could hardly risk its future on a worthless promise by the Nazis.

Some French ships did defect – and with no retribution at all from Germany. These amounted to a couple of battleships, two light cruisers, eight destroyers and five submarines. There were also a number of French capital ships at Alexandria, a British-controlled port, which were immediately demobilized, and others at Toulon, Cherbourg and Brest. The bulk of the Fleet, however, sailed, as instructed by Amiral Darlan, to Mers-el-Kébir near Oran in French Algeria. Darlan had originally intended to send them to Dakar in West Africa or to Martinique in the Caribbean and for them to fight alongside the Allies, but then he was made Minister of Marine in Pétain's government and changed his mind.

There the Fleet sat in Mers-el-Kébir, the French sailors twiddling their thumbs, the British agonizing over what to do. On 28 June, the War Cabinet made up their mind. Force H, part of the Mediterranean Fleet, would blockade the French Fleet at Mers-el-Kébir and give them an ultimatum to surrender or be destroyed.

The unenviable task of dealing with the French Fleet was given to Vice-Admiral James Somerville, who arrived with his force on 2 July and immediately issued the ultimatum. The French commander, Amiral Marcel-Bruno Gensoul, was completely taken aback, not least because he and his men wanted to continue to fight alongside the Allies, but it was a big call to make on behalf of a lot of men and ships. He tried to play for time, but none the less rejected the British demands. At 5.45 p.m., with time having run out, Somerville gave the order to open fire. Of the five French capital ships in harbour, all but one was immobilized; the battleship *Bretagne* was sunk with the loss of 977 of her crew. One battlecruiser limped away to Toulon. A few days later, the battleship *Richelieu* was also put out of action at Dakar. In all, 1,297 men were killed and a further 351 wounded. If anyone had doubted Britain's ruthless determination to fight on, the tragedy of Mers-el-Kébir demonstrated otherwise. There would be a price to pay: the further enmity of Vichy, the hatred of many French; but the threat of the French Fleet falling into enemy hands had gone.

The loss of France and the growing strength of totalitarianism on the Continent, meant that Fascist Spain was now a threat too. British Gibraltar, the tiny island lying on the very south-west tip of the Iberian peninsula and at the mouth of the Mediterranean, was now perceived to be particularly vulnerable. The last thing Britain needed was for General Franco to come into the war on Germany's side, yet despite the political sympathy between Spain and the Third Reich, it was reckoned to be unlikely. After the civil war, Spain was impoverished and in any case was rather too dependent on British supplies to risk further war. In fact, Britain was adopting a cleverly orchestrated game of carrot and stick with the Spanish, offering enough aid to the war-worn country while at the same time making it very clear that the tap would be cut off and made worse with a brutal blockade by the Royal Navy should Franco declare war.

The second way in which Britain's situation had significantly altered was in the loss of so many European trading partners. Most of its timber had come from Scandinavia, a large proportion of its iron ore from Sweden and French North Africa, foodstuffs from Holland and Denmark, oil from Romania. All these trading routes were now closed, although for Oliver Lyttelton, still the Government's Controller of Metals, the fall of France was something of a relief. 'Everyone seemed to have had a burden lifted from his shoulders,' he noted. 'The sense of unity was unmistakable: Britain was one country again.' On one level, this was a ridiculous attitude, but on another it was perhaps understandable. Britain had an unmistakable arrogance and sense of superiority born from having been the pre-eminent global power for some time and from having the world's largest empire. What Lyttelton was really saying was that Britain's war leaders no longer had to play second fiddle to the French; they were back in control of their war strategy without having to pay lip service to an ally about whose temperament and attitude they had grave doubts.

Furthermore, as far as Lyttelton was concerned, Britain could cope with the loss of North African and Swedish iron ore. 'The defeat of France brought no new or startling problems,' he noted. 'Our supplies of metals were brought across the sea from Canada, Australia, Burma and America.' This meant that although Britain had to rethink where many essential resources would come from, this could be done comparatively easily, for not only did Britain have huge overseas interests, but it was also able to benefit from those of other newly conquered countries. The Belgian and Dutch governments-in-exile were now in Britain and brought with them the trading links with their considerable overseas possessions; the Belgians had large copper mines in the Congo, for example, and the Dutch had oil and rubber in the Far East. Not only could these be drawn upon by Britain and its allies, but they could also be denied to Germany. Almost all Norway's merchant fleet had also sailed to Britain; since it possessed the third-largest tanker fleet after Britain and the USA, this was no small fillip. The biggest problem arising from this dramatically altered situation was time – or, rather, round-voyage time, which on average rose by between 30 and 40 per cent after the fall of France. Even short-haul trips, such as coastal shipping around Britain, would soon have to be altered; the Channel, as it increasingly came within range of the Luftwaffe, was too dangerous a passage; the tip of Kent became known as 'Hell's Corner' because shipping passing through was also in range of German guns on the French coast. The alternative was to sail all the way around the top of Scotland instead.

Germany's deal with Romania on 27 May cut off Britain's oil supply in an instant, while providing Hitler with a much-needed source of fuel. However, the USA was the world's largest oil producer, while Venezuela was the second-biggest. The latter's oilfields on Lake Maracaibo shipped crude oil straight to the Dutch West Indies. Instead of purchasing fuel from Romania, Britain could get it from the Americas instead. The supply of oil to Britain, while taking up large amounts of shipping, was not, nor never would be, a major issue, and thus British plans for expanding the Air Force and Navy and for making their fifty-five-division Army entirely mechanized would never be under threat due to a shortage of fuel.

Undoubtedly, though, the single most important nation to Britain's chances of survival was the United States of America, in both the short and the long term. Recognizing the growing popular support for both rearming and keeping Britain in the fight, President Roosevelt delivered an important speech on 12 June. 'We will extend to the opponents of force the material resources of this nation,' he told his audience in Charlottesville, Virginia, 'and, at the same time, we will harness and speed up the use of those resources in order that we ourselves in the Americas may have equipment equal to the task of any emergency and every defence.'

This, of course, was exactly what the British wanted to hear and was followed by renewed requests for all manner of goods and materials, not least the fifty destroyers. FDR still felt unable to release those, but he did promise to do all he could to ensure the sale of aircraft, anti-aircraft guns, ammunition and steel. Also top of Britain's shopping list were machine tools, and large numbers were bought and shipped across the Atlantic – by the end of 1940, some 11,000 would be sent over, all of which would be invaluable for Britain's rapidly growing numbers of factories.

None the less, for the immediate replacement of the losses in Dunkirk, Britain would have to largely rely on its own production. The USA could immediately provide steel, oil and machine tools, but in most other respects America was regarded as much more of a long-term project. The key, as Roosevelt was also keenly aware, was to get US industry building towards all-out war production just as quickly as possible, and in this Britain had a crucial role to play; British orders meant Roosevelt could oversee rapid expansion in the armaments industry without laying himself open to accusations of preparing the US for war. With the election in November and with FDR gearing up to stand for a historic third term, this was of vital importance.

Yet getting American industry operating at the scale Roosevelt was now thinking of was proving to be fraught with any number of obstacles. News of the formation of the National Defense Advisory Commission had not been well received. Officially, it came under the authority of not only the President but the Cabinet as well. For New Dealers, still suspicious of big business, it smacked of a return to the bad old days. For big business, it seemed these industrialists and businessmen called in by the President were still not being given the necessary room to manoeuvre.

Bill Knudsen, in charge of industrial production, tried to ignore these concerns and get on with the task he had been set, which was, in essence, to try and find a way to turn the USA's predominantly consumer manufacturing industry into one that could make weapons. He had begun by assembling a team of men he knew, trusted and respected from his long career, all of whom, like himself, agreed to give up their well-paid jobs and come to Washington to work for nothing more than patriotism. These would become known as the 'One-Dollar-a-Year Men'. Knudsen also went and talked to people, including the Army Chief of Staff, General George Marshall, who pulled no punches about the enormous task now facing them. 'Our greatest need,' Marshall told him, 'is time.' But how much time? That was not clear.

Knudsen was given a better indication of the scale the War Department was thinking about by the third week of June, when it was agreed that the Army would rise to 1 million men by 1 October 1941, 2 million by 1 January 1942, and 4 million by 1 April 1942. It was also expecting an annual production capacity of 9,000, 18,000 and 36,000 aircraft in the same time frame, plus 13,500 planes for the Navy by April 1942. These figures would change, but they were something for Knudsen to go on – a ballpark figure at least.

Such was the state of the armed forces, the US was effectively having to start from scratch. Back in 1918, it had been the leading supplier in the world of TNT explosive, for example, but now produced almost none. Some weapons would have a longer cycle of manufacturing than others, such as tanks and aircraft and even TNT. Others, such as trucks and clothing, had a shorter cycle. Clearly, it needed to set the ball rolling on the longer-cycle items first.

Equally clear was just how clueless the Army was about how this should be done, something Marshall had recognized. Ideas such as economies of scale did not even feature in its planning. There was also an industrial-mobilization plan already in existence, dating back to 1919, which would, theoretically, be launched on Mobilization Day, or M-Day. Rather like Hitler's Z-Plan, it was both woolly and pie-in-the-sky stuff; the very idea of having a mobilization day was ridiculous, because it was self-evidently impossible to simply switch from consumer to military production on a grand scale with the click of a finger.

'Democracy must wage total war against totalitarian war,' Harry Hopkins had written in a memo for the President. 'It must exceed the Nazi in fury, ruthlessness, and efficiency.' He was quite right, and Knudsen understood that perfectly, but it gradually dawned on him that both the Government and the leaders of the armed forces were looking to him and his colleagues to answer those questions about just how far US industry could go.

That was the great unknown. No one could doubt that America had great potential as an armaments producer, but potential is one thing; making it actually happen was quite another, and there were a large number of obstacles in the way.

One of the problems was the attitude of the New Dealers still dominating Washington, and their suspicion of capitalists and big business. Something of a witch-hunt of US armament manufacturers had taken place in the early 1930s. These firms were accused of having deliberately urged America into the last war purely so they could profit as a result. Encouraged by Roosevelt himself, Senator Gerald Nye had led an investigation that heavily criticized leading companies like Du Pont, General Electric, General Motors, Curtiss, Boeing and others, claiming they had been 'merchants of death' driven by greed, lies and hypocrisy. It had been chastening for those under scrutiny and a number, such as Du Pont, had simply turned their back on armaments manufacture as a result; it simply wasn't worth the hassle. This was one of the reasons the US now had almost no explosives.

Furthermore, as a consequence of the Nye Committee, a number of new restrictions and tax laws had been introduced to prohibit any future war profiteering. No firm manufacturing armaments was allowed to make more than 8 per cent profit, which was acceptable, but firms were also to be audited to ensure such a cap *before* a contract was awarded. The problem, though, was that since most companies embarking on arms production would be new to it, they would have no idea what the costs and profits might be until they'd started the work. Second, it was now law that the amortization rate was a staggering sixteen years. This meant no company expenses – such as machinery, labour and so on – could be offset against tax for that period of time. In other words, any company embarking on arms production in 1940 could not claim back any tax breaks until 1956. Finally, anyone who wanted a government contract not only had to go through a lengthy bidding process, but also had to stump up the costs of doing so. This might mean building a prototype tank, for example. Why would any firm invest that amount of money, time and energy for a contract it might never win? Nor would it ever be reimbursed for those costs even if it did win the contract.

The intentions of the Vinson–Trammell Act, which had introduced these tight new laws, were all very noble, but there were now far too many reasons for American industry not to touch arms manufacturing with a barge pole. What was desperately needed at this dramatic moment were plenty of incentives. The trouble was, both the President and the New Dealers had built their administration on tackling big business and curbing the kind of greed and profiteering that was widely believed to have been responsible for the Depression. To cast those ideals – and laws – aside now would be a giant political volte-face.

Knudsen, however, was not a political animal and cared little for such considerations. In a further meeting with FDR, Knudsen asked him, 'Mr President, do you want statistics, or do you want guns?'

Roosevelt laughed. 'What do you mean?'

Knudsen told him – it was a question of choice: the President could keep his laws but then there was little hope of the mass rearmament now being proposed. Instead, he urged the President to axe the pre-contract audit and change the amortization rate – he had to explain to FDR what amortization was – and suggested introducing a letter of intent, something he had picked up from the British. The Army or Navy would send a pre-contract letter of intent to a company, which would protect that manufacturer on any expenditure it made before the contract was actually signed. In other words, the company could get going right away, without tedious bidding, without waiting for a formal contract to be drawn up, and safe in the knowledge it was not investing any time, money or effort for nothing. Any money it put in would be reimbursed.

Roosevelt was initially doubtful, but Knudsen again stressed the importance of clearing paths through red tape. To make the kind of arms in the numbers envisioned required nothing less than a major overhaul of legislation. General Marshall had stressed the battle against time. Tough decisions would have to be made.

The President listened, although not only to Knudsen, but also to his new Secretary for War, Henry L. Stimson, now seventy-two but a grandee of American politics. It had been clear for some time that FDR needed to bring new men to the key offices of War and the Navy. Woodring, Stimson's predecessor, was an isolationist and notoriously ineffective. Edison at the Navy was not much better, yet Roosevelt had always been curiously reluctant to sack people. The axe had finally fallen on both men, however, in June, with France heading for unavoidable defeat and with Britain sending ever more desperate signals for help. Disaster on the other side of the Atlantic had been the spur that had forced FDR to finally take action. Even so, the appointments astounded many of Roosevelt's supporters. Both Stimson and Frank Knox, the new Secretary of the Navy, were Republicans and fervent critics of the New Deal. It showed, as Churchill had also realized, that the focus now had to be on getting ready to tackle Hitler and the potential threat from Imperial Japan. The all-out preparation for war – and war itself should it come to that – had to transcend domestic politics. What Roosevelt now understood was that he needed the best men for the job – whether they be men from big business or Republicans. With public opinion swinging rapidly in favour of rearming, he now felt able to take the political risks needed to see the job done.

Tall, lean and erudite, the Colonel, as Stimson was known, was not only a man of vision, but had served under Presidents Taft and Hoover, was a devout Christian, was highly cultured and had a wide geo-political understanding that many other leading political figures in the United States lacked. Moreover, he had long recognized that the United States needed to be ready for war and had for years taken every opportunity, whether it be speeches, radio broadcasts or newspaper articles, to sound the warning call. That the President was now desperate to make up for lost time was music to his ears. He also recognized in Bill Knudsen not only a kindred spirit but a man who was talking sense. 'My impression of Mr Knudsen's ability and his tact grows with each time I see him,' Stimson noted in his diary. And, like Knudsen, he recognized that big business needed to be able to make money out of rearming. There was no time for any more hysteria about war profiteering. He urged the President to listen to Knudsen's proposals. Within a few days, the letter of intent had been accepted by Congress and the Vinson–Trammell Act suspended. It was another very important step towards rearming.

Meanwhile, across the Atlantic, the great air battle that would surely come had still not started. June had given way to July. The Luftwaffe had begun attacking Channel shipping, but these were skirmishes, as much to draw the RAF out over the sea as anything. For many in Britain, this delay seemed little short of a miracle rather than rooted in hard logistical pragmatics.

Time, General Marshall had pointed out, was their greatest commodity, but this was especially true for Britain, whose shipyards and aircraft factories were now working harder than ever before. 'Today is supposed to be the day on which the German bomber force should be ready and refitted,' scribbled Jock Colville on 8 July. 'I have the impression that Germany is collecting herself for a great spring; and that is an uncomfortable impression.' He did not say on what he was basing this view. The next day, he wrote, 'The invasion and great attack is now said to be due on Thursday.' Again, he did not mention who was saying this. A month later, it *still* hadn't come. 'We still await "The Great Invasion",' noted Gwladys Cox from her flat in Hampstead. By then, invasion fever was calming down somewhat. As the days and weeks passed, so Britain was beginning to breathe just a tiny bit more easily.

But the air attack, at least, would come. And soon.

CHAPTER 29

Indecision

THE ARMISTICE in France had come into effect at 1.35 a.m. on the morning of 25 June. France would be partitioned – the northern half, including Paris, occupied by Germany, the southern two-thirds run by Pétain's new government. By 10 July, the new French Parliament, based at the small Auvergne spa town of Vichy, voted overwhelmingly to give full powers to the Maréchal. After decades of fractious democracy, of one government after another, France had become a totalitarian state under the control of one of its greatest war heroes. For most in France, that seemed like quite a good outcome, all things considered. It wasn't so good for Reynaud and many in his government, however. Daladier and other senior ministers had decided to make a run for North Africa and sailed on 21 June, and in so doing defied Pétain's orders for all Frenchmen to remain in France. On arriving at Casablanca they were promptly arrested. Meanwhile, Paul Reynaud and his mistress, Madame de Portes, were driving south when their car ran off the road and hit a tree. Madame de Portes was killed instantly and Reynaud taken to hospital unconscious. He recovered only to be arrested too.

For many Germans, the swift conquest of France signalled what they assumed was the end of the war. There was widespread relief accompanied by celebrations in Germany, and Hitler was certainly happy to take all of the credit. He took Speer and others on an early-morning tour of Paris and then happily told his acolyte and chief architect it was time to resurrect their plans to transform Berlin. 'Berlin is to be given the style commensurate with the grandeur of our victory,' he assured Speer. 'I regard the accomplishment of these supremely vital constructive tasks for the Reich as the greatest step in the preservation of our victory.'

Hitler had almost skipped for joy at the signing of the armistice and yet, despite this astonishing victory, he was troubled. A new Führer headquarters was set up deep in the Black Forest near Kniebis, codenamed 'Tannenberg', and here, in the forest, Hitler spent much time in contemplation, wondering what to do about Britain. He returned to Berlin on 6 July and paraded through the capital awash with ecstatic crowds and thousands of swastikas fluttering gently in the summer sun. By this time, Hitler had told his inner circle that he intended to make a speech in which he would offer Britain a chance for peace, although he would not say when precisely he would make it. The following day, Count Ciano arrived in Berlin for talks. 'He is rather inclined to continue the struggle,' recorded Ciano, 'and to unleash a storm of wrath and steel upon the English.' From Berlin, Hitler went to Munich for meetings with the Hungarians, then withdrew once more, this time to the Berghof, his villa in the Bavarian Alps.

During the next ten days, Hitler remained at the Berghof, far from the centre of government, as a parade of his senior commanders trooped through, all giving their opinions on what to do about Britain. Preparing appreciations and plans for a variety of differing scenarios should have been the task of the OKW and, specifically, Warlimont's operations team at Section L; after all, that was what they were supposed to do, but this was not the case. Warlimont had tried to discuss some ideas with Jodl, but had been given short shrift. Unbeknown to Warlimont, Jodl had already presented a memo to Hitler outlining his personal thoughts on what to do with Britain. In it, he began with the assumption that victory over Britain was only a matter of time, so a policy of minimizing risks and economizing forces was sensible. Jodl suggested the first task was for the Luftwaffe to destroy the RAF and its factories, then there should be co-ordinated sea and air attacks against British shipping, combined with occasional terror attacks against British cities. An invasion would be the *coup de grâce* when the British will to resist had been broken. Jodl expected this final phase to take place some time in August or September.

Hitler approved the basis of this plan initially on 2 July and then, two weeks later, issued more detailed instructions. In between, he saw Raeder and his naval staff, who gave him their views about an invasion of England, von Brauchitsch and Halder, who discussed with him their opinions on the Army's requirements, then Göring and the Luftwaffe. There were also visits from Admiral Wilhelm Canaris, head of the Abwehr, the Wehrmacht's intelligence service, and others. It was very clear that each of the services had very different views and expectations. The Army, for example, were thinking that the invasion would involve landings from Lyme Regis in the south-west to Deal in Kent, and stretch over a hundred miles. The Kriegsmarine was thinking of something entirely different and wondering how it was going to get enough shipping for an invasion front of just a few miles in Kent alone. None of the various parties appeared to be talking to one another. 'My impression is that the Führer is now more irresolute than ever,' noted Major Gerhard Engel, Hitler's Army Adjutant, in his diary, 'and does not know what to do next.' Engel also wondered whether Hitler was ever now going to make the much-vaunted speech.

He did, eventually, on 19 July, to a packed Reichstag in Berlin. Hitler never liked to say one word when a dozen would do, and he went on for some two and a half hours. Twelve new field marshals had been appointed and Göring elevated to Reichsmarschall, the world's first and last six-star general. Eventually, he turned to Britain. 'I only know clearly,' he told his audience, 'that the continuation of this struggle can end only with the entire destruction of one of the two opponents.' In this, he was spot on; he meant it would be Britain, of course. He then made an 'appeal of reason and common sense' to Britain to come to the negotiation table. He could not, he said, see any reason why the war should go on.

Most felt the Führer's speech lacked its usual fire. A lacklustre performance was, perhaps, not so surprising, coming from a man whose normal clarity of vision and purpose had deserted him. Hitler was spectacularly poorly travelled for a major national leader, and while it is true he had read lots about Frederick the Great and other Prussian military types, his choice of reading was selective to say the least. As a result, his geo-political understanding was poor, as was the case with most of the leading Nazis. He was a continentalist and thought as such. The army was everything and so was land warfare. He did not understand naval power and did not accept that Britain's approach to war was very different. The attack in the West was a battle his forces had trained and were prepared for, but military action against Britain was not. The Channel changed everything. He had expected Britain to sue for peace; expectation had then turned to hope. But the stony silence from Britain in the wake of his Reichstag speech was followed by a broadcast by Halifax, known to Germany as the leading British dove, three days later. 'Hitler may plant the Swastika where he will,' Halifax announced, 'but unless he can sap the strength of Britain, the foundations of his Empire are based on sand.' With that, all hope had been dashed. Hitler finally accepted that he would have to fight Britain after all.

All the while, the Luftwaffe had been preparing landing grounds and anti-aircraft defences, and gradually moving units up towards the Channel coast. Bomber units, with their greater range, could be spread further – Hajo Herrmann and KG4, for example, could remain where they were at Schiphol in Amsterdam – but fighter units with their small fuel tanks needed to be clustered together as close to southern and south-east England as possible. The bulk were being prepared in the Pas-de-Calais. Fighter Command airfields, by contrast, were spread quite widely, which was another small advantage for the RAF. Bombing accuracy was not good, but the Pas-de-Calais was fast becoming such a target-rich environment, Bomber Command could hardly miss.

British bombers were still, almost daily and nightly, flying over and bombing the Reich, much to the consternation of Göring and the Luftwaffe command; RAF Bomber Command mounted no fewer than fifty-eight separate operations in July, of which forty-one were directed at Germany itself.

With this in mind, Oberst Josef Kammhuber was given the task of setting up a night-fighter group using both Me110s and Me109s. Among those drafted in were the fighter pilots of 4/JG2, commanded by Macky Steinhoff. Based at an airfield near Bonn, no one had really thought about how night-fighter operations might work. The use of radar would eventually be brought in, but, to begin with, the pilots were expected to use their wits, their instrument panels and not much more. Steinhoff hated it and thought it a waste of time – he could just about fly all right but could rarely see a thing. 'All the German cities had their lights off,' he said. 'We weren't very successful at it and it's a miracle in itself that I survived at all.'

The rest of JG2, however, was operating from airfields in Normandy. Siegfried Bethke and his *Staffel* were based at Beaumont-le-Roger, and spent most of their time either off duty or at readiness waiting to intercept any marauding RAF bombers. 'We do not notice that England is already constantly being attacked by bombers as the Wehrmacht news said yesterday,' he scribbled at the end of June. He was not wrong. The Luftwaffe was sending bombers over but mostly to attack British coastal shipping and to lay mines in harbours and shipping channels; few bombs were actually landing on British soil. A fortnight later, on 12 July, he wrote, 'Apparently negotiations are underway. The large-scale concentration of troops is apparently completed. Supplies and everything else are apparently in order. In Germany, apparently thousands of very simple ten-man boats are being built for the invasion. All rumours.' Then he wrote, 'What is really happening: bomb attacks from both sides every day and night.' The Luftwaffe would up the ante in July, but even then there were only eight night raids on land targets of any note – the rest of the effort was again directed at shipping.

Because the Luftwaffe was not using radar, the only way to meet the frequent bombing raids by the RAF was to have several pilots strapped into their Messerschmitts and ready to take off the moment an intruder was spotted or reported. In fact, Bethke and his comrades were experiencing much the same as British and French pilots had back in May and early June, albeit at not quite such a frenetic rate. Bethke flew just five times in all July and, as the month wore on, became increasingly frustrated. 'When will it finally start?' he asked on 24 July. 'According to rumours,' he scribbled two days later, 'it should start soon.' But as July gave way to August, the 'attack of the eagles', as Göring had decided to call his air assault, had still not been launched.

Among those from Bomber Command attacking German targets was Tony Smyth, now recovered and back with 101 Squadron. The squadron had been attached to 2 Group but in reserve until 1 July, when it returned to operational flying once more. Based at West Raynham in Norfolk, it was joined by the battered remnants of 18 Squadron, which like 101 operated with Bristol Blenheims. 18 Squadron had returned from France with just three pilots still standing and tension quickly arose between the two, as the 18 Squadron survivors resented the reserve status 101 Squadron had enjoyed during the Battle of France. However, it was precisely because of the mauling of the Blenheim squadrons that Bomber Command had decreed that, in future, they would only operate over the Continent at night or with either a fighter escort or a decent amount of cloud cover for protection.

As a result, Smyth had a number of operations cancelled at the last moment, and it wasn't until 1 August that he flew operationally once more. His primary target was in the Ruhr, while the secondary was Leeuwarden airfield in northern Holland. Discovering the cloud was too sparse over the Ruhr, Smyth made for Leeuwarden instead, which he soon found. Diving from just 2,000 feet to 1,000, he delivered his two 250lb bombs and a stick of 40lb bombs, photographing the drop as they roared over. With no ground fire at all, they had dropped their bombs and were on their way and back into the safety of the cloud. 'Feeling highly elated,' he noted, 'we set course for home.' That same day, another 101 Squadron crew hit Schiphol and one other attacked Waalhaven. All managed to hit something, although even at 1,000 feet it was difficult to be really accurate. In any case, a lone Blenheim was hardly going to cause mass destruction. These were really just nuisance raids – or 'Rhubarbs', as the bomber boys called them.

At the same time, the Luftwaffe fighter squadrons were being sent over from the Pas-de-Calais, but for the most part, the Luftwaffe command was happy to let bomber formations operate independently; there was a sense of preserving strength for the main event. Hajo Herrmann and his *Staffel*, for example, had operated several times laying mines at the mouths of British ports and attacking specific targets such as the Vickers factory in Newcastle, which they bombed on 2 July. Like those in Bomber Command, however, Herrmann did not find it easy to hit the target. His entire *Staffel* had attacked the Vickers works – some nine Junkers 88s – but none of them hit it. Accurate bombing with little by way of navigational aids and using primitive bomb sights was very, very difficult.

The Stukas were also discovering that operations on British shipping were becoming ever more fraught, with British fighters descending on them as soon as they neared their targets. On 25 July, Helmut Mahlke, now *Gruppenkommandeur* of the newly designated III/StG 1, had been attacking a convoy with his *Gruppe* when they were attacked in turn as they emerged from their dives. On this occasion, the arrival of their own fighter escort saved them, but although his entire *Gruppe* landed back down again at Théville, one gunner had been killed and another wounded and many of the Stukas were badly damaged. 'One thing was already abundantly clear,' noted Mahlke, 'Britain's fighters were beginning to make our job ever more difficult and dangerous.'

Meanwhile, the squadrons of Fighter Command were trying to resist the urge to follow the Luftwaffe out to sea and using the time not only to meet the threat but also to recover from the intense battles over Dunkirk and in France. One squadron licking its wounds from Dunkirk was 609. A pre-war auxiliary squadron, in ethos rather like a Territorial Yeomanry regiment, it had been filled with young landowners and professionals from the West Riding in Yorkshire. They had been a tight-knit bunch, many of whom had known each other most of their short lives. Over Dunkirk, they had lost three killed and one wounded, and two more were still missing. In a squadron of nearly two dozen pilots, these were grievous losses and especially so since most were all such good friends.

At the end of June, 609 Squadron had been posted from Northolt in west London to Middle Wallop, near Salisbury, as part of 10 Group. It was also given a new CO, Squadron Leader George Darley, who since his return in June had been posted as a supernumerary squadron leader to a Spitfire squadron operating from Hornchurch in Essex.

Darley had taken one look at 609 Squadron and, realizing they were low on morale and feeling sorry for themselves, had decided a kick up their backsides was what they needed. Calling the pilots together, he took off his jacket, rolled up his sleeves and said that if anyone disagreed with anything he was about to say, he would see them outside and sort it out man-to-man. He then told them they were a miserable and ignorant lot, but they were not going to stay that way. He promised to lick them into shape. Having then grilled them about their experiences thus far, he set to work. 'To me it was apparent that the main causes,' he said, 'were too rigid a formation and no knowledge of deflection shooting.'

At the time, Fighter Command squadrons were trained to follow set-piece formation attacks, which looked impressive in practice but simply did not work in the cut-and-thrust of aerial combat. Gunnery was a problem for both sides since there was no effective way of practical training; however, the principles of deflection shooting – that is, aiming at a point where bullets and target would meet – could be taught, as could a variety of combat manoeuvres. Darley also dismissed the standard firing range of 400 yards and insisted on a maximum range of 250 yards.

Spitfires and Hurricanes were armed only with .303 Browning machine guns, which were little more than pea-shooters. The actual bullet that was fired was the size of a fingernail and, unless fired at close range, packed a very small punch indeed. Back in 1925, a report had pointed out that 'a .303' bullet has but little effect on any aeroplane'. This was at a time when aircraft were still made predominantly of wood and doped linen.

By 1940, it was even less effective, and, furthermore, Spitfires and Hurricanes had just 14.7 seconds of ammunition compared with the 55 seconds of the Me109. Machine guns could be harmonized so that the bullets of all eight converged at a certain distance, and as those who had fought in France and over Dunkirk had learned, the only way Brownings could be effective was by getting as close as possible. The closer a pilot opened fire, the more effective he would be; the more effective, the less time spent hammering away at a target, which in turn made him vulnerable and quickly used up his meagre supplies of ammunition.

Setting up a programme of practice attacks, with himself as the elusive target, they soon began to dramatically improve. Darley had recognized that the older auxiliary pilots were depressed about the loss of their pals, and this atmosphere was doing nothing for the morale of the younger pilots. 'The basic need,' he said, 'was to restore morale by improving the kill/loss ratio.'

However obvious this may sound, it was men with experience such as George Darley and others sprinkled through Fighter Command who were now licking many of the fighter squadrons into shape. The Luftwaffe had learned much from those who had experienced the Condor Legion in Spain, and then from Poland; Fighter Command was now benefiting from those who had seen combat in France.

Darley also had them both training and operating as a full squadron of twelve aircraft, divided into the standard 'vics' of three. But Darley would lead with one vic, and with one either side, spread out and above, and with a further vic some 500 feet above them. He taught them all to constantly look around, repeatedly shift their position and to keep up-sun as far as possible. Each pilot was rotated to fly every single position too. He also taught them to try and disperse any enemy formation – the key was to get the bombers to drop their loads away from their target, which was best achieved by flying head-on towards them, no matter how overwhelming the enemy numbers.

The squadron lost two more pilots during July and were frustrated by orders to fly standing patrols over Channel convoys, but by August were in good shape. The learning curve had been steep, but a month of comparatively light operational flying had allowed them the time to improve their fighter skills dramatically. Morale had risen too. Darley, widely loathed initially, had won his squadron over. They had accepted he was a man who knew what he was talking about and respected the fact that he was looking after them in the air and on the ground. On one occasion, they had been operating from the forward base at Warmwell on the Dorset coast. When the Mess staff had refused to make them breakfast at 3 a.m. in the morning, Darley had gone into the kitchens and made bacon and eggs for his pilots himself. It was a gesture that had gone down well.

On 8 August, when they were scrambled to intercept a formation of Stukas and their fighter escort heading to attack Warmwell, the squadron were able to put all the training into practice. They shot down three Me110s and two Stukas in that one engagement. Darley himself, weaving in and out of cloud after the initial contact, followed an Me110, then dived down and opened fire at 250 yards, then closed to just 75 yards. Breaking to starboard, he watched the aircraft plunge down into the sea. 'We soon sorted them out,' said Darley, 'and only one or two managed to lob their bombs on to the sacred airfield.'

Watching the unfolding air battles with keen interest was Colonel Carl Spaatz, or 'Toohey' as he had been known ever since picking up the nickname at West Point. Officially, Spaatz was in Britain as an Assistant Air Attaché, but to General 'Hap' Arnold, the US Chief of the Army Air Corps, he had described himself as 'a high-class spy'. His role was in part to observe and to study RAF training and tactics, and also to unofficially discuss British aircraft requirements.

Spaatz was nearly forty-nine when he reached Britain on the last day of May, having travelled via ship to Italy and then by train across France and finally boat again. With France collapsing and the Dunkirk evacuation at its zenith, he had arrived in London to find Britain in deep crisis. An experienced air man with combat experience from the last war, Spaatz had risen up the ranks of the Air Corps to become Chief of Plans at the Office of the Chief of the Air Corps, and as such had been intimately involved in trying to both modernize US air forces and increase their size. One of his frustrations had been that while the President had, back in November 1938, told Arnold that he wanted an Air Force of at least 20,000 aircraft with a production capacity of 2,000 planes a month, Spaatz had been unable to do much to realize those lofty aims – not least because British and French orders kept taking precedence. By the time he had left for Britain, combined British and French orders had been placed for 14,000 aircraft. Spaatz rather felt the US should build up its own air forces before handing them over to another country.

BATTLE OF BRITAIN, July–October 1940

KEY

RAF

⊙ command headquarters
⊕ group headquarters
○ sector station
⚓ fighter base
⚐ low-level radar station
⚑ high-level radar station
🌿 towns bombed

LUFTWAFFE

✝ fighter base
𝄪 bomber base

Glasgow
Turnhouse
Belfast
Newcastle
Sunderland
Usworth
Middlesbrough

Irish Sea

LUFTFLOTTE 3
from Norway and Denmark

Range of high-level radar

North Sea

Range of low-level radar

FIGHTER
COMMAND
GROUP 13
Church Fenton
Hull
Liverpool
Manchester
Kirton in Lindsey
Sheffield
Digby

BRITAIN

Nottingham
Wittering
FIGHTER COMMAND
GROUP 12
Birmingham
Coventry
Duxford
Norwich

Amsterdam

NETHERLANDS
Rotterdam
Antwerp

Swansea
Cardiff
Bristol
Filton
Ipswich
Debden
North Weald
FIGHTER
COMMAND
GROUP 10
Stanmore
Northolt
Uxbridge
LONDON
Kenley
Hornchurch
Biggin Hill
Canterbury
Ghent

BELGIUM

Middle Wallop
Southampton
Portsmouth
Tangmere
FIGHTER COMMAND
GROUP 11
Calais
Lille

Exeter
Plymouth

English Channel

Range of low-level radar

Cherbourg
Le Havre

Amiens

LUFTFLOTTE 2

LUFTFLOTTE 3

PARIS

Rennes

FRANCE

Range of high-level radar

N

| 0 | | 100 km |
| 0 | | 100 miles |

Spaatz was stockily built, with piercing blue eyes which revealed both a great sense of humour but also a toughness and a natural air of authority. By his own admission, he was no air power intellectual; rather, he depended on his own instinct and intuition and the persuasiveness of those he respected. Fiercely loyal, he was quick-witted, pragmatic and cool-headed. These attributes had served him well, and continued to do so now that he was in Britain. He immediately struck up an important rapport with his opposite number, Air Commodore John Slessor, and as he toured RAF facilities around the country their friendship grew.

During the second half of July, Spaatz spent time with RAF Bomber Command, including nine days on a Wellington bomber station. The British bomber crews were quite frank with him about how inaccurate their bombing was. Pre-war US air doctrine was firmly glued to daylight bombing, and his observations of British night-time bombing operations did nothing to change his mind.

On the other hand, by the beginning of August, he was fairly certain the Luftwaffe could not hope to destroy the RAF, even though Göring's main assault had yet to start. 'Unless the Germans have more up their sleeve than they have shown so far,' he wrote to Arnold, 'their chance of success in destroying the RAF is not particularly good. In air combat, German losses in daylight raids will be huge. In night attacks, the accuracy of their bombing is of very low order.'

Meanwhile, Britain's Dominions and Empire were showing the mother country it was not alone. Britain was still aiming for an army of fifty-five divisions and expected twenty-one of those to be provided by its Dominions and the Empire. One Canadian division had already reached Britain and another was on its way. Australia and New Zealand as well were sending troops to help, earmarked for the Middle East. An Indian Army Division, the 4th, had also been formed in Egypt.

A plan had been undertaken, too, to dramatically increase the number of air-training schools. The problem facing Britain was that the country was geographically small, lay in the firing line, and had inconsistent weather. These constraints did not apply to Canada, where the Empire Air Training Scheme had been established. A large number of training schools were being built with the aim of producing some 24,000 pilots and aircrew a year from across Britain's Dominions. The first courses had begun that April, and now new schools were being set up in Rhodesia and South Africa.

But there were also others reaching Britain: Poles, Czechs, Americans, South Africans, Norwegians, Danes, Dutch, French and Belgians – some just to flee the Nazis, others to continue the fight. Général de Gaulle had returned to France on 17 June only to fly back to Britain along with Edward Spears. In fact, it had been Spears who had helped arrange the last-minute flight from Bordeaux, and it was Spears who had taken him to a small flat in Curzon Street that would be his temporary home and then on to see Churchill. On 18 June, de Gaulle had made a broadcast on the BBC, announcing that 'the flame of French resistance must not be extinguished and will not be extinguished.' The following day, he made a second broadcast, announcing that he was speaking in the name of France and urging Frenchmen to rally to his call. Few heard it in France, while most of the 150,000 French troops evacuated to Britain would choose to return home. This was perhaps not so very surprising. To the majority of beleaguered French servicemen, it seemed better to get out of the war, and to head back to their families and what they thought would be peace, than to stay on and fight from a country that looked as likely to fall as France. At any rate, if de Gaulle's broadcast was the first flame of resistance, it was a very small one.

Yet there were still large numbers of French desperately trying to escape, including Capitaine Barlone, who was stuck in Bayonne urgently trying to work out how to get to England.

Also escaping France was a nineteen-year-old Parisian, Jean-Mathieu Boris. On 10 May, he had been studying for entry to the École Polytechnique, but the arrival of the Germans put paid to that. With no news from his father, who was away fighting with Georges's Northern Armies, on 13 June his mother decided they should all leave Paris and head south to her sisters-in-law. It was there, in Rennes, that Boris left his brothers and mother and continued south. 'I decided,' he said, 'not to accept the defeat.' Rather, he planned to travel on to Algeria to join the Army of Africa. On 23 June, he eventually reached Saint-Jean-de-Luz, a small port on the French–Spanish border, where he saw some Polish soldiers leaving. They had left their uniforms on the quayside, but because Pétain had already declared that no Frenchman could leave the country, he took a Polish uniform, put it on and managed to get through the French officials and on to a British ship, the *Baron Nairn*, that was leaving the port. 'You don't look very Polish,' one of the officials said to him, but Boris pretended he did not understand and was eventually waved through.

Also on the *Baron Nairn* with Boris were three American pilots, one of whom was a lanky, ginger-haired 23-year-old, Eugene 'Red' Tobin. He had made the trip to Canada and then across the Atlantic after originally quitting his job flying MGM Studio's stars around the States to go and fly for the Finns. When news reached him that Finland had ended the war with the Soviet Union, he was stuck with no job and wondering what to do next. A week later, he had been approached by a nameless French contact and asked if he would fly for the French Armée de l'Air instead. Tobin agreed, as did two fellow Americans who had made the trip with him: Andy Mamedoff, the debonair son of White Russian émigrés, and Vernon Keogh, who at just four feet ten was, unsurprisingly, always known as 'Shorty'.

Giving up his glamorous Hollywood job and heading off to fight in another country's war was, on many levels, a brave decision. Tobin's job for MGM had given him the chance to fly pretty much every day in skies clear of enemy aircraft trying to shoot him down, while volunteering to fight for a foreign country's armed forces was illegal in the USA. If caught, he faced a large fine, a jail sentence and having his passport torn up. But he was young, thirsting for adventure and desperate to fly fast, modern fighter aircraft like the Supermarine Spitfire, which, as far as he was concerned, was the 'sweetest little ship in the world'. In any case, he reckoned America would get drawn into the war eventually, and he certainly didn't want to get drafted into the Army as a soldier. A much better option, he reckoned, was to head over to Europe right away and get flying.

By the time he, Mamedoff and Keogh had finally reached Paris at the beginning of June, it seemed the huge gamble they had all taken had been for nothing. The agent they were supposed to contact had disappeared; at the French Air Ministry no one seemed able to help them; and France faced imminent defeat. On 11 June, they had decided to leave Paris, along with half the capital, and had caught a packed train to Tours. There, they had finally been cleared to fly, but then the airfield had been bombed and when they tried to hijack an aircraft with two Czech pilots, they had been shot at by French troops and had fled. They had reached Saint-Jean-de-Luz the same day the armistice had been signed. Unlike Jean-Mathieu, they simply pushed their way on to the *Baron Nairn*.

Jean-Mathieu Boris had thought the boat would take them to North Africa, but instead it sailed to Plymouth in England. From there the young Frenchman made his way to London and, after being screened by British intelligence, he and several others he had travelled with made their way to de Gaulle's new headquarters, intending to join the Légion de volontaires français, as this embryo force was being called. He was given the number 850, then they were sent to a makeshift camp at the Exhibition Hall at Olympia in west London. On 11 July, some 500 of them left Olympia and were sent to the British Army camp at Aldershot. Here they would begin their training as soldiers.

Red Tobin and his two fellow Americans, meanwhile, had safely landed in Britain and made their way to London. There, they were told in no uncertain terms by the US Embassy that they should head back to America as soon as possible. However, on the ship to Plymouth, they had befriended an English lady who had promised to help if they ever needed it.

Now taking up that lifeline, strings were pulled and soon after they were being interviewed by an RAF recruiting officer and told that so long as they swore allegiance to King George VI, they would be accepted. In effect, they were being asked to give up their American citizenship, but all three made the pledge readily enough; they were young, had travelled a long way, and had crossed the Atlantic to fly. Now that the possibility of actually getting into a Spitfire was within touching distance, they were not going to forego the chance over some trifling matter of citizenship. On 9 July, the three of them were posted to No. 7 Operational Training Unit (OTU) at Hawarden. 'Well,' said Tobin, 'we'd made it! We were in at last!'

A few days later, on 15 July, Jean Offenberg and his friend Alexis Jottard reached England too, arriving in Liverpool on board the freighter *Har Sion*. It had been a long journey from France that had meant defying orders and stealing a French plane, flying to Corsica, then Maison Blanche, Algiers and Casablanca, before finally catching the boat to England. Two days later, after being sent to London for medicals, they were posted to 6 OTU to carry out their conversion to British fighter planes. They were among fifteen Belgians who would be joining RAF Fighter Command, and a further fourteen that would be posted to Coastal Command.

Offenberg and Jottard trained on Hawker Hurricanes. They were not as fast as the Spitfires and were very much a progression of earlier Hawker biplanes, with their doped-linen-covered fuselages. Nor were they as quick to climb as either the Me109 or the Spitfire, but they were none the less robust, provided a solid gun platform, and were highly manoeuvrable. Perhaps more importantly, there were a lot more of them than Spitfires, and as a weapon to take on German bombers and Me110s they were more than adequate. At any rate, they were a vast improvement on the obsolescent Fiats the Belgians had been flying. Offenberg found flying the Hurricane 'a piece of cake'. By the end of July, both men had been given commissions in the Royal Air Force Volunteer Reserve and been posted to 145 Squadron at Drem, near Edinburgh, in 13 Group.

Throughout July, the Luftwaffe had barely used 10 per cent of its strength. It had lost some 185 aircraft, while Fighter Command had lost 91. In the same time, Messerschmitt had produced 240 new Me109s, while the Ministry of Aircraft Production had built 496 Spitfires and Hurricanes. It was a ratio that would not improve for Germany any time soon.

The question for Air Chief Marshal Dowding and Britain's war leaders, however, was whether the gains made since the fall of France would be enough when Göring unleashed his eagles.

CHAPTER 30

Adler-Angriff

AFTER THE EUPHORIA of victory, the German armies went back to training. In July, 7. Panzerdivision, for example, transferred to an area west of Paris, where it began preparing for Operation SEALION, the codename for the planned invasion of Britain. 'This,' noted Leutnant Hans von Luck, 'was the start of wearisome weeks and months of preparation.' On the River Seine, it practised loading and unloading converted barges over and over. The young paratrooper Martin Pöppel, meanwhile, having been briefly posted to Norway to support the troops at Narvik, was now back in Germany at a training camp at Gardelegen north of Magdeburg. For his actions in Holland on 10 May, he had been awarded both the Iron Cross First and Second Class and promoted to *Oberjäger*, the equivalent to a sergeant. He was also now a machine-gunner in a newly formed machine-gun battalion. If they were training for the invasion of Britain, however, no one said so. The *Fallschirmjäger*, part of the Luftwaffe, came under Göring's command, and he had so far refused to commit them to SEALION.

In Britain, it was the prospect of massed formations of German paratroopers suddenly falling out of the sky that was among the greatest fears of many. A. G. Street was hard at it farming by day – he had ploughed up 90 acres of grassland and had begun the year's grain harvest – and keeping watch for enemy parachutists by night, having joined his local Home Guard. By the beginning of August, there were still not enough uniforms and weapons to go round, but the situation was improving. 'Observation duty,' he wrote, 'had now settled down to a regular feature of every man's everyday life, while the evening and Sunday morning drill had turned what had been an unsoldierly rabble into a body of men who could obey simple orders without question, and who now yearned for less drill and more weapon training.' The Home Guard has traditionally been seen as part of the amateurish backs-to-the-wall approach of Little Britain, but for the most part these units quickly sorted themselves out into a valuable second-string force, mixing former soldiers from the last war, who knew a thing or two about army discipline and front-line experience, with those in reserved occupations. In the country, farmers, especially, tended not only to be good shots, but also knew the land like the backs of their hands. Some were too old to fight in the Regular Army, but recruiting older men was not unique to Britain; Germany was doing so too, and most of what the OKH termed Third and Fourth Wave troops were reservists with little training or former 1914–18 veterans. These amounted to some 1.6 million men, so a similar number to those now in the Home Guard.

Meanwhile, the Regular Army troops were recovering from their ordeal in France. Bill Cheall and the survivors of his battalion of The Green Howards were sent to Cardiff, where they were fattened up and given the chance to regain their strength, then, on 18 June, to Cornwall, to a Nissen hut camp near Launceston. Here the battalion was rapidly brought up to strength and transferred to the newly formed 50th 'Tyne Tees' Division. Cheall was also impressed with the swiftness at which all their equipment, left in France, was replaced. 'We were given a full complement of Bren guns, Bren carriers, anti-tank weapons, 15 cwt trucks plus all the backing the division could now provide,' noted Cheall. 'We had anything we needed to enable us to take offensive action.'

By early July, they were on the move again, this time to the south coast, near Bournemouth, on anti-invasion duty, which, for the most part, was enjoyable enough. They were based near Highcliffe Castle, and, as batman to the company commander, Cheall was given a room in the castle itself. Most of their daily tasks were preparing beach defences: building gun emplacements and laying wire and mines. 'We felt very confident of our ability to give a good account of ourselves should the enemy try to set foot on our part of the coast,' Cheall wrote. 'Our earlier confrontations with the Germans had given us the confidence – we had been well blooded in warfare.'

Also now serving with The Green Howards was Hedley Verity, the England cricketer, who had been given a commission and was an officer

MIGHTIER YET!

Every day more PLANES
Every day more PILOTS

Above left: Britain was keen to tell its people that factories were working full-tilt. And so they were – out-producing Germany in aircraft, tanks and ships by the summer of 1940.

Above right: Britain's new Prime Minister, Winston Churchill. His geo-political understanding was crucial to Allied fortunes.

An Allied trans-Atlantic convoy. On any given day, more than 2,000 merchant ships were sailing on Britain's behalf. Even with European markets cut off, Britain's access to the world's resources was at a level of which Germany could only dream.

Top: Hitler salutes a triumphal procession. The Germans were still giddy with victory in July 1940, and most believed the war was all but over.

Above left: Teddy Suhren, 1WO on the U-boat *U-48*.

Above right: Squadron Leader George Darley, brought in to shake up 609 Squadron and lick them into shape following their losses over Dunkirk.

Left: Donald Macintyre, destroyer captain and Escort Group commander, protecting trans-Atlantic convoys.

Left: A British merchant ship is struck by a torpedo and sunk.

Below: *U-48* returning from a successful patrol. With much of the British Home Fleet on invasion watch, leaving convoys under-protected, the summer and autumn of 1940 became known as the 'Happy Time' for the small band of U-boats operating in the Atlantic.

Bottom left/right: The President of the United States, Franklin D. Roosevelt (*left*), speaking on 10 May 1940, and his friend and advisor, Harry Hopkins (*right*).

Above: The Wiltshire farmer, A. G. Street.

Left: General Adolf von Schell, the man given the unenviable task of trying to streamline the German motor industry.

Above/below: Britain and Germany were Europe's biggest meat consumers. Britain's national meat was mutton, a more practical source of meat as sheep had multiple benefits and did not compete with humans for foodstuffs. The same could not be said for pork, which was Germany's national meat.

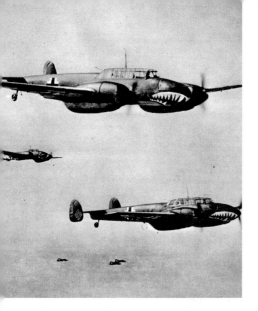

Above left: The Me110 'Destroyer': armed to the teeth, but ill-suited to air-to-air combat.

Above right: A Chain Home radar station, one cog in Britain's very effective air defence system.

Right: A Heinkel 111 bomber flies over southern England.

Below: Spitfires of 609 Squadron taking off from Middle Wallop airfield, August 1940.

ARMY FIELD UNIFORMS
Noncommissioned Officers and Enlisted Men

Above left: The Italian Fascist leader, Benito Mussolini.

Above right: Italian uniforms: elaborate, varied and impractical for a cash-strapped, resource-poor nation.

Left: Italian cavalry. Compared with Germany and Britain, Italy was badly behind the times in terms of modern military equipment.

Below: Parades such as these hid innumerable shortcomings in the Italian military.

Above/below: The world's only six-star general Reichsmarschall Hermann Göring was an effective politician and businessman but a poor military commander. His mismanagement of the Luftwaffe over Dunkirk and during the Battle of Britain cost Germany dear. The painting below by Paul Nash shows a scene common over the southern English skies in August and September 1940.

Above left: The construction of Rolls-Royce Merlin engines. Britain was producing more than double the number of aircraft per month than Germany during the Battle of Britain.

Above right: A Luftwaffe bomber crewman on operation over England.

A downed Ju88 in southern England. The Luftwaffe never really recovered from the huge losses it suffered during the long summer of almost constant operations in 1940.

in the 1st Battalion and helping to train troops at the Green Howards' depot at Richmond in Yorkshire. He had quickly gained a reputation as a strict disciplinarian, but a fair-minded one too. Not only that, but he was happy to bowl to his men in the cricket nets at the end of the day's training. Many of them already idolized him for his cricketing prowess; bowling to them helped create an even greater sense of loyalty.

There could be no invasion, however, without control of the air – the risks to the troops crossing the Channel and the support operations of the Luftwaffe in containing British defences would otherwise be too great. No matter how disparate the plans of the German Army, Navy and Air Force, there was no dispute over this essential prerequisite for SEALION. The RAF had to be destroyed.

By the beginning of August, the Luftwaffe had three air fleets ready and raring to go. There were Luftflotte 5 in Norway, Luftflotte 3 in Normandy and the largest, Luftflotte 2, in northern France and the Low Countries. The last was commanded by a former Luftwaffe Chief of Staff, Feldmarschall Albert Kesselring, who had proved himself a far more able air commander than administrator during the battles for Poland and France and had been promoted to five-star rank as a result. Together, these three air fleets amounted to 3,358 aircraft on the various *Staffeln* and *Gruppen* lists, and a serviceable number, ready to fly, of 2,550 of all types.

On 1 August 1940, Hitler issued his latest War Directive, No. 16, 'On preparations for a landing operation against England'. Raeder had told him the Kriegsmarine would not be ready for the invasion before 15 September, and in fact they were still arguing with the OKH over the size and breadth of the potential invasion front. This date, however, became the deadline for which all preparations had to be completed, and that included not only defeat of the RAF but also containment of the Royal Navy and creating a corridor through the English Channel that had been swept clear of mines.

Incredibly, Göring had still not asked his air fleet commanders for their own thoughts on the forthcoming air battle, but, with Hitler's directive now issued, he ordered them to submit their own plans the same day. Again, the idea of sitting round a table and working a solution out together does not appear to have occurred to him. Hitler's directive had been quite specific: civilian targets were to be avoided, and the attack was to focus on destroying the RAF in the air and on the ground, yet even with those guidelines the plans then submitted by the air fleets were all quite different. Not until 6 August had they been ironed out into a co-ordinated plan, but then the weather intervened. Göring reckoned it would take just four days in all to knock out the RAF, but the caveat was four continuous days. Not until 13 August did the weather appear to be playing ball. This, then, was to be *Adlertag*, 'Eagle Day' – the launch of the 'Attack of the Eagles'.

Up to this point, Göring was confident of victory and that his four-day time frame was a reasonable appreciation. This was largely due to the Luftwaffe's intelligence picture, which was some way off reality, to say the least. The Luftwaffe had a number of different intelligence units, but it was the 5th and the 3rd Abteilung that were the most important. The former was run by Oberst 'Beppo' Schmid, who was a good party man, had been at the Beer Hall Putsch in 1923, and served on Göring's personal staff as well as commanding the 5th Abteilung, whose task was to gain information about enemy air forces. Schmid had never travelled, spoke no foreign languages, had never learned to fly, but was shrewd and cunning and knew how to keep in Göring's good books. The 3rd Abteilung, on the other hand, was a signals unit and radio-listening service and was run by General Wolfgang Martini. Despite Martini's superior rank, how-ever, there was no question that Schmid had considerably more influence. Because intelligence meant power in Nazi Germany, rival units were not very good at sharing information, which did not help when trying to create a full intelligence picture of the enemy.

In fact, for the most part, German intelligence was not especially good. Göring's Forschungsamt had been very helpful in the run-up to war because many of the key players were communicating from within the Reich – such as the French and British ambassadors – and their communi-cations were easy enough to both tap and intercept. This was no longer the case, so while the Forschungsamt remained critically important for Göring in keeping a check on his rivals and enemies within Germany and the Axis, it was less useful in adding to the broader intelligence picture.

Elsewhere, intelligence was split between the Nazi party security service and intelligence within the Wehrmacht. The security service, the Sicherheitsdienst, or SD, which included the Gestapo, the secret police, was concerned mainly with internal security within the Greater Reich and all occupied territories rather than specifically military intelligence.

Under the control of the OKW, there was the Foreign Information and Counter-Intelligence Service, the Abwehr. This was commanded by Admiral Canaris, who, since Hitler's move on Czechoslovakia, had turned against the Führer and the regime; he had even been co-operating with the British to keep Fascist Spain neutral. Under him there was also a Foreign Information Division and a Press Evaluation Group, as well as a cipher branch. The Kriegsmarine had its own intelligence service and its own signal intelligence branch, the B-Dienst.

This meant very little of German intelligence was in any way joined up; the lack of co-operation within the Luftwaffe's own intelligence department was symptomatic of the German intelligence organization as a whole. The reality was that the only time this intelligence came together was at the very top – that is, with Hitler himself.

It was perhaps, then, not surprising that it was Colonel Beppo Schmid, not General Martini, who on 16 July submitted to Göring the principal intelligence appreciation of the RAF, which became the basis for the Luftwaffe General Staff's plans. He underestimated the strength of squadrons, claiming they were eighteen aircraft strong, when in fact they had between twenty-two and twenty-four aircraft. He also stated that only a limited number of airfields could be considered operational with modern maintenance and supply installations, which was nonsense. He badly underestimated current aircraft production figures to the tune of about 50 per cent and claimed there was 'little strategic flexibility', when, in fact, Dowding's air defence system provided exactly the opposite. The Me110, he claimed, was a superior fighter to the Hurricane. Even more glaring were the omissions. The Luftwaffe had no concept of how the air defence system worked, no concept of there being three different commands – Fighter, Coastal and Bomber – and no understanding of how repairs were organized. 'The Luftwaffe is clearly superior to the RAF,' he concluded, 'as regards strength, equipment, training, command and location of bases.' He was correct in terms of strength only. The rest of his claims were utter twaddle. On the eve of *Adlertag*, Schmid further reassured the Luftwaffe General Staff that some 350 British fighters had been destroyed since the beginning of July and that they were already being shot down faster than they could be produced. In fact, up to 12 August, 181 had been destroyed and more than 700 new fighter aircraft built. The gulf between fact and fiction was quite startling.

*

The British, by contrast, had a far more joined-up intelligence organization even though, like Germany, each of the armed services had its own intelligence structures. There was also the Secret Intelligence Service, or MI6, which handled foreign intelligence, as well as MI5, which handled home security and counter-intelligence. There were also further units such as MI9, formed in December 1939 to help foreign resistance fighters in enemy-occupied territories.

As far as Air Intelligence was concerned, the biggest source of information came from 'sigint' – signal intelligence. Since 1935, the RAF had maintained a radio intelligence service known as the 'Y' Service, for listening in to and collating low-grade wireless traffic, usually between aircraft, low-grade radio and telephone traffic, and other signals traffic such as navigational beacons. More recently, the service had acquired high-grade ciphers encrypted by the German Enigma coding machines. The Government Code and Cypher School (GC&CS) at Bletchley Park, north of London, had grown rapidly since the outbreak of war, and the intelligence work there had benefited from the recruiting of brilliant young mathematicians such as Alan Turing and Gordon Welchman, both from Cambridge University. GC&CS was its own entity but within its structure had teams dedicated to decoding ciphers on behalf of the three different services.

The Germans had assumed that their Enigma machines were infallible. In fact, thanks to information passed on by the Poles before the war, GC&CS had begun to break general Enigma traffic regularly during the Norwegian campaign and the Luftwaffe key fairly regularly since January. Luftwaffe Enigma traffic was not yet being deciphered with any great speed, but, combined with Y Service sigint, it had enabled Air Intelligence at the Air Ministry in London to build up a fairly accurate picture of the Luftwaffe, its structure and dispositions, as it built up strength for the air assault on Britain. As with Dowding's air defence system, the components of British intelligence added up to much more than the sum of their individual parts. It was certainly the case that dictatorships were more likely to produce highly disciplined militaristic societies, but democracies were more conducive to efficient intelligence.

One of those trying to advise Dowding and the British war chiefs on the Luftwaffe's strength was Group Captain Tommy Elmhirst. Aged forty-five, diminutive and quietly spoken, Elmhirst had sharp, twinkly eyes and uncommonly bushy eyebrows that lent him an air of experience and wisdom that was not without foundation. His background had been the Royal Navy – from ships he had been transferred to airships in the last war, and then switched again, to the newly formed RAF in 1918. Although he had become an experienced pilot, since 1925 he had served in intelligence, first on the Middle East Section and most recently as Air Attaché at the British Embassy in Turkey.

Now he was Deputy Director of Air Intelligence and head of the German Section, which also gave him a seat on the Joint Intelligence Committee. This met daily, and was where all the various intelligence agencies came together and drafted intelligence summaries for the Chiefs of Staff and War Cabinet. The Germans had no equivalent joint organization.

His task was twofold. In the first instance, he had to advise on suitable bombing targets, for which he created a committee formed of representatives of Bomber and Coastal Commands, the War Office, the Admiralty and the Ministry of Economic Warfare, the latter having been formed to fan the fires of resistance in the occupied territories. By pooling data and information, they were able to provide Bomber Command HQ with a weekly directive.

Elmhirst was dubious about how effective Bomber Command's bomber force was, and not as confident as many of his colleagues that there were key targets in Germany's industrial heartland in the Ruhr region in the western Reich which, if destroyed, would paralyse the German war machine. If for him the glass was half empty as far as the RAF's bombing capability went, it seemed to have nothing left in it at all when he contemplated the Air Force's ability to resist the German onslaught when it finally came. The last weeks of July were mostly glorious summer days, but for Elmhirst and his colleagues at Air Intelligence they were 'one long nightmare'. He tried to hide his pessimism, but he was pretty certain they had a clear picture of the Luftwaffe's order of battle, and that made him far from sanguine. Throughout July, his department watched the grouping of the enemy Air Force as it moved airfields near to the coast in Norway, Denmark, Holland, Belgium, Flanders, Normandy and Brittany. By the beginning of August, they knew there were three air fleets now ranged against them; they knew the numbers of bomber, fighter and other groups, as well as the details of squadrons and other units. The only thing they were not so clear about was the individual unit strengths. However, based on the premise that a German *Staffel* was the same size as an RAF squadron, i.e. around 20–24 aircraft strong, they had quickly arrived at a figure of about 4,500 aircraft, of which around 3,000 were perceived to be combat-ready. With Fighter Command's daily combat-ready strength at less than 700 aircraft, this was a terrifying disparity. 'Uppermost in my thoughts,' Elmhirst noted, 'was the question of whether we should have sufficient fighter aircraft to beat off the German attack when it came.'

Elmhirst warned his superiors to expect heavy attacks on RAF airfields and an attempt to destroy the Air Force on the ground. It would, he believed, be a battle of attrition. 'And the outcome would depend on whether each of our pilots could destroy three enemy aircraft for the loss of one of their own.' This was the stark equation as far as Elmhirst was concerned. It was one that made him feel sick with worry, because those odds, following on from defeat on the Continent, seemed too high. 'We, in my Department,' he noted flatly, 'could not be optimistic.'

Elmhirst's prediction about Luftwaffe strategy was bang on the money, although before Göring finally launched *Adlertag* on 13 August 1940, there had been some important softening-up operations. General Martini was well aware of the British radar chain but was uncertain exactly how it was being used. A series of attacks on radar stations all along the south coast were carried out. Ventnor was knocked out, but impulses were then sent out from a mobile transmitter that gave the impression it was still working. Otherwise, Pevensey was up and running again within a few hours and the rest were largely undamaged. Airfields at Lympne and Manston on the south-east tip of Kent were hit and believed to be permanently knocked out. In fact neither was. Part of Dowding's preparations had been to establish not only secondary Operations Rooms, but also huge piles of soil and scalpings with which to fill in bomb craters.

Adlertag itself, when the great day dawned at long last, was something of a damp squib. The bombers of KG2 took off early to attack RAF airfields only to discover they had no fighter escort. In fact, low cloud had prompted cancellation of the operation but while the fighters had received this information, the bombers had not. Once they were airborne and incommunicado, there was no way of recalling them and so they pressed on, were attacked twice, lost a number of planes, and eventually bombed Eastchurch, a Coastal Command airfield with no fighters. Despite this, KG2 claimed ten Spitfires destroyed on the ground. Eastchurch itself was fully operational again within ten hours, even though, like Lympne and Manston, Oberst Beppo Schmid had crossed it off his list as another airfield the Germans no longer needed to worry about.

Further attacks were made throughout the day, including by a formation of around thirty Stukas escorted by some forty fighters, which were heading for an attack on Middle Wallop airfield. The intention had been to achieve complete surprise and smash the aircraft on the ground. However, their progress across the Channel had been picked up and 609 Squadron had been scrambled to meet them. Leading the squadron into battle was Squadron Leader George Darley. Leaving one section up-sun and high in the sky to cover any attack by fighter escorts, he led the rest of the squadron straight into the middle of the Stuka formation. They hurtled through, firing as they went, and Stukas began falling out of the sky or hurriedly dropping their bomb loads and heading for safety. The squadron claimed thirteen enemy aircraft that day for no loss of their own. It would not always be so one-sided, but this one engagement was symptomatic of a day that had not panned out nearly so well as Göring had hoped and expected.

Certainly, Britain's war leaders were rather underwhelmed by the Luftwaffe's efforts of the past few days. 'The question everyone is asking today,' scribbled Jock Colville, 'is what is the motive of these gigantic daylight raids, which cost so much and effect so little? Are they reconnaissance in force, or a diversion, or just the cavalry attack before the main offensive?'

As it happened, Churchill was more concerned that day with issues further afield. Chief of these was what to do about the Middle East, where Britain had considerable interests. Middle East Command was huge, incorporating Egypt, the Suez Canal, Palestine, Iraq, Persia, Aden, East Africa, Transjordan and the island of Malta. Even though Egypt was officially a 'protectorate' and not part of the Empire, it was the hub of this huge swathe of land. General Headquarters, Middle East, was based in a leafy Belle Époque suburb of Cairo called Garden City. Hand-in-hand with Middle East Command was Britain's considerable naval presence. The Royal Navy had been the dominant power in the Mediterranean since Nelson's day, with key ports at either end – Gibraltar in the west, Alexandria in Egypt in the east, and with tiny Malta slap bang in the middle, some sixty miles off the south coast of Sicily. The French armistice, however, had massively changed the picture. No longer was north-west Africa in the hands of an ally. The French also had colonies in Lebanon and Syria, all of which were now Vichy- and thus Axis-controlled.

Now the Royal Navy, already stretched despite its size, would have to take on the Italian Navy and Regia Aeronautica alone, while between Gibraltar and Malta the seas were almost entirely hostile. Supplying the Middle East would be difficult and realistically would mean, for the most part, a long route via South Africa and the Suez Canal, which might take three months. Time counted a great deal in supplying a war. With the Mediterranean closed it was now 13,000 miles instead of 3,000, while to Bombay it was now nearly 11,000 instead of just over 6,000. Malta itself, a crucial staging post and critical offensive base for operations against the Italians, was also now in grave danger – so much so that the Mediterranean Fleet had already moved to Alexandria, which was not much better placed and was highly vulnerable to attack.

In terms of land forces, the British had a mixed body of British, New Zealand and Indian troops in Egypt amounting to roughly two divisions, i.e. around 36,000 men. There were 27,500 men in Palestine, including the Sherwood Rangers Yeomanry, while there were three British battalions in Sudan as well as the Sudan Defence Force, and a couple of brigades in East Africa. RAF Middle East, meanwhile, had just over 200 aircraft of all types.

Across the border from Egypt in Libya, the Italians now had an entire Ninth Army, and it was clear as day that it was only a matter of time before it made a move on Egypt and the Middle East. Churchill was a great admirer of Admiral Andrew Browne Cunningham, C-in-C Mediterranean Fleet, who had just the kind of bullish fighting spirit of which he approved, but was less sure about General Sir Archibald Wavell, who was widely respected for his intellect, but who the PM suspected lacked mental vigour and resolve. In this, however, he was largely alone, as among others Wavell had a very high reputation. The truth was, Wavell's command was enormous and he simply did not have the means to effectively defend all of it. What Churchill took for defeatism in Wavell's signals was actually just realism.

'The PM is very much on edge,' noted Jock Colville on 13 August, 'concerned with the quickest method of sending reinforcements to the Near East before the expected attack on Egypt.' Certainly, on paper,

Britain's position did not look promising. The Mediterranean Fleet had just one aircraft carrier and lacked escorts and minesweepers, while the land and air forces were similarly understrength. With the Mediterranean route now all but closed, any reinforcements would take months to arrive. 'Thus,' noted Churchill, 'we might easily rob the Battle of Britain without helping the Battle of Egypt.' It was a conundrum, but one Britain decided to tackle. After all, if British forces surrendered there, the Mediterranean and Middle East would be gone for good; on the other hand, if they fought on, they might well hold out against the Italians. In fact, they might do better than that.

However, if they were going to defend the Middle East, it would need commitment and that meant sending reinforcements. To do this at the very moment the German aerial onslaught over home soil was beginning was a big call, but one Churchill and his war chiefs were prepared to make.

There was good news from the USA, where the President had at last notified Churchill that America would be prepared to hand over the fifty destroyers in return for leases on British bases in the Western Atlantic. By this time, Roosevelt had declared that he would stand for re-election for a historic third term. It is not clear when exactly he decided, but it was no coincidence that he had spent four days at his house at Hyde Park, New York, just as France was signing the armistice and the crisis in Europe looked at its bleakest. Hopkins had been urging it upon him since the previous year. Massive rearmament was just in the process of beginning, but would another president see this through? Who else had the vision and authority needed to protect the USA from Nazi hegemony? This was not immodesty on FDR's part; this was a pragmatist realizing he was best placed to fulfil the task, even though his Republican opponent, the suave and charismatic Wendell Willkie, was no isolationist.

With the third-term issue now settled, with growing support to aid Britain, and with Willkie assuring Roosevelt he would offer no objection, what had been politically impossible two months earlier was now acceptable. Legal technicalities were overcome, and although there was some negotiating and small print yet to resolve, the destroyers would be handed over to the Royal Navy.

Red Tobin and his two fellow Americans had all been posted to 609 Squadron at Middle Wallop, and, much to their relief, this had meant flying Spitfires. Tobin's first flight had not been a disappointment – never before had he felt such power in an aircraft. 'For the first time in my life,' he said, 'I had a real taste for speed.' Since joining George Darley's new-look squadron at the beginning of August, however, all three had yet to be allowed to fly operationally. Much to Tobin's annoyance, he had missed out on the big fight on 13 August, but a day later Darley asked him to fly his own damaged Spitfire to be repaired. Tobin was strolling over to Hangar 5 with another pilot when a lone Ju88 swooped in low and dropped a stick of bombs. Both men dived to the ground. 'My head was spinning,' said Tobin. 'It felt as though I had a permanent ringing in my ears. I felt the blast go over me as I lay there flattened on the ground.' As the blast subsided, they staggered to their feet and ran towards the wreckage of Hangar 5. One man was lying there with his foot and half a leg blown off, while another was writhing in agony with an arm missing.

Effective though this attack was, moments later another 609 Squadron pilot, Sergeant Feary, was airborne and, shortly after the bombs had fallen, managed to shoot down the marauding Junker. Therein lay the conundrum for the attackers: to cause effective damage, bombers needed to attack from a low height; but to do so was risky in the extreme.

The weather in August was not quite so clear and perfect as Göring would have liked, but the Luftwaffe continued to come over, bombing airfields and getting into tussles with Fighter Command. The trouble was, lots of cloud badly hampered the ability to bomb accurately.

On 15 August, Göring summoned all his senior commanders to Carinhall, north of Berlin and thus away from the battle front. He told them there was no point in attacking British radar sites and that all efforts should be directed at the RAF and nothing else – no ships or factories. So worried was he about Stuka losses, he also told them that from now on they had to attach at least three fighter groups to each Stuka group – one to attack with the Stukas, one to fly ahead over the target, and one to protect the entire attack from above. He insisted Stukas should be escorted all the way. He also berated them for misusing his precious Zerstörers, which were also getting a pasting.

Having told them all this to their faces, it was then written down formally as a directive. It was, frankly, madness. Radar was key to the British ability to successfully intercept German attacks. Me109s and 110s were not dive-bombers and flew at very different speeds; by keeping close escort they were negating one of their very great advantages: speed. Nor were there enough fighters to consistently provide escorts at a rate of three to one.

A huge air battle developed on Sunday, 18 August. Jock Colville witnessed some of it, as he was spending the weekend with friends near Chichester in Sussex. Sitting out on the terrace of the house, looking towards the sea and to Thorney Island, he and his friends watched as anti-aircraft guns opened fire, puffs of smoke peppering the sky. Then they heard the roar of engines and the sound of machine guns. Suddenly, a number of aircraft were engaging in the sky above them, black dots spiralling and twirling. A bomber came hurtling down trailing smoke, then a parachute opened and dropped gracefully down through the whirling mêlée. Two minutes later it was over, the aircraft having moved on across the sky. In all, some sixty-seven German planes were shot down that day, the Luftwaffe's worst losses since 10 May; Fighter Command lost thirty-three.

The air fighting continued, with the Stukas and Me110s, especially, continuing to be hit hardest; every day the Luftwaffe came over, it continued to be pecked at by Spitfires and Hurricanes – twelve here, half a dozen there, occasionally two dozen at once, but harrying the German planes for much of the time they were over English soil. Helmut Mahlke's *Gruppe* had only flown a couple of times, but they had also worked out that while there was no avoiding the risk of enemy fighters during the attack, by diving to the deck and flying back as low as possible they were at least fairly safe on the return trip. He had been enjoying watching terrified Brits on the ground diving for cover as they hurtled over. 'But unfortunately,' he noted, 'not every Stuka unit has escaped as lightly as us. StG 2, in particular, had suffered disproportionately high losses.' In fact, they had lost twenty-five aircraft in the week following *Adlertag*, a loss rate of around 30 per cent.

Meanwhile, British squadrons were developing ways of getting the Me110s. As soon as they came under attack, the Zerstörers tended to put themselves into a defensive ring. George Darley, for example, had worked out that if he flew straight over this ring, firing as he went, it tended to break up and then they were easy pickings. 'But not only did the chaps manage to get the 110s,' said Darley, 'the most important thing was that the bombers were left unescorted, and therefore became easier meat.'

On 19 August, Göring summoned not only his air fleet commanders but also some of his younger fighter commanders, berating them for not protecting his bombers better. Just a month earlier he had issued orders insisting fighters be allowed to fly freely in order to maximize their advantages; now he was telling them to close-escort bombers all the way to the target and back again. For the Me109 pilots, this meant flying so slowly they were almost dropping out of the sky; it also made them very vulnerable to attack from Spitfires and Hurricanes.

Fighter Command had been suffering too, however. Although only one airfield in all of Britain had so far been put out of action for more than twenty-four hours, the main fighter airfields of southern England were in a sorry state. Hangars had been destroyed, buildings wrecked, and Operations Rooms put out of action, and the airfields themselves were now pockmarked with hastily filled-in bomb holes. An attack on Kenley, to the south of London, on 18 August, was symptomatic of the kind of damage these front-line airfields were suffering. Just nine low-flying raiders attacked at 1.10 p.m., zooming over at just one hundred feet off the ground. Ample warning had been given, but their approach was masked by trees and hangars and, although two were shot down, the damage they inflicted was heavy. Shortly after, a further fifty bombers attacked from 10,000 feet, of which twelve were reported as being shot down. This attack was less effective than the low-level raid, but overall nine people were killed on the ground and a further ten wounded at Kenley that afternoon. Four Hurricanes were destroyed and two Hurricanes and three Spitfires damaged. Twenty vehicles and ten trailers were also destroyed, as were eleven hangars, the sick quarters, two married quarters and part of station headquarters. A number of other buildings were badly damaged. Nearby Biggin Hill and Croydon were also attacked; damage at Biggin was similarly severe.

Aircraft and pilot losses were also mounting throughout August. Fighter Command suffered 176 pilot and aircrew casualties in the month and 389 aircraft. Production of new aircraft, combined with a truly astonishing number of repaired and returned aircraft, ensured that losses were being more than met, but it was pilot casualties that were really concerning both Dowding and Air Vice-Marshal Keith Park, whose 11 Group was bearing the brunt of the battle. Many squadrons were operating at only 75 per cent strength, a figure that both men believed was unacceptably low.

In the same period, the Luftwaffe had lost 993 aircrew and 694 aircraft;

that was a ratio of not even 2:1 in favour of Fighter Command. In other words, in terms of aircraft losses, the ratio that Tommy Elmhirst and those at Air Intelligence believed was necessary in order to win was not being met.

Tommy Elmhirst was not alone in fearing the worst. As August gave way to September, Dowding, Park and Britain's war leaders were beginning to worry about just how much longer Fighter Command could hold out. The Battle of Britain appeared to hang very much in the balance.

While the very visual air battles were raging over southern England, and while daily newspapers and BBC reporters were gleefully announcing the numbers of downed German aircraft as though they were cricket scores, there was another battle going on out at sea, and one about which, for the most part, the average member of the British public was largely ignorant.

It certainly suited the purposes of the Government and the Ministry of Information not to shout too loudly about it, because the losses of Allied merchant ships since June had been horrendous: 134 sunk in June, 102 in July and 91 in August, amounting to over a million tons. These successes were a huge relief to Dönitz, who had agonized over what to do about the defective torpedoes suffered in Norway: should he send his crews back out into the Atlantic with the problem still not fully rectified or wait until all the torpedo problems had been solved? The former could wreck morale even more, but the latter risked letting Britain off the hook at a vital moment.

In the end, he had decided to order a maximum effort in the Atlantic, although he banned the use of magnetic pistols and instead switched to using torpedoes with new improved contact pistols. It had proved a wise decision; his U-boat force was still some way short of the 500,000 tons per month he had reckoned they needed to sink to bring Britain to its knees, but these small numbers of U-boat crews lurking off the Western Approaches started to call this the 'Happy Time'. Morale was certainly no longer an issue.

One of the U-boats cashing in was *U-48*. After Narvik, Kapitänleutnant Herbert Schultze had been taken ill and was relieved by Hans-Rudolf Rösing, who was then thirty-five and had an already long naval career behind him. Certainly Teddy Suhren rated him highly, and there is no doubt that although there were barely ever more than a dozen U-boats operating in the Atlantic at any one moment during the summer of 1940, this band of brothers were at least commanded and manned by extremely experienced men.

On Rösing's first patrol with *U-48*, they sank no fewer than eight ships. The favoured way to attack was to do so at night, when they could usually operate on the surface. The Mk VII U-boats operated at speeds of around 17 knots on the surface, which was faster than any convoy; on the other hand, when submerged, the best they could manage was around 7 knots. Because they were usually lower in the sea than the vessels they were stalking, they tended to blend in with the darkness of the water and therefore could often get so close they could hardly miss. However, it required nerve, cunning and skill to get away quickly once a successful attack had been made.

On 20 June, however, *U-48* pulled off an astonishing shot at a distance which reflected both the skill and the high confidence of the crew. Any underwater attack was handled almost entirely by the captain, but if on the surface it was the 1WO, the torpedo officer, who tended to carry out the shooting, and on *U-48* that was Teddy Suhren.

It was a little before 5.30 p.m. when Suhren had been up in the bridge and had spotted a large tanker in the distance, travelling at a decent speed. There was no chance of catching it, but having made calculations of the distance, course and speed of the tanker, and having then combined these with their own position and worked out the angle at which a torpedo would need to run, he called out, 'Eels at the ready!'

Rösing was deeply sceptical, however. Surely, he thought, the distance was too great. But Suhren thought otherwise. 'Don't let's waste time talking about it,' he told the Kapitänleutnant, or 'Kaleu'. 'If we don't get the torpedo off soon, the opportunity will slip through our fingers.'

With some reservations, Rösing agreed to let him take the shot, which Suhren reckoned was a massive 5,000 metres away.

Just before firing, he made a last-minute adjustment by 0.6 degrees then gave the order. 'No one believed it would hit,' noted Suhren. Tension grew as the minutes passed – one, then two, three and even four, but nothing. Those up on the bridge grinned at him resignedly, then turned away. Rösing shrugged.

But after five minutes they suddenly saw an enormous fireball in the distance and following that the sound of an explosion as the sound finally reached them. The men were dumbstruck, while Rösing shook his head, gave Suhren a quizzical look, then left the bridge. 'But the Kommandant,' noted Suhren, 'never queried my judgement again.' The ship they had sunk had been a Dutch tanker, the *Moordrecht*, one of the many merchant vessels from now occupied countries that had chosen to continue sailing on behalf of the Allies. At 7,493 tons it was a big ship and had been carrying more than 10,000 tons of fuel at the time. No wonder it had been such a big explosion. Of the twenty-nine crew, only four survived, picked up five days later.

CHAPTER 31

Crossing the Water

STILL IN ENGLAND was the US Army Air Force's Colonel Toohey Spaatz, who was there officially as 'Assistant Air Attaché'. He had been spending some time with Bomber Command, basing himself on a Wellington station where its squadrons were not just attacking Luftwaffe airfields, but rather had been spreading their net pretty wide into Germany itself. On 10 June, the day Mussolini declared war, British bombers had wasted no time in flying all the way to Italy to attack targets there, and had done so again on the night of 15–16 August, when more than sixty Wellingtons had been sent to attack Germany, but thirty-five Whitleys had flown to Turin, Italy's most industrialized city. Italy had so far played no part in the air battle over Britain but was talking tough and threatening Egypt. A key part of Bomber Command's policy was to show that Britain was not simply going to sit back.

The Whitleys included those from 10 Squadron, now commanded by Wing Commander Sydney Bufton, who had successfully made it home from France, where he'd been a staff officer for the Advanced Air Striking Force. Based at Leeming in Yorkshire in the north of England, they refuelled at an airfield further south en route and headed off. Safely flying over France, they found the city lights of Switzerland helped guide them, then slid past Mont Blanc – Bufton could see its ice cap glowing in the darkness and thought its vastness seemed to dwarf their plane. There was cloud in the Po Valley, but it was clearer over the target.

As they flew over the city, the navigator could clearly see the Fiat factory and dropped the flare with unusual accuracy. 'Crumbs! Navigator to Skipper,' he said, 'the flare has dropped plumb on to the factory roof. It's lighting it up like day!'

That certainly made life a lot easier for them as Bufton swept around and began his run at only around 4,000 feet.

'Hold her there, Skipper,' called out the Navigator. 'Bomb doors open.'

The aircraft lurched then steadied as the bomb bay opened, while the Navigator continued to give Bufton instructions to move right a bit, then steady, then right again, then left until eventually he called out, 'Bombs gone.' The aircraft lifted with the lightening of the load and they began to climb and head back for home. From fifteen miles away, the tail gunner reported he could still see fires. They landed back down again at around 6.30 a.m. having been airborne for nine hours and forty-five minutes, but it had been a successful raid, with most of the attackers hitting their target.

Bomber Command had been predominantly targeting factories, ship-yards and airfields but had never worried too much if civilian houses got in the way. In contrast, Hitler had strictly forbidden any attacks on civilian targets in Britain because he believed it was a policy more likely to induce the British to come to the peace table, and Göring had, since *Adlertag*, repeatedly stressed the need to focus on destroying the RAF. None the less, at night, and with many aircraft equipped with only unsophisticated navigational tools, it was all too easy to bomb the wrong target, and on the night of 24–25 August several German bombers, aiming for the aircraft factory in Rochester, had mistakenly hit parts of east and north-east London instead.

Churchill and his War Cabinet decided to retaliate immediately and instructed Bomber Command to hit Berlin that very night. The targets were the Klingenberg power station, the Henschel airframe factory and Tempelhof Airfield in the heart of the city. Some 103 Wellingtons and Hampdens were sent to the German capital, including Guy Gibson and his crew. At Scampton, the news had been received with great excitement. 'We had been waiting for this for a long time,' noted Gibson. 'Now we were going to get our chance.' As it happened, there was a strong headwind that night, many of the aircraft struggled to reach such a distance and over Berlin itself there was cloud cover. One of Gibson's fellow crews in 83 Squadron ran out of fuel and had to ditch off Flamborough Head, taking to their dinghy. 'The raid was in fact lousy,' noted Gibson. Despite this rather ineffective first raid, Bomber Command returned three more times over the next week, much to the fury and outrage of the Nazis. Goebbels denounced the raids as cowardly, and Hitler immediately ordered the construction of several huge flak towers – large concrete edifices containing air raid shelters and on top of which were placed anti-aircraft guns. It was a personal humiliation for Göring, too, who had repeatedly boasted that the RAF could never reach Berlin.

None of the raids caused a huge amount of damage, but actually, at this point in the war, that didn't matter so very much. What they were demonstrating was defiance and reminding both Germany and the rest of the world that the war was far from over, no matter how emphatic the German victory over France had been. Nor was Britain expecting Hitler to turn the other cheek, and that had been another reason for carrying out the raids. The War Cabinet wanted to lure the Luftwaffe away from attacks on airfields.

Furthermore, in the air battles still raging over southern England, the British picture was not quite so bleak as Dowding and Park – and Elmhirst, for that matter – feared. By the first week of September, Fighter Command was still able to climb up and meet everything the Luftwaffe sent over. What's more, such had been the casualties among the Stukas that the entire force had been completely withdrawn from the battle. Nothing could have demonstrated more starkly the terrible misjudgement by the Luftwaffe General Staff of putting so much emphasis on dive-bombing; not only did the Luftwaffe's bomber development programme now lie in tatters, but it also starved the attackers of a proportion of its bombing force.

While British commanders, with the responsibility of defending Britain, were following the air battle's developments with a healthy dose of pessimism, others were able to stand back and observe with a little more objectivity. Certainly, one person who still fancied the RAF's chances was Toohey Spaatz. Now that the air battle had intensified, he had not changed his views either on the RAF's chances of denying the Luftwaffe or on the efficacy – or lack of it – of current bombing operations. Also in Britain was another of the President's 'special envoys', William J. Donovan, a friend of FDR's as well as a decorated war hero. He, too, had been sent to assess Britain's chances of holding out, and when, during a breakfast meeting at Claridges, that London hotel so favoured by Americans, Spaatz made it clear he thought the Luftwaffe had no chance of defeating the RAF, Donovan rather agreed.

When Spaatz had arrived back at the very end of May, the British had been reluctant to show him or any Americans secret information about radar, IFF or Huff-Duff, or even to reveal the detailed mechanics of their Operations Rooms or how Dowding's system functioned. On 3 July, it had been agreed that it was time to be more open with the Americans, however, and so, since then, Spaatz had been given full and open access to pretty much all areas, including the Royal Aircraft Establishment at Farnborough, where detailed assessment of downed and captured German aircraft was undertaken. Reports on these aircraft were sent back across the Atlantic to General 'Hap' Arnold. As for Luftwaffe bombing, Spaatz reported that it continued to be 'particularly lousy'. He was also increasingly convinced that a modern, well-dispersed and organized air force like the RAF could not be destroyed on the ground.

In a further attempt to gain a realistic impression of the war, Roosevelt had authorized Rear-Admiral Robert L. Ghormley, the US Assistant Chief of Naval Operations, to head an American military delegation that would begin joint talks with the British. These began on 29 August, and in the interest of not arousing isolationist suspicion back in the States were both secret and given the cover name of the 'Standardisation of Arms Committee'. Leading the British delegation was Sir Cyril Newall, the Chief of the Air Staff, who told Ghormley and the US delegation in no uncertain terms that Britain would fight on and win. 'Our whole strategy is based on the assumption that we should withstand attack,' he told them, 'and it is the fixed determination of the whole nation to do so.' This was certainly the case, and his outward confidence was in fact in no way misplaced even if it was not entirely representative of all Britain's senior commanders.

In fact, he told Ghormley, Germany's only chance of avoiding decisive defeat lay in either ending the war very soon or somehow breaking the blockade and obtaining new sources of outside supplies. In this, Newall was reflecting over-optimistic assumptions about Germany's paucity of supplies and miscalculating the Germans' ability to make do with less than Britain imagined was possible. None the less, the various American visitors that were being sent across the Atlantic were all getting very much a united view about Britain's determination to fight on – a view, frankly, that was being backed up very clearly by what they were witnessing with their own eyes.

The truth was, for all the shock and awe it had created since the start of the war, the Luftwaffe simply wasn't strong enough for the task that had been set it. Its two-engine bombers could carry a maximum of around 4,400 pounds – two tons – and despite the damage caused to places like Kenley, Biggin Hill and even Middle Wallop, by September still only one airfield in all of Britain had been put out of action for more than twenty-four hours, and that was Manston on the south-east tip of Kent and thus the closest airfield to France. For the most part, Fighter Command's aircraft were able, because of the early-warning system, to get airborne before the raiders arrived. And because the aerodromes were grass and at least a hundred acres in size, the fighters were then able to get back down again – simply by dodging the potholes, which would then be hurriedly filled in again. What's more, because secondary Operations Rooms had been set up a couple of miles from the airfield, destroying the main one did not paralyse future flying.

In other words, to destroy one of Fighter Command's grass airfields, the Luftwaffe needed a lot more bombers and a lot more bombs. Its strategy had been to destroy the RAF on the ground, as far as was possible; and it had been confidently expected that any which escaped the onslaught would be easily picked off the moment they tried to get airborne. The Luftwaffe's over-confidence, the enormous gaps and errors in its intelligence picture, and consistently faulty tactics were all conspiring against it.

However, while Dowding and Park were pleased with the way their preparations and the defence system were standing up, their number one concern was pilot shortage and the fact that so many front-line squadrons were, by the first week of September, operating at 75 per cent strength.

In fact, they need not have been quite so concerned. Unlike the Luftwaffe intelligence, which had underestimated RAF strength, Group Captain Tommy Elmhirst and his team had overestimated the strength of the Luftwaffe. While their intelligence picture in terms of numbers and locations of formations was fairly accurate, they had assumed that German *Staffeln* were the same as RAF squadrons in structure, when they were not at all. The Luftwaffe consisted of *Geschwader*, *Gruppen* and *Staffeln*, which Elmhirst and his colleagues in Air Intelligence had, understandably, assumed were the equivalent to the RAF's group, wing and squadron. In the RAF, a fighter squadron would have an immediate establishment of sixteen aircraft and up to twenty-four pilots, which would provide a comfortable excess that enabled two flights of six to be airborne at any given time. A German *Staffel*, by contrast, had a theoretical establishment of just twelve aircraft and pilots, but more often than not an operational number of nine. In other words, German formations were generally at least 50 per cent smaller than RAF squadrons. This meant that Air Intelligence had greatly overestimated Luftwaffe strength.

This also meant that when Park reported a squadron's strength at just 75 per cent, he did not mean he had nine pilots left but, rather, fifteen or sixteen. This, both he and Dowding agreed, meant pushing their pilots too hard. Had the Luftwaffe fighter pilots heard this, they would have been astonished that British commanders were so concerned about the welfare of their pilots; certainly, British pilots had it a lot easier than their German counterparts. By the first week of September, German fighter pilots were regularly flying up to four times a day and sometimes as many as seven. Most flights were rarely longer than an hour, but combat flying was utterly exhausting, both physically and mentally, not least because the pilot had to have unparalleled levels of concentration if he was to have any chance of survival, and because during a flight he suffered repeated changes in air pressure, experienced numerous moments of abject terror, and had adrenalin pumping through his blood. Most German fighter squadrons had fewer than five operational aircraft at this stage and some had days when they had none at all. Not one was operating at full strength. At the end of August, there was such a shortage of fighter planes, I/JG2 was moved to the Pas-de-Calais. 'I only have five planes here,' recorded Siegfried Bethke on 2 September. 'The other squadrons only have six–seven machines at the moment.' Three days later, he noted, 'We now take off with only three planes; that is my whole squadron.' The entire *Gruppe* had just eighteen planes, and one nearby Zerstörer *Gruppe* had just twelve aircraft in all.

Dowding and Park had no idea about this. They also believed very strongly in preserving the fighting strength of each squadron. Pilots were given twenty-four hours off every week and forty-eight hours every three weeks. As much as possible, squadrons were not left in the front line for protracted periods either but, rather, regularly rotated. Usually, British fighter pilots would not fly more than three times a day and often less; four times was rare. The Luftwaffe enjoyed no such sensitive handling. Pilots and aircrew were rarely given leave and instead were expected to fly and fly and fly. By September, they were exhausted. Göring was expecting them to fly ever more escort missions, yet their numbers were declining, which meant those still standing had to fly even more. Morale was being sapped.

Also being depleted was faith in their senior commanders, and Göring in particular. Fighter leaders like Adolf Galland were appalled by the tactics imposed upon them, and this inevitably filtered down. Macky Steinhoff's disgust at the C-in-C reached new heights at the beginning of September. He had been flying as an ineffective night fighter since the end of June, but after the RAF hit Berlin, he had been summoned to Carinhall along with several senior commanders. They sat around an enormous table, with Göring holding forth, smoking a huge cigar as he spoke. 'What he said sounded like the script of a movie about World War I,' wrote Steinhoff. 'Biplanes looping, attacking from below, flying so close that pilots could see the whites of their enemy's eyes. I couldn't stand it any longer.' Daringly, Steinhoff raised a hand. There was an aghast silence from the others, but Göring allowed him to speak, so Steinhoff told him some home truths: that aviation was different now, that they operated at much higher altitudes in different machines, and were night-flying with no navigational aids.

'Young man,' said Göring, 'you still have a lot of experience to gain and a lot to learn before you think you can have your say here. Now why don't you just sit back down on your little rear end.' Steinhoff was incensed. 'At that moment,' he wrote, 'I realized that the man was obviously an amateur and I began to hate him.' Immediately afterwards, he was posted away from night-fighting and sent to the Pas-de-Calais as *Staffel* commander of 4/JG52.

Nor was it just Göring's junior commanders who were losing faith in his command. So too was Hitler. The Führer's right-hand man and Air Force chief had promised to destroy the retreating British at Dunkirk, but had failed; he had also promised to destroy the RAF swiftly over England, and had not yet managed that either. Hitler wanted quick victories not battles that dragged on. And, in any case, he was on unfamiliar ground with this aerial clash. Hitler preferred land warfare, where there were maps with lines denoting the scale of advance.

On 10 August, Major Engel had flown to the Berghof to see Hitler. The Führer had just received detailed reports from General Guderian, who had spent time with the Red Army the previous autumn. 'Reported very unfavourably about Soviet armaments and morale,' recorded Engel. 'Especially tanks, old and obsolete. Signals system also very backward.' Later, Hitler spoke at length about Guderian's report. 'If we get to grips with this colossus the right way first time,' he told his assembled party, 'then it will collapse far quicker than the world expects. If only we can destroy it.' Hitler had always planned to turn East at some point. Now, with Britain failing to play ball, and still flush with the astonishing victory in the West, he was beginning to think that moment might come very much sooner.

Meanwhile, Dowding and Park had to conduct the battle with the information they were given, and while the situation in the air might have been far rosier than they perceived, top of their current concerns was how to bring in new pilots. Already cuts had been made in training at the Operational Training Units, the final stage of a pilot's passage to becoming a fully fledged fighter pilot. The trouble was, because of the very limited gunnery experience, and because new pilots were arriving in squadrons with usually no more than twenty-five hours on Spitfires or Hurricanes, they tended to be lambs to the slaughter when sent up into the fray. In practice, however, few squadron commanders would let these rookies into the action until they had built up some hours and had a few training sessions with experienced pilots.

Sergeant Cyril 'Bam' Bamberger was a case in point. Brought up in the Wirral, near Liverpool, Bamberger had joined the Auxiliary Air Force as a ground staff member of 610 Squadron back in 1936, when he had turned seventeen. Two years later, he was given the chance to train as a pilot, an opportunity he jumped at, although it was not until just before the outbreak of war, when 610 Squadron was fully mobilized, that he began his full-time flying training. Training was thorough and extensive, so Bamberger was not awarded his precious wings until 8 June. His time at OTU, however, was spent still flying biplanes, so that when Sergeant Pilot Bamberger arrived back at 610 Squadron at Biggin Hill on 27 July, his squadron commander was unimpressed and immediately insisted he go back to OTU and convert on to Spitfires. His first flight was on 7 August, and ten days later, having amassed just twenty-five hours on Spits, he returned to Biggin Hill. He did not fly for three days and then was on his own on station defence while the rest of the squadron were scrambled to engage the enemy.

Between that day and the end of August, Bamberger flew thirty operational sorties. Some of these were to and from forward operating airfields at Hawkinge, near Folkestone, but there was plenty of contact with the enemy too. Like so many fighter pilots, Bamberger found the endless waiting the hardest thing to bear. They would be up before dawn, down at Dispersal for first light and on standby all daylight hours. He found it very difficult to ever relax, and only once scrambled and running for his Spitfire, strapping himself in and then hurtling off into the sky, did he feel more at ease. Very quickly he learned some life-saving tricks. The moment they came under fire from behind, he would break into a tight turn. 'For a new boy, this manoeuvre frequently resulted in a confused and frightening situation,' he recalled. 'One minute you were safely part of a squadron, the next second you are alone in an apparently empty sky.' He also rapidly learned the handling qualities of the Spitfire as well as his own capabilities and limitations. On 24 August, he was involved in dog-fights twice; four days later, he flew four times and claimed a 'probable' Me109; the next day, Pilot Officer Webster, with whom he had joined the squadron and with whom he had trained, was killed. On 31 August, they were rotated out of the action and posted to Acklington in Northumberland. Here, they were to intercept any marauding bombers stationed in Norway, while in between Bamberger was able to use the time to train and build up his flying hours. Even during the most intense air fighting, Dowding insisted the entire country be given fighter cover, not just the south.

Meanwhile, Britain's defences were rapidly improving so that by the end of August the United Kingdom was a lot stronger than might have been expected considering the shock of Dunkirk just a couple of months earlier. General Brooke had taken over from General 'Tiny' Ironside as C-in-C United Kingdom Home Forces. Ironside had favoured a static coastal defence, but Brooke had torn up that plan in favour of placing a lighter force all around the coast and a more mobile defence in depth inland.

Britain now had twenty-seven infantry divisions and two independent groups of brigades. Most had all their troops, small arms such as rifles and machine guns, most of their mortars, and much of their field artillery and mechanized transport (M/T). It was anti-tank guns that most were short of, although this was by no means universally the case.

The Home Guard had also now risen to around 600,000 men, most of whom were equipped with American rifles and some 25,000 Browning automatic rifles – which were, effectively, light machine guns – as well as 22,000 Browning heavy machine guns. By the beginning of September, most were also now kitted out with uniforms and steel helmets. They were also equipped with a number of rapidly emerging devices, from Molotov cocktails to No. 74 grenades, known as 'sticky bombs', and the McNaughton tube, an underground pipe mine that could be used for blowing bridges, roads and railway lines. These men now formed a network of defended villages and local towns. Together with the Regular troops in Britain, they amounted to the best part of two million men.

By this time, Britain also had an impressive stock of chemical weapons, which Brooke and Portal, the C-in-C of Bomber Command, had agreed would be dropped by air. Sixteen squadrons were earmarked for the task, which would include spraying gas and dropping chemical bombs. Thanks to the huge reserves of fuel, new flame-throwing weapons were also being developed. One such was a 'flame fougasse', which was a barrel filled with a mixture of oil that, when detonated, would cover a large area with burning liquid. On 24 August, trials had been held along the coast near Fareham in which oil was pumped into the sea and then ignited, producing a giant wall of flame and smoke that rose thousands of feet into the sky. Details of these trials were then spread by intelligence networks, all part of an attempt to raise doubt in the minds of German invasion planners.

In addition, new Auxiliary Units had been formed by Colonel Colin Gubbins, who served in the SIS and was attached to Military Intelligence (Research). The idea was that if the invasion took place, these Auxiliary Units would lead Britain's resistance, carrying out acts of sabotage, fanning the flames of resistance and generally doing all they could to disrupt the invaders. In setting up these Auxiliary Units, Britain was the only country in the war so far to have prepared a resistance movement in advance of conquest by the enemy. Although they came under the jurisdiction of General Headquarters, Home Forces, they were equipped as members of the Home Guard. The units were formed into patrols of between four and eight men, which were then organized regionally. The men recruited tended to be gamekeepers and farmers – people who had country skills and knew the lie of the land. Most were young, and each had to swear an oath to keep the existence of the Auxiliary Units secret. Training took place at Coleshill House in Wiltshire, where they were taught about sabotage, unarmed combat, demolition and other skills.

Each patrol then had a secret base, often hidden underground in a wood or accessed via a secret trapdoor through a farm building. Here weapons, supplies and ammunition were stored.

One of those recruited that summer was Lieutenant Norman Field, who was recovering from his wounded hand with his mother and step-father in Somerset when he was visited by his friend Peter Wilkinson. At the time, Field was feeling frustrated and anxious to do something. 'To think those bloody Germans were going to come here!' he said. 'I'd had plenty of time to think whilst I was recovering and I was hoping I might get an undercover job and get back into action quicker than might other-wise be the case.' As Wilkinson was leaving, Field said to him, 'I don't know what you're doing and I am not going to ask, but whatever it is, if there might be any opportunities for me, bear me in mind.' Two days later a telegram arrived.

After an interview at Coleshill, he was given a medical, promoted overnight to captain and then posted to Garth, a large country house in Kent. On arrival he met Peter Fleming, who was running the network there, codenamed XII Corps Observation Unit. Field's job initially, he learned, was to recruit men for these teams of patrols and help set up their OBs – operational bases. The key, he quickly realized, was to find a good patrol leader and then be guided by him. After all, their lives would depend on their associates. It was all somewhat bewildering, but Field had fulfilled his wish – he was now actively doing something to help defend his country.

While Britain was rapidly improving its land defences, the seas around it were still protected by the Senior Service, the Royal Navy. Most of the Home Fleet was now massed in the south and south-east of England, but there was also the Royal Navy Patrol Service, better known as 'Harry Tate's Navy', drawn from Royal Navy Reserve men and crewed by fishermen, tugmen and lightermen. 'Harry Tate' was slang for being inefficient and amateur, but these men were nothing of the sort. Rather, they were tough, weather-beaten and generally men born to the sea. Their primary role was minesweeping in their adapted trawlers and keeping invasion watch. While they swept German minefields, naval minelayers were putting down ever greater numbers of their own mines. Since the Kriegsmarine was never able to send out more than fourteen U-boats at any one time at any point throughout all of 1940 and was concentrating on merchant shipping, the only means the Germans had of combating this mass of British naval forces was by their own inadequate numbers of surface vessels or by *Schnellboote*, or E-boats, as the British called them. These were incredibly powerful in terms of both arms and speed but were very complicated to build and as a result both costly and time-consuming. This meant there were just two flotillas of *S-boote* along the Channel coast amounting to only sixteen vessels. There had been extravagant plans to build up the *S-boote* force, but these too had been casualties of the axed pre-war naval expansion, the Z Plan. The Luftwaffe was the only other means of attacking British naval power, but it was busy tackling the RAF.

On 29 August, Göring's intelligence chief, Beppo Schmid, had reported that the RAF's fighter strength now stood at about a hundred. In fact, Fighter Command had 701 serviceable aircraft on 1 September. Although British fighter aircraft strength was broadly rising as the battle progressed, Dowding and Park were still deeply concerned by what they perceived to be the pilot crisis.

At the end of August, Tommy Elmhirst had been promoted to Air Commodore and posted to Fighter Command HQ, but before he left Air Intelligence he was asked to make an assessment of how long the battle might continue. He concluded the Luftwaffe would keep going until at least the third week in September. 'The greatest query was, however,' he noted, 'whether our fighters could continue their present volume of effort and sustain their present rate of losses for another three weeks.'

Dowding and Park met on Saturday, 7 September, to discuss the pilot shortage along with Sholto Douglas, the Deputy Chief of the Air Staff, and Douglas Evill, Dowding's Senior Air Force Officer, at Bentley Priory. Dowding confessed that, as far as he was concerned, Fighter Command was going downhill because it was losing pilots at a rate of 120 a week, which could not be sustained as it was a higher figure than for those coming through the OTUs.

A solution of sorts, however, came from Park, who suggested a system of squadron categorization into classes A, B and C. Class A would be those squadrons in the front line in 11 Group and some in 10 and 12 Groups, such as 609 Squadron. These would be fully operational and would have at least sixteen combat-ready and experienced pilots. Class B would contain up to six non-operational pilots and would be near the front line but not in the thick of things. Class C would have at least three experienced and combat-ready pilots while the rest would be greenhorns. These would be in 13 Group away from the main battle zone.

It was a simple but very sensible plan that enabled Park to keep his own group up to strength while allowing new pilots time to gain flying hours, learn some skills and become combat-ready. Because all airfields were structured the same way, a squadron could move from one part of the country to another in the time it took to fly there.

That same day, the Joint Intelligence Committee warned the Chiefs of Staff that invasion was once again imminent, and at 8.07 p.m. General Alan Brooke, now commanding United Kingdom Home Forces, gave the signal 'Cromwell', the code that warned all troops to go to their invasion battle stations.

For those in charge of Britain's defence, the huge barriers the Germans would have to overcome if they ever attempted SEALION did not seem quite so formidable. Dowding found himself in an almost perpetual state of gloom as more and more of his precious pilots were being wounded or killed. For General Brooke, the pressure was almost overwhelming. He, for one, felt the threat of invasion was a very real one. Having seen the effectiveness of the German military machine at first hand, he was not prepared ever to be even remotely complacent. 'All reports look like invasion getting nearer,' he wrote in his diary on 7 September. He was fully aware of the mass of barges collecting across the Channel and that the Stuka *Gruppen* had been moved to the Pas-de-Calais. Although they had been withdrawn from the battle, British intelligence had assumed, understandably, that they were concentrating for the invasion. A number of German spies had also been captured trying to infiltrate England – four Dutchmen acting as German spies were captured at Dungeness on 3 September. Another German spy had parachuted into Northamptonshire that same morning, 7 September. He had, however, been hit by his wireless set as he landed and suffered concussion, and was promptly captured. Other Secret Intelligence Service reports suggested the invasion was imminent.

'The responsibility of feeling what any mistakes or even misappreciations may mean in the future of these isles and of the Empire,' recorded Brooke, 'is a colossal one and one that rather staggers me at times!' He wished he had more adequately trained formations – some he had inspected were in very good shape, but others were woefully short of training. The weight on his shoulders was immense, but such was the burden of high command.

For Private Bill Cheall, on the other hand, invasion watch was all rather boring. His 6th Green Howards were now covering the south coast around Studland and Swanage. They were patrolling the cliffs, watching for enemy parachutists and invasion barges, but there were none to be seen, despite Brooke's fears to the contrary.

There were, however, more than 2,000 barges all along the Channel ports, as Guy Gibson had seen with his own eyes. By pulling river barges from the Rhine and plundering harbours, rivers and canals throughout Germany and the newly occupied territories, the German Navy had amassed a large number ready for the invasion. 'Every port from Antwerp to Dieppe,' noted Gibson, 'was packed like lumber floating in a river with thousands of these invasion barges.' 83 Squadron were given Antwerp as their main target. They loaded up with as many small bombs as possible and then fought their way through intense flak and hoped they would manage to get home again. Luck was with Gibson, but squadron casualties were mounting. Gibson found himself flying alongside one bomber that was on fire. 'It was a nasty sight,' he noted, 'because I could see it was one of our own.' Eventually, one man baled out. Gibson hoped he could swim.

Saturday, 7 September, also marked the day the Luftwaffe changed tactics and bombed London. Four RAF raids against Berlin were too much of an insult and needed to be avenged, as Hitler had announced to a packed crowd at the Sportpalast in Berlin on 4 September. The first bombers arrived over London just before half past four in the afternoon, but further waves followed throughout the night.

A. G. Street had been in London that day for a broadcasting engagement and had been at his club. He carried on playing bridge through the first raid and was later walking to dinner with a naval friend when the air raid sirens went off again. 'But we both agreed that as this might be our last chance of oysters, the thing to do was to walk on to Bentley's,' wrote Street. There they were told they could have their oysters for as long as they were prepared to pay for them. 'So we did our best,' added Street, 'and a good best it was.' Later he returned to his club and continued playing cards in the basement.

From her flat in Hampstead, Gwladys Cox watched the raids with horror. Large volumes of smoke seemed to cover the East End and much of London all the way to St Paul's, and as darkness fell she could see a red glow from the fires. 'All evening we have been looking out of the windows at the terrible conflagration in the city, covering a great distance,' she scribbled in her journal at midnight. 'Planes are over and around us all the time. One violent thud in the west, presumably a bomb, shook my chair . . . The eastern sky glows redder.'

Colonel Toohey Spaatz was another in London that day, dining with a fellow American, the journalist Drew Middleton, at Rules restaurant. As the first bombs fell, Spaatz said to Middleton, 'By God, that's good, that's fine. The British are winning.' He recognized that the Luftwaffe had changed tactics – and that night attacks on London were not going to help the Germans beat the RAF. 'The British have got them now,' he continued. 'They've forced them to bomb at night. The Krauts must be losing more than we know.'

Middleton suggested that night-bombing might not destroy the RAF but could bring the Brits to their knees instead. 'Not in a million years,' said Spaatz. 'I tell you, the Germans don't know how to go about it.'

The bombers came back the next day, and the next and the next day and night after that. No matter how awful it was for Londoners, however, the Luftwaffe could not be hitting RAF airfields if it was attacking London. It was an odd change of tack. As the invasion date was getting closer, so it needed to be stepping up its efforts to destroy the RAF; a couple of heavy raids on London to show Germany would not take an attack on Berlin sitting down would have been one thing, but to relentlessly keep hitting the capital and Britain's other major cities every single day made no sense at all, especially as Londoners were showing no sign whatsoever of crumbling under the strain. Even Göring seemed to sense this. During a conversation with Jeschonnek, he asked, 'Do you think that Germany would cave in if Berlin was wiped out?'

'Of course not!' replied Jeschonnek immediately, then realizing what he'd said, added, 'British morale is more brittle than our own.'

'That's where you're wrong,' said Göring. He may have been wrong about how best to handle his Air Force, but in this he was unquestionably right.

CHAPTER 32

The Approach to Battle

A T FORT BENNING in Georgia, the US 1st Infantry Division continued to train its men and incorporate new recruits. The 'Big Red One', as it was known, was one of only four Regular divisions that had remained in full service following the end of the First World War. In truth, the division was not so very different from the outfit it had been twenty years earlier. They still used the same bolt-action 1907 Springfield rifles they had back then; still wore the same British-style steel Tommy-helmet; still wore thigh-length wool service coats; and when not wearing their tin hats, wore the same beaver-coloured Boy Scout wide-brimmed hat. Tactically, they had not progressed much either. Manoeuvres were carried out every year, but these large-scale training exercises involved little integration with other arms, such as artillery and cavalry, most of the latter, in any case, still mounted on horseback rather than inside a tank. 'In our summer training for war,' wrote Lieutenant Gerald Clarke, a young officer new to the division, 'we had broomstick handles for practice because rifles weren't available. To represent cannons, we had logs mounted between two old wooden wagon wheels. Everything was simulated. Our military was really in a hopeless condition to start fighting a war.'

Two other new men were Tom and Henry 'Dee' Bowles, who had joined back in March. Identical twins, they were from America's Deep South, in north-west Alabama. The Bowleses were poor, although both Dee and Tom were happy enough growing up, always with plenty to eat and enough going on to amuse themselves. Life had been tough, though.

They lost first a brother and then their mother when they were just twelve years old. Their father was a farmer, growing fruit and vegetables that he would then load on to a cart and sell in town, but being a smallholder in the Depression-era Deep South was hardly lucrative, and so, soon after their mother died, the family moved to the cotton mill town of Russellville. The twins left school and went out to work – the extra bucks they brought home made all the difference.

By 1940, however, the cotton mill in Russellville was already in terminal decline, even though the rest of the country was lifting itself out of the Depression. 'We wanted to go to work,' said Tom Bowles, 'but there wasn't no work around.' They'd applied for places in the Civil Conservation Corps – one of the New Deal schemes that had been set up, and which was an attempt to combat massive soil erosion and declining timber resources by using the large numbers of young unemployed. But they were turned down. Instead, in March 1940, two months after their eighteenth birthdays, the twins decided to enlist into the Army. Of the two, Tom tended to be the decision maker, so he was the first to hitch a ride to Birmingham, the state capital, in order to find out about joining up. Since they were only eighteen, their father had to give his consent. 'I remember his hand was pretty shaky when he signed that,' said Tom. Four days later, on 9 March, Dee followed. 'We hadn't heard from Tom,' said Dee, 'so I told Dad I was going too. He said, "Son, make good soldiers", and we always tried to remember that.' After being given three meal tickets in Birmingham and a promise of eventual service in Hawaii, Dee was sent to Fort Benning, one of the country's largest training camps. He still wasn't sure where his brother was – or even if he had actually enlisted – until eventually he got a letter from his father with Tom's address. It turned out they were only a quarter of a mile apart and that both were in 1st Infantry Division, even though Tom was in 18th Infantry Regiment and Dee the 26th.

Unsurprisingly, their basic training had been just that. On arrival at Benning they were told to read the Articles of War, then they were given a serial number and told to make sure they never forgot it. After eight weeks' training – drill, route marches, occasional rifle practice and plenty of tough discipline – they had been considered to be soldiers. They were living in pup tents but eating more than enough food and surrounded by young lads of a similar age, so as far as the Bowles twins were concerned life in the Regular Army seemed pretty good, and a lot more fun than back home in Russellville, Alabama.

Training continued. More marching – three-mile hikes, then ten-mile, then twenty-five-mile hikes with a light pack and eventually thirty-five miles with a heavy pack. A mile from home, they were greeted by the drum and bugle corps, who played them the last stretch back into camp. But while this was doing wonders for their stamina and levels of fitness, they were hardly ready to fight a modern war, should it ever come to it.

Those running both the country and the US Army were all too aware of these shortcomings. The new Secretary of War, Henry Stimson, had wasted no time in pushing for a massive increase in the size of the Army, and to achieve that it needed personnel as well as equipment. Quite simply, he argued, if Congress wanted an army large enough to defend the country, it had to introduce compulsory service. In much the same way as Chamberlain had resisted calls for conscription right up until the spring of 1939, so now did the President. Since the American Revolution, military conscription in peacetime had been considered deeply un-American. It didn't matter that Stimson was a Republican; an election was just around the corner, and FDR was reluctant to scupper his re-election chances over the issue.

The Selective Service Bill was introduced by a Republican and a Democrat rather than by Stimson, and immediately caused an outcry from isolationists, college students, labour leaders and others, but it was Stimson who pushed hardest. Roosevelt got around the quandary it caused him by largely keeping out of the debate and letting Congress decide, and, despite the outcry in certain quarters, by mid-August polls suggested at least 65 per cent of the nation were in favour. Soon after, the bill was approved in both houses and finally signed by the President on 16 September. It was an important step.

Now that the Army was about to dramatically increase in size, structures were needed to enable this to happen. At the end of July, a new General Headquarters, US Army, was established at the US Army War College in Washington to oversee the command of these enlarged field forces and, most importantly, get them trained.

Chief of Staff of GHQ was General Leslie 'Buck' McNair and among his new team was Lieutenant-Colonel Mark Clark, who had impressed General Marshall, in particular, with the training exercises he had devised for 3rd Division. Now he and his family were heading to Washington, where Clark would take on the position of G-3, responsible for the training of troops.

Clark was forty-four, six feet two inches tall and a career soldier. He had served in France in 1918 and been wounded, but had returned and proved a most capable and dependable staff officer and trainer of men. Promotion since the end of the last war had been slow for most officers, and Clark was no exception; he had spent fifteen years as a captain. He had, however, since been earmarked for higher things, having been sent to the staff course at the War College. Now, under McNair, and with Marshall having already singled him out, he had the chance to help shape the future of the US Army as it began its exponential growth. 'Our goal, of course,' wrote Clark, 'was to integrate and speed up training in order to develop an Army for combat in the shortest possible time.' Just how this was to be done was for McNair and Clark, especially, to work out.

Over southern Britain, the air battles continued, with a particularly heavy day on Sunday, 15 September, the original date for SEALION; the invasion, however, had already been postponed, as the sky was self-evidently not clear of the RAF. One of those flying that day was a twenty-year-old Luftwaffe fighter pilot called Hans-Joachim Marseille, although he was always known as 'Jochen'. The son of an army general, he had been raised in a strict military family in Berlin, but despite the best efforts of his parents their son had been a tearaway. Always in trouble, and with a blatant disregard for any kind of authority, this bright, good-looking young man had been a hopeless student and had only begun to show his considerable brains when he had managed to get into the Luftwaffe as a trainee pilot – and that had only been after strings had been pulled by his father.

Marseille had immediately shown enormous natural aptitude, but his acrobatic stunts had repeatedly got him into trouble. In fact, he had excelled at every aspect of flight school except for discipline, but despite this he had still managed to graduate with honours for gunnery and aerobatics on 18 July. Posted to I (Jagd) Lehrgeschwader 2, he had joined his unit at Calais-Marck three days before *Adlertag* and had shot down his first British fighter, a Hurricane, two weeks later. However, in doing so, he had left the man he was supposed to have been protecting, and also without warning; these were cardinal sins, and he was duly roasted by his *Staffel* commander. Of far greater concern to Marseille, however, had been the thought that he had killed a man. 'Today, I shot down my first opponent,' he wrote to his mother. 'It does not sit well with me. I keep thinking about how the mother of this young man must feel when she gets the news of her son's death.'

Since then, he had shot down two more, and had run out of fuel and crash-landed on the beach in Calais; he had also received the Iron Cross Second Class and a further reprimand for leaving his comrades. Marseille, it seemed, was immune to discipline. It was a dilemma for his commanding officer because he was also clearly an exceptional pilot.

On Sunday the 15th, he was flying over London and 'bounced' – surprised – a Hurricane over the River Thames and saw it go down. This, however, was after he had once again become separated from his *Schwarm* – his four-aircraft flight – although, for once, he managed to rejoin them.

Also in action that day were 609 Squadron, who had been scrambled early to patrol over London and had then been sent up again mid-morning. Both Squadron Leader George Darley and the American pilot officer 'Red' Tobin were in action. Their principal task was to take on the escorting Me109s, and on this second occasion they were soon being dived on by around fifty of the German fighters. A desperate mêlée followed. Tobin, who had now been fully operational for around a month and already had one kill to his name, now managed to escape the 109s, then shot down a Dornier 17, and saw it crash-land on farmland near Sevenoaks in Kent. Circling overhead, Tobin saw the German crew clamber out dragging a wounded man with them. A short distance away, both a Spitfire and a Hurricane had also crashed. 'But the white billowy folds of two parachutes nearby showed that their pilots were safe,' said Tobin. 'Crashed planes were a dime a dozen.' He had still been watching this scene when tracer sped past him. Quickly looking around, he realized it was meant not for him but another Spitfire, and saw above him a 109 and a Spitfire duelling a few thousand feet higher. Tobin climbed up to help, but by that time the Me109 had been sent down in a long sickening spin and suddenly the air was clear.

The squadron had been scrambled twice more that day, but Tobin, whose Spitfire had been damaged, had not been able to get a replacement until the following morning, and so had been forced to sit out. Darley, though, had twice more led 609. During the fighting, he had made just one claim: opening fire at extreme range and from the starboard quarter, he had pulled off an extraordinary full-deflection shot that had hit a bomber in the starboard engine. The squadron had shot down four confirmed that day, but had lost one of their own, a blow that was felt keenly in this close-knit unit. 'Today was the toughest day,' jotted Tobin in his diary that night. 'We were in a terrific battle over London. Geoffrey Gaunt, one of my best friends, is missing. I saw a Spitfire during the fight spinning down on fire. I sure hope it wasn't Jeff.'

It had been another big day for air fighting. Park, especially, was continuing to marshal his forces with an exceptionally deft hand, yet despite this an argument had begun to develop between him and Air Vice-Marshal Trafford Leigh-Mallory commanding 12 Group. Leigh-Mallory, at the urging of one of his squadron commanders, Douglas Bader, had been proposing using 'Big Wings' of massed Spitfires and Hurricanes to intercept the enemy as they crossed the Channel. The problem was that it took too long to get the five or so squadrons needed for a Big Wing in formation so that the enemy had already crossed and was over London by the time they arrived on the scene. The truth was that Big Wings were more about the egos of Leigh-Mallory and Bader, both of whom wanted to get more involved in the battle, than about introducing sensible new tactics.

In fact, the one person who was doing that was Park, who was continually trying to hone tactics and improve 11 Group's kill/loss ratio. The Luftwaffe's switch to London allowed him to do this very effectively. Massed formations heading for London were far easier to predict, and his answer was to allow them to get near the capital, which gave him more time to send up squadrons, now operating in pairs, ever higher. Hurricane squadrons would attack the bombers, while the Spitfires, at 25,000–30,000 feet, would get the sun behind them and dive down and attack the fighters as they were turning for home and thus short of fuel. It meant London was being pummelled, but it was saving fighters. In September 1940, that was more important. Occasionally, the Duxford Big Wing would arrive on the scene, as it did on 15 September. Regardless of the flawed tactic, it none the less proved to the Luftwaffe that the RAF was far from defeated. It had been assured that the British were on their last legs. The battles on that day and over the fortnight that followed proved otherwise.

The Luftwaffe was also sharpening its tactics. There was a far greater culture of talking shop in the Luftwaffe than there was in the RAF, and *Staffeln* and *Gruppen* would spend a lot of time analysing actions, writing reports and sharing ideas. Regardless of the orders from higher up, fighter leaders were still able to influence how they fought at the tactical level.

Adolf Galland adopted a system of sending one or two *Schwärme* of four fighters each some twenty minutes ahead of the rest of the fighters and operating at high altitude. These were designed to draw the RAF up. Once this happened, these scouting fighters would engage, drawing the enemy fighters away from the bombers. Just as the Spitfires and Hurricanes were getting low on fuel, the rest of the fighters would arrive. 'That was when we in the second wave had the advantage with a reserve of fuel,' said Macky Steinhoff. 'That was how many of us scored kills.'

Spitfires and Hurricanes had nothing like the punch of Me109s, nor the fuel injection, which meant that when they dived, the sudden downward force pushed the fuel to the top of the float chamber and the carburettor would then flood with fuel. This caused the engine to cut out. This would quickly right itself but gave the Me109 precious seconds to get away or catch up, depending on the situation.

Despite the superiority of the Me109, Göring's tactical interference hindered the fighter pilots and meant they could not always get the best from their machines. There were, however, a number of other dis-advantages. If they were shot down over England, they would be baling out or crash-landing into captivity, whereas British fighter pilots could be airborne again within hours. There was also the Channel, which looked very small and insignificant from high up but was unfathomably huge if a pilot found himself bobbing about on the surface. The chances of ever being picked up were slight. Siegfried Bethke hated flying over the Channel and especially when he was based in Normandy. 'I have to admit that the thought of the Channel and everything behind it made my stomach churn,' he noted on 10 August. A week later, it wasn't getting any easier. 'Our conversations now revolve almost solely on the Channel and all that water,' he wrote. 'It is so terribly disagreeable to us all.'

Nor was there ever much chance to let their hair down. In the evening, there were reports to write, while sleep was often interrupted by sirens, anti-aircraft guns and the arrival of British bombers. British fighter pilots were able to head off base should they wish to – more often than not to the nearest pub, where they were slapped on the back and generally made to feel like heroes. By contrast, German aircrew, if they had time for a drink, could expect no such gratitude from the local, and recently conquered, Frenchmen.

One of the means of improving pilot numbers was for Dowding to overcome earlier reservations about foreign pilots and bring them into

front-line squadrons. Two Polish squadrons, and one Czech, were introduced and they quickly proved themselves to be first-class and particularly
determined pilots, so much so that 303 (Polish) Squadron soon became
the top-scoring squadron in the Battle of Britain. Others, like Jean
Offenberg, were still up in Scotland in 13 Group, but by the latter half of
September the benefit of Park's squadron categorization was beginning to
be felt. Heading south on 17 September, for example, was Bam Bamberger,
who having had over a fortnight in the north was now posted to 41
Squadron based at Hornchurch in Essex. Between then and the end of
the month, he completed twenty operational sorties, and he felt that with
each one he was adding to the sum of his experience and therefore
increasing his chances of survival. 'But,' he admits, 'I was still scared.' On
one sortie, he was hit by an Me109, and after he had taken drastic action
to get himself clear, the Spitfire shuddered and then began to dive, spiralling towards the ground. Thinking he should bale out, he unfastened his
harness and was ready to jump, then changed his mind, determined to
try and get out of the spin. Much to his relief, he managed it, the plane
levelled out, and although it was damaged he was still able to nurse it
back to base. His skill and experience were growing.

On Friday, 13 September, the Italian Tenth Army in Libya, under
Maresciallo Rodolfo Graziani, had crossed into Egypt after repeated
chivvying from Mussolini. The Marshal, who had earlier served in East
Africa, had been sent to replace Italo Balbo, who had been killed at the
end of June when he had been shot down over Tobruk, hit by over-excited
Italian gunners who mistook his plane for an enemy aircraft.

The Duce, still concerned that Italy would miss out on the spoils of a
negotiated German peace with Britain, had been chomping at the bit
every day since he had declared war. So anxious was he not to miss out
that he had even offered an Italian expeditionary force to help in the
attack on Britain, which went against his plans for a parallel war. Hitler,
however, had turned down the offer.

Both Maresciallo Badoglio and Graziani did their best to postpone any
attack on Egypt, rather as the OKH had done with Hitler the previous
autumn, but by the beginning of September Mussolini was insisting. 'If
Graziani does not attack on Monday,' noted Count Ciano on Saturday,
7 September, 'he will be replaced. He has also given orders to the Navy to
make a move to seek out the British fleet and give battle.' The Regia

Marina was every bit as reluctant to pick a fight as the Army, however; back in July, it had tentatively ventured out of port and had clashed with the British Mediterranean Fleet at Calabria and received a bloody nose for its trouble, which had done little to instil confidence.

Like Hitler, Mussolini believed battle should be joined and won purely through his own will. The difference was that for all the shortcomings of the German armed forces, in terms of size, tactics and discipline – if not machinery – they were still better than any other in 1940. Italy was a very different kettle of fish in terms of military prowess.

The country was, like Germany, young, founded a decade earlier than its ally in 1861, but it remained, even in 1940, more of a geographical concept than a tightly unified nation state. Among the young in the larger cities there was a fairly broad degree of enthusiasm for Fascism, but Italy was still a predominantly agrarian society, which had never undergone either an agricultural or an industrial revolution, and was riven by more regional patois than any other country in Europe. A third of the population were illiterate, not least because more than half the population did not speak true Italian but regional versions of it; nearly 18 per cent had never finished elementary school.

To make matters worse, Italy had fewer natural resources than Germany, and despite demonstrating an early love affair with the motor car had just eleven vehicles for every thousand people. Also like Germany, Italy suffered from producing too many models of different types of vehicle in insufficient quantities, with all the ensuing logistical headaches that brought about. The lack of industrialization, of education and of technological know-how meant that Italy was fifty years behind Germany in becoming an industrial society. This was not good news for a dictator who believed Italy would become a new Roman empire with himself as its new Caesar.

Mussolini's other problem was keeping the people sweet. Although a dictator and the political leader of Italy, because of the King and the Army generals he knew he still needed to maintain a groundswell of popular support, not least among Italy's fledgling industries. Even with the declaration of war, workers in the industrial north were kept on peacetime working conditions, rather than being placed on a wartime footing, and so what armaments factories there were still operated without the urgency that any nation in a time of war requires. Moreover, in his concern for his workers, the Duce resisted foreign investment and turned to companies like Fiat to make tanks and aircraft. Fiat and its partner, Ansaldo, then created a monopoly in armoured military vehicles, which would not have mattered had they been any good; unfortunately, they were not. Under-powered, under-armoured and under-armed, they were already massively out of date by the time Italy entered the war.

Money had poured into the armed services throughout the 1930s, and especially into the Army, which accounted for over two-thirds of all military expenditure. Much of this money was then washed down the drain again, lost amid a labyrinthine military bureaucracy. Each and every new piece of equipment required the approval of the different arms and departments of the military that would be using it, as well as the relevant part of the ministry, the inspectorate branch concerned, the training section and then the Ministry Secretariat. If any modification was proposed, the whole process had to start all over again. In July 1940, a month after war had been declared, the Ministry Secretariat, the mechanism of government, proposed a return to the traditional daily closing hour of 2 p.m. This was approved. Meanwhile, at Pinerolo, the horse cavalry school continued to absorb nearly 4,000 men, none of whom were doing anything to further the war effort but were simply a drain on Army coffers.

The Army itself was commanded by ageing marshals and generals who steadfastly refused to embrace any kind of advancement in tactics and technology. Maresciallo Badoglio, the Chief of Staff, rigidly believed that infantry in vast numbers was the key to modern warfare. Handed a perceptive intelligence analysis of the German tactics during the 1940 Battle of France, he said, 'We'll study it when the war is over.' There were seventy-one divisions in the Italian Army in 1940, of which a mere four were armoured, i.e. with any tanks at all. Even Generale Ettore Bastico, one of very few commanders with experience of using armoured units in combat, questioned the tank's importance. 'The tank is a powerful tool,' he said, 'but let us not idolise it; let us reserve our reverence for the infantryman and the mule.'

The Italian Air Force, the Regia Aeronautica, was similarly riven with a lack of vision and foresight. As a result, Italy entered the war with light-weight and obsolete two- and three-engine bombers that simply did not have the range, speed or payload to make any significant impact, while most fighter aircraft were biplanes. Right after the declaration of war, Maggiore Publio Magini had been told the flying school would be closed down immediately. The Major could scarcely believe it, but he and the other instructors were assured the war would be won quickly, so what they needed right now was pilots, not instructors.

The day after the declaration of war, the Regia Aeronautica had sent over bombers to attack Malta, one of the most important pieces of real estate in the entire Mediterranean. From Malta, Britain had the potential to strike at Italian convoys heading to North Africa. It was also an important staging post. For Italy, the swift capture of Malta would have been a hugely important stepping stone, one that would not only have denied Britain its use, but would also have offered an important asset for its own operations. In the summer of 1940, Malta had been poorly defended, with a shortage of anti-aircraft guns and, initially, just a handful of Gloster Gladiator biplanes to protect it.

Within a short time, Britain had sent over precious Hurricanes as reinforcements, but even so these were hardly enough to stave off a concerted attack. Yet the offensive against this tiny island had been pathetic. Bombers had flown over too high, had half-heartedly dropped their bombs and that had been it. No attempt at suppression had been made, no plan to invade. Malta was getting stronger by the week; a golden opportunity to take it had been passed over due to a lack of proper forward planning and a lack of offensive drive from the military.

The only beacon of modernity was the Italian Navy, although it had been designed in the belief that future naval engagements would be much like they had been in the last war: at long range using big guns. There were no aircraft carriers and there was a shortage of torpedo boats. There were, however, plenty of submarines – some seventy-one in June 1940, which was more than anyone else had at the time, but that they were operating in often clear Mediterranean waters in which they could easily be seen from the air by British planes does not appear to have occurred to pre-war planners. By the end of July, thirteen of these precious submarines had been sunk. Because of its modernity, the Navy did attract some of the best volunteers – men like the dashing and highly intelligent aristocrat Valerio Borghese – but for the most part the Regia Marina was undermanned and lacked the experience that formed the bedrock of the Royal Navy.

At every level, ineptitude and a lack of foresight ran riot through Italy's armed forces. As in Germany, image was all-important, so uniforms were varied and elaborate. Italian troops also used a staggering array of headwear: Alpine hats, pith helmets, tin helmets, fezzes, peaked caps, tropical *bustina*s, continental *bustina*s, sidecaps, leather helmets; the options were many. Nazi uniforms might have been extravagant, but they did at least convey the right image; it was hard to say the same for an Italian wearing a helmet with black cockerel feathers stuck on one side.

Even something as straightforward as arming the infantry with rifles and machine guns was made more complicated than it needed to be. Italian rifles were made by a firm called Carcano and were a pre-1914 design that came in three versions: the standard rifle and two shorter carbines. All three used a 6.5mm bullet, which was too small a calibre for modern war, so in 1937 a new, more powerful 7.35mm calibre rifle was introduced. Unfortunately, not enough were manufactured in time to equip more than a small portion of the Army by June 1940, and the new rifle programme was shelved as a result. Both rifle and carbine types were now in circulation, which, of course, required two types of ammunition. To complicate matters more, an 8mm carbine was introduced, which meant yet another calibre of bullet, while the Fascist Youth units were given a further type of carbine, which fired a 5.5mm bullet. As if that were not enough to make the supply authorities' heads spin, Italian forces were also equipped with variety of 9mm and 10.35mm calibre pistols and revolvers.

Breda made a superb sub-machine gun, but it required an altogether different type of round to its handgun equivalents. In contrast, the Breda Model 30 light machine gun was not as good as most others coming into action at the time, not least because it also fired the underpowered and smaller 6.5mm calibre bullet and was prone to jam because the type of lubricating oil it used was thick and tended to pick up grit and dirt. Like the MG34, it also tended to overheat rapidly, although it had a rate of fire of only 400 rounds per minute. It also had no carrying handle, but, unlike German machine-gunners, Italian soldiers were not issued with asbestos mitts. These technical issues were significant because they caused both endless logistical headaches as well as questionable performance.

Artillery, by which Badoglio and his fellow senior commanders set great store, was largely 1914–18 vintage and in terms of both velocity and range came nowhere near to being as powerful and effective as most British equivalents.

Training was basic and rigid, and initiative was stifled. Many middle-ranking officers were reserves, hastily re-recruited, and were frequently too old and as unversed in modern fighting techniques as the senior commanders. In almost every regard, the Italian armed forces were woefully out of date, and while the young men of the cities – lads like William Cremonini – were well indoctrinated and highly motivated, and understood concepts of honour and discipline, they were a comparative minority in a highly regionalized and still predominantly rural society.

In any case, William Cremonini and his comrades were not heading anywhere just yet. Having been trained, some 25,000 of these young volunteers found that their battalions had been dissolved and they were ordered home, part of some 600,000 fighting men who were released from active service because of the endemic lack of arms and equipment. 'We were so disillusioned,' says Cremonini, 'we staged the funeral of the Fascist Party.' Collecting some packing crates, they stacked them high, draped them in black sheets and set them on fire, singing funeral marches as the flames took hold.

Graziani had been citing a lack of equipment as his reason for holding off attacking Egypt, but in fact he had plenty: 8,500 motor vehicles and over 300 tanks (albeit not very good ones). His two armies of around 167,000 men were all equipped with rifles, machine guns and other small arms, and although their guns and armour lagged behind those of Britain, he still had a sizeable force at his disposal, which should have been confident of taking on the 36,000 British troops in Egypt.

There was, however, a pronounced lack of will and tactical ingenuity that began at the top with Graziani and went all the way down. His officer corps were disconnected from their men and lived in lavish style compared with the troops they commanded, eating pasta and parmesan and drinking wine, all of which took up valuable shipping space.

Few Italians in North Africa were interested in taking on the British – only Mussolini, it seemed, had the will for a scrap. And so Graziani's Tenth Army marched into Egypt and, after lethargically advancing forty-odd miles to Sidi Barrani, then stopped.

CHAPTER 33

Science, Money and Resources

ALTHOUGH HITLER had postponed SEALION on 17 September, less than a month later, on 12 October, he pushed it back again until the spring. The air fighting continued, but the days were drawing in, the weather was worsening, and the RAF was stronger than it had been when Göring had launched *Adlertag* back on 13 August. The Luftwaffe had lost the Battle of Britain and, as a result, there would be no invasion of England in 1940.

Shipping was now released, and barges were sent back to the Rhine. The air fighting would continue, but by this time the Luftwaffe was exhausted and a shadow of the confident, brash and all-conquering force it had been long ago back in May. The Me110s had been decimated and the Stukas withdrawn, and there were now only a few hundred Me109s remaining. By that time, bomber pilot Leutnant Hajo Herrmann had flown nearly a hundred combat missions with KG4 and in recent weeks had repeatedly flown over London and other English cities, sometimes for three nights in a row; he had carried out twenty-one attacks on London alone. RAF Bomber Command would never consider sending their crews out on consecutive nights, but then the Luftwaffe had never thought much about aircrew care; after all, in a short lightning war, tours of duty were not really a consideration. On 18 October, he was taking off as Schiphol came under attack by British bombers. One of his tyres was burst by shrapnel, he lost control of the plane and crashed, his bomb load still on board. The Junkers, however, did not explode, although Herrmann was badly injured. He was psychologically damaged too, mentally and physically spent after flying without a break since 10 May.

Herrmann was now given an enforced break, but the same could not be said for the rest of the German bomber force. The Luftwaffe was still coming over in daylight hours when conditions allowed but had realized, after a night attack on Liverpool back in August, that Britain's fighter defence was designed for daylight operations and that the only real danger facing them at night was British anti-aircraft guns, which, by September, were still not as numerous as they might have been.

Assisting them to their night-time targets was a system of navigation beams, known as *Knickebein* and *X-Gerät*. While the Luftwaffe had not made the most of radar technology for defensive purposes, or done much to develop radio communication within aircraft, it had used pulse radio technology to create beams that could converge on a particular target and thus home bombers in on it with some degree of accuracy. British intelligence had cracked *Knickebein* but not *X-Gerät*, so as the Luftwaffe began its night campaign, its planes were well placed to both hit their targets and get back home again without excessive risk.

The problem was that it was unable to make the most of this advantage, as it continued to strike rather pointlessly at London every single night, once, on 15 October, with around 400 bombers, but usually with no more than around 160 and often fewer than that. In October, it dropped 6,500 tons of high explosive, which was enough to wreck houses in almost every borough, to cause major interference to London's rail network and to damage many of the East End docks and other public utilities.

On 2 October, bombs hit Gwladys Cox's flat in Hampstead. 'The bottom of our world has dropped out!' she recorded. 'Last night, most of our home, together with the whole top floor of Lymington Mansions, was destroyed by incendiary bombs.' They had been in the air raid shelter below at the time but had actually heard the sound of the falling incendiaries. Her husband, Ralph, had rushed out and grabbed an ARP warden, and initially they could see no sign of damage. Incendiaries, however, were designed, as their name suggests, to create fires and were often delayed-action bombs. Soon smoke was pouring from the roof of No. 11. Gwladys, worried she would end up trapped for ever in the shelter, decided with the others that they would be safer above ground. Grabbing their cat, Bob, she looked up the shaft steps and saw nothing but tongues of flame streaming out of one of their neighbours' flats. Above ground, she found Ralph. 'For God's sake,' he said, 'come quickly – the whole of the top storey is on fire!' The fire brigade had now arrived and were battling to put out the rapidly worsening conflagration. Ralph hurried Gwladys – and Bob – away, stumbling over the numerous hoses, to another shelter at the top of Sumatra Road.

There, Gwladys felt as though she and the other refugees from Lymington Mansions were like ship-wrecked mariners. Cigarettes were lit and they smoked and smoked, still numb with shock. 'I felt Ralph's hand,' she wrote, 'it was feverishly hot and he coughed painfully.' ARP wardens came in at regular intervals, taking roll calls and shouting out names of missing people. Firemen also looked in to report on the progress of the blaze.

No matter how shocking and traumatic this was for people like Gwladys and Ralph Cox and their neighbours, no one was panicking, while the ARP wardens and firemen were, for the most part, handling the situation with swift and calm efficiency. Elsewhere, this sustained assault was hardly causing mortal injury to the capital. Even the bombing of the docks was considered 'serious but not crippling'. Nor was the bombing breaking the morale of the people.

Despite this, it was disconcerting to say the least, even for old hands at being shelled like the newly promoted Major-General John Kennedy. Since returning from France, he had been Chief of Staff to the C-in-C Northern Ireland. Part of the job entailed preparing defence plans for a possible German invasion of the Irish Republic, no matter how unlikely this might be. Churchill had hoped the Irish might join the war on Britain's side, but the Irish President, Éamon de Valera, had made his position clear: if the Germans invaded, he wanted Britain's help to drive them out again; if Britain moved in first, however, Ireland would fight them instead.

On 9 October, and with a German invasion of Ireland looking unlikely, Kennedy had received a telegram appointing him Director of Military Operations, a key posting at the War Office and one that would see him playing a crucial role at the heart of Britain's wartime military strategy. It was also a job that he accepted with a certain degree of misgiving, knowing how difficult and fraught it would prove to be.

On his first evening back in town, he had been dining at his club when a bomb had demolished the neighbouring Carlton Club just a couple of hundred yards away. The blast bellied out the curtains and he was covered in a shower of dust. Later, as he sat drinking coffee, a further bomb fell on nearby Waterloo Place, and this time a shower of bricks and broken glass fell among him and his companions. With the electricity then knocked out, he took a candle and went up to bed, only to be kept awake by the thud and crash of yet more bombs falling and the light of parachute flares. 'I thought to myself that this was really too much,' he noted. 'It was bad enough having to put up with the horrors of life in the War Office without having the horrors of war as well. I had not heard such a din since the Battle of Passchendaele.'

On 27 September, Japan signed a tripartite pact with Germany and Italy, and also forced an agreement with the Vichy government in French Indo-China for facilities there for bases in its ongoing war with China. Although there was no question of its declaring war on anyone else at this moment, the move was a threatening one to British, American and Dutch interests in the Far East. Yet it also offered a cause for hope for Britain. Each member of the pact had pledged to aid one another militarily and economically should one of them be attacked by a power not already involved in the European or Sino-Japanese war. This was clearly directed at the United States, and from the British point of view, anything that further wedded America to the Allied cause was to be welcomed.

For this reason, the news of the American Draft, as it was widely known from the outset, was also a step very much in the right direction, as were other ties developing between the two countries. Britain was still paying with cash, and vast amounts of it too, but such was the scale of its requirements, this could not last for ever; British reserves of gold and dollars were beginning to run short. Fortunately for Britain, however, the Americans recognized not only that supplying Britain was massively helpful for its own rearmament, but also that the longer Britain could keep going on its own, so much the better for the United States.

In the summer and autumn of 1940, however, British cash was still helping to fund the development of the new armaments business, which was great for Roosevelt because to a certain extent he could use British requirements and cash to really aim big without being accused of secretly planning to send American boys to war.

Back in June, the battleship HMS *Nelson* had arrived with the precious blueprints of the Rolls-Royce Merlin engine. It was an already highly proven aero engine and better than anything being produced by American

manufacturers at the time. The idea was that a US company would produce them under licence for both the British and for American aircraft
too. It was Bill Knudsen who was given the task of finding a
manufacturer. Already he was realizing that mass aircraft production was
going to be the hardest task for American industry. The President had
demanded that the USA produce 27,000 aircraft by 1 October 1941 and a
further 36,000 by 1 April the year after, but, for the US, warplanes were
still something new. When he spoke to potential manufacturers about
aircraft production, he realized they were mostly talking nonsense. Most
of the existing aircraft manufacturers were small companies who could
not possibly make the numbers needed. 'The number of people who
talked, without having the faintest idea of the technical problems involved,'
said Knudsen, 'beggared all description.' The blueprints of the Merlin
were unquestionably an extremely valuable asset, and Knudsen immediately thought of Ford as the obvious company to make them. True, Ford
was primarily an automobile manufacturer, but it had some experience of
aircraft manufacturing, not least its Trimotor commercial plane. Henry
Ford, however, an ardent isolationist, refused point-blank to make any
engines for the British. Furious at this rebuttal, Knudsen then turned to
the Packard company, a small manufacturer of top-end motor cars.
Unlike Ford, it jumped at the chance, even though there were a host of
obstacles now confronting it. Every single blueprint, with thousands of
parts, had to be converted into US measurements, while the company
also had to develop and design a means of production that would allow
for mass production from a largely unskilled workforce, a third of whom
were women newly recruited by Packard. Again, this would not happen
overnight.

Important though the Merlin deal was, it was as nothing compared
with the riches brought by the Tizard Mission that September. Sir Henry
Tizard was an academic, chemist and scientist, and was chairman of the
Aeronautical Research Committee, and in this latter role had been instrumental in the development of British radar. Tizard himself had flown to
the United States in August to make preliminary arrangements and was
later followed by the rest of the mission, a mixture of officers from all
three services as well as scientists.

The Tizard Mission offered a wealth of new technology, including
power-driven turrets, gyroscopic gunsights, details of jet engine technology then beginning to be developed in Britain, engine superchargers,

plastic explosives and, perhaps most significantly, the Frisch–Peierls memorandum on the feasibility of an atomic bomb, radar and specifically the newly developed cavity magnetron. The Americans had developed their own radar, but nearly all this other technology was new to them; Americans knew how to build large numbers of cars, fridges, vacuum cleaners and other exciting new domestic products but were lagging behind in terms of military technology. This was hardly surprising considering the intensely isolationist approach since the end of the last war. Now, however, they needed to catch up not just in terms of tanks and aircraft and men in uniform, but in terms of science too.

The cavity magnetron was hugely important to the future development of radar, because it allowed for shorter-wavelength radars, which in turn meant detection of smaller objects from smaller antennas. This was part of the process of drastically reducing the size of radar sets, so that British scientists were now developing sets that could be put into aircraft and anti-submarine escort ships. While the Americans had nothing like the cavity magnetron, they were, however, further ahead in terms of receiver technology – it was one development the Americans were able to share in return. The Bell Telephone Company began making cavity magnetrons almost immediately, while as a direct result of the Tizard Mission the National Defense Research Committee set up the Radiation Laboratory at the Massachusetts Institute of Technology with the brief to research and develop better radar and radio navigation systems.

These secrets handed over by the British would have had huge commercial value in peacetime, and they still did now, although perhaps in a different way. Handing over such secrets had risks, but in doing so the British were killing two birds with one stone: they were finding someone else to supplement their own production and research, and at the same time forging ever closer ties and unity of purpose. And when Britain's cash did finally run out, as it surely would now that exports had been sacrificed for war production, these would be of critical importance.

It wasn't only Britain that was tapping into new sources of supply. So too was Nazi Germany, now undisputed masters of Europe. A vast Greater Reich now lay in Hitler's grasp, almost as big as the United States in terms of size and much bigger in terms of population – some 290 million people now looked up to see the swastika fluttering over them. It was almost as many as those living under the Union Flag and within a stone's throw too, rather than scattered around the globe. Also now in German hands was an enormous booty of cash, raw materials and war materiel. From France alone, the Nazis plundered 314,878 rifles, 5,017 artillery pieces, nearly 4 million shells and 2,170 tanks – all of which would be put to considerable use in the future; the Germans were never, ever shy of using second-hand goods.

Adolf von Schell and his comrades in the Reichsbahn also received a bonanza of extra vehicles, steam locomotives and rolling stock. Hundreds of thousands of captured and requisitioned military and civilian vehicles passed into German hands, bolstering the inventories in no small way. Over 4,000 locomotives and a staggering 140,000 railway wagons considerably helped Germany's freight shortcomings. As for raw materials, from France came 13 billion francs' worth, including 81,000 tons of all-important copper. Germany was also significantly better off in terms of zinc and nickel. The rapidly diminishing oil and fuel stocks had also been given a much-needed surge. The oil deal with Romania at the end of May was one huge headache solved, but Germany was now able to add to this goldmine with substantial supplies from the newly conquered European territories.

A further problem apparently alleviated was the shortage of foreign exchange. For too long it had been largely one-way traffic in Germany with only armaments leaving the country in any significant numbers, which, of course, meant they could not be used by the Wehrmacht. Not only did Germany plunder foreign banks – justified as 'reparations' and then renamed 'occupation costs' – but it also established a centralized clearing system. What this meant, in very simple terms, was that a company in France might still export to Germany and be paid for it, except that payment would be made by the French central bank, not that of Germany. The French would then in turn bill the Germans, but that would be squirrelled away in a folder marked 'never to be settled' and forgotten about. This way, the foreign suppliers still received their money, Germany got its goods and the only ones to lose out were the vassal governments of the newly occupied territories, as the governments in Vichy France, Belgium, Holland and elsewhere were discovering. That was the more than fair price of defeat as far as Nazi Germany's economists were concerned. This clearing system took on another level when it became clear that France could not keep up the 20 million Reichsmarks a *day* 'occupation costs' demanded by Germany. To help them out, Germany offered to take payment in shares of French companies; Vichy France managed to largely resist this kind offer but did sell – at much reduced rates – French interests in eastern and south-eastern Europe, where France had invested heavily in Poland, Yugoslavia and Romania, including a large stake in the Romanian oil and Yugoslavian copper industries. New oil 'multinationals' such as Kontinentale Öl AG and the copper mining operation Mines de Bor, superficially private concerns, fell under the increasingly large web spread by Reichsmarschall Göring, whose business interests were now gargantuan and made him the largest single industrialist in Europe, if not the world.

However, if the Nazis had been initially giddy as schoolboys with all this new-found plunder, it was, in reality, little more than a short-term fix, especially since the war was clearly far from over. In any case, the victor's booty was still as nothing compared to the resources Britain could call upon, while hovering in the background, ever-more ominously, was the United States. The combined might of Britain *and* America had the kind of global reach, purchasing power and access to every conceivable raw material that was the stuff of Nazi dreams.

Germany's incredible victories had persuaded Hitler that he really was a military genius. He was, of course, nothing of the sort. Selective reading of military history and four years in the trenches were not the qualifications for being a supreme military commander. As Warlimont and his staff had long ago realized, Hitler had neither an understanding of nor interest in staff work. What he *was* interested in were men with dash and verve, who could rapidly implement his will and fulfil the true destiny of the Third Reich. Curiously, though, he was also then prone to sudden bouts of doubt and prevarication. Plans would be embraced and ordered with absolute certainty – his directives for both Norway and the attack on the West were testimony to this – but then he would fret, interfere and be overcome with anxiety once those attacks began. A true psychopath would have had no such anxieties.

Rather, Hitler was more a fantasist and schizophrenic than a psychopath. The Third Reich was little more than a projection of his warped fantasies: one in which he was the leader, in charge of a world that harked back to a magical, mystical time. He was obsessed with the stories of Arminius's defeat of Varus's legions. The myths of Arminius as a freedom fighter who had liberated the pure Aryan German peoples from the tyrannical yoke of Rome became a source for Nazi ideology. Blurring into this was his love of Wagner, whose operas similarly harked back to a mystical time of old. Hitler had mixed these passions to create a German heritage that had virtually no basis in reality but which, because of his will, became truth. Most of the leading Nazis bought into this, not least Heinrich Himmler, the head of the SS, who had even created a special cult headquarters at the Schloss Wewelsburg, near Paderborn, in which there was even a stone round table. In this mish-mash of ancient myths, there was, it seemed, even a place for the British – and mythological – King Arthur.

It was almost as though Hitler existed in a kind of parallel world: one of Aryan purity, in which there were enemies that needed to be eradicated for the good of the world. He was the master, and because of him and his iron will Germany was rising again, greater than ever. Vast buildings were being erected, enemies were being slain, while marching to his tune were millions of uniformed men. There was ceremony, there was the cult of his own being, and there were endless banners of blood-red, black and white. The people saluted him, cheered him, idolized his brilliance. He was their Führer – their guide. Their inspiration. Their key to greatness.

Hitler's fantasy world was becoming a reality, but his world-view, so warped, was also very narrow, which was all too evident in his strategy for global domination, this was a major problem. Hitler was a continentalist, and his strategic outlook reflected that. He was born nowhere near the sea and rarely visited the coast; after all, there were no seafaring stories among the myths of the Teutonic Knights. In fact, he had barely travelled outside Germany since becoming Chancellor – the odd trip to Italy and Austria, a brief spot of sightseeing in Paris, but that was about it. Even his forward headquarters tended to be surrounded by trees, so even when not ensconced in his Führerbunker he could hardly see much. His boyhood nickname had been Wolfi; wolves were important symbolic creatures to him, which might explain the penchant for forests and for being underground.

He also judged others by his own standards and shallow perspectives. The British were has-been imperialists, the Americans degenerates and in the grasp of the Jewish conspiracy. His outlook was not just warped and deranged but infantile – like a schoolchild calling another names because they have big ears. Had he ever bothered to understand his would-be enemies better, his strategic judgements might have been more carefully considered, but that was not in Hitler's capacity.

The air assault on Britain had been an unmitigated disaster. True, it had not seemed that way to those in Britain who had been watching the sky blacken with German aircraft, or who had suffered the blitzes on London and other cities, but it was now abundantly clear that the Luftwaffe had never had nearly enough aircraft to achieve what was needed: total control of British air space. The Luftwaffe had been mighty enough when operating against an enemy air force that was, to all intents and purposes, operating blind, and when flying in support of the ground forces, but it was in no way near large enough to destroy the RAF over its home turf. The number of times more than a hundred bombers had flown together over England on a single raid could be counted on one hand. Usually, twenty or thirty bombers was more like it. The Italian Generale Douhet, the prophet of Armageddon, had been wrong, while Guernica, Warsaw and Rotterdam had given a false sense of strength and what might be achieved with a few hundred twin-engine bombers. The RAF, on the other hand, had demonstrated quite clearly that the bomber would not always get through if you had a half-decent fighter force backed up by an equally half-decent co-ordinated air defence system, something that had not existed when the Condor Legion had flown in Spain, or when the Luftwaffe had been operating over Poland and France. And Britain's air defence system had proved not just half decent, but very decent indeed.

Perhaps Göring – and indeed Hitler – could be forgiven for not appreciating the scale of air assault that would be needed, since no air force had ever attempted such a large-scale operation before or come up against such concerted defence, but the tactical and especially the intelligence failings had demonstrated a much bigger chink in the armoury.

The Luftwaffe had shown a complacency born from easy aerial successes against much weaker enemies that had outweighed the greater experience it had gained than that of the RAF; the lack of proper ground control, the failure to harness technology such as radio and radar, and the shocking over-confidence had worked seriously to undermine its chances of success. Meanwhile, men like Beppo Schmid continued to pedal baloney to his boss, telling the Reichsmarschall what he wanted to hear rather than the truth. To enter a major aerial battle with Britain and still not know that the RAF was divided into three home commands, or not understand the importance of radar, or insist that two-engine fighters were better than single-engine models in air-to-air combat was breath-takingly foolhardy. How could Göring really have thought that? How could Milch, Kesselring, Jeschonnek et al. let him think that? Did they never bother to ask those kinds of questions? And how was it that poor old Ernst Udet was still convinced that dive-bombing was the way forward? Until the Battle of Britain, the Luftwaffe had shone a beacon for Nazi might. Its pilots were among the pick of Germany's finest young men: bright, dashing and brave, and the leading aces were the Reich's biggest pin-ups; but over southern England they had suffered a rude awakening. Publicly, the Luftwaffe was as dashing and exciting and *modern* as ever; but in Hitler's eyes, Göring's men had suffered a dent to their reputation they would never make good.

Already, Britain on its own was out-producing Germany in numbers of aircraft, a decisive factor in the air battle that had raged in the summer. Some 15,049 aircraft were built in British factories in 1940, and a further 1,069 had arrived from America, a number which was due to increase significantly in 1941. If Roosevelt was to be believed, Germany faced the spectre of 50,000 new American aircraft a year being added into the mix. Germany, in contrast, produced only 10,826 aircraft, almost a third less than Britain alone.

Even worse, America's shipyards were also now busy building large fleets of destroyers, cruisers and, most ominous of all, aircraft carriers. The proposed expansion of the German Navy, the Z Plan, had called for aircraft carriers; but this was no longer possible. It was, however, not only possible for the US Navy, but was already becoming a reality. For that matter, it was a reality for the Royal Navy too, even if it was not quite on the scale of those planned for the United States. British shipyards were none the less busy building more ships too. In all, 1 battleship, 2 aircraft carriers, 7 cruisers, 27 destroyers, 15 submarines, and over 50 corvettes were completed in 1940, as well as 810 merchant vessels, along with nearly 2,000 vessels converted for war service. In contrast, the Kriegsmarine added just 22 new U-boats to the BdU in 1940. At no time in the 1920s and 1930s had the British armaments industry ever gone to sleep, but now, with the war a year old, it was positively humming.

Which was more than could be said for the captured shipyards and aircraft factories in the newly conquered territories. The number of aircraft built in French factories was tiny, because unlike those in America they were drastically short of coal and oil, and its workers of food.

Plundering booty and demanding crippling occupation costs had, unsurprisingly, had an adverse effect on the French economy. Its oil had been taken and its vehicles requisitioned, and without fuel and vehicles there was little way of moving food and supplies around the country. By the end of 1940, France's level of automobile ownership, previously the highest in Europe, had dropped by 92 per cent – and all those vehicles had been swept up by Germany.

Moreover, all these occupied territories needed governing and defending. Admittedly, half of France had been left to the new Vichy Government, but Poland, Holland, Belgium, Denmark, Norway and the other half of France all had to be occupied and *run* on a day-to-day basis, with military commanders and security forces. This dispersed manpower, weapons and resources, and after the initial flow of bounty was beginning to cost Germany more than it was gaining.

To cap it all, the rain that had prevented Göring from having the four clear days of good weather over southern England he needed had also affected the harvest. After stripping France and the other conquests of their riches and reserves, Germany was discovering that these countries were now drawing on resources rather than providing them.

When Hitler had triumphantly returned to Berlin at the beginning of July, it must have seemed as though the war was won and all his dreams and ambitions in the West had been fulfilled. By October, the long, attritional war that all Germans had so dreaded appeared now to be a reality.

And with the poisoned chalice of Italy for an ally, Hitler's headaches were about to get a whole lot worse.

CHAPTER 34

The Grey Atlantic

O N MONDAY, 2 SEPTEMBER, a young ship designer called Robert Cyril Thompson had been asked to come to London for a meeting at the Admiralty to discuss an important mission to the United States. This, he was told when he got there, was to persuade the Americans to build merchant ships on behalf of the British. It was explained that this was of vital importance. U-boats were sinking ships headed to Britain at rates of more than 350,000 tons a month. At present, the Admiralty could cope with this: at the end of June, Britain had had some 18,911,000 deadweight tons of shipping – that is, the weight when fully loaded – under its control, and by the end of September that figure would be 18,831,000, barely much of a difference at all. However, that figure might easily start to drop rather quickly if the U-boats kept sinking ships at similar rates. The problem was that British shipyards were simply not building enough merchant ships quickly enough, and were further constrained by the blackout, which because of the size of these vessels and the outdoor nature of the work meant construction work had to stop during the hours of darkness. Only the US had the ability to build the kind of numbers needed, which, in the first instance, was a minimum of sixty new vessels, each of around 10,000 deadweight tons. The Admiralty wanted Thompson to head this mission and to go to America right away. He accepted on the spot.

It showed enormous good judgement on the part of the Admiralty to single out Cyril Thompson, who was only thirty-three, worked for a family firm that had been struggling to survive just a few years earlier, and might easily have been overlooked for someone of both greater years and experience. Yet, despite his comparative youth, and despite owing his position at Joseph L. Thompson to family connections, he had none the less gained a deserved reputation as one of Britain's leading and most dynamic shipbuilders. In 1935, he had won a Gold Medal from the North-East Coast Institute of Engineers and Shipbuilders for producing a pioneering paper on how to increase the service speed of merchant ships without an increase in power. And at six feet three inches tall, and broad as well, Thompson was a big man physically as well as in character, blessed with a touch of genius and a determination that had been quickly respected not only within the firm but within the industry as a whole.

Joseph L. Thompson had been founded the previous century at North Sands on the mouth of the River Wear at Sunderland in the north-east of England, and Cyril was one of two sons who both joined the family business. After Cambridge and an apprenticeship with Sir James Laing & Sons, another Sunderland business, he had joined the family firm at twenty-three and become a director a year later. The 1930s had been a lean time for shipbuilding; however, Cyril Thompson was convinced that the way to revive British merchant shipbuilding was to design and construct cheaper and more economic-to-run vessels. With this in mind, he drew up a number of designs, testing models thoroughly at the National Physical Laboratory's test tanks at Teddington, until finally settling on a distinctive new hull form that caused less drag and, when put together with a more efficient engine, would create a ship that required significantly less power to achieve a decent speed. With a further eye on economy, he reckoned these designs could be built for less than £100,000.

At any rate, someone at the Admiralty had clearly been taking note, which was why, on 21 September, following on from his meeting in London, Thompson set sail for the United States, accompanied by Harry Hunter of North-Eastern Marine Engineering, the firm that had designed the more efficient engines now powering the new Joseph L. Thompson ships. At no point did the Admiralty ever specify that the ships should be built to a British design. None the less, as the designated Head of the British Shipbuilding Mission, Thompson was told that he had to personally approve the technical details concerning the designs, and with this in mind he crossed the Atlantic with blueprints for a new ship that was just beginning construction at Thompson's shipyard at North Sands.

The Admiralty had made it crystal clear just how vital it was that he bring home the deal. Whether the Americans would play ball, however, was another matter; US shipyards were already known to be working at capacity constructing their own naval and merchant shipping requirements.

Much rested on Thompson's shoulders.

Out in the Atlantic, the U-boats were continuing to wreak havoc, and not least *U-48*, which, in two patrols with Kapitänleutnant Hans-Rudolf Rösing, had accounted for twelve ships, amounting to some 60,000 tons of shipping; this was indeed proving a 'Happy Time' for the U-boat and her crew. After the U-boat's eighth patrol, however, Rösing had been posted to become U-boat liaison officer to the Italians based at Bordeaux, so his place was taken by Heinrich 'Ajax' Bleichrodt, who had yet to command his own U-boat. By this time, the entire 7th Flotilla was based at Lorient, and the U-boat arm was making the most of the newly conquered Atlantic ports, which saved a time-consuming trek through the Baltic, North Sea and out over the north of Scotland; now they could head straight out of the Bay of Biscay and into the Atlantic.

Nor were there any signs that the change of commander was about to have an effect on *U-48*'s ongoing success. Bleichrodt was inexperienced and, as far as Suhren was concerned, it showed. However, the rest of the crew, Suhren included, knew all the tricks and were able to compensate; after all, it was Suhren, as torpedo officer, who was responsible for most of the shooting in any case. And ten days into their patrol they had sunk four ships, including an 11,000-ton liner, the *City of Benares*, which tragically had been carrying a large number of children who were being evacuated to Canada. Those on *U-48* had been unaware of this, although Hitler had already declared that all Allied or neutral shipping was fair game.

On 20 September, the submarine was off the west coast of Ireland when it received a coded message from *U-47*, commanded by Günther Prien, already famous throughout the Reich for his exploits, not least sinking the *Royal Oak* in Scapa Flow almost a year earlier. Prien had spotted a large eastbound convoy heading to Britain, and since *U-48* now had the latest, most advanced radio equipment, he asked her to report this news to Dönitz at his command post in Lorient, who immediately ordered them to 'Proceed to beacon.' This meant *U-47*'s beacon – *U-48* was to join *U-47* and the two were to operate together. Then, at 5.15 p.m., they received another signal, directing four more U-boats towards *U-47*. Now *U-48*, *U-65*, *U-43*, *U-99* and *U-100* were to assume attack formation.

Dönitz was ordering them to form a wolfpack, and more specifically a 'stripe', which meant stretching themselves out in a line on the surface across which the convoy was expected to pass. The U-boats would be approximately five miles apart. Such tactics were not new, but only with the new improved radio technology they were now using could this be effectively put into practice. At any rate, by the morning of 21 September, all five were converging on Prien's *U-47*.

Just after 3 a.m. on the morning of 21 September, *U-48* had the convoy HX72 of forty-three ships from Halifax to Liverpool in sight. Just over two hours later, they picked up an SOS from a ship called *Elmbank*, a large freighter, carrying timber and sheet metal, which had been hit by Otto Kretschmer's *U-99* amidships and had gone down in just forty seconds. Peering through the periscope, Bleichrodt had seen flashes and the sound of dull explosions. Half an hour later, they were also in position to fire. Suhren missed with their first torpedo, but the second, fired twenty minutes later, hit, the detonation sending huge columns reaching high into the air. They had hit the *Blairangus*. Fires now broke out on the ship as her cargo began to explode. Lifeboats were hurriedly launched, but the skies were grey with squally showers and, after a while, the stricken ship disappeared from view. *U-48* now turned her attention to a tanker, although, again, the torpedo missed. Another immediate shot was not possible because they discovered one of the torpedo fins had been dented. Turning around, they now took over from *U-47* as the convoy shadow, radioing position reports to the other U-boats.

All day, *U-48* kept up with the convoy, waiting for darkness, as were the others in the wolfpack. Several were low on torpedoes, *U-47* and *U-48* included, but at twenty minutes before midnight Suhren attacked with his last tube, hitting *Broompark*, which soon began to list.

That night the carnage really began as HX72 struggled on, the wolfpack snapping at its heels. *U-99* sank two, including a 9,200-ton tanker. *U-47* then surfaced, and with *U-99*, used their guns to finish off the *Elmbank*, which had limped on all day. In a move that was typical of the very best U-boat captains, *U-100*, commanded by another ace, Joachim Schepke, then manoeuvred into the heart of the convoy and sank three more. All through the next day, the wolfpack continued to keep up with the convoy, picking off one ship after another, *U-100* sinking a further four. By the time *U-48* turned for home, eleven ships had been sunk and a further two badly damaged – more than a quarter of the entire convoy.

There were a number of reasons for these extraordinary successes. The first was the experience and skill of the tiny U-boat force crews, who in this first year or so of war really were an elite band. Bleichrodt might have been new to the U-boat arm, but men like Suhren were, by this time, old hands, who were able to combine innate skills with a kind of sixth sense born of experience. The biggest aces of all – Prien, Schepke and Kretschmer – were similarly hugely experienced. All were still young men but had served in the German Navy for many years – Schepke and Kretschmer had joined in 1930 and Prien in 1931 – and they had learned their craft on sailing ships and surface vessels before joining the U-boat arm. The sea was in their blood.

The second reason was the lack of escorts for transatlantic convoys – that is, destroyers, which had been developed specifically for hunting U-boats in the last war, and smaller sloops and corvettes. In part this was because of the loss of a sizeable number during both the Norway campaign and the evacuation from Dunkirk, but principally it was because the Admiralty had decided these escorts should be taken off convoy duty to strengthen the southern commands. They were to be added to the constant anti-invasion patrols, to harass and bombard the enemy's build-up of shipping gathering in the Channel ports, and to be on hand to attack the invasion fleet should it ever attempt the crossing. There were a number in the Admiralty who were rather hoping the Germans would attempt it, confident as they were that a mass of barges carrying troops and only very lightly escorted would be easy meat and decimated as a result. Their confidence probably wasn't that misplaced.

Yet if this policy was understandable enough, it was none the less militarily rather illogical, as Admiral Forbes, C-in-C Home Fleet, repeatedly tried to point out. Forbes correctly argued that no German invasion was going to happen while the RAF was still flying, and therefore concentrating so many surface vessels in the Thames and on the south coast was completely unnecessary. Minesweepers, minelayers and capital ships were one thing, but escorts were wasted there. As it was, the Royal Navy had around 700 minesweeping vessels operating in the Channel by September. In any case, it was inconceivable that Britain would not know up to twenty-four hours beforehand that invasion was imminent – the time it would take any escort from the Western Approaches to reach the south-east.

Forbes, however, had not won the argument, and so most convoys had been crossing the Atlantic with barely any escorts at all; in fact, ocean convoys averaged just two escorts at this time. As a consequence, if a convoy ran smack into the path of a stripe of U-boats, carnage would follow, as it had with HX72 and then as it did again during two more, SC7 and HX79. In a matter of weeks, three convoys had suffered forty-three losses. A decent number of escorts accompanying these convoys would have certainly made a big difference.

Despite Forbes's entirely understandable concerns, however, these disasters were still rare. After all, the Atlantic Ocean was a big place and, with barely more than a dozen U-boats operating at one time, it was more than likely a convoy would slip past undetected. As it happened, by the end of 1940, a staggering 692 convoys had arrived and 17,882 ships had been sailed, of which just 127 had been sunk in convoy; this amounted to a mere 0.7 per cent of the total. Or, to put it another way, 99.3 per cent of ships sailing in convoy were getting through.

Yet a further 865 ships had been sunk in 1940, and that was rather too many. All of these had been hit when sailing independently from convoys. There were, however, good reasons for sailing ships independently, no matter how compelling the convoy statistics. To begin with, many neutrals chose not to sail as part of the convoy system, but from June Hitler had announced that all ships were fair game, neutral or not. Others were simply too slow for convoys or even too fast. A large number became stragglers – that is, they might develop some problem and then find themselves lagging behind. Escorts, especially when in such small numbers, could not afford to risk leaving the many to protect the lone lame duck.

But a further reason was because convoys were only escorted part way across the ocean and then tended to disperse. Up to July, escorts only had the range to accompany outward-bound convoys as far as 17°W, which was roughly due south of Iceland. In October, this was then increased to 19°W. Air cover from Britain was also limited. The U-boat aces like Prien, Kretschmer and Schepke scored most of their hits on independently sailing ships. The *Moordrecht*, sunk by Teddy Suhren's 'supershot', was travelling independently, for example, having dispersed from convoy

HX49 heading to Halifax, Nova Scotia, and steaming on her own to a different port.

The truth is, the Admiralty had been caught out by the dramatic events of the summer. Like the rest of Britain's war leaders, they had not expected France to collapse so quickly and in their pre-war appreciations had assumed that any U-boat campaign would be largely coastal and so had planned accordingly.

A major rethink was needed, and swiftly too. In the Battle of the Atlantic that was now unfolding, neither side could afford to stand still for a moment. This was becoming a battle both of wits and of resources, and one in which the stakes could not possibly have been higher.

The U-boat arm may have been demonstrating its lethality all too clearly, but the same could not be said for the submarines of the Regia Marina, the Italian Navy. Although it had boasted the world's largest submarine force, it had managed to lose no fewer than thirteen since Italy had declared war back in June. A little too late, it seemed, they had discovered the clarity of the Mediterranean waters worked against them, as RAF aircraft were able to see them even when they were as deep as 70 metres below the surface. Their German allies had repeatedly attempted to pass on practical advice on a range of military matters, and had warned them of British developments in anti-submarine warfare and the use of aircraft in this role, but it had gone unheeded. As it was, time and again, the RAF had caught Italian submarines on the surface and in daylight. Considering how hard it was to hit a submarine from the air, even if perfectly visible, the loss of thirteen was reckless, to say the least.

Nor was the Italian battle fleet winning any points either. After the embarrassment of the action at Calabria in July, the fleet had left its base in Taranto on 31 August in an attempt to intercept the British Mediterranean Fleet as it escorted a convoy to Malta. Bizarrely, however, Amiragglio Cavagnari, C-in-C of the Regia Marina, ordered the fleet to turn back for port if no contact had been made by dusk. Rather than heading for home at dusk, however, Cavagnari ordered it to do so at 4.30 p.m., and an hour later it complied. As a result, it missed an understrength British fleet by half an hour. Nothing could have demonstrated Cavagnari's defensive mindset more. The Italian Admiral still hoped the British would evacuate the Mediterranean of their own accord and lacked confidence in the seamanship of his men, so the move out to sea from Taranto and back was a placatory nod to Mussolini's aggression. Cavagnari was going to do everything he could to avoid a scrap, even when the odds were stacked in his favour. So far, the Italians had managed to capture a largely undefended British Somaliland, advance a few miles into Egypt and half-heartedly bomb Malta. Mussolini was beating his chest and talking of Italy's military destiny, but the Comando Supremo, the Italian Chiefs of Staff, and his senior commanders were not hearing him.

In London, over 120 American correspondents had been covering the Battle of Britain and now the Blitz. These men and women were providing a rich diet of newspaper and magazine articles, newsreels and radio broadcasts for a population that was increasingly fascinated by the dramatic events taking place on the far side of the Atlantic. One of the radio men in London was Eric Sevareid, who had only just managed to escape from southern France and make it back to England. He was now one of a number of men gathered around Ed Murrow, the man responsible for CBS's entire war coverage.

Everything in Eric Sevareid's education, upbringing and liberal beliefs told him that war was to be avoided at all costs. Even during the battle for France he had remained convinced that the United States should keep out. Now, however, after that long and unforgettable summer, he had reached a crossroads and was taking a turning he had never expected. It was, he believed, the experience of being in London, with Britain attacked daily, that had changed his mind. 'The course was quite clear now,' he wrote. 'The duty was to fight with every means available, even though the better future of men was not guaranteed by success in the fighting. But success in the fight would give the future a chance at least.' The alternative, he believed, was a new age of barbarism creeping across the planet. 'There was no possible living with Fascism,' he added, 'even for a strong America; neutrality was quite impossible.'

By this time, Sevareid was a sick man and in need of rest. He had accepted, as Ed Murrow had accepted, that it was the task of radio men like himself to convince Americans that the fate of Britain and the United States were inextricably linked. But they didn't need him personally; Murrow was doing that job sublimely and without equal, so he asked to go home. Murrow acquiesced but asked him to make one last broadcast before he left. Sevareid agreed.

'When all this is over,' he told his listeners, 'in the days to come, men will speak of this war, and they will say: I was a soldier, or I was a sailor, or I was a pilot; and others will say with equal pride: I was a citizen of London.' As he was saying this, he couldn't help a catch in his throat. Afterwards, he felt it had been mawkish and was embarrassed to think that anyone could have heard him, yet over and over he was told how it had brought a lump to the throat of listeners too. In these tense, difficult times, in the midst of a war that was unlikely to end anytime soon, and in which everyone, it seemed, was expected to keep calm and carry on, a little bit of revealed emotion had hit a chord. 'In contribution it was a mite,' he wrote, 'but apparently it helped.' Propaganda, as all those fighting the war were keenly aware, was an invaluable tool.

Britain's determination to keep fighting was throwing Mussolini's war plans awry and showing up the shortcomings of both the armed forces and Italy's ability to wage war. The Navy was proving feckless, so too was Graziani in Egypt, and the country was already running short of food. On 2 October, Generale Ubaldo Soddu, the Under-Secretary for War and effectively Mussolini's military Chief of Staff, issued a directive calling for a mass demobilization, which would begin on 10 November and last four days. The many peasant soldiers from the countryside were needed back on the land, helping with the harvest now that sea imports of food had been cut off; rationing had already begun, on cooking oil and fats. There were some 1.5 million men under arms at the time; 750,000 of them were to be sent home.

For Maresciallo Badoglio, who was all too aware of Italy's military shortcomings, this was good news, even though the demobilization, based on class, would cause mayhem as men were pulled from their units. The reason for his magnanimity was his assumption that there could no longer be any more talk of invading Yugoslavia or Greece, which both Mussolini and Ciano had been gunning for in recent weeks. In fact, having so feared Italy's entry into the war, Ciano had become the leading hawk with regard to an invasion of Greece. Not only had he overseen the bribing of certain Greek generals and politicians, but he was convinced that Greece, militarily weak, would be a walkover. 'Two hundred airplanes over Athens,' he said, 'would suffice to make the Greek government capitulate.' By invading Greece and occupying all the Greek islands of the Aegean, Italy could dominate the eastern Mediterranean and strengthen its position against the British with both ports and airfields.

Badoglio had been quite wrong in his assumption, however. On 12 October, the Italians learned that German armed forces were moving into Romania. In fact, the Romanian Government had only invited Luftwaffe units in to protect its oilfields, but it stung Mussolini's paranoia about German domination, especially since Hitler and von Ribbentrop had repeatedly warned Ciano and Mussolini about not making a move against Greece or Yugoslavia until Britain had been defeated. 'Hitler places me in front of a fait accompli,' he railed. 'This time I am going to pay him back in his own coin. He will find out from the papers that I have occupied Greece.' Mussolini's pride was further dented by Graziani, who had replied to orders to advance in Egypt in the middle of the month with another request for a postponement.

This was Mussolini's worst nightmare: a bullying, dominant ally with a raft of victories already under its belt, and his own useless generals lacking any kind of get up and go; and all the while the British, who were supposed to be dead and buried already, were getting stronger, not weaker. This was not how it was supposed to be, and now the Germans appeared to be invading his patch. Mussolini wanted a parallel war in which the Germans butted out and where the British were so weak, his victories would be ridiculously easy, but which would make him, and Italy, look good and the leading world player he thought they should be. So far, nothing had gone to plan at all, but a swift victory over the feeble Greeks could change all that. Mussolini outlined his new directive for an attack on Greece on 15 October. Neither Cavagnari nor Pricolo, heads of the Navy and Air Force, were present, which was odd considering the part their services would be expected to play. Badoglio was present, as were Ciano and General Soddu, Mussolini's military toady. Another absentee was Cesare Amé, the head of SIM, the secret intelligence service, whose views on Greek weakness were not so confident as those of Ciano's staff.

The invasion would take place in two phases, Mussolini told them – first against the whole southern coast of Albania and the Ionian Islands, and then a swift knockout blow against the mainland by troops already stationed along the Bulgarian border. Bulgaria would go along with the plan and its own forces even advance towards Salonika, because it was in their interests to do so. At that point, Bulgaria had not been told any of this, but Mussolini airily assured them he would write to King Boris and fix it. He reckoned 70,000 troops should suffice, and he was confident it would be a cake-walk. It was to be launched no later than 26 October, i.e. in nine days' time.

The recklessness of this plan put anything Hitler had proposed into the shade. Hitler at least had a large, experienced and highly disciplined Army and Air Force to help him. This should have become all too apparent in the days that followed, but nothing, it seemed, could now deter Mussolini from the path on which he had set himself. Badoglio implored Ciano to back down, reporting that all three service chiefs were against it, and to Soddu threatened his resignation. By the time he faced Mussolini, however, he had decided to keep his objections to himself. In fact, as the invasion date grew closer, he appeared to become more enthused, latching on to Mussolini's idea for a co-ordinated two-pronged assault into Greece and Egypt. None of them appeared to appreciate the huge logistical difficulties: the lack of adequate ports in Albania, the mountainous terrain, almost no proper roads, the potential poor weather that could easily come their way. But even when King Boris of Bulgaria replied thanking Mussolini for his kind offer but firmly stating he would pass on an invasion of Greece this time, the Duce was not to be deterred, even though it meant the invasion would now have to take place entirely through Albania and without Bulgarian support.

On 19 October, he wrote to Hitler, dismissing German suggestions that France should join the Axis, rejecting a recent offer of troops in North Africa, showing no interest at all in getting Spain to join the war, and warning him of his intentions towards Greece. 'In short,' Mussolini told him, 'Greece is to the Mediterranean what Norway was to the North Sea, and must not escape the same fate.' His anger at German dominance, his paranoia and his determination not to be thwarted any more in his quest for glory had ensured that Mussolini's grip on reality had now entirely deserted him.

CHAPTER 35

The Humiliation of Mussolini

BACK IN SEPTEMBER, Mussolini had approved sending the 3. Corpo Aereo Italiano (CAI), amounting to some 175 aircraft, to Belgium to support the Luftwaffe's operations against Britain. It was blatantly a ruse to ensure Italy was seen to be playing an active part in Britain's downfall, but so obsessed was the Duce with making a good impression on the Luftwaffe that the men were issued with special new grey-blue uniforms and anything that seemed faintly old-fashioned, such as puttees and baggy breeches, was put to one side. They couldn't hide, however, the fact that most of the planes were Fiat CR.42 biplanes or outmoded bombers.

Maggiore Publio Magini was among those sent to Belgium, even though the Major was still in the process of setting up a flying school in Bologna when he was posted. During its time in Belgium, the CAI was unable to shoot down a single English aircraft, while it lost two dozen of its own and, as time passed, became increasingly beset with problems as the aircraft it had brought were not really designed for operating in cold and damp conditions.

For Magini, this rather pointless involvement in the air battle against Britain made him question what on earth Italy was doing in the war. Assailed by a crisis of conscience, he realized he was increasingly against Italy's involvement. 'It was criminal,' he wrote, 'to throw away the lives of our folk with such casualness, and to risk the fate of a nation in a contest, in which, sooner or later, our military and industrial weakness would make itself felt.' The stress helped bring on a stomach ulcer. On a radio he bought in Mons, he listened to Churchill's speeches, which had been translated into Italian and were broadcast by the BBC. These only alarmed him further.

Neither the RAF pilots who came up against them nor their counterparts in the Luftwaffe were terribly impressed by these Italian aviators. Most were good enough pilots, but they lacked any modern technology, achieved very little, and would have been far better off elsewhere, such as defending their homeland or in Libya.

Meanwhile, the RAF was now sending more pilots, aircrew and aircraft out to the Middle East, including Flight Lieutenant Tony Smyth, who was posted at the end of September. Since it was now recognized that Blenheims were obsolete for daylight work over Europe, it had been decided that each squadron should send a proportion of its strength to the Middle East theatre.

After leave in London – in which he was amazed to discover so many people sheltering in the Underground and shocked by the overpowering stench – Smyth reported to Thorney Island on the south coast, to lead a flight of six Blenheims to Malta, where they would stop and refuel, and then fly on to Egypt. Already painted in desert camouflage, they were equipped with extra auxiliary fuel tanks, but it was still a long trip to Malta, straight across France and down past Sardinia and Sicily, of some 1,400 miles with little margin for error.

It was mid-October when they left, and thankfully for Smyth and his fellows the journey to Malta was an uneventful one. The most fraught part was as they neared the island and so were within easy range of Italian fighters on Sicily, but they saw nothing and successfully landed at Luqa airfield at nine in the morning after a flight of eight hours and twenty minutes, and with just 51 gallons of fuel left. That wasn't a lot for a twin-engine Blenheim.

Smyth stayed twenty-four hours in Malta, where he discovered the Italians had already stopped any daylight raids and hadn't bombed the island once in a fortnight. One of the crews remained to join the burgeoning 431 Reconnaissance Flight, but Smyth and the rest then flew onwards a further thousand miles to Egypt, and to sunshine, food, drink and no blackout. Smyth, who had a love for travelling and adventure, was in his element.

*

At sea in the Mediterranean, an audacious British plan was developing to hit the Italian Fleet with a single devastating attack. The lack of martial drive on the part of the Italian Navy had been picked up only too clearly by the C-in-C of the Mediterranean Fleet, Admiral Andrew Browne Cunningham, a tough, gritty terrier of a sea dog if ever there was one. Cunningham, known to all simply as 'ABC', was unusual among flag-rank commanders in that his background was with smaller, agile destroyers rather than capital ships. He'd been a captain of a destroyer in the Mediterranean during the last war and then a destroyer flotilla commander, before being appointed Rear-Admiral Destroyers in the Mediterranean in 1933. It was a part of the world he knew intimately and cared about passionately, and he had absolutely no intention whatsoever of giving the Italians – or anyone else for that matter – an inch. A man of action rather than one careful with his paperwork, his orders tended to be brusque and to the point, and he firmly believed, as many in the Royal Navy did, that skill and superior seamanship counted for a very great deal.

His offensive spirit had been apparent from the start of hostilities against Italy. He had willingly engaged at Calabria and had been distraught when the Italians had turned away, and had supported the troops on the ground with a series of bombardments of Italian coastal forts at Sollum and Fort Capuzzo. It had also been on his watch that the French Fleet at Mers-el-Kébir had been attacked.

Unlike Cavagnari, Cunningham also readily understood that warfare was something that never stood still and that any commander had to constantly look forward and improve not only fighting skills but the means of achieving those skills. The Italian Navy might have had some of the most modern capital ships in the world, but it had no aircraft carriers, for example; Britain, on the other hand, had built its first, HMS *Argus*, back in 1918. The Royal Navy had long ago recognized that air power was a crucial element of sea power, yet in the Mediterranean Cunningham, much to his frustration, had just one aircraft carrier, the *Glorious*, at the beginning of June. 'You may be sure that all in the Fleet are imbued with a burning desire to get at the Italian Fleet,' he had written to the First Sea Lord, Dudley Pound, back on 6 June, 'but you will appreciate that a policy of seeking and destroying his naval forces requires good and continuous air reconnaissance.'

Indeed, the entire Mediterranean Fleet was understrength for the task demanded of it: to destroy the Italian Fleet as soon as possible, to provide an all-important convoy escort as Britain strove to build up the defences of Malta and Egypt, and to support land operations too. 'Out here in the Mediterranean,' wrote ABC, 'we were also having to contrive and improvise to make bricks with very little straw.' That was perhaps overstating the case, but Cunningham felt it more keenly now that France had gone; the Mediterranean was more than 2,000 miles long. It was a big area for him to cover.

Yet reinforcements were arriving, despite the nervousness of those defending the British Isles. A second aircraft carrier, HMS *Illustrious*, brand new and armed with modern Fairey Fulmar fighter aircraft, had joined the Fleet, and it was during a conversation with Rear-Admiral Lumley Lyster, the newly arrived commander of the Carrier Squadron, that the idea of attacking the Italian fleet in harbour arose. Lyster was proposing using carrier-based aircraft to bomb and torpedo the Italians as they lay in Taranto, and Cunningham now gave him every encouragement. In a short time, a plan began to take shape. Codenamed Operation JUDGEMENT, it was to take place on 21 October, which suited Cunningham as it was Trafalgar Day and he was fiercely proud of Britain's naval tradition. Then a fire on one of *Illustrious*'s deck hangars forced a delay until the next time there would be a suitable moon. That was the night of 11 November.

It quickly became apparent that for such an attack to have any chance of success, close co-operation would be needed with the RAF based on Malta. Since 10 June, the tiny island fortress had been greatly reinforced with some 2,000 troops, many more light and heavy anti-aircraft guns, as well as Hurricanes, bombers and, crucially, reconnaissance aircraft – or rather, just three reconnaissance aircraft, US-built Glenn Martin Marylands taken over from the French and seconded from 22 Squadron Coastal Command back in England. These three planes now made up what was 431 Reconnaissance Flight, and on the face of it they did not appear to be the pick of the RAF's best pilots. One, Pilot Officer Adrian Warburton, had proved so hapless he had almost been fired from the RAF – and during the Battle of Britain, too, when trained pilots were at a premium. Utterly feckless, he had managed to get himself married to a barmaid, run up debts and proved to be so bad at taking off and landing that those in 22 Squadron had wondered how he had ever passed his wings examination. Between joining the squadron in the summer of 1939 and being posted to Malta, Warburton had been allowed to fly barely an hour and even on the trip out to Malta had been brought along as a navigator rather than as a pilot.

However, the flight was so small and the demands on them so extensive that when they lost a pilot to illness, there was no other option but to give Warburton his chance. His first flight back in the pilot's seat was due to have been a reconnaissance trip to Corfu but 'was abandoned owing to hydraulic failure and aircraft crashed on landing'. This was a polite way of saying Warburton had zig-zagged so badly on take-off that a wheel had come off. It was repairable, but by giving Warburton his chance, the Flight had temporarily lost one of its precious planes.

Had Warburton still been in England, he would almost certainly have been axed after this, but the far-flung nature of the Empire had ensured that mavericks could often find their place, and on Malta, where every piece of equipment and every serviceman counted, that was doubly true. Given a second chance, Warburton managed not only to get himself airborne, but also to land without mishap. Furthermore, he showed that in the air he was a highly skilled pilot and one blessed with phenomenal eyesight. On his first trip to Taranto, where he was back as navigator not pilot, he surprised his CO by picking out all the ships, which were later confirmed by careful examination of the photographs.

On 30 October, he was once again in the pilot's seat. The weather was poor over Taranto, so he flew in low to take a series of oblique photographs of the Fleet. Anti-aircraft fire was not slow in opening up, but he and his two other crew members still got their pictures. On the return trip, they even shot down an Italian seaplane. By this point, plans for Operation JUDGEMENT were at an advanced stage, which meant further reconnaissance photographs were essential – any small change in the harbour at Taranto had to be known about, and, indeed, a balloon barrage and anti-torpedo nets had recently been added to the anchorage.

In America in that last week of October, Harry Hopkins, Roosevelt's friend and the architect of his presidential campaign, was starting to fret. The President had been ahead in the polls, but his opponent, Wendell Willkie, was gaining ground, and while he and the vast majority of the nation were now only too happy to send aid to Britain and China, very few supported US entry into the war. But that, Willkie was telling audiences, was exactly what would happen if Roosevelt was re-elected.

Matters were not improved when Roosevelt appeared at the War Department ceremony to pick the first number of the 800,000-man draft. 'This fellow Willkie,' said Hopkins, 'is about to beat the Boss.'

Meanwhile, Hitler had been on the move, having made trips to see Pétain and General Franco, the Spanish dictator. Both meetings had been unsatisfactory. Hitler had stressed to both the importance of bringing the war to a speedy conclusion, but both Pétain and Franco made it clear that actively joining Germany in the war would require generous territorial and material concessions. This was not bargaining but the stark truth: both countries were so impoverished, they would have been worse allies than Italy. Franco even told Hitler that he thought there was little chance of the war ending swiftly. Hitler had wanted complete support from both but was simply not prepared to give them even a fraction of what they wanted. Consequently, not much was achieved, and Hitler, already in a foul mood, flew into an even bigger rage when he received Mussolini's bellicose letter telling him the Italians were about to invade Greece.

Diverting his train to Florence, he pulled into the station on the morning of 28 October, to be met by a beaming Mussolini. 'Early this morning,' the Duce told the Führer, 'in the dawn twilight, victorious Italian troops crossed the Greco-Albanian border.' Face to face, Hitler remained cordial enough with Mussolini, but to Major Engel, his Army Adjutant, he was less circumspect. 'F. in a rage,' noted Engel. 'Observed that this occurrence had spoiled many plans he had in mind . . . and doubted if the Italians would be able to defeat Greece.'

This quickly proved to be the case, as the campaign unravelled in spectacular style. In addition to the 70,000 Italian troops already in Albania, more were sent over by ship, but because of the demobilization and the ridiculous speed with which the campaign had been put together, most of these were only partially trained and poorly equipped. The majority were deposited at Durazzo, the only port big enough, but there they found the docks already full of Italian ships unloading marble for building projects in Albania. Consequently, troops were packed off to the front but were separated from much of their equipment. It soon began to rain, and roads – unmetalled – quickly turned to mud. Troops were sent to the wrong places, supply lines were stretched, and morale swiftly plummeted. Nor was it improved when a consignment of boots was sent to the front – all left-footed.

Mussolini was paying for his hubristic impatience, and Ciano his breathtaking arrogance. Both men had chosen to believe what they had wanted to hear rather than listening to more measured advice – including that from SIM, the secret intelligence service, which had compiled a 200-page report that was, in fact, pretty accurate. Rather than having just 30,000 troops as claimed by the hawks, the Greek Army was ten times that size, just as SIM had warned. In terms of equipment, it was about on a par with the Italians. Added to that was their far greater motivation to defend their country, as well as home advantage. But the report had been ignored. Furthermore, the attack came as no surprise to the Greeks, who recognized the Italians had been spoiling for a fight, had mobilized some weeks before, and were ready to meet that aggression.

By 1 November, a huge hole had been blown in the Italian line. That same day, Ciano had joined in, flying a 'spectacular' bombing mission to Salonika. On his return, he was attacked by Greek fighter planes. 'Two of theirs went down,' he commented, 'but I must confess that it is the first time that I had them on my tail. It is an ugly sensation.' It was not as ugly as the slaughter of Italian troops on the ground below. By 4 November, Italian forces were being driven back into Albania.

On Friday, 1 November, Jock Colville had travelled in Churchill's car to Chequers, the PM's country retreat. Churchill was in a good mood and optimistic about the forthcoming presidential election in the US, telling Colville that Roosevelt would win by a far greater majority than most had been predicting. He also thought America would come into the war. As it turned out, Churchill was quite right about the election.

On that election day, the President had returned to his home at Hyde Park with his wife and sons, Harry Hopkins, and a few other close friends and colleagues. After supper at Eleanor Roosevelt's cottage, they drove back through the woods, a favourite spot of the President's, to Springwood, the 'Big House'. There, FDR pitched camp around the cluttered dining room table, while Hopkins went upstairs to his bedroom, where he listened to the results on a cheap radio set and began noting them down on a chart. At first, Willkie appeared to have made some gains; Hopkins was still worried. He needn't have been, however. By 9 p.m., the big industrial states had voted for FDR, and by ten o'clock it was clear he was heading for victory. By midnight, it was not only victory but a big victory: 55 per cent of the popular vote but 449 Electoral College votes to Willkie's 82.

Roosevelt would be President for a historic third term. More importantly, he would be President for the next four years. No president was ever as powerful as in his first year, and what a critical year it was to be. For so long, Roosevelt had had one arm tied behind his back, but now the spectre of the election was over and he was free to oversee America's full commitment to rearmament. The United States had always had the potential to become the biggest armaments manufacturer the world had ever known, but Roosevelt's vision for an army of millions, for 50,000 aircraft a year, for huge military aid to Britain, to China and elsewhere, was now a massive step closer to becoming a reality.

Roosevelt's re-election and the disastrous Italian campaign in Greece were two events for the British to cheer about as Luftwaffe bombs continued to batter its cities on a nightly basis. Its war leaders hoped there might be more to celebrate soon in the Mediterranean and the Middle East, as two quite separate operations were about to be launched.

The first was Operation JUDGEMENT, the Royal Navy's attack on the Italian Fleet at Taranto, for which reconnaissance from Malta-based aircraft continued to be critical. Adrian Warburton flew over Taranto again just a few days before the attack. The weather over southern Italy was just as poor as over Greece, but he insisted on going. When they reached Taranto, having flown below the dense cloud all the way, Warburton and his crew saw the balloon barrage had been lowered; the Italians were not expecting visitors. Making the most of their surprise arrival, they circled twice, calling out the names of the ships as the camera clicked. By the time they had completed the second circuit, the ack-ack was firing at them furiously, but as they skimmed away, they realized they had counted six battleships when the previous day there had been only five reported. Undeterred, Warburton turned around and flew over the harbour again, this time so low they were almost touching the water. They counted five – they had mistaken a cruiser for a battleship.

Incredibly, they got away a second time, although they were pursued by four Italian aircraft. They shot down one, the other three then turned for home, and Warburton and his crew safely made it back to Malta, where they discovered part of an aerial from one of the ships caught in the tail wheel. They flew over once more on the 7th of November, and again on the 10th, and finally on the 11th, the afternoon of the planned attack, by which time a sixth battleship had arrived. In addition, there were fourteen cruisers and twenty-seven destroyers – rich pickings indeed if the attack could possibly be made a success.

At 6 p.m. that evening, Cunningham sent a good-luck message to Rear-Admiral Lyster and his men, now 170 miles off Taranto. 'As may be imagined,' noted Cunningham, 'we spent the night on tenterhooks.' The plan was to attack in two waves of twelve Fairey Swordfish, naval biplanes known as 'Stringbags'. They were hardly modern, but they were highly manoeuvrable and very robust, so were ideal for the kind of attack planned. At 8.35 p.m., the first squadron of Swordfish took off with the moon high and clear. It was just before 11 p.m. when they were approaching the harbour. The plan was that these first aircraft would drop flares to light up the battleships in the outer harbour, then dive-bomb the cruisers and destroyers in the inner harbour. As they reached Taranto, the anti-aircraft guns both on the warships and around the harbour immediately opened up, yet most of the attackers managed to complete their runs successfully and then make good their escape. Around midnight, the second wave of Swordfish arrived and were also able to complete their mission as planned. Just two were lost, and reconnaissance photographs the following morning showed that three battleships had been sunk or damaged, and a cruiser and two destroyers damaged. Half the Italian battle fleet had been put out of action in one go. To lose one battleship was disastrous; but to lose three of these most expensive, enormous and powerful warships at once was little short of catastrophic, and while two of them would eventually be recovered, it was only at great cost of money and time.

'Admirably planned and most gallantly executed' was Cunningham's view of the attack; from his flagship, HMS *Warspite*, he signalled with his flags, '*Illustrious* manoeuvre well executed', which he admitted was something of an understatement.

Yet while there can be no doubt that Warburton and his fellows in 431 Flight and the Fleet Air Arm did gallant and sterling work, the Italians should never have let it happen. No matter how intense the anti-aircraft barrage was at Taranto, it was nothing like adequate; it was not, for example, even as intense as that now guarding the harbours of Malta, where the Mediterranean Fleet was not even based. Co-ordination between searchlights and flak was also poor, and some weeks earlier Maresciallo Badoglio had already suggested to Count Ciano that the Fleet should be moved. Three weeks later, with the moon high and

OPERATION COMPASS, December 1940–February 1941

MEDITERRANEAN SEA

Gulf of Sirte

LIBYA

EGYPT

Qattara Depression

Cyrenaica

Jebel El Akhdar

Graziani's Advance (13–16 Sept, 1940)

Wavell's Offensive (9 Dec 1940–7 Feb 1941)

El Agheila
Benghazi
Soluch — 7 Feb
Msus
Beda Fomm — 5 Feb
Agedabia
Mechili — 3 Feb
Bir Hocheim
Derna
Timimi
Acroma
El Adem
Tobruk — 22 Jan
Gambut
Bir El Gobi
Bardia — 16 Dec
Fort Capuzzo — 13 Sep
Sidi Barrani — 10 Dec
Sollum — 5 Jan
Halfaya
Sofafi
Sidi Omar
Buq Buq
Nibeiwa
Maddalena
Mersa Matruh
El Daba
El Alamein

KEY
→ Allied attacks
→ German attacks
⇢ German withdrawals
| German positions

N

0   100 km
0   100 miles

with the British Fleet clearly out at sea, nothing had been done.

'A black day,' Ciano noted on 12 November. It was, and by then the Army was already suffering an even greater humiliation.

The second British operation was a planned attack against Maresciallo Graziani's forces now halted thirty miles inside Egypt. Codenamed COMPASS, this was to be the first major land attack against the Italians and had evolved after many long discussions between London and Cairo. In July, Wavell had flown to London for strategy discussions, and then in October Anthony Eden, the Minister of War, had flown out to Cairo for more talks. From the outset, Churchill had made it clear to Wavell that he should not sit on the defensive for long – he wanted action against the Italians just as soon as it was feasible. On the other hand, Wavell, while every bit as keen to act, was also hamstrung by the vastness of his command and the varying demands upon him.

The strategic importance of the Middle East and Mediterranean to Britain had only increased since the fall of France and the entry of Italy into the war. On the face of it, Britain's insistence on continuing the fight there might seem misplaced. 'Atlantic trade,' the First Sea Lord had signalled to Admiral Cunningham back in June, 'must be our first consideration.' In this, he was unquestionably right. Keeping the supply chains open was the most important factor for any nation now caught up in this war. Without those key ingredients, there could be no strategy, no tactical developments. As such, the battle raging at sea in the Atlantic, now, at the end of 1940, had to be the most important priority for Britain.

So why was Britain already focusing so much energy on the Mediterranean and the Middle East? After all, the oilfields of Abadan in Iran and Kirkuk–Mosul in Iraq were not its prime supplier and were nothing like as significant as those in Baku in the USSR, or in Venezuela or the United States, the biggest producer of all. Even if Axis forces had reached the oilfields of Iraq and Iran, they would have been able to make little use of them as they would be unable to ship the oil by sea and there was no way they could transport a significant amount of the stuff across land; pipelines were still in their infancy and did not exist in these far-flung parts of the world. The British oil facilities in Iraq and Iran only really supplied Britain's forces in the Middle East. If the armed forces weren't there, Britain wouldn't need the oil.

British protection of the Middle East was not, then, about oil, as has so often been claimed. There were, however, other important consider-ations. While no strategy should have been allowed to compete with the Atlantic supply lines, Britain was none the less not in the war to survive. It was in the war to win – and primarily to beat Germany and rid the world of Nazism. Back in Britain, it was now clear that the threat of invasion had, for the time being at any rate, passed. That being the case, and with the Battle of Britain won, there was no longer any immediate threat to its sovereignty, and while ground troops were still needed for the defence of the United Kingdom, its war leaders could release div-isions for other theatres. More importantly, they could also afford to send tanks, artillery, transport and other equipment, as well as air and naval forces. Even back in July, the War Cabinet and Chiefs of Staff had agreed to sending 150 tanks to the Middle East. This has always been seen as an incredibly brave decision considering the threat from Germany, yet it was also a calculated and measured risk based on the assumption that, although Britain's position was precarious, a successful German invasion attempt was still very unlikely. Furthermore, the Middle East was the one part of the war where Britain could most easily concentrate the assets of the empire, whether manpower or supplies – from India, Ceylon, Australia, New Zealand and South Africa.

The first objective was to use the Middle East and Mediterranean to blunt Italian ambitions, then to make the Italians even more of a liability to Germany, and then to defeat them. Britain had hoped to create an eastern Mediterranean bloc with Turkey – by far the strongest power in the region – Greece and Yugoslavia, but after agreeing mutual friendship, Turkey had then stopped short of an alliance and in June had declared itself resolutely neutral. Britain's failure to secure Turkey as an ally had merely reinforced the importance of Egypt as the cradle of British strategy. From here, Britain could possibly push into Vichy-held Syria too and influence Franco's Spain. It was already holding Franco's broken country to ransom with the threat of cutting off its much-needed supplies, but Gibraltar – British, and the gateway to the Mediterranean – remained vulnerable owing to its proximity to Fascist Spain. Then there were the Balkans; the closer Britain could get to Ploeşti in Romania, now Germany's prime source of crude oil, the better.

It was, then, a largely opportunistic approach, but in the circumstances it made very good sense. After all, following a largely defensive land strategy in the first year of war had not done the Allies much good.

The second part of Britain's overall strategy was to continue to grow the bomber force and strike back ever harder at the Reich from the air. Finally, Churchill hoped to undermine Nazi occupation and help those now under the German yoke to rise up. There were the Commandos, formed in early July, who would carry out harassing raids, and there was the Special Operations Executive, or SOE, under the control of a new Ministry of Economic Warfare. SOE would foster resistance, carry out sabotage, and spread dissent and chaos. It would, Churchill hoped, set Europe ablaze.

But first it was time to test the water in the desert, so to speak. For some weeks, British forces had been harrying the Italian positions. Patrols and larger formations had been probing Italian defences and even getting right behind their series of makeshift forts and disrupting supply lines. Certainly, the men of 2nd Rifle Brigade had been busy through much of October. Part of the recently formed 7th Armoured Division, the Rifle Brigade had been created during the Napoleonic Wars as scouts, skirmishers and sharpshooters; somewhat confusingly, they were not a brigade at all, but rather a regiment, and now, in Egypt's Western Desert, they were once more carrying out exactly what they had originally been formed to do.

For Albert Martin, a young man from Poplar in London's East End, these forays had been an ideal means of completing his training. After arriving in Port Suez in September, he been sent on a hardening course to prepare him for life in the desert, and had then been sent to join A Company. Normally, each platoon had three sections of ten men, but 2RB was divided into four sections of six instead – and each six-man section was assigned a single 15 cwt Morris truck, stripped of any glass or excess fixtures and fittings. 'Our truck was a friendly haven,' he wrote. 'We ate with it, slept with it, travelled in it, crawled under it for shade, hung equipment to its side. It was also a mobile larder and an occasional social centre.' Four of the men in his section were pre-war Regulars who had served in Palestine, India, the Northwest Frontier and elsewhere; these men knew a whole host of tricks about how to make food and water last, navigating using the sun and the stars, how to barter with Bedouins, making a mug of tea in two and a half minutes using a cut-in-half tin and lighting petrol-soaked sand, and how to cleverly camouflage their truck so that from a hundred yards it could barely be seen at all.

What Martin and his fellows also learned very quickly was that the

Italians were obviously not embracing the desert in the same way. The platoon found it all too easy to pluck prisoners from Italian positions and realized that their enemy was unlikely to venture from the forts created to the south of Sidi Barrani. One night, they were supporting an attack on an Italian strong point at Maktila on the approach to Sidi Barrani. Leaving their truck, they then approached on foot, only to come under intense machine-gun fire. Martin was rather mesmerized by this, his first time under enemy fire. One of his mates pulled him to the ground, but he needn't have worried – the Italian firing was way too high. They were easily able to advance and helped take the position with no casualties at all.

After this, they were formed into larger mobile columns. An entire company of trucked infantry would be joined by two troops of mobile 25-pounder field guns, a troop of 2-pounder anti-tank guns, armoured cars and supporting sappers (engineers), signals and field ambulances. These columns would then rove further south and west, outflanking the Italian positions and attacking any supply vehicles they saw feeding the Italian troops at the front. 'We had total freedom of movement,' noted Martin, 'the Italians preferring to stay in their defensive enclaves and, when they did venture out, travelling close together along well-defined tracks and presenting themselves as tasty targets.'

These raids were all part of the softening-up process for the main assault. Martin and his mates knew something was brewing by the volume of traffic, the assembly of tanks and supporting vehicles, and the growing number of field guns arriving a short way behind them. Large fuel and ammunition dumps were also created. On the night of 8 December, Martin and the rest of the column moved out, assembling in a patch of desert now called Piccadilly Circus, about thirty-five miles south of Sidi Barrani. 'And believe me,' noted Martin, 'it really was like Piccadilly Circus. I had never seen so many of our troops, armour and vehicles in one place.' Commanding this force of 7th Armoured and 4th Indian Divisions was Major-General Richard O'Connor. His plan was to punch a hole fifteen miles wide. Half of 7th Armoured would strike at a series of forts above an escarpment thirty miles from the coast, the rest of the division – including Martin's A Company – would drive straight for Buq Buq, fifteen miles beyond Sidi Barrani, and so cut the coast road, while 4th Indian turned towards the town itself and other forts closer to the coast. At the same time, a further column, called Selby Force, would strike west directly along the coast. Meanwhile, the RAF had blasted Italian airfields on the 7th and 8th, while fighter patrols shooed away any Italian reconnaissance planes.

As first light crept over the desert, O'Connor's Western Desert Force smashed into the Italian positions, achieving complete surprise. At one fort, Nibiewa, 4th Indian attacked from the rear as the Italians were barely rousing. Generale Pietro Maletti, wounded as he tried to rally his troops, retreated to his tent with a machine gun and was firing from his camp bed when he was killed. Nibiewa was captured in just half an hour. The story was repeated elsewhere. Two days later, on 11 December, it was all over: the forts destroyed, Sidi Barrani taken, Albert Martin and 2nd Rifle Brigade in Buq Buq as planned, and some 38,300 prisoners in the bag, along with 237 guns and seventy-three Italian tanks. Rarely could a battle have gone so completely to plan.

CHAPTER 36

Change of Tack

THE BRITISH SHIPBUILDER, Cyril Thompson, and the marine engineer, Harry Hunter, had reached New York on 3 October and had immediately been met by Sir Walter Layton, the Director of Programmes at the Ministry of Supply, who was already Stateside, and Arthur Purvis, a Scottish businessman who had made his fortune in Canada and since the beginning of the war had been head of the British Purchasing Commission. Layton and Purvis briefed them on the two men they had to convince: Rear-Admiral Emory 'Jerry' Land, the Head of the US Maritime Commission, and his deputy, Commander Howard Vickery.

Admiral Land, however, was already under fire for not having overseen a rise in shipbuilding big enough to meet American needs and quickly made it clear that, while the US wanted to help, it was a tricky time. In fact, under Bill Knudsen's direction, the National Defense Advisory Commission had already cleared contracts for a staggering 948 naval vessels, including 292 warships and twelve 35,000-ton aircraft carriers. The British mission would, he told them, be welcome to approach American shipbuilding firms, but would need US Government clearance before a deal was struck. Furthermore, he also made it clear that not only would new shipyards have to be built specifically for the British orders, but Britain would have to also fund their construction. Since Thompson had set sail with the strict brief not to exceed £10 million for the entire order, it was already looking like the mission was facing an uphill struggle.

None the less, armed with Land's blessing-of-sorts, Thompson and

Hunter began a three-week whistle-stop tour of shipyards and marine-engineering works in the United States and Canada, but at every single one the message was much the same: they were working at full capacity already. Furthermore, it was clear that most people they met thought Britain was a busted flush. 'We got the impression,' said Thompson, 'that they thought they were being invited to back a losing cause.'

Finally, however, on 23 October, Thompson and the mission's fortunes appeared to take a turn for the better. On that day, at Portland, Oregon, Thompson met Henry Kaiser. Fifty-eight years old, bald and round, Kaiser was none the less a firebrand entrepreneur with a nose for money-making opportunities and a can-do attitude to life that had, so far, served him very well. Although he was not a qualified engineer, he had headed a number of construction businesses, and back in 1931 had set up a consortium called Six Companies Incorporated which had built the Boulder Dam in Colorado and followed that by constructing the massive Hoover Dam. Kaiser knew only a little about building roads and dams, but he understood how to harness new technology to make construction cheaper and easier. It had been his idea, for example, to add a plough to the front of a tractor, which he named the Caterpillar, and which soon became a standard piece of construction equipment. He strongly believed that no one should be afraid to do things a new way; innovation was exciting and to be embraced. And he also knew how to build good relations with local, state and federal officials. Bureaucrats and red tape were not barriers: they were something to be oiled, charmed and won over.

Kaiser had got wind of the British Shipbuilding Mission and was excited by the opportunities it might present. He had little experience of shipbuilding, but his Six Companies Incorporated had recently entered a partnership with Todd Shipyards to build and operate a new yard near Seattle. When he met Thompson, Kaiser told him emphatically that if the British gave him the backing, he would build 200 ships during 1942. Both Thompson and Harry Hunter were impressed, and were even more so after visiting the Kaiser–Todd shipyard at Seattle. With Kaiser's drive and Todd's know-how, they had already produced two ships and built a yard from scratch in just eleven months. This was the kind of dynamism and speed Thompson had been looking for; what's more, at last, in Kaiser he had found someone who actually wanted the contract.

There were, however, three big issues to resolve. The first was deciding on the design of the ships that would be built. In the interest of speed of production, it clearly made sense to build just one design, and a provisional agreement was struck that Kaiser's consortium would build the ships using the plans Thompson had brought with him. Through early November, Thompson and the engineers at Todd worked on those designs, making just a few modifications. It was agreed that the US-built ships would be welded, rather than riveted, partly because it was quicker and partly because there was a lack of trained riveters in America. They would also be powered by British-style coal-fired steam engines, with which British crews were familiar.

Then came a setback. 'Cable from London,' noted Thompson in his diary on 16 November, 'changing size of all ships. Oh Hell.' Despite the work already put in with Todd, the Admiralty now wanted the new ships to follow a further design of Thompson's, a slightly larger version, which the shipyard back at North Sands was planning to start building early the following year. The plans of these, however, were back in England. None the less, enough had been agreed for the time being. More important in the immediate term was the securing of US government approval from Rear-Admiral Jerry Land. Wedded to this was the building of new shipyards and deciding just where they might be. Kaiser had made it clear that they could not be built in Seattle; he would build the new shipyards, but these would need to be near a major conurbation with a large potential workforce and good inland transport connections, and also near deep-water channels. The USA had a big coastline, but finding two, if not three, such locations was easier said than done.

Kaiser, however, soon came up with three options. The first was at Richmond, California, on the eastern side of San Francisco Bay, and he took Thompson and his party to see the site. There was nothing there but a mass of dismal mud flats. 'It's true you see nothing now,' Kaiser told them, 'but within months this vast space will have a shipyard on it with thousands of workers building the ships for you.' This yard would be constructed and run by the newly formed Todd California Shipbuilding Corporation. The second would be constructed at Portland in Maine, on the east coast, by the Todd Corporation in association with Bath-Iron. In this case, Thompson had much greater involvement in the choice of site. Here it was decided to create a series of shallow dry docks blasted out of the rock. The third was planned for Mobile, Alabama, in the Gulf of Mexico.

On 1 December, Admiral Land informed the British Shipbuilding Commission that the US Government had given its blessing to the building of the two new yards at Richmond and Portland, but not Mobile, and the construction of thirty vessels at each, but there was still a third issue to be overcome, and that was the cost. The deal Thompson had provisionally agreed would cost £24 million, more than double the authorized expenditure. While the Admiralty and British Government had been kept in the loop throughout Thompson's mission, getting this vastly inflated sum approved was another matter. It was time, Thompson believed, to head back to Britain and argue the case in person. So, armed with the draft contract and a number of other documents in a safely locked briefcase, he boarded the cargo liner *Western Prince* at New York on 6 December and set sail for home.

Meanwhile, back across the Atlantic, the Battle of Britain had been won. The Luftwaffe had not destroyed the RAF, it had not won air superiority over Britain, and there had been no chance of Germany launching an invasion across the Channel. However, whenever the weather permitted, daily clashes in the air still occurred, although at nothing like the intensity of the summer and early autumn. Jochen Marseille had been posted away from LG2 to JG52 – largely for disciplinary reasons – and there came under the command of Macky Steinhoff. He had arrived a day late after spending the night with a French girl, but sauntered in to see his new CO as though he had done nothing wrong at all.

'What the hell is this?' Steinhoff asked him, holding up his personnel record. 'It's almost as thick as a telephone directory!' Despite Steinhoff's warnings, Marseille seemed unwilling to change his ways. In combat, he invariably shot off on his own without warning. Steinhoff had him grounded for a week, but it never occurred to him to restrict his errant pilot to barracks. 'He stole my car,' said Steinhoff, 'went into town and came back drunk, with two girls in varying degrees of undress, also drunk, and one was driving the car. I was beyond angry.' Steinhoff now restricted him to base for a month. It says much about the autonomy which these Luftwaffe *Gruppen* were allowed to exercise that in such a disciplined and militaristic totalitarian state as Nazi Germany someone so wayward as Marseille could survive.

While Steinhoff was struggling to contain Marseille, the Luftwaffe's bombers continued to pound Britain, although mostly now by night. In fact, they had been bombing Britain every night since the first attack on London back on Saturday, 7 September. The aim was no longer to destroy the RAF but to cause as much damage as possible and to break the morale of the British people. The British had dubbed this bomber assault by the Luftwaffe 'the Blitz'.

Unsurprisingly, civilian casualties were mounting. For all the swift efficiency that Gwladys Cox had witnessed when her flat was destroyed, Britain was not as prepared for aerial bombing as it might have been. There were spaces in public shelters for only around half the nearly twenty-eight million people living in the major cities, and most of these were not, in 1940, deep reinforced concrete bunkers but, rather, tended to be basements in the public buildings, such as church halls. Many people never bothered going to these in any case. The Government had also tried to persuade people to build their own shelters. This could mean reinforcing the cellar or basement, placing a cage or box under the kitchen table, or building an Anderson shelter in the garden. These shelters, named after the engineer David Anderson, involved digging a trench into the ground, covering it with curved but solidly thick corrugated-iron strips, then layering it with the already excavated soil. None of these shelters would protect from a direct hit, but the Anderson shelter, especially, protected its inhabitants from almost anything other than that. These unquestionably saved many lives, but casualties were still quite high: 6,968 deaths and 9,488 serious casualties in September, 6,313 and 7,949 in October, 5,004 and 6,247 in November. The British people had never suffered a violation like this, and not since the plague of 1665 had the public been in such personal danger.

In London, people had taken to using Underground stations as shelters which were, for the most part, bombproof. Initially, this was prohibited, although the ban was quickly lifted. Other cities, though, did not have this unexpectedly effective facility, and, as October had given way to November, so the Luftwaffe began to widen its net.

On the night of 14 November, Coventry, an industrial cathedral city in the Midlands, was hit by an unusually large number of bombers – some 450, led by KG100 equipped with *X-Gerät*. Attacking in two waves in perfect bombing conditions and with a mixture of high explosives and incendiaries, the gap in the waves was timed to perfection, with the second fanning the flames of the first. The target had been the city's motor factories, but the centre was devastated. The cathedral and the medieval heart of the city were destroyed. The attack was the worst so far in the Blitz and was a psychological and physical blow that shocked both the wider public and Britain's war leaders. Coventry would not be forgotten – neither the method of the attack nor its effects.

RAF Bomber Command wasted no time in striking back, however. The following night, over a hundred bombers attacked Hamburg and Dutch airfields used by the Luftwaffe. The Hamburg raid caused a number of fires and heavy damage to the Blohm & Voss shipyard and was unquestionably the most successful RAF raid so far; the same conditions that had helped the Luftwaffe over Coventry had worked for Bomber Command too.

Striking back was all very well, but there was a growing feeling that not enough was being done to combat the Luftwaffe's night raids. The incredibly successful fighter defence of Britain had been based entirely on daylight operations. Air Chief Marshal Dowding was frantically working on a system of night interception, in which fighters would rely entirely on their instruments to fly and be guided to targets by onboard radar. Yet although the cavity magnetron had revolutionized the potential of radar and made much smaller sets possible, it was not something that could be perfected overnight.

Fighter Command also needed night fighters. It was clear that most who were told to convert from day to night operations both loathed it and found it very difficult to acclimatize to the change. The obvious answer was to draw new night-fighter pilots from Bomber Command, whose pilots were used to operating in the dark, and when Air Marshal Sholto Douglas, Deputy Chief of the Air Staff, asked Air Vice-Marshal Arthur Harris, C-in-C of 5 Group, Bomber Command, for some recommendations, he had no hesitation in putting forward Flight Lieutenant Guy Gibson, whom he considered one of the most dogged, determined pilots to have served in his command.

In fact, Gibson had already been packed off to 14 OTU as an instructor at the end of September, having flown thirty-seven operations, during which time he had lost no fewer than sixty-two of his colleagues. Gibson had taken the chance of some leave to get engaged to his girlfriend, Eve Moore, a dancer seven years his senior, with whom he was quite infatuated.

He had barely started at 14 OTU, however, when Harris contacted him and told him he was being posted to 29 Night Fighter Squadron. In return,

Harris promised that after doing this stint he would bring him back and give him the best squadron in Bomber Command he could. Gibson was only too happy to chuck in the instructing but was less than enamoured of RAF Digby, a soulless and bleak airfield in the Lincolnshire fens.

The atmosphere in the squadron was as bleak as the setting. They had shot down just one enemy in five months, but one of their own planes had been mistakenly blasted out of the sky by a Hurricane. To make matters worse, they were regularly dispersed in penny-packets of three to different airfields, had been flying totally unsuitable Blenheims and were fed up that the day fighter boys were getting all the accolades. The only solace was the arrival of new Beaufighters in recent weeks – a twin-engine aircraft based on the Blenheim, but which could fly at well over 300 mph and was armed with both 20mm cannons and machine guns. None the less, when Gibson turned up from Bomber Command to take over A Flight, he was given a surly reception.

On his second day with the squadron, he was taken to the Operations Room to see the techniques of ground control. By chance, the enemy raid he followed from the dais was that on Coventry. As the plots developed and were moved across the map table, Gibson watched and listened as night fighters were ordered into the sky, but during the entire two waves of raids only one fighter even so much as spotted an enemy bomber. Earlier in the summer, Macky Steinhoff had discovered exactly the same difficulties were facing the Luftwaffe: without an effective means of homing aircraft in on a target, night-fighting was never going to work.

Dowding and the Air Ministry Research Establishment were making progress, though, and had recognized that night-fighting was now the prime task in the air defence of Great Britain. The Beaufighter was gradually coming into service and was a good machine: rugged, packing a punch, faster than any bomber and big enough to carry the kind of equipment and weapons needed. A new onboard radar was also coming into service, Air Interceptor (AI) Mk IV, which had a greater range than earlier versions, although of still only a few miles.

The biggest headache facing Dowding and his scientists had been how to track enemy bombers once they flew past the static screen of radar stations along the coast. This, too, had now been solved by the development of a Ground Control of Interception (GCI) radar. Fully rotational, it was tested successfully the same November that Gibson joined 29 Squadron. Such was the speed of technological advancement in this war.

✳

In Bill Knudsen's office in the marble Federal Reserve building in Washington DC, he had fixed up a static radial engine for him to look at and to help him keep his focus. A man in a hurry, he had insisted – as Lord Beaverbrook had insisted at the Ministry of Aircraft Production in Britain – that the normal methodical means of doing business were thrown out the window. All contracts, he demanded, had to be boiled down to a single typewritten sheet, while his own stamp was a single 'K' written in blue ink. This was jumped on in a feature in *Time* magazine in early October when 'Motormaker' Knudsen was the cover story under the question, 'How are we doing?' 'The answer last week,' concluded *Time*, 'was about as well as a democracy in peacetime could be expected to do. No one pretended that a peacetime democracy could hope to take on a totalitarian war machine – yet.'

Despite the hint of cynicism in the piece, Knudsen would agree with the magazine that time was most definitely the biggest challenge. He was making progress, though, and not least with the automobile business. Packard was in the process of making Merlin engines, Pontiac was making Oerlikon cannons, and Chrysler was making the new M3 tank for both the US and the British, but by October Knudsen was realizing that all US car firms should be working on war production. After all, collectively, they were America's biggest employer, with more than a thousand factories and manufacturing facilities worth $3 billion. While other areas of American industry had become run down, the motor car industry was the one area above all others still in rude health. With his biggest problem still how to mass-produce aircraft, and with a dangerous bottleneck developing, he hoped the automobile moguls would provide the answers.

On 29 October, he had gathered all the US automobile executives in New York and introduced them to a panel of Air Corps officers and aviation people, who then explained to them the process of making aircraft, how they were used, the different types, and the level to which they needed to be produced in double-quick time.

To a man, the motor execs agreed to help and out of that conference formed the Automotive Committee for Air Defense. Annual model changes were suspended, which would give them time for retooling to make aircraft parts. The key, Knudsen knew, was to let the aircraft manufacturers continue to make aircraft, but to get the motor manufacturers to mass-produce parts. So Chrysler and the Hudson Motor Car Company agreed to make airframes for the B-26 Marauder medium bomber, while GM, among others, would make parts for the B-17 Flying Fortress heavy four-engine bomber. GM would also help with the B-25 medium bomber and Ford was one of those who agreed to make parts for the B-24 Liberator heavy bomber.

Yet it was also two steps forward, one step back. Knudsen was utterly apolitical, and he viewed the process purely from the perspective of the businessman and practical economics. The deal with the automobile manufacturers had outraged union leaders, and he had been widely criticized for giving the biggest contracts to the biggest firms. Once again, they railed, Big Business was winning at the expense of the little guy. Knudsen, however, had stuck to his guns, pointing out that it was the biggest companies who had the capacity as well as the best engineering staffs. There was, he argued, plenty for small business too, but as subcontractors.

The criticism of Knudsen and the NDAC was still rumbling on when on Tuesday, 3 December, Henry Stimson had invited Knudsen, Ed Stettinius and Donald Nelson, the ex-president of Sears and Roebuck and now Stettinius's deputy, to an emergency lunch. (Nelson's *Time* magazine photo caption had been: 'From safety pins to 16-inch guns.')

They drove up to Woodley, Stimson's grand house at Rock Creek Park, where they found not only Stimson, but Frank Knox, the Navy Secretary, and Cordell Hull, the Secretary of State. Hull was not optimistic. Britain was being bombed to blazes, too many ships were being lost, British cash was running out. If they weren't careful, Britain could be out of the war before they knew it. Somehow, Stimson told them, they needed to stir up the business people of America, who, as far as he was concerned, were still asleep.

Afterwards, Stimson drove with Knudsen and Knox to the Treasury to see Henry Morgenthau. On a large blackboard, Morgenthau had chalked up Britain's remaining gold and reserve assets, which showed the UK would owe $3 billion by 1 June 1941 but most likely be around a billion short.

'I'm rather shocked at the depth we're getting into,' said Stimson.

Knox said, 'We are going to pay for the war from now, aren't we?'

'Well, what are we going to do?' said Morgenthau. 'Are we going to let them place more orders, or not?'

'Got to,' replied Hull. 'No choice about it.'

'We can make it,' said Knudsen, 'if it can be financed.'

As it happened, Roosevelt had already been thinking about this conundrum and had on 9 December received a letter from Churchill expressing his concerns that before long British cash would run out, yet pointing out the urgent need to keep shipping orders, especially, coming their way.

At the time, Roosevelt was on board the heavy cruiser *Tuscaloosa*, along with his inner circle, for a restorative trip around the Caribbean. Naturally enough, Harry Hopkins was with him and noticed FDR read and re-read Churchill's lengthy letter. Then, on the night of the 11th, he explained to Hopkins his idea. America would simply 'lend' Britain all the materiel it needed. 'He suddenly came out with it,' said Hopkins. 'The whole programme.' Obviously, the US would in effect be giving Britain this materiel, as realistically the US was unlikely to want it back after the war. But that wasn't the point. Rather, it was about ensuring Britain kept fighting so that America didn't have to for as long as possible, and making certain that this was tied to a legal framework, however spurious.

It was the genesis of what would be called Lend-Lease.

In the Western Desert, an Australian war correspondent, Alan Moorehead, had listened to a briefing from General Wavell early on 9 December and then had hurried up into the 'blue', as the desert was known, and later that day reached the carnage. The first Italian strongpoint he and his colleagues reached was Nibiewa and they were stunned by the scene of chaos and devastation. Walking from one tent to another, and through trenches and subterranean tunnels, Moorehead marvelled at the work and effort that had gone into the position only for the British to go through it as easily as a knife through butter. They found Generale Maletti, beribboned, bearded and bloodied, sprawled on his bed. 'Extraordinary things met us wherever we turned,' wrote Moorehead. 'Officers' beds laid out with clean sheets, chests of drawers filled with linen and an abundance of fine clothing of every kind. Uniforms heavy with gold lace and decked with the medals and colours of the parade ground.' They walked into at least thirty dugouts and everywhere Moorehead was overcome by the quality of the leatherwork, the intricacy of their kit. He had never seen an army so well supplied with personal comforts. Nor had he ever seen so many letters. He picked up a number, scanning them briefly. All talked of home, of lovers or family. 'God watch and keep our beloved Federico and Maria,' he discovered in one, 'and may the blessed Virgin preserve them from all harm until the short time, my dearest, passes when I shall press thee into my arms again. I cry. I weep for thee here in the desert at night and lament our cruel separation.'

He also discovered others that showed a surprising understanding of their situation. 'We are trying to fight this war as though it is a colonial war in Africa,' one officer had written. 'But it is a European war in Africa fought with European weapons against a European enemy. We take too little account of this in building our stone forts and equipping ourselves with such luxury. We are not fighting the Abyssinians now.'

They had hardly covered themselves in glory in that conflict in any case. The endless bits of paper, the broken equipment, the scattered supplies and other detritus at Nibiewa demonstrated a terrible truth, plain to almost all but Mussolini and his acolytes, that neither was Italy ready for modern war and nor did the Italian troops have the stomach for it. The vast majority of them wanted to be back at home cuddling Maria and Federico.

Nor did the defeat at Sidi Barrani mark the end of the British charge. Flushed with success, they pushed on. Sollum and Fort Capuzzo were captured on the 17th, and three days later the Italians were swept from Egypt. By now, 6th Australian Division had entered the fray and taken the lead, and had swiftly surrounded Bardia in Libya. Mussolini had not just taken on Britain, but the British Empire and the Dominion countries as well.

In his report to Mussolini of his meeting with Hitler at the Berghof in the middle of November, Count Ciano put a fairly good gloss on things, although he was more honest with himself. 'Hitler is pessimistic,' he noted, 'and considers the situation much compromised by what has happened in the Balkans. His criticism is open, focused and final.' Ciano couldn't get a word in edgeways.

Hitler was pessimistic because he now had a lot of problems on his hands, all stemming from Britain's very infuriating insistence on continuing to fight. If only Britain had seen sense and sued for terms back in the summer! Now, British factories were churning out ever-more war materiel, and so too was the United States, and the two Western democracies were beginning to cosy up to each other to a worrying degree. How to beat Britain and curb the threat of the USA had been exercising his mind since June and although he had been perfectly willing to go ahead with an invasion of England, he was not going to let his troops be slaughtered in mid-Channel before they had fired a shot.

Conscious that a war across a sea was not a strategy he felt comfortable with, Hitler had very quickly reverted to the German default plan for engaging in war: a lightning strike that would bring about a swift and crushing victory, and on land, which was what the Wehrmacht was primarily designed for. This meant an attack not against Britain, but against the Soviet Union.

General Walter Warlimont first heard of Hitler's plan at the end of July, when he and others in Section L were called together by General Jodl, by then recently promoted three ranks from major-general to full general. It was his reward for being the unfaltering mouthpiece of the Führer's will. And now he told his senior staff that, once and for all, Hitler was going to rid the world of Bolshevism. They would invade no later than May the following year.

To a man, they were horrified and immediately offered a whole host of objections, not least the opening up of the situation most feared above all: a war on two fronts. Jodl countered them all: a collision with Soviet Russia was going to happen at some point, so it was better, he argued, to do it now, while the Red Army was still weakened by Stalin's purges and Germany was at the peak of its military powers. There was, in fact, something in this; Stalin had no more intention of keeping the pact in place than Hitler did, and there was no doubt that the much weakened Red Army had been rather embarrassed by Finland. And while it was true that the Soviet Union was much larger than France and therefore would bring about certain logistical headaches, no one could claim the Reds were a better military machine than the French, who had been despatched in a mere six weeks. So how hard could it be? Hitler had gambled in Norway and won, gambled in France and victory had followed. He would crush the Soviet Union in a war of annihilation too.

Warlimont's consternation was entirely understandable, but the truth was, Hitler's worst decision had been invading Poland in the first place and then not having a properly thought through Plan B if Britain didn't sue for peace. What were the alternatives to a swift pre-emptive strike on the Soviet Union? Attack in a few years' time, by which point Britain and America would be overwhelmingly strong and the Soviet Union stronger too? Or sit back and wait? That wasn't the German way of war at all; when cornered, the Prussian–German way, as it always had been, was to take advantage of superior training and the *Bewegungskrieg*, and attack.

Because of the huge scale of an invasion and because, as Napoleon had discovered back in 1812, winters in the Soviet Union were appalling, this operation really did need Germany's unwavering focus, which was why Hitler was far from pleased to find the Balkans now under threat. He could not afford to have a war on a third front to Germany's south, nor to have Italy knocked out of the war, nor to have the Romanian oilfields threatened. It was clear the Italian Fleet no longer had any chance of defeating the Royal Navy and now, to make things worse, it looked as though Italy might be kicked out of North Africa altogether. Britain had guaranteed the independence of Greece back in April 1939, and Ioannis Metaxas, the Greek Prime Minister-cum-dictator, had wasted no time in asking the British to honour that promise. And Britain had done so, sending naval and air support and troops and naval forces to Crete. Troops, Churchill had pledged, would follow.

This meant Germany had to intervene. This had become more practicable since Hungary, Romania and Slovakia had joined the Axis in the third week of November, and Yugoslavia looked as though it might well sign up as well; all feared the encroaching spread of Soviet Communism more than Nazism, and it was clear that cosying up to Germany, whose armies appeared so unstoppable, seemed like a shrewd move. For Hitler, these new Axis partners helped him shore up a crucial southern bloc. Greece, however, could not be allowed to defeat Italy, nor be a portal for Britain to re-enter Europe. As a result, Hitler accepted that he had to intervene with his own troops. The Greeks would have to be defeated.

He also recognized that he needed to do something to curb the strength of the Royal Navy in the Mediterranean. Warlimont's Section L had been preparing a plan to capture Gibraltar, but Franco had refused to countenance such a move. The alternative was to send some Luftwaffe units to Sicily, from where they might attack the British fleet; Mussolini had rejected such offers of support before but no longer, and Luftflotte X was duly posted to the Mediterranean in the middle of December.

On 14 December, Hitler issued a directive for the invasion of Greece, and four days later a further directive for Operation BARBAROSSA, the invasion of the Soviet Union. Immediately, von Brauchitsch spoke to Hitler's Army Adjutant, Major Engel, asking whether he thought Hitler really meant to invade the Soviet Union or whether he was bluffing. 'I am convinced that the Führer still does not know what will happen,' wrote Engel. 'Distrustful of his own military leaders, uncertainty about Russian strength, disappointment over British stubbornness continue to preoccupy him.' It was hardly an encouraging assessment. Despite this, a recent detailed report had suggested Russian forces were as weak as Hitler had hoped. 'Hopes English will relent,' added Engel, 'does not believe USA will enter war. Big concerns about Africa and the Italians. Astonishing faith in the capabilities of the Luftwaffe.' The long and short of it was this: Hitler was facing an appalling conundrum made very much worse by the ineptitude of his number one ally. One thing was certain, however: time was not standing still and Germany could not expect to hold on to its military dominance for ever. And just as Britain was running out of cash, so Germany would soon enough be running out of resources. Britain was turning to the USA; Germany would have to snatch the resources it needed from Russia. For all Hitler's ongoing prevarication, he really did have no alternative.

One young Luftwaffe pilot who had every intention of repaying Hitler's faith was Heinz Knocke, who had at long last completed his flying training and on 18 December, the very day Hitler had issued his BARBAROSSA directive, was to see the Führer in person at the Sportpalast in Berlin. Knocke was one of 3,000 future officers from all three services and the SS who had been assembled. In just a few months, he would be a fully fledged officer and sent to the front. Knocke couldn't wait.

The ceremony began with Göring appearing on the vast stage. The errant young pilot Hans-Joachim Marseille, had none the less made a name for himself during the air fighting over Britain, and was now presented to the Reichsmarschall, after which a few minutes passed and then the crowd was brought to attention. Arms were outstretched in salute and then there he was, Hitler himself, flanked by Raeder and Keitel. Absolute silence reigned, then the Führer began to speak.

Knocke could not imagine the world had ever known a more brilliant orator. 'His magnetic personality is irresistible,' he enthused. 'One can sense the emanations of tremendous will-power and driving energy. We are 3,000 young idealists. We listen to the spell-binding words and accept them with all our hearts. We have never before experienced such a deep sense of patriotic devotion towards our German fatherland.' Whipped up to a frenzy, Knocke and his fellows happily pledged their lives to the battles ahead. At the end, Knocke was left feeling profoundly moved. 'I shall never,' he added, 'forget the expressions of rapture which I saw on the faces around me today.'

The following day, Knocke received his posting: to JG52 – one of the most successful fighter wings in the Luftwaffe.

While young, impressionable men like Heinz Knocke, who had been indoctrinated since their early teens, were keen as mustard to head off and fight for Führer and Fatherland, many older Germans were increasingly tiring of both the war and the iron grip of the party.

Else Wendel was a young housewife in Berlin who was losing her enthusiasm for both Hitler and the Nazis. Rations were getting smaller and smaller. Berlin, she thought, looked forlorn and abandoned – there were no lights and no Christmas trees showing through the blackout curtains; no getting away from the war.

Wendel had been brought up in Charlottenburg, an affluent suburb of Berlin, but, although educated and intelligent, had remained largely apolitical. She had married and had two sons, and then her husband had run off with another woman; because Nazi ideology denigrated the Church and religion, it had become much easier for men to divorce without any obligations to their families. Severing all ties with his wife and sons, he had completely abandoned them. Else had been left with no choice but to look for work and foster out her two boys, a decision she had understandably found heartbreaking. She did, however, have a good job – working for the Department of Art in Kraft durch Freude (KdF), part of the German Labour Front. She and her boss, Herr Wolter, had to organize art exhibitions in factories, all part of the Nazi cultural plan.

Despite her personal difficulties, Wendel enjoyed her work and like most people had been swept along by the astonishing victories earlier in the year; and like many, back in the summer, she had assumed the war would soon be over. Even so, she was keenly aware of the ever-watching eyes of the party. She would not, for example, dare tell derogatory jokes about the regime, and at her middle sister's recent engagement party had been shocked to hear her future brother-in-law telling gags about 'Wotan's Mickey Mouse'; he had meant Goebbels. She had been further shocked to hear the plight of her younger sister, Erna, and the demands made upon her as a youth welfare worker in Königsberg, where the party dominated all they did. 'All you have to do today,' Erna had told her, 'is kneel down and worship Hitler – you don't want any other qualifications for your job of work at all.' Rules, ludicrous demands and endless threats were making it almost impossible for Erna to do her job efficiently.

Others were more virulently against the regime – and not just those who were victims of persecution like Jews or other minorities. Hans Schlange-Schöningen was a landowner and farmer in Prussia who had fought throughout the last war and dabbled in right-wing politics before the Nazis came to power. Now farming once more, he had, since the war began, been writing down his growing disgust as 'a documentary record for a people who so easily forget,' but added, 'I am writing this today under constant threat from the Gestapo . . . I am writing in the name of innumerable old war comrades who proved their love of country for four long years and shed their blood. I am writing in the name of millions of people who cannot raise their voices, but who can say with full justice that they do not want, and never have wanted, what is happening now.'

As far as he was concerned, at Christmas 1940, Germany was a beleaguered fortress, now responsible for feeding the greater part of Europe and saddled with a pathetic ally attached to Germany like a convict's ball and chain. At home, food shortages were increasing. As a farmer, he was suffering from the shortage of fodder supplies. 'Exchange in kind is flourishing illegally,' he wrote. 'Cold and hungry people get up tired from disturbed nights in the air-raid shelters to queue up in front of food shops in the early morning.' No matter how fervent an admirer of Hitler one might be, no one could claim that life was easier now that the war was entering the New Year.

Ardent admirers, the apathetic and the antis – they were all there in Nazi Germany. Only the ardent admirers, however, would dare to openly profess their feelings.

In Britain, the improvements in night-fighter technology had come too late to save Air Chief Marshal Dowding, who was forced to relinquish command on 24 November. It was Lord Beaverbrook, the Minister for Aircraft Production, who effectively wielded the axe, despite his enormous respect for the Fighter Command chief. Dowding's dismissal has caused a lot of grumbling ever since, but it had been a very long summer, he had already carried on past his due retirement day twice and he was unquestionably exhausted, and getting some fresh blood in to tackle what was a quite different challenge to that of daylight defence was probably, on balance, a sensible move.

It marked a month of changes, however. When Dowding left Fighter Command, so too did Keith Park, who had handled the Battle of Britain with such skill and ingenuity. In their place came Sholto Douglas and Air Vice-Marshal Trafford Leigh-Mallory, two very different animals; they had big boots to fill. But November 1940 was also the month that a giant of British politics passed away. On the 9th, Neville Chamberlain died of cancer. He'd been ill for some time, probably – and unknowingly – even during the crisis of April and May 1940. He was not a martial man, yet when he had been Chancellor of the Exchequer, he had backed rearmament and the build-up of the Air Force and the Navy. After Munich, he had shown he would not be duped by Hitler again, and at the end of May he had sided with Churchill, not Halifax, in what probably turned out to be the most important decision of his life.

The attack on Coventry, the sacking of Dowding and the passing of Chamberlain: at home in Britain, a turning point had been reached as the New Year approached. The Battle of Britain was over; the country's sovereignty appeared safe. Victory over its enemies, was, however, a quite different proposition. No one was doubting that ahead lay long years of war.

PART IV

THE WIDENING WAR

CHAPTER 37

The Vanquished and the Defiant

Q UEEN WILHELMINA of the Netherlands had escaped to England during the collapse of her country, along with her daughter, Princess Juliana, and her German son-in-law, Prince Bernhard, and members of her Government, and had formed a government-in-exile in London. During her long reign, which had begun when she was a ten-year-old girl in 1890, she and the Royal Family had been widely accepted and broadly popular without ever being especially cherished, and her leaving had been a cause of controversy; King Leopold of the Belgians, in contrast, had chosen to stay with his sinking ship.

Leopold had been widely criticized for surrendering, while Wilhelmina had faced the same charge for making good her escape; only King Haakon of Norway, who had eventually escaped to Britain, appeared to have avoided such censure. Being monarch of a country overrun by the Nazis was, it seemed, a thankless job.

Be that as it may, Queen Wilhelmina had wasted no time in establishing both a government-in-exile and making herself the focus of future Dutch resistance to Nazi rule, despite having a German mother and son-in-law and despite the many close ties between Germany and the Netherlands. Although a constitutional monarch, she also put herself very much in charge; when she clashed with her defeatist Prime Minister, Dirk Jan de Greer, who was urging collaboration with Germany, she forced him to resign and appointed Pieter Gerbrandy, an outspoken anti-collaborator, instead.

The Queen was also the wealthiest woman in the world, and when, that summer, Lord Beaverbrook introduced the Spitfire Fund, a scheme for individuals and organizations to 'purchase' a Spitfire for £5,000, she bought an entire squadron. She also used the BBC to broadcast in Dutch on Radio Oranje to her subjects across the sea in the Netherlands.

Listening to her first address, on 28 July, had been Gerrit den Hartog, who although not found by his wife back in May had returned home a few weeks later after being released as a prisoner of war. Physically, he was none the worse for his ordeal, although he had become even quieter and suffered recurring nightmares as a result of what he'd witnessed. 'My compatriots,' she told den Hartog and the many others clandestinely listening, 'because the voice of the Netherlands could and should not remain silent, I, at the last moment, made the decision to take myself and my government, as symbols of our nation, to a place where we can continue to work as a living power and make our voice heard.' For den Hartog, who had remained as wedded to the news on his radio as ever, it was a significant moment. Disliking the Nazi propaganda and endless martial marches blaring out from the Dutch radio, he tried to listen to the BBC and the new Radio Oranje as often as he could.

Yet although he resented the Germans and was a loyalist to the Queen, den Hartog was hardly stirred to join the early resistance movement. Rather, with a family to feed and a further son born on 5 December, he had continued with his market-garden business and found he had never been in greater demand. It made him and his wife uncomfortable to think they were growing food to feed the bellies of the Germans, and yet what other choice did he have? If he refused, he'd have ruined himself.

Initially, the Netherlands had been given a military administration, appointed by the C-in-C of the Army, with General Alexander von Falkenhausen as Governor. Von Falkenhausen, who had advised the Chinese leader, General Chiang Kai-shek, in the mid-1930s, was known for being critical of the Nazi regime, so initially there were hopes in Holland that German occupation would be conducted in tune with international law. Hitler was having none of it, however, and instead appointed Reichskommissar Arthur Seyss-Inquart as head of all civil administration and charged him with creating a closer economic collaboration with Germany. Seyss-Inquart was Austrian but a die-hard Nazi and protégé of Himmler, and a further indication of the rule of steel that would be imposed was the appointment of Brigadeführer Hanns Albin Rauter as Senior SS and Police Leader. Their brief was to win over the 'kindred-blood' population and to govern the Netherlands through 'considerate' treatment. This meant the Dutch would not be treated like *Untermenschen* – that is, racially inferior – as the Poles had been, for example, but Germany still meant to take its fair share of plunder and booty from the Netherlands and to treat the Dutch with an iron fist in terms of security.

And the troops and SS police remained an intimidating presence, as the den Hartogs soon discovered. One Sunday, they had been out walking with friends when their visitors' teenage son was called over by some German troops, blindfolded and a pistol pressed into his cheek – all in full view of both families. He was soon released, but it was hardly the kind of action to win over the Dutch to Nazi rule. And no matter how lenient by Nazi standards, the occupiers still had every intention of bleeding the Netherlands dry.

It had taken quite a while for the French officer Capitaine Daniel Barlone to reach England, by way of Spanish Morocco and Lisbon, but he had eventually got there at the beginning of October, just as the last French servicemen were voluntarily heading in the opposite direction back to France. Barlone had marvelled at the naivety of so many of his fellow Frenchmen, not least the Maréchal himself. 'Do Pétain and Weygand think that Great Britain is incapable of both defending herself and of winning the war with her 500,000,000 subjects, her unlimited powers of purchasing arms from America, and her Dominions who have thrown themselves body and soul into the struggle?' he asked in his diary back in July. Barlone, however, was in the minority in thinking rationally about Britain's strengths at that critical moment in the summer.

The new regime appalled him and he was utterly horrified that the press had been subdued into being little more than a Nazi mouthpiece. 'It must not speak of our defeat and abasement,' he wrote, 'nor of the hard times ahead. It must keep us beaten and dejected, persuade us there is no hope . . . But above all they must keep us in the stupor and torpor of the hopelessly vanquished. That probably is the "New Order" so noisily promised by Hitler and Mussolini. But not for me, thank you.'

None the less, it was clear that there was little appetite for continuing the struggle, and Capitaine Barlone, Jean-Mathieu Boris and others who had made their way to England and vowed to follow de Gaulle's flag were in a minority. Edward Spears, now Churchill's liaison officer for de Gaulle, had accompanied the general to Liverpool soon after the armistice, where they had done their best to persuade some 15,000 French sailors not to leave. Spears offered them wages in return for basic labour, but to a man they refused. 'As for what might happen to England,' said Spears, 'they couldn't have cared less.'

The Nazi- and Vichy-controlled press made much of any returning French servicemen who were prepared to speak out against Britain and in support of Pétain. One such was Gonthier de Basse, a former pilot in the Armée de l'Air who had been disgusted after the attack at Mers-el-Kébir to have been offered money to serve Britain. It would, he claimed, have been treason. 'Frenchmen, comrades,' he announced, 'it is our duty to follow our leader, Maréchal Pétain, to restore our defeated France to her place in a New Europe, so that our French prisoners may return home soon.'

Despite the overwhelming desire of most Frenchmen to get home, get their heads down and get on with life in the new France, some colonies had opted to show allegiance to de Gaulle's Free French. France had considerable possessions in Africa. There were Algeria and French Morocco, as well as West Africa and French Equatorial Africa. And while the North African territories and West Africa had chosen to fly the Vichy flag, much of French Equatorial Africa, which incorporated Congo and Cameroun, had chosen to side with the Free French.

With this strong African support, the British and Free French under Général de Gaulle decided to try and spread their influence into West Africa. To fly the Cross of Lorraine, the new Free French flag, over French West Africa would, it was felt, send out a powerful message and from a practical point of view would also offer the Allies a far better staging port at Dakar than at Freetown in Sierra Leone. Furthermore, the gold reserves of both the Bank of France and those of the Polish government-in-exile were stored in Dakar. All in all, winning Dakar over to the Free French cause would bring many benefits.

Launched on 23 September, the assault was, however, a failure. Free French planes flew from the British aircraft carrier *Ark Royal* and after landing at the airfield at Dakar were promptly captured. An attempt to land troops was met with stiff gunfire, so de Gaulle recalled them. Two Vichy submarines and one destroyer were sunk, while the British battleships *Barham* and *Resolution* were damaged by shore defences. When Admiral Cunningham, who was aboard *Barham*, suggested to de Gaulle that they should cut their losses, the Free French leader could only agree. The operation's failure meant a loss of face for the British but was a grievous setback for de Gaulle. 'I went through what a man must feel,' he noted, 'when an earthquake shakes his house brutally and he receives on his head the rain of tiles falling from his roof.'

On the back of this setback for de Gaulle, there was a danger other Free French possessions might change sides to Vichy. None did, however. In fact, in November, Gabon, the lone Vichy outpost in French Equatorial Africa, was successfully taken by Général Philippe Leclerc and his Free French forces. That was something at least, but the failure of Dakar had shown that there would be no massed uprising in the Vichy colonies let alone Metropolitan France any time soon. It was a blow for de Gaulle and it was a blow for Churchill, who had set such store by Britain fanning the flames of resistance. It was another reminder, if any were needed, that there could be no quick or easy victory over the Axis.

Yet the failure at Dakar did not mean the colony was pro-Nazi or that, in time, the majority would not change their mind. The truth was, Vichy was, as a rule of thumb, more popular the further people were from occu-pied France. There were no swastikas in French West Africa and no German soldiers. Furthermore, many in France had been happy to leave the country's future in the hands of one of the most revered of Frenchmen. 'Maréchal Pétain stood in my country's history,' wrote René de Chambrun, 'as a symbol of integrity, patriotism, and military glory.' There were plenty who thought France was better off without corrupt, fractious politicians who could agree on and do nothing. In Algeria, where Général Weygand had been appointed delegate, there was a widespread belief that it was perfectly possible to be broadly right wing, pro-Pétain and still anti-German. Weygand, who had urged an armistice in June, had done so in the belief that it was possible to salvage some honour and then fight back; he remained quite openly anti-German. In fact, Vichy North Africa was allowed to keep 30,000 troops in service, a figure that was then permitted to rise to 120,000 following the British attack on Mers-el-Kébir; the Germans thought it a small price to pay to ensure those possessions remained pro-Vichy. Germany hardly wanted the hassle of manning France's overseas territories. For those in North Africa, however, it seemed as though life had not really changed very much at all.

The same, of course, could not be said for Metropolitan France, although many returning from Britain had assumed otherwise. Only around two-fifths of France remained in the hands of the Vichy Government. The town itself was chosen as something of a stopgap; most had thought in the summer of 1940 that Britain would soon be out of the war, the Germans would go back to Germany, and France would be returned to the French, with the Government moving back to Paris. Having overseen this smooth transition, Pétain, who was, after all, in his mid-eighties, would resign, his task complete.

Britain fighting on rather changed all that, and there was no doubt enthusiasm was waning for the Pétain regime by the New Year, particularly since there was no sign whatsoever of the French POWs being returned home any time soon. Even so, disgruntlement was not the same as abhorrence. Moreover, Vichy was perceived around the world to be a legal government, and crammed into the tiny spa town in the Auvergne were more than forty embassies, including those of Russia and the United States. Admittedly, Britain had broken off diplomatic relations but still allowed a Canadian life assurance firm to continue to pay the Maréchal a pension.

But while Vichy France meant living under the legitimate dictatorship of Pétain, more than half the country was occupied and that included the Atlantic coast, the north and many of France's major cities, including Paris. The north, including the Pas-de-Calais and the Channel ports, was incorporated into a 'Forbidden Zone' that was governed not from Paris but from Brussels. In Paris itself, there were curfews, severe rationing, almost no vehicles and different rules for both civilians and different German ranks. There was a military commander in Paris, from October General Otto Stülpnagel, who was effectively a military governor and was allocated troops for policing and to keep order.

Among those now in Paris was the young Austrian Jew Freddie Knoller. Since being arrested in May and sent to the internment camp at Saint-Cyprien, he had had mixed fortunes – but at least he was still alive and now at liberty, even if not exactly free. In the camp, he had been nearly raped by a Senegalese guard, but having kneed the soldier in the crotch and run had been determined to swiftly escape the camp before suffering any retribution. This he had done on 11 August by simply crawling under some loose wire at night and making his way to the town of Gaillac, where he was taken in by some cousins there and given some forged papers and a new name: Robert Metzner.

In sleepy Gaillac, however, he had quickly become restless and with the callowness of youth had determined to make his way back to now occupied Belgium and find and rescue his cello. Equipped with a pass from the town *Mairie* to cross the demarcation zone, and with more false papers declaring him to be on his way to his home in Metz in Alsace, he made it to Belgium and then to Antwerp to see the Aptes, the family who had looked after him when he had first arrived back in 1938. They were no longer there, however, and he later learned they had made it to England. Making his way to Eksaarde, he found the Jewish Centre ransacked and, of course, there was no sign at all of his cello. From there, he went to Brussels and bought a train ticket to Paris. It had been a mad idea: he was a young, largely penniless Austrian Jew, heading straight to the heart of the German-occupied city, and yet for Knoller Paris held an extraordinary allure. He was young, virile and sex-starved, and the thought of Montmartre and the illicit clubs there had drawn him to the place like a moth to a light.

And he had been lucky – taken in by a Jewish restaurateur, who fed him and gave him a job out of sight in the kitchen cleaning dishes. There was another young Viennese Jew working there clandestinely too, called Otto. They quickly struck up a rapport and Knoller agreed to share Otto's simple flat with him. It was on the top floor of an old building – just one room with twin beds, a cupboard, a couple of chairs and a wash basin. 'If the Germans come,' Otto told him, 'we can easily climb from the balcony on to the roof.'

Whenever they had the chance, Knoller and his new friend would head over to Pigalle and the red-light district. One evening, Knoller had watched a smartly dressed young man with Mediterranean good looks accompanying German soldiers to the doors of cabarets. Once they were in, he would then return to the street. Clearly, the man was making money, and it occurred to Knoller that if he managed to create a similar role for himself, he would not only get money but, more importantly, provide himself with a cover. Another night he spotted the man again and, steeling himself, brazenly walked up to him. 'Look, I'm a refugee from Metz,' Knoller said to him. 'I'm penniless here in Paris. My German is very good, so I think I can be of some use to you. I've been watching you and understand how you make a living. To be frank, I need some money.'

The man looked him up and down, then said, 'Come with me.' Knoller was led to a nearby bistro. There the man sat him down and told him his name was Christos and that he was Greek. He made his living by introducing Germans to the clubs, who then gave him a percentage of their take. Knoller proposed working for Christos and giving him a percentage of his own take. A deal was struck and the details soon worked out. 'Just a little warning,' Christos told him. 'If you try to cheat me, I have certain friends who will take care of things.' On the other hand, he said, if they were to become friends then there were certainly more than enough Germans for both of them. 'I can't handle them all,' he admitted. He even invited Knoller to share his flat. Knoller agreed and in so doing simply walked out on Otto and the Jewish restaurant. He sensed that to survive, he had to think about himself and separate himself from his Jewish identity. With fair, wavy hair and a round, youthful-looking face, he certainly did not look obviously Jewish. He had recognized that he needed to make the most of what few advantages he had.

Christos bought him a suit, a shirt and a tie, took him to several brothels and introduced him to the madams, and with that he had begun his new life as a pimp. The lie he had created came surprisingly effortlessly, he discovered; he was a natural at his new job, steering a succession of Germans straight into the brothels. 'I was rudderless, virtually friendless, and in constant danger of discovery,' he wrote, 'but I felt like a bird released from its cage. I had found my ingenuity and independent spirit.'

Also still in Paris was Andrée Griotteray, who had kept her job at the Police HQ, where French policemen and Germans were now operating side by side. She was also once more living with her entire family, who had been unable to get on board a boat to England and so had returned home. Andrée and her younger brother, Alain, were also involved in very embryonic resistance work. Now at the Sorbonne, Alain and a few friends had begun writing and circulating a resistance bulletin called La France. Andrée had agreed not only to type it up but also to use the printing facilities at the office to run off copies for them to circulate. Doing this at police headquarters was not only brave but, frankly, rather reckless.

As the 11 November Armistice Day commemorations approached, Alain and his friend Noël Le Clerq decided to organize an anti-German demonstration on the Champs-Élysées. 'Résistez l'envahisseur,' they printed in La France. 'L'Étoile vers 16 heures.' It was an unqualified success, with some 3,000 students gathering on the day, shouting defiance and singing the 'Marseillaise'. Both police and German troops moved swiftly to break up the demonstration. Alain Griotteray managed to escape the arrests and cross over the Seine, and spend the night in a friend's flat. As German troops moved in to break up the crowds, Andrée linked arms with a girlfriend and quietly headed away. Neither was stopped.

Although Paris was run entirely by Germans, Vichy did have representatives in the city. One of the key intermediaries was Otto Abetz, curiously the German Ambassador in a part of France that was occupied and governed by Germany. Abetz was still good friends with Jean Luchaire, who had been made editor of the pro-German daily newspaper *Le Matin*. Also now back in Paris was his daughter, the film star Corinne Luchaire, who had returned to France after completing her film in Italy, only to flee to Saint-Brieuc in Brittany with a Jewish girlfriend in an effort to escape the fighting. Corinne had still been there some time after the armistice when the German commander in the area had called her in and told her she was suspected of being a spy. He pointed out that she had travelled a great deal, spoke several languages and was now living near the Atlantic coast. It was, she was told, deeply suspicious. Thus warned, she had left for Paris immediately, where she had been reunited with her father.

She worried, however, about the ongoing friendship between her father and Abetz. 'I don't know why,' she wrote, 'but I felt uneasy about that.' Jean Luchaire was not only a friend of Otto Abetz, but also of Pierre Laval, twice Prime Minister in the thirties, a former minister and now Pétain's deputy. As such, Luchaire was uniquely placed to be not only a pro-regime newspaper editor, but also an intermediary between Paris and Vichy. It was an unofficial post but often took him to Vichy. Crossing the occupied zone required special passes, but he was able to secure the relevant paperwork to take his daughter with him on one occasion.

Vichy was buzzing, with many familiar faces from Paris hovering around the main hotels where the Government now resided. Pétain had rooms in the Hôtel du Parc, and proximity to his rooms was considered a sign of power. Corinne dined and lunched with many of the new members of the Government, all of whom, it seemed, wanted to both talk to her father and be seen with her. 'Everybody,' she wrote, 'was carefully listening to his advice and opinions. When he was in Vichy, he was eagerly expected in Paris. And when he was in Paris, he was eagerly expected in Vichy.' He was clearly revelling in being at the heart of the new politics; Corinne, though, wondered whether her father was being a little naive. 'He didn't know,' she added, 'that success brings jealousy.'

It was largely jealousy that caused the downfall of Pierre Laval in

December. Pétain had never really liked him and was concerned that his deputy was making too many pro-German decisions off his own bat. Laval also had a habit of blowing smoke in his face, which the Maréchal disliked intensely; it lacked deference as much as anything. In December, Pétain asked all his ministers to write their letters of resignation. Laval did so, thinking it was a trick to axe René Belin, the Minister of Labour. It wasn't; it was a trick to sack him. A stunned Laval was promptly arrested and then not long after, in what was a truly bizarre episode, was dramatically rescued by German troops who stormed into the 'free' zone and whisked him to Paris.

Laval's sacking came shortly after a series of talks between General Warlimont and Abetz on the German side and several leading Vichy ministers, Amiral Darlan included, about closer co-operation, or, to put it another way, the possibility of Vichy joining the Axis. That Mussolini was against such a move was no longer of any concern to his German allies. Warlimont was fully aware that Laval had been the driving force on the French side, but his arrest, seen by Hitler as a slight on Pétain's part, effectively killed the talks. Hitler's contempt for France had not changed since the armistice, as had been made clear by the brutal reparations demanded. 'According to Hitler's plans,' said Warlimont, 'France was to have a minor role in the New Europe led by Germany . . . He picked up his ideas on France from books that were probably biased and which he never bothered to question. Thus he pictured a decadent France that would go on declining forever.' Pétain and his Government could puff around the unoccupied zone believing they had done what was best for France and thinking they had real power, but it was largely illusory. They were Hitler's puppets, and as the war continued, life in France was only going to get tougher.

As yet, though, Vichy France was free of bombing raids, which was more than could be said for Britain, Germany, Italy or any other countries where the war was continuing. Bad weather in December had dogged the Luftwaffe's bombing efforts over England, but it was clear enough on 29 December and the bombers had returned to London with a vengeance. On Goebbels's suggestion, the Luftwaffe liked to try and put in a good, heavy raid whenever Roosevelt was about to make a big statement, in the hope that news of the destruction they had caused would dilute the effect of the President's words.

Roosevelt had made a point of discussing the war while delivering his 'Fireside Chats' to the nation, and in this last one of 1940 he pulled no punches. 'We cannot escape danger,' he told Americans, 'or the fear of danger, by crawling into bed and pulling the covers over our heads.' The only peace that could be achieved with the Nazis could come at the price of total surrender, he said. There could be no dealing with these people, and no compromise. Rather, it was up to the United States to help Britain and its allies win the war. The United States, he told his listeners, had to become 'the arsenal of democracy'.

Around the time Roosevelt was recording his 'chat', another American was watching the bombing of London. Ernie Pyle was a newspaperman, rather than a broadcaster, who had already revolutionized the way in which a journalist might write. His style was simple: to talk to people, observe life around him, and write as though he were talking to someone standing next to him. His columns were informal, ponderous, sensitive, often funny and often rather moving too. He'd made a name for himself travelling around America recording everyday life, and his pieces, syndicated through the Scripps Howard chain of newspapers, made him seem like a friend to his millions of readers. Funny, intelligent, but prone to depression, he was a complicated man with a profound fear of failure, despite his originality and apparently effortless skill. As his readers were discovering, this intimate, informal approach was bringing alive the experiences of the British as the Blitz continued.

His arrival had coincided with the lull in the heavy bombing, and he was impressed by how little effect the Blitz had had up to now. 'So far,' he wrote in one of his first despatches, 'the blitz on London is a failure. London is no more knocked out than the man who smashes a finger is dead.' On the night of 29 December, however, he was awestruck by what he saw. With some friends, he climbed up on to a high darkened balcony that gave him a view directly towards the City and the East End. 'There was something inspiring just in the awful savagery of it,' he wrote. Fires were springing up, leaping into the air, as bombers droned over, 'like a bee buzzing in blind fury'. The biggest fires seemed to be directly in front of them, around St Paul's Cathedral, the flames licking hundreds of feet into the air and smoke ballooning up around the gigantic dome.

Also watching these raids was Gwladys Cox, who had just about recovered from the trauma of losing her flat. They had rented a shabby and depressing place for a month, then retreated to the Lake District and had only just returned to the capital, renting a ground-floor flat in Honeybourne Road, close to their old home. It had taken all that time to have their furniture restored or replaced and carpets dried and cleaned.

Invited by a Dutch neighbour to view the unfolding attacks, they had watched with mesmerized horror. 'Volumes of rose-pink smoke and many coloured flashes from explosions pierced again and again the blood-red clouds,' she recounted in her diary. 'We could only guess at the destruction wrought by each flash or explosion.' She feared for the Wren churches, the libraries, the Guildhall and other historic buildings. 'We sensed numbly that London would have known no such dire experience as this since the Great Fire of 1666.'

For Ernie Pyle, closer to the scene, the site of London burning was, he was ashamed to confess, a beautiful sight. 'St Paul's was surrounded by fire,' he wrote, 'but it came through. It stood there in its enormous proportions – growing slowly clearer and clearer the way objects take shape at dawn. It was like a picture of some miraculous figure that appears before peace-hungry soldiers on a battlefield.'

Columns like these, broadcasts, film reels and even photographs by the likes of the fashion photographer Cecil Beaton showing injured girls in their hospital beds on the front of *Life* magazine – it was all grist to the mill in helping Roosevelt to sell the idea of aid to Britain.

The President had announced his intention to 'lend' Britain the aid it needed on 17 December at a White House press conference following his trip on the *Tuscaloosa*. This would be put to Congress as a bill that he hoped would soon become law. The best defence for the US, he said, was the success of Britain in defending itself. What he was proposing was to get Britain the help it needed without a big dollar sign before it. 'Let me give you an illustration,' he told the assembled reporters. 'Suppose my neighbour's home catches fire, and I have a length of garden hose and connect it up with his hydrant, I may help him put out his fire. Now what do I do? I don't say to him, "Neighbour, my garden hose cost me fifteen dollars; you have to pay me fifteen dollars for it." No! I don't want fifteen dollars. I want my garden hose after the fire is over.' The neighbourly analogy was a masterstroke as it was the kind of language – as Ernie Pyle had discovered – that Americans responded to. Heated debates in Congress would ensue, but the combination of shifting public opinion, a president newly re-elected with a whopping majority and an administration that was united behind Roosevelt was going to be hard for the isolationists to deny.

At the beginning of January, the President sent Harry Hopkins to Britain. He arrived by flying boat, landing at Poole Harbour on the south coast from Lisbon on 9 January, and was met by Brendan Bracken, one of Churchill's inner circle and his Parliamentary Private Secretary. Hopkins was suffering after the long trip, but as they took the train to London he peered out of the window and said, 'Are you going to let Hitler take these fields from you?'

'No,' came Bracken's succinct reply.

Hopkins finally met Churchill the following day after a tour of 10 Downing Street. 'A rotund – smiling – red faced gentleman appeared,' he wrote to Roosevelt that night, 'extended a fat but none the less convincing hand and wished me welcome to England.' They then lunched together in a small dining room in the basement, talking for three hours.

The two men quickly developed a rapport, with Churchill going out of his way to make as much of a fuss of him as possible, and with Hopkins winning friends with his wit, charm and ability to cut to the chase; he got on especially well with Churchill's wife, Clementine, who often took a while to take to someone new, but was both drawn to Hopkins's mordant humour and touched by his frailty.

His visit included weekends at Chequers, lunch with the King and Queen, and trips to see the Home Fleet at Scapa Flow, the guns and defences at Dover, and the bomb damage at Portsmouth. There were other lunches and dinners too. On Saturday, 11 January, Churchill had taken him to Ditchley, near Oxford, for a typical aristocratic weekend in the country. Also on hand were not only Oliver Lyttelton, but also Jock Colville, and after dinner Churchill launched into one of what Lyttelton called his 'majestic monologues'. 'We seek no treasure, we seek no territorial gains,' said Churchill, 'we seek only the right of man to be free; we seek his right to worship his God, to lead his life in his own way, secure from persecution.' He continued in similar vein, then paused and asked, 'What will the President say to all this?'

Hopkins paused before answering, then in his Midwest drawl said, 'Well, Mr Prime Minister, I don't think the President will give a damn for all that.' He paused again, and Lyttelton was beginning to cringe. Then Hopkins added, 'You see, we're only interested in seeing that that Goddam sonofabitch Hitler gets licked.' Lyttelton, along with everyone else, could not help laughing loudly.

On Sunday, 8 February, Hopkins spent his last full day in England at Chequers, where news arrived that the Lend-Lease Bill had been passed in the House of Representatives by 260 votes to 165. All that remained was getting it through the Senate.

The following day, Hopkins left for America, having written a last, hand-scrawled note to Churchill. 'I shall never forget these days with you,' he wrote, 'your supreme confidence and will to victory. Britain I have ever liked – I like it the more.'

CHAPTER 38

Saved from the Deep

O N 14 DECEMBER, the *Western Prince*, a British 10,000-ton passenger and cargo ship, had been some 250 miles south of Iceland when the ship was struck by a torpedo fired from *U-96*. Among the sixty-one passengers was Cyril Thompson, returning to Britain with the draft contract of the shipbuilding deal struck with Rear-Admiral Land and Henry Kaiser in his black briefcase. The torpedo hit the vessel forward of the bridge on the port side with a huge explosion, and a vast column of water shot up and cascaded down upon the decks. Then the ship shuddered and began tilting downwards from the bows. Immediately, the captain ordered everyone to the lifeboats.

It was around 6.40 a.m., and Thompson, in his cabin, quickly threw on more clothes, grabbed his all-important despatch case and hurried to the lifeboats as they were being cleared ready for lowering. The ship was already dangerously low in the water, but he hoped she would stay afloat for a little while more. Clambering into one of the lifeboats, he and the other passengers and crew were lowered on to the water and began rowing for all they were worth, Thompson using his size and rugby player's build to pull on his oar as hard as he could.

Suddenly, the U-boat emerged, surfacing sixty yards away and several of the crew clambered on to the bridge and took photographs of the stricken vessel. Unbeknown to them, the captain of the *Western Prince* and a couple of other crewmen had suddenly remembered the ship's Spitfire Fund Collection was still in the safe and so returned to fetch it. They were still aboard when *U-96* fired the fatal *coup de grâce*. A second huge explosion erupted, this time with a sheet of flame. Very soon after, the ship sank beneath the waves, its whistle blasting mournfully as it did so.

Thompson and the other passengers now found themselves alone in a dark, grey, empty Atlantic, on a rising swell and with a cutting Arctic wind. It was freezing cold. The prospects did not look good for the survivors.

The sinking was announced by German radio, causing huge concern at the Admiralty and a terrible couple of days for Thompson's wife, Doreen, who happened to hear the news on a German broadcast and understandably feared the worst. Yet her husband was not only still alive, but had the contract still with him. For nine hours, he kept rowing, and then, just as the survivors were bracing themselves for a long and dreadful night, they spotted a freighter and sent up flares. To their enormous relief, the ship spotted them and turned. This was the *Baron Kinnaird*, and was clearly crewed by men of extreme courage: at just 9 knots, she was too slow for convoy work and so had to sail alone, a far more dangerous means of crossing the ocean. To stop and pick up survivors of another ship was also extremely hazardous, and yet all the survivors of the *Western Prince* were safely picked up, and instead of continuing to Halifax the *Baron Kinnaird* turned and headed back to Scotland. It safely reached port at Gourock on the River Clyde at around 10 a.m. on 18 December.

It may well be that the British Government would have signed those somewhat sodden papers anyway, but the fact that Thompson arrived in London straight after his ordeal can hardly have done any harm. After all, it was a reminder, if any were needed, that a way was urgently required to build more merchant ships. On 20 December, the historic deal was signed. Kaiser and his corporations would build the two new shipyards and the ships. What's more, the ships they would be building would be Cyril Thompson's latest design, to which he had given the provisional name 'Hull No. 611'. When completed in the Thompson yard it would be called the *Empire Liberty*, and it was from this that the term 'liberty ship' was coined.

Meanwhile, in the Western Desert, General Richard O'Connor's Western Desert Force, now renamed XXX Corps, was continuing to make short work of the Italian Tenth Army, and with good help from the RAF. The air forces available were still not huge, although they had been helped by the opening up of the Takoradi route, pioneered before the war and which involved shipping aircraft to Takoradi in West Africa and then flying them across the continent via staging posts to Khartoum in the Sudan and finally up to Egypt. By the end of the year, a further 41 Wellingtons, 87 Hurricanes and 85 Blenheims had reached RAF Middle East since September.

Tony Smyth was now A Flight commander in 55 Squadron, and on the last day of the year had attacked Bardia, now almost surrounded by the 6th Australians, who had taken over from 4th Indian Division, not only dropping bombs but also hurling out empty beer bottles in the hope that the loud whistle of their drop might further damage Italian morale. After all eleven aircraft safely made it back, they flew back over group HQ and dropped a message saying, 'We have just wished Bardia a Happy New Year. Same to you.' After landing back at Fuka, some eighty miles west of Alexandria, they were rung by Air Marshal Arthur Tedder, newly arrived as Air Officer Commanding Middle East Air Forces, to thank them personally. 'This was somewhat different,' remarked Smyth, 'from the distant and severe atmosphere of Bomber Command.' As he was discovering, the atmosphere in the Middle East, with its distance from home, the sand, and extremes of heat and cold, and the necessity of making do with less, was understandably less formal than it was back at home.

For the most part, it was the problems of sand and operating far into the desert that were causing the biggest issues for the air forces in North Africa, but on 4 January, as they were attacking Tobruk, Smyth was hit in the starboard engine and turret and was frantically assessing the damage when his CO, having released his bombs, turned in towards him and they nearly collided. Fortunately, the damage to his Blenheim was manageable, and they flew back without further mishap, passing over a tank battle raging below them near Bardia.

One of those fighting on the ground below was Sergeant Alf Parbery, thirty years old and from Woolgoolga in New South Wales. He and his younger brother, Reg, had both volunteered on the outbreak of war, reaching Egypt the previous February, and both were attached to J Section of 6th Division Signals. Casualties were fairly light, but Parbery found the experience bad enough, with the shelling incessant. Part of their task was to lay field telephone wire, which meant getting out from their hastily dug trenches and running across open land. Even though they did this at night as much as possible, it was still a difficult task, especially with shells exploding around them. Parbery was particularly shaken by the death of their popular company commander, Captain Stewart, who was hit in the head and heart by shrapnel and killed instantly.

Later in the day, Parbery went forward to examine some captured Italian guns only to come under shellfire once more. 'All our nerves were on edge after such a day,' he scribbled in his diary. 'There had been so many near things and the concussion from each shell close by made the head thump.' He eventually got his head down in a dirty Italian trench and wrapped himself in a dirty Italian blanket.

The following day, the Australians captured Bardia, along with 45,000 Italians and 130 tanks. The Aussies suffered just 500 casualties. Two days later, Tobruk was surrounded, and by 22 January that garrison had also run up the white flag with a further 25,000 Italians, 208 guns and 87 tanks captured, as well as a number of fuel dumps and other stores. With this, General Wavell was ordered to instruct O'Connor to keep going and push on around the bulge of Cyrenaica. The next stop would be Benghazi, one of the larger ports in Libya.

During Operation COMPASS and the subsequent pursuit of the Italians across the desert, General O'Connor had always known he had limited resources. On the other hand, he had a high opinion of his divisions, knew they were well trained and that they were well equipped with vehicles, while those raids and patrols beforehand had shown him that the Italians were low in morale and training despite their vast numbers. 'It was essential in my mind,' he said, 'that we had to make some plan that would throw them off their balance and prevent them from getting full advantage from the large superiority of their numbers.' He was also helped by their defences, which were in makeshift forts that, while reasonably well fortified, were not mutually supporting.

In fact, COMPASS followed precisely the same principles used by General Guderian during his attack across the Meuse and through France the previous May. In advance of the attack, enemy airfields had been neutralized and then mobile troops had rushed forward, achieving complete surprise. Leading elements had charged onwards, ignoring their flanks and aiming to sever Italian lines of supply. Greater intent, morale, motivation and equipment had overwhelmed a tactically moribund enemy complacently stuck in a defensive mindset. The parallels could not have been more obvious. Similarly, the tactics adopted by O'Connor were not only the right ones but also the obvious solution, dictated by the situation in which Britain found itself at the time. Germany did not have a monopoly on the *Bewegungskrieg* approach to fighting battles.

Reaching Tobruk just a few days after it had fallen were Ted Hardy and the rest of 2/3rd Field Company of the Australian Engineers. They had reached Suez at the end of December, had spent a couple of weeks training and acclimatizing at Amariya camp near Alexandria, and then were sent along the desert road equipped with bridging, mines, wire and explosives, and attached to 20th Australian Infantry Brigade, part of 9th Australian Division that had been released from England and was now arriving in theatre.

Hardy was only just eighteen, having joined up when he was still only seventeen the previous summer. Born and brought up in Columbia Bay, a small township south of Sydney, he had left school at fourteen and was working in a small engineering factory. Having heard about Dunkirk, he decided to enlist. His boss, who had served in the last war, let him go, even though he was underage. It took Hardy a few attempts, but eventually the recruiting officer accepted his false age and he was in. After training for the best part of five months, he found himself on board the *Aquitania*, a liner now converted into a troopship, and heading to the Middle East. These were all new experiences, but he took them in his stride. Hardy was a phlegmatic and laid-back fellow.

At Tobruk, he was surprised to see Italians still wandering about. 'They were waiting in groups,' he said. 'There was masses of junk all over the place.' The engineers unloaded, set up their HQ at the side of a hill near the road to the south of the town, and began repairing the road, which was strewn with broken Italian aircraft and potholes from the Royal Navy's offshore bombardment.

Back at the base depot of Geneifa near Cairo was Albert Martin of 2nd Rifle Brigade. Just after the lightning strike on Buq Buq, he had come down with sandfly fever and been briefly hospitalized. He was long recovered, but had been sent on a 'hardening' course to build up his strength and fitness before being sent back up to the 'blue'. He was quite enjoying the course, although he was less keen on the guard duty they had to perform looking after the thousands of Italian POWs. 'So far none of them have tried to escape,' he noted in his diary. 'In fact, they all seem very cheerful.'

By the end of the month, Martin was feeling as fit as a fiddle and desperate to rejoin the battalion. By 1 February, he was expecting a draft back up the line at any moment. 'The news from the front,' he scribbled, 'though vague, suggests that our advance is progressing favourably.' And so it was. The Australians had captured Derna and were hurrying towards Benghazi.

Despite this success, however, there were disagreements rumbling on between Whitehall and GHQ in Cairo. Churchill was not just a Prime Minister, he was a war leader too, and from the outset had regularly bombarded field commanders with instructions, suggestions and even what effectively amounted to orders. The trouble was, Churchill hadn't been overly impressed with the cut of Wavell's jib, and he worried that he didn't have enough drive. As far as Churchill was concerned, precious supplies and men were being sent to the Middle East and not enough was happening. First South African Division was now in Kenya, 4th Indian had been moved to Sudan, there were two more West African brigades in East Africa, plus what was now in North Africa and Palestine. Churchill felt that as soon as these men and tanks were in theatre they should be in action, but Wavell, the man on the spot, recognized that equipment needed to be made ready for desert conditions, and men trained and 'hardened'. There was a massive difference between basic training in England and fighting in Libya or Eritrea.

Caught up in this battle of wills between Churchill and Wavell was not only the Chief of the Imperial General Staff, now General Sir John Dill, but also the Director of Military Plans, Major-General John Kennedy. Since taking up this post in October, Kennedy had discovered that everyone in Churchill's immediate circle had to dance to the Prime Minister's eccentricities, him included, whether it be sudden whims and ideas for new strategies or his impossible working hours. Churchill liked to work in bed in the morning, had a siesta in the afternoon, tended to have meetings with the Chiefs of Staff and anyone who was with him at around 9.30 p.m. and often kept them up until one or two in the morning. In this, he was not so very different from Hitler. At the weekend, Churchill always tended to disappear to the country.

Kennedy, to cope with this relentless routine, put a bed into his room in the basement of the War Office. After dinner in the evening, he would go back there, work for a few hours, then have a discussion with Dill around 10 p.m. The CIGS, Kennedy noticed, was becoming increasingly exhausted by the combination of Churchill's demands and daily routine.

A huge argument between the two, for example, had erupted in December over Churchill's insistence on capturing the Italian island of Pantelleria, to the south-west of Sicily. It was an idea the PM had been pressing for some time, but which had little strategic benefit and would potentially tie up a lot of resources. The policy of the General Staff, agreed upon by both Dill and Kennedy, was to build up resources both at home and in the Middle East and to avoid any unnecessary operations. 'We wished to do nothing,' noted Kennedy, 'that would postpone decisive action; we considered it rash to risk unnecessary reverses merely for the sake of doing something. Churchill, on the other hand, thirsted for action.' Dill, especially, who was first in the firing line, found dealing with Churchill quite a battle in itself.

One of the biggest causes of disagreement between Wavell and Churchill, however, was over East Africa, where large numbers of Italian troops commanded by the Duke of Aosta were, to a large extent, marooned; so while a quarter of a million troops sounded quite a lot, there was every reason to suggest they might be even less of a proposition than those in Libya, who were at least still linked to Italy by the Mediterranean sea lanes. Ironically, Churchill's view was that the combination of blockade and internal revolt sponsored and supplied by Britain would probably see off Mussolini's East African empire. Wavell, however, disagreed and felt that, as things stood, the Italians were still a threat to Kenya, with its key staging ports, and Sudan, with its links to Egypt. He preferred to do it the proper way. That, however, meant using troops which Churchill believed could be better employed elsewhere, especially since he had assured the Greeks that Britain would send troops to help them.

For the time being, the Greeks were doing just fine without them, so, by January, Wavell's initial plans to gently probe forward into East Africa from Kenya and Sudan had developed into a more full-scale offensive. On 19 January, General Platt attacked in the north of Abyssinia from Sudan with two Indian divisions. The following day, the Emperor Haile Selassie, in exile since the Italian conquest, re-entered Abyssinia with a force of 'Patriots' – Abyssinian troops reinforced with the Sudan Defence Force and with a maverick young British major hand-picked by Wavell called Orde Wingate.

Meanwhile, in the south, General Alan Cunningham, brother of the admiral, was mounting a series of harassing raids with a combination of

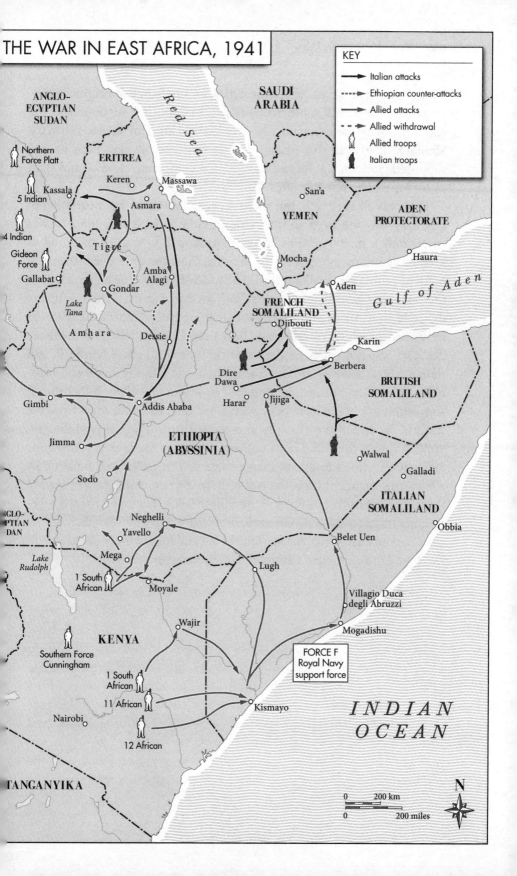

THE WAR IN EAST AFRICA, 1941

KEY

→ Italian attacks
⇢ Ethiopian counter-attacks
→ Allied attacks
⇢ Allied withdrawal
⛏ Allied troops
⛏ Italian troops

SAUDI ARABIA

Red Sea

ANGLO-EGYPTIAN SUDAN

Northern Force Platt
Kassala
5 Indian
4 Indian
Gideon Force
Gallabat

ERITREA
Keren
Massawa
Asmara
Tigre

San'a

YEMEN

Mocha

ADEN PROTECTORATE
Haura

Aden

Gulf of Aden

Amba Alagi
Gondar
Lake Tana
Amhara
Dessie

FRENCH SOMALILAND
Djibouti

Karin

Berbera

BRITISH SOMALILAND

Gimbi
Addis Ababa
Harar
Jijiga
Dire Dawa

Walwal

Galladi

Jimma

ETHIOPIA (ABYSSINIA)

ITALIAN SOMALILAND

Sodo

Obbia

Neghelli
Yavello
Mega
Moyale
1 South African

Lugh

Belet Uen

Villagio Duca degli Abruzzi

Mogadishu

ANGLO-EGYPTIAN SUDAN
Lake Rudolph

Wajir

FORCE F
Royal Navy support force

KENYA
Southern Force Cunningham

1 South African
11 African
12 African

Nairobi

Kismayo

INDIAN OCEAN

TANGANYIKA

0   200 km
0   200 miles

N

South African and East African troops. Cunningham had originally proposed to launch his southern offensive in May, but so poor was the resistance to his harassing raids he decided to bring it forward to February. Similarly, Platt was also finding Italian resistance weaker than he had supposed. Suddenly, it looked as though a comparatively easy and swift victory might be possible after all.

That was all very well, but looming very heavily by the beginning of February was the need to intervene in Greece, especially since it was surely only a matter of time before Germany did. And for that, and to keep momentum going in North Africa at the same time, every man and piece of equipment available would be needed. It was true enough that in the last war General von Lettow-Vorbeck had led the British a merry dance in East Africa and tied down far more troops than Britain would have liked, of which Wavell would have been all very aware; but the Duke of Aosta was not cut from the same cloth as von Lettow-Vorbeck, and Italian troops were not imbued with the same fighting spirit and ingenuity as the Germans. In the present circumstances, Churchill's original suggestion might not have been such a bad one. After all, apart from the Italians' capture of the virtually undefended British Somaliland the previous summer, there had been nothing to suggest the Duke of Aosta was any more inclined to attack than Graziani. The truth was, Italian East Africa was cut adrift from the rest of Italy with no real means of supply, the morale of its troops was low, and there were plenty of Africans eager to exact revenge. With this in mind, it's hard to see why Wavell could not have parked East Africa for the time being and fought more pressing battles first. On this matter, Churchill had probably been right.

CHAPTER 39

Developments at Sea

O N 13 FEBRUARY, one of Dönitz's new Type VII U-boats left Kiel for its first patrol. *U-552* was commanded by Erich Topp, who, after leaving *U-46* the previous June, had then commanded the smaller Type IIc *U-57*, before it had been rammed by a Norwegian steamer and sunk. Topp had sunk seven ships with *U-57*, but when he had lost his boat, along with six of his crew, it had hit him hard.

So far, he had not had a great deal of luck in his U-boat career, but with his new boat he was hoping for a change of fortune. It worried him, though, that his chief navigator, normally so cheerful and lively, appeared to be particularly quiet and subdued. They were already out in the North Sea when Topp asked him what the matter was, but only when he pressed him did his navigator confess.

'Sir, it is not important, but I forgot something at home,' he told Topp.

'What did you forget?'

Reluctantly, his navigator told him. On all his other patrols, he said, he had brought his wife's wedding wreath with him, which he kept under a glass cover. It was his good-luck mascot, but this time he had left it behind.

Topp realized he could not have one of his key crew members spending long weeks in a state of mounting despair – they lived and worked too close together for that – so he immediately ordered their return to base. There, the talisman was collected and they set off again, this time for nearly four weeks. 'This much I had learned from my experience on *U-57*,' wrote Topp. 'The personal feelings of my men – faith, superstition – play a vital role in exercising command successfully.'

At any rate, soon after finally reaching the Atlantic, on the night of 1 March, they managed to sink a large British tanker, *Cadillac*, which had been carrying a massive 17,000 tons of fuel. Struck by two torpedoes, the tanker vibrated violently and began listing to starboard, then the fuel caught fire. Moments later, there was a massive explosion. As the ship began to sink, an emergency lifeboat was lowered, but it was swamped as it was let down too quickly. Most of the twenty-six survivors then managed to abandon ship in a second lifeboat, but the waters were on fire, and most of the men, surrounded by a wall of flame and smoke, were struggling to breathe and panicked. Some were crying out for help, others praying, but most jumped over the side and were either burned or drowned. Just five survived and were later picked up.

Being a crewman on a transatlantic oil tanker was a particularly unenviable job.

Such dramas out at sea appeared to have little impact on either Hitler or the OKW. General Warlimont and his Section L were busy with other areas of possible operations, for although they had little to do with the planning for the Soviet Union, they were now pursuing other possibilities on the orders of the Führer – and all were to do with trying to destroy the British in the Mediterranean theatre.

The OKW was curious in that although it was a combined services group, the senior officers were nearly all Army, Warlimont included, and the lack of any naval plans was conspicuous. Yet even the Kriegsmarine's own staff seemed to have become obsessed with the Mediterranean. 'The naval staff regards the British Fleet as the decisive factor for the outcome of the war,' Grand Admiral Raeder told Hitler in a staff appreciation at the end of the year. 'It is now no longer possible to drive it from the Mediterranean as we have so often proposed. Instead a situation is now developing in Africa which is most dangerous both for Germany and Europe.' Certainly, the British Mediterranean Fleet was proving a thorny enemy; Fliegerkorps X had attacked the aircraft carrier *Illustrious* repeatedly out at sea and then in Grand Harbour, Malta, while it underwent repairs, but had been unable to sink it and the ship successfully escaped to Alexandria. Malta, so weak back in June, now had one of the most densely placed anti-aircraft barrages in the world.

What was conspicuous by its absence was much mention of the Atlantic. Warlimont appeared to have barely given it a thought. Hitler issued 'Directive No. 23: Directions for operations against the English war economy' on 6 February, which was more of a situation report than anything and was breathtaking in its tone of over-confidence and its refusal to consider the wider context of the war at sea. While it admitted there had been little obvious effect on British morale by the night-bombing offensive, the damage to merchant shipping and port installations had been considerable, it claimed, and heavier than had earlier been appreciated. These losses would increase still further, the directive asserted, with ever-more U-boats coming into service, 'and this can bring about the collapse of English resistance within the foreseeable future'.

What was so striking about the directive was the very limited nod to the British response to all this. That the 'Happy Time' for the U-boats was largely due to the lack of escorts, which were busy on anti-invasion duty, does not appear to have been considered. Nor does the fact that in the United States, Britain and Canada shipyards were already producing large numbers of merchant ships at a level that was far outstripping U-boat production. It was as though British merchant shipping production were standing still while German shipyards continued to build more submarines.

Nor was there any acceptance that technology and tactics were moving forward too. The Mediterranean and the Middle East were an important theatre, but Germany would not defeat Britain by destroying its military forces there. Rather, there was only one way Britain would lose the war and that was with the destruction of its overseas supply lines. While the forthcoming invasion of the Soviet Union was understandably now the greatest focus, the mess the Italians had made of things in the south was drawing Germany into an ever-more resource-heavy commitment to a theatre that had never originally been part of its grand strategic design, and so much so that its leaders were taking their eye off a far more important theatre of war.

By the beginning of 1941, much had changed in the battle for the Atlantic. With the threat of the invasion over, not only had the Royal Navy made more ships available for Western Approaches Command and for escort duty, but more smaller escorts were emerging from Britain's shipyards too. There were also those fifty US destroyers, renamed Town-class destroyers, or 'four-stacks', and given British names instead of their original American ones. All had undergone major refits, and so had been put to sea far too late to solve the crisis in which the deal had been made.

However, fifty destroyers were not to be sniffed at, and they still had an important role to play.

At any rate, by the beginning of 1941, there were some 126 destroyers, 39 sloops and 89 corvettes attached to Western Approaches Command, and losses among convoys were falling dramatically. It was not only ships that had been released from anti-invasion duty, but aircraft too. RAF Coastal Command was now spending less time patrolling the Channel and more off the west coast on anti-shipping warfare.

Many of Coastal Command's Avro Ansons had been replaced by American-built Hudsons, which had a greater range of around 350 miles, while there were also a number of Sunderland flying boats, which could fly as far as 600 miles. Most were also now equipped with a small search radar, the ASV Mk I and then Mk II, which had a range of around twenty miles at 2,000 feet. These were also beginning to be fitted to escort vessels such as the Type 286. These advances in the scale and conduct of Coastal Command pushed the U-boats further west. At the same time, routings were pushed north and thus further away from the Biscay ports from which many of the U-boats now operated.

Back out in the Atlantic was the recently promoted Commander Donald Macintyre and his Hunt-class destroyer, HMS *Hesperus*. For Macintyre it had been a great relief, as he had had a horror of spending the war bogged down on a Fleet destroyer, always operating at the beck and call of the capital ships. However, the autumn and winter of 1940 had been disappointing. The weather had been truly atrocious and the tactics employed were, as far as he was concerned, hopeless. There was no proper organization, and so they had been repeatedly sent on one wild goose chase after another, following reports of the latest sinkings and reaching the spot only to find the U-boat long since gone from the scene. Macintyre had not been impressed.

In February, however, things began to look up, not least with the appointment of Admiral Sir Percy Noble as C-in-C of Western Approaches Command, who wasted no time in streamlining the organization both ashore and afloat and bringing new thinking to the battle plan in the Atlantic.

One of the first big changes was moving Western Approaches HQ from Plymouth to Liverpool. This had actually been anticipated by Churchill when he had still been First Lord and had ordered the development of Derby House, a new office block behind Liverpool's Town Hall, into a massive bombproof and superbly equipped operational control centre. Only now, in February 1941, was Derby House finally ready, although Liverpool had, since early the previous year, become Britain's most important ocean convoy port. It had a vast dock system stretching around seven miles on the northern, Liverpool, side of the River Mersey and considerable further facilities on the southern side in Birkenhead as well.

The same month that Admiral Noble took over, he also chose to go out into the Atlantic to see for himself how escorts were operating and what improvements might be made. Throughout the trip, he experienced first hand the endless interferences from shore staff that Macintyre had found so frustrating – interference that stifled initiative and effectiveness. On his return, he vowed to overhaul the entire system. Macintyre was delighted to hear it. 'A new feeling of intelligent purpose was in the air,' he noted.

In Libya, the Italians were still reeling from the shock of defeat and now were preparing defences around Tripoli. Few doubted the British would try and push on – it seemed the obvious move to kick an enemy when he was down and make sure he never got up again. New reinforcements were still arriving in Libya, including Sergio Fabbri, who was now a *sotto-tenente* – second lieutenant. He and the rest of 2nd Light Artillery Regiment reached Tripoli in January, even though he'd only been called up the previous month and given a commission immediately because of his education and professional background of working in a bank. Joining the regiment in Ferrara, he had done little training, although he and his fellow officers had dined well and spent a fair amount of time riding and hunting; a sum had even been deducted from his wages to pay for the upkeep of the Mess silver.

By the time they reached Tripoli, he still hadn't even seen an artillery piece let alone fired one, but on arrival they were allocated a number of antiquated 105/28 field guns. Fabbri was placed in a battery of four with thirteen men under his command. The guns were in a bad state, covered in rust and sand, and getting them clean again was difficult because, incredibly, they didn't have enough oil or rags. They solved this by surreptitiously stealing pennants from Arab grave markers at night and pinching cooking oil from the military kitchens. It wasn't ideal, but it would have to do.

By the end of January, they had the guns working and had organized themselves into some kind of order, and were then posted to Benghazi. No sooner had they reached there, however, than it was clear the town was about to be overrun, and so they were promptly sent back to Tripoli, where they were ordered to help prepare a giant anti-tank ditch that was to reach all around the city. They discovered that each tract had been divided up between different units, but Fabbri quickly realized that officers were reporting they had dug and lined with stone a greater part of their allotted section than was actually the case. Thus a platoon commander would report that his men had lined nine metres of the ditch when in fact they had dug just three. The battalion commander, using the same method, would then multiply this by the number of his platoons, and then, for good measure, round it up. 'The best, or perhaps it was the worst, thing,' commented Fabbri, 'was that everyone knew the truth of the matter, but no one said anything officially, because the ditch was no use anyway.'

While still getting ready to defend Tripoli, they were given new guns, although these were actually older models, 120/25s, taken from the French after the armistice and to be used, they were told, in an anti-tank role, despite being hard to manoeuvre and not designed for such a task. 'I don't rule out the possibility that, in special circumstances,' wrote Fabbri, 'a group of heroic volunteers, willing to lay down their lives, could succeed in scoring the odd hit on a tank with a 120/25, but to pretend that normal soldiers, recently civilians, could, with a hopelessly antiquated weapon, properly take on an anti-tank role, in my opinion must only be madness, stupidity, or, worse, sabotage.'

Help, however, was now arriving for these beleaguered Italians. While German planning for Operation MARITA, the invasion of Greece, was taking place, the Comando Supremo, the Italian Chiefs of Staff, had accepted that some assistance in North Africa from their ally would be, in fact, much appreciated. More to the point, Hitler believed it was essential; he could live with the loss of Libya, but he didn't want Italy being knocked out of the war, leaving Britain to roam free in the Mediterranean and to threaten his southern flank. Therefore the rot had to be stopped. The man he appointed to take over the command of this new German corps for Libya was Generalmajor Erwin Rommel, who had so impressed him during the Battle of France.

Rommel was to have one light mechanized and one panzer division,

5. Division and 15. Division respectively. Shipping entire divisions to Tripoli was not straightforward, especially since there was not only limited Axis shipping but very limited large shipping; so although the first formations would be sent over in February, it was not expected that Rommel would have all his forces until the end of May.

Covering this shipping would be Fliegerkorps X, still based on Sicily and, in February, reinforced by the arrival of StG 1 at Trapani. The focus of their attacks would be the island fortress of Malta, and to respond to any sign of the Royal Navy forces at Gibraltar heading towards the eastern Mediterranean. Malta was already proving to be quite a thorn in the Axis side; not only were Adrian Warburton and the Reconnaissance Flight (now 69 Squadron) still operating but so too were Royal Navy submarines, Fleet Air Arm torpedo-bombers and RAF bombers, all of which were attacking Axis shipping, while from the island Tripoli was also well within range of the bombers.

Malta had also been strengthened with Hurricanes, including the recently formed 261 Squadron, although this was by no means at full strength. By the beginning of January, there were just sixteen on the island. These had been just about enough to cope with the half-hearted forays by the Regia Aeronautica, but were most certainly not when more than 140 aircraft of Fliegerkorps X reached Sicily.

The problems of maintaining decent numbers of aircraft on Malta were numerous. Once there, they had to be maintained with limited parts and facilities and kept in fuel, both of which, for the most part, were delivered across hostile seas. There were also the difficulties of getting them there in the first place, as Cyril 'Bam' Bamberger had discovered at the end of November. He had been one of thirteen pilots posted overseas and put aboard the aircraft carrier HMS *Argus* in Glasgow. They had then sailed to Gibraltar, where they had been met by Flight Lieutenant James MacLachlan, who had already made the trip in August and was there to brief them. They then realized that with the arrival of Bamberger there were now thirteen pilots and twelve Hurricanes, so someone had to miss out.

Since Bam Bamberger had come from a Spitfire squadron and had just one hour on Hurricanes, he was told to stay ashore on Gibraltar and catch a lift to Malta with the Royal Navy. Bamberger was depressed and frustrated by this, but, as it happened, it most likely saved him from a watery grave, for only four of the twelve Hurricanes made it to Malta

– the rest of the pilots ended up ditching in the sea and all but one of them was drowned. With the Italian fleet rumoured to be at sea, the escort commander had ordered them off at the earliest possible point eastwards. Inexperience, strong winds and poor weather had conspired against them; one of the Hurricanes that had made it had run out of fuel on landing.

After a pleasant – and safe – passage to Malta onboard the destroyer HMS *Hotspur*, Bamberger joined the survivors of the understrength 261 Squadron. It had been quiet in December, and he had gained the distinct impression that the fighter force on the island was little more than a token effort, there mainly to show the flag. The arrival of the damaged aircraft carrier *Illustrious* and the appearance of the Luftwaffe in force put him and his colleagues under extreme strain. On 18 January, for example, he flew four times. 'Only one hour's operational flying,' he noted, 'but as almost every minute involved combat, or more likely, the threat of being shot down, it was the equivalent in stress to being airborne for four hours during the Battle of Britain.' Bamberger managed to shoot down a Stuka that day but was far more interested in keeping alive than in racking up scores.

For Bamberger and his fellows, there was little let-up in the intensity of air fighting, even once the *Illustrious* had successfully slipped out of port. Usually just four or six of them were scrambled at a time. There was radar on the island but it lacked the support network available back in Britain – there was no 'system' on the island as there was for Fighter Command. The Luftwaffe's Messerschmitt fighters always had the advantage of height and speed and numbers. One of the debates Bamberger was having with his fellow pilots was whether it was better to be strapped into their Hurricanes when on readiness. If they were, it meant they could be scrambled into the air more quickly, which, because of the comparatively slow rate of climb of the Hurricane, gave them just a bit more time; on the other hand, if the airfield was attacked by low-flying marauding Messerschmitts, swooping in under the radar, then it was much harder to get out quickly and run for cover.

These were the kinds of dilemmas facing the outnumbered Malta fighter pilots when Hauptmann Helmut Mahlke and his *Gruppe*, III/ StG 1, first flew over the island at the end of February. And it was the island's airfields, and specifically Luqa, the largest, that they had been ordered to attack just a few days after their arrival. After flying down to

Catania on the south-east coast of Sicily to refuel, they took off at 1.15 p.m. on 26 February, the entire *Gruppe* flying in close formation at around 14,000 feet and escorted by a *Staffel* of Me109s and some Italian Macchi 200 fighters.

After weaving through the thick flak around the harbour, they moved into line astern and prepared to dive. Mahlke picked out an aircraft pen, tipped over into a 70-degree dive, centred the target in his sights and kept it there as the ground hurtled towards him and his siren screamed. At 1,200 feet, he let go his bombs, then easing out of the dive looked around for a possible second target to attack with his machine guns. Right over the airfield, and at just 600 feet, he was hit by Luqa's anti-aircraft gunners. A massive jolt, an ear-splitting crash, and a hole burst open in his starboard wing. It was as much as Mahlke could do to keep his Stuka flying at all, such was the wind resistance on his damaged wing.

By now his height had dropped and he was barely twenty feet off the ground and heading straight for a hangar. Desperately, Mahlke tried to pull the plane up and gradually it began to climb so that he just missed the top of the hangar by a matter of inches.

'Boy, that was close!' called out his gunner, Baudisch.

They managed to clear the island and head out to sea, only for Baudisch to call out, 'Hurricane approaching from astern!'

'Well, shoot it down then, Fritzchen,' Mahlke replied as calmly as he could. He knew they were a sitting duck. Baudisch opened fire, but the Hurricane quickly gained on them and opened fire itself. 'Once again,' wrote Mahlke, 'I was conscious of a series of metallic popping noises as a fresh crop of tiny holes sprouted in both wings.'

It looked certain that they were done for, but then another Stuka appeared, seemingly from nowhere, and flying right across the Hurricane's nose forced it to break away. It was a courageous move because the Stuka was riddled with bullets as a result. Neither pilot nor gunner was hit, however, much to Mahlke's relief. The Hurricane was now lining up for yet another shot, with Mahlke's Stuka barely flying and Baudisch's machine gun jammed. Mahlke was bracing himself for the worst when suddenly an Me109 dived on the unsuspecting Hurricane. 'The 109's opened fire!' yelled Baudisch. 'Going full pelt – and at extreme range . . . But he's got him! Still firing . . . the Hurricane's been hit! He's on fire . . . He's going in! He's shot him down!'

Mahlke exhaled – he realized he'd been holding his breath. 'Escaped by the skin of our teeth again, Fritzchen,' he said. The Hurricane pilot was Eric Taylor, Malta's top-scoring ace with seven victories, but he was shot down by Joachim Müncheberg, the leading German ace on Sicily.

Mahlke and Baudisch's nightmare was not over yet, however. With no flaps, they were facing another crash-landing and sure enough, as they touched down, way too fast, the Stuka bounced and touched down again, careering across the field until finally coming to a halt a stone's throw from the far perimeter. As they clambered out, Mahlke took a photograph of the astonishing amount of damage. In addition to the gash in the wing, they counted no fewer than 184 bullet holes. 'The aircraft,' noted Mahlke, 'looked like a colander.'

It was one of the Luftwaffe's heaviest raids on the island to date. The defenders shot down five Stukas and one Ju88 in addition to those, like Mahlke's, that were damaged, but the damage to Luqa was considerable. Furthermore, five Hurricanes were lost and three pilots killed. Unlike during the Battle of Britain, these could not be readily replaced. Luftwaffe attacks on this scale were thus a more effective means of subduing the RAF on Malta than they ever had been the previous summer over England.

It meant Rommel's forces were, for the most part, safely reaching Tripoli. Rommel himself had arrived on 12 February and immediately had taken command of all Italian motorized units as well as his own, with orders to form a blocking force near Sirte, well to the east of Tripoli. His immediate superior was Generale Gariboldi, who had just taken over from the recently resigned Graziani.

Rommel set about his business with his usual energy, which came as something of a shock to the colonial Italians, who were used to a much more languid way of doing things. On his orders, unloading of ships at Tripoli continued through the night, something that was unheard of on the Italian watch; reconnaissance flights were made, two Italian motorized divisions were hurried east, as were the German troops newly kitted out in tropical uniforms. Generale Gariboldi was dubious about this whirlwind of dynamism but appeared happy to let Rommel take the lead. 'Everything's splendid with me and mine in this glorious sunshine,' Rommel wrote to his wife on 17 February. 'My lads are already at the front, which has been moved about 350 miles to the east.' As far as he was concerned, the British couldn't reach them too soon. Rommel had been given strict instructions to simply block the British advance, but already he was eagerly spoiling for a fight.

On the same day that Rommel reached Tripoli, O'Connor's forces took a further 20,000 Italian prisoners, 200 guns and 120 tanks. As Anthony Eden, the new Foreign Secretary, waggishly noted, 'Never has so much been surrendered to so few.'

At the beginning of March, Commander Donald Macintyre was shocked to discover that he'd been ordered to give up his command of *Hesperus* and take over command of HMS *Walker*, an ageing destroyer that, although since refitted, had first seen action back in 1916. Not only was he sorry to bid farewell to his sharply honed crew on *Hesperus*, but it felt like a backward step to be given an older ship that had been originally designed for North Sea operations and had limited range and poor sea-keeping qualities.

However, a large degree of gloss was added by his appointment as Senior Officer Escort (SOE) commanding one of the new Escort Groups that were now being introduced. These were flotillas of destroyers and other escorts that operated together in conjunction with the convoy commodore and with little interference at all from shore.

As SOE, Macintyre had a critical role. In the rapidly expanding Royal Navy, experience had to be spread, and all SOEs and most ship's captains tended to be Regular Royal Navy officers, while First Lieutenants were quite often Royal Navy Reserve (RNR), and the rest of the new officers tended to be drawn from the Royal Navy Volunteer Reserve. These latter men had to learn quickly from men like Macintyre, while the seamen aboard had to similarly draw on the experience of Regular RN sailors.

In any transatlantic convoy there would be between forty and eighty merchant ships. There were three main convoy routes to Britain. 'Fast' convoys could travel between 9 and 14.9 knots, and across the Atlantic they were routed from Halifax, Nova Scotia, and called 'HX'. 'Slow' trans-atlantic convoys operated at 7.58 knots and began at Sydney, Cape Breton Island, north-east of Halifax, and were called 'SC' convoys. 'SL' convoys were also slow, and came up from Freetown in Sierra Leone. Many of the ships in these had earlier sailed independently from Australia, Ceylon, India and South Africa, for example, before reaching West Africa. However, some ships could not even sail at 7 knots and so had no choice but to sail independently. Others, such as neutrals, were also initially kept apart from convoys.

Convoys heading back across the Atlantic to North America were called 'ON(F)' – fast – and 'ON(S)' – slow. And it was ON convoys that Macintyre and his escorts were taking from Liverpool that spring. The convoy would steam in two columns as much as ten miles long until clear of the Irish Sea. While this was going on, each ship would test lamp and radio communications, as well as guns, while the escorts beetled about like sheepdogs. Macintyre's 5th Escort Group consisted of his own ship, two V-class destroyers, *Vanoc* and *Volunteer*, the S-class destroyers *Sardonyx* and *Scimitar*, and the Flower-class corvettes *Bluebell* and *Hydrangea*. These seven vessels would escort one convoy.

Destroyers came in different sizes, signified by the different classes; V-class destroyers, for example, had greater ranges than most. Corvettes were much smaller and therefore more manoeuvrable, but were not as fast as destroyers, which, depending on their class, could sail at speeds of up to 40 knots. Corvettes could usually manage 18–20 knots, which still made them faster than a U-boat operating on the surface. The other advantage of corvettes was that being smaller they were quicker and easier to build.

Night-time brought new challenges to the convoy as for obvious reasons it had to operate in a blackout. Nor, in early 1941, was there any radar, so navigation had to be carried out by compass and the human eye. As land fell away, the convoy commodore, usually a retired senior naval officer now with the RNR, would organize the ships into eleven or twelve lines covering an area around six miles wide and two deep. It was then Macintyre's job as SOE to organize his escorts into a ring around three to five miles outside the convoy, which meant a perimeter of as much as forty-five miles, putting each escort about eight miles apart. Each escort would then have her own section of this ring to patrol. The golden rule, rather as with a fighter plane, was never to stay on the same course for more than a couple of minutes, and instead to weave and zig-zag constantly, although at night, with little or no moon, there was no alternative but to cling closely to the rest of the convoy and pray that the following morning the ships would still all be there. This became even harder in rough weather with ships pitching and rolling and with giant waves drenching the decks and the open bridge and all those there.

Control of the force was not easy, because the escorts were still operating with high-frequency radio sets, which had very long range and so could easily be picked up by submarines. Radio signals therefore had to be laboriously coded and decoded, while tactical signals between the escorts and convoy tended to be made during daylight only and by using lamps to transmit Morse. Communications at sea was a key area in which the Royal Navy had to urgently find improvements.

Macintyre delivered his first convoy safely to the 19°W point in the Atlantic, then successfully managed to rendezvous with another inbound on 15 March. This was convoy HX112, and as they began to steam eastwards Macintyre had received warnings to suggest they were being shadowed by a wolfpack. 'I warned my ships to prepare for an attack after dark,' wrote Macintyre, 'and a cloak of tense expectancy settled over the convoy.'

For the U-boat arm, the past few months of early 1941 had been frustrating. Dönitz had moved his headquarters from Paris to Lorient, and the Organisation Todt had started building immense U-boat 'pens' at Brest, Lorient, La Pallice and Saint-Nazaire, but there were still nothing like enough U-boats. Dönitz was painfully aware of just how big an impact a sizeable U-boat fleet would have made during the 'Happy Time'. 'I was still of the opinion that only very greatly increased monthly sinkings could make Britain ready for peace,' he noted. 'And as before, I still maintained that the building of a powerful U-boat fleet was the German Navy's most urgent task.'

It must, then, have been almost as frustrating for Dönitz as it was the British when, back on 5 November, the pocket battleship *Admiral Scheer* had slipped unseen through into the Atlantic, sighted a North Atlantic convoy, sunk the sole escort vessel, and then sunk five more merchant ships, amounting to 47,300 tons. Outraged, the British Home Fleet sent a mass of four battleships and heavy cruisers out to try and catch her, and at the same time took the drastic step of suspending further convoys for the best part of a fortnight. Despite this, *Admiral Scheer* managed to elude her pursuers.

Meanwhile, Dönitz's U-boats had almost nothing to attack and did not sink a single vessel between 5 and 21 November, the longest dry spell of the war to date. Adding to Dönitz's frustrations had been the uselessness of the Italian submarines. Mussolini had offered thirty of his submarines to help in the Atlantic, an offer Dönitz could hardly refuse. Operating from Bordeaux, where Rösing had been posted as liaison officer, they quickly proved they were totally ill-suited to the task. During October and November, they sank only one ship, of just over 4,000 tons. In the same period, Dönitz's few U-boats sank eighty, at 435,000 tons. The boats themselves were unfit for the tough operational conditions of the Atlantic, while their crews were insufficiently trained. By December, Dönitz had accepted they were more hindrance than help. 'I felt obliged,' he noted, 'for the time being to dispense with close Italian co-operation.'

Equally unhelpful was the Luftwaffe. Dönitz had been expecting considerable assistance in locating convoys, but the disconnect between the German armed services was rearing its ugly head once more. Göring had long ago insisted that anything that could fly would belong to him, so although the Kriegsmarine had air support, run usually by former Kriegsmarine officers, it none the less answered to the Luftwaffe. Since Göring, like Hitler, was continentalist in outlook, the Kriegsmarine was never very high on his priority list, something that was reflected in the Luftwaffe General Staff. A *Fliegerführer Atlantik* had been created, under the command of Luftflotte 3, and included a number of bomber *Gruppen* specifically earmarked for supporting the U-boats, but whenever requests were made, help was invariably not forthcoming. One entire *Gruppe* of Focke-Wulf Condors, for example, based near Bordeaux, could only provide one aircraft per day. It was not good enough.

Back in November, Otto Kretschmer, the leading U-boat ace, had been awarded the Oak Leaves to his Knight's Cross and invited to Berlin to be given them by Hitler in person. In the Reich Chancellery, the Führer invited him to sit down and then asked Kretschmer about how the U-boat war was progressing. For a moment, Kretschmer wondered how frank he should be, then decided he should not hold back. Many more U-boats and decent aerial reconnaissance were what was needed and right away, he told Hitler.

'Thank you, Kommandeur,' the Führer replied. 'You have been admirably frank, and I shall do what I can for you and your colleagues.' He then invited Kretschmer to stay for lunch. It turned out to be a torturous occasion. Not only was the naval man served a vegetarian meal, but he was not allowed any alcohol and was not given permission to smoke. Kretschmer, like almost every man in the U-boat arm, was a full-blooded smoking, drinking carnivore.

Dönitz, too, repeatedly pressed his case with regard to better co-operation from the Luftwaffe, urging Raeder to do something. How much it was because of Dönitz, or whether Kretschmer's plea had made a bigger impression, Hitler personally intervened and on 7 January went over

Göring's head and authorized the placing of KG40, equipped with Condors, specifically under the BdU's direct control. Göring was incensed and tried his best to reverse the decision, but to no avail, and in the process Dönitz made a lasting enemy; Göring was not a man to forget such a slight. None the less, in the short term, the U-boat arm would reap the benefits. 'This order,' noted Dönitz in his war diary, 'is a great step forward.' It may have been, but that month he had just eight U-boats operating in the Atlantic. It was nothing like enough.

Teddy Suhren had been awarded the Knight's Cross, usually the preserve of U-boat commanders. However, his captain, Kapitänleutnant Heinrich Bleichrodt, had urged his superiors to give the award to Suhren, recognizing the part his 1WO had played in sinking some 200,000 tons of enemy shipping. Suhren had been delighted.

That had been in November, and soon after he had been posted away from *U-48*. He had hoped he might get his own command, but Dönitz had insisted no one under the age of twenty-five could be a commandant, and since Suhren still had six months to go until he reached that age, he was posted, much to his chagrin, as a torpedo instructor at Memel. However, the winter was so bad, the course eventually had to be abandoned – it was impossible to train men to fire torpedoes effectively when their passage was repeatedly blocked by ice floes.

As it turned out, Suhren did not have to wait six months. His birthday was on 16 April, but some weeks before that orders had arrived telling him to take command of *U-564* on 1 March, which would, by then, be complete and ready for trials. 'That was it!' noted Suhren. 'At last I had my own boat and a brand-new one too!'

The United States may yet to have formally entered the war, but any outside observer could have been forgiven for thinking otherwise. In February, top-secret talks had taken place in Washington to discuss potential joint future war plans against the Axis, which, since the signing of the Tripartite Pact back in September, included Japan. This was an astonishing move and had come on the back of closer ties since Roosevelt's re-election. The result was an agreement called 'ABC-1', eventually signed on 27 March, in which it was accepted that should the USA be drawn into war, then the priority would be to defeat Germany. Admittedly, these talks and the subsequent agreement had been kept secret, but it demonstrated that America's leaders were now working on an assumption that it was a matter of when, not if, the USA would enter the war. For Britain's war leaders, ABC-1 was an enormous boost.

Important though this was, even more significant in the short term was the American acceptance that they needed to help in the Battle of the Atlantic. To this end, part of the ABC-1 agreement was that the US would take responsibility, along with the Royal Canadian Navy, of helping to escort convoys to Britain. In order to make such support a reality, Roosevelt authorized the establishment of the US Navy's Atlantic Fleet under the command of Admiral Ernest J. King, and under him the Support Force, Atlantic Fleet, commanded by Admiral Arthur L. Bristol.

The caveat was that, because the USA was still not officially at war, no US naval forces should operate from American soil, so the Support Force would operate from Argentia, in Placentia Bay in Newfoundland, handed over to the US as part of the bases-for-destroyers deal the previous September. In addition to this, a deal was done with the Danish government-in-exile to develop further air and naval bases on Greenland and Iceland. The aim was to have the Support Force up and running by April.

Following fast on the footsteps of the dramatic ABC-1 agreement came Lend-Lease, which had been passed by the Senate and finally became law on 11 March, plus a host of further concessions. Ten US coastguard cutters, what the British called sloops, were handed over to the Royal Navy. Fifty first-class oil tankers were added to Britain's merchant fleet, as were seventy-five Norwegian and Panamanian tankers then under US charter. US shipyards were also building a new, smaller aircraft carrier to be known as an 'escort carrier' for the British, while from now on British warships could enter US shipyards for repairs and refits. All of this amounted to a major boost for the British, both materially and psychologically. In terms of the Battle of the Atlantic – the one battle that mattered above all in the war in the West – the United States was fast becoming a neutral in the loosest sense only.

CHAPTER 40

Sea Battles

IT WAS IMPOSSIBLE for anyone in Britain not to be aware of the vital importance of shipping, which its existence had for centuries depended upon, but never more so than now. It is hard to see how Britain could have been brought to its knees with the naval and air forces at Germany's disposal, but they might, possibly, have affected its ability to wage war, as Churchill was keenly aware. In recent weeks, long-range Condors had sunk a number of ships, proving their worth, including one attack that saw them sink seven ships in convoy. Furthermore, the pocket battleship *Admiral Hipper* had also slipped back out into the Atlantic, sinking one straggler and then catching a slow convoy from West Africa, SL(S)64, and, in a furious display of firepower, sending seven of the convoy's nineteen ships to the bottom of the ocean. U-boats were also continuing to add to their tally. In all, sixty-four ships were sunk in January, a hundred in February and a further 139 in March.

Adding insult to British injury had been the failure of Bomber Command to attack the U-boat pens as they were being built along the Atlantic coast, and the appearance of the battle cruisers *Gneisenau* and *Scharnhorst* in the Atlantic. Throughout February and into March, they harried stragglers, disrupted convoy routes and played cat-and-mouse with the British Home Fleet, repeatedly evading their British pursuers by a whisker. At the end of March, they slipped successfully into the safety of Brest and, as their British pursuers followed, the *Admiral Hipper* was able to pass through the British blockade and reach the Baltic for refits. These operations were a stinging blow to British naval pride.

It was with these battles in the Atlantic in mind that Churchill, at the beginning of March, formed the Battle of the Atlantic Committee, with himself as chairman. The committee would meet once a week and was designed to focus minds on how to deal with the mounting threat to British shipping trade. On 6 March, the PM distributed a directive listing thirteen crucial steps they needed to take. Key among these was the urgent transfer of more RAF Coastal Command forces to the Western Approaches. These were now to come under the direct command of Admiral Noble and his headquarters at Derby House, demonstrating an inter-service co-operation that was manifestly lacking in the Wehrmacht. Merchant ships were to be given anti-aircraft guns, all western British seaports were to be given a priority for anti-aircraft defence, and a large amount of the 2.6 million tons' worth of merchant shipping currently idle in British ports was to be made urgently seaworthy.

A further step was to allow any 'fast' merchant vessel of 12 knots or more to sail independently. This went against the advice of the Admiralty but was based on Churchill's desire to speed up the turnaround time of merchant ships, for while there was no doubting the improved safety of ships travelling in convoy, such a system did cause problems, because suddenly a mass of ships would arrive in port at once and all need unloading at the same time. Then they would head out to sea again and the ports and the stevedores would be idle once more. In other words, it was rather an inefficient way of loading and unloading. If faster ships could travel independently, then much time would be saved. On the other hand, with U-boats able to travel at 17 knots on the surface, the risks of independent sailings were high.

Finally, Churchill was determined that more U-boats should be destroyed. Only six had been confirmed as sunk since the beginning of September and not one since December. Escorts needed to be better trained, and much improved anti-shipping devices were urgently required. No stone was to be left unturned in pursuit of these goals. 'The U-boat at sea must be hunted,' Churchill announced, 'the U-boat in the building-yard or dock must be bombed.' The Focke-Wulf, he added, 'must be attacked in the air and in their nests'. The Battle of Britain was over, he proclaimed, but the Battle of the Atlantic had begun.

In this battle, the Prime Minister was about to get some much better news, and sooner than he could have dared to hope.

*

At the War Office in Whitehall, London, General John Kennedy was as busy as ever with the myriad amounts of planning that were needed and the constant juggling of resources. He still found time to dine most evenings at his club or elsewhere about town, however, and an increasingly good friend and dinner partner was Colonel Raymond Lee, the US Military Attaché. Lee had been in Britain since the summer and, unlike Joe Kennedy, the American Ambassador throughout the first year of war, was both an ardent Anglophile and a believer in Britain's ability to fight back. Urbane and charming, Lee had quickly won friends in Britain, and while Kennedy had since been recalled to the US and replaced by John Winant, Lee was still very much a fixture at the US Embassy.

Even at the beginning of 1941, part of General Kennedy's job was to look ahead and begin to shape a long-term strategy, which included a return to France. Yet while he was certain Britain could plan for not losing the war, how to win it was another matter. Like Churchill, he was convinced that American help was essential. Over dinners with Lee, the two would often discuss America's own strategy and what the chances were of the US eventually joining the fight more emphatically. On one occasion, Lee asked Kennedy whether he had read Ernest Hemingway's *Death in the Afternoon*, with its vivid descriptions of bullfighting. The principle of bullfighting, Lee told him, was to wear the bull out gradually. Every move was planned for the eventual killing of the beast by getting him to exhaust himself. It was considered a bad mistake to attempt to deliver the *coup de grâce* too soon. The Germans, Lee suggested, were rather like the bull, and the following day sent Kennedy a copy of Hemingway's novel, which he duly read.

The analogy, Kennedy thought, was a good one, but he also thought it worth pointing out it only applied up to a point. Wearing down the enemy was one thing, but, as far as he was concerned, there was no benefit to dragging out the fight longer than necessary. 'If you regard Hitler as a bull, and this war as a bullfight,' Kennedy wrote, 'then I regard you as a man in the front row of the stalls with a machine gun. I want you to press the button now and shoot the bull.'

At the forefront of his mind in the opening months of 1941 was the rapidly escalating situation in the Mediterranean and Middle East, where Germany was now making its presence increasingly felt. It was certainly the case that this was leading Hitler to spread his forces further and was even more of a critical diversion of resources for the Germans than it was for the British; but neither Kennedy nor any of Britain's war leaders knew then about German plans for the Soviet Union, so the situation seemed more fraught as a result. It was no wonder Kennedy was wishing the USA would declare war right away.

British forces were slowly but surely being built up, and there were now as many as 300 ships at any one time ploughing their way back and forth to the Middle East. This still wasn't enough for a theatre of truly enormous scale. In this massive expanse of scrub, desert and sea, the British needed to force a rapid end to Axis resistance in North and East Africa, prevent German forces sweeping down into Greece, make sure Malta survived, and help ensure that the Mediterranean Fleet was kept strong and that further trouble did not erupt in Iraq and elsewhere at the extremities of the theatre. Part, or even most, of those commitments could be achieved – but not all, and certainly not all at once. And it was the potential commitment to Greece that was causing Kennedy his biggest headache.

Back in January, when General Wavell had flown to Athens for talks with the Greeks, the Prime Minister, General Metaxas, had declined the British offer of troops. The artillery and tank regiments on offer were not, he felt, enough to be decisive, while they might easily merely provoke an attack by Germany and even Bulgaria. He would, he told Wavell, welcome the help of British troops should the Germans cross the River Danube and move into Bulgaria, the obvious route through which they might advance.

This gave the British command a welcome breathing space, but, in Kennedy's view, Britain stood far more to gain by pushing the Italians out of North Africa altogether than by denying Greece to the Germans. He also reckoned – and Dill agreed – that it would mean a commitment of at least twenty divisions to give them even a chance of making a difference. Twenty divisions was an amount they simply did not have, so to his mind the Greece venture was a non-starter.

However, a month later, the Greeks decided that maybe the time for British intervention was drawing near after all. Any German attack would be resisted to the utmost, they insisted, but they felt that, depending on the size of force the British could send, Yugoslavia and Turkey might also be encouraged to join their struggle against Nazi aggression. Churchill then sent a telegram to Wavell suggesting that four divisions be made available to Greece. When Dill told him all troops were already fully employed in the Middle East, the Prime Minister exploded. Once again, Churchill was looking at paper statistics, not making a realistic appreciation of his forces' capability. The two were quite different, something he stubbornly refused to accept.

At any rate, it was thought sensible to go and talk face to face with the Greeks, and with this in mind Churchill sent Anthony Eden and Dill to Athens for talks, along with Tedder and Cunningham, the service chiefs in the Middle East. With Eden and Dill on their way, Churchill invited Kennedy to stay with him for the weekend of 15–16 February at Ditchley, a country house that belonged to a friend and was considered safer than Chequers. On the Sunday morning, with the PM still in bed and wearing an elaborate silk dressing-gown, Kennedy was summoned to give him his current appreciation of the situation. Their talk lasted three hours and, when he left him, Kennedy felt confident the Prime Minister had both listened to and accepted his *tour d'horizon.*

Back in London, he followed it up with a memo, summarizing in writing all that he had said to him. 'Hitler has in fact made many mistakes,' he wrote, 'and doubtless he will make more. His biggest mistake, of course, was in starting the war without a navy.' In this, Kennedy was, of course, absolutely right. He then went on to discuss each commitment in turn, but gave especial warning about Greece. 'Nothing we can do can make the Greek business a sound military proposition,' he wrote. The Greeks did not have enough reserves and were, he believed, too far forward in Albania. In any case, in the build-up of supplies – the key to fighting any campaign – the Germans would always win in Greece. 'The locomotive and the petrol engine will always beat the ship,' he pointed out, 'especially when the ship has to go round the Cape.' He also pointed out that anything they put into Greece they should be prepared to lose, because, really, there was almost no chance of victory with the addition of four divisions sent in piecemeal. 'But the point is that if we use up four divisions and a large quantity of reserves in Greece,' he told him, 'our power of offensive action is gone until we can replace them.' The loss of Greece, he added, would be an embarrassment but not a strategic disaster. What was a strategic imperative was safeguarding sea communications, something that would be improved with the capture of Tripoli. 'It is essential,' he concluded, 'to cling to the things that matter and not waste our strength on things that are not vital to our strategy.'

Churchill seemed to have listened, because he now sent Eden a signal.

'Do not consider yourselves obligated to a Greek enterprise,' he warned them, 'if in your hearts you feel it will only be another Norwegian fiasco.'

Despite this, both Dill and Wavell now began to change their minds. Instead of using the PM's message as the much-needed excuse to extricate themselves from Greece, they instead told the Greeks they would send four divisions so long as it happened right away. There were two further provisos: first, that four full-strength divisions be sent; second, that the Greeks abandon Thrace and Eastern Macedonia and fall back to what was called the 'Aliákmon Line', a narrow strip of about fifty miles between the Yugoslav border and the northern Aegean. It meant sacrificing Thrace and Eastern Macedonia, but, they believed, it was a feasible place from which to defend the rest of the country. Suddenly, the Greek venture was back on.

It was already considered too late to move troops from East Africa, which was a shame because the two Indian divisions now there were suited to mountain warfare; in fact, the topography in Abyssinia and Eritrea was not very different to that of northern Greece. So that left taking troops already in the Middle East and those newly arriving into the theatre, such as the New Zealand Division.

The demands of potentially fighting in Greece as well as in East Africa and Libya forced Wavell to radically rejig his forces and caused him and his staff at GHQ a massive logistical headache. The Sherwood Rangers Yeomanry, for example, had arrived in Palestine in early 1940 complete with their chargers for what was essentially pre-war colonial policing duties. After a cavalry charge with sabres drawn and then two embarrassing stampedes, they had been ordered to send their horses home and, much to their general disgust, had been trained up as artillery; it was not intended, however, to keep them in that role for ever. The obvious course for a cavalry regiment was to mechanize them and put them into tanks, but there simply weren't enough to go round – not yet, at any rate.

They were, however, keen to learn and anxious to play their part, and had trained hard since sending their steeds home. Officers like Stanley Christopherson had been packed off on one course after another, learning various new skills, which he was then expected to impart to the men; few of these training courses had much to do with artillery, however.

At the end of January, with the new demands facing Wavell's command, the Sherwood Rangers were finally needed at the front. Their old squadrons were now batteries, and while two batteries were being sent to Crete as part of the island's new defences, two others were posted to the recently captured port of Tobruk, where they were told they would be operating 2-pounder anti-tank guns on the coast, ready to intercept any Italian torpedo boats or other vessels that might appear.

'Y' Battery, to which Stanley Christopherson had been attached, reached the tiny port, which was tucked in behind a long, narrow inlet already strewn with the wrecks of half-submerged Italian ships, on Saturday, 1 February. On the quayside, no one seemed to know anything about them. Eventually, they were taken to see the captain of HMS *Terror*, a small gun monitor, who explained that their task was to defend Tobruk with their 15-inch guns, but that they needed men on the coast to operate an OP, or observation post, and fire the guns there if it came to it. 'We then explained,' noted Christopherson, 'that our gunnery experience consisted of a three-week course six months ago, and we did not remember much about it!'

The Sherwood Rangers were precisely the type of unit Churchill was looking at on his paper list and thinking should be more readily employed, but Wavell was quite right: they were simply not ready to be thrown head-long into battle. It was only due to the extreme demands now being placed upon his command that they had been sent to Crete and Tobruk. It was hoped they would not be required to do much for some time yet, even though by the time the first troops were being shipped to Greece they were aware that German troops had landed in Tripoli. Wavell was working on the assumption that the German lines of supply were far too great for them to make any counter-attack for some time yet. 'Tripoli to Agheila is 471 miles and to Benghazi 646 miles,' Wavell signalled Churchill on 27 February. 'There is only one road, and water is inadequate over 410 miles of the distance; these factors, together with the lack of transport, limit the present enemy threat.' It was not an unreasonable assumption, and, as it happened, mirrored both the German view and Rommel's corresponding orders to establish a blocking force east of Tripoli, not east of Sirte.

By this time, O'Connor's advance had run out of steam. There was a good case for pushing on to Tripoli and smashing the Axis in North Africa for good, but what was true for German and Italian forces heading eastwards was doubly true for British forces trying to push west. Had Wavell not been fighting a full campaign in East Africa, and had he not agreed to send troops to Greece, attempting the drive to Tripoli would have been worth the risk. In the suddenly altered circumstances, however, it simply was not. Rather, their advance ended at El Agheila, to the west of Cyrenaica.

On 8 March, Alf Parbery and J Section Signals left Tobruk as the entire Aussie 6th Division was being shipped to Greece. First, though, they had to drive all the way back along the coast, a distance of some 600 miles, which took longer than it might due to accidents on the single road, sandstorms and mechanical problems. They reached Alexandria on the 14th, spent the next couple of days preparing the trucks and kit for shipping, and finally sailed on 17 March, reaching Piraeus four days later after an uninterrupted journey. Alf took all this moving about in his stride. After a day of unloading, he and his mates in J Section Signals set off for the 16th Brigade camp on the evening of 22 March. 'Going through the streets,' he noted, 'the people gave us a great welcome – cheered and shouted as we went through.' Naturally inquisitive, he enjoyed the chance to visit the Parthenon, but was slightly taken aback to see a long column of Greek troops just back from the front marching through the city. 'Many had frost-bitten feet,' he noted, 'and were crippled with it.'

While such scenes demonstrated the hazards of fighting in the mountains in winter with insufficient supplies, there was further trouble brewing to the north. As Parbery and his mates began the slow journey up through Greece he thought the scenery was some of the best he had ever seen. He was, however, completely unaware that the British plan agreed with the Greeks was already unravelling – just as John Kennedy had feared.

In fact, even before he had left Tobruk, Bulgaria announced that it was joining the Axis. The next day, 2 March, German troops crossed the Danube and immediately began their approach march towards the Greek border. At the same time, Anthony Eden was flying back to Athens from Ankara, where he and General Dill had been talking to the Turks, who approved of the plan to defend Greece and promised they, too, would fight, should Germany turn on it next.

On board a Royal Australian Air Force Sunderland flying boat, Eden was up front next to the pilot and had been given permission by the Turks to fly over the Dardanelles, the scene of such bitter fighting in the last war. Taking control, Eden had flown low to take a good look.

Having flown on to Athens, they found bad news awaiting them. The Greeks had not, as planned, been given orders to fall back to the Aliákmon

Line. Rather, General Papagos, the Greek C-in-C, told them it was now too late because of the risk to his troops of being caught on the move. What followed was what Eden reckoned resembled the most painful haggling at an oriental bazaar, and ended with a compromise fudge. Papagos would keep his forces at the front in Macedonia but would send three of his divisions to the Aliákmon Line, which was about a third less than the British had been originally expecting.

A braver decision would have been to turn around and head straight back to the Middle East, but Eden, Dill and the Middle East C-in-Cs all believed that to abandon Greece would not only lead to its certain and rapid defeat, but would also have a disastrous effect throughout the Near and Middle East, as well as throughout the Empire and the United States. More than that, nine RAF squadrons were already in Greece, and troops were embarking. The decision made, while recognized to be far from ideal, was considered the least dangerous, overall, of the options available. 'By this time,' wrote Eden, 'Dill and I felt that the die was cast.' None the less, they had made a political decision, not a military one, and, on his return to London, Dill confessed to Kennedy that he thought they had made a bad mistake. 'I tried to console him,' noted Kennedy, 'by saying that, even if things went wrong, it would only be an incident – we must regard this as a defensive phase, and hang on until we were stronger.'

There was, however, better news for Britain coming from the Atlantic. On 7 March, U-47, commanded by the ace Günther Prien, was lost during an attack on an outbound convoy, OB 293. Officially, the claim went to the destroyer *Wolverine*, but some debate remains about precisely how and when U-47 went to the bottom. It may well be that a depth-charge attack did bring about the fatal blow that same day, or the following morning as claimed. What is certain is that Prien's last signal came on the morning of 7 March and that nothing more was ever heard of the U-47, her brilliant commander or any of the crew.

Also involved in that engagement had been Otto Kretschmer's U-99, but a week later his boat, that of another ace, Joachim Schepke's U-100, and the U-30 were converging on another convoy, this time HX112 from Halifax to the UK.

Escorting HX112 on their first homeward leg were Commander Donald Macintyre and his Escort Group, EG5. Just before midnight on 15 March, Macintyre was on the bridge when the night was ripped apart by a blinding flash of flame, followed moments later by the sound of an explosion. This was the 10,000-ton tanker *Erdona*, and it was the first time Macintyre and his men had seen a ship like this erupt. They were shocked into silence by the spectacle and assumed no one could possibly have survived. Immediately, alarm bells clanged through the ship and men ran to their action stations. In the glare of the burning ship, Macintyre strained through his binoculars for the sign of a U-boat as the destroyer zig-zagged widely in an effort to cover as much sea as possible. The only real instrument to help them was their ASDIC, effectively sonar, which transmitted impulses that could be heard as a 'ping'. If these impulses hit an object, they would be reflected back with a further ping, the response time being shorter the closer the object was.

The problem with ASDIC was that the version used at the time, the 120 series, had a range of only 2,500 yards in perfect conditions, and conditions were rarely that, making the range usually more like 1,500 yards. Compounding the problem was the fact that it was effective in a cone of just 16 degrees below the horizontal of the surface, which meant it could not detect to any great depth. Usually, by the time an escort was in a position to drop depth charges, it was doing so on a hunch rather than from any help from the ASDIC. As it was, depth charges had been set on pre-war assumptions that submarines would not be able to dive very deep; in fact, U-boats could dive much further than the British had expected, so could generally get beneath any depth-charge explosion.

At any rate, Macintyre and his escorts were picking up nothing on their ASDIC sets and nor was there any way of telling from which direction the torpedo had been fired. In the wide, dark Atlantic, it was like looking for a needle in a haystack. Despite this, the destroyer *Scimitar* had spotted the U-boat, which was *U-110*, a new Type IXB commanded by Fritz-Julius Lemp, who had sunk the *Athenia* on the first day of the war, and tried to ram it. Before it could do so, *U-110* dived to safety.

After a fruitless search, no further attack developed that night. Dawn broke and with it came a respite, yet Macintyre couldn't help worrying about what might happen when night fell once more. That one U-boat had clearly escaped, now knew the location of the convoy, and would most likely not only attack again but very possibly have drawn in others. He was well aware that U-boats now tended to operate in packs.

Then, shortly before dusk, *Scimitar* flashed a signal that a U-boat had been spotted some six miles ahead. This was not Lemp in *U-110*, which had now headed in the wrong direction, but Joachim Schepke in *U-100*. Ordering full-speed ahead, Macintyre was joined in the pursuit by both *Vanoc* and *Scimitar*. As they closed, however, the U-boat dived. Still, Macintyre hoped they now had a good chance of catching the boat, so in a line a mile and a half apart they swept the area. To his disappointment, they detected nothing and, leaving the other two destroyers to continue the hunt, Macintyre ordered *Walker* to rejoin the convoy, confident that with the U-boat submerged and therefore unable to travel at more than 7 knots, and with the convoy making a dramatic change of course, there was now little chance of the German boat attacking that night.

Unbeknown to Macintyre, however, there were now other U-boats trailing the convoy, including *U-99* and *U-37*. Earlier, Lemp in *U-110* had reported seeing only two destroyers, so it was a surprise to the new arrivals, Schepke included, to discover the convoy had an escort of no fewer than seven destroyers and corvettes.

It was Kretschmer in *U-99* who began the attack that night, sailing right into the middle of the convoy, as was his way, and firing torpedoes from his eight tubes. One missed but seven others hit six merchantmen, the first shortly after *Walker* had rejoined the convoy. 'I was near to despair,' noted Macintyre, 'and I wracked my brains to find some way to stop the holocaust.' His one real hope was to sight the tell-tale white wake of a U-boat, then give chase and hopefully pick it up on the ASDIC and then pummel it with depth charges. Putting *Walker* into a curving course and with his binoculars glued to his eyes, he prayed he would spot their elusive attacker.

Suddenly, he spotted the wake of what could only be a U-boat and, urgently ordering an increase of speed to 30 knots, bolted towards the sighting. Spotting them almost too late, the U-boat crash-dived, but *Walker* was over her moments later and could still see the swirl of phosphorescence and sent a pattern of ten depth charges. Macintyre was certain they could hardly have missed, and soon after the charges exploded they heard a further explosion from below and an orange flash briefly spread across the water. Was this their first U-boat kill? Macintyre hoped so, especially since there was no further ping on the ASDIC.

It was not, however; the U-boat in question, *U-37*, was badly damaged but not destroyed. In the ensuing confusion, it was able to quietly slip away and head back to Germany for repairs. Meanwhile, as *U-37* was limping away, *U-110* and a fifth boat, *U-74*, had seen the explosions on the horizon and had turned back in the right direction. Approaching the convoy, they could see the full number of escorts weaving back and forth, letting off depth charges and firing star shells into the sky to illuminate any U-boat on the surface.

Forty minutes after the attack on *U-37*, *Walker* finally picked up U-boat contact on the ASDIC once more and assumed it must be the original boat he had already thought killed. In fact, it was *U-100*, which had still not managed to fire any of her torpedoes. Calling *Vanoc* to help, Macintyre then ordered both ships to make repeated sweeps over where he thought the U-boat had dived, and to set salvoes at a variety of ranges from 150 to 500 feet. The trouble was, the depth-charge explosions affected the ASDIC readings so, with no apparent sign of success, Macintyre swept *Walker* around to pick up survivors of the SS *J. B. White*.

Under the sea, however, *U-100* was in trouble as the depth charges had caused flooding and smashed a number of instruments, so that by 3 a.m. Schepke had no choice but to surface. This was picked up almost immediately by *Vanoc* using her new Type 286M radar – the first confirmed radar contact with a U-boat of the war. Seeing both *Vanoc* and *Walker* now hurrying towards them, Schepke ordered the boat into a firing position, but the engines wouldn't start and by the time they finally did it was too late. Believing *Vanoc* would miss them, Schepke was manning the bridge, but this was to prove a fatal miscalculation. *Vanoc* was steaming directly towards the stricken U-boat.

'Abandon ship!' Schepke yelled, and a moment later he was crushed to death as *Vanoc*'s bow smashed into the conning tower. *U-100* sank moments later. 'Have rammed and sunk U-boat,' signalled *Vanoc*, then managed to scoop up just six survivors.

'What a blissful moment that was,' noted Macintyre, 'the successful culmination of a long and arduous fight.'

But it was only the culmination of one particular fight, for soon after 3.30 a.m. *Walker*'s ASDIC picked up the ping-ping of a contact.

'Contact, contact!' called out Backhouse, the ASDIC operator.

At first, Macintyre dared hardly believe it, but Backhouse was insistent. 'Contact definitely submarine,' he told his skipper.

This was Otto Kretschmer's *U-99*, which had surfaced and suddenly found itself within yards of *Walker*. The watch officer on the bridge, assuming they must have been seen, ordered a crash-dive. In fact, they had not been, but now, by diving, they had been picked up on *Walker*'s

ASDIC; had they held their nerve, they may well have got away.

As the destroyer swept over the U-boat, Macintyre ordered another salvo of depth charges, which smashed air, fuel and ballast tanks. Water was pouring in and, realizing they had no chance of surviving under water, Kretschmer ordered them to surface, still hoping they might escape in the darkness. It was not to be. Picked up by *Vanoc*, which signalled the sighting to *Walker*, the stricken U-boat was hit with a searchlight and fired on with their 4-inch guns. The firing was pretty wild, but, soon after, the U-boat signalled in poor English, 'We are sunking.' Kretschmer had ordered *U-99*, the most successful U-boat of all, to be scuttled and for the men to abandon her.

Walker pulled up to her, lowered nets and helped pull the men aboard. 'Some of them,' noted Macintyre, 'were in the last stages of exhaustion from the cold of those icy northern waters by the time we got them aboard.' The last man to come aboard was the U-boat's captain, Otto Kretschmer, still wearing his prized Zeiss binoculars, one of only a few made on Dönitz's orders for his greatest aces. At the last moment, Kretschmer tried to throw them into the sea, but he was not quick enough and they were taken from him and handed over to Macintyre – a prize he would cherish.

The next day, Kretschmer was spotted looking at the ship's crest, a horseshoe. 'This is a strange coincidence,' he said in perfect English. 'My ship also sailed under the sign of the horseshoe.' His though, he said, was shown pointing down not up.

'Well, Captain,' replied Osbourne, *Walker*'s Chief Engineer, 'in our belief a horseshoe that way up allows the luck to run out.' Kretschmer laughed ruefully.

On a small vessel like a destroyer, it was impossible to keep prisoners and survivors of the *J. B. White* apart, and Macintyre had his work cut out preventing fights. Despite this, it was not long before Osbourne had organized a bridge four between himself, two of the *J. B. White*'s officers and Kretschmer, an extraordinary occurrence in the circumstances. Apart from showing his skill at cards, Kretschmer revealed little except that he'd studied at Exeter University before the war, appeared largely apolitical, and was resentful that conflict had ever broken out between the two countries.

A few days later, they reached Liverpool, where they were met by Admiral Noble and many of the Western Approaches staff, all anxious to congratulate Macintyre and his EG5, and to see the great U-boat ace. Kretschmer, wearing his own clothes and Captain's white-covered cap, strode down the gangway. There was silence as he stepped ashore, and for a brief moment he paused and looked at Macintyre and the group of officers standing around Admiral Noble, then gave a slight nod to his adversary and stepped towards the waiting car, with a soldier now at each elbow.

CHAPTER 41

Mixed Fortunes: I

Now PUSHED BACK into the mountains of Albania, the Italians were continuing to struggle, fighting a war not only against the Greeks but also against the conditions and their own inadequate supply chain. Gino Cappozzo, aged twenty-three, was a gunner in 17th Battery of 3rd Alpine Artillery Regiment Julia. Ever since they had come under surprise attack at the end of December, he and his comrades had been on the back foot, battling to escape the Greeks as they pressed forward and losing mounting casualties. They were also largely rudderless as too many officers and senior NCOs had been lost; in early January, they had even lost Colonnello Tavoni, shot dead during yet another engagement. In early February, they were withdrawn from the front line and given fifteen days' rest. 'By now,' noted Cappozzo, 'we were reduced to extremes: barefoot, ragged, puttees wrapped around our feet rather than boots, hungry and deathly cold.' Their brief respite over, they were sent back – still without their new allocation of boots.

Towards the end of February, they crossed the Plain of Tepelenë, then climbed a 1,300-metre peak, carrying the guns, ammunition and supplies with them. There they would remain for the next thirty days. 'It was a month of hellish fights,' noted Cappozzo, 'at all hours of the day and night. The mountain resembled an erupting volcano.'

Others were returning home, albeit briefly. Pace Misciatelli-Chigi was absolutely horrified to see the state of her husband when he appeared one day in February at their home in Siena, on leave from the Albanian front: he was gaunt, ill and depressed. She also worked twice a week in the military hospital in Siena, writing letters for them and reading aloud. 'They had lost all that was most in life,' she noted, 'in a cause for which they felt nothing.'

Meanwhile, more recruits were being processed through the training camps, most of which continued to be poorly equipped and run. Giuseppe Santaniello was a twenty-year-old law student who had been called up and posted to a recruitment barracks near Naples. He arrived with a sense of pride at joining the Italian Royal Army and was excited by the prospect of serving his country; war, he had thought, was rather a glorious business. He was, however, in for a devastating shock at what he found there. His things were stolen, and the barracks were filthy and squalid. 'The worst place,' he noted, 'was the lavatories. A choking, foetid stench provided an advance warning of their state, the floor covered in a layer of stinking piss smeared with excrement on which sandals slipped and slithered all too easily. An inventor of tortures could not have dreamed anything worse.' Nor did any of the uniforms they were given fit. Santaniello was desperate. 'Very soon,' he added, 'our hopes and dreams crumbled, replaced by the awful reality of having to live in the midst of this filth and surrounded by criminals.'

Conditions were far more savoury in the Regia Marina, however, which, despite its humbling at Calabria and during the attack at Taranto, still boasted a good number of modern warships. Now serving on one of its biggest was Walter Mazzucato, aged nineteen, who had joined the battleship *Vittorio Veneto* at La Spezia back in January after two years' training as a naval cadet. 'It made my heart thud seeing such a vast ship for the first time,' he noted. Mazzucato had joined the Navy at seventeen; sailing the seas and serving his country was something he had set his heart on ever since he was a boy. In February, he'd sailed on his first trip out to sea on the mighty battleship, taking his position as an anti-aircraft gunner on one of the ship's twenty 37mm cannons.

Putting to sea had been prompted by news that Force H, the Royal Navy's force based at Gibraltar, had moved into the Mediterranean. Amiragglio Iachino, the admiral commanding the Italian Fleet, had done so in an effort to confront the British, but Force H had evaded the Italians and gone on to bombard Genoa and Livorno and mine the entrance of La Spezia. In terms of material damage, the attacks had not achieved a great deal, but they had further dented the morale of the Italians.

The Admiral's failure to intercept the British had not gone down well with the Germans and particularly with the naval staff. In March, with the Royal Navy responsible for ferrying British forces across the Aegean, they put renewed pressure on the Italians to act and take the offensive. Finally, on 26 March, they put to sea, with a force that included the battleship *Vittorio Veneto*, the heavy cruisers *Trento*, *Trieste* and *Bolzano*, and seven destroyers.

The aim was to try and disrupt British shipping to Greece, but unbeknown to Amiragglio Iachino, his counterpart, Admiral Cunningham, had got wind of this move. Having been spoiling for a battle at sea ever since the brief engagement off Calabria the previous July, ABC immediately put to sea.

This intelligence had come from the decrypts of German Enigma machine traffic carried out by the code-breakers at the Government Code and Cypher School at Bletchley Park. Many of these decrypts, codenamed 'Ultra', were cracked too intermittently and slowly to be much use, but in this case, however, news of the movement of the Italian Fleet had been picked up swiftly and the decrypts relayed to Cunningham. The Admiral was one of just a very few of Britain's war leaders to have been given clearance to receive Ultra decrypts.

In order to ensure British knowledge of Enigma traffic remained secret, the RAF then flew reconnaissance missions to give the impression that these were the source of the intelligence. Still flying from Malta were Adrian Warburton and his fellow photo reconnaissance crews of 69 Squadron. Warburton was sent to take photographs of the Italian Fleet, which he duly did, and then, while he and his crew were still flying high above them, he tried to relay the information back via radio. However, because of the numerous naval ships at sea, his message could not be received. Warburton eventually used a high-priority prefix, which indicated the sender was an air marshal, not a junior officer. This did the trick and the reply then asked him to try and identify as many Italian ships as possible. This Warburton did by flying so low the aircrews could read off the names.

Admiral Cunningham thus had a very clear picture of both where the Italian Fleet was and also its size and precise numbers. The nub, however, was how to force an engagement, because he was pretty certain Amiragglio Iachino had no intention at all of picking a fight, and that, rather, their putting to sea was more about paying lip service to their ally. Slipping out of Alexandria with his flagship, *Warspite*, Cunningham agreed to rendezvous with his second-in-command, Vice-Admiral Pridham-Wippell, and his cruiser force the following morning, by which time he would have assembled his battle fleet, along with a further force of destroyers.

Despite this, ABC had bet one of his staff officers ten shillings they would not even spot the enemy, so he was delighted when, the following morning before they had met up with Pridham-Wippell's force, he received a signal from his second-in-command saying he had sighted the Italian Fleet. Pridham-Wippell was now trying to lure it towards Cunningham and the battle fleet. This was a dangerous game because the nine 15-inch guns of the *Vittorio Veneto* had the power to make short work of Pridham-Wippell's cruiser force. The key was to draw the Italians to Cunningham without getting blasted themselves.

On board the *Vittorio Veneto*, the crew were all now at battle stations, Walter Mazzucato included, as the cruiser force chased its British counterparts and tried to bring them within range of the *Vittorio Veneto*. Eventually, the battleship was close enough to open fire, her huge 15-inch guns firing their shells from some fifteen miles.

On *Warspite*, Cunningham realized his cruiser force was now in dire need of help and so ordered off the torpedo-bombers from *Formidable* to attack and harry the Italians and the *Vittorio Veneto* especially. By the time these aircraft attacked, the Italian battleship had already fired ninety-four shells, although none had hit their target, and as Walter Mazzucato fired away at their aerial attackers, the big guns fell silent and the battleship began to withdraw. This was just what Cunningham had feared, and now he knew that the only chance of catching the Italians was if more aerial attacks could slow down their retreat.

While the Fleet Air Arm attacked twice more, so the cruiser force also continued to lob shells. At 3.19 p.m., Mazzucato was still firing when he saw three torpedo-bombers release their missiles. 'The aircraft that was almost aligned with the bow of the ship,' he remembered, 'attacked with extreme resolution and a spirit of self-sacrifice in the face of a hail of anti-aircraft fire. Hit by it, the plane fell into the sea and disappeared.' Moments later, however, Mazzucato was jolted as the torpedo scraped the stern and exploded outside the housing of the steering gear. Suddenly, water was pouring in, the helm became useless and the ship came to a halt. Mazzucato felt utterly bewildered as the ship began to lean, then looking up at the sky was absolutely convinced he then saw an image of the

Madonna. 'I was speechless,' he wrote. 'I stood looking at it for a few moments, then suddenly it disappeared and the light went, leaving behind a light grey cloud that slowly dissolved into the air.' Whatever it was he had seen, he felt reassured that the ship would be saved. Sure enough, her engineers soon managed to get her going again, although using just one screw, which meant sailing at half-speed.

Cunningham now gave chase, conscious he had no chance of catching them before nightfall and that by the following morning the Italian Fleet would be within range of its own air forces. This meant that his only chance of a fleet engagement was to launch a night attack, a notoriously difficult and high-risk tactic. ABC's staff officers were against it – the risk of collision and battle damage at a time when there were so many other demands on them seemed too great. 'You're a pack of yellow-livered skunks,' he told them. A night battle was on.

Whether the Madonna had come to the rescue of the Italian battleship or not, she most certainly had deserted the cruiser *Pola*, which had been hit and stopped in the water. Amiragglio Iachino had not anticipated that his adversary would possibly attempt such an action, so while the *Vittorio Veneto* sailed on to Taranto, his two other cruisers and their destroyers were ordered to remain with the stricken *Pola*. These were picked up on Pridham-Wippell's radar, so the British battle fleet was able to stealthily close in to about 4,000 yards – effectively point-blank range – and then swing around their mass of heavy guns. 'Director layer sees target,' Cunningham heard from the director tower. 'Never,' he wrote, 'have I experienced a more thrilling moment.' They opened fire moments later, as searchlights were turned on and lit up the Italian ships like rabbits in headlights. It was a massacre; all three cruisers were sunk. By morning, all that remained was a mass of debris, bobbing corpses and a film of oil, while the British fleet had picked up 900 Italian sailors. The Battle of Cape Matapan, as it quickly became known, had ensured that the threat of the Italian fleet was finished once and for all. For Mussolini, it was yet another humiliating blow.

None the less, however much the British might have been whipping the Italians, the Germans were now moving into the theatre. Over Malta, the Luftwaffe was hammering the tiny RAF defences, while, in Libya, General Rommel had launched a limited offensive, ignoring, in traditional Prussian style, the orders from his superiors to provide a blocking force and no more. With their forward positions weakened, the British had hastily withdrawn, first from El Agheila and then to Agedabia.

Meanwhile, as the two fleets had been chasing around the Mediterranean, extraordinary events were taking place in the Balkans. On 25 March, Yugoslavia stunned the free world by joining the Axis, but then in a coup two days later by a group of Air Force officers, Prince Paul, the Regent, and the Government were overthrown and the pact was revoked.

Hitler was already becoming increasingly frustrated and agitated by developments in the Balkans, which were proving a worrying distraction and diversion from his plans for invading the Soviet Union. On 30 March, Feldmarschall Erhard Milch, the deputy chief of the Luftwaffe, had been in Berlin to be harangued by Hitler. The Führer had given him and other generals a classic three-hour rant, in which he had repeatedly argued that the Western theatre – that is, the war against Britain – was still the most important one, and that the attack on the Balkans was, unfortunately, a vital prerequisite to the defeat of Britain. Also witness to this growing agitation was Major Gerhard Engel, his OKH Adjutant. Already, the Balkan situation had forced the Führer to accept postponement of BARBAROSSA. 'By themselves,' jotted Engel in his diary, 'a couple of weeks earlier or later are not necessarily so bad, but we do not want to be surprised by the Russian winter.' This was Warlimont's concern too; already the Wehrmacht was spread so widely that logistical issues and the problems of supply, and the vast geographical range, meant that it was too late to change strategy in any way; thus any new problem had to be dealt with by being slotted into the existing strategic framework.

The news of Lend-Lease added further to German agitation and the grating sense that the clock was ticking. Britain was getting stronger; America was hovering in the shadows; they couldn't get into Russia soon enough. Hitler was incensed and prone to go off repeatedly on long tirades against the Americans, Roosevelt in particular, and American Jewish high finance. His only solace was that it gave him the excuse to declare war, should he feel like it – as if he didn't have enough enemies to contend with already.

So news of the Yugoslavian coup on 27 March 1941 went down particularly badly with the Führer. His response was to order the immediate invasion and crushing of the Yugoslavians. Again, it was left to the Army – and General Halder and his staff – rather than the OKW to devise a

Left: British Commander of the Mediterranean Fleet, Andrew Browne Cunningham.

Right: Adrian Warburton. Few pilots can have appeared so unpromising, yet from Malta he swiftly developed into one of the best reconnaissance pilots in the RAF.

Below left: General Richard O'Connor (*left*), whose tiny Western Desert Force routed the Italians, and his C-in-C, General Sir Archibald Wavell.

Above right: Maresciallo Rodolfo Graziani, who understood that his Italian forces were ill-trained and -equipped to take the offensive.

Below: In Libya, in Greece and in East Africa columns of Italian POWs became a common site. These are just some of the 133,000 captured during Operation COMPASS.

Left: Indian troops in East Africa. Most British troops in the Middle East theatre were from India and the Dominions, which made geographical good sense.

Below: Italian 105/28 field guns, dating from 1913. Rusting versions of these were given to Sergio Fabbri on his posting to Tripoli.

Above left: General Rommel, who reached Libya in February 1941.

Above right: A German and an Italian share a smoke. Most Germans had little more than contempt for their Axis allies.

Left: Hermann Balck (*centre*), in his Panzer Mk III in Greece in April 1941.

Above: The Operations Room at Derby House, Liverpool, HQ of the Royal Navy Western Approaches and the hub of an increasingly sophisticated shipping and anti-submarine warfare operation.

Above: The open bridge of a British destroyer. Once the invasion threat was over, convoy protection increased significantly.

Left: Otto Kretschmer was one of the most successful U-boat aces, but he was captured in March 1941. Two others, Günter Prien and Joachim Schepke, were killed that same month.

Right: Erich Topp, another of the pre-war U-boat force.

The Bowles twins, Henry and Tom, at Fort Benning in 1940.

Kit inspection at Fort Benning. The US Army was still tiny and poorly equipped in 1940.

Left: Hajo Herrmann, whose unauthorized bombing of Piraeus harbour was stunningly successful.

Right: A wrecked British Blenheim in Greece.

Below: British forces on the retreat again. Most British troops were safely evacuated, but, as at Dunkirk, much of their equipment was left behind.

General John Kennedy, the British Director of Military Operations.

Above: Stanley Christopherson (*centre*), with fellow Sherwood Rangers at Tobruk.

Below: A German soldier points to a map of Tobruk, which was surrounded and besieged.

RITORNEREMO!

Above: An Italian poster attempting to put a gloss on the loss of East Africa, centrepiece of Mussolini's pre-war empire. It promises a return and victory.

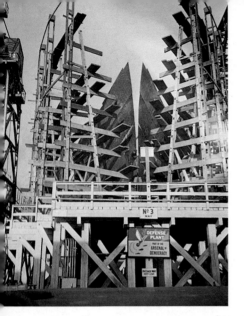

Above right: Bill Knudsen, giant of the US car industry, was brought in by the President to help kick-start US rearmament.

Left and above left: Liberty ships under construction, designed by Cyril Thompson in the UK and adapted for production in the US. Construction king Henry Kaiser managed to build two new shipyards on either side of the US in just five months.

Below: Oliver Lyttelton, brought into government by Churchill, visits a British factory. 'Steel not flesh' was one of Britain's overriding strategies for war.

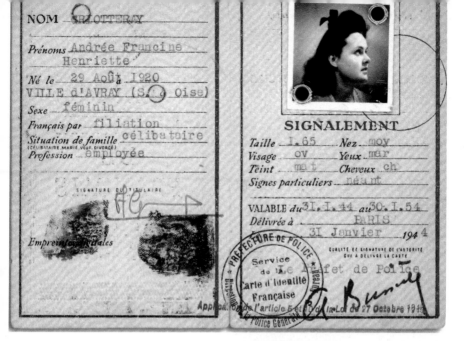

Above: The ID card of Andrée Griotteray, the young Parisienne working in French police headquarters.

Right: Freddie Knoller and family in Vienna in happier times before the war. Freddie is sitting with his beloved cello.

Below: Firefighters tackle a blaze in London. The Blitz began in September 1940 and continued until May 1941. The damage was considerable but not sufficient to seriously affect Britain's war effort.

Top: Hitler with his generals. The Führer's meddling and micro-managing of military operations was disastrous for Germany and often made no strategic sense.

Above left: General Bernard Freyberg VC. His courage could not be doubted, but he had been over-promoted and his misjudgement on Crete helped lose the island.

Above right: German *Fallschirmjäger* dropping on Crete as a Ju52 falls in flames.

Left: The evacuation of Crete cost the Mediterranean Fleet dear. Here HMS *Jackal* comes under attack.

plan of action in lightning-quick time. Fortunately for them, this was more straightforward than it might have been: with Bulgaria, Hungary and Romania all now in the Axis camp, and with planning for Operation MARITA, the invasion of Greece, at an advanced stage, the forces needed were pretty much in position. The German 2. Armee, already in Austria, swiftly moved south into Hungary and, with the Italians on its right and the Hungarian Third Army on its left, on 6 April struck with a *Schwerpunkt* of three large mechanized columns, all driving towards the capital, Belgrade. This was following the classic Prussian principle of *Bewegungskrieg*: to head towards an objective the enemy simply could not afford to lose and would therefore have to defend. At the same time, a further mechanized force headed to Zagreb, while in the far south General von Kleist's panzer group drove north from Bulgaria.

The Luftwaffe crushed the Yugoslav Air Force, mostly on the ground, in about twenty minutes, losing just two aircraft itself in the process. Meanwhile, the Yugoslav Army, a million strong but stretched around an impossibly long border of nearly 2,000 miles, and badly short of modern equipment, crumbled in just a few days under this clinical perfection of what had become known to the wider world as 'Blitzkrieg': lightning war.

On the same day that the Germans stormed into Yugoslavia, they also struck Greece, attacking with 12. Armee from Bulgaria and then splitting, with one force striking west then south from Yugoslavia and another bludgeoning its way towards the Aliákmon Line. Among those storming into southern Yugoslavia was Günther Sack, now a *Feldwebel* and in charge of ten men and a quick-firing light flak gun of 86. Light Anti-Aircraft Battalion. 'I started this morning!' he scribbled breathlessly in his diary. 'We crossed the border at the craziest speed I've ever seen. We saw our Stukas, about thirty planes, accompanied by twenty fighters flying towards the enemy. Then we heard their detonations in the distance and saw them circle over the enemy. It was a fantastic image of modern war.' The following day, they reached Skopje, and Sack was shocked by the levels of destruction caused by the Luftwaffe. 'Our population at home should be very thankful that they do not have to experience a war in their own country. We are seeing horrible pictures here.'

Air power was once again leading the way for the Germans. The battle for Yugoslavia had begun with the almost instant obliteration of the Air Force, but in Greece it was not the Stukas Sack had been watching, but a

INVASION OF YUGOSLAVIA AND GREECE, April 1941

N

AUSTRIA

WEICHS
Graz
XLIX
LI
XLVI

Budapest

HUNGARY

HUNGARIAN

Szeged

ROMANIA

Zagreb
Karlovac
14
8
XLI

Banda
Luka
16

Belgrade

Bucharest

Italian
Ambrosio
Travnik
Sarajevo
Uzice

YUGOSLAVIA

Nis
11

XI

BULGARIA

1 Panzer
KLEIST

Dubrovnik

*Adriatic
Sea*

Skopje

5
XIV
Sofia

XL

Plovdiv
16
Erdirne

ALBANIA

Bitola

XVIII

XXX

ITALY

Brindisi

Berat

Sérrai
Kilkis
Edessa

Drama
Xanthi
Thasos
Komotini
Alexandroupo

3

Kozani
Katerine

Salonica

Samothrace

Corfu
Ioannina

GREEK

GREEK
Arta

1

Larisa
Trikkala

2
5

GREEK

Lemnos

TURK

*Aegean
Sea*

Lesbos

Lamia
2

Missolonghi

GREECE

Khalkis
Marathon
Athens
Corinth

Khios

Andros

5
Pyrgos
Tripolis

Tinos

Naxos

Kalamata

4

KEY

→ German attacks
-→ Allied evacuation
--- German front line
●●● Allied fortified front line
Allied troops
German troops
1 German front line 16 April
2 German front line 20 April
3 German front line 23 April
4 British evacuation 22–28 April

Monemvasia

Crete

0 ___ 100 km

0 ___ 100 miles

Luftwaffe strike on the largest port, Piraeus, which did untold damage to the Allied cause.

Among those attacking Piraeus that night were Ju88s of 'Adlergeschwader' III/KG30, based at Gerbini in Sicily on the plain of Catania. One of the *Gruppe's Staffel* commanders was Oberleutnant Hajo Herrmann, who had recovered from his injuries at Schiphol and been based in Sicily, attacking Malta and British targets in Cyrenaica, for the past couple of months.

Their task that night was to lay mines at the narrow entrance to the harbour with the hope that they would sink ships as they entered and then block ships trying to both go in and out. Each Ju88 was to be loaded with two mines each, but, during his recent operations against Malta, Herrmann had surreptitiously ordered his ground crew to increase the bomb load as well. Now, as he sat beneath the olive trees early that evening listening to the sound of his aircraft being warmed up, it occurred to him that two parachute mines seemed a bit feeble. With this in mind, he told his ground crew to add two 250kg bombs to the payload in addition to the mines.

It was around 450 miles to Piraeus, and with the extra load they would have enough fuel for 900; so it was cutting it a little tight, but Herrmann was confident it would be all right. Heading over to his aircraft, he watched the ground crew putting the bombs in place and then discussed with the other crews the plan of attack; they had done many such mine-laying operations by moonlight before and this latest one was nothing for them to be overly concerned about.

Herrmann had hoped that darkness would fall before the commander, Major Arved Crüger, would come around and see the bombs hanging under each wing, but his hopes were in vain. 'I thought as much,' Crüger told him. 'I'm telling you – take them off! You know very well what the weather's like: heavy cumulus over Greece up to a great height. We'll have to overfly them, and it can't be done with the extra load.' Reluctantly, Herrmann told his chief mechanic, Oberfeldwebel Lorenz, to take off the bombs. Then, once Crüger had gone, Lorenz stood there looking at Herrmann, not moving. There was clearly a choice to be made: Herrmann could defy his commander or do as he had been ordered. Silently, he stared at Lorenz, and, as he put his foot on the first rung of the ladder up into the aircraft, a moment of silent understanding passed between them. The bombs would stay.

They took off shortly before sunset, at intervals of a minute or two, and headed due east to avoid any night Beaufighters from Malta, climbing to around 2,500 feet. Crüger had suggested that because of the predicted cloud, once over Greece they should climb above it and fly directly to Piraeus using the light of the half-moon, but Herrmann, with his heavier load, decided to opt for a low approach beneath the cloud and through the Gulf of Patras and the Isthmus of Corinth. In any case, he always preferred a lower approach if at all possible; he disliked wearing an oxygen mask and nor did he like wearing the heavy overalls and fur boots needed for higher-altitude flying: they made him sweat during take-off, which then turned icy cold once aloft.

Key to their chances of safely negotiating this lower route and not flying into a mountain was going to be hitting the coast at a precise point, and, despite Herrmann's mounting anxiety as they crossed the sea, they managed it perfectly, although they immediately hit a thunderstorm as a blinding flash of lightning lit the sky. Of course, Herrmann thought to himself: they were in the land of the ancient Gods. They flew on, across the isthmus and over Plataea and Marathon, and then there was Athens in the pale moonlight. For the first time in his life, Herrmann was looking at the places so familiar to him from his schoolboy studies. 'Wonderful scenes,' he noted, 'made living by youthful memories.'

They circled low, then turned towards the harbour, knowing there was no better navigational aid than the enemy's displays of searchlights and flak. The key was to weave from side to side and constantly adjust speed. And because the harbour entrance was so narrow, they had to fly low to drop the mines: the trick was to head straight in then perform a break-neck half-turn, and all at the reduced speed of around 200 mph to ensure the parachute mines opened as planned.

Herrmann turned the aircraft and prepared to make his run. As they approached the harbour entrance, they were bathed in light as search-lights hit them from ahead and both sides. Tracer and rapid-firing flak were flashing past them, glowing chunks of metal. Then the mines were dropped, as the crew's machine-gunners fired for all they were worth. Someone said, 'Whose idea was this operation anyway?' as Herrmann put them into a full-throttle climb. They were out over the harbour again. Herrmann knew he now had to wait until the rest of his *Staffel* finished the mining job before he could return and use the bombs he had added. They could see a long line of ships moored alongside the quay, and agreed that a low horizontal approach gave them the best chance of hitting a target. After the navigator had made his careful calculations, Herrmann circled them out over the island of Salamis and then made his approach. As they got closer, flying in softly towards the west, the flak and search-lights had become more subdued, but they were still there. Herrmann reminded himself that it was not the red glow of tracer lines they needed to worry about but the afterglow left on the retina; if you were hit flying through flak, it was just bad luck. One had to be fatalistic; the more one was, the less one had to draw on reserves of courage.

They dropped low, now flying straight and level towards the harbour. 'Ten seconds to go,' said Schmetz, the observer and bomb aimer. Herrmann flattened out some more, opened the throttles a fraction and gave his instruments one last brief glance. His mouth was dry. Then the bombs were released, the Ju88, suddenly lightened, rose up, and Herrmann put the aircraft into a steep turn to port, waiting for the fifteen-second delay until the bombs detonated.

Suddenly, there was a massive bright flash, then a further explosion, and wild gusts of turbulence hurled the aircraft about violently. Rapidly regaining control, Herrmann turned out to sea and below in the port they could see yet more explosions and white glowing masses hurling them-selves into the night sky. What had happened? They had merely aimed for the largest ship; never had they seen a couple of bombs have such a devastating effect.

As they were escaping the fray and setting a course for home, a lone light anti-aircraft gun hit them with a hefty thump. Moments later, coolant began to leak and the temperature in the port engine began to rise. Herrmann cut the engine immediately to stop a possible seizure or, worse, a fire, and they had to continue on their way with just one engine, no easy task in a Ju88. 'Gloom took over,' Herrmann wrote, 'but the best way to get rid of it was by activity. So: throttle back. Ignition off. Propeller feathered, and press on one engine.'

After a long and fraught journey, they eventually made it to Rhodes, an island in the Dodecanese seized by the Italians back in 1912, and their prearranged emergency landing strip. It was also in completely the opposite direction, lying as it did just off the coast of Turkey. By the time they finally touched down, Herrmann had been struggling with cramps in his right leg for much of the journey. It was hardly a smooth landing: visibility was minimal, and they had no idea when the field might run out, but at last they came to a halt – alive and in one piece. For a moment, no one spoke. Herrmann just sat there then switched off the ignition for the starboard engine. In all his many combat operations, he had never felt happier to be back on hard ground. Then eventually he said, 'Out you get, men.'

Little did they realize it at the time, but the last-minute decision of Oberfeldwebel Lorenz and Herrmann to fly with those two bombs effectively sealed the fate of the Greeks on that opening night of the German invasion. The bombs struck the 12,000-ton freighter *Clan Fraser*, which had just arrived with a convoy and was carrying 350 tons of explosives. Only a hundred had been offloaded at the time it was hit. The explosion shattered windows in Athens seven miles away, *Clan Fraser* was obliterated and ten other ships totalling 41,000 tons were also destroyed in the massive explosion. Even worse, this almost seismic explosion wrecked the port so that no further ships could use the harbour for several months. In one chance strike, Greece's main port and the only one that could feasibly be used to supply the British was wiped out. No other single attack of the war had so far caused such astonishing levels of destruction.

It was a blow from which the British, and the Greeks, would not recover in Greece, and came just as British fortunes were turning against them in North Africa as well, where Rommel was refusing to be tamed. Once again, German commanders were ignoring the orders of their seniors. On that night in Piraeus, such insubordination had paid off spectacularly.

CHAPTER 42

Forwards and Backwards

STAFFELKAPITÄN MACKY STEINHOFF had taken a pretty dim view of night-fighting, and when Helmut Lent had discovered his entire *Gruppe* were about to join the newly formed *Nachtjagd-Division*, or Night-Fighter Division, the previous August, he had not been too happy about it either. 'We are currently converting to night-fighting,' Lent had written to his parents at the end of August. 'We are not very enthusiastic. We would sooner head directly for England.' I/ZG 76 had left Stavanger on 29 August and headed to Bavaria for training, where they became II/NJG 1 – the second *Gruppe* of Nachtjagdgeschwader 1.

Steinhoff had found the single-engine Me109 was not well suited to night-fighting, but the Me110 Zerstörer was ideal. Perhaps unsurprisingly, both the RAF and Luftwaffe were drawing similar conclusions about night-fighting. Both, for example, were discovering that firepower not speed was a key ingredient, while the greater size of a twin-engine aircraft meant there was more opportunity to accommodate extra equipment such as onboard radar.

Both sides had also discovered just how hard it was to intercept enemy raiders without onboard radar and a system of ground control. The Luftwaffe had used its highly effective Freya radar to pick up British bombers, but then had no real way of directing the night fighters to close in. A system called *Helle Nachtjagd* was developed whereby fighters were scrambled and then patrolled behind a belt of searchlights, which would, in theory, light up the enemy bomber so the night fighters could then see it and open fire. It wasn't very effective.

In October, Lent was posted to command 6/NJG 1, based at Deelen, an airfield just north of Arnhem, in Holland, with nine night-fighter crews under his command. Not until January did they score their first aerial victory, however. The *Geschwader* as a whole was doing better, but most successes were achieved by long-distance attacks on British bomber bases and hitting them either on the ground or as they took off.

In February, 6/NJG 1 got a second kill, a Wellington bomber, but Lent himself felt he was getting nowhere and asked the commander of NJG 1, Major Wolfgang Falck, if he could be transferred back to daylight operations. Falck asked him to be patient. Give it another four weeks, he told him. If he hadn't shot down an enemy plane by then, he promised he would give him his transfer.

Meanwhile, in England, Guy Gibson was finding it almost as hard to shoot down night raiders as Helmut Lent. The weather had not helped; in Lincolnshire it seemed that the almost continuous fog would never end. Everyone on the squadron was getting a bit low, so the CO, Wing Commander Charles Widdows, decided to hold a party towards the end of February, which took place at the Lincoln City Hall. Gibson and his fellows thought it a great success; the local council, on the other hand, thought it a disgrace, as drunk airmen caroused and sang and made a nuisance of themselves. Still, it was a fillip for the squadron and appeared to mark a change of fortune: the weather lifted, the Beaufighters were running smoothly and they were at last getting enough flying to train with the new Air Interceptor radar equipment and Ground Control of Interception.

Night-fighter successes were still not significant, although they were improving, but further strides had been made against the Luftwaffe's navigation beams. R. V. Jones, a scientist at Air Intelligence, had been largely responsible for cracking *Knickebein* and by the end of the year had worked out counter-measures for *X-Gerät* as well. Essentially, *X-Gerät*, also codenamed *Wotan*, was, like *Knickebein*, a system of converging radio beams, although they operated at a much higher frequency. This was understood early on, but not until a Heinkel 111 using *X-Gerät* was shot down and its equipment recovered in November was it discovered exactly what frequency it was using. This then enabled Jones and his team to adjust their jamming counter-signals accordingly. Also, because the Germans tended to set up their beams on a target the afternoon before an attack, it was now possible to pick these up and insert a false beam instead.

In this battle of the beams, the Luftwaffe quickly responded by setting the converging beams later in the day; this gave the British less time to insert a false beam, but it also made *X-Gerät* less effective. A further British counter-measure was 'Starfish' – an elaborate series of decoy fires controlled from a single bunker and set up around four miles from an obvious target such as a major factory, port or city centre. The idea was for the Starfish fires to simulate a fire-bombed town so that the night bombers would drop their ordnance there instead of the intended target.

As a further sign of rapid technological development, anti-aircraft fire was also improving, with the help of gun-laying radar. This was a small mobile radar system that could determine the height, direction and range of aircraft, which meant anti-aircraft guns could operate both more accurately and without searchlights. It was estimated that it took 20,000 rounds of ack-ack to shoot down an enemy bomber in September, but this had dropped to 3,000 by February. Even so, that was a lot of iron that was being pumped into the sky.

And German raids were still coming over. Following on from Hitler's War Directive No. 23 in February, more attacks were directed towards Britain's ports. Between 19 February and the second week of May, there were sixty-one attacks of more than fifty bombers, of which forty-six were directed against ports. Liverpool and Birkenhead were repeatedly attacked, for example. Some 316 bombers hit Merseyside on the night of 12 March, in an attack that lasted six hours. More than 500 people were killed and large numbers of houses were destroyed, as were a number of stores, maintenance sheds and dock facilities. A more minor casualty was Commander Donald Macintyre's car, much to his intense disgust.

That night, Guy Gibson and his observer, Sergeant James, were scrambled to try and intercept the raiders, and with the help of the new improved Mk IV AI set and ground control interception they managed to get on to the tail of one and open fire. Gibson noted 'one Hun destroyed' in his logbook, but he was probably mistaken; at least, there are no records of a German plane being shot down anywhere near him that night.

The next day, the Luftwaffe returned, making good use of fine weather. Others in 29 Squadron managed to shoot down a couple of bombers, including the CO, Wing Commander Widdows, whose cannon fire made the Ju88 he was attacking break up mid-air. Later, Gibson and James took off and from the ground were directed on to the tail of a Heinkel 111 heading towards Glasgow. Gibson spotted it visually from about 400 yards then stalked it, keeping below so that he could see the Heinkel's profile but not reveal his own. Closing to around 100 yards, he then opened fire, only for the guns to jam. The Heinkel immediately turned back towards the sea, but Gibson stuck to him and, having cleared the stoppage, managed to attack again and this time knocked out the port engine, then the starboard one as well, although the Beaufighter was hit by bits of debris which dented its wing. The Heinkel was now out of control and plunging towards the sea. 'When I first saw him I had screamed over the R.T. full of excitement,' recalled Gibson. 'When he was gliding down completely helpless I felt almost sorry for him.' The Heinkel came down just off Skegness and all the crew were killed. The following day, Gibson helped collect the tail assembly, which had come down on land and which they wanted to keep as a squadron trophy. In Skegness, the chief constable cheerfully told them one body had been found – an officer. 'Head nearly shot off by a cannon shell. Care to see him?' he asked Gibson.

'I was nearly sick,' wrote Gibson. The body had also been stripped of the pilot's Iron Cross and watch.

Terrible though the Blitz continued to be, the Luftwaffe was still no nearer to bringing Britain to its knees. The loss of life was tragic; the loss of facilities was frustrating and disruptive – but it was not making a decisive difference. Ships were still being unloaded; more war materiel was being produced than ever before; the British people were not suffering from a lack of food. And, all the while, the Luftwaffe's strength was being depleted. Some 3,132 aircraft had been lost between the beginning of August and the end of March, of which 2,265 had been to enemy action. In the same period, 8,121 German pilots and crew had been killed, wounded or taken prisoner. These were big numbers, especially since so many of those were men of experience and since the number of training schools had still not been sufficiently increased. Every operation over Britain – or North Africa, or Malta or Greece for that matter – meant risking men and machines that might be used in Hitler's latest go-for-broke gamble: the invasion of the Soviet Union.

Meanwhile, in the desert of Libya, Generalleutnant Erwin Rommel had further exceeded his orders. Despite quite explicit instructions from Generale Gariboldi, his new Italian superior in the theatre, and even Hitler himself, to hold firm and not go on the offensive, he had set off hell for leather and after easily taking El Agheila decided to press on further. Mersa Brega had been abandoned without a fight; then Agedabia fell as well. It was now clear to him that he had unhinged the entire British defences in Cyrenaica. He was quite right. Wavell had judged that the newly arrived Germans were unlikely to attack any time soon, and had they been led by almost any other commander that assumption would have been spot on. Because of the demands of East Africa and Greece, XIII Corps had been pulled out and replaced by the skeleton and essentially static Cyrenaica Command under General Sir Philip Neame. O'Connor had been promoted and given the job of overall commander of British troops in Egypt. His original force, 7th Armoured Division, which included Albert Martin and 2nd Rifle Brigade, had been sent back to Egypt. The result was that the only troops left in Libya were those new to North Africa, rather inexperienced, and a mish-mash of units like the split-up Sherwood Rangers Yeomanry.

Having studied the British methods against the Italians with keen interest, Rommel decided to ape those tactics – which in turn had mirrored his own approach during the French campaign – and split his force in three prongs, one heading along the coast while the other two dashed directly across the bulge of Cyrenaica.

Benghazi fell on 4 April 1941, then Derna on the 7th. Huge supply dumps at Msus and Mechili were taken too. Wavell responded by despatching O'Connor back up into the desert and taking over from Neame, who had no experience of desert fighting. O'Connor, who believed a golden opportunity to wrap up all of Libya had been missed, already blamed himself for not pushing on to Tripoli when he'd had the chance. It was too late for that now, but he did still hope Rommel could be stopped. His plan was to help organize defences further east, then, because he thought it would be a bad idea to replace Neame so soon and in the field, he suggested instead that he act as the latter's advisor and subsequently return to Egypt.

Unfortunately, after he had joined Neame at the front, they were both in a car miles behind what they thought was the front line, heading towards the new headquarters being set up at Timimi, when they were intercepted by a German reconnaissance patrol and promptly captured. 'It was a great shock,' said O'Connor. 'By sheer bad luck we drove into the one bit of desert in which the Germans had sent a reconnaissance group and we went bang into the middle of them.'

*

Wavell was distraught at the loss of O'Connor – so much so that he suggested to London that an offer of six Italian generals be made in exchange for his return. It was turned down, but this left only two British generals in the field and one of those, Gambier-Parry of the rookie 2nd Armoured Division, was then captured at Mechili, having held up Rommel's forces for a couple of days. Some of the troops at Mechili managed to successfully break out before they were overrun, and the slight delay certainly allowed General Leslie Morshead and his 9th Australian Division to fall back to Tobruk.

Still Rommel pressed on, his supply lines back to Tripoli ever more stretched. Tobruk was surrounded while other formations were sent on, capturing Bardia and then reaching the Egyptian border at Sollum. While these troops were still eating up miles of largely barren desert scrub, the rest of his forces were battering their heads against Tobruk, with its wide perimeter defences, wire and minefields.

Among the defenders desperately trying to hold back the Axis forces were Lieutenant Stanley Christopherson and Y Battery of the Sherwood Rangers Yeomanry. On 10 April, he and others from the battery had been formed into an ad hoc mobile patrol consisting of a mixture of trucks mounted with captured Breda machine guns, fifty-odd naval personnel and six tracked Bren carriers. The following day, the 11th, Christopherson was sent out to lead a patrol of three carriers, an 8 cwt truck and one 15 cwt truck. Having never operated with Bren carriers before, he decided to treat them like cavalry and sent two out as advance points, with the trucks following behind. Reaching the key point of El Gubi, he paused with one of the carriers and then sent the others off on single patrols. 'We saw nothing,' he noted in his diary, 'except some Arabs on camels whom we rushed across to inspect, thinking they be parachutists in disguise.' Later that day they were ordered back to Tobruk itself. The attack appeared to have been beaten off.

Rommel wasn't finished yet, however, and renewed his efforts to break through the following day. 'The battle still goes on around Tobruk,' wrote Christopherson. Artillery fire continued throughout the day. From the battery's position on the northern side of the Tobruk inlet, Christopherson was witnessing the confusion of battle first hand and for the first time, as piecemeal news reached them alongside even more rumours. Apparently, five German panzer attacks had been repulsed. Another rumour was that

German and Italian attacks had been engaging each other. 'I am not surprised,' jotted Christopherson, 'as we, the Germans and Italians are all using Italian tanks!' Enemy aircraft flew over and bombed them, among them Helmut Mahlke and the Stukas of III./StG 1. One was brought down, crash-landing with the pilot and air-gunner unhurt. The two Germans were brought to Navy House and assured their captors the war would be over by November.

The following day, 13 April, was Easter. There were three raids, the worst in the evening. Later, listening to the BBC news from London on their wireless, Christopherson and his friends in the battery learned they were now surrounded. More rumours arrived the following day: twelve tanks had supposedly broken through, but ten had been destroyed and more than 200 Germans captured. 'On the news tonight,' wrote Christopherson, 'we hear that Bardia and Sollum have both been captured by the Huns. But still,' he added, 'he has a hell of a line of communication to maintain.'

He was exactly right. It is interesting how much Rommel has been fêted for his performance in North Africa, and there is no doubt that the myth began with these stunning series of little victories. In just over a fortnight he had advanced 600 miles, which certainly caused consternation back in Britain and was an achievement leapt upon with glee by Goebbels and his propaganda people in Germany. The Germans had arrived in Libya with plenty of cameras and cine film, and Rommel was a man who enjoyed the attentions of the media; reporters and film units were never far away.

In the 1930s, there had been four main news film companies in Germany, including the German offshoot of Twentieth Century Fox, but after the fall of Poland Goebbels had brought them all under one – more manageable – umbrella, led by Universum Film AG in Berlin. The following year, to make the most of the string of victories, he established *Die Deutsche Wochenschau* – the 'German Weekly Newsreel' – the new title for the news films charting the progress of the war. All opened with stirring martial music, including a riff on the 'Horst Wessel Song', and used a fanfare motif derived from Liszt's *Les Préludes*. Then came the action, thick and fast, with narration by the voice-over artist Harry Giese. The *Wochenschau* films were shown repeatedly in every cinema, and when the propaganda machine decided to focus on an individual, he or she soon became a national hero.

Rommel was a gift. He was smashing the arrogant *Engländer*, who, as everyone knew, was the most dangerous enemy. Africa looked exotic, and Rommel had captured a pair of British sand goggles, which he consciously perched above the peak of his cap; it gave him an extra bit of raffish flair. The Nazis and wider German public were enthralled by the news of this dashing panzer commander.

Not everyone in Germany was so seduced, however, not least General Halder, Chief of Staff of the Army, who was incensed that Rommel should have blatantly disobeyed orders and been frittering away troops for not very much gain – and not just any old troops. One of those lost in the attempt to take Tobruk was General Heinrich von Prittwitz, commander of 15. Panzerdivision. Rommel's forces were now 900 miles from Tripoli and there was no question of going any further while Tobruk still held. Isolated on the mainland it may have been, but there was no reason why the town could not be supplied by sea indefinitely. All Rommel had gained was a lot of strategically unimportant desert, but he had over-stretched his supply lines and lost far too many men and too much materiel. British forces had suffered too, but for the most part they had scuttled back without heavy casualties; they had certainly not been destroyed as the Italian Tenth Army had been. And this was the point: the main purpose of taking land in the Western Desert was as a means of destroying the enemy, but if all the advance did was make that enemy scamper backwards and at the same time make your own supply situation that much harder, there really was very little point to the exercise. From Britain's perspective, the loss of O'Connor was a blow and pride had taken a dent, but there was little intrinsic value to the large tract of land between Alexandria and Tripoli; the coastal towns in between were really just staging posts. Holding on to Tobruk was a brake on Rommel – a means of preventing him pushing further into Egypt.

In any case, Rommel's advance had meant a diversion of important air resources. Helmut Mahlke and his Stukas could not attack Tobruk and Malta at the same time; Hajo Herrmann could not bomb Piraeus and Valletta at the same time. With the Luftwaffe now concentrating on North Africa and the Balkans, Fortress Malta was able to strike back, with its bombers and submarine flotilla attacking those all-important convoys from Italy that provided the Axis with its only real link to North Africa.

It was for this reason, as well as Rommel's spurious wasting of precious resources, that Halder and senior staff at the OKH were so annoyed.

'Rommel hasn't given us a clear report for days,' he added that same day. 'I have a feeling something's wrong. All the comments I read in the officers' reports or in personal letters indicate that Rommel is in no way up to his leadership task. He storms around all day long with formations strewn all over the place, launches reconnaissance missions, fritters away his troops.' In fact, Halder thought Rommel had gone mad and so despatched his Quartermaster General, General Friedrich Paulus, to fly to North Africa and talk some sense into him. At a time when Halder really needed Paulus to focus on BARBAROSSA, this was a further unwelcome distraction from the main event.

Of much greater importance to Britain that April was ensuring that something was salvaged from the disaster looming in Greece, and that Iraq, where there had been a pro-Axis coup led by Rashid Ali al-Gaylani at the beginning of the month, was swiftly stabilized once more. There was also the small matter of the ongoing war in East Africa, which was going altogether much better but was still a drain on troops and resources.

In fact, both sides were being drawn into battles they did not want to fight as Germany was being sucked ever more into the Mediterranean and Middle Eastern theatre. The difference, of course – although Britain did not know it at the time – was that Germany was just a couple of months away from the biggest land operation on which it had ever embarked. For Britain, however, the Middle East and the Mediterranean was the only theatre in which its troops were actively engaged in anything other than clandestine operations.

Among those leading the charge into Greece was Oberst Hermann Balck, who in December had been posted away from 1. Rifle Regiment, promoted and given command of 3. Panzerregiment instead, part of 2. Panzerdivision. Its task was to strike west across the Bulgarian border and into Yugoslavia, then turn south, following the Strumica River, and head towards Kilkis–Salonica. In so doing, they were effectively outflanking the well-built defences of the Metaxas Line that covered Macedonia from Bulgaria but not Yugoslavia.

They crossed the border then followed 2. Panzerdivision's right column, which had overrun the Yugoslavian defence. Thereafter, however, the roads worsened and it seemed to Balck that all he and his men were good for was shifting vehicles from the quagmire. Communication with other units was also difficult with radio systems failing; the difficulties of operating in tough, mountainous terrain and with very limited roads were becoming all too apparent.

None the less, with Yugoslavia now no barrier, the Greek defensive plan had rapidly come unstuck; the German units that had struck the western end of the Metaxas Line had hit a brick wall, such was the strength of the defences. Those now pushing south from Yugoslavia – such as Balck's 3. Panzerregiment – were discovering that apart from mud, mountains and packs of feral dogs, there was little to stop them driving straight for Salonika and in so doing encircling the 60,000 men of the Greek East Macedonian Army, which had now surrendered.

It was this terrible realization that had made the Greek Army command in Athens order them to lay down their weapons: the outflanking of their position, combined with heavy air attacks from the Luftwaffe, meant there was no chance of escape. Even so, Balck was surprised – to him, the Germans' own situation appeared far from good: the conditions were getting the better of them and they were desperately low on fuel. 'The old adage is never give up in war,' wrote Balck. 'The enemy is at least as bad off as you are.' It was certainly the case in this instance.

Balck and his men entered Salonika on 9 April to a rapturous reception. Crowds were shouting 'Heil Hitler!', throwing flowers and raising their arms in salute. Balck was utterly nonplussed. The Greeks' biggest fear appeared to be that they would be handed over to the Italians or Bulgarians.

Balck's 3. Panzerregiment halted for several days, a snow-capped Mount Olympus now within sight. He found the view of the mountain rather overwhelming in its beauty. 'I sat, pensively in awe,' he wrote, 'holding my copy of Homer that I had brought along. I never put him away while I was in Greece.'

The Germans had been genuinely surprised and impressed by the extensive defences of the Metaxas Line and next to bar their way was the Aliákmon Line, not so heavily constructed but a strong position nevertheless. On paper, both these positions had appeared to be very strong, but they revealed the fundamental weakness of linear defence: that if the plan went awry, they quickly came undone.

The rapid defeat of Yugoslavia changed everything. Not only could the Metaxas Line be outflanked within a few days, but so too could the Aliákmon Line, as the bulk of the remaining Greek forces were still facing the Italians on the Albanian front. Realizing this, Greek and British forces hurriedly tried to move the Aliákmon position south and west in an effort to block this second southward thrust. It was, of course, too little, too late, even though bad weather spared them from the Luftwaffe. The Greek divisions, which had the furthest to travel, also struggled to fall back through the mountains. Cohesion was lost, but, in any case, the British and Greek divisions had almost no chance of stopping the full force of the German 12. Armee, now advancing in two giant thrusts, one from Salonika and the other from the central southern Yugoslavian border, not least because not all the British units had reached the front yet.

Flying into this maelstrom was Pilot Officer Roald Dahl, a 24-year-old who had only recently been passed fit to fly after suffering a near-fatal crash. At the time of the accident, he had just been posted to his first operational squadron and had been on his way to join them when he had crash-landed in the desert, cracking his skull and nose, knocking out several teeth, and then narrowly avoiding almost complete incineration.

Having been declared fit to fly once more, he had been posted to RAF Ismailia in Egypt and told to take a Hurricane to join the rest of 80 Squadron at Eleusis in Greece. Rather worryingly, he had never flown a Hurricane or any kind of monoplane fighter before; he had been in a Gloster Gladiator biplane when he'd had his accident. Moreover, the only way he could fly to Greece was by using auxiliary fuel tanks. If they failed him halfway across the Mediterranean, that would have been that; there would be no one to rescue him. All in all, it was a daunting proposition.

Dahl was given two days to familiarize himself with the Hurricane then off he went on 13 April. At six feet six inches tall, he quickly discovered that whether the drop-tanks would work was the least of his problems. For the best part of four and a half hours he flew with crippling cramps as his legs were wedged into the narrow and shallow cockpit. By the time he finally reached Eleusis, he was so doubled up he had to be pulled out of the aircraft by two members of the ground crew.

One of these men was unimpressed to see him arrive with a brand-new Hurricane that had been shipped from England to the Middle East and then to Greece. What was going to happen to it, he kept asking Dahl rhetorically.

'What *is* going to happen to it?' Dahl replied.

'Crash bang wallop!' replied the corporal. 'Shot down in flames! Explodin' in the air! Ground-strafed by the One-Oh-Nines right 'ere where we're standin' this very moment! Why, this kite won't last one week in this place!'

Dahl was rather taken aback by this and wondered why the corporal was being such a prophet of doom. It was because, the corporal explained, they were so badly outnumbered. They had just fourteen Hurricanes left at Eleusis – fifteen now that Dahl had arrived. At first Dahl refused to believe him, but he soon after learned to his horror this was indeed the truth.

In fact, the RAF contingent sent to Greece comprised four Blenheim bomber squadrons (now considered obsolete back home in Britain), one Blenheim night-fighter squadron (ditto), three fighter squadrons (not all equipped with Hurricanes) and one Army Co-operation squadron. Against this, the Luftwaffe had Fliegerkorps VIII, supported by Fliegerkorps X on Sicily, which were bristling with Me109s, Me110s, Stukas and Ju88s, and which had amounted to the best part of a thousand aircraft by the end of March, in addition to 160 Italian aircraft in Albania and a further 150 in Italy. British planes had amounted to just eighty in total. By the time Roald Dahl touched down at Eleusis, there were about half that figure remaining. He was entering the fray with just seven hours on Hurricanes and no combat experience whatsoever. Sending him to Greece was a ridiculous posting.

None the less, on his first combat sortie on 15 April, he did manage to shoot down a Ju88. Having spotted a formation of six of these aircraft, he tore after them, and although their rear-gunners immediately opened fire, the mountains near Khalkis suddenly narrowed, forcing them into line astern, which meant there was now only one plane firing at him, not six. Closing in, Dahl pressed his thumb down on the gun button, felt the Hurricane shudder as the eight Brownings spat out bullets and was astonished to see bits of metal falling and black smoke start pouring from the bomber's engine. Slowly, the Junkers rolled over and then a string of airmen jumped, their parachutes billowing open moments later. 'I watched spellbound,' he wrote. 'I couldn't believe that I had actually shot down a German bomber. But I was immensely relieved to see the parachutes.'

That same day, Günther Sack and his flak battery were advancing towards the Aliákmon Line, travelling along winding tracks through craggy, shrub-covered hills. Eventually halting, they set up their platoon on a hill overlooking the Aliákmon River, from where they could see the entire valley. From his position, he watched columns of British vehicles being shelled by German artillery. 'Next to us a 8.8cm takes up position,' he scribbled. 'On the other side of the valley, thirty Stukas and just as many HS123s are bombing a pass. It is an awe-inspiring spectacle.' Neither Stukas nor 88mms could dislodge the defenders, however. An attempted river crossing failed, and the following day Sack was marvelling at how the Tommies could withstand an attack by thirty Stukas.

Meanwhile, Roald Dahl had managed to shoot down another enemy plane the following day. None the less, while he was helping the RAF put up what fight it could, a further plan was being drawn up between the British and the Greeks to withdraw all forces further south from Mount Olympus all the way across the country, but for the Greeks in Albania, this was a crushing blow. Having pushed the Italians back out of Greece with such determination, to then give up those gains without a fight was more than many were prepared to stomach. The battle for Greece was fast going wrong, and it was only the fuel shortages, bad weather and difficulties of terrain that were holding back the Germans and giving the Allies even the smallest of breathing spaces.

The weather soon took a turn for the better, however – or for the worse as far as the Allies were concerned. Alf Parbery and his fellows in J Section, 6th Division Signals, were dug in beneath the shadow of Mount Olympus, and by 14 April they were coming under heavy and sustained air attack. Parbery was making a mental note of the numbers: twenty on one raid, then fifteen, all dive-bombing repeatedly and strafing too. 'Today, like yesterday,' he jotted on the 15th, 'the German aircraft have been bombing at will. The sky is never without a plane.'

Already, this new, wider, hastily conceived second Aliákmon Line was beginning to crumble; the German strike south through the centre from Yugoslavia had completely unhinged their position before it had been properly formed. There was now little choice but to pull back across the Plain of Thessaly to the south of Olympus and to fall back to the next defence line, which, for the British, was Thermopylae, where in 480 BC the Spartans had made such an heroic defence against the Persians.

Alf Parbery and J Section pulled out on the 16th. The following day, they were halfway across the Plain of Thessaly and sheltering from the seemingly ceaseless air attacks in Larissa. Parbery saw one man killed and the company commander wounded that day but despite the incessant nature of the air attacks, casualties were proving surprisingly slight. Hitler had made it clear he wanted the British forces in Greece encircled and annihilated; so far, however, they appeared to be getting away.

One of the reasons for this was the stout defence by the rearguard making good use of the naturally defensive terrain. Oberst Balck and his men had been held up first by the stoic defence of the New Zealanders and then in the narrow Tempe Valley Pass, which led into the Plain of Thessaly, by the Australians. On one side was a railway, which was of little use to them in their tanks, half-tracks and armoured cars; on the other was a road. In between was a torrential river, while from the hills the Australian rearguard were firing at them. Balck decided to risk sending a panzer across the river and to his relief it worked. Painfully slowly, one panzer after another gingerly made the crossing. Two were lost in the process, but eventually, by the end of the 18th, his leading company was over the river and able to push the rearguard back and clear of the pass. By the 19th, they too had reached Larissa.

By that time, Alf Parbery and much of 16th Brigade had left, travelling down congested roads throughout the night. They were still heading south on the 20th when Parbery learned that two of his best mates had been hit during an attack by a dive-bomber. Harry Searle had been killed and his great pal Tiny Dunbar had lost a leg. With incredible heroism, Dunbar had managed to drag himself over to the mortally wounded Searle in an effort to administer aid. It had been in vain.

With the German 12. Armee more mechanized than had been the case the previous year, its men were discovering how easily congestion built up, especially on narrow roads that had been repeatedly bombed and with bridges collapsed and blown up. Furthermore, the British rearguard, using their artillery to good effect, were also able to hold them up further, which allowed the main body to escape south.

The decision to evacuate had come at the urging of the Greeks. On the evening of the 21st, the Greek Army of Epirus, on the western side of the country, had surrendered and the King and Government now accepted that further sacrifice of British troops was pointless; the Greek Army was exhausted after six long months of winter fighting. The German attack had been a battle too far. Surrender was now the only option.

For Germany, that was another country conquered, another foe vanquished. Greece was now in their hands, the shambles created by the Italians put right, and yet, by 1 May, nearly all the British troops had got away. All Hitler's enemies had so far succumbed to his will, but not the British, his most dangerous enemy. Once again, they had escaped to fight another day.

CHAPTER 43

Gains and Losses

IN MARCH 1941, five U-boats had been sunk, and the loss of the three greatest aces within a fortnight was a particularly harsh blow, which Dönitz and all his staff at BdU felt keenly. It was a blow for Goebbels too. Nazi Germany was proud of its heroes and whether they were dashing generals or panzer commanders, or fighter and U-boat aces, these men were pin-ups, famous throughout the Reich and featured regularly in magazines and newsreels. This, of course, was all very well and inspiring while they continued to shoot down Spitfires or sink ever-larger numbers of merchant vessels, but was rather humiliating – not to say tragic – when they were either killed or taken prisoner. As much as anything, it reminded Germans that the war, apparently won the previous summer, was not over at all. Rather, it was going on, and would continue to do so, plucking ever more of the Reich's young men and heroes.

For Dönitz, men like Prien, Schepke and Kretschmer were quite simply irreplaceable. The pool of men who had long years of experience both of the sea and on U-boats before the war ever began was diminishing fast. Time and time again, Dönitz found himself rueing the fact that the U-boat arm of the Kriegsmarine had come so low in the pecking order compared with other services and even other naval requirements. Had it been larger before the war, more men of the calibre of Kretschmer et al. could have been drawn to it, and with the successes the U-boats had had in the last war, this was such an obvious policy. If Britain was its greatest enemy, as Hitler had repeatedly claimed in the build-up to war, then why had he not thought to build up his U-boat fleet as a priority for the Kriegsmarine? Even in the summer of 1940, when U-boat production was set at twenty-five per month, Göring had wilfully restricted the Kriegsmarine's allocation of steel, which had, in turn, ensured even this number was unachievable; as it was, the Kriegsmarine received only 5 per cent of the Reich's total steel production. As a result, new U-boats were reaching the BdU at a rate of just six per month in the second half of 1940 and had risen to only thirteen in the first few months of 1941; on one level this was a good number, but with the rule of thirds – a third at sea, a third heading back, and a third undergoing training or repairs – this meant a monthly operational increase of only four or five.

There was worse to come, however, not that Dönitz and his staff were aware of it at the time. On 9 May, Fritz-Julius Lemp, commander of *U-110*, who had on his previous patrol escaped from Donald Macintyre and EG5's grasp, was caught attacking convoy OB 318. Surfacing after being heavily depth-charged, the boat was then pummelled with gunfire and Lemp killed. Rather than ram the U-boat, however, Commander Addison Joe Baker-Creswell of the destroyer *Bulldog* decided to board the boat and took off *U-110*'s codebooks and its Enigma coding machine.

Up until this point, both sides had sporadically been breaking the other's codes. The German decryption service, the Beobachtungsdienst, or B-Dienst, had begun solving parts of the British naval codes before the war, and during the Norwegian campaign, for example, had managed to garner useful information about the movements of Allied forces at sea. The British changed their codebooks in August 1940, and it took several months again before the B-Dienst could decrypt both the Naval Cypher No. 1 and the Naval Code, and even then often too slowly to have any effect. This eventually amounted to around one third of the intercepted messages, some of which were used for directing U-boats.

By August 1940, British cryptanalysts at the Government Code and Cypher School at Bletchley Park had managed to gain all eight of the rotors used in the naval Enigma M-3 machine. Five had been handed over by the Poles back in 1939, while rotors VI and VII had been captured when *U-33* was sunk, and finally VIII was captured in August the previous year. Despite this, they were cracking only around 10 per cent of the Kriegsmarine's naval traffic. A major step forward occurred with a Commando raid on German shipping in the Lofoten Islands in the north of Norway, in which the latest cipher materials were captured.

Further cipher material was captured when a British navalforce boarded a German weather trawler in fog off the Dutch coast at the beginning of May. Then, just two days later, came the Aladdin's cave of *U-110*. The potential intelligence breakthrough this might bring was enormous.

There was, however, another sign of Britain's growing advantage in the Atlantic, where the reach of its naval escorts was dramatically increasing. In the opening eighteen months of the war, a lack of mid-Atlantic refuelling bases combined with a shortage of escorts had meant there was a large section in the middle of the ocean where the convoys were on their own, and, as a consequence, increasingly vulnerable. In April 1941, however, naval and air bases had finally opened in Iceland, which ensured the British from then on could escort convoys as far as 35°W, a huge improvement. Then, on 20 May, the Royal Canadian Navy agreed to close the final gap that ran from 35°W to Newfoundland.

This was already another crucial marker in Canada's huge commitment to the war. Its Navy had effectively had to grow from scratch, and it had, by May, some eighty corvettes either in service or nearly built. Canadian crews lacked the training and experience of the Royal Navy, but this was hardly surprising considering the speed of growth. The importance of the Newfoundland Escort Force – or NEF, as it was called – was that it meant convoys could be escorted from one side of the ocean to the other for the very first time. Under operational control of Western Approaches Command and following the Western Approaches Convoy Instructions (WACIs) as issued by Admiral Noble and his staff in April, they increased the strength and scale of the Allied escort forces in the Atlantic massively.

Under this new arrangement, Canadian Escort Groups would hand over to British ones at the Mid-Ocean Meeting Point, or MOMP, then head to Iceland for refuelling and rearming, before rejoining a westbound convoy heading back. The RAF also handed over a number of flying boats to the Royal Canadian Air Force, while its own Coastal Command had also significantly grown by the middle of the year, with more than 200 maritime patrol aircraft operating from Iceland in addition to those based in the west of the United Kingdom.

For the crews, anti-U-boat patrols were thankless: they meant long hours airborne, endlessly scanning a vast and often empty sea, and battling the capricious harshness of the Atlantic weather. But they were making a difference. Dönitz was forced to push his U-boats ever further west to the one gap that still existed in the Atlantic defences: the area in the mid-Atlantic where aircraft could not yet reach.

Meanwhile, in the Mediterranean, Admiral Cunningham's fleet had successfully evacuated almost all the British forces from Greece. Alf Parbery had left early in the morning on 27 April, the same day German troops marched into Athens, and by 4.30 a.m. they were under attack from the Luftwaffe. 'We had miraculous escapes,' recalled Parbery, 'and so did other ships. The explosions would hide half of the ships at times.' Their gunners never stopped firing and Parbery reckoned they had shot down nine aircraft. More importantly, they all managed to make it safely to Alexandria. In all, 58,364 men had been transported to Greece and 50,732 were brought out. Some were Greeks and Yugoslavians, but, in all, the British had suffered just 12,000 casualties, many of whom were sick and wounded and later returned to active service. The British also lost 8,000 trucks, 209 aircraft and two Royal Navy ships and four transports.

These were significant losses, but, all things considered, Britain had got off lightly. It had honoured its treaty pledges to the Greeks and had caused the Germans a massive logistical headache by making them divert so many men and resources to a theatre so close in time to their planned invasion of Russia, which Hitler had already been forced to delay by a month from May to June. Admittedly, this had given General Adolf von Schell the time to get more trucks coming off the production line to the forward units massing in Poland, but there was no denying it would have been best to use every possible day in the Soviet summer. By delaying BARBAROSSA until the third week of June, they had denied themselves almost two months of the campaigning season.

In London and Cairo, however, this was unknown. In fact, General John Kennedy's appreciation had been almost perfect: Greece had ended in failure and Britain had consequently lost the initiative in North Africa. None the less, as he had consoled Dill, it had not proved disastrous in the big scheme of things, and that night Churchill, in his broadcast to the British nation, also pointed out that while the setbacks in North Africa and Greece were hard to bear, it was important to keep a sense of proportion.

In this he was surely quite right. Together Britain and the United States possessed command of the oceans, 'and will soon obtain decisive superiority in the air'. The USA, he added, possessed more wealth and more technical resources, and made more steel, than the rest of the world put together. This was undeniable. Certainly, his speech gave heart to Gwladys Cox, who always, like the vast majority of Britons, listened to Churchill's broadcasts. 'Really, he is a remarkable person!' she noted. 'He has a great grasp of his subject, as he has of his audience.'

Nor was it all bad news for the British in any case, even though defeat in the recent battles in North Africa and in Greece had caused doom and gloom back home in Britain. By the end of the month, it looked certain that the East African war was nearing its end. Asmara, the capital of Eritrea, had been captured, Emperor Haile Selassie's British-mentored forces had captured key Italian forts and the British 11th African Division had taken Addis Ababa along with 8,000 Italian prisoners. On 2 May, Haile Selassie returned triumphantly to his old capital, five years after he had been forced to leave. Another part of Mussolini's short-lived empire was about to crumble for good, which meant one less problem for Britain to worry about.

Moreover, even though Rommel had rather pointlessly pressed on through Sollum and the Halfaya Pass – or 'Hellfire Pass', as it was now known – he had again run out of steam. Egypt was not under threat. This meant that Wavell could deal with an emerging rebellion in Iraq and start thinking about confronting Vichy-held Syria too. Securing both East Africa and the Middle East would make the British situation in Egypt much stronger, despite the loss of Greece.

There were, however, two inescapable lessons from Greece. First, the intervention of the Germans had proved beyond question that on land, at any rate, there was no army to touch them; Britain still had a very long way to go before it could compete, even though this was, in the spring of 1941, entirely understandable. Britain's Army was growing, but it would take time to build to a strength that could compete with Germany.

The second was with regard to air power. During their advance south, Balck and the whole of 2. Panzerdivision, to which his regiment was attached, had been left virtually untouched by the RAF. Balck had been amazed. 'Had they done so,' he wrote, 'they would have had plenty of targets of opportunity and we would have learned a hard lesson on how not to take panzer divisions through mountainous terrain.'

Of course, the RAF had been in such small numbers it had been all the pilots could do to watch their own backs. Roald Dahl had faced an extraordinary baptism of fire. The depleted squadron had lost Flight-

Sergeant Cottingham and Flight-Sergeant Rivelon on 17 April, and Pilot Officer 'Oofy' Still the following day, which left them with just twelve aircraft and twelve pilots. They were the only remaining Hurricanes in Greece. On the 20th, Dahl had flown four times, and during the first sortie that day he found himself caught up in a large, swirling dogfight in which they were colossally outnumbered. Half the time he was simply trying to avoid a collision, and by the time he pulled away and dived for home, he'd fired off all his ammunition and was struggling to control a sluggish fighter plane that had obviously been hit. When he finally touched down, he remained sitting there for a minute gasping for breath and overwhelmed to discover he was still alive. One mechanic said to him, 'Blimey mate, this kite's got so many 'oles in it, it looks like it's made out of chicken wire.' The Germans had got five of their twelve Hurricanes in that particular scrap, killing two experienced pilots in the process.

On the 21st, two more Hurricanes had been destroyed, both as they were taking off, and one of the pilots killed. Finally, two days later, the last five were flown to Greece and the spare pilots, Dahl included, taken by a Lockheed Hudson back to Egypt. 'We really had the hell of a time in Greece,' Dahl wrote to his mother once safely back in Alexandria. 'It wasn't much fun taking on half the German Airforce with literally a handful of fighters.'

As the RAF had discovered in France, there was little that could be achieved in the air if there was no effective way of directing those air forces towards or away from the enemy. Trying to second-guess massed formations of enemy bombers and fighters did not work. Nor could much be achieved when massively outnumbered, because pilots then spent their time desperately trying to save themselves rather than actually achieving anything helpful in terms of what was going on below.

It was no simple matter getting aircraft all the way to the Middle East, but Admiral Cunningham, for one, was with Roald Dahl and the men of 80 Squadron in believing many, many more were needed. ABC had been demanding more aircraft ever since the Italians had entered the war; he wasn't alone. So too had Air Marshal Arthur Longmore and Air Marshal Tedder, his successor as Air Officer Commanding Middle East. For Cunningham, the exhilaration of victory at sea at Cape Matapan had long been replaced by the gloom born of his great responsibilities and diminishing resources, primarily the lack of air support. 'If our deficiencies in the air could not be made good, and quickly,' he noted, 'I foresaw we should have to face some very unpleasant alternatives in the Middle East. Why the authorities at home apparently could not see the danger of our situation in the Mediterranean without adequate air support passed my comprehension.'

There was no question that all three British services were now greatly overstretched and that a huge amount was being expected of the Mediterranean Fleet. Yet it was also ever thus that commanders in theatre needed more than they had. The build-up of the RAF in the Middle East and on Malta had actually been reasonably impressive, especially considering that Britain had a critical air battle to fight at home. Furthermore, the decision to send Hurricanes and Blenheims, which were being gradually replaced by the home commands, made perfect sense when the only opposition were the Italians. The Hurricane, for example, was more than a match for anything the Regia Aeronautica had at that time. What's more, it was an easier aircraft to maintain than the Spitfire, and that was an important consideration out in the Middle East, where there were not the easily available repair and maintenance workshops that there were back in Britain.

Of course, it was a different kettle of fish when coming up against the latest Messerschmitt 109s and the overwhelming numbers of the Luftwaffe. It was also much easier for the Luftwaffe to move between theatres than it was for the RAF, as all it had to do was fly down from existing bases in the Greater Reich and occupy pre-existing airfields in Italy or other parts of the Balkans. It was always a logistical headache to move a *Staffel* or *Gruppe*, but this was as nothing compared with the problems facing the British in getting air forces across seas and continents to the Middle East.

And, in any case, the Air Ministry had reacted swiftly to the arrival of the Germans, and from March more significant numbers of aircraft were sent to the Middle East – 109 Hurricanes in March and April, 72 Blenheims, and 27 Curtiss Tomahawks from the USA, ordered the previous summer and now being shipped directly to the Middle East. Again, by sending these new American single-engine fighters direct and only to the Middle East made good sense; there was no sense in splitting shipments, spare parts and even mechanical knowledge. These figures would increase dramatically in the coming months as Britain's war leaders accepted the need to regain the initiative in North Africa and the Middle East.

*

Meanwhile, back in Britain, RAF Fighter Command continued to grow in strength as production of Spitfires increased. Most of the day squadrons of Fighter Command were equipped with Spitfires by the spring of 1941, and that included 145 Squadron. They had been sent south to Tangmere, near Chichester in Sussex, on 10 October and had seen plenty of action right up to the end of the year; the Luftwaffe had continued to make daylight raids both with bombers and with fighters in what the German pilots called *Freijagd* – free hunts. Jean Offenberg now had four confirmed kills to his name plus several probables and damaged claims as well. He was now completely fluent in English and accepted by his peers, but these had nevertheless been long, lonely months, especially since his great friend, Alexis Jottard, had been killed at the end of October. 'It was one of the saddest moments of my life,' Offenberg wrote in a letter to Jottard's family. 'We were very close and we were like brothers.'

Since then, there had been many changes for Offenberg and 145 Squadron. In early January came the news that they would be handing over their Hurricanes and converting to Spitfires. They were also told they would be going on the offensive, although much to Offenberg's frustration he was not allowed to fly over the Continent; in part this was because it was considered too risky for foreign nationals in the RAF to do so, and in part it was because the Secret Intelligence Service feared some of these men might be spies and would take their machines and knowledge and go over to the other side. There was, however, little evidence to support this. Nearly all, like Offenberg, were flying in the hope that they would be helping to liberate their countries.

This restriction had not lasted long. On 21 February, it was lifted, and Offenberg was able to join his fellows in the squadron in carrying out sweeps across the Channel. A policy of 'leaning forward into France' had been proposed by Air Chief Marshal Sholto Douglas soon after he had taken over as C-in-C Fighter Command, approved by the Air Staff and embraced by Air Vice-Marshal Leigh-Mallory, now commanding 11 Group. The aim of this strategy was to give the Luftwaffe no rest and to wear it down: British fighters were to destroy enemy aircraft in the air and on the ground, to shoot up and even bomb airfields, and, most importantly, to keep plenty of Luftwaffe formations in France and the Low Countries at the expense of the Mediterranean and North Africa. It was also felt important to take the offensive and to imbue the men of

Fighter Command with a sense of superiority in the air. For so long, the Luftwaffe had seemed to be the top dogs; it was felt important to show the Germans and those in occupied France that Britain's air forces still had plenty of fight and, moreover, were growing all the time.

For Offenberg, who had been restless and bored during the long winter, this more offensive policy was welcome news, and particularly so once he was allowed to join in. Even so, Fighter Command's efforts to lean forward into France were fairly lukewarm to start with as short days and bad weather hampered efforts. It wasn't until 13 March that Offenberg flew his first sortie back over France; bad weather and convoy protection had prevented them heading over sooner. Crossing the Channel at 30,000 feet, they had flown towards Arras and then spotted twenty or so Me109s away and below them, but the enemy fighters had scuttled off as soon as they saw the Spitfires. In between had been a mixture of patrols and coastal-convoy protection.

And so it continued: patrols and frustrating sweeps over France in which the enemy was spotted but rarely engaged. The large sweeps, with entire wings of squadrons heading over en masse in formations of over a hundred fighters, were known as 'circuses'. Smaller, lower-level raids were called 'rhubarbs'. For Offenberg, life was made more difficult by the arrival of a new flight commander called Stevens, whom he had not taken to and who kept trying to stop him flying more than the rest of the flight. 'I get more and more browned off with life in this squadron,' he recorded on 4 May.

Offenberg was not the only foreign pilot getting fed up. So too was Red Tobin, who just four days after the big air battles of 15 September 1940 had been posted with Keogh and Mamedoff to 71 'Eagle' Squadron, an all-American unit; such was the number of US volunteers now in Britain. A radio reporter had visited the Eagles a few weeks after they had been formed and had asked Tobin why he was flying for Britain. 'Well,' Tobin had told him, 'at first I just felt I wanted to fly some of these powerful machines, so I just came over . . . I guess one's views change a little once one is over here. The British are a swell people. This is a nice little country and I don't mind fighting for it one little bit.' The trouble was, he wasn't doing much fighting any more. Posted to Church Fenton in Yorkshire, Tobin and his fellows from 609 had soon come to resent being palmed off to a quiet backwater and missed their old pals. Tobin had come over to fly for the RAF, not sit on his backside all day.

Morale wasn't much better among the Luftwaffe units still in northern France. Siegfried Bethke had, like most fighter pilots, found the ongoing air battles of the autumn of 1940 a difficult time. So much had been expected of them and yet so many had been lost. A massive blow had been the death of Helmut Wick, one of the most highly regarded aces not only of JG2, but of the entire Luftwaffe. Wick had been shot down into the Channel on 28 November by John Dundas of 609 Squadron.

In February, Bethke had finally been given some leave and had become engaged to his girlfriend, Hedi; they planned to marry in June. All too soon, however, he was back at the front, carrying out fighter-bomber missions over England, a task he disliked intensely; flying over the Channel had not got any easier on his nerves, while such missions meant flying in and out at low altitude. This was also more dangerous: the lower the aircraft, the less room there was for manoeuvre should anything go wrong.

By the beginning of May, his *Staffel* were based at Théville at the tip of the Cherbourg peninsula. On the 12th, Bethke carried out another fighter-bomber mission to attack a British airfield. Flying low over the Channel once more they reached England but were unable to find the airfield. Instead, they attacked some British shipping. Bethke couldn't really see whether they had been successful or not but hoped they had caused some damage. The rest of the time they sat around the airfield at readiness, waiting to be scrambled to meet the British fighters. Losses were mounting and yet he had survived. For how much longer, though, he was unsure. 'One always thinks about what will come, concerning the flying,' he noted. 'I think about the future with Hedi.' He hoped they had one.

Meanwhile, on 5 May, Jean Offenberg was given permission for a brief solo flight. However, instead of flying calmly around Tangmere, Offenberg flew across the Channel towards the Cherbourg peninsula. Avoiding the flak around the port, he dived to around 1,000 feet and was off the coast near Barfleur when he spotted two Heinkel 60s, small biplane seaplanes. Opening fire, he hurtled past and banked and climbed to see the first crash into the water. He had barely time to think about the second Heinkel when two 109s appeared. Offenberg turned north and realized he and the first Messerschmitt were converging almost head-on. Firing first, he pulled up at the last moment and avoided a collision, then climbed on a right-hand turn, and as one of the Messerschmitts crossed his gunsight opened fire. From the corner of his eye, he could see it in shallow dive trailing white smoke. 'I thought it best to get away as quickly as possible from these waters and make for home,' he remembered. 'I skimmed over the water beneath a cloudless sky.' He knew he was going to be in big trouble, but despite Stevens's wrath, Group Captain 'Woody' Woodhall, the Station Commander at Tangmere, gave him little more than a slight rap on the knuckles, made him promise not to do it again, and told him he had been recommended for a Distinguished Flying Cross, a DFC.

In Churchill's speech of 27 April, he had also pointed out that it was the Battle of the Atlantic that should hold the first place in their thoughts. It was here, he said, and in the men sailing the world's sea lanes, that the responsibility for victory lay. Again, he was quite right. He also reminded his listeners – and it was not just the British who tuned in but people from all around the world – that Britain never had fewer than 2,000 merchant ships afloat at any one time. This was a truly impressive number and was why so much materiel was still pouring into Britain and elsewhere despite the threats lurking above and below the waves.

The point was this: the Middle East and Mediterranean were a theatre of strategic opportunity for Britain; but the Atlantic was one of strategic necessity. If Greece or even Egypt fell, Britain would survive; if it lost the war in the Atlantic, it would not.

Conversely, it was all very well Germany demonstrating its strength against weaker opponents on land, but these victories should not have been masking the setbacks at sea. These were mounting, for if the loss of the aces in March had signalled a change in German fortunes in the Battle of the Atlantic, the loss of *U-110*'s codebooks and Enigma really marked the end of an era. For all the disappointments Britain would face in 1941 – and there were many – at least its all-important sea lanes remained open. Just so long as more and more supplies continued to come its way, Britain could continue to fight. As such, first the failure of the Luftwaffe the previous summer and now the U-boat arm's setback in the Atlantic marked major turning points in the war in the West.

As the second summer of war arrived, the critical factor for Britain, however, was whether enough supplies would reach it. Uncertainty about the United States and its ability to send supplies in time to make a significant contribution constantly played on the minds of Britain's war leaders, and not least Churchill himself. 'Battles might be won or lost,' wrote the PM, 'enterprises might succeed or miscarry, territories might be gained or quitted, but dominating all our power to carry on the war, or even keep ourselves alive, lay our mastery of the ocean routes and the free approach and entry to our ports.'

It was not U-boats but German surface vessels that were at the forefront of both the Kriegsmarine's and Churchill's thoughts that May, however. On the night of the 19th, the heavy cruiser *Prinz Eugen* and the monster battleship and pride of the German fleet, the *Bismarck*, burst through the British naval blockade and out into the Atlantic. After the humiliations of the *Admiral Hipper* and *Admiral Scheer*, and the raids made by the *Scharnhorst* and *Gneisenau*, the Royal Navy had vowed to not let these pesky German capital ships make fools of them again. The RAF had since then been bombing Brest regularly and had managed to hit *Gneisenau* in dock, but the *Bismarck* now promised to be an unbeatable prize.

Needless to say, the Home Fleet sent HMS *Hood* and the fast battleship the *Prince of Wales* to join the cruiser force already in the Atlantic in an effort to track down the *Bismarck* and the *Prinz Eugen*. Early on 24 May, the two big British ships sighted their German adversaries and opened fire, even though together they had half the large 15-inch guns of the *Bismarck* and *Prinz Eugen*. All four ships opened fire just before six in the morning. A few minutes later, one particularly lucky shot from the *Bismarck* did for *Hood*. Although she was a heavy battle cruiser rather than a battleship, *Hood* was none the less one of the oldest and best-known capital ships in the entire Royal Navy. She had been due a major refit in 1939, but war arrived too early, so that by 1941 standards neither her guns nor her armour were quite sufficient for the role she was expected to play. Hit probably in her magazine, she exploded and sank, killing all but three of her 1,418-strong crew.

However, *Bismarck* had been hit as well, although not fatally. But the damage to her fuel tanks was serious enough for her to have to immediately turn and make for Brest, a voyage that was dogged all the way by radar-equipped British vessels and aircraft. It was a Fairey Swordfish, the same ageing naval aircraft that had struck such a blow to the Italian fleet at Taranto, that produced the fatal hit in the end. A torpedo dropped by one of these biplanes hit her stern and jammed her rudder, leaving the giant battleship circling like a wounded whale. Other British battleships and cruisers closed in for the kill, including *Rodney* and *George V*, repeatedly hitting the stricken vessel. Admiral Lütjens, who had orchestrated the series of raids by his surface fleet, was killed, and with most of her guns out of action, her decks aflame, she was abandoned. The *coup de grâce* came from a torpedo fired by the heavy cruiser *Dorsetshire*.

While it was the end for the *Bismarck*, her consort, however, the *Prinz Eugen*, had managed to scurry back to Brest. The British, milking the propaganda value of this victory at sea for all it was worth, felt the loss of *Hood* had been avenged. More importantly, it marked the end of the Kriegsmarine's surface fleet as a fighting force in the Battle of the Atlantic. Not one capital ship ever dipped into those grey, bitter seas ever again.

CHAPTER 44

Mixed Fortunes: II

WHILE CHURCHILL may have been right to call for a sense of proportion when considering the defeat in Greece, that was easier said than done if you were the troops involved or if you were Wavell and the service chiefs. For Admiral Cunningham, the next operation on his agenda was the protection of Crete, where it was accepted that the island had to be held and where it was expected the Germans would strike. At the same time, he faced the ongoing challenge of supplying the besieged fortress of Tobruk and doing what he could to help protect it. Losses in small ships and minesweepers were mounting. 'These losses,' he noted bitterly, 'were the price we had to pay to the almost complete lack of air cover.' However, more Hurricanes and a newly arrived squadron had reached Malta, and although it had taken a hammering in the first months of the year, with the beginning of the German attack on Greece the pressure had lifted.

And as the pressure on Malta had lifted so the ability of this tiny island fortress to disrupt Axis shipping lines had increased. A destroyer force under Captain Philip Mack of the *Jervis* was sent briefly to Malta and while using the island as a base sank five Axis merchant ships and three Italian destroyers in just one action. Malta-based Fleet Air Arm aircraft were also mining the harbour entrances at Tripoli and Benghazi in turn, and the island's 10th Submarine Flotilla was also starting to prove its worth. On 24 May, the submarine HMS *Upholder*, in a daring attack that was worthy of the U-boat aces, manoeuvred inside a destroyer screen and sank the 18,000-ton troopship the *Conte Rosso*. Thirteen hundred Axis troops were lost as the ship went down. Furthermore, it was clear that the Luftwaffe was now leaving Sicily altogether, as Adrian Warburton and the reconnaissance crews of 69 Squadron had been reporting.

Clearly, it was not only the British who were struggling to have sufficient forces in a multitude of different places at the same time. The Luftwaffe was preparing for the invasion of the Soviet Union, maintaining forces in north-west Europe and on the Atlantic coast, as well as supporting Rommel in North Africa and the operations in the Balkans and the Mediterranean. With Greece subdued, there was clearly an imperative to get troops away from the theatre without delay. What John Kennedy had sagely noted about prioritization of effort applied just as readily to the Germans, especially with Operation BARBAROSSA looming.

Despite that, during the campaign in the Balkans, General Warlimont's Section L had been asked to produce an appreciation of whether, in terms of future strategy in the Mediterranean, it was better to attack Crete or Malta. The simple answer was that in May 1941 probably neither justified any further diversion of resources with BARBAROSSA now planned for the third week of June. However, of the two, Crete was of little strategic value and certainly posed no obvious threat to Axis forces occupying Greece, or supply lines to Tripoli or even Benghazi. However, the Luftwaffe was arguing that the island could be used as an air base for attacks on Egypt, and then as a springboard into Syria and Iraq; agents had already been at work in Vichy Syria, scouting airfields. Furthermore, the Italians were suggesting that Malta was a difficult nut to crack – certainly, it would be harder to invade than the open door it had presented back in June 1940.

But neither Crete nor airy thoughts directed at Iraq were of critical importance at this time. If Rommel ever managed to reach Alexandria, British naval forces on Crete would become irrelevant; effectively, the island would have been bypassed. The only threat to German interests was the build-up of British air forces on the island; these, potentially, could attack targets in Greece and even the oilfields in Romania, but already Ploești was ringed with air and anti-aircraft defences, and the chances of British bombers successfully interrupting the flow of oil into the Reich was slim. On the other hand, an operation against Malta would rid the Axis of a major thorn in its side. Moreover, by capturing the island, Axis forces would not only be denying it to the British, but would benefit from having it themselves. If they were to continue operations in North Africa, there was much to be said for neutralizing Malta. 'It becomes increasingly clear,' noted General Halder at the beginning of May, 'that without Malta we'll never have a safe supply route to North Africa.'

The key question was really how important the Mediterranean and Middle East theatre was to Germany. Rommel had pushed British forces back into Egypt, and Tobruk remained besieged. The British had also been forced out of Greece. In other words, for the time being, neither North Africa nor the Balkans were under any threat of being suddenly overrun; German intervention had bought them time.

The two most important theatres were the Atlantic, where there were clearly not enough U-boats operating, and the Soviet Union, for which Germany was amassing large forces, with plenty of experience to draw upon. BARBAROSSA remained a huge gamble, but there could be no mistaking the urgency to get moving right away and with 100 per cent focus. If the Germans were victorious in the Soviet Union, as Hitler believed they would be, there was absolutely no need to spend a moment longer in the Mediterranean. Crete, Malta, North Africa, the Suez Canal – all could be dealt with later, with overwhelming force and in the flush of a further victory. It was like Norway all over again: important, but not necessary right now.

This, however, was not what Warlimont's Section L had been asked to examine. Their task was to offer an answer as to which was a better option: an attack on Malta or Crete. They unanimously concluded it was the former. Hitler, however, insisted an attack be launched on Crete, using a mass of airborne troops, which could have been put to far better use in Russia, and, more importantly, using yet more air transports, the strength of which had still barely recovered from the debacle of 10 May 1940. The idea had been proposed by Göring and the Luftwaffe, and particularly General Kurt Student, the founder of the *Fallschmirmjäger*, who envisioned a series of island hops using his airborne troops. Crete would be followed by Cyprus, which would then put pressure on Turkey and help quash British influence in the eastern Mediterranean. This, however, was all very speculative and would, of course, require even more commitment of forces in that theatre. It was one of the curses of having airborne troops: having taken the time and trouble to build up a force of elite troops there was then an imperative to use them.

They could, however, still have been used in BARBAROSSA, and more importantly so could the vital transport aircraft, which were going to be of absolutely critical importance over the vast distances of the Soviet Union. The proposed Cretan venture was given the codename MERCURY and was initially set for the second week of May 1941 – that is, just a month before BARBAROSSA.

It was, however, an astonishing decision, because regardless of whether it resulted in victory or failure, it made no strategic sense whatsoever considering its proximity to the invasion of the Soviet Union. In fact, on a chart of possible future operations, Crete and the potential opportunities that might follow should have been pretty low in the pecking order, and way below even the capture of Malta. MERCURY revealed, once again, Hitler's woeful lack of geo-political understanding; his Directive 28, issued on 25 April 1941, demanded the capture of Crete 'as a base for air warfare against Great Britain in the Eastern Mediterranean'. More than that, however, it also showed his essential paranoia about threats to his flanks and also that critical Romanian oil supply. Already, Hitler had shown greater interest in and concern about this southern theatre than Germany's current situation warranted.

Curiously, however, no matter how warped his logic for an invasion of Crete may have been, no one appears to have pointed this out. Göring was delighted to be in charge, and the rest of his staff, Warlimont included, offered not a word of dissent. Such was the iron will of the Führer.

While the Germans were congratulating themselves on their swift and crushing victories in Yugoslavia and Greece, Wavell was once more juggling the many balls that had been thrown into his hands as a result of his enormous command. In Iraq, Rashid Ali al-Gaylani, the former prime minister, had, at the beginning of April 1941, seized power from the Regent, Emir Abdul-Ilah, the uncle of the boy king, Faisal II. While Adbul-Ilah had been openly pro-British, al-Gaylani most certainly was not; rather, he was an ardent nationalist and had repeatedly tried to get German support to both overthrow the Emir and undermine British influence in the region. The German response had been lukewarm, largely because Iraq was still beyond their effective sphere of influence, but this had not stopped al-Gaylani plotting to murder Emir Abdul-Ilah. Learning of the plot, Abdul-Ilah had fled the country, and the following day, 1 April, al-Gaylani had launched his *coup d'état* and promptly reinstated himself as Prime Minister once more.

While the oil from Iraq was important for British operations in the

Middle East, so too was the port of Basra, an important bridge between the Middle East and India, so for Iraq to have an openly hostile political leader who was known to be consorting with both Germany and Italy was intolerable. Churchill immediately asked both Wavell and General Claude Auchinleck, the C-in-C India, what forces they could provide for a challenge to Rashid Ali al-Gaylani. Wavell replied that he had none and suggested a diplomatic solution. Of this response, Churchill took a rather dim view. In contrast, Auchinleck offered a brigade from 10th Indian Division followed by the balance as soon as the shipping could be provided. They would be sent straight to Basra.

On hearing of the coup in Iraq, Hitler had immediately ordered the OKW to give al-Gaylani all possible help, but there was almost none available – German forces in the region had their hands full with Greece and the Balkans, not to mention North Africa and the preparations for BARBAROSSA. If al-Gaylani had seriously expected German help, he had timed the coup poorly. Even Hitler accepted this.

Unfortunately for al-Gaylani, however, the die had been cast and with news reaching him of the arrival of the lead brigade from India, he was forced to play his hand and so sent Iraqi troops to demand the surrender of the RAF base at Habbaniya, to the west of Baghdad. Having anticipated this move, Air Vice-Marshal Harry Smart, the RAF air officer commanding, had already fitted bomb racks to his miscellaneous training aircraft and created a rudimentary defence force with 1,000 British airmen, 1,200 locally raised Iraqi and Assyrian levies, and several thousand more civilians. While al-Gaylani's forces dug in, 300 men from the Indian brigade now at Basra were flown in, as were eight Wellington bombers. Al-Gaylani was told to withdraw his forces, and when he refused the Wellingtons and AVM Smart's makeshift force went on the attack. By 6 May, the Iraqis had abandoned their positions, but while the siege of Habbaniya was over, the rebellion was not.

Churchill now repeated his request for help to Wavell, who once more recommended a diplomatic solution. This time, Churchill overruled him and after scratching around his forces in Palestine, Wavell managed to cobble together 'Habforce', which included local Arabs as well as mechanized infantry. The sole German contribution was to send a few aircraft to attack this force as it struck across the Iraqi desert in blistering temperatures of over 120 degrees. The Iraqi rebels then hardly did themselves any favours by accidentally shooting down Major Axel von

Blomberg, son of a German field marshal, as he came in to land at Baghdad.

As Habforce was heading across the desert, the Indian brigade was also striking north from Basra with the assistance of nearly sixty RAF bombers that had flown in to support it. On 19 May, Fallujah was taken, opening the road to Baghdad. Al-Gaylani's coup had almost run its course.

'Rather a hectic day,' scribbled Captain Stanley Christopherson on Thursday, 1 May. 'The Germans launched their largest attack so far against Tobruk and penetrated our outer perimeter.' Word reached the Sherwood Rangers at their battery command post, or CP, at 8.30 in the morning. They were immediately ordered to 'stand to' and soon after to be ready to shoot landwards. Christopherson and two other officers hurried off in a wireless truck to division HQ, where they discovered a large number of war correspondents listening to a German interpreter calmly telling them about types of enemy prisoner. Soon after, Christopherson and his colleagues went back, listening to the sounds of intense artillery fire all the way. 'The perimeter has come in for some very formidable dive-bombing and machine-gunning from the air,' added Christopherson. 'We get a very clear view from our position and it is certainly a grim spectacle to see 40 or 50 dive-bombers hurtling down.'

Despite this, Rommel's latest attempt to break Tobruk failed, which he blamed in part on the stubborn resistance of the Australians and partly on the lack of Italian drive. Even with his urging, he could not get the Ariete Armoured Division to push far enough forward. 'With British artillery fire sweeping the whole area,' he recorded, 'the Italians crept under their vehicles and resisted all their officers' attempts to get them out again.' Rommel, like many Germans, had scant regard for his Axis allies. The reality, however, was that he had not had enough supplies to keep going, and the arrival of the *khamseen*, a notoriously vicious desert storm, the following day, put paid to any further action.

By now, General Friedrich Paulus had reached North Africa to try and talk some sense into the errant commander of the newly formed Deutsche Afrikakorps, or DAK, as it was known. Paulus subsequently wrote up his observations on 12 May, in a report which was promptly intercepted by British intelligence. In it, he claimed that Rommel's supply situation was terrible and that strong action was needed if a crisis was to be avoided. Better defences for Tripoli and Benghazi were needed, as was protection of sea lanes. Further anti-aircraft guns and aircraft should preferably be German not Italian. Paulus reported that the joint Axis forces in North Africa now required 50,000 tons of supplies a month, but the total monthly capacity for coastal shipping was only 29,000 tons, which meant a large amount would still need to travel overland all the way from Tripoli, which, of course, used up more fuel in resources; it was a thousand miles from Tripoli to Tobruk. 'By overstepping his orders,' Halder noted sourly, 'Rommel has brought about a situation for which our present supply capabilities are not sufficient.' In other words, Germany was going to have to reinforce North Africa further, with yet more resources – and especially mechanized transport – being directed away from BARBAROSSA, or the mission would end in failure.

Everyone unfortunate enough to be up in the 'blue' when the *khamseen* struck suffered. The high winds and swirling sand battered everyone and everything, no matter what the nationality. Men were left gasping for water, but nothing could move. The suffocating heat and stinging sand on a sweaty body was a grim kind of torture. 'Today has been really dreadful,' scribbled Albert Martin in his diary. 'The stifling heat has sent everyone nearly crazy. The only small consolation is that the Germans must be suffering too.'

Martin was now not only completely fit once more, but after intense training with the battalion and the rest of 7th Armoured Division had returned to the desert, where he and his mates were now expecting action any moment. Once the *khamseen* had cleared, he and the rest of 2nd Rifle Brigade were busy patrolling on the top of the escarpment above Sollum. On the 12th, he watched British gunners shelling a gathering of German trucks, which later were withdrawn, and with the large amounts of vehicles, tanks and troops now gathering, it was clear the attack was imminent. In fact, some 240 tanks had reached Egypt along with more troops, and so, with details of Paulus's report on Rommel's dire supply situation ringing in his ears, General Auchinleck decided to make a move.

The border was marked by a long, steep escarpment that curved in towards the coast just before Sollum. This gave any troops on top of it far-reaching views back along the Egyptian coast. There was certainly some sense in trying to clear the area of Axis forces before launching any further significant operation; the key, though, in any action in the desert, was to make it count.

Operation BREVITY was launched on 15 May and involved three separate drives. In a wide sweep some fifteen miles inland, 7th Armoured Brigade pushed around the back of Fort Capuzzo, while closer to the top of the escarpment came a drive from 22nd Guards Brigade. Meanwhile, Albert Martin and 2nd Rifle Brigade were to advance along the coast in an effort to take Sollum and the lower end of the Halfaya Pass, the only route up on to the escarpment.

The entire operation was commanded by Brigadier William 'Strafer' Gott, forty-three years old and with an impeccable career already behind him. He had got his nickname in the last war from the German phrase 'Gott strafe England' – 'God punish England'; it had stuck but although he was a genial and easy-going fellow, the nickname did rather suit his cut-and-thrust approach to battle. However, although the plan looked sound enough on paper, two brigades were not enough to deal a decisive blow. Rommel's forces may have been too stretched for further offensive action, but in the open expanses of the desert, all they had to do was position their guns judiciously and open fire. It only needed a handful with greater range and velocity than those of the British and any break-through would be denied.

In a nutshell, that was what happened. The Rifle Brigade managed to take the lower Halfaya Pass but could not push on. Albert Martin, how-ever, was sanguine. They had not lost many men or vehicles – no one had as it happened – and, as he pointed out, that was what really mattered. 'What counted,' he noted, 'was the destruction of the enemy and his ordnance. That was more important than travelling 100 miles in an unopposed advance.' On 16 May, Martin and the rest of the Rifle Brigade received orders to pull back. 'There was no sense of defeat or despondency,' he wrote. 'This was just another move in a grand game of chess played out on a giant board.' Nevertheless, it was a setback. Routing the enemy in North Africa was no longer quite so easy, not even one that was as overstretched as Rommel's Afrikakorps.

On the other hand, where the British were facing only the Italians, the war news was altogether more encouraging, and certainly by the middle of May the East African campaign appeared to be drawing to a close.

The war correspondent Alan Moorehead had just landed at Nairobi when he was given a communiqué from GHQ, Cairo, that Emperor Haile Selassie had re-entered Addis Ababa a few days earlier. Soon after, he took off again, flying over the northern expanse of Kenya and on over the Juba River and into Italian Somaliland. From there he and his colleagues took off again, this time towards the green mountains and lakes of Abyssinia, and suddenly the sun had gone and rain was slashing down against the aircraft. At long last, after an incredible sunset against deep, thunderous clouds, they landed in a field near the town of Herar.

Because of the rain, there was no truck to meet them and so they trudged across a mile of mud and eventually to the RAF Mess on the edge of town. The news was good: the Duke of Aosta, the general commanding Italian forces, had sent an envoy into Diredawa declaring it would be an open and undefended town; an armistice now seemed very close. Moorehead was desperate to get to Addis Ababa, but he soon discovered at first hand the difficulties of getting from A to B in what was still a remote part of the world. To reach Diredawa involved a long and tortuous drive down a 2,000-foot drop into an immense gorge and along roads blasted out by the Italians. From there, they drove on, climbing once more on to a high plateau some 7,000 feet above sea level.

When he eventually reached the capital, Moorehead thought it seemed like a complete madhouse, with marauding Ethiopian troops out for revenge lurking with knives and spears at every corner. In one outlying Italian settlement, the settlers had spread out a huge notice imploring the British to come and rescue them. Moorehead learned that British armoured cars had fought their way through the tribesmen to save the Italians at another settlement.

Back in Addis Ababa, Moorehead booked himself into the Albergo Imperiale, where he found lots of truculent Italians still occupying the lounge and listening to Radio Roma and cheering the news of Axis successes. 'I can conceive of no other people in the world emerging so quickly from fear to impudence,' wrote Moorehead. 'I know of no people except the British who would accept such a slight with such indifference.'

Later, however, he witnessed a more sober assessment from an Italian officer, now in plain clothes. 'We knew the end was coming,' he told Moorehead, producing a copy of an Italian newspaper, 'when they stopped saying we were invincible and started printing things like this.' He handed it to him. 'Consider as light the burdens you are enduring today,' Moorehead read, 'and the bigger burdens you must expect to endure tomorrow.'

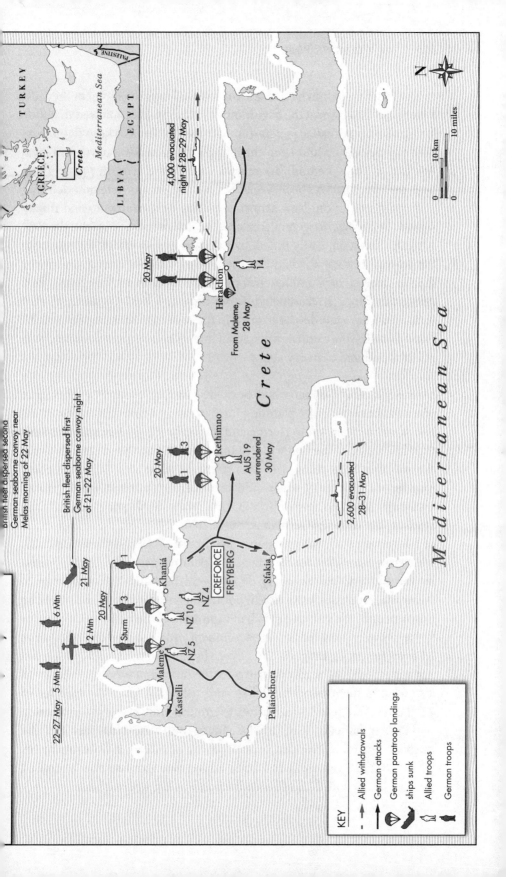

TURKEY

GREECE

Crete

Mediterranean Sea

PALESTINE

LIBYA   EGYPT

British fleet dispersed second
German seaborne convoy near
Melos morning of 22 May

British fleet dispersed first
German seaborne convoy night
of 21–22 May

22–27 May   5 Mtn

6 Mtn

21 May

20 May

2 Mtn

Sturm

Maleme

Kastelli

NZ 5

NZ 10

1

Khaniá

3

NZ 4

CREFORCE
FREYBERG

Sfakia

Palaiokhora

2,600 evacuated
28–31 May

20 May

1

3

Rethimno

AUS 19
surrendered
30 May

Crete

20 May

Herakleion

From Maleme,
28 May

14

4,000 evacuated
night of 28–29 May

N

0   10 km
0   10 miles

Mediterranean Sea

KEY

Allied withdrawals

German attacks

German paratroop landings

ships sunk

Allied troops

German troops

The Italian told him he had known it was all over the moment they lost Keren; that had been at the beginning of February. He confessed that they had drawn up armistice papers, but had been ordered to keep fighting to hold the British up and keep their forces from moving north to Libya. 'We had to obey,' he told Moorehead. And so the armistice papers had been torn up. That had been weeks ago, but the Italians were now defeated and could not go on. New armistice papers were drawn up and finally signed on 20 May. To a certain extent, the Italian had been right: the East African campaign, badly timed, had tied up British efforts for too long. But in turn the Italians had lost the best part of 400 aircraft and more than a quarter of a million troops. More than that, Mussolini's East African empire – so trumpeted before the war – was now gone; all that remained were a few defended posts in the eastern mountains. For Britain – and Wavell – the campaign was to all intents and purposes over and was one less problem to worry about.

Meanwhile, the Germans had been discovering a number of further potential hazards in the planning for Operation MERCURY. First of all, planning had been left to Göring and the Luftwaffe, which, after the hash they had made of the Battle of Britain, ought to have been enough to get the warning bells going. However, General Alexander Löhr, the commander of Luftflotte IV, who would be in overall command, was untainted by the air campaign against Britain. Under him, he also had General Kurt Student, the father of German airborne troops. Student was commander of Fliegerkorps XI, with its transport aircraft and *Fallschirmjäger* units, which was earmarked for the attack. The paratroopers would be supported by the fighters and bombers of Fliegerkorps VIII. *Gebirgsjäger* of 5. Gebirgsjägerdivision were also to bolster the invasion force and would be flown in once the paratroopers had captured key airfields.

Delays were incurred moving equipment and personnel of Fliegerkorps XI from Romania, Bulgaria and Greece by rail and then truck, which did not augur well for the reverse trip once the campaign was over. There was also an argument between Halder and the OKW over the transfer of 22. Luftlandedivision – a Luftwaffe ground unit currently protecting the Ploești oilfields – by trucks. 'Using our road transport for this purpose,' grumbled Halder, 'would rob us of 602nd MT Regiment for BARBAROSSA, where it has been apportioned among the armoured groups.' In the end, 22. Luftlandedivision was left where it was.

Even though the weather had dramatically improved, the logistical difficulties of getting troops, equipment and supplies down to airfields and bases in Greece were still legion. Not until 14 May were the 500 Ju52 transports in place in Greece; in all, some 1,280 aircraft would be involved in what was becoming a very large operation indeed. The Luftwaffe – and the Führer – had to hope it didn't lose too many of these precious transport planes in particular. There were then still further difficulties in establishing the supply system for MERCURY, which put back the launch date yet further. From a planned launch of 10 May, it moved to the 16th, then the 18th, and then there was a further postponement to the 19th. Delays in the shipment of fuel meant it was not finally ready for launch until 20 May. BARBAROSSA was set for 21 June, a little over four weeks away. This was cutting things very fine.

On 19 May, Oberjäger Martin Pöppel and the rest of his 2. Company, 2. Fallschirmjägerregiment, received their orders for an attack on Crete the following day. Now at Tanagra, near Khalkis, to the north of Athens, after a long journey south via train and truck, they were encamped in British tents, left behind during the British retreat, among the olive groves. After preparing their kit and cleaning weapons, Pöppel and his comrades gathered under a giant olive tree and drank beer and sang songs. For most of the men it would be their first combat jump; Pöppel was an old hand.

The following day, they would be among the second wave to be dropped over Crete; the 502 Ju52s available were not enough to take the thirteen battalions of more than 9,000 paratroopers in one drop. The distance from Crete, the number of transports and other logistical considerations all played their part in the planning. In the end, it was agreed that the first wave would be directed on Canea in the north-west of the island and the nearby airfield of Maleme, which was considered the key objective. This part of Crete was closest to the Greek mainland and still within range of Me109s. It was also agreed that as soon as the drop had been made on Canea and Maleme, the transports would turn around right away and pick up the remaining paratroopers. These would then drop on the airfields at Crete's two other major towns, Rethymnon and Heraklion – the idea was that by attacking these two other airfields and swiftly capturing them, they would deny the British the chance to reinforce. Then, on D-Day plus 1, the lightly equipped airborne troops would be reinforced by Generalmajor Julius Ringel's 5. Gebirgsjägerdivision, flown into the captured airfields. A further smaller assault force would be landed by sea.

On this eve of battle, Martin Pöppel was conscious that he and his friends were singing not only the usual cheerful soldiers' songs, but also more nostalgic ones about home. Even so, spirits were high. The *Fallschirmjäger* considered themselves to be the elite: they were all volunteers, highly motivated to a man and well-trained. They had been told that there were now some 10,000 Commonwealth troops on Crete and the remnants of a handful of Greek divisions. 'We reckoned,' noted Pöppel, 'that such a small island wouldn't be a problem for us.' The following day he would find out whether his prediction had been right.

CHAPTER 45

Mercury Falling

THROUGHOUT THE SPRING and into May 1941, the Luftwaffe had continued to pound Britain, focusing particularly on ports. Liverpool
was severely and repeatedly hit in the first week of May, with nearly 700
bombers flying over. Sixty-nine out of 144 cargo berths were put out of
action, the cathedral was hit and some 6,500 homes were completely destroyed. In all, there were 2,895 casualties. Clydebank near Glasgow was
also heavily bombed, as too were Belfast, Hull, Cardiff and Plymouth.
The centre of Portsmouth was devastated by five nights of bombing.
None the less, all these ports, and also Southampton, which had been
badly hit earlier in the Blitz, continued to function.

On the night of 10–11 May, London was also heavily hit once more, by
571 bombers dropping 800 tons of bombs. Some 1,436 people were killed
and a further 1,800 seriously injured. The next night, the bombers
returned and hit Westminster Abbey, the Law Courts and even the
Chamber of the House of Commons. Much of London's traffic, both on
the roads and on the railways, was paralysed.

For those still concerned with defending Britain, the continued attacks
were doubly sinister because, with the arrival of longer days and better
weather, the conditions for a German invasion were improving. There
was no real intelligence to suggest that this was likely to happen in the
immediate future, but preparations to repel the invader were at once
stepped up. In north London, Gwladys Cox received a pamphlet through
her letterbox on 24 May called 'Beating the Invader'. 'It tells us what to do
in the event of an invasion by answering fourteen questions such as,

"What do I do if fighting breaks out in my neighbourhood?" and "What does it mean when the church bells are rung?"' she noted in her diary, then added, 'More and more unreal!'

It did no harm to be prepared for the worst, although in fact the worst was over. The attacks on London in the second week of May were the last major ones for the time being. By the third week in May, Luftflotte 2 had been largely withdrawn in preparation for BARBAROSSA, leaving a depleted Luftflotte 3 to continue the raids against Britain – attacks that would be carried out with far less vigour than before. The Blitz was over – for the time being, at any rate.

The Luftwaffe's bombing of Britain had failed in its objective. The morale of the British had not collapsed, nor had its infrastructure been fatally damaged. In all, just 0.1 per cent of the population had been killed and a further 0.15 per cent had suffered serious injury. Forty thousand deaths were a lot, but the number fell way short of the picture of Armageddon many had predicted before the war. Many of the damaged houses had been repaired within a matter of weeks; by March 1941, for example, of the 719,000 houses that had suffered bomb damage in London, only 5,100 were still awaiting repair. Food supplies had also been maintained throughout. It had been calculated by the Ministry of Home Security that of the 6,699 economic 'key points' – that is, industry, food stocks, oil depots, armaments and so on – only 884 had been hit, and just eight out of 558 factories had been destroyed beyond repair. Weekly outputs of steel continued to rise throughout the Blitz. Aircraft production took a small dip in the last quarter of 1940, but by May 1941 was higher than at any point in the war so far. British society had been a very long way from disintegrating.

On the other hand, the Blitz had been disruptive enough, had been very expensive for the Government, and had tied up more than 600,000 men on military and civil defence who could otherwise have been employed elsewhere; managing Britain's war effort had been made just that bit more difficult. On the other side of the fence, it had cost the Luftwaffe around 600 bombers, which most certainly could have been used elsewhere. It had also taught the British much about aerial bombing – what worked and what was less effective. Most of all, it taught Britain's air chiefs that to cause really substantial damage to the enemy, a significantly bigger air force was needed than the one the Luftwaffe had been sending over. Britain had every intention of creating one.

*

After taking the unusual decision to fly on operations for the Regia Aeronautica, Count Galeazzo Ciano was back in Rome and once more resuming his duties as Foreign Minister and right-hand man to the Duce. Generally speaking, the Italians were rather ungrateful to Hitler for baling them out of a tight spot in both the Balkans and North Africa. Both humiliated and chastised, they were grumbling and back to their bitchiest best regarding their Axis partner, while at the same time resentful that Hitler was not involving them more now that the fighting in mainland Greece and Yugoslavia was over.

High on Ciano's list of priorities was annexing some part of Yugoslavia and ensuring they, the Italians, not the Greeks, governed Greece. The Germans had made vague noises about the Italians being given a free hand in Croatia and along the Dalmatian coast. 'But,' noted Ciano, 'up to what point are they sincere?'

There was also mounting consternation at the way German commanders were treating the Italians in the field. Ciano had heard reports that Rommel was threatening Italian divisional commanders with military tribunals if they didn't show more gumption, while in Albania the bad feeling between the two forces was equally palpable.

When Hitler made a Reichstag speech on 4 May, in which he ranted about Churchill and the Jewish conspiracy, Mussolini dismissed it as 'useless' and told Ciano it would have been better if he'd not bothered. A couple of days later, en route to Monfalcone to talk to Ante Pavelić, the new Fascist leader of Croatia in Yugoslavia, Ciano noticed Mussolini was rapt in thought. 'We speak at length of the future prospects of the war,' noted Ciano. 'I cannot say that now he has cast aside his optimistic view of a rapid end, he has any clear idea of the future.' It was not surprising. Mussolini's pride had taken a huge beating over the past months.

Far better news for both men was the stunning revelation that Rudolf Hess, one of the leading Nazis and Hitler's appointed Deputy Führer, had flown to Scotland for what he claimed were clandestine peace talks with the Duke of Hamilton. The Duke, although an aristocrat and RAF Wing Commander, had little if any political influence and was certainly not an anti-war appeaser as Hess appeared to believe. At any rate, after being chased by various British night fighters, Hess's Me110 finally ran out of fuel, so he bailed out and was promptly caught and arrested. For several days, the British kept the news of his capture secret as they tried to make head or tail of what on earth Hess had been trying to achieve. In the meantime, Hitler sent von Ribbentrop to Rome to announce the news to Mussolini. He was clearly stunned by what had happened, and Ciano, for one, enjoyed his discomfiture enormously. 'The tone of the Germans is one of depression,' wrote Ciano. 'Von Ribbentrop repeats his slogans against England with that monotony that made Göring dub him "Germany's No. 1 parrot".' Later, after von Ribbentrop had taken off for the flight home, von Bismarck, the German councillor at the embassy, said, 'Let's hope that they will all crash and break their necks.' Ciano was amused. 'That's German national solidarity for you!'

It was against the backdrop of battles at sea, preparations for BARBAROSSA, negotiations with the Greeks and strange peace missions by a deranged Nazi Deputy Führer that Operation MERCURY was finally launched.

On the long, narrow and mountainous ancient island of King Minos, the morning of 20 May dawned calm and cloudless; the rains and bad weather that had been a feature of the Greek spring had made way for summer. From his billet in the village of Galatas, just to the west of Canea and between the town and the airfield at Maleme, Colonel Howard Kippenberger was shaving when first a reconnaissance plane appeared followed soon after by a fighter, which roared over the main street in the village strafing with its guns. Kippenberger, forty-four years old and commander of the New Zealand 10th Brigade, thought this was unusual and, hurriedly finishing his shave, cautiously looked out of his first-floor window. He now saw there were other fighter aircraft thundering overhead and towards Canea but, having decided there was little he could do about it, went down to have some breakfast.

While there were mainly fighters over Galatas, elsewhere Dornier 17s and Ju88s were giving the defenders yet another demonstration of air power. So long as those on the receiving end were in slit trenches, these attacks killed comparatively few, but they were frightening, the blast of bombs was deafening and disorientating, and psychologically they were also a reminder of the lack of support in the air from the RAF.

Kippenberger had been largely unperturbed by their latest visit, but he worried it was affecting the cooks, who had produced an especially bad bowl of watery porridge that morning. But he had barely begun to eat, however, when someone gave a loud exclamation. From the open courtyard where they sat, they could see four menacing gliders, the first they had ever seen, while from the north was a growing thunderous roar.

'Stand to your arms!' shouted Kippenberger, then ran upstairs for his binoculars and rifle. By the time he had run back down to the courtyard, the roar overhead was deafening and scores of troop carriers were flying low overhead. Running down to brigade HQ in what was known as Prison Valley, hundreds of enemy paratroopers were dropping out of the sky directly over the 10th Brigade positions. Gunfire was crackling loudly. Kippenberger sprinted to the command post, a small pink house on a knoll, and had just dashed through a gap in the cacti when a burst of gunfire spattered the cactus either side of him. Jumping sideways, he rolled down a slope, twisted his ankle, then, hobbling, crawled up the track and into the back of the house, where he saw the German. Fortunately, he had not been seen in turn, so he stalked around the house and then shot him cleanly through the head from ten yards. 'The silly fellow was still watching the gap in the hedge,' wrote Kippenberger, 'and evidently had not noticed me crawl into the house.'

With the CP back in his possession he quickly caught up with his Brigade Major, Captain Brian Bassett, and his signallers, and made a quick assessment of the situation. Discarded parachutes covered the landscape; Kippenberger could also see that Germans had fallen among the two Greek battalions attached to his brigade and men were running about all over the place. As more bullets tore through the surrounding cactus, it was clear they needed to move their HQ a little way north. Taking a sub-machine gun and a pistol from the dead German, Kippenberger and the others set off to their new CP, which was to be in a hollow just to the north of Galatas, where a field telephone had already been set up. By the time he got there, the fighting had quietened down. A number of Germans had been shot and a lot more rounded up. The rest had gone to ground, presumably trying to group themselves back into some kind of organized formation. One of Kippenberger's New Zealand battalions reported killing more than 150 paratroopers. For Kippenberger, it was now time to take stock. He had two Greek regiments under his command, one of which, the 6th, had not been issued with any ammunition, so it wasn't until they began capturing the weapons of dead Germans and their ammunition arrived that they could start fighting back. Enemy fighters were still about; snipers were taking potshots in and around Galatas; more transports were dropping supplies. But otherwise, their area, at least, was calm. By midday, at any rate, there was no sign that he could see to suggest the airborne invasion had been even remotely successful.

It had been agreed with the Greek Government that the moment the Italians showed any sign of aggression towards them, British and French forces would occupy Crete as a means of denying it to the enemy. With the French out of the war by the time Italy invaded Greece, that task was left to the British only. As far as Admiral Cunningham was concerned, Suda Bay, just to the east of Canea, would make a useful refuelling post for his smaller vessels and so a small base was established there, some anti-aircraft guns were brought in, and a landing ground was created at Maleme for Fleet Air Arm fighters which could then defend the harbour. At Heraklion, roughly in the middle of the 160-mile-long northern coast-line, a further RAF airfield and staging post was established.

As a base, Crete had been little used – not, at least, until the fall of Greece, when it had become the first port of call for many of the evacuating forces. Thanks to Ultra decrypts of German Enigma traffic at Bletchley Park, the British knew about the German invasion plans for the island, and Wavell appears to have had no question marks at all over his determination to defend the island. There was certainly some sense in trying to keep this base in the Aegean, and in any case, on paper, it looked like a hard nut for the Germans to crack. It was true that its defences were poor: almost no air forces, poor communications and road links, and few anti-aircraft guns, all of which its small force had repeatedly flagged up since they had arrived there the previous autumn. However, arming Crete to the teeth had not been a high priority – or even a necessity – and had only become a higher one with the threat of the German invasion of Greece. Even now, its strategic importance remained limited.

None the less, on balance, it was worth defending, especially since Cunningham's fleet remained the dominant naval presence in the Mediterranean and because there were now some 32,000 British, New Zealand and Australian troops on the island, as well as a further 10,000 Greek troops; once again, German intelligence had been woeful, mis-judging the real size of the garrison by a margin of four to one. True, this force of over 40,000 was not well-equipped in terms of tanks or motor transport – most of which had been left in Greece – but the very nature of airborne operations meant that the Germans would be even more lightly equipped. The rule of thumb in battle is that attackers need at least a 3:1 advantage in manpower. Making an initial assault with 1:4 *dis*advantage made dubious military sense.

In fact, there were so many troops now on Crete that there was barely time to evacuate them in any case. Furthermore, the Greek King, George II, had evacuated Athens to Crete; there were thus important political reasons for keeping the island out of Axis clutches.

The man given the job of defending the island was Major-General Bernard Freyberg, commander of the New Zealand Division. Brought up in New Zealand, he had come to Britain in 1914 and volunteered to fight. Serving in the Royal Naval Division, he had fought with immense bravery both at Gallipoli and in Flanders, was wounded numerous times and won a Victoria Cross. After the war, he remained in England, married well and was a good friend of Churchill, who was fascinated by Freyberg's deeds of arms and self-effacing nature. At one country-house weekend, Churchill urged Freyberg to strip off his shirt to allow him to count all his wounds and totted up no fewer than twenty-seven. Freyberg pointed out that it wasn't really that number as one bullet usually created an exit as well as an entrance mark. In fact, Freyberg retired from the army in 1934, largely because of a heart condition, and by the outbreak of war was gearing up to stand as a British Member of Parliament; he had put his military days behind him. However, with the start of hostilities, Churchill urged the New Zealand Government to recall him to lead the country's expeditionary force. In truth, there was no other candidate. Freyberg, despite having little ambition for such a post, accepted it as his duty.

He accepted this new task too, even though he had been hoping to get his division back to Egypt and properly reorganized and trained. The shortcomings on Crete, and especially the poor communications and almost total lack of air cover, worried him considerably, which he voiced to Wavell, but he was not a man to flinch from duty. In fact, he was in every way a noble, fearless and quite extraordinary bear of a man, and as an inspirational figure he was well suited to commanding the dogged New Zealanders. This, however, could not disguise the lack of intellect or deep military understanding missing at higher levels of command; good staff officers could protect him from these shortcomings, but unfortunately, when he arrived to take command of 'Creforce' on 29 April, he barely had a staff at all.

Freyberg responded to the Ultra details of the German plan by concentrating his forces along the very narrow northern strip between the
mountains and the coast. The New Zealand Division – of which
Kippenberger's 10th Brigade was part – were between Suda Bay, Canea
and Maleme, while the Australians were at Rethymnon and the British at
Heraklion. This was all in keeping with the revelations of German plans.
Nevertheless, Freyberg also felt hidebound by Ultra. He wanted, for
example, to further reinforce Maleme but felt that to do so would risk
exposing their intelligence. He was also unduly worried by details of a
seaborne landing. This was clearly only part of the subsequent reinforcements and in any case was taken note of by ABC and his naval forces, yet
Freyberg interpreted it differently as a major threat concurrent with the
airborne forces. The general had witnessed the power of the Luftwaffe
first hand over Greece, but otherwise his experience and understanding
of air power were extremely limited; those years out of the army, at a time
when air power was developing, had left him behind the times.

Yet despite the shortage of communications, the lack of heavy weapons
and air power, and Freyberg's own somewhat muddled interpretation of
German intentions, there was much reason for the defenders to feel confident as those first *Fallschirmjäger* began falling among the scrub, cactus
and rocks of northern Crete that May morning. After all, one of the key
ingredients for a successful *coup de main* operation was surprise, yet it
was not an advantage Operation MERCURY could claim.

While Colonel Kippenberger had been shaving that morning, just a
few miles away Freyberg was having his breakfast at his villa overlooking
Creforce HQ on the edge of Canea. A young officer from the British
Military Mission to the Greek Army arrived with a message, and Freyberg
invited him to stay. They were sitting on the veranda when the invasion
began. Suddenly, the sky was full of gliders and Ju52s spewing thousands
of paratroopers.

'Well,' muttered Freyberg, 'they're on time.'

Around midday, as the German paratroopers around Maleme and Canea
were struggling to recover from catastrophic losses that morning, Martin
Pöppel and the rest of 2. Fallschirmjägerregiment were being driven over
to their transports, now returned, refuelled and in many cases repaired
after their first trip to the island. The result was an inevitable delay in
launching the second wave. For the men, it was dusty and hot, and

especially so since they had all their jump equipment. Pöppel noticed his Ju52 already had a number of bullet holes over the wings and fuselage. Around 1 p.m., with the men all loaded, they were off at last, climbing high initially and then dropping low over the wine-dark sea. It was over two hours to Rethymnon, so Pöppel decided to use the time to get some sleep. 'It's a blessed ability,' he noted, 'one that I can use at any time of day or night.'

As they approached Crete, he awoke and checked his equipment one more time. As they crossed the coast, the order 'Prepare to jump!' was given. Moments later, they were out; it was now 3.40 p.m. Pöppel looked around as he floated down – the drop zone, he reckoned, had been judged perfectly: about seven miles to the east of Rethymnon and with nothing to meet them other than a few threatening shots. Landing in an olive tree, he managed to quickly free himself and was soon clear and on firm ground once more. The heat was intense, and after gathering the weapons containers and grabbing their kit, they collected themselves together and tried to acclimatize for a moment before heading towards the airfield, their day's objective.

The area had been bombed just before their drop but not very effectively, and while Pöppel saw little gunfire as they floated down, elsewhere the defenders responded more bullishly; seven transports were brought down on land and a number disappeared in flames into the sea. Nor was the drop as accurate as Pöppel had thought. A number of *Fallschirmjäger* fell straight into the sea and drowned, while about a dozen had the misfortune to land among bamboo and become impaled on the stalks. Others suffered injuries on the rocky ground. In fact, only Pöppel's company and one other were dropped in the right place.

The drop at Rethymnon had involved some 1,500 troops. One group headed towards Rethymnon itself, with the town and port their objective, but soon came up against the 800-strong Cretan gendarmerie there and were beaten back. A second force of some 200 *Fallschirmjäger* landed mostly right in front of one of two Australian battalions and were beaten off by nightfall with eighty-eight Germans captured and a number of weapon canisters captured.

Meanwhile, Martin Pöppel and his overheating comrades, under the command of Major Kroh, headed either side of the coast road towards the airfield only to be stopped in their tracks by Australians protecting the landing ground from the rocky hills to the east, known by the defenders as Hill A. Forced to take cover in the vineyards next to the coast road, they pushed forward tentatively as dusk began to fall, calling out the password 'Reichsmarschall' in loud whispers as more *Fallschirmjäger* managed to join them.

The third drop took place around the ancient town of Heraklion and fared little better. It was also even later, not arriving until after 5.30 p.m. Once again, the drop was badly dispersed, many paratroopers were killed as they fell, and here the Bofors light anti-aircraft guns had more success against the lumbering Ju52s. Transports were still coming over after 7 p.m., at which point no fewer than eight were reported as falling in flames at the same time. And as at Rethymnon, counter-attacks by the defenders around the airfield were swift, determined and largely successful.

A further group of *Fallschirmjäger* had been dropped to the west of the town, and as darkness fell these now attempted to storm the massive Heraklion city walls around the Canea Gate. Once again, the town itself had been left in the hands of local Cretans and Greek troops. In what became a battle of furious close-quarter fighting, the Germans broke through into the city but were eventually forced to pull back for lack of ammunition and through mounting casualties; bullets quickly ran dry when a magazine had just three seconds of fire-time.

As night descended over Crete like a shroud, it seemed clear to most that the airborne assault had been a costly failure, yet one of the most striking characteristic features of the fighting was its confused nature, and it was confusion, or, rather, the fog of war, that had the final say.

Indeed, that Colonel Howard Kippenberger, a brigade commander, had been both actively involved in the fighting and had shot a man in the head from a matter of yards said much about the nature of the battle that day. Even when undertaken in daylight, airborne drops were rarely as accurate as those conducting the airlift would have liked. As a result, the normal practice of infantry warfare was swept aside as paratroopers landed largely willy-nilly, sometimes several miles away and in other places literally on top of the defenders. It was disorientating for all concerned: the defenders never really knew whether there might be a *Fallschirmjäger* lurking behind any cactus or olive tree, while the attackers had to work out where they were, then more often than not found themselves fighting alongside unfamiliar comrades.

Nowhere had the confusion been more marked than in the New

Zealanders' sector around Canea, Galatas and Maleme. It was 22nd Brigade that was defending Maleme and the key low Hill 107 that overlooked the airfield. The *Fallschirmjäger* of the Storm Regiment that had landed there had been badly mauled: the New Zealanders had been told to aim at the paratroopers' feet because of their deceptively swift descent and many had been killed before they even hit the ground. A number of commanders were either killed or wounded, which led to further confusion; in one Storm Regiment battalion, no fewer than sixteen officers died and seven were wounded. The attackers were also shocked to find themselves confronted by groups of Cretans, including women and boys; near the little port of Kastelli Kissamou, to the west of Maleme, fifty-three out of seventy-two *Fallschirmjäger* were killed by locals and the rest taken prisoner. A number of the corpses were hacked at by these locals, many of whom had been armed only with axes and spades.

Around Galatas and Prison Valley, the confused nature of the fighting had continued all day. Unfortunately, the Germans had managed to capture the prison itself – Kippenberger's men had been positioned around and overlooking the valley rather than defending the prison building – which gave the paratroopers there a firm base as well as water. None the less, the defenders largely had the area under control, and the German occupation of the prison would have counted for nothing had the *Fallschirmjäger* there remained unable to be reinforced.

None of the German objectives had been taken: not Canea, not Maleme, not even the tiny port of Kastelli Kissamou. In all, 1,856 *Fallschirmjäger* had been killed on the first day – a huge number of the attacking force. Many others had been wounded, so that total casualties for the day were around 4,000 out of the roughly 14,000 paratroopers available for the entire operation. Back in Athens, as piecemeal reports reached them, it seemed clear to General Löhr that Operation MERCURY had failed and would have to be aborted.

That it was not was largely due to the inability of the defenders to properly communicate with one another. As in France in May 1940, field telephone lines were cut, runners were unable to get through, and Colonel Leslie Andrew, the commander at Maleme, was left with an increasingly unclear picture of what on earth was going on. His request for support from the neighbouring battalion was refused by Colonel James Hargest, 5th Brigade's commander, and with darkness falling Andrew felt he had no choice but to withdraw.

The beleaguered, battered *Fallschirmjäger* around Maleme and Hill 107 had been bracing themselves for a major British counter-attack, but it never came. Colonel Andrew never received the reinforcements he so urgently needed. Just one battalion, maybe even one company, to help Colonel Andrew might have made all the difference.

Near the landing ground to the east of Rethymnon, Major Kroh's force of paratroopers attacked uphill through the vineyards in the grey light of early dawn. The men were all exhausted, hungry and thirsty, and, unbeknown to them, the Australian commander, Colonel Campbell, recognizing the hill was the key objective for the Germans, had thrown all his reserves into reinforcing the position, including two Greek regiments, one on either flank. Martin Pöppel and his comrades were soon pinned down by heavy Allied fire. He spotted one *Oberjäger* holding his torn guts with both hands and hurried over to help, but the man told him to press on and come back and help him later. 'It's no good,' noted Pöppel. 'People are getting hit all around us, and the air is full of their groans and cries of pain. We're forced to withdraw from this hill of blood and so fail to achieve our objective.' Pulling back, they found some cover on a reverse slope and then occupied a lone house, where the wounded were tended by the medical orderlies. The rest scrambled over a road and into a shallow hollow. There were only thirty or so men. A heated debate followed. Should they surrender? 'Quite out of the question,' grunted one *Feldwebel*. Moments later, they heard vehicles and British voices. Crouching low, they waited for them to pass then scurried away, back down the coast road and discarding everything but their weapons, ammo and other essentials.

Eventually, they stopped in a hollow. Of Major Kroh, there was no sign. Another officer, Oberleutnant Anton von Roon, began to organize another battlegroup from the remnants of their shattered unit. A friend handed Pöppel a much-needed cigarette. 'Tired and dispirited,' he recorded, 'we sit with bowed heads.' Short on ammunition, with many of their comrades dead or wounded, and with almost no communications, their chances of reversing this dire situation looked bleak indeed.

Yet while it was hard for the besieged *Fallschirmjäger* around Heraklion and Rethymnon to envisage a way out, the news was better at the western end of the island. Back on mainland Greece, General Kurt Student was still under pressure to abort and was keenly aware that unless he was able to start landing 5. Gebirgsdivision by the end of play that second day, it was all over. Throwing caution to the wind, he ordered one of his staff, a pilot, to fly to Crete and then touch down and take off at the western side of Maleme. This he did, and although he was able to report some light firing, none of it had been direct. This told Student what he needed to know: the western side of Maleme, at any rate, was no longer being defended. Immediately ordering his reserve troops under the command of Colonel Gerhard Ramcke to take off and drop to the west of Maleme, and two further companies to be dropped east of the airfield, he also told the *Gebirgsjäger* to be on standby to fly to Crete at a moment's notice.

Although the 28th Maori Battalion massacred the paratroopers dropped to the east of Maleme, by 5 p.m. the first *Gebirgsjäger* units were landing at Maleme. As many as twenty Ju52s were hit or crashed, but they kept going: disgorging troops, taking off again, and then more landing among the wreckage. At one point, they were landing and the men jumping out in around seventy seconds. By the time a counter-attack was finally launched, it was early in the morning of 22 May, and they were up against fresh and now well-armed mountain troops and revitalized para-troopers. Consequently, it failed.

Still occupying the ground around Galatas, Colonel Kippenberger and his men were holding up rather better, and a concentrated attack by the *Fallschirmjäger* around the Prison Valley was forcibly beaten back not by the New Zealanders, but by a horde of Cretans led by a British officer of the Military Mission. Later, Kippenberger's 'Composite' Battalion, made up of troops hurriedly brought together before the invasion began, found another forty-odd German paratroopers in the village of Agio Goannino, where they were 'nearly all disposed of'. Kippenberger noticed that most of the Germans they came across were armed only with sub-machine guns, the MP40, or 'Schmeisser', as it was known to the British. These had an effective range of little more than 75 yards and were best at distances of 30 yards or less. And while the Germans had some light mortars and machine guns too, really there was absolutely no reason at all why any soldiers armed with rifles and Bren guns that were lethal at 400 yards should lose.

Nor would they have done, so long as Creforce had only the *Fallschirmjäger* units to deal with. Martin Pöppel and his comrades at Rethymnon would have soon been overrun for good, and so too would those German para-trooper units at Heraklion. Unfortunately for the defenders, however, now that more and more fresh troops were being landed at Maleme, this was no longer the case. The *Gebirgsjäger* were equipped with mainly rifles, machine guns, mortars and even small artillery pieces. After the Germans had been a whisker away from defeat, Freyberg and his senior commanders had allowed the enemy a lifeline, one that their training and determination had allowed them to rapidly exploit. Suddenly, the Allied defence of Crete was unravelling. Of all the setbacks Britain had faced so far in the war, this was surely the most unnecessary and inexcusable.

On the 23rd, Freyberg ordered his forces to fall back to a new line around Galatas, while more German reinforcements were landing at Maleme and further paratroopers were being dropped around Heraklion. When the RAF arrived and bombed Maleme, they destroyed twenty-four all-important Ju52s, but as far as saving Crete was concerned it was too little, too late. On the 26th, the Canea–Galatas line was broken, the defenders pushed back yet further. 'The news from many quarters,' noted Kippenberger, 'made it plain that the end was near and I was unashamedly pleased in the evening when orders came to set off on the march over mountains to Sphakia and there embark.'

In fact, the order for the evacuation was not given until the following day, the 27th, and while the defenders might have been relieved to get away from the place, Admiral Cunningham, whose Mediterranean Fleet would have to perform this latest miracle, was far from happy. Many of his ships were already in the vicinity, however. In fact, the attempted German effort to reinforce the invasion by sea had been swiftly intercepted by ABC's forces and largely sunk. One battalion of German mountain troops, travelling in traditional Greek sailing boats, was almost entirely wiped out.

The Luftwaffe, however, had struck back, and on 22 May two cruisers, the *Gloucester* and *Fiji*, were sunk, along with four destroyers, while two battleships and two further cruisers were damaged. Among those carrying out attacks were Helmut Mahlke and his Stuka *Geschwader*, who had been posted to Greece from Sicily that same day and had added to Admiral Cunningham's woes by sinking a merchant vessel in Suda Bay.

The naval losses, especially, were severe blows to the British. In his office in Alexandria, near the war room where all the movements of his ships were carefully plotted, Cunningham followed the events with a heavy heart. 'I came to dread every ring on the telephone, every knock on the door,' he noted, 'and the arrival of each fresh signal.' That night, 22 May, he had signalled to all his ships at sea, 'Stick it out. Navy must not let Army down. No enemy forces must reach Crete by sea.'

Nor did they, but, sadly for ABC and all his men, their valiant efforts had been for nothing. Now, less than a week later, they had to attempt to rescue Creforce with the Luftwaffe still ruling the skies. Sphakia was little more than a small fishing village on the south side of the mountainous island, and an evacuation from there was unquestionably going to be difficult and made worse by the near-exhaustion of many of the men being picked up and the crews who had to carry out the lift. 'We were not really in favourable condition to evacuate some twenty-two thousand soldiers,' wrote Cunningham with some understatement, 'most of them from an open beach, in the face of the Luftwaffe. But there was no alternative.' A plan was hastily formed. Troops from Canea and around Suda Bay would make their way south, through the mountains, while a blocking force held off the enemy. They would be evacuated from Sphakia. Those from Rethymnon would, it was hoped, be picked up from Plaka Bay, near the town, while a further lift would be carried out in one night from Heraklion. In the event, they were unable to reach Rethymnon, and the Australians there either took their chances and went into the mountains or surrendered. More than 700 did the latter. At Heraklion, the evacuation was altogether more successful, and on the night of 28–29 May some 4,000 were taken off the island in one lift, and without lights and without disturbing the enemy. It was no small feat.

In all, some 16,500 men were safely evacuated, including Colonel Kippenberger. For all involved, it was a devastating blow, not least because a number had to stay behind as a rear-party to cover their departure. One of his fellow brigade commanders, Jim Burrows, had volunteered to remain and command the New Zealanders. 'I spoke as reassuringly as I could to the rear-party,' wrote Kippenberger, 'shook hands with Jim, and went off very sadly.' After tramping several miles to the beach, they later boarded the Australian destroyer *Napier*, safely reaching Alexandria the next day.

Crete was surrendered at 9 a.m. on 1 June. Although some 5,000 British and Commonwealth troops were left behind, and some 3,500 were casualties, once again, the bulk of British forces had escaped. The naval losses had been hard for the British, and ABC especially, to bear. Three cruisers and six destroyers were sunk and sixteen further vessels damaged, some badly so. With it had come the loss of more than 2,000 lives. 'Once again,' wrote Cunningham, 'it had been borne in upon us that the Navy and the Army could not make up for the lack of air forces.' He had a point and reckoned, not unreasonably, that three squadrons of long-range fighters might have saved Crete. And a few radios would have helped too.

But the losses to the Germans had been worse. In Rethymnon, Martin Pöppel spent the day of victory helping to bury the dead. 'We put up crosses with names and dates,' he wrote, 'but what good are crosses to our comrades? Young lads, like ourselves, cheerful and happy in Tanagra such a short time ago. Now they lie here, far from home.' The *Fallschirmjäger*, among the best troops in the Wehrmacht, had lost around 6,000 men, more than half those dropped. These were catastrophic casualties for one of Hitler's most prized spearheads, and a cautionary tale for any military thinking that airborne operations were some kind of panacea. Perhaps even more critically, the losses of transport aircraft had been terrible too: 143 had been destroyed and eight were missing, while a further 120 were severely damaged and 85 more had suffered lesser damage. More than 50 bombers and fighters had also been lost.

With BARBAROSSA now just three weeks away, it was the loss of transport aircraft, however, that would hurt Germany most. Greece and Crete had been won, but whether the prize had been worth it was another matter.

CHAPTER 46

Midsummer Heat

T O MUCH OF THE WORLD, Germany's latest victory in Crete, especially when the British defenders appeared to hold all the aces, merely added to the sense of military invincibility. German propaganda made sure that the modern mechanized juggernaut was on full display: *Die Deutsche Wochenschau* newsreels showed diving Stukas, columns of panzers and armoured cars, and troops firing powerful machine guns. Guns pounded enemy positions, just as viewers were pounded with imagery of military might. Suddenly, the failure of the Luftwaffe in the Battle of Britain was a distant memory. Nazi Germany was back on form doing what it did best: smashing one country after another with overwhelming air and land power.

There was, however, less footage of the all-important war at sea, where Germany was not faring anything like so well, and nor was anyone questioning whether charging into the Balkans and on to Crete made good strategic sense. Nor would they when BARBAROSSA remained a secret.

Yet the fact remained that with the exception of the astonishing victory against France, crushing a string of weaker opponents masked the huge challenges still facing Germany. The British had been defeated in Flanders, in Greece and on Crete, and been given a bloody nose in Libya, but as convoys and supplies continued to stream across the oceans, so its Army was growing with every passing day, and so too were its air forces. Britain was not only still very much in the war, but as a threat its power was increasing, not falling away.

In fact, the blitzkriegs hid from the world the very brittle foundations on which those German victories were based. Because of the chronic shortages of resources, and because Britain was still in the war, invasion of the Soviet Union was the only chance of remedying the situation. And nothing less than total victory would suffice. Yet despite German confidence, that was a very tall order because the German way of war was based on a comparatively small operational reach – one that worked very effectively in countries such as Norway, Greece or even France but would be tested more fully in the vast expanses of the Soviet Union.

In the Balkans, the Wehrmacht had demonstrated a more refined version of the *Bewegungskrieg* tactics employed in France, and it was certainly the case that 12. Armee, used in Yugoslavia and Greece, was more proportionally mechanized than any German army of 1940. Yet, for BARBAROSSA, the number of fully mechanized divisions remained alarmingly low: panzer divisions had more than doubled to twenty-one, and motorized divisions to thirteen, but that still made only thirty-three in all out of an expanded army of over 200 divisions.

Nor were all these divisions available for BARBAROSSA. Despite Mussolini's and Ciano's fears, it was agreed that occupation of Greece would largely be in the hands of the Italians (although German forces would remain on Crete), but elsewhere Germany had to maintain occupation forces: in the occupied zone in France, in the Low Countries, in Denmark and Norway, as well as the Greater Reich. There were also the increasing demands of the North African theatre, which most certainly did require motorization and was a further drain on General Adolf von Schell's motor pool. It meant that instead of twenty-one panzer divisions being available for the Soviet Union, there were only seventeen – i.e. seven more than had been used in France for a country that was thirty-seven times the size.

Key to the success of *Bewegungskrieg* was overwhelming force at the main points of attack combined with speed of operations. The trouble was, this combined weight of force and speed could only be maintained so far – in fact, a distance of around between 300 miles and 500 miles at the absolute most.

Overseeing the operational plan for BARBAROSSA was General Halder, the army's Chief of Staff, who was well aware of the German operational reach and so was basing the plan of attack on smashing Soviet resistance very quickly and on the assumption that the Red Army would crumble under the weight of the initial blow. A number of premises were assumed, including, perhaps most importantly, that the Red Army could be crushed close to its western borders – that is, along the line of the Dnieper and Dvina rivers, which ran north–south for some 500 kilometres, or 300 miles, from the German–Polish border, and was thus within the German operational reach. As it was, Adolf von Schell was forced to create a complicated system of dumps and motor pools in order to supply fuel to panzer and motorized divisions that far forward. The danger, as Halder was keenly aware, was of hold-ups for lack of supplies; it was no good cutting a swathe and then being forced to halt, because then the Red Army would be able to retreat and reorganize; unlike the French Army, it had thousands of miles to play with. And unlike its counterpart in France, it had effectively a limitless source of manpower. The latest German intelligence suggested that the Red Army had more than 170 divisions and a large arsenal of weapons and tanks. Their intelligence, as usual, was wrong: the Russians had even more than that, some 303 divisions, over 4.7 million men in uniform, and more waiting in the wings.

The key was to destroy as much of the Red Army as quickly as possible, to the point where it would be incapable of further resistance. 'Speed! No stops!' Halder noted in his diary, echoing Guderian's mantra from the previous May. 'The continuous operation depends on motor transport.' A few days later, he added, '*Motor vehicle* must accomplish everything.'

It has been repeatedly argued that the postponement of BARBAROSSA was not caused by the campaigns in the Balkans, North Africa or Crete, and that, rather, the delay allowed for the further production of trucks. It has also been pointed out that the German Army benefited from the numerous British trucks captured in Greece. Be that as it may, the campaigns none the less used up a great deal of precious fuel. The campaign in the Balkans, General Georg Thomas pointed out at a meeting of the War Economy Department in April, had influenced the fuel situation 'through the additional amounts that have to be taken from the Reich for these ventures'; these were amounts that could not then be used in the East.

Fuel, or the lack of it, was a never-ending headache that so far Germany had failed to solve. Having plundered the existing stocks of conquered territories, the only other means of getting crude oil was from the Ploeşti oilfields and then sending it by rail. The alternative was synthetic fuel, a process pioneered in Germany during the last war which involved gasifying coal or converting a mixture of carbon monoxide and liquid hydrocarbons. At any rate, both processes needed coal, which meant it could not be used for steelmaking and other industrial processes.

Leading the way in Germany's synthetic fuel production was Carl Krauch, chairman of the advisory board of IG Farben, the chemical industry conglomerate, and also the Plenipotentiary of Special Issues in Chemical Production. By the end of 1940, Krauch had begun the process of dramatically increasing production particularly of synthetic aviation fuel, with the expansion of three existing plants and the creation of a fourth facility at the small town of Auschwitz in Poland, which was served by good railway connections. This latter plant, which would produce all manner of synthetic fuels, including methanol, used for aviation fuel and explosives, was mapped out over an area of eight by three kilometres, with a budget of a staggering 776 million Reichsmarks – that is, about £6 billion in today's money. Even so, this new plant would take time to bear fruit. Factories of this size were not built overnight, and not in a matter of months either – at least, not in the Third Reich. A further alternative was using gas, and General von Schell reckoned that in May they had around 65,000 vehicles running with gas generators. The long and short of it was this: that unless the Germans defeated the Soviet Union swiftly and then were able to plunder the oilfields at Baku in the Caucasus, the oil shortage was only going to get worse, regardless of state-of-the-art new factories at Auschwitz. However, since they would have had no means of transporting the oil even if they did get there, this was all rather academic. Without pipelines and without shipping, the oil at Baku would remain tantalizingly where it was – and that was if the Red Army did not destroy it first, before the Germans could get their hands on it.

While the distractions in the Balkans, Greece and North Africa were undoubtedly using up fuel Germany could ill afford to burn, those campaigns were also a sap on another crucial supply as BARBAROSSA loomed. General von Schell had been valiantly trying to reduce the number of different types of motor vehicles, but fresh booty kept adding to the pool. The trouble was that every vehicle needed spare parts, and every vehicle variant needed different spare parts. With Halder repeatedly stressing the importance of trucks in maintaining a swift blitzkrieg in the Soviet Union, building up a stock of spares was clearly of paramount importance. 'The Balkan campaign,' wrote von Schell, 'left a large hole in the stock of supplies, because the vehicles of motorized troops that had taken part in it had suffered badly in the mountainous terrain, and they had to be re-equipped for action in the East in four weeks.'

The truth was, those same old problems that had plagued Prussia and then Germany for centuries had not gone away: the lack of natural resources and the geographical isolation from the world's sea lanes meant the Reich had to avoid long, attritional conflicts at all costs. The booty plundered from the early victories had provided a short-term fillip and not much more, so that by midsummer 1941 Germany was growing short of all manner of materiel – even manpower. There were now 7.3 million men in the Wehrmacht, including teenagers, who accounted for some 660,000 recruits a year, but that was it as far as trained young men of military age was concerned; by June 1941, the manpower barrel was beginning to be scraped, and because BARBAROSSA was yet another do-or-die, go-for-broke gamble, the best available manpower was now either committed to the initial assault or already in action elsewhere, such as North Africa and the Mediterranean. Reserves for the Army amounted to 385,000 men. Since planners were assuming casualties would be around 275,000 during the 'frontier battles' and possibly a further 200,000 in September, the supply of trained reserves would therefore be exhausted by October. This was fine, just so long as the battle was over every bit as quickly as hoped – and expected.

Production of small arms (rifles, machine guns and so on), as well as tanks and artillery pieces, had considerably increased because due to Hitler's major drive to increase ammunition the previous year, there was now a vast stockpile. This allowed steel allocations that had been made for ammunition to be redirected elsewhere. It was an inefficient waste of factories and machine tools, but it did allow a dramatic increase in armaments, and not least tanks. Panzer production was hardly efficient, however. There were no giant factories like that planned by IG Farben at Auschwitz; rather, they were being produced in what the British might call 'shadow factories' around the Reich – at Alkett and Daimler-Benz in Berlin, for example, or at MAN in Nuremberg. Dispersal was not good for economies of scale and meant materials had to be shipped all over Germany, but by using existing plants and expanding those factories, at least capacity could be swiftly increased. Also important was the increasing fear of the RAF; dispersal was seen as an important deterrent, and for all the withering criticism that has been flung at RAF Bomber Command ever since this period, their not-very-accurate bombing efforts were most definitely playing on German fears and affecting how the Reich was both defended and how it produced war materiel.

By the first half of 1941, these factories were producing some 140 Panzer Mk IIIs a month, each armed with a 50mm gun, a figure that was steadily rising, and around thirty Mk IVs with a 75mm gun. This meant, however, that although the Wehrmacht had around 3,000 tanks in June 1941, still only 1,600 of those were Panzer Mk IIIs and IVs.

A further increasingly worrying shortage was in food and animal feed-stuffs. The 1940 harvest had not been good, while there was now such a shortage of manpower in the Reich itself that Polish prisoners had been brought in to help on the land. Nor had the occupied territories remotely solved the problem, for although Germany had wasted no time in demanding considerable amounts of agricultural riches, all of these countries, whether France, the Netherlands or elsewhere, were, like Germany, dependent on food imports themselves; Norway, for example, was reliant on imports for 57 per cent of its food, all of which was now cut off by the British blockade, which had been in place against all occupied countries since the previous August. By the summer of 1941, this was being felt increasingly keenly. Rationing was stringent in Germany and considerably harsher than it was in Britain, which was positively bursting with food in comparison. Nor was oil the only fuel needed for the Army; BARBAROSSA would not only involve more than three million men who all needed to be fed, but some 600,000 horses requiring fodder.

Herbert Backe's Battle of Production had not been the hoped-for success, but the invasion of the Soviet Union was expected to solve a lot of the food shortage problems. In fact, the need for food was a driving force in Hitler's plans for *Lebensraum* in the East. Yet Backe was aware that for all the vast tracts of grain that grew across the Ukraine each year, only a small surplus was exported. The rest was used to feed the urban population, which had grown by around thirty million since the revolution back in 1917. There was, however, a solution that Backe now proposed – one that would, as far as he was concerned, kill two birds with one stone. As a man imbued with the same warped racial ideology as the Führer, Backe saw the war as a struggle of race as much as a battle of resources. Quite simply, Backe was proposing to divert food away from

Russian cities and straight to Germany and the Wehrmacht instead.

In a meeting called by General Georg Thomas on 2 May 1941, it was quite calmly accepted that the mass starvation of millions of Soviets was the only solution to Germany's food shortage. 'The war can only be continued if the entire Wehrmacht is fed from Russia in the third year of the war', it was minuted matter-of-factly. 'If we take what we need out of the country, there can be no doubt that many millions of people will die of starvation.' This stunning admission suggests Thomas and his colleagues were aware there was a choice; indeed there was, and all chose to save Germany. For Thomas, it was about survival not ideology; for Backe, it was both. The SS was also making preparations to exterminate vast numbers of Jews and *Untermenschen*, but the Hunger Plan, which was expected to result in the deaths of 'umpteen millions', was being coolly endorsed by the Wehrmacht. Like the SS, its leaders too were becoming architects of genocide.

In fact, Thomas, by instinct anti-Nazi, was turning himself into something of a monster, with his ruthless pragmatism getting the better of him. Earlier in the year, he had been gloomy about the potential for exploitation in the East, which was increasingly being painted in Nazi quarters as a panacea; he was aware, for example, that when Germany had captured Ukraine in 1917, it had reaped few rewards. Yet, by May, he had completed, openly at any rate, a volte-face and began embracing the possibilities for exploitation to be found in the Soviet Union. In a private memo in June, however, he was once again more circumspect. Russia was undoubtedly rich in raw materials and foodstuffs, but, he noted, 'as experience teaches, a really significant increase, however, can only occur over a period of several years.' This, he added, was especially the case in the East, because of the primitive infrastructure. 'In conclusion,' he added, 'the core problem of German warfare cannot be completely avoided through access to Russian territory. Relief is only in certain areas and only partially within those areas.'

In other words, Thomas suspected Germany was doomed.

CHAPTER 47

Industrial Potential

'THE VIRTUAL ENTRY into the war of the United States at England's side,' wrote General Thomas in June 1941, 'has resulted in all probability that what lies ahead is an economic war against Germany of indefinite length.' Certainly, Thomas was not alone within the Third Reich in fearing the lurking threat of the USA; Hitler was also very aware of it. Back in the 1920s, when the USA had been Germany's saviour, there had been every reason to hope that America and Germany would be economic and industrial allies for the foreseeable future, but, after Munich, Roosevelt's rhetoric against the Nazis had left Germans in no doubt where his sympathies lay. Since the changes in the US Neutrality Act and the growing armaments production of the USA on behalf of Britain, the threat from America had grown alarmingly, no matter that US polls still showed there was little appetite for war.

This was just another reason why Hitler needed to win the war swiftly. It was also why Britain continued to fight – the USA, whose military strength was only growing, would have that all-important springboard from which to attack the Greater Reich. And not only was the United States vast, with access to the kind of resources Nazi Germany could only dream about, but it had the right conditions in which to build up military strength too. 'The Americans can manufacture in peace,' Feldmarschall Milch would tell a gathering of German industrialists. 'They have enough to eat, they have enough workers, with still over five million unemployed, and they do not suffer air raids. American war industry is magnificently organized by a man who really knows his business, Mr Knudsen of General Motors.'

Compared with the chaos and personality clashes of the German armaments industry – and nowhere was this more evident than in the Luftwaffe – it was true that US rearmament suffered few of the hindrances that beset German industry, yet in June 1941 Bill Knudsen might have argued that he still had problems a-plenty. No one could doubt America's rearmament potential, but a year on from leaving his position at GM and answering the President's call, Knudsen was still struggling to ensure that potential was realized.

The problems had really begun to emerge following his deal with the US car manufacturers to make aircraft the previous autumn. In many circles in Washington and throughout the media, Knudsen was lambasted for allowing big business to scoop up most of the largest defence contracts. No matter how much Knudsen pointed out that it was those biggest companies that had the power and wherewithal to see those contracts through, and no matter how often he argued that there were still plenty of jobs for smaller subcontractors, the criticisms persisted.

Knudsen was, of course, looking at the situation with a purely businessman's hat on; capitalism had served the American car industry well, and he had been given a brief to increase armaments production exponentially. He could take the criticism – he cared not a fig for politics – but whether the President could was another matter. Another gripe was that the car makers were still making motor vehicles for commercial sale, while also taking on war contracts. This, it was argued, was surely outrageously greedy and typical of fat-cat big businesses – and the criticism was certainly a concern to the President, who called Knudsen in to explain why civilian production was continuing when massed war production was of such urgent importance and the car manufacturers had been given millions of dollars to carry them out.

Knudsen explained. The key was to keep production in the plants going. If civilian production was shut down, the plants would stop producing anything for months. 'If they are shut down for months,' he told FDR, 'the toolmakers will scatter.' And if they did, it would be very hard to get them back swiftly again. What he was proposing was this: to bury the automobile manufacturers under defence orders – to the tune of three times as much as they could make with their existing facilities. This would keep them busy and force them to expand their facilities. And as their facilities expanded, so they would be able to keep their toolmakers. The government could force the automobile makers to stop manufacturing civilian automobiles, but not until the new facilities were in place. Successfully forcing them to switch to war manufacturing could only happen if there was continuity of production in their plants.

Roosevelt accepted these arguments; after all, it was for precisely this kind of knowledge of the industry that Knudsen had been hired in the first place. However, it was clear that the National Defense Advisory Commission was not working; its brief was too woolly, its authority too undefined. In December, the NDAC had been shut down and replaced with the Office of Production Management (OPM). Knudsen was appointed its Director General alongside Sidney Hillman, who had also served on the NDAC. Knudsen, Roosevelt announced, would lead American business, while Hillman would head up American labour. The OPM would also be a four-man board with Stimson and Knox, the Secretaries for War and the Navy, joining Knudsen and Hillman. To all concerned apart from Roosevelt, it felt like a bit of a fudge, but at least Knudsen was now working to a legal position, unlike his role with the NDAC, which had never been given any formal authority as such.

In the months that followed, the US rearmament commitments grew and grew. Lend-Lease did not help, because suddenly the British were ordering even more, for which the capacity somehow had to be found. Knudsen reckoned British orders were adding 60 per cent more man-hours to the original US war production programme. Suddenly, they were looking at orders worth $150 *billion*, yet Congress's defence authorization for the following year remained just $10 billion. The truth was, no one, not even Bill Knudsen, knew what American business could achieve, so in the early summer of 1941 these vast numbers of contracts and dizzying figures really were just a lot of numbers on pieces of paper.

One thing, however, was certain: American potential would not be realized if the labour unions continued to agitate in the way they had begun to do. Roosevelt had repeatedly called for unity of purpose, but the American unions were coming to the fore, and the Fair Labor Standards Act of 1938, in which it was decreed there should be a maximum forty-hour week, had only just come into being in October 1940, just as the demand came for massively increased productivity. The unions were keen to protect this privilege. 'The hard difficulty now,' commented the *Saturday Evening Post*, 'is to reconcile our newly conceived national labor policy with the imperatives of an unlimited defense program.' Added to this was the CIO, the Congress of Industrial Organizations, dominated by Communists, who resented US involvement in war production as they viewed the conflict as a bourgeois struggle from which the US should steer clear. Yet not all unions were dominated by the Communists and, in fact, the CIO's new president, Philip Murray, was not even a Communist; his prime concern was to secure a greater share of the defence-boom profits for those in the union and to ensure they were protected as and when the boom was over. At any rate, one way of making these gripes and concerns heard was to go on strike. The first to do so were workers at the Vultee aircraft plant in San Diego in November 1940, and the action then spread like wildfire. By March, there were some fifteen strikes at aircraft factories alone. This loss of man-hours was beginning to badly affect the US's ability to rearm – Knudsen reckoned it was slowing war production by as much as 25 per cent. 'When I realize that the hours lost might produce engines and bombers, guns, tanks, or ships,' he told the National Press Club, 'then I hope for guidance – divine guidance – to get some sense into all our heads and to realize this thing must stop.' Sidney Hillman, the OPM labour head, seemed powerless to do anything about it, and the situation was made worse by John L. Lewis, leader of the United Mine Workers (UMW) union, who had a personal vendetta against Hillman, was a virulent isolationist, and encouraged miners to repeatedly strike over issues of both pay and union shop. Hillman and Knudsen suggested the creation of a national defence mediation board, to which the President agreed, but it made no difference. Nor was the President prepared to take any radical action; instead, the glut of strikes was simply allowed to run its course.

Despite this, armament production was rising, and, more to the point, the huge increase in the production of machine tools, a process that took at least around nine months, was about to take effect. With these crucial weapons of any industrial process in place, production could at last accelerate, even with ongoing labour issues.

Union strikes were not affecting all corners of war production, however. Henry Kaiser's workers, for example, showed no inclination to strike; rather, workers were queuing up to sign on. Labourers from some sixteen different craft unions applied for work and were quickly taken on – which was one of the reasons why Kaiser had been able to confound predictions over the speed with which his new shipyard at Richmond, California, would be up and running. By calling upon many of the key men who had helped build his large road and dam projects and understood how to think big, he completed the foundations for the new yard not in the six months predicted, but in just three weeks. Gargantuan amounts of mud and silt were dredged and replaced by rock and gravel, and then the concrete was added, at the rate of a staggering 700 concrete piles a day. Seven slipways were built, each with a large assembly area at the head where sections of ship could be prefabricated and then lifted by giant cranes into position.

Cyril Thompson had returned to the States – this time flying – to see the work in progress and had been amazed. 'Progress in California was astonishing,' he noted. 'Kaiser went about the task in a big way.' In Portland, the second new shipyard was being built almost as quickly as that at Richmond. Incredibly, the first keel was laid in the Todd–Kaiser yard on 14 April 1941, while the first at Portland was put down on 24 May. The transformation at both places – from nothing to bustling shipyard – was truly staggering and a vindication of Thompson's choice of Kaiser as the right man to fulfil Britain's urgent demand for more shipping.

On this second trip to America, Thompson had also brought with him the blueprints for his latest merchant ship design, and, with Admiralty approval, these were given to Gibbs & Cox, a firm of naval architects. The project was given to William Gibbs, one of the firm's partners, and it was hoped initially that under his guidance the firm would fill the gap caused by the lack of design and drawing offices at the two new yards, but very quickly they took on the added role of purchasing all necessary materials needed to build both the ships and their engines. Under the guidance of Thompson, they were to produce an entirely new set of plans, based on the original ship design but modified for welding rather than riveting and to suit US ship-building practices. Far greater detail was needed than was ever expected in a British shipyard. 'In other words,' said Thompson, 'nothing whatever was left to be arranged on the ship. This practice saved endless time and argument in the shipyards, where local surveyors were responsible only for seeing that all plans were exactly followed.'

By the time Thompson flew back to Britain during the first week of June, he had already seen the first Liberty ships emerging at both Richmond and Portland. These vessels, created by harnessing British and American design, expertise and construction acumen in almost perfect co-operation, were an achievement that could not have been realized anywhere else in the world. And since shipping, as much as any other factor, was shaping Britain's ability to fight the war, and preventing Germany's defeat of its most dangerous enemy, the free world had reason to thank Cyril Thompson, William Gibbs and Henry Kaiser, especially.

Far across the oceans, at GHQ in Cairo, the British were once again able to temper bad news with good. Crete had fallen, but the more important island of Malta had been enjoying a respite from the Luftwaffe and had been causing havoc to Axis convoys bound for Tripoli. The coup in Iraq had also been successfully quelled and a new pro-British government formed in Baghdad. The Greek government had formed in exile in Cairo, and fresh supplies, including more aircraft, had reached Egypt. Greece and Crete had been lost, but the British position in the Middle East was reasonably safe in the short term, at any rate.

However, one serious further threat was now emerging, and that was from Vichy-controlled Syria, where the governor, Général Henri Dentz, had been entertaining German agents who had come to Syria in the hope of securing some Luftwaffe air bases. Général de Gaulle had got wind of this news and requested facilities, which were granted from London, to visit Cairo and see his representative there, Général Georges Catroux. With General Edward Spears in tow, de Gaulle reached Egypt only to learn from Catroux that Syria was ready to cast aside Vichy and fly the Cross of Lorraine, but only if Free French troops arrived in force. Currently, though, there were some 30,000 Vichy French forces in the Levant; de Gaulle could call on just 6,000. This meant he needed British help. On 15 April, in Cairo, de Gaulle, with Spears's support, then appealed to Anthony Eden, who was broadly sympathetic but pointed out that it could not afford to fail; therefore a force had to be put together that could ensure success. When he put this to the Chiefs of Staff, however, they ruled out such a venture absolutely. Wavell was equally dogmatic. 'If de Gaulle's people do anything,' he told Spears, 'it must be a success.'

For de Gaulle, this was more than frustrating. He both wanted and needed his Free French movement to gather momentum, and despite the failure at Dakar the forces flying his banner had kept hold of their successes in Central Africa. Free French units had fought alongside the British in East Africa too, while back in December they had successfully attacked an Italian outpost in southern Libya. From Chad, de Gaulle had ordered one of his best lieutenants, Général Philippe Leclerc, to march on the oasis at Kufra, which, after a month's siege, had been taken along with 300 Italian prisoners. On the other hand, de Gaulle's offer to send troops to fight alongside the British in Greece had been declined, while his approach to Weygand, still in Algeria, had been ignored. What's more, he was extremely frustrated at being beholden to the British, all of whom seemed to him to be patronizing and unwilling to share his vision for the Free French. The person he found most annoying of all was General Spears; the two wanted the same ends but increasingly were struggling to rub along together.

Rashid Ali al-Gaylani's coup, however, changed everything, although it should have changed nothing. German intentions in Syria and Iraq were speculative and, following the losses on Crete, unrealistic, but the swathe of dynamic German successes had clouded British judgement; even John Kennedy, equally unaware of German plans for the Soviet Union, was in favour of an immediate move into Syria, partly to stop German interference there, but also because RAF possession of Syrian airfields would counteract any Luftwaffe presence on Crete; Alexandria was equidistant between the two.

Yet, in reality, not even the Führer was prepared to divert more resources to the Middle East with BARBAROSSA around the corner. Furthermore, Hitler was so appalled by the casualties to the *Fallschirmjäger* that he had even announced that, henceforth, there would be no more airborne assaults. However, since the British only knew about the German build-up of forces in the East but no details of any offensive plan, the security threat from Vichy Syria now appeared to be growing, not lessening – or, at least, it seemed that way to Churchill and the Chiefs of Staff back in London. De Gaulle had moved to Brazzaville in Central Africa in a fit of anti-British pique and had threatened to pull out Général Catroux, his representative in Palestine. On 14 May, Churchill signalled to de Gaulle, urging him to keep Général Catroux in Palestine and inviting him to return to Cairo. A joint assault on Vichy Syria was suddenly very much on the cards. De Gaulle's reply, his first and only one in English, was succinct:

1. Thank you.
2. Catroux remains in Palestine.
3. I shall go to Cairo soon.
4. You will win the war.

Général Catroux, who had remained in Palestine, then insisted he had intelligence that the Vichy French were about to move into Lebanon and hand over the rest of Syria to the Germans. Turkish troops, meanwhile, were reported to be moving towards the Syrian border. Catroux's information was nonsense, however, and, needless to say, Wavell, took a dim view of both Churchill's latest interference and London's willingness to gobble up the French general's claims. Wavell's reluctance to send troops to Syria was compounded by the imminence of Operation BATTLEAXE, his latest attempt to push back Rommel and relieve Tobruk, which had similarly been pushed on to him by Churchill. For any joint British and Free French operation in Syria to have a chance of success, Wavell would have to scrape back together the forces he had sent into Iraq and also pull more from BATTLEAXE.

His objections fell on deaf ears, however. The attack on Syria, code-named EXPORTER, was on, and would launch on 8 June. BATTLEAXE, meanwhile, would begin on 15 June, just a week later. The timings were hardly complementary, and had Wavell had a better relationship with Churchill, the obvious and right course of action would have been to postpone the latter. Even without the Syrian venture, British forces in the Western Desert were not ready for battle. It was true that the Tiger convoy of 240 tanks had been safely delivered, but they had arrived in bad shape, having been damaged by careless stowage, and in any case 7th Armoured Division needed training time to get used to the new, fast Crusader tanks.

However, by the kind of juggling at which Wavell was by now becoming expert, he managed to get a force for Syria in place which included most of 7th Australian Division, a 5th Indian Brigade group, fresh back from East Africa, some Free French forces and a few units of armour and cavalry. Admiral Cunningham promised some offshore naval support too.

The assault on Syria opened with a proclamation broadcast by Catroux and leaflet drops, and with the Australians advancing up the coast and the Indian Brigade heading north from Transjordan into central southern Syria. The Free French then took up the advance from the Indians and soon found themselves facing the bitter realities of civil war as they came up against Vichy French troops to the south of Damascus. Meanwhile, the Australians were also facing dogged resistance as they tried to cross the Litani River north of Tyre. With a battalion of Commandos, they managed to eventually get across the river, but, five days into the campaign, it was clear reinforcements were going to be needed. Despite Free French intelligence to the contrary, the Vichy defenders apparently had no intention of tamely giving up.

Wavell's attack in the Western Desert began, as planned, on 15 June, and was in essence an enlarged version of BREVITY a month earlier. Both sides were fairly evenly matched with a similar number of men, tanks and guns; attacking the Italians without a material advantage was one thing, but doing so against Rommel's Afrikakorps was another. Nevertheless, British intelligence about German dispositions was pretty accurate – the Italians were keeping up the siege of Tobruk, Rommel's 15. Panzerdivision was up at the Egyptian–Libyan border, while his second division, 5. Leichte Division, was further back resting and retraining. The key was going to be overrunning 15. Panzer immediately before 5. Leichte Division could enter the fray. Even so, that still only gave the British a two-to-one advantage at the *Schwerpunkt*, and the plan called for 4th Indian Division to do most of the head-on assault on 15. Panzer around Sollum and 'Hellfire' Pass, while 7th Armoured carried out another wide sweep to the south in an outflanking manoeuvre that was also intended to block 5. Leichte Division.

Sadly for the British, however, the plan was simply too ambitious. In three days of fighting, fortunes ebbed and swayed, but by the 17th the British were forced to break off the battle and withdraw to refit, leaving behind roughly half of the 200 tanks with which they had begun the fighting. The Germans had lost about half that number but were in no position to push the British any further. Once again, stalemate descended over the Western Desert.

For the soldiers involved, BATTLEAXE had once again been a battle of dizzying confusion. At the best of times, the desert was disorientating. Apart from the large escarpment overlooking Sollum and the coast, the land appeared flat; but this was deceptive. The horizon would appear short, but then would suddenly widen again as the top of an imperceptible ridge was reached. Distances were incredibly hard to judge in this vast, bleached and, in June, fearsomely hot landscape. For miles and miles there was nothing: no houses, no infrastructure, no obvious landmarks. The difference from fighting in France, for example, could not have been greater.

And once the fighting started, and sand was whipped up and the air

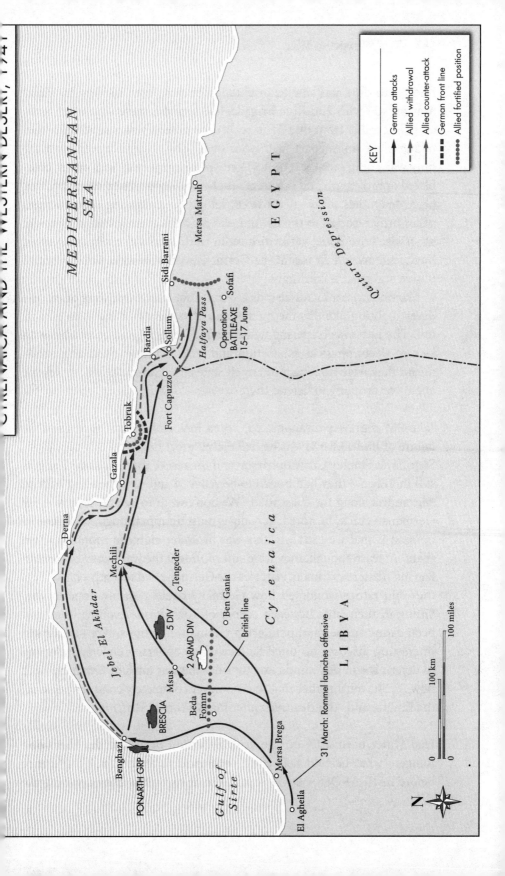

CYRENAICA AND THE WESTERN DESERT, 1941

KEY

German attacks
Allied withdrawal
Allied counter-attack
German front line
Allied fortified position

MEDITERRANEAN SEA

EGYPT

Qattara Depression

Mersa Matruh

Sidi Barrani

Sofafi

Operation BATTLEAXE
15–17 June

Halfaya Pass

Sollum

Bardia

Fort Capuzzo

Tobruk

Gazala

Derna

Mechili

Jebel El Akhdar

Tengeder

5 DIV

Ben Gania

British line

Cyrenaica

2 ARMD DIV

Msus

BRESCIA

Beda Fomm

Benghazi

PONARTH GRP

LIBYA

Mersa Brega

31 March: Rommel launches offensive

El Agheila

Gulf of Sirte

N

100 km
100 miles

filled with dust and smoke, orientation became even harder. As Albert Martin, still with 2nd Rifle Brigade, had learned, there was never really any discernible front line. 'The reality,' he noted, 'was a series of battles taking place miles apart, with your own private conflict seemingly the only war going on at the time. Then your engagement was either completed or broken off and you were sent to lend support in an action taking place ten miles away.' Because it was all so confusing, commanders necessarily resorted to the use of radio more frequently than they might otherwise have done, yet British radio traffic was too easily intercepted by the enemy, which meant the Germans were able to anticipate British moves and react accordingly.

Martin and his mates also discovered that after three days of intense desert fighting like this the mental and physical strain began to take its toll. The heat was blistering, which sapped energy, and combined with lack of sleep, physical exhaustion and lack of proper food and drink, meant they were no longer in any fit state either adequately to attack the enemy or properly to defend themselves.

'The PM is gravely disappointed,' noted Jock Colville at the news of the failure of BATTLEAXE, 'as he had placed great hopes on this operation.' So too was Stanley Christopherson and the rest of the Sherwood Rangers still in Tobruk; they had hoped to be relieved and to be heading back to Alexandria along the coast road. 'We don't seem to be able to give these Germans a crack,' he noted. 'It really is most disappointing . . . the general opinion is that we can't win this war in under eighteen months or two years.' At least, though, they were still confident the war *would* be won. In fact, no matter how many victories the Germans had recently chalked up, they still rather wondered how Germany could possibly hope to win. Sitting in their little besieged corner of Tobruk one evening, they had been eating supper and pondering German intentions. 'We had a most interesting discussion,' jotted Stanley Christopherson cheerfully, 'trying to determine in our minds exactly what the war aims of Germany were now . . . She must realize that she can never completely conquer England, the Empire and America, even after many years of struggle.'

Had Hitler been a fly on the wall, he would have told the Sherwood Rangers what he told his senior commanders at the final conference before BARBAROSSA on 14 June. Germany would win by invading the

Soviet Union and decisively beating the Red Army. Russia's collapse, he assured them, would induce Britain to give in. There was absolutely no evidence to support this, and no reason whatsoever why Britain would even consider it in the short to medium term, but that was what Hitler told them and he was sticking to his guns.

Three vast army groups, each of a million men, were now lined up ready for the invasion, although, as with the invasion of France and the Low Countries, it was the thirty panzer and motorized divisions that would be leading the charge. Along with nearly 3,000 tanks, General von Schell had managed to muster around 600,000 motorized vehicles to support this vanguard. There were also 7,000 artillery pieces, which was fewer than for the attack on the West, and 2,252 combat-ready aircraft, compared with 2,589 the previous year.

There was also some sense of mission creep over what the objectives were for BARBAROSSA. The Führer had made it clear from the outset that it was about making the most of the Soviet Union's economic, industrial and agricultural resources, while at the same time fulfilling his racial ideology. This meant turning north to secure the Baltic coastline and south into Ukraine. For Halder, however, the most important objective was Moscow, and striking quickly and capturing the capital was his prime goal. This was fraught with risk because it would mean driving a massive wedge through the heart of the Soviet Union, leaving German flanks very much more exposed than they ever had been in France. On the other hand, by turning north and south, they would be allowing the Russians a chance to fall back and protect the capital. However, since Hitler was even more powerful a military leader than he had been before the fall of France, Halder had been forced to acquiesce.

For the men now waiting to flow into the Soviet Union, the mood was mixed. Günther Sack, back from the Balkans and part of Army Group Centre, remained as unwavering in his zeal as ever. 'My belief in God is still strong and unshakeable,' he jotted, 'and also my belief in Germany and my love for the Führer.' But there was understandable apprehension too, although it was the war against Britain, not Russia, that was most on his mind. 'What the near future will bring me is unclear,' he added. 'Probably, it will take me somewhere where we will confront the English as well. But then, the war will last many more years.'

Oberst Hermann Balck was also feeling contemplative. 'We are at a decision point in the war,' he noted in his journal. It worried him that the

British were still in the Mediterranean – they would have to be driven out. And then there was the Soviet Union. At the beginning of June, he was still unaware that an invasion was imminent, but he was with Hitler in thinking a showdown with Russia was unavoidable and that the sooner it happened, the better. 'Once Russia is subdued,' he wrote, 'an encirclement and blockade of Germany becomes impossible. And at that point we can ignore any ups or downs in the public opinion on the home front. We will have a free rein then to crush England.'

For Hans von Luck, the biggest apprehension was over the size of the Soviet Union, which was so vast as to be incomprehensible. 'The Ural Mountains,' he wrote, 'which are nearly 2,000 miles away, were merely the end of the European part.' Among his comrades, the earlier euphoria had given way to a more sober view. And would Germany be able to cope with a second front? Would Britain exploit the fact that the bulk of the German armed forces were now in the East? He was ready to do his duty, but he felt in a strange frame of mind. 'We were not actually afraid,' he wrote, 'but neither were we sure what our attitude should be toward an opponent whose strength and potential were unknown to us, and whose mentality was completely alien.'

On the eve of BARBAROSSA, there were, then, several major question marks remaining: about the ongoing war with Britain, about how much plunder could realistically be taken from the Soviet Union, over whether Hitler's or Halder's strategy was the correct one, and whether German qualitative superiority was enough to smash the quantitative superiority of the Red Army. Finally, did the Germans have enough mechanized forces and air power to deliver the lightning crushing of the Russians that was so essential to German success?

BARBAROSSA was launched in the early dawn on 22 June.

CHAPTER 48

Trouble at the Top

B Y THE SUMMER of 1941, the Canadian contribution to Britain's war effort was already proving quite exceptional. An entire division had reached Britain in the summer of 1940, and another had followed. Entire wings of Canadians were in Britain, serving with Fighter Command, while further Canadian squadrons were serving in Bomber Command, and pilots and aircrew were sprinkled liberally through all parts of the RAF, both in the UK and overseas. All Canadian servicemen were volunteers. Other Canadian volunteers had chosen to join the rapidly growing Royal Canadian Navy; it did not have the large core of pre-war professionals that had enabled the smooth addition of so many civilians into the Royal Navy, and in terms of its overall professionalism the RCN was definitely a work in progress, but both its command and its rapidly growing crews were all more than answering the call; certainly, what they lacked in training and equipment, they made up for in determination and dedication to the cause. The first few corvettes of what was called the Newfoundland Escort Force – or NEF – left Halifax, Nova Scotia, on 23 May in what was a significant moment. Henceforth, convoys would be escorted from one side of the Atlantic all the way to the other. 'The Royal Canadian Navy,' said Admiral Noble, 'solved the problems of the Atlantic convoys.' Their role was to escort convoys to what became known as the 'Mid-Ocean Meeting Point', or 'MOMP', to the south of Iceland. There they would hand over their charges to British Escort Groups. NEF Escort Groups, under the overall control of Western Approaches Command, would refuel in Iceland, then sail back to the MOMP to meet the next convoy headed back west.

It was into this improving situation for Britain in the Atlantic that *U-564* crept out of the 1st Flotilla's base at Lorient in Brittany on the Atlantic coast on 17 June. The U-boat's commander, Oberleutnant Teddy Suhren, was delighted to be getting this first patrol underway and had deliberately done everything he could to make it operationally ready as quickly as possible. How long a new boat took to work up to readiness depended entirely on the experience of the commander and how well he could control both the U-boat and his crew. In Suhren's case, there was no shortage of experience or confidence, and he was quick to demonstrate both attributes to his new crew, as well as a relaxed but no-nonsense attitude; certainly, no one on *U-564* was left in any doubt as to who was boss. Suhren was clearly more than up to the challenge, but command of a U-boat required a considerable number of different skills: a mind that could quickly calculate equations of distance, speed and time; a profound understanding of the sea; an immense imperturbability; an ability to maintain the morale of fifty men of differing characteristics and ages in an intensely confined metal tin; and a sixth sense that could only be won through experience. Since the BdU had begun the war with only 3,000 men, one of the challenges facing Dönitz as U-boat losses mounted and more new vessels and crews entered service was how to maintain the necessary standard of training among officers and particularly commanders.

Once out at sea, U-boats were directed by the operations team at BdU HQ at Kernével, a small village some twenty-five miles inland from Lorient, where Dönitz had chosen to set up his command post. The oceans were mapped out and divided into squares, which were in turn subdivided into smaller squares, which served as position locators. On this first patrol, *U-564* was ordered by radio signal, encoded by the Enigma machine, to head north-west in the hope of intercepting a Halifax convoy heading to Britain across the North Atlantic.

They had barely reached their station when they managed to intercept convoy HX133. In the early hours of 27 June, they sank two ships and severely damaged a third. Two nights later, they spotted and sank a third ship, an independent, which went down in just two minutes. Three confirmed sinkings within two weeks of their first patrol was an encouraging start.

Dönitz's frustrations were mounting, however. Time and again both the military and political leadership demonstrated a complete lack of understanding as to the essential nature of submarine warfare. Repeatedly, Dönitz found himself being issued orders from on high that interfered with his command of the BdU. The operations of the Kriegsmarine's surface vessels, for example, had been, to his mind, a useful supplement to the work of the U-boats, but it had been a complete waste of time to use his force as escorts for these much faster vessels. None the less that was what they had been ordered to do. The Luftwaffe insisted that two U-boats should be stationed as weather watchers at all times; it was only two, but if they were spending their days issuing weather reports, they couldn't be sinking ships, and effectively that meant four U-boats because they had to rotate.

Then with the launch of BARBAROSSA, no fewer than eight U-boats were ordered, over and above Dönitz's head, into the Baltic, although why they were there and what they were supposed to achieve was not made clear to him. Certainly, they sank nothing in that time. At the beginning of July, a further six U-boats were ordered to the Arctic, even though the Allies had not yet sent a single convoy to Murmansk or Archangel. 'The decisive factor in the war against Britain is the attack on her imports,' he wrote to the OKW through gritted teeth. 'The delivery of these attacks is the U-boats' principal task and one which no other branch of the Armed Forces can take over from them. The war with Russia will be decided on land, and in it the U-boats can play only a very minor role.'

Even more frustrating was the priority the surface fleet continued to take over the U-boat arm. At this crucial moment in the war, the High Command insisted on withdrawing some 800 U-boat maintenance workers and posting them to Brest to work on the damaged *Scharnhorst* and *Gneisenau*. This made absolutely no sense whatsoever and led to long delays in the refitting and repair of U-boats, which in turn had an adverse effect on Dönitz's under-resourced force. Dönitz was incensed but powerless. He could fire off one outraged memorandum after another, each clearly laying out watertight reasoning for greater focus on the BdU, but he had no direct line to the Führer and was constrained by the overwhelmingly continentalist approach to warfare that was such a feature not only of Hitler's mindset but also of almost all the senior Nazi leadership.

And this was not about to change any time soon.

*

On 21 June, Churchill finally wielded the axe on Wavell, demanding that he swap commands with General Claude Auchinleck and move to India and Auchinleck take on the mantel of the giant Middle East theatre. Moving Wavell was unquestionably the right decision. Churchill had never had much faith in him, and, regardless of whether that was fair or not, it meant Wavell was always battling uphill to get his perspective across; this was important, because on those few really crucial matters he needed to make his point and for Churchill both to trust his judgement and to accept it. That never happened. 'He sounds a tired and disheartened man,' Churchill had told Jock Colville at the end of May, and so he was, as he admitted to Dill when he was fired.

Yet so too was Dill. As CIGS, he had also found it hard to deal with Churchill, but there was also a creeping pessimism that was affecting his judgement. Exhaustion usually feeds negative thinking. On the same day that Wavell was axed, Kennedy had gone to see Dill after a week's leave. 'I suppose you realize we shall lose the Middle East?' he told Kennedy. Despite the losses in Greece and Crete, and despite the check on BATTLEAXE, there was no real reason for such a gloomy prediction. They were aware of the German withdrawal of troops from the Balkans and the build-up in the East; the Germans – and Italians – had almost nothing like the naval forces and shipping with which to conduct a war across the Mediterranean on any significant scale, and, as British intelligence was well aware, Germany was already increasingly stretched. Meanwhile, supplies were continuing to pour into Britain and out again across the world's oceans – between April and June that amounted to 3,294 ships. Ever more factories were now in operation in Britain; the UK was out-producing Germany in terms of tanks and aircraft. More pilots were being trained in Canada, the USA and Southern Africa than Germany could ever hope to process. Farmers across Britain, A. G. Street included, had begun an agricultural revolution that was producing food to a level of efficiency that Germany could not match. Of course, transferring this to the battlefield took time; Britain's Army had been tiny when compared with that of Germany and remained very small a year after the fall of France. The responsibility bearing down on the shoulders of men like Dill was immense, but there was much that should have given him reassurance. The Middle East was not in imminent danger of being lost; and nor, more importantly, was the Battle of the Atlantic. In the West, at any rate, a wider perspective was needed when assessing Britain's situation in the war.

And there was good news in the Middle East as well. On that same day, Damascus had fallen; after stiff resistance, the battle for Syria was going the Allies' way, particularly now that BATTLEAXE was over and more forces could be released to support this second campaign. Further hard fighting followed, but on 11 July the Vichy commander, Général Dentz, asked for an end to hostilities. The formal surrender was signed three days later. To a large extent, the occupation of Syria – and airfields there – was a counterweight against the loss of Crete.

The RAF had contributed two and a half fighter squadrons and two of bombers, as well as two Fleet Air Arm squadrons. These had operated particularly successfully, destroying a number of Vichy air forces in the air and even more in a concentrated series of attacks on Syrian airfields. German bombers operating from the Dodecanese Islands had also been attacked and destroyed, and all at a remarkably small cost. It was a reminder, as if any were needed following the German victories, of the enormous benefits of plentiful air support for any ground operations.

Back on 6 June, General John Kennedy had produced a highly perspicacious appreciation, in which he called for far greater air forces to be diverted to the Middle East theatre. 'When we operate our air cover is never sufficient,' he noted, echoing the words of ABC. 'The necessity for adequate air support has been rubbed in time and time again. Without such support neither the Navy nor the Army can operate with full effect.' He also speculated that the next phase of the war would see great efforts on each side to produce the heaviest scale of bombardment on the other. Certainly, he was thinking in terms of the mass bombing of German cities. 'The execution of this policy,' he added, 'demands the building up of a very large force of bomber aircraft, but the numbers required are all well within the capacity of British and American production.'

Bomber production was certainly on the increase, including new four-engine heavy bombers, of which Britain was currently producing two: the Short Stirling and the Handley Page Halifax. By the end of June, 179 had been built in Britain so far that year, along with 1,276 medium bombers and 4,049 fighters of all kinds; more and more Spitfires were being built, and the new, much-improved and cannon-firing Mk V was entering service too, but Hurricanes had still been built in large numbers early in the year.

Among the first squadrons to receive the new four-engine Halifax was 76 Squadron, newly formed in April at Linton-on-Ouse in Yorkshire, under the command of Wing Commander Sydney Bufton. The Halifax had some teething issues – they were grounded at Linton for a while because of frequent hydraulics failures, for example – but Bufton was delighted with them: the increase in size and payload was a big leap from the Whitleys they had been flying.

Bufton may have been pleased with his new bombers, but the Command as a whole was struggling. Bombing Germany had been an important part of Britain's war strategy, and in his first signal to Marshal Stalin on 7 July 1941 Churchill promised the Soviet leader that Britain would help Russia by bombing German industry. Germany would thus be fighting on two fronts, even though Britain could not invade Nazi-occupied Europe on the ground. There was also a sense of increased urgency on the part of Churchill and Britain's war leaders in their desire to start making Germany hurt. The Luftwaffe's Blitz on Britain had only just ended, but there was no telling when it might start again. If Hitler won his quick victory, the Germans might return with all the fury of a mighty Luftwaffe reinvigorated and grown with the riches of the East.

The trouble was, Bomber Command was not really growing, much to the frustration of Churchill and Air Chief Marshal Sir Charles Portal, who had been promoted to Chief of the Air Staff in October 1940. Britain's bombers were supposed to be in the vanguard of its fight-back, and yet high losses combined with the slow build-up of bomber production and the arrival into service of new, bigger bombers had ensured it was hardly any larger in the summer of 1941 than it had been in the summer of 1940.

Even more serious, however, were the ongoing problems of success-fully navigating at night, often in cloud, to the right target and the subsequent inaccuracy of bombing. In July, Churchill's friend and chief scientific advisor, Professor Frederick Lindemann, asked Air Marshal Sir Richard Peirse, the C-in-C Bomber Command, whether he might under-take analysis of bombing accuracy using photographs taken during operations. This was agreed, so Lindemann charged one of his staff at the Statistical Section, David Bensusan-Butt, to analyse 650 photographs taken from one hundred bomber raids between 2 June and 25 July. That Bomber Command had conducted so many raids in less than two months demonstrated the effort and commitment that were going into bomber operations. The subsequent Butt Report, however, demonstrated that in terms of accuracy Bomber Command had a long, long way to go. The statistics were terrible: just one in five aircraft managed to get within five miles of the target. On cloudy nights that dropped to one in fifteen. 'It is an awful thought,' Churchill wrote to Portal, 'that perhaps three-quarters of our bombs go astray.'

The revelations of the Butt Report were a severe jolt and a blow to both pride and British hopes. The answer was more bombers and bigger bombers capable of carrying much larger payloads, but the heavy-bomber programme had been set back by Beaverbrook's entirely justifiable decision to limit the number of aircraft models the previous year. That restriction had long since been lifted but it took time to build up strength, not least because the bigger the piece of machinery, the more parts there were and the longer it took to make. As German defences increased, so bombing became harder and casualties, both to crews and to aircraft, steadily rose.

And the demands for ever-more numbers of aircraft never stopped, not least from the Middle East. Wavell – before he was fired – Admiral Cunningham and the new AOC Middle East, Air Marshal Arthur Tedder, were all calling for more aircraft. Of the three, Tedder was the only one urging far closer tri-service co-operation, and these cries for aircraft reinforcements tended to reach London separately. It would have been better if, instead, they had got their heads together and made a joint plea, with a united and agreed strategy for their application as Tedder had suggested. Different pleas and different suggestions for the use of air power did not help. Wavell, for example, had sent recommendations to the War Office demanding the creation of an army air component. To those commanders on the ground, it seemed only right that the RAF should be at their beck and call, providing a constant air umbrella and being on hand to provide aerial artillery any time a suitable target appeared. This was unrealistic on a number of levels but was certainly a very ineffective and inefficient use of air power, and Tedder, quite rightly, severely criticized Wavell's suggestions, as did the Air Ministry.

Tedder turned fifty-one in the second week of July, and was tall, lean and rarely without a straight-stemmed pipe sticking out of the corner of his mouth, which gave the impression that his entire face was somewhat skewed to whichever side of his mouth his pipe was jammed. A Scot by birth, he had originally planned to become a diplomat but with the start of the First World War joined the Dorset Regiment and after service in France returned to Dorset where he badly damaged his knee. This put an end to his career as an infantryman and instead he applied for and was granted a transfer to the Royal Flying Corps. Gaining his wings, he returned to France and went on to command 70 Squadron over the Western Front before ending the war helping to develop bomb-dropping techniques in Egypt. After the war, he remained with the RAF and steadily climbed the ladder. A stint as AOC Far East was followed by a return to Britain to be Director-General of Research and Development, a role in which he was a dynamic and forward-thinking influence; it was on his watch that the Air Ministry approved the development of four-engine bombers and new fighter aircraft such as the Spitfire came into service. By the autumn of 1940, he was working with Beaverbrook at the Ministry of Aircraft Production, although the two did not get on. He managed to escape by being posted to the Middle East to serve as Deputy AOC. When Longmore was recalled at the beginning of June, Tedder took over.

The RAF had not only done well in Syria but had also performed valiantly during BATTLEAXE, protecting the advance of the ground troops to the front and harrying the enemy on the ground. Tedder, however, was realistic about the inevitable recriminations. 'One thing is clear,' he noted in his journal about BATTLEAXE, 'and that is the whole thing is a complete flop. The only bright spot is that our chaps have been simply grand and have done more than even the Army could have called for. There'll certainly be a witch hunt for scapegoats after this and I know we were marked down as the prospective sacrifice – but I don't think that will come off this time!'

And nor did it, as it was Wavell who was sacked. 'Well, it's probably a good thing to have a change of bowling,' Wavell told Tedder. 'And I have had one or two sixes knocked off me lately.' Tedder had liked him well enough, but as far as he was concerned, in the future, the RAF and Army needed much closer co-operation and communication. Proper training, especially in signals communications, was what was needed for the Army, and more combined-operations training for his air forces. With Auchinleck newly installed as C-in-C, there was an opportunity to over-haul this increasingly important partnership. Most of all, however, there was a need for more aircraft. Reinforcements were arriving – not least a further 394 aircraft of all kinds, including 204 Hurricanes in June alone, which showed what could be done. Hurricanes were all very well, but they had been outclassed in 1940 and were even more so in 1941. Still, the June deliveries were an important step in the right direction. In the

Middle East, at any rate, both Tedder and now Auchinleck understood that the RAF had a key role to play, both as a strategic bomber force and in providing tactical close air support to the troops on the ground. Land operations such as those in Greece and Crete, where air support had been virtually non-existent, would never happen again.

Jock Colville was staying at Chequers for the weekend when, on the morning of Sunday, 22 June, he was woken by a telephone call announcing that Germany had invaded the Soviet Union. He hurriedly went around the bedrooms breaking the news, including to the PM, who greeted the revelation with a smile of satisfaction. Also staying was John Winant, the US Ambassador, who wondered whether it was a put-up job by Hitler and Stalin. As the day unfolded, it became clear that was not the case. Over dinner, the PM said that Russian peasants were now being slaughtered; Britain should forget about Communism and extend its hand to fellow human beings in distress. Later that night, as Churchill went to bed, he repeated how wonderful it was that Russia had come in against Germany. Within a few weeks, Britain and the Soviet Union would sign, on 12 July, a mutual-assistance pact; if only they had been able to do so two years earlier, how differently matters might have turned out.

In the United States, Harry Hopkins had heard the news late on the night of the 21st. His first reaction was one of elation, but then he immediately began worrying about the inevitable demands for Russian aid. Meanwhile, Henry Stimson, the Secretary of War, decided to mull over this highly significant news and then consult with General Marshall and the War Plans Division. He was delighted to discover his and their views chimed perfectly. In a nutshell, they recognized that over the next few weeks and even months Germany would have its hands full in the Soviet Union and that gave the US the ideal opportunity to really start pushing aid across the Atlantic to Britain. 'By this final demonstration of Nazi ambition and perfidy,' he wrote to Roosevelt, 'the door is wide open for you to lead directly towards the winning of the battle of the North Atlantic.'

While Roosevelt did not disagree, most in Washington seemed to think that Russia would be swept aside. Nevertheless, while the initial German advances certainly appeared to be impressive, Roosevelt was not convinced the Soviet Union would crumble and preferred to take a more measured approach; before rushing into anything, he wanted to know exactly what aid Russia needed and how that might be delivered. At any rate, by this second week of July, it seemed to Roosevelt that there was much else to consider too; there was, for example, also the imminent involvement of the US Navy in the Battle of the Atlantic, agreed at the ABC-1 talks but still to be put into practice. During a long discussion with Hopkins in the White House study on the evening of 11 July, he told his friend he wanted him to cross the Atlantic once again to visit the British. What's more, Roosevelt had decided it was, at long last, time for him to meet Churchill face to face. In London, Hopkins was to fix up such a meeting, preferably on a ship some place.

The United States had still not declared war; nor was there any move towards creating a formal alliance with Britain. But a partnership was unquestionably being forged, and one that shared the same aim: the defeat of Nazi Germany.

Glossary

AASF	Advanced Air Striking Force
AI	Air Interceptor
AOC	Air Officer Commanding
ARP	Air Raid Precautions
ASDIC	British naval vessels' onboard sonar
Auftragstaktik	mission command
BdU	*Befehlshaber der U-boote* (C-in-C of German submarines)
BEF	British Expeditionary Force
Bewegungskrieg	operational war of movement
Bren	British light machine gun
chasseurs alpins	French mountain troops
CIGS	Chief of the Imperial General Staff
C-in-C	Commander-in-Chief
CIO	Congress of Industrial Organizations
CO	Commanding Officer
CP	Command Post
EG	Royal Navy Escort Group
Fahnenjunker	officer cadet
Fallschirmjäger	German paratroopers
Feldwebel	German non-commissioned officer equivalent to sergeant
GC&CS	Government Code and Cypher School (Bletchley Park)
Gebirgsjäger	German mountain troops
Geschwader	Luftwaffe group of squadrons (*staffeln*)
He	Heinkel
HF/DF	High Frequency Direction Finding
Huff-Duff	slang for HF/DF
HX	North America to UK convoy route
IFF	Identification Friend or Foe

JG	*Jagdgeschwader* – fighter group
Ju	Junkers
KG	*Kampfgeschwader* – bomber group
Kriegsmarine	German Navy
leaguer	night-time tank formation – a rough circle usually
Lehrgeschwader	training group
Luftwaffe	German Air Force
Me	Messerschmitt
MG	machine gun
MG34	*machinegewehr* or German machine gun, first built in 1934
MOMP	Mid-Ocean Meeting Point
MP40	*machinepistole* or German sub-machine gun, first produced in 1940
NCO	non-commissioned officer
NCS	Naval Control of Shipping
NDAC	National Defense Advisory Commission (US)
NEF	Newfoundland Escort Force
NJG	*Nachtjagdgeschwader* – night fighter group
Oberjäger	most junior NCO in the German airborne and mountain divisions
OKH	Oberkommando des Heeres – Supreme Army Command
OKM	Oberkommando der Marine – Supreme Naval Command
OKW	Oberkommando der Wehrmacht – Combined Operations Staff
ON(F)	British to North America fast convoy route
ON(S)	British to North America slow convoy route
OPM	Office of Production Management
OTU	Operational Training Unit
Panzer	German term for a tank. There were a number of variants or 'marks', usually written as Mk I, Mk II, etc
RAD	Reichsarbeitsdienst – Reich Labour Service, for teenage boys between school and joining the military.
RCN	Royal Canadian Navy
Regia Aeronautica	Royal Air Force (Italian)
Regio Esercito	Royal Army (Italian)
RNR	Royal Navy Reserve
RNS	Reichsnährstand – Department of Food and Agriculture
RWM	Reichswirtschaftministerium – Reich Ministry for Economic Affairs
SC	North America to UK slow convoy route
Schmeisser	Allied slang for a German sub-machine gun
Schwerpunkt	main point of attack

SIM	Servizio Informazioni Militari – the Italian Military Intelligence Service
SL	Sierra Leone to UK slow convoy route
SOE	Special Operations Executive
SOE	Senior Officer Escorts
sortie	individual operational flight by a pilot, so a squadron of e.g. twelve aircraft could fly up to twelve sorties at any one time
Spandau	Allied slang for a German machine gun
Staffel	German squadron
StG	*Sturmkampfflugzeuggeschwader* – Stuka bomber group
Sturzkampfflugzeug	Stuka dive-bomber
TA	Territorial Army
UMW	United Mine Workers
WACI	Western Approaches Convoy Instructions
Wehrmacht	German armed forces
1WO	1st Watch Officer
Zerstörer	Destroyer. Luftwaffe name for the Messerschmitt 110
ZG	*Zerstörergeschwader* – Messerschmitt 110 fighter group

Naval Strength at the Outbreak of War

(showing principal war vessels only)

	Numbers on 1 Sept 1939	Under Construction on 1 Sept 1939
GREAT BRITAIN		
Battleships	15	9
Aircraft Carriers	7	6
Heavy Cruisers	15	–
Light Cruisers	41	9
Anti-aircraft cruisers	8	16
Minelayer Cruisers	1	1
Modern Destroyers	113	24
Older Destroyers	68	–
Modern Submarines	53	11
Older Submarines	12	–
Escorts (Corvettes etc.)	54	80
Fleet Minesweepers	44	10
Gun Monitors	2	–
FRANCE		
Battleships	7	4
Aircraft Carriers	1	–
Heavy Cruisers	7	–
Light Cruisers	12	3
Destroyers	78	27
Submarines	81	38
Minesweepers & Gunboats	56	30
GERMANY		
Battleships	2	11 (*only* Bismarck *completed*)
Older Battleships	2	–
Pocket Battleships	3	–
Aircraft Carriers	–	2 (*neither completed*)
Heavy Cruisers	2	3 (*only 1 completed*)

GERMANY *contd*

	Numbers on 1 Sept 1939	Under Construction on 1 Sept 1939
Light Cruisers	6	6 (*none completed*)
Destroyers	22	12
Torpedo Boats (*S-boote*)	20	13
Submarines	62	50

ITALY

Battleships	6 (*4 under refit*)	–
Aircraft Carriers	–	1
Heavy Cruisers	7	–
Light Cruisers	12	3
Fleet Destroyers	61	–
Escort Destroyers	73	–
Submarines	116	–
Torpedo Boats	67	–

Comparative Military Strengths
(on 10 MAY 1940)

Actual Total Combat Strength of Aircraft

France	3,097
Britain	1,150
Belgium	140
Netherlands	82
TOTAL	4,469
Germany	3,578

Tank Strength

Germany	2,439
France	3,254

Artillery Strength

Germany	7,378
France	10,700
Britain	1,280
Belgium	1,338
Netherlands	656

Divisions at Front

Germany	135
France	117
Britain (BEF)	13
Belgium	22
Netherlands	10

Source: Blitzkreig Legend *by Karl Heinz-Frieser*

Aircraft Production 1940

SINGLE-ENGINE FIGHTERS
(monthly averages)

	Germany	Britain	United States
1939			
Monthly Ave.	128	85	–
1940			
1st Quarter	113	159	–
2nd Quarter	197	342	12
3rd Quarter	210	480	91
4th Quarter	89	447	156
1941			
1st Quarter	160	486	146
2nd Quarter	326	557	152

TWIN-ENGINE AIRCRAFT
(monthly averages)

	Germany	Britain	United States
1939			
Monthly Ave.	219	151	–
1940			
1st Quarter	264	151	24
2nd Quarter	435	288	24
3rd Quarter	470	365	28
4th Quarter	369	339	20

TWIN-ENGINE AIRCRAFT *contd*

	Germany	Britain	United States
1941			
1st Quarter	366	375	51
2nd Quarter	353	428	106
3rd Quarter	454	438	169
4th Quarter	373	407	224

FOUR-ENGINE AIRCRAFT

	Germany	Britain	United States
1940			
1st Quarter	3	–	5
2nd Quarter	3	1	–
3rd Quarter	3	3	6
4th Quarter	3	11	9
1941			
1st Quarter	5	25	17
2nd Quarter	5	34	18

Sources: BA-MA ZA3; The Strategic Air Offensive Against Germany 1939–1945 Volume IV, Appendix XXIV; GSWW Vol. II, Table IX.III

Armaments Production 1939 – May 1940

PRINCIPAL ARMY WEAPONS,
GERMAN & BRITISH, SEPTEMBER 1939–MAY 1940

WEAPONS *German / British*	Sept–Dec 1939	Jan–April 1940	May 1940
Rifles (1000s)	279 / 18.7	310.4 / 26.8	101.6 / 11.1
Machine guns (1000s)	12.7 / 6.9	14.7 / 7.4	5.2/2.9
Field Artillery	773 / –	675 / 51	217 / 63
Heavy Anti-aircraft	192 / 224	317 / 234	86 / 94
Tanks	247 / 314	283 / 287	116 / 138

GERMAN & BRITISH TANK PRODUCTION

	Germany	Britain
Pre-War	3,503	1,148
Sept–Dec 1939	370	314
1940	1,888	1,093
1941	3,263	4,841

Source: British War Production, *Table 25, and BA-MA RH8/v3743*

Armaments Production 1940–41

(in US $1 billion 1944 prices)

	1940	1941
USA	1.5	4.5
Britain	3.5	6.5
USSR	5.0	8.5
Germany	6.0	6.0
Japan	1.0	2.0

Source: GSWW Vol. V/IA, Table II.V.4

Increase in Armaments Production 1940–41

(percentage of preceding year)

	1940	1941
USA	150	200
Britain	250	86
USSR	52	70
Germany	76	0
Japan	–	100

Source: GSWW Vol. V/IA, Table II.V.1

The Effects of the Blockade on Germany:
Imports of Raw Materials into Germany
(1938 = 100)

1939		1940	
July	109	January	17
August	99	February	30
September	66	March	13
October	49	April	24
November	44	May	17
December	57	June	29

Source: GSWW Vol. V/IA, Diagram II.II.3

The Effects of the War on British Trade:
Imports & Exports
(1938 = 100)

	1938	1939	1940	1941
Imports	100	97	94	82
Exports	100	94	72	56

Source: Fighting With Figures, Table 9.4

TIMELINE
August 1939 – June 1941

──────────── **1939** ────────────

AUGUST

23 Molotov–Ribbentrop Pact signed in Moscow.

24 British Govt passes Emergency Powers Act.

SEPTEMBER

1 German invasion of Poland.
   Evacuation begins in Britain.

2 Ultimatums delivered to Germany by Britain and France.

3 Britain and France declare war on Germany, as do Australia, New Zealand, Canada and all British Dominions.
   Chamberlain forms new War Cabinet with Churchill back as First Lord of the Admiralty and Eden as Sec. of State for Dominion Affairs.

5 USA declares neutrality.

6 South African Prime Minister Jan Smuts declares war on Germany.

9 British Expeditionary Force begins to land in France.160,000 men and 24,000 vehicles arrive throughout September.

17 Soviet invasion of Poland.
   British aircraft carrier HMS *Courageous* sunk by *U-29* off southwest Ireland.

18 Warsaw surrounded.

19 German and Soviet forces link up at Brest-Litovsk.

27 Hitler's senior commanders are told to prepare for an offensive in the West as soon as possible.

OCTOBER

6 Last Polish resistance ceases.

9 Hitler issues order for attack on the West.

14 HMS *Royal Oak* sunk by *U-47* at Scapa Flow.

NOVEMBER

4 USA – changes to the Neutrality Act allow belligerent states to purchase arms from private suppliers on a cash-and-carry basis, using own shipping to deliver arms.

30 Soviet forces invade Finland.

DECEMBER

13 RN heavy cruiser *Exeter* and light cruisers *Ajax* and *Achilles* engage pocket battleship *Graf Spee* at the mouth of the River Plate in Argentina.

17 *Graf Spee* scuttled.

1940

February

11 Soviet–German economic agreement.

16 *Altmark* incident.

March

12 Soviet–Finnish peace treaty.

28 Britain and France agree not to make any separate peace. From 5 April, they also plan to mine Norwegian waters to force German ships carrying Swedish iron ore out into the open sea. This is delayed until 8 April.

April

9 German invasion of Denmark and Norway. First use of airborne troops in assault on Oslo. German cruiser *Blücher* sunk by Norwegian shore guns with loss of over 300 lives.
    Gneisenau badly damaged by HMS *Renown*. Cruiser *Karlsruhe* sunk in Kristiansand by a British submarine.

10 Royal Navy's attack on German ships at Narvik.

11 First British contingent sails for Norway.

15 British landings near Narvik.

16 Allied landings at Namsos.

21 Lillehammer falls to Germans.

22 Allied landings at Åndalsnes.

26 Allied decision to evacuate southern Norway.

28 French *chasseurs alpins* reach Narvik.

May

6 3,000 French Foreign Legion reach Narvik.

9 Vote of Confidence in House of Commons. Polish Brigade reaches Narvik.

10 **Germany launches attack on West.**
    Chamberlain resigns and Churchill becomes Prime Minister.

13 Guderian crosses Meuse at Sedan, and Reinhardt at Monthermé. Rommel crosses Meuse at Dinant.
    Churchill's 'blood, toil, tears and sweat' speech.

14 Luftwaffe bombs heart of Rotterdam.
    British Govt (Eden) broadcasts message for Local Defence Volunteers.

15 French 1st Armoured Division destroyed by 5. Panzerdivision.
    Beginning of RAF's strategic air offensive against Germany.
    Dutch capitulate and entire Meuse front collapses.
    Reynaud tells Churchill, 'We have lost the battle.'
    Churchill appeals to Roosevelt for loan of destroyers.

16 Churchill flies to Paris for meeting with Reynaud and Général Gamelin.

17 Germans enter Brussels.

18 Gamelin sacked and replaced by Général Weygand.

19 General Gort begins to consider evacuation of BEF. Churchill orders that no more fighters should be sent to France.

20 Germans reach Amiens and Abbeville and then the Channel coast.

21 British counter-attack at Arras.
  Hitler turns his thoughts towards England when he discusses invasion with Raeder.

23 King George VI broadcasts to the people and calls for National Day of Prayer on Sunday.

24 Hitler issues halt order to his panzer spearhead.

25 Churchill sacks General Ironside. General Brooke takes over as CIGS.
  Boulogne falls to Germans.

26 National Day of Prayer in Britain.
  Reynaud flies to London for meeting with British.
  Churchill and Halifax clash.
  Calais falls to Germans.
  Operation DYNAMO begins.
  First troops from Dunkirk brought back to UK.

27 King Leopold of Belgium decides to surrender.
  Dunkirk receives heaviest day of bombing.
  Halifax threatens to resign.

28 Churchill secures support of Cabinet to fight on at all costs.
  Allies capture Narvik.

29 President Roosevelt invites Bill Knudsen to the White House.

31 OKM begins work on planning the invasion of Britain.

JUNE

3 Operation DYNAMO ends.

3–7 Evacuation of British troops from north Norway.

4 Churchill's 'never surrender' speech.

5 Germans launch Case RED.

10 Mussolini declares war on Britain and France.
  Churchill flies to France for talks with French Govt, now at Briare.

10–11 First Bomber Command raid on Italy (Turin).

12 Spain declares non-belligerency.
  Général Weygand urges Reynaud to seek armistice.

13 Churchill flies to France again.

14 Germans enter Paris.
  Keitel issues OKW directive for war against England and reduction of German Army to 120 divisions.

15 Operation AERIAL begins to bring back remaining BEF troops in France from Cherbourg, Saint-Malo, Brest, Saint-Nazaire and La Pallice.

16 Reynaud resigns and Pétain takes over.

17 French Govt asks Germany for an armistice.

18 De Gaulle's first broadcast.
  Churchill makes 'finest hour' speech.

18–20 Port of Brest destroyed and French Fleet sails – most to North Africa.

Hitler meets with Mussolini and Ciano – talks in private about land and air assault of England.

22 French sign surrender – French fleet to be demobilized and disarmed.

23 HMS *Ark Royal* and *Hood* arrive in Gibraltar.

24 OKH issues order for regrouping of Army and 'preparations against England'.
France signs armistice with Italy.

25 Last fighting in France ends.

26 Turkey announces it will remain non-belligerent.

28 US National Defence Act passed.
De Gaulle recognized as leader of Free French.

30 Germans land on Channel Islands.

July

1 Halder enthusiastically embarks on planning of invasion – meeting with Admiral Schniewind.

2 Hitler orders appreciation and preparations to begin for Operation SEALION.
French government settles in Vichy.

3 Operation CATAPULT – destruction of French Fleet at Mers-el-Kébir.

4 Diplomatic relations between Britain and Vichy severed.

6 Hitler returns in triumph to Berlin.

9 Naval action off Calabria in the Mediterranean between British and Italian Fleets.

10 French National Assembly votes full powers to Pétain.
Hitler demands that coastal artillery should be trained on Britain.

11 Raeder reports to Hitler at the Berghof about preparations for invasion of England.
Pierre Laval becomes Prime Minister of France.

13 Halder and von Brauchitsch report to Hitler at the Berghof on invasion of England.

14 Russia incorporates Baltic states into Soviet Union.

17 Hitler's Operation SEALION Directive cancelled.

19 Hitler's peace offer to Britain.

21 Hitler's first mention of attack on Russia.

22 Halifax gives speech rejecting Hitler's peace offer.
Constitution of SOE.

25 Heavy and repeated attacks on shipping off Dover by Luftwaffe.
RAF frequently outnumbered.

August

1 Halder receives Hitler's Directive No.16 for air war against Britain.

2 Göring issues order for *Adlertag*.

3 Actual strength of Luftwaffe against Britain: single-engine fighters: 760; twin-engine fighters, 230;

bombers 823 (inc. Norway);
dive-bombers, 343.

4 Italians invade British Somaliland.

13 *Adlertag*. Co-ordinated attacks
on airfields in southern England.
  Britain decides to send tanks to
Middle East.

14 Britain and USA agree in principle
on Destroyers for Bases deal.

17 Hitler declares total blockade of
British Isles.

18 The Hardest Day. Losses: RAF
Fighter Command 33 / LW 67.
Co-ordinated attacks on aerodromes
in south and south-east England.

20 Churchill's 'Never in the field of
human conflict . . .' speech.

23 Local Defence Volunteers
become the Home Guard.

25 Night: First RAF Bomber
Command raid on Berlin.

SEPTEMBER

2 Destroyers for Bases agreement
ratified between Britain and USA.

7 Black Saturday – Luftwaffe bomb
London in afternoon and evening
with more than 300 bombers.
  Operation SEALION postponed
until 24 September.

11 Luftwaffe raids over London and
Southampton.
  Italian invasion of Egypt.

15 More than 200 bombers raid
London and 30 target Portland and
Southampton. Losses: RAF 31 / LW 61.

16 USA – Congress passes Selective
Service Act USA.

21 *U-48* and four other U-boats join
U-47 to make largest wolfpack ever
concentrated against a convoy.
  Cyril Thompson and British
Shipbuilding Mission set sail for
the United States.

23 British and Free French attack
on Dakar.

27 **Tripartite pact signed between
Japan, Germany and Italy.**

28 Admiral Forbes's final appeal to
be able to use his Home Fleet more
offensively.

OCTOBER

12 Operation SEALION deferred
until spring 1941.

17 Air Ministry meeting in which
Dowding gets knifed in the back.

23–24 Hitler meets Franco and
Pétain.

28 **Italians invade Greece.**

29 Bill Knudsen gathers US
automobile executives in New York.

NOVEMBER

4 Greeks drive Italians back into
Albania.

5 **Roosevelt re-elected for third term.**

11–12 British attack on Italian Fleet
at Taranto.

12 **Hitler orders German invasion
of Greece.**

14 Luftwaffe attack Coventry.

20–24 Hungary, Romania and Slovakia join Axis.

DECEMBER

9 British mount counter-offensive in Egypt – Operation COMPASS. Royal Navy bombards Maktila and Sidi Barrani.

11 Sidi Barrani captured.

13 Hitler issues directive for occupation of Balkans.

18 Hitler issues directive for invasion of Russia.

19 Mussolini asks for German help in North Africa.

1941

JANUARY

1 Western Desert Force renamed XXX Corps.

2 RN bombards Bardia.

5 Australians capture Bardia – General Bergonzoli surrenders 45,000 Italians, 130 tanks. Just 500 Australian casualties.

6 Churchill orders Wavell to release troops for Greece.

7 Tobruk surrounded.

20 Emperor Haile Selassie re-enters Abyssinia.

22 Tobruk surrenders – 25,000 Italians captured, plus 208 guns and 87 tanks. Combined British and Australian casualties 450. Wavell ordered to capture Benghazi.

24 General Cunningham's Southern Force invades Italian Somaliland from Kenya.

FEBRUARY

3 British forces attack Keren in Eritrea.

12 Italians surrender 20,000 men, 200 guns and 120 tanks to just 3,000 British troops. Eden: 'Never has so much been surrendered by so few.'
    Generalmajor Erwin Rommel arrives in Tripoli.

25 Mogadishu taken by British Nigerian forces.

MARCH

1 Bulgaria joins Axis.

4 British Commando raid on Lofoten Islands.

7 British ground troops arrive in Greece.
    Günther Prien and *U-47* lost at sea.

11 Lend Lease becomes law in USA.

16 British troops from Aden land and strike towards Berbera in British Somaliland.

17 Joachim Schepke killed and *U-100* sunk; Otto Kretschmer captured and *U-99* sunk.

24 Rommel makes limited offensive to capture El Agheila.
British Somaliland cleared of Italians.

25 **Yugoslavia joins Axis.**

27 **Coup in Yugoslavia and pact revoked.**
ABC-1 Agreement between Britain and USA signed.

27–9 British Mediterranean Fleet takes on Italian Fleet at Battle of Cape Matapan.

APRIL

1 General Platt's Northern Force captures Asmara, capital of Eritrea.
Rashid Ali al-Gaylani, in pro-Axis coup, seizes power in Iraq.

4 Rommel takes Benghazi unopposed.

6 **Germany invades Yugoslavia and Greece.**
Haile Selassie's forces capture Italian forts at Deba Markos.

9 Rommel takes Bardia.

12 Rommel's forces complete encirclement of Tobruk.

17 Yugoslavia surrenders.

27 Germans enter Athens.

MAY

2 British attack Iraq from Palestine.
Haile Selassie returns to Addis Abbaba, five years after start of Italian occupation.

9 Fritz-Julius Lemp killed and *U-110*'s Enigma machine and code-book captured.

19 Fallujah in Iraq retaken.

18 Formal Italian surrender in East Africa.

20 German airborne forces land in Crete.

24 HMS *Hood* sunk by *Bismarck*.

27 *Bismarck* sunk.

30 Revolt in Iraq collapses.

JUNE

1 Germans secure Crete.

2 Greek Govt in Exile formed in Egypt.

8 British and Free French forces launch Operation EXPORTER, attacking Vichy Syria and Lebanon from Palestine.

15 Operation BATTLEAXE launched to relieve Tobruk.

17 BATTLEAXE called off – 91 tanks lost.

22 **Operation BARBAROSSA launched.**

Notes

Abbreviations used in notes

AI   Author interview
BA-MA   Bundesarchiv-Militärarchiv, Freiburg, Germany
CCA   Churchill College Archives, Cambridge, UK
DTA   Deutsches Tagebucharchiv, Emmendingen, Germany
FADN   Fondazione Archivio Diaristico Nazionale, Pieve Santo Stefano, Italy
GSWW   Militärgeschichtliches Forschungsamt: *Germany and the Second World War*
IWM   Imperial War Museum, London, UK
NARA   National Archives and Records Administration, Washington DC, USA
TNA   The National Archives, Kew, London, UK
WSC   Winston Churchill, *The Second World War*

Introduction

4   'Where they came from and how they got there . . .': AI with Tom Neil.
4   'We just went back to Echelon . . .': AI with David Render.

Part I: War Begins

1. Countdown

9   'Before the ceremonies began . . .': John E. Skinner, Rutgers Oral History Archives.
10   'For the past two weeks . . .': Lou Gehrig's farewell, Historic Films Archive, YouTube.
12   'The United States must go in . . .': cited in Dallek, *Franklin D. Roosevelt*, p. 11.
15   'a negative compromise . . .': cited in Reynolds, *Creation of the Anglo-American Alliance*, p. 57.
15   'It was a great blow to me . . .': Ciano, *Diary*, 26/6/1939–2/7/1939.
17   'He can be Führer as much as he likes . . .': ibid., 21–23/5/1939.
17   'However, it is clear to me . . .': ibid.

2. Diplomacy

27   'What will the British do?': cited in Irving, *Göring*, p. 256.

29   'a silent witness to the Empire': Beaufre, *1940*, p. 97.

30   'It would be difficult . . .': ibid., p. 100.

30   'If the crisis comes . . .': Ciano, *Diary*, 6/8/1939.

30   'implacable': ibid.

30   'I am certain . . .': ibid., 11/8/1939.

31   'France and England will certainly . . .': Muggeridge, *Ciano's Diplomatic Papers*, 'First Conversation with the Fuehrer', 12 August 1939.

31   'They have betrayed and lied to us . . .': ibid., 13/8/1939.

31   'arouse in him every possible . . .': ibid., 14/8/1939.

3. Running Out of Time

33   'Remember that we are faced . . .': cited in Spears, *Assignment to Catastrophe*, p. 18.

34   'I understand your point of view perfectly . . .': Beaufre, *1940*, p. 123.

34   'With the Germans we risk the loss . . .': ibid.

34   'I have them! I have them!': Speer, *Inside the Third Reich*, p. 234.

35   'All I wanted was for this great man . . .': cited in Sereny, *Albert Speer*, p. 186.

35   'To see the names of Hitler and Stalin linked . . .': Speer, *Inside the Third Reich*, p. 234.

35   'This is very bad news, isn't it?': Spears, *Assignment to Catastrophe*, p. 23.

37   'We are faced . . .': cited in Kershaw, *Hitler: 1936–1945, Nemesis*, p. 208.

37   'Act brutally . . .': *GSWW*, Vol. II, p. 75.

38   'That's exactly the man . . .': cited in Warlimont, *Inside Hitler's Headquarters*, p. 13.

39   'Grave . . . Not just over Poland . . .': Engel, *Heart of the Reich* (diary, 24/8/1939).

40   'Looks like a great deal of blood . . .': Speer, *Inside the Third Reich*, p. 234.

40   Monthly aircraft production figures: Postan, *British War Production*, Apps. 2 and 4; *GSWW*, Vol. I, p. 699.

4. The Point of No Return

42   'The day is charged with electricity . . .': Ciano, *Diary*, 23/8/1939.

42   'This evening the Duce is favourable to war . . .': ibid.

43   'peasants . . . damn Germans . . . We must therefore . . .': ibid., 24/8/1939.

43   'No greater mistake could be made . . .': *Documents on the Origin of the War*, No. 454.

44   The British Government . . .: ibid., No. 456.

44   'No foreign propagandist bent upon blackening . . .': *The Times*, 11/11/1938, http://www.thetimes.co.uk/tto/archive

46   'He fears the bitter judgement of the Germans . . .': Ciano, *Diary*, 25/8/1939.

48   'make friendship . . . lasting understanding': *Documents on the Origins of the War*, No. 463.

49   'mobilisation of mind and spirit': cited in Noakes and Pridham (eds.), *Nazism*, Vol. 2, Doc. No. 267.

49   'We did not lose the war . . .': cited in ibid.

50   'Radio must reach all . . .': cited in Grunberger, *Social History of the Third Reich*, p. 507.

50   *Völkischer Beobachter*: figures are from Hale, *Captive Press*, p. 144.

51   'The Polish atrocities against the German minority . . .': Knocke, *I Flew for the Führer* (diary, 31/8/1939).

51   'The anger that I felt inside . . .': Herrmann, *Eagle's Wings*, p. 54.

51   'September 1, 1939, was no day . . .': Topp, *Odyssey*, p. 56.

51   'We were not hungry for war . . .': Luck, *Panzer Commander*, p. 26.

5. War Declared

54   'Remember – many things are more painful . . .': Chambrun, *I Saw France Fall*, p. 26.

55   'The events against which we had fought . . .': TNA, CAB 23/100.

56   'Speak for England!': cited in Spears, *Assignment to Catastrophe*, p. 31.

56   'The moment we look like weakening . . .': cited in ibid., p. 32.

56   'I shall never forget . . .': Cox, diary, IWM 2769.

57   'The sky was heavy . . .': ibid.

58   'It had an excellent private. . .': Colville, *Fringes of Power*, Vol. 1, p. 20.

59   'That's it . . . war has been declared': Bradford White, *Andrée's War*, p. 15.

59   'We are now at war . . .': ibid., p. 45.

61   'In fact, we were coming in so low . . .': AI with Eric Brown.

61   'I'm afraid you'll have to come with us . . .': ibid.

62   'This is the way the world ends . . .': Goodson, *Tumult in the Clouds*, p. 13.

6. All at Sea

65   'Once again we must fight . . .': WSC, Vol. 1, p. 365.

65   It was comfortably the world's largest . . .: these figures can be found in Roskill, *War at Sea*, Vol. 1, and in *GSWW*, Vol. II.

66   And for all this . . .: details of Britain's global reach can be found in Edgerton, *Britain's War Machine* and *Warfare State*, as well as in Howlett, *Fighting With Figures*, Table 8.3, p. 183.

67   '. . . actual and prospective': Howlett, *Fighting With Figures*, p. 377.

68   'A war against Britain . . .': Carls, cited in *GSWW*, Vol. I, p. 475.

69   'He would ensure that . . .': Doenitz, *Memoirs*, p. 42.

69   'Seldom indeed . . .': ibid., p. 47.

70   'Now I came back to life . . .': Suhren and Brustat-Naval, *Teddy Suhren*, p. 55.

70   'Stop at once and show papers!': cited in Suhren, p. 63.

71   'Good God, what do we do now?': cited in ibid., p. 63.

71   'It all went according to plan . . .': Suhren and Brustat-Naval, *Teddy Suhren*, p. 64.
71   'To Mr Churchill . . .': cited in Blair, *Hitler's U-Boat War*, Vol. 1, p. 85.

7. Offensive Reconnaissance
74   'On take-off she swung like hell . . .': Gibson, *Enemy Coast Ahead*, p. 35.
74   'Good luck, sir, give those bastards . . .': Gibson, *Enemy Coast Ahead*, p. 38.
76   another Battle of Verdun: cited in Horne, *To Lose a Battle*, p. 141.
76   'How should we come off . . .': Barlone, *French Officer's Diary*, 2/9/39.
76   'We skirt huge earthworks . . .': ibid., 5/9/39.
77   'The attack is on the point . . .': ibid., 11/9/39.
77   'We are all burning with desire . . .': ibid.
78   'Poland is done for . . .': ibid., 19/9/39.
78   'X Platoon tried to continue . . .': cited in Horne, *To Lose a Battle*, p. 141.
78   'The Germans did not react . . .': Beaufre, *1940*, p. 147.
80   'We shall prevail . . .': Reynaud, *Thick of the Fight*, p. 241.
81   'We are glad to observe . . .': Spears, *Assignment to Catastrophe*, p. 51.
81   'We have heard of the sinking . . .': IWM 6854.
82   'The former made us very popular . . .': Macintyre, *U-Boat Killer*, p. 9.
83   'Of course. What can I do about it?': AI with Norman Field.
84   The Regular British Army had been small . . .: these figures are cited by Dennis, *Decision by Default*, p. 27.

8. Vehicle Shortages
88   'You've taken my books . . .': AI with Eric Brown.
88   In 1935, there was one vehicle for every 65 . . .: these figures can be found in *Whitaker's Almanack* for 1940 and 1942, and in DiNardo, *Germany's Panzer Arm*, p. 42.
90   General Georg Thomas . . .: The WiRüAmt changed its name to the Economics and Armaments Office (Wirtschafts- und Rüstungsamt) from Office of Economics (Wirtschaftsstab) at the start of the war.
91   no fewer than 131 different types of truck . . .: cited in Schell, 'Grundlagen der Motorisierung'.
91   'Once this has happened . . .': BA-MA RW18/822.
93   'You mean they still pull the artillery . . .': Knappe, *Soldat*, pp. 99–101.
94   Fully trained Regular troops . . .: figures from NARA RG 0498-UD205-1222 and from *GSWW*, Vol. II.
94   most were between 14,000 and 17,000 men strong . . .: figures from US Army Technical Manual TM-E 30-451, *Handbook of German Military Forces*.
95   'Even though we were technically at war . . .': Knappe/Brusaw, *Soldat*, p. 158.

9. The Modern Army
101   'It was a vast improvement . . .': AI with Norman Field.

104   'We were slightly apprehensive . . .': Christopherson, diaries, BA-MA.

10. Leading the Nation

107   'It was all the same . . .': Sevareid, *Not So Wild*, p. 114.
109   'Post's jush down the nex' turn . . .': ibid., p. 116.
109   'The only interest here . . .': Roll, *Hopkins Touch*, p. 125.
109   The first wartime poll . . .: polls cited in ibid., p. 127 and in Dallek, *Franklin D. Roosevelt*, p. 201.
109   'We in the Americas . . .': cited in Roll, *Hopkins Touch*, p. 126.
111   'Our acts must be guided . . .': Roosevelt, *Public Papers and Addresses*, p. 512.
112   'Such lack of foresight . . .': Warlimont, *Inside Hitler's Headquarters*, p. 54.
112   'to serve as a base . . .': cited in Trevor-Roper, *Hitler's War Directives*, p. 50.

11. Attention to Detail

115   The basic infantry light machine gun . . .: machine guns are discussed by Daniel Musgrave in his encyclopedic tome, *German Machineguns*, pp. 283–4.
116   nearly 50 kilograms of iron was needed . . .: BA-MA RH6/v2806.
116   It cost 312 Reichsmarks . . .: ibid.
117   'Shooting more than 250 shots . . .': *Ausbildungsvorschrift fur die Infanterie*, Heft 2a, 1941.
120   no fewer than 323 different companies . . .: BA-MA RH56/354.
123   'On the one hand . . .': Luck, *Panzer Commander*, p. 20.

12. Case YELLOW

125   'When I recall . . .': Churchill, *War Speeches*, Vol. 1, p. 115.
125   'The latest German claim . . .': Colville, *Fringes of Power*, Vol. 1, 8/11/1939.
126   'The wireless has just given . . .': IWM 96/59/4.
127   'He was absolutely right . . .': Suhren and Brustat-Naval, *Teddy Suhren*, p. 71.
128   'Kapitän, on the bridge!': the description of this attack and counter-attack is in ibid., pp. 73–80.
134   'Suprise may now be regarded . . .': Halder, *Halder War Diary*, 18/2/1940.

13. Home Front

137   'Our clothes were always too small . . .': Dos and Lieff, *Letters From Berlin*, p. 56.
139   One tractor for every 1,000 acres . . .: figures are from Farquharson, *The Plough and the Swastika*, p. 175.
140   Germany had 4 million sheep . . .: figures are from *Whitaker's Almanack*, 1940.
140   food was the most urgent problem . . .: cited in Collingham, *Taste of War*, p. 30.

141   'German policy . . .': *Documents on German Foreign Policy*, Series D, Vol. 10, No. 19.

142   'Now we're not even allowed . . .': Dos and Lieff, *Letters From Berlin*, p. 59.

142   Wheat prices: cited in Paxton, *French Peasant Fascism*, p. 14.

143   Seventy-eight per cent of French milk . . .: cited in ibid., p. 28.

144   'War was just an accident . . .': Luchaire, *Ma drôle de vie*, p. 84.

145   'So once again in a time . . .': Street, *Hitler's Whistle*, p. 12.

146   two-thirds of what it had been in 1801: cited in Langlands, 'The Battle for Food', in Ginn, Goodman and Langlands, *Wartime Farm*, p. 17; and in Short, Watkins and Martin, *Front Line of Freedom*, p. 4.

146   25 per cent fewer farm workers: cited in Stapledon, *Way of the Land*, p. 245.

147   'No weapon ever invented . . .': *Land at War*, p. 7.

148   'In this instance . . .': Street, *Hitler's Whistle*, p. 27.

149   'Whenever I see an aeroplane . . .': ibid., p. 13.

150   'Colder than ever! . . .': Cox, diary, 20/1/1940.

150   Petrol rationing: figures are from Zweiniger-Bargielowska, *Austerity in Britain*, p. 192.

150   'the butcher, Atkinson, . . .': Cox, diary, 18/11/1939.

150   'Today, butter, sugar and bacon . . .': ibid., 8/1/1940.

14. Iron in the Soul

153   'the hours were numbered . . .': cited in Fullilove, *Rendezvous With Destiny*, p. 49.

153   'most of what Nazidom . . .': Self, *Neville Chamberlain Diary Letters*, 16/3/1940.

154   'The minute hand . . .': Roosevelt, *Public Papers and Addresses*, Vol. IX, 16/3/1940.

154   'I have had too many dealings . . .': Ciano, *Diary*, 26/2/1940.

154   'I feel that you cannot simply . . .': cited in MacGregor Knox, *Mussolini Unleashed*, p. 68.

155   80 per cent of Italy's raw materials . . .: figures are cited in ibid., pp. 69–72.

156   'I have the pleasure . . .': cited in Ciano, *Diary*, 18/1/1940.

156   'Everybody knows and understands . . .': ibid., 16/12/1939.

156   'The Duce must be aware . . .': ibid., 18/1/1940.

156   'It is hard for me . . .': ibid.

157   'It is not possible that of all people . . .': cited in ibid., 6/3/1940.

157   'A coup de théâtre . . .': ibid., 8/3/1940.

159   'I had little dreamt . . .': Lyttelton, *Memoirs of Lord Chandos*, p. 152.

160   less than 1 per cent of all Allied . . .: these figures can be found in Grove, *Defeat of the Enemy Attack*. Losses in convoys were even lower – about 0.3 per cent. For example, 2,224 ships sailed in coastal convoys between 3 September and 31 December 1939, of which just seven were sunk.

160   22 million tons . . .: figures for German iron ore imports are from Butler, *Grand Strategy*, Vol. II, p. 91.
160   'basic demand of the Wehrmacht': *GSWW*, Vol. II, p. 189.
162   'The French are becoming excited . . .': Colville, *Fringes of Power*, Vol. 1, 29/1/1940.
164   'I could hardly believe . . .': Kennedy, *Business of War*, p. 47.
164   'I think the whole thing . . .': ibid., p. 48.
165   'You know it wasn't my fault . . .': ibid., p. 50.
165   'I learned how futile . . .': ibid., p. 51.

15. All Alone

167   3,500 tons demanded . . .: figures cited in Ciano, *Diary*, 22/2/1940.
167   Germany had suffered an 80 per cent reduction . . .: Tooze, *Wages of Destruction*, p. 332.
168   Göring had warned . . .: IWM EDS 1571.
169   'Fine, but the best thing . . .': Barlone, *French Officer's Diary*, 18/2/1940.
170   'During four years . . .': Chambrun, *I Saw France Fall*, p. 63.
170   'But nothing was done . . .': Beaufre, *1940*, p. 170.
171   'But the Germans . . .': Spears, *Assignment to Catastrophe*, pp. 80–1.
172   'Neither have begun to realise . . .': ibid., p. 86.
172   'It sounded ominous . . .': ibid., p. 87.
173   'The stake in total warfare . . .': Reynaud, *Thick of the Fight*, p. 261.
173   'A submarine is designed . . .': Topp, *Odyssey*, p. 62.
174   'You have to have been with us . . .': ibid., p. 63.
175   'Lord Halifax does indeed seem . . .': Cox, diary, 28/1/1940.
175   'wreck our economy . . .': Colville, *Fringes of Power*, Vol. 1, 2/2/1940.

Part II: Germany Triumphant
16. Operation WESERÜBUNG

178   'One could speculate . . .': Hinchliffe, *Lent Papers*, p. 60.
178   'It was to be the most daring . . .': ibid., p. 61.
180   'rashest undertakings in the history . . .': cited in Kersaudy, *Norway 1940*, p. 49.
182   'salad in a colander . . .': Spears, *Assignment to Catastrophe*, p. 103.
182   'The two men detested . . .': ibid.
182   'What will centuries to come say . . .': cited in ibid., p. 106.
182   'The PM for his part . . .': Colville, *Fringes of Power*, Vol. 1, 6/4/1940.
183   Hitler had missed the bus . . .: Self, *Neville Chamberlain Diary Letters*, p. 415.
184   'Majesty, . . .': cited in Kersaudy, *Norway 1940*, p. 68.
186   'For the first time . . .': Hinchliffe, *Lent Papers*, p. 61.
186   'I dive, pull up, turn . . .': ibid.
188   'Everyone I met . . .': AI with Gunnar Sonsteby.

17. The Battle for Norway

190   'broke all the rules . . .': Warlimont, *Inside Hitler's Headquarters*, p. 76.
191   'Despite tremendous anti-aircraft fire . . .': Topp, *Odyssey*, p. 67.
191   'witches' cauldron . . .': ibid., p. 69.
192   'It's just an exercise . . .': Kynoch, *Norway 1940*, p. 12.
195   'I've had enough . . .': cited in Smyth, *Abrupt Sierras*, p. 85.
195   'I went to bed . . .': ibid., p. 86.
195   'To say that we were all keen . . .': Gibson, *Enemy Coast Ahead*, p. 62.
195   'Everyone was very optimistic . . .': ibid., p. 63.
196   'We were only about one hundred feet . . .': ibid., p. 65.
198   'We continually saw burned farms . . .': Sonsteby, *Report from No. 24*, p. 15.
199   'Whatever else had been on the *Cedarbank* . . .': Kynoch, *Norway 1940*, p. 25.

18. The Go-for-Broke Gamble

201   Frederick the Great . . .: cited in Frieser, *Blitzkrieg Legend*, p. 329.
202   'And then what . . .': cited in Guderian, *Panzer Leader*, p. 92.
203   'You will be creeping by . . .': cited in Frieser, *Blitzkrieg Legend*, p. 98.
204   'But we won't be able . . .': cited in Emilio Faldella, *L'Italia e la seconda guerra*, p. 734.
204   'and we shall all asphyxiate inside': ibid.
205   'Mussolini read the letter . . .': Ciano, *Diary*, 24/4/1940.
205   'I was proud to go everywhere . . .': Luchaire, *Ma drôle de vie*, p. 92.
205   'I, only, remained sitting . . .': ibid., p. 94.
208   'Geddown and lie flat!': Kynoch, *Norway 1940*, p. 52.
209   'I have an uneasy feeling . . .': Colville, *Fringes of Power*, Vol. 1, 24/4/1940.
210   'Their height, combined with the narrowness . . .': Wight-Boycott, diary, 2/5/40, IWM 6854.
210   'I turned and took one last look . . .': Kynoch, *Norway 1940*, p. 148.
211   'in spite of his amateurish interventions': Warlimont, *Inside Hitler's Headquarters*, p. 79.

19. Attack in the West

215   'Anton 2 to Anton . . .': Mahlke, *Memoirs*, p. 83.
215   'The general feeling . . .': ibid., p. 84.
217   'Go to hell . . .': Offenberg, *Lonely Warrior*, p. 12.
217   'Don't worry . . .' ibid., p. 13.
218   'The old Fiat vibrated . . .': ibid., p. 15.
219   'Missed the bus! . . .': Holland, *Battle of Britain*, p. 49.
222   'General. The battle has begun . . .': Reynaud, *Thick of the Fight*, p. 287.
224   'The Nazi lieutenant . . .': Chambrun, *I Saw France Fall*, p. 69.
225   'Il faut qu'on gagne . . .': ibid., p. 71.

20. Race to the Meuse

226   'It was hard to believe . . .': Alanbrooke, *War Diaries*, 10/5/1940.
227   'Sixty-three Dutchmen . . .': Pöppel, *Heaven and Hell*, p. 34.
227   'Night fell mercifully . . .': Offenberg, *Lonely Warrior*, p. 16.
228   'There was a feeling . . .': AI with Billy Drake.
229   'On the one hand, I had no idea . . .': Knoller, *Living with the Enemy*, p. 52.
230   'As the air cleared . . .': ibid., p. 74.
232   'But all the communications . . .': George Darley, IWM 15184.
233   the Army had shrunk to just 119,913 . . .: figures are cited in Cardozier, *Mobilization of the United States*, p. 73.
234   'He knows instinctively . . .': cited in Klein, *Call to Arms*, p. 34.
235   'We younger ones . . .': Luck, *Panzer Commander*, p. 37.

21. Smashing the Meuse Front

237   'All of you are enemies . . .': Knoller, *Living with the Enemy*, p. 77.
239   'If ever the success . . .': cited in Frieser, *Blitzkrieg Legend*, p. 107.
240   'To use an analogy . . .': ibid.
242   'My whole attack . . .': Guderian, *Panzer Leader*, p. 101.
243   'All the work of the past nine months . . .': CCA, Bufton Papers, diary, 15/5/1940.
243   'We're almost disappointed': Bethke, diary, 13/5/1940, DTA, 652.9.
244   'Still the 110 was shooting at me . . .': Drake/Shores, *Fighter Leader*.
245   'What was easy today . . .': Balck, *Ordnung im Chaos*, trans. David Zabecki.
245   'Ask General Doumenc . . .': cited in Beaufre, *1940*, p. 183.
245   'Our front has been broken . . .': ibid.
246   'All our doctrine . . .': ibid., p. 185.
247   'I know exactly what he would say . . .': cited in Pogue, *George C. Marshall*, pp. 30–1.
248   'If you don't do something . . .': cited in Herman, *Freedom's Forge*, p. 10.
248   'The small countries . . .': Lowenheim, Langley and Jonas, *Roosevelt and Churchill*, Doc. 8, 15/5/1940.
249   'These are ominous days . . .': Roosevelt, *Public Papers*, Vol. 9, pp. 198–202.
249   'Boot them, don't slap them!': Guderian, *Panzer Leader*, pp. 105–6.
249   'Keep going . . .': cited in Luck, *Panzer Commander*, p. 37.

22. Encirclement

251   'The sudden revelation . . .': Reynaud, *Thick of the Fight*, p. 302.
251   The Luftwaffe was losing . . .: figures for aircraft and air personnel losses come from Cornwell, *The Battle of France Then and Now*. The books in this series are widely accepted as the most authoritative on this matter.
251   'This 14 May . . .': Mahlke, *Memoirs*, p. 89.
253   'We are beaten . . .': Reynaud, *Thick of the Fight*, p. 320.

254 'My dear Siegfried!': Bethke, diary, 15/5/40, DTA, 652.9.
255 'Apparently the French . . .': Colville, *Fringes of Power*, Vol. 1, 16/5/1940.
255 'Then I will find other roads': Hartog and Kasaboski, *Occupied Garden*, p. 64.
256 'Where is the strategic reserve?': WSC, Vol. II, p. 42; Reynaud, *Thick of the Fight*, pp. 323–5; Spears, *Assignment to Catastrophe*, p. 150.
256 'We found the plane's serial number . . .': Sevareid, *Not So Wild*, p. 139.
257 'Unfortunately they did not know . . .': Offenberg, *Lonely Warrior*, p. 23.
257 'These sights on the Belgian roads . . .': Chambrun, *I Saw France Fall*, p. 77.
258 'With our reconnaissance battalion . . .': Luck, *Panzer Commander*, p. 39.
258 'No plan, no thought of a plan . . .': cited in Horne, *To Lose a Battle*, p. 572.
259 The populations of Tourcoing . . .: cited in Vinen, *Unfree French*, p. 30.
259 'The army retreated . . .': IWM 15814.
259 'very powerful armoured forces . . .': Liddell Hart, *Rommel Papers*, p. 32.
259 'A critical moment . . .': cited in ibid., p. 34.
260 'He seemed to everyone . . .': Reynaud, *Thick of the Fight*, p. 340.
260 'The morning he took over . . .': Beaufre, *1940*, p. 190.
261 'I learned that the smell . . .': Knappe/Brusaw, *Soldat*, p. 168.
261 'It was devastating . . .': ibid., p. 170.
262 'This being the state of affairs . . .': Warlimont, *Inside Hitler's Headquarters*, p. 98.

23. Britain's Darkest Hour
265 'Everything depends upon the sequence . . .': cited in Beasley, *Knudsen*, p. 54.
265 'Accuracy is the only straight line . . .': ibid., p. 59.
266 'Mr Knudsen, the President has asked . . .': ibid., p. 237.
267 'You are to try and get to Paris . . .': Chambrun, *I Saw France Fall*, p. 86.
268 'I was a little browned off . . .': Cheall, *Fighting Through*, p. 10.
268 'some good boys': ibid., p. 16.
268 'But we were determined . . .': ibid., p. 15.
268 'So we are encircled! . . .': Barlone, *French Officer's Diary*, 23/5/1940.
269 'We would have a few skirmishes . . .': AI with Norman Field.
270 'As I realized . . .': Spears, *Assignment to Catastrophe*, pp. 190–6.
272 'Herr Hitler has the whip hand . . .': TNA CAB 65/13/21. Transcripts of the entire War Cabinet meetings on these crucial days can be found online too at the National Archives website.

24. Getting Away
275 'At some distance . . .': Barlone, *French Officer's Diary*, 29/5/1940.
275 'That is all that remains . . .': ibid., 30/5/1940.
276 'Tears came to my eyes . . .': AI with Norman Field.
276 'I believe that my unexpected return . . .': Chambrun, *I Saw France Fall*, pp. 98–9.

277   'I realized I'd been clobbered . . .': AI with Norman Field.
278   'BEF evacuated . . .': cited in Gardner, *Evacuation from Dunkirk*, Appendix T.
279   'A painful conference . . .': Ciano, *Diary*, 28/5/1940.
280   agriculture was still the biggest employer . . .: figures come from *Whitaker's Almanack*, 1940 and 1942, and from *Italy, Vol. II: Geographical Handbook Series*.
280   'The decision has been taken': Ciano, *Diary*, 30/5/1940.
281   'curiously calm . . .': Cox, diary, 2/6/1940.
281   'Even though large tracts . . .': cited in Colville, *Fringes of Power*, Vol. 1, 4/6/1940, and Churchill, *War Speeches*.
283   'What ship? What ship?': Kirchner, *Erinnerungen: Mein Lebenslauf*, DTA 700, IX.
283   'As we approached . . .': ibid.

25. The End in France
285   'He thought any war with Britain . . .': Magini, memoir, FADN.
286   'An hour appointed by destiny . . .': translation at http://globalrhetoric. wordpress.com/mussolini-speech-of-the-10-june-1940-declaration-of-war-on-france-and-england/
286   'People of Italy! . . .': ibid.
286   'I got up calmly . . .': 'The Wartime Journal of Pace Misciatelli-Chigi 1939–1945', in Cartwright-Hignett, *Three Ladies of Siena*.
287   As far as the Führer was concerned . . .: Engel, *Heart of the Reich*, p. 93.
287   'The declaration of war . . .': Sergio Fabbri, memoir, FADN.
287   'We were full of enthusiasm . . .': AI with William Cremonini.
287   'In those days . . .': ibid.
288   'The news of the war . . .': Ciano, *Diary*, 10/6/1940.
288   'Captain, your breakfast . . .': Luck, *Panzer Commander*, p. 43.
289   'Bravo, von Luck': ibid., p. 4.
290   'Paris lay inert . . .': Sevareid, *Not So Wild*, p. 147.
290   'The latest news . . .': cited in Bradford White, *Andrée's War*, p. 29.
290   'All my friends have gone . . .': ibid., p. 30.
290   'I beg you . . .': cited in Reynaud, *Thick of the Fight*, p. 478.
291   'The country will not forgive you . . .': cited in ibid., p. 489.
292   'France is finished! . . .': cited in Sevareid, *Not So Wild*, p. 149.
292   'A day I will remember . . .': cited in Bradford White, *Andrée's War*, p. 31.
293   'I for once forgot . . .': recordings for the *The World at War*, IWM 2712.
293   'L'homme du destin': cited in Williams, *Last Great Frenchman*, p. 100.
294   'The Cabinet meeting turned . . .': Colville, *Fringes of Power*, Vol. 1, 16/6/1940.
294   'He was transfigured with joy . . .': Spears, *Assignment to Catastrophe*, p. 589.
294   'It did not occur to us . . .': ibid., p. 590.
294   'She is ugly, dirty, nasty . . .': cited in ibid., p. 578.

295   'He seemed to regard . . .': Sevareid, *Not So Wild*, p. 153.
295   'We learn by wireless . . .': Barlone, *French Officer's Diary*, 18/6/1940.
296   'The German Government solemnly . . .': Reynaud, *Thick of the Fight*, p. 562, and Butler, *Grand Strategy*, Vol. II, p. 205.
296   'They walk around as if . . .': cited in Bradford White, *Andrée's War*, p. 35.
296   'It is pouring . . .': ibid., p. 36.

26. Air Power: I

297   'An eerie sight . . .': Bethke, diary, 30/5/1940, DTA, 652.9.
298   'I'm extremely ambitious . . .': ibid., 6/6/1940.
298   'I'd made it': Herrmann, *Eagle's Wings*, p. 60.
298   'What's happened back there? . . .': Mahlke, *Memoirs*, p. 96.
299   'We'd had the devil's own luck . . .': ibid.
300   'I looked at these men . . .': Steinhoff, interview in Heaton and Lewis, *German Aces Speak II*.
304   'He described this mission . . .': cited in Suchenwirth, *Command and Leadership*, p. 160.

Part III: War in the Air and on the Sea
27. Air Power II

309   'At last we were out of it all . . .': Gibson, *Enemy Coast Ahead*, p. 79.
311   this had risen to 300 per week . . .: aircraft production figures are from the Beaverbrook Papers, House of Lords Archives.

28. Not Alone

314   'Very well, alone': *Evening Standard*, 18/6/1940.
318   'Everyone seemed to have had . . .': Lyttelton, *Memoirs of Lord Chandos*, p. 160.
319   'The defeat of France . . .': ibid.
320   'We will extend . . .': cited in Hancock and Gowing, *British War Economy*, p. 226.
321   'Our greatest need . . .': cited in Beasley, *Knudsen*, p. 242.
321   'Democracy must wage total war . . .': cited in Herman, *Freedom's Forge*, p. 73.
324   'My impression of Mr Knudsen's . . .': Henry Lewis Stimson Papers, Manuscripts and Archives, diary, 25/7/1940, Yale University Library.
325   'I have the impression . . .': Colville, *Fringes of Power*, Vol. 1, 8/7/1940.
325   'The invasion and great attack . . .': ibid., 9/7/1940.
325   'We still await "The Great Invasion"': Cox, diary, 7/8/1940.

29. Indecision

326   'Berlin is to be given . . .': cited in Speer, *Inside the Third Reich*, p. 249.
327   'He is rather inclined . . .': Ciano, *Diary*, 7/7/1940.
328   'My impression is that the Führer . . .': Engel, *Heart of the Reich* (diary, 15/7/1940).

328 'I only know clearly . . .': original transcript in the Author's Collection.
329 'Hitler may plant the Swastika . . .': cited in Roberts, *Holy Fox*, p. 249.
329 'All the German cities . . .': cited in Steinhoff, Pechel and, Showalter, *Voices from the Third Reich*, p. 80.
329 'We do not notice . . .': Bethke, diary, 30/6/1940, DTA, 652.9.
330 '*Apparently* negotiations are underway . . .': ibid., 12/7/1940.
330 'When will it finally start? . . .': ibid., 24–26/7/1940.
331 'Feeling highly elated . . .': Smyth, *Abrupt Sierras*, p. 99.
331 'One thing was already . . .': Mahlke, *Memoirs*, p. 120.
332 'To me it was apparent . . .': George Darley, IWM 15814.
332 'a .303 bullet has but little effect . . .': cited in Irons, *Relentless Offensive*, p. 61.
333 'The basic need . . .' cited in Ziegler, *Story of 609 Squadron*, p. 99.
334 'We soon sorted them out . . .': ibid, p. 118.
334 'a high-class spy': letter from Spaatz to Arnold, 27/8/1940, Spaatz Papers, Library of Congress.
336 'Unless the Germans have more . . .': letter from Spaatz to Arnold, 31/7/1940, cited in Davis, *Carl A. Spaatz*, p. 48.
337 'I decided . . .': AI with Jean-Mathieu Boris.
338 'sweetest little ship . . .': cited in Kershaw, *The Few*, p. 5.
339 'Well, we'd made it! . . .': 'Yankee Eagle over London', *Liberty* magazine, 5/4/41.
340 'a piece of cake': Offenberg, *Lonely Warrior*, p. 42.
340 Messerschmitt had produced . . .: Me109 figures are from BA-MA RL XXX; Ministry of Aircraft Production figures are from the Beaverbrook Papers, House of Lords Archive.

30. Adler-Angriff

341 'This was the start . . .': Luck, *Panzer Commander*, p. 58.
341 'Observation duty had now settled . . .': Street, *From Dusk till Dawn*, p. 42.
342 These amounted to some 1.6 million men . . .: NARA RG 0498/UD205/1222.
342 'We were given a full complement . . .': Cheall, *Fighting Through*, p. 26.
342 'We felt very confident . . .': ibid., p. 27.
343 amounted to 3,358 aircraft . . .': figures are from Wood and Dempster, *Narrow Margin*, Appendix 20.
345 'The Luftwaffe is clearly superior . . .': cited in ibid., pp. 43–4.
345 up to 12 August . . .: casualty figures are from Ramsey, *Battle of Britain: Then and Now*; new fighter aircraft figures from BBK and *GSWW*, Vol. II, p. 382.
347 'one long nightmare': Elmhirst, *An Airman's Life*, CCA.
348 'Uppermost in my thoughts . . .': ibid.
348 'We, in my Department . . .': ibid.
349 'The question everyone is asking . . .': Colville, *Fringes of Power*, Vol. 1, 13/8/1940.

350 'The PM is very much on edge . . .': ibid., 13/8/1940.

351 'Thus we might easily rob . . .': WSC, Vol. II, p. 370.

352 'For the first time in my life . . .': cited in Kershaw, *The Few*, p. 76.

352 'My head was spinning . . .': ibid., p. 117, and Ziegler, *Story of 609 Squadron*, pp. 124–5.

353 they had lost twenty-five aircraft . . .: figures are from Ramsey, *Battle of Britain: Then and Now*.

353 'But not only . . .': George Darley IWM 15814.

355 134 sunk in June . . .: figures are from Grove, *Defeat of the Enemy Attack*. Table 13.

356 'Eels at the ready! . . .': Suhren and Brustat-Naval, *Teddy Suhren*, p. 86.

356 'No one believed it would hit': ibid., p. 87.

356–7 'But the Kommandant . . .': ibid., p. 88.

31. Crossing the Water

358–9 'Crumbs! Navigator to Skipper . . .': Bufton Papers, CCA.

359 'We had been waiting for this . . .': Gibson, *Enemy Coast Ahead Uncensored*, p. 102.

359 'The raid was in fact lousy': ibid.

361 'particularly lousy': cited in Davis, *Carl A. Spaatz*, p. 51.

361 'Our whole strategy is based . . .': cited in Butler, *Grand Strategy*, Vol. II, p. 342.

363 'I only have five planes here . . .': Bethke, diary, 2–5/9/1940, DTA, 652.9.

364 'What he said sounded like . . .': Steinhoff, Pechel and Showalter, *Voices from the Third Reich*, p. 81.

364 'Young man . . .': ibid.

364–5 'Reported very unfavourably . . .': Engel, *Heart of the Reich* (diary, 10/8/1940).

366 'For a new boy . . .': Bam Bamberger, private manuscript.

368 'To think those bloody Germans . . .': AI with Norman Field.

369 Fighter Command had 701 serviceable aircraft . . .: daily figures can be found at www.raf.mod.uk/bob1940/september1 (no longer extant, but information provided by Air Historical Branch)

369 'The greatest query was . . .': Elmhirst, *An Airman's Life*, CCA.

370 'All reports look like invasion . . .': Alanbrooke, *War Diaries*, 7/9/1940.

370 'The responsibility of feeling . . .': ibid., 8/9/1940.

371 'Every port from Antwerp to Dieppe . . .': Gibson, *Enemy Coast Ahead Uncensored*, p. 104.

371 'But we both agreed . . .': Street, *From Dusk till Dawn*, p. 57.

372 'All evening we have been looking . . .': Cox, diary, 7/9/1940.

372 'By God, that's good, that's fine . . .': cited in Middleton, *Sky Suspended*, p. 147.

372 'Do you think that Germany . . .?': cited in Irving, *Göring*, pp. 295–6.

32. The Approach to Battle

373   'In our summer training': cited in Baumer and Reardon, *American Iliad*, p. 4.

374   'We wanted to go to work . . .': AI with Tom Bowles.

374   'We hadn't heard from Tom . . .': AI with Henry Bowles.

376   'Our goal, of course . . .': Clark, *Calculated Risk*, p. 13.

376   'Today, I shot down . . .': cited in Heaton and Lewis, *Star of Africa*, p. 16.

377   'But the white billowy folds . . .': *Liberty* magazine, 29/4/1941.

378   'Today was the toughest day . . .': Tobin, diary, 15/9/1940, cited in Kershaw, *The Few*, p. 188.

379   'That was when we in the second wave . . .': Steinhoff, interview in Heaton and Lewis, *German Aces Speak II*, p. 134.

379   'I have to admit . . .': Bethke, diary, 10–16/8/1940, DTA, 652.9.

380   'But I was still scared . . .': Bamberger, private manuscript.

380   'If Graziani does not attack . . .': Ciano, *Diary*, 7/9/1940.

382   'We'll study it when the war is over': cited in Knox, *Hitler's Italian Allies*, p. 57.

382   'The tank is a powerful tool': cited in ibid., p. 55.

385   'We were so disillusioned . . .': AI with William Cremonini.

33. Science, Money and Resources

387   'Last night, most of our home . . .': Cox, diary, 2/10/1940.

388   'I felt Ralph's hand . . .': ibid.

388   'serious but not crippling': cited in Collier, *In Defence of the United Kingdom*, p. 256.

389   'I thought to myself . . .': Kennedy, *Business of War*, p. 60.

390   'The number of people who talked . . .': Beasley, *Knudsen*, p. 262.

392   the Nazis plundered . . .: figures are cited in Tooze, *Wages of Destruction*, p. 385.

396   15,049 aircraft . . .: figures are from Hall and Wrigley, *Studies of Overseas Supply*; Howlett, *Fighting With Figures*; and *GSWW*, Vol. II.

34. The Grey Atlantic

398   Britain had had some 18,911,000 . . .: figures are from Behrens, *Merchant Shipping*, Appendix VIII, p. 69.

403   a staggering 692 convoys . . .: figures are from Grove, *Defeat of the Enemy Attack*, Tables 10 and 12.

405   'The course was quite clear now . . .': Sevareid, *Not So Wild*, pp. 181–2.

405   'When all this is over . . .': ibid., pp. 179–80.

406   'Two hundred airplanes . . .': cited in Burgwyn, *Mussolini Warlord*, p. 45.

407   'Hitler places me . . .': cited in Ciano, *Diary*, 12/10/1940.

408   'In short, Greece is to the Mediterranean . . .': cited in Burgwyn, *Mussolini Warlord*, p. 50.

35. The Humiliation of Mussolini

409   'It was criminal . . .': Magini, memoir, FADN.

411   'You may be sure . . .': cited in Cunningham, *Sailor's Odyssey*, p. 232.

412   'Out here in the Mediterranean . . .': ibid., p. 233.

413   'was abandoned owing to hydraulic . . .': TNA AIR 27/606.

413   'This fellow Willkie . . .': cited in Roll, *Hopkins Touch*, p. 71.

414   'Early this morning . . .': cited in Burgwyn, *Mussolini Warlord*, p. 51.

414   'F. in a rage . . .': Engel, *Heart of the Reich* (diary, 28/10/1940).

415   'Two of theirs went down . . .': Ciano, *Diary*, 1/11/1940.

416   'As may be imagined . . .': Cunningham, *Sailor's Odyssey*, p. 285.

417   'Admirably planned and most gallantly executed': ibid., p. 286.

417   'A black day.': Ciano, *Diary*, 12/11/1940.

419   'Atlantic trade': Cunningham, *Sailor's Odyssey*, p. 241.

419   After all, the oilfields of Abadan . . .: for this assessment, I am grateful to David Edgerton and to Klaus Schmider, 'The Mediterranean in 1940–1941: Crossroads of Lost Opportunity?' *War & Society*, 15 (1997), 2, pp. 19–41.

421   'Our truck was a friendly . . .': Martin, *Hellfire Tonight*, p. 37.

422   'We had total freedom . . .': ibid., p. 48.

422   'And believe me . . .': ibid., p. 50.

36. Change of Tack

425   'We got the impression . . .': cited in Elphick, *Liberty*, p. 41.

426   'Cable from London . . .': cited in ibid., p. 47.

426   'It's true you see nothing now . . .': cited in Heiner, *Henry J. Kaiser*, p. 117.

427   'What the hell is this?': cited in Heaton and Lewis, *Star of Africa*, p. 21.

427   'He stole my car . . .': ibid., p. 23.

428   6,968 deaths and 9,488 seriously injured . . .: figures are from TNA HO 191/11.

431   'How are we doing?': *Time*, 6/10/1940.

432   'I'm rather shocked . . .': cited in Langer and Gleason, *Undeclared War*, pp. 228–9, and Blum, *From the Morgenthau Diaries*, Vol. 2, pp. 202–3.

433   'He suddenly came out with it . . .': Sherwood, *White House Papers of Harry L. Hopkins*, Vol. I, p. 223.

433   'Extraordinary things met us . . .': Moorehead, *African Trilogy*, p. 62.

433   'God watch and keep . . .': ibid., p. 64.

434   'We are trying to fight . . .': ibid., p. 66.

434   'Hitler is pessimistic . . .': Ciano, *Diary*, 18–19/11/1940.

436   'I am convinced that . . .': Engel, *Heart of the Reich* (diary, 18/1/1940).

437   'His magnetic presence . . .': Knocke, *I Flew for the Führer* (diary, 18/12/1940).

438   'All you have to do . . .': Wendel, *Hausfrau at War*, p. 93.

439   'a documentary record . . .': Schlange-Schöningen, *Morning After*, p. 137.

439   'Exchange in kind is flourishing . . .': ibid., p. 159.

Part IV: The Widening War
37. The Vanquished and the Defiant

445   'My compatriots . . .': cited in Hartog and Kasaboski, *Occupied Garden*, p. 80.

445   'kindred-blood', 'considerate': *GSWW*, Vol. V/IA, p. 79.

446   'Do Pétain and Wegand think . . .': Barlone, *French Officer's Diary*, 3/7/1940.

446   'It must not speak . . .': ibid., 5/7/1940.

447   'As for what might happen . . .': cited in Marcel Ophüls, *The Sorrow and the Pity*, p. 58

447   'Frenchmen, comrades . . .': ibid.

448   'I went through what a man . . .': de Gaulle, *War Memoirs: 1940–1942*, p. 133.

448   'Maréchal Pétain stood in my country . . .': Chambrun, *I Saw France Fall*, p. 106.

450   'If the Germans come . . .': Knoller, *Living with the Enemy*, p. 92.

451   'I was rudderless . . .': ibid., p. 103.

452   'I don't know why . . .': Luchaire, *Ma drôle de vie*, p. 107.

452   'Everybody was carefully listening . . .': ibid., p. 112.

453   'According to Hitler's plans . . .': cited in *Le Chagrin et la pitié* (film).

453–4 'We cannot escape . . .': cited in Sherwood, *White House Papers of Harry L. Hopkins*, Vol. I, p. 227.

454   'So far the blitz on London . . .': Pyle, *Ernie Pyle in England*, p. 27.

454   'There was something inspiring . . .': ibid., pp. 31–2.

455   'Volumes of rose-pink smoke . . .': Cox, diary, 30/12/1940.

455   'St Paul's was surrounded by fire . . .': Pyle, *Ernie Pyle in England*, pp. 31–2.

455   'Let me give you an illustration . . .': cited in Sherwood, *White House Papers of Harry L. Hopkins*, Vol. I, and Roll, *Hopkins Touch*, p. 76.

456   'Are you going to let Hitler . . .': cited in Sherwood, *White House Papers of Harry L. Hopkins*, Vol. I, p. 235.

456   'A rotund – smiling . . .': cited in Roll, *Hopkins Touch*, p. 83.

456   'majestic monologues . . .': This episode is recounted in Lyttelton, *Memoirs of Lord Chandos*, pp. 165–6.

457   'I shall never forget . . .': cited in Roll, *Hopkins Touch*, p. 97.

38. Saved from the Deep

460   'We have just wished Bardia . . .': Smyth, *Abrupt Sierras*, p. 125.

460   'This was somewhat different . . .': ibid., p. 125.

461   'All our nerves were on edge . . .': Parbery, *Alf's War*, p. 37.

461   'It was essential . . .': IWM 2912/02.

462   'They were waiting in groups . . .': AI with Ted Hardy.

462   'So far none of them . . .': Martin, diary, 8/2/1941, BA-MA.

463   'The news from the front . . .': ibid., 1/2/1941.

464   'We wished to do nothing . . .': Kennedy, *Business of War*, p. 62.

39. Developments at Sea

467   'Sir, it is not important...': Topp, *Odyssey*, p. 74.

468   'The naval staff regards...': cited in Warlimont, *Inside Hitler's Headquarters*, p. 128.

469   'Directive No. 23': Trevor-Roper, *Hitler's War Directives*, p. 102.

470   126 destroyers...: figures from David J. Lyon, 'The British Order of Battle' in Howarth and Law, *Battle of the Atlantic*.

471   'A new feeling of intelligent...': Macintyre, *U-Boat Killer*, p. 19.

472   'The best, or perhaps it was...': Fabbri, memoir, FADN.

472   'I don't rule out the possibility...': ibid.

474   'Only one hour's operational flying...': Bamberger, private manuscript.

475   'Boy, that was close!': This episode is recounted in Mahlke, *Memoirs*, pp. 165–72.

476   'Everything's splendid with me...': Liddell Hart, *Rommel Papers*, p. 103.

477   'Never has so much...': Anthony Eden, speech to the House of Commons, 12/2/1941.

479   'I warned my ships to prepare...': Macintyre, *U-Boat Killer*, p. 29.

479   'I was still of the opinion...': Doenitz, *Memoirs*, p. 113.

480   'I felt obliged...': ibid., p. 148.

480   'Thank you, Kommandeur...': cited in Robertson, *Golden Horseshoe*, 1937.

481   'This order is a great...': cited in Doenitz, *Memoirs*, p. 137.

481   'That was it!'...: Suhren and Brustat-Naval, *Teddy Suhren*, p. 96.

40. Sea Battles

484   'The U-boat at sea...': WSC, Vol. III, p. 107.

485   'If you regard Hitler as a bull...': Kennedy, *Business of War*, p. 66.

487   'Hitler has in fact made many mistakes...': this memorandum is produced verbatim in ibid., pp. 83–5.

487   'Do not consider yourselves...': WSC, Vol. III, p. 63.

489   'We then explained...': Christopherson, diaries, 2/2/1941, BA-MA.

489   'Tripoli to Agheila is 471 miles...': cited in WSC, Vol. III, p. 175.

490   'Going through the streets...': Parbery, *Alf's War*, p. 44.

491   'By this time...': Avon, *The Eden Memoirs: The Reckoning*, p. 214.

491   'I tried to console him...': Kennedy, *Business of War*, p. 90.

493   'I was near to despair...': Macintyre, *U-Boat Killer*, p. 35.

494   'Abandon ship!': cited in Blair, *Hitler's U-Boat War*, Vol. 1, p. 257.

494   'Have rammed and sunk U-boat...': Macintyre, *U-Boat Killer*, p. 37.

494   'What a blissful moment...': ibid.

494   'Contact, contact!': ibid.

41. Mixed Fortunes: I

497   'By now we were reduced...': Gino Cappozzo, *Breve racconto...* Archivio Provinciale di Trento.

497   'It was a month of hellish fights . . .': ibid.
498   'They had lost all . . .': Cartwright-Hignett, *Three Ladies of Siena*, p. 90.
498   'The worst place . . .': Santaniello, memoir, FADN.
498   'It made my heart thud . . .': Mazzucato, *Un Marinaio*, FADN.
500   'The aircraft that was . . .': ibid.
501   'I was speechless . . .': ibid., p. 11.
501   'You're a pack of . . .': Commander Geoffrey Barnard quoting
       Cunningham, cited in Winton, *Cunningham*, p. 142.
501   'Director layer sees target . . .': Cunningham, *Sailor's Odyssey*, p. 332.
502   On 30 March, Feldmarschall Erhard Milch . . .: recounted in Irving, *Rise
       and Fall*, p. 118.
502   'By themselves a couple of weeks . . .': Engel, *Heart of the Reich* (diary,
       24/3/1941).
503   'I started this morning! . . .': Günther Sack, diary, 7/4/1941, DTA.
503   'Our population at home . . .': ibid., 8/4/1941.
505   'I thought as much . . .': the following episode is described in Herrmann,
       Eagle's Wings, pp. 102ff.

42. Forwards and Backwards
509   'We are currently converting . . .': Hinchliffe, *Lent Papers*, p. 85.
511   'one Hun destroyed': TNA AIR 4/37.
512   'When I first saw him . . .': Gibson, *Enemy Coast Ahead Uncensored*,
       p. 127.
512   'Head nearly shot off . . .': ibid., p. 128.
512   3,132 aircraft had been lost . . .: figures from *GSWW*, Vol. II, p. 400.
513   'It was a great shock . . .': IWM 2912/02.
514   'We saw nothing . . .': Christopherson, diaries, 1–11/4/1941, BA-MA.
514   'The battle still goes on . . .': ibid., 12/1/1941.
514–15 'I am not surprised . . .': ibid., 12/4/1941.
515   'On the news tonight . . .': ibid., 15/4/1941.
516   'Rommel hasn't given us a clear . . .': Halder, *Halder War Diary*,
       23/4/1941.
518   'The old adage . . .': Balck, 'The Greeks Surrender', in *Ordnung im Chaos*,
       Chapter 11.
518   'I sat, pensively in awe . . .': ibid., 'Salonika'.
519   'What *is* going to happen . . .?': Dahl, *Going Solo*, p. 123.
520   'I watched spellbound . . .': ibid., p. 138.
520   'Next to us a 8.8cm . . .': Günther Sack, diary, 15/4/1941, DTA.
521   'Today, like yesterday . . .': Parbery, *Alf's War*, 15/4/1941.

43. Gains and Losses
526   'We had miraculous escapes . . .': Parbery, *Alf's War*, p. 52.
526   'and will soon obtain decisive . . .': Churchill, *War Speeches*, Vol. 1,
       27/4/1941.

527   'Really, he is a remarkable . . .': Cox, diary, 27/4/1940.
527   'Had they done so . . .': Balck, 'Larisa', in *Ordnung im Chaos*, Chapter 11.
528   'Blimey mate, this kite's . . .': Dahl, *Going Solo*, p. 152.
528   'We really had the hell of a time . . .': ibid., p. 185.
528   'If our deficiencies . . .': Cunningham, *Sailor's Odyssey*, p. 351.
529   109 Hurricanes in March . . .: figures from Playfair, *Mediterranean and the Middle East*, Vol. II, Appendix 7.
530   'It was one of the saddest moments . . .': Offenberg, *Lonely Warrior*, p. 69.
530   'leaning forward into France': cited in Richards, *Royal Air Force*, Vol. I, p. 383.
531   'Well, at first I just felt I wanted . . .': cited in Kershaw, *The Few*, p. 205.
532   'One always thinks about . . .': Bethke, *Erinnerungen*, p. 139, DTA.
532   'I thought it best to get away . . .': Offenberg, *Lonely Warrior*, 5/5/1941, p. 106.
533   'Battles might be won or lost . . .': WSC, Vol. III, p. 98.

44. Mixed Fortunes: II
536   'These losses were the price . . .': Cunningham, *Sailor's Odyssey*, p. 361.
538   'It becomes increasingly clear': Halder, *Halder War Diary*, 6/5/1941.
539   'as a base for air warfare . . .': Trevor-Roper, *Hitler's War Directives*, p. 117.
541   'Rather a hectic day . . .': Christopherson, diaries, 1/5/1941, BA-MA.
541   'With British artillery fire . . .': Liddell Hart, *Rommel Papers*, p. 132.
542   'By overstepping his orders . . .': cited in Playfair, *Mediterranean and the Middle East*, Vol. II, p. 157.
542   'Today has been really dreadful . . .': Martin, diary, 9/5/1941, BA-MA.
543   'What counted was the destruction . . .': Martin, *Hellfire Tonight*, pp. 74–5.
544   'I can conceive of no other people . . .': Moorehead, *African Trilogy*, p. 128.
544   'We knew the end was coming . . .': ibid., p. 131.
546   'We had to obey': ibid.
546   'Using our road transport . . .': Halder, *Halder War Diary*, 2/4/1941.
548   'We reckoned that such a small island . . .': Pöppel, *Heaven and Hell*, p. 54.

45. Mercury Falling
549   'It tells us what to do . . .': Cox, diary, IWM 24/5/1941.
551   'But up to what point . . .': Ciano, *Diary*, 24/4/1941.
551   'We speak at length . . .': ibid., 6/5/1941.
552   'The tone of the Germans . . .': ibid., 13/5/1941.
553   'Stand to your arms!': Kippenberger, *Infantry Brigadier*, p. 52.
553   'The silly fellow . . .': ibid., p. 54.
556   'Well, they're on time': cited in Woodhouse, *Something Ventured*, p. 13.
557   'It's a blessed ability . . .': Pöppel, *Heaven and Hell*, p. 55.
560   'It's no good . . .': ibid., p. 56.
560   'Tired and dispirited . . .': ibid.
561   'nearly all disposed of': Kippenberger, *Infantry Brigadier*, p. 59.

562   'The news from many quarters . . .': ibid., p. 71.
562   'I came to dread . . .': Cunningham, *Sailor's Odyssey*, p. 372.
563   'We were not really . . .': ibid., p. 380.
563   'I spoke as reassuringly . . .': Kippenberger, *Infantry Brigadier*, p. 76.
564   'Once again, it had been . . .': Cunningham, *Sailor's Odyssey*, p. 389.
564   'We put up crosses . . .': Pöppel, *Heaven and Hell*, p. 66.

46. Midsummer Heat
567   'Speed! No stops!': Halder, *Halder War Diary*, 28/1/1941.
567   '*Motor vehicle* must accomplish everything': cited in *GSWW*, Vol. IV/I,
       p. 297.
567   'through the additional amounts . . .': BA-MA RW19/165, S.295.
568   'The Balkan campaign . . .': Schell, 'Grundlagen der Motorisierung',
       pp. 210–29.
570   these factories were producing . . .: figures are from BA-MA RH8/v1427.
570   Norway, for example, was reliant on . . .: figures are cited in Collingham,
       Taste of War, p. 35.
571   'If we take what we need . . .': cited in Tooze, *Wages of Destruction*, p. 479.
571   'umpteen millions': cited in Collingham, *Taste of War*, p. 37.
571   'as experience teaches . . .': BA-MA RW19/473, S.167.

47. Industrial Potential
572   'The virtual entry into the war . . .': BA-MA RW19/473, S.167.
572   'The Americans can manufacture . . .': cited in Irving, *Rise and Fall*,
       p. 127.
573   'If they are shut down . . .': Beasley, *Knudsen*, p. 270.
574   'The hard difficulty now . . .': cited in Klein, *Call to Arms*, p. 137.
575   'When I realize that the hours . . .': cited in Beasley, *Knudsen*, p. 307.
576   'Progress in California . . .': cited in Elphick, *Liberty*, p. 54.
576   'In other words, nothing . . .': ibid., p. 56.
577   'If de Gaulle's people do anything . . .': cited in Spears, *Fulfilment of a
       Mission*, p. 37.
578   '1. Thank you . . .': cited in ibid., p. 77.
582   'The reality was a series . . .': Martin, *Hellfire Tonight*, pp. 79–80.
582   'The PM is gravely disappointed . . .': Colville, *Fringes of Power*, Vol. 1,
       1/6/1941.
582   'We don't seem to be able . . .': Christopherson, diaries, 19/6/1941,
       BA-MA.
582   'We had a most interesting . . .': ibid., 13/6/1941.
583   'My belief in God . . .': Günther Sack, diary, 1/6/1941.
583–4 'We are at a decision point . . .': translation by David Zabecki
       (unpublished).
584   'Once Russia is subdued . . .': Balck, 'Russia', Chapter 11, translation by
       David Zabecki (unpublished).

584   'The Ural Mountains . . .': Luck, *Panzer Commander*, p. 65.

48. Trouble at the Top

585   'The Royal Canadian Navy . . .': cited in Milner, *Battle of the Atlantic*, p. 65.

586   Three confirmed sinkings within . . .: in Suhren's memoirs, he confuses his first patrol with his third. The description of the attack on the Gibraltar convoy did, in fact, take place during the forty-seven-day third patrol begun on 16 September.

587   'The decisive factor in the war . . .': Doenitz, *Memoirs*, p. 153.

588   'He sounds a tired and . . .': Colville, *Fringes of Power*, Vol. 1, 29/5/1941.

588   'I suppose you realize . . .': Kennedy, *Business of War*, p. 133.

589   'When we operate our air cover . . .': ibid., p. 130.

590–1 'It is an awful thought . . .': cited in Overy, *Bombing War*, p. 267.

592   'One thing is clear . . .': Tedder, *With Prejudice*, p. 126.

592   'Well, it's probably a good thing . . .': cited in ibid., p. 133.

592   a further 394 aircraft . . .: figures from Playfair, *Mediterranean and the Middle East*, Vol. II, Appendix 7.

593   'By this final demonstration . . .': cited in Sherwood, *White House Papers of Harry L. Hopkins*, Vol. I, p. 304.

Selected Sources

PERSONAL TESTIMONIES
Author Interviews

Beamont, Roland 'Bee'
Bob, Hans-Ekkehard
Boris, Jean-Mathieu
Bowles, Henry D.
Bowles, Tom
Brothers, Peter
Brown, Eric 'Winkle'
Burbridge, Ralph
Byers, Bill
Carter, Bob
Cremonini, William
Davies, Alf
Drake, Billy
Field, Norman
Halloran, Walter
Hardy, Ted

Herrmann, Hajo
Jackson, Andrew
Klein, Josef 'Jupp'
Laity, Bill
Maassen, Franz
Martin, Albert
McInnes, Bill
Munro, Les
Neumann, Julius
Reed, James
Roberts, Eldon 'Bob'
Semken, John
Shaw, Peter
Sonsteby, Gunnar
Wellum, Geoffrey

Imperial War Museum, London

Behrendt, Hans-Otto
Cavalero, Francesco
Clark, Mark
Cormeau, Yvonne
Darley, Horace 'George'
Dönitz, Karl
Finch, Thomas
Galland, Adolf
Gilhesphy, John
Herget, Wilhelm
Hilse, Rolf

Kehrl, Hans
Kretschmer, Otto
Maloubier, Robert
Neary, Tom
O'Connor, Richard
Poulsson, Jens-Anton
Pullini, Emilio
Roberts, Gilbert
Speer, Albert
Warlimont, Walter

Rutgers, State University of New Jersey

Bruyere III, Walter
Kinaszczuk, Thomas
Skinner, John E.

UNPUBLISHED MEMOIRS, DIARIES, ETC.

Archivio Provinciale di Trento

Cappozzo, Gino, *Breve racconto*

Churchill College Archives, Cambridge

Bufton, Air Vice-Marshal Sydney, Papers, memoir, diary
Chandos, Oliver Lyttelton, Lord, Papers
Cunningham, Admiral Viscount Hyndhope, Papers
Elmhirst, Air Marshal Sir Thomas, Papers and *An Airman's Life*
Lewin, Ronald, Papers

Fondazione Archivio Diaristico Nazionale, Pieve Santo Stefano

Fabbri, Sergio, Memoir
Magini, Publio, Memoir
Marchese, Luigi, Memoir
Mazzucato, Walter, Memoir: *Un Marinaio: Una storia*
Santaniello, Giuseppe, Memoir

Imperial War Museum, London

Cox, Gwladys, Diary
Milch, Field Marshal Erhard, Diary and papers
Montgomery, Field Marshal Bernard, Papers
Tuker, General Sir Francis, Papers
Wight-Boycott, Vere, Lieutenant Commander, Diary and papers

Deutsches Tagebucharchiv, Emmendingen

Bethke, Siegfried, *Erinnerungen*, diary, logbook
Kirchner, Hans-Hellmuth, *Erinnerungen: Mein Lebenslauf bis zur Familiengründung*
Lamm, Adolf, *Erinnerungen*
Sack, Günther, Diary
Schild, Heinrich, Untitled memoir and diary

United States Army Heritage Center, Carlisle, Pennsylvania
US Army Historical Division, Foreign Military Studies Series

Blumentritt, Günther, Thoughts on World War II
Göring, Hermann, *An Interview with Reichsmarschall Hermann Göring: German Military Strategy*
Holtzendorff, Hans-Henning von, *Reasons for Rommel's Successes in Africa, 1941–42*
Müller-Hillebrand, Hermann, *German Tank Strength and Loss Statistics*
—, *Germany and Her Allies in World War II: A Record of Axis Collaboration Problems*
Piske, Dr Arthur, *Logistical Problems of the German Air Force in Greece, 1941–43*
Rath, Hans-Joachim, *1st Stuka Wing*
Reinhardt, Hellmuth, *Utilization of Captured Material by Germany in World War II*
Ringel, Julius, *Capture of Crete*
Rommel, Lucie, Interview
Warlimont, Walter, *An Interview with Gen. Art. Walter Warlimont: Norway, North Africa, French Resistance, German–American Relations, Dieppe, Sitzkrieg*

Unpublished Memoirs, Doctorates, etc.

Giffard, Hermione S., *The Development and Production of Turbojet Aero-Engines in Britain, Germany and the United States, 1936–1945*
Hansen, Chester B., Diary
Harper, George C., Recollections
Marsh, Robert, Notes

Others

Bamberger, Cyril 'Bam', *Three Jumps at the Pantry Door and a Slide Down*, and logbook
Christopherson, Stanley, Diaries
Ellis, Ray, *Once a Hussar*
Elmhirst, Air Marshal Sir Thomas, KBE, CB, AFC, Recollections
Fairbairn, John, The Diary of an Ordinary Fighter Pilot
Marks, John, Papers
Martin, Albert, Diary
Semken, John, Diary, album
Smyth, A. J. M., *Abrupt Sierras*

CONTEMPORARY PAMPHLETS, BOOKLETS AND TRAINING MEMORANDA

The Air Battle for Malta, HMSO, 1944

Army Life, War Department Pamphlet 21-13, US Government Printing Office, 1944

Army Training Memorandum, No. 39, April 1941, War Office

Army Training Memorandum, No. 42, January 1942, War Office

Army Training Memorandum, No. 43, May 1942, War Office

Army Training Memorandum, No. 44, October 1942, War Office

Ausbildungsvorschrift für die Infanterie, Heft 2a, 1941

The Battle of the Atlantic: The Official Account of the Fight against the U-Boats, 1939–1945, HMSO, 1946

The Battle of Britain, August–October 1940, Air Ministry, HMSO, 1941

Bomber Command, Air Ministry, HMSO, 1941

Bomber Command Continues, Air Ministry, HMSO, 1942

Brief Notes on the Italian Army, Prepared by GSI, GHQ, Middle East Forces, August 1942

Coastal Command, HMSO, 1942

Combat Instruction for the Panzer Grenadier, Helmut von Wehren, 1944, English translation by John Baum

Combined Operations 1940–1942, HMSO, 1943

Company Officer's Handbook of the German Army, Military Intelligence Division, US War Department, 1944

The Development of Artillery Tactics and Equipment, War Office, 1951

Der Dienst-Unterricht im Heere, Dr jur. W. Reibert, E. S. Mittler & Sohn Berlin, 1941

Documents Concerning German–Polish Relations and the Outbreak of Hostilities between Great Britain and Germany on September 3, 1939, HMSO, 1939

Documents on German Foreign Policy 1918–1945, Series D, Volume IX, HMSO, 1957

Documents on German Foreign Policy 1918–1945, Series D, Volume X, HMSO, 1957

Documents on the Origin of the War, Auswärtiges Amt 1939 No. 2, Berlin, 1939

East of Malta, West of Suez, Prepared by the Admiralty, HMSO, 1943

Field Service Pocket Book, various pamphlets, War Office, London, 1939–45

Final Report by The Right Honourable Sir Nevile Henderson on the Circumstances Leading to the Termination of his Mission to Berlin, September 20, 1939, HMSO, 1939

The Fleet Air Arm, Prepared by the Admiralty, HMSO, 1943

France, Volume II, Naval Intelligence Division, 1942

France, Volume III, Naval Intelligence Division, 1942

Front Line 1940–1941, HMSO, 1942

German Infantry Weapons, Military Intelligence Service, US War Department, 1943

The German Squad in Combat, Military Intelligence Service, US War Department, 1944

German Tactical Doctrine, Military Intelligence Service, US War Department, 1942

German Tank Maintenance in World War II, Department of the US Army, June 1954

Germany, Volume III, Naval Intelligence Division, 1944

The Gunnery Pocket Book, 1945, Admiralty, 1945

Handbook of German Military Forces, TM-E 30-451, US War Department, 1945

Handbook on the British Army with Supplements on the Royal Air Force and Civilian Defense Organizations, TM 30-410, US War Department, September 1942

Handbook on the Italian Military Forces, Military Intelligence Service, US Army, August 1943

His Majesty's Minesweepers, HMSO, 1943

Home Guard Manual 1941, War Office, 1941

Infantry Training, Part VIII: *Fieldcraft, Battle Drill, Section and Platoon Tactics*, War Office, 1944

Infantry Training: Training and War, HMSO, London, 1937

Instruction Manual for the Infantry, Vol. II: *Field Fortifications of the Infantry, 1940*, H.Dv. 130/11, English translation by John Baum

Instruction Manual for the Infantry, Vol. 2a: *The Rifle Company, 1942*, H.Dv. 103/2a, English translation by John Baum

Instruction Manual for the Infantry, Vol. 3a: *The Machinegun Company, 1942*, H.Dv. 130/3a, English translation by John Baum

Italy, Volume I, Naval Intelligence Division 1944

Italy, Volume II, Naval Intelligence Division 1944

Kampf um Norwegen, Oberkommando der Wehrmacht, 1940

Land at War, HMSO, 1945

The Mediterranean Fleet: Greece to Tripoli, HMSO, 1944

Merchantmen at War, Prepared by the Ministry of Information, London, HMSO, 1944

Notes from the Theatres of War, No. 1: *Cyrenaica, November 1941*, War Office, February 1942

Notes from the Theatres of War, No. 2: *Cyrenaica, November/December 1941*, War Office, March 1942

Notes from the Theatres of War, No. 4: *Cyrenaica, November 1941/January 1942*, War Office, May, 1942

Notes from the Theatres of War, No. 6: *Cyrenaica, November 1941/January 1942*, War Office, July 1942

Notes from the Theatres of War, No. 10: *Cyrenaica and Western Desert, January/June 1942*, War Office, October 1942

Notes on the French Army, War Office, 1936

Peace and War: United States Foreign Policy 1931–1941: The Official American

Document Issued by the Department of State, Washington, HMSO, 1943

Pilot's Notes General, Air Ministry, 1943

RAF Middle East: The Official Story of Air Operations, Feb 1942–Jan 1943, HMSO, 1945

The Rise and Fall of the German Air Force (1933–1945), Air Ministry, 1948

R.O.F.: The Story of the Royal Ordnance Factories, 1939–48, HMSO, 1949

Roof Over Britain: The Official Story of the A.A. Defences, 1939–1942, HMSO,1943

Der Schütze-Hilfsbuch, 1943, Oberst Hasso von Wedel and Oberleutnant Pfafferott, Richard Schröder Verlag, Berlin, 1943

Shooting to Live, Capt. W. E. Fairbairn and Capt. E. A. Sykes, 1942

Statistics Relating to the War Effort of the United Kingdom, HMSO, November 1944

Tactics in the Context of the Reinforced Infantry Battalions, Generalmajor Greiner and Generalmajor Degener, 1941, English translation by John Baum

TEE EMM: Air Ministry Monthly Training Memoranda, Volumes I, II, III, Air Ministry, 1939–45

The Tiger Kills: The Story of the Indian Divisions in the North Africa Campaign, HMSO, 1944

Transport Goes to War: The Official Story of British Transport, 1939–1942, HMSO, 1942

Truppenführung: On the German Art of War, Bruce Condell and David T. Zabecki (eds.), Stackpole, 2009

We Speak from the Air: Broadcasts by the RAF, HMSO, 1942

What Britain Has Done 1939–1945, Ministry of Information, 1945

Whitaker's Almanack, 1940

Whitaker's Almanack, 1942

Whitaker's Almanack, 1944

OFFICIAL HISTORIES

American Battle Monuments Commission, *American Armies and Battlefields in Europe*, US Government Printing Office, 1938

Aris, George, *The Fifth British Division 1939 to 1945*, Fifth Division Benevolent Fund, 1959

Behrens, C. B. A., *Merchant Shipping and the Demands of War*, HMSO, 1955

Butler, J. R. M., *Grand Strategy*, Volume II, HMSO, 1957

Cody, J. F., *28 (Maori) Battalion*, War History Brand, Wellington, 1956

Collier, Basil, *In Defence of the United Kingdom*, HMSO, 1957

Court, W. H. B., *Coal*, HMSO, 1951

Craven, Wesley Frank, and James Lea Cate, *The Army Air Forces in World War II*, Volume II: *Europe: Torch to Pointblank*, University of Chicago Press, 1949

Derry, T. H., *The Campaign in Norway*, HMSO, 1952

Douglas, W. A. B., Roger Sarty and Michael Whitby, *No Higher Purpose: The Official Operational History of the Royal Canadian Navy in the Second World War 1939-1943*, Volume II, Part I, Vanwell, 2002

Duncan Hall, H., and C. C. Wrigley, *Studies of Overseas Supply*, HMSO, 1956

Echternkamp, Jörg (ed.), *Germany and the Second World War*, Volume IX/I: *German Wartime Society 1939-1945: Politicization, Disintegration, and the Struggle for Survival*, Clarendon Press, 2008

Fairchild, Byron, and Jonathan Grossman, *United States Army in World War II: The Army and Industrial Manpower*, Office of the Chief of Military History, 1959

Foot, M. R. D., *SOE in France: An account of the work of the British Special Operations Executive in France, 1940-1944*, HMSO, 1966 (original first edition)

Gibbs, N. H., *Grand Strategy*, Volume I, HMSO, 1976

Greenfield, Kent Roberts, et al., *United States Army in World War II: The Organization of Ground Combat Troops*, Historical Division Department of the Army, 1947

Grove, Eric (ed.), *The Defeat of the Enemy Attack on Shipping, 1939-1945: A Revised Edition of the Naval Staff History*, Volumes 1A and 1B, Ashgate, 1997

Hancock, W. K., and M. M. Gowing, *British War Economy*, HMSO, 1949

Hastings, Major R. H. W. S., *The Rifle Brigade in the Second World War 1939-1945*, Gale & Polden, 1950

Hinsley, F. H., *British Intelligence in the Second World War*, HMSO, 1993

—, et al., *British Intelligence in the Second World War*, Volume I: *Its Influence on Strategy and Operations*, HMSO, 1979

Howard, Michael, *Grand Strategy*, Volume IV: *August 1942-September 1943*, HMSO, 1972

Howe, George F., *United States Army in World War II: Northwest Africa: Seizing the Initiative in the West*, Office of the Chief of Military History, 1957

Howlett, Peter, *Fighting With Figures: A Statistical Digest of the Second World War*, prepared by the Central Statistical Office, HMSO, 1995

Institution of the Royal Army Service Corps, *The Story of the Royal Army Service Corps 1939-1945*, G. Bell and Sons, 1955

Knickerbocker, H. R., et al., *United States Army in World War II: Danger Forward: The Story of the First Division in World War II*, Society of the First Division, 1947

Lee, Ulysses, *United States Army in World War II: The Employment of Negro Troops*, Office of the Chief of Military History, 1966

Lindsay, T. M., *Sherwood Rangers*, Burrup, Mathieson & Co, 1952

Matloff, Maurice, and Edwin M. Snell, *United States Army in World War II: Strategic Planning for Coalition Warfare 1941-1942*, Office of the Chief of Military History, 1953

Maughan, Barton, *Australia in the War of 1939-1945: Tobruk and Alamein*, Collins, 1987

Militärgeschichtliches Forschungsamt, *Germany and the Second World War,* Volume I: *The Build-Up of German Aggression,* Clarendon Press, 2003

—, *Germany and the Second World War,* Volume II: *Germany's Initial Conquests in Europe,* Clarendon Press, 2003

—, *Germany and the Second World War,* Volume III: *The Mediterranean, South-East Europe, and North Africa, 1939–1941,* Clarendon Press, 2008

—, *Germany and the Second World War,* Volume IV: *The Attack on the Soviet Union,* Clarendon Press, 2009

—, *Germany and the Second World War,* Volume V: *Organization and Mobilization of the German Sphere of Power,* Part 1: *Wartime Administration, Economy, and Manpower Resources, 1939–1941,* Clarendon Press, Oxford, 2000

—, *Germany and the Second World War,* Volume V: *Organization and Mobilization of the German Sphere of Power,* Part 1B: *Wartime Administration, Economy and Manpower Resources, 1942–1944/5,* Clarendon Press, 2003

—, *Germany and the Second World War,* Volume VI: *The Global War,* Clarendon Press, 2001

—, *Germany and the Second World War,* Volume VII: *The Strategic Air War in Europe and the War in the West and East Asia, 1943–1944/5,* Clarendon Press, 2006

Morison, Samuel Eliot, *History of the United States Naval Operations in World War II,* Volume I: *The Battle of the Atlantic, September 1939–May 1943,* Naval Institute Press, 2010

—, *History of the United States Naval Operations in World War II,* Volume II: *Operations in North African Waters, October 1942–June 1943,* Little, Brown and Co., 1990

Murray, Keith A. H., *Agriculture,* HMSO, 1955

Nicholson, Lt-Col. G. W. L., *Official History of the Canadian Army in the Second World War,* Volume II: *The Canadians in Italy 1943–1945,* Department of National Defence, 1957

Orpen, Neil, *South African Forces, World War II,* Volume III: *War in the Desert,* Purnell, 1971

Palmer, Robert R., Bell I. Wiley and William R. Keast, *United States Army in World War II: The Procurement and Training of Ground Combat Troops,* Historical Division Department of the Army, 1948

Parker, H. M. D., *Manpower: A Study of War-Time Policy and Administration,* HMSO, 1957

Playfair, Major-General I. S. O., et al., *The Mediterranean and the Middle East,* Volume I: *The Early Successes against Italy,* HMSO, 1954

—, *The Mediterranean and the Middle East,* Volume II: *The Germans Come to the Help of Their Ally 1941,* HMSO, 1956

—, *The Mediterranean and the Middle East,* Volume III: *British Fortunes Reach Their Lowest Ebb,* HMSO, 1960

Postan, M. M., *British War Production,* HMSO, 1952

—, D. Hay and J. D. Scott, *Design and Development of Weapons*, HMSO, 1964
Richards, Denis, *Royal Air Force 1939–1945*, Volume I: *The Fight at Odds*, HMSO, 1953
—, *Royal Air Force 1939–1945*, Volume II: *The Fight Avails*, HMSO, 1954
—, *Royal Air Force 1939–1945*, Volume III: *The Fight is Won*, HMSO, 1954
Rissik, David, *The D.L.I. at War: The History of the Durham Light Infantry 1939–1945*, The Depot: Durham Light Infantry, n.d.
Roskill, Captain S. W., *The War at Sea 1939–1945*, Volume I: *The Defensive*, HMSO, 1954
—, *The War at Sea 1939–1945*, Volume II: *The Period of Balance*, HMSO, 1956
Savage, C. I., *Inland Transport*, HMSO, 1957
Scott, J. D., and Richard Hughes, *The Administration of War Production*, HMSO, 1955
Stevens, Lieut.-Colonel G. R., *Fourth Indian Division*, McLaren & Son, 1949
Voss, Capt. Vivian, *The Story of No. 1 Squadron S.A.A.F.*, Mercantile Atlas, 1952
Wardlow, Chester, *United States Army in World War II: The Transportation Corps: Movements, Training, and Supply*, Office of the Chief of Military History, 1956
Webster, Sir Charles, and Noble Frankland, *The Strategic Air Offensive Against Germany, 1939–1945*, Volume I: *Preparation*, Naval & Military Press, 2006
—, *The Strategic Air Offensive Against Germany, 1939–1945*, Volume II: *Endeavour*, Naval & Military Press, 2006
—, *The Strategic Air Offensive Against Germany, 1939–1945*, Volume III: *Victory*, HMSO, 1961
—, *The Strategic Air Offensive Against Germany, 1939–1945*, Volume IV: *Annexes and Appendices*, Naval & Military Press, 2006

MEMOIRS, BIOGRAPHIES, ETC.

Agius Ferrante, Anne, *No Strangers in the Silent City*, Andrew Rupert, 1992
Alanbrooke, Field Marshal Lord, *War Diaries 1939–1945*, Weidenfeld & Nicolson, 2001
Aldridge, Arthur, with Mark Ryan, *The Last Torpedo Flyers*, Simon & Schuster, 2012
Allaway, Jim, *Hero of the Upholder*, Airlife, 1991
Ambrose, Stephen E., *The Supreme Commander: The War Years of Dwight D. Eisenhower*, University of Mississippi, 1999
Ardizzone, Edward, *Diary of a War Artist*, The Bodley Head, 1974
Atkins, Peter, *Buffoon in Flight*, Ernest Stanton, 1978
Aubrac, Lucie, *Outwitting the Gestapo*, University of Nebraska Press, 1985
Avon, The Rt Hon. The Earl of, *The Eden Memoirs: Facing the Dictators*, Cassell, 1962
—, *The Eden Memoirs: The Reckoning*, Cassell, 1965

Badoglio, Marshal Pietro, *Italy in the Second World War*, Oxford University Press, 1948

Balck, Hermann, *Ordnung im Chaos*, Biblio, 1981

Ball, Edmund F., *Staff Officer with the Fifth Army*, Exposition Banner Book, 1958

Barlone, D., *A French Officer's Diary: 23 August 1939 to 1 October 1940*, Cambridge University Press, 1943

Barnham, Denis, *One Man's Window*, William Kimber, 1956

Baruch, Bernard M., *Baruch: My Own Story*, Henry Holt and Company, 1957

Beamont, Roland, *My Part of the Sky*, Patrick Stephens, 1989

Beasley, Norman, *Knudsen: A Biography*, McGraw Hill, 1947

Beaufre, General André, *1940: The Fall of France*, Cassell, 1967

Beauvoir, Simone de, *Wartime Diary*, University of Illinois Press, 2009

Behrendt, Hans-Otto, *Rommel's Intelligence in the Desert Campaign*, William Kimber, 1985

Below, Nicolaus von, *At Hitler's Side: The Memoirs of Hitler's Luftwaffe Adjutant 1937–1945*, Greenhill, 2004

Bennett, Donald, *Pathfinder*, Goodall, 1998

Bennett, Donald V., and William R. Forstchen, *Honor Untarnished: A West Point Graduate's Memoir of World War II*, Forge, 2003

Bigland, Tom, *Bigland's War: War Letters of Tom Bigland, 1941–45*, Printfine, 1990

Binder, L. James, *Lemnitzer: A Soldier for His Time*, Brassey's, 1997

Birrell, Dave, *Big Joe McCarthy: The RCAF's American Dambuster*, Nanton Lancaster Society, 2012

Blum, John Morton, *From the Morgenthau Diaries*, Vol. 2: *Years of Urgency, 1938–1941*, Houghton Mifflin, 1965

Bob, Hans-Ekkehard, *Betrayed Ideals: Memoirs of a Luftwaffe Fighter Ace*, Mönch, 2004

Boelcke, Willi A. (ed.), *The Secret Conferences of Dr Goebbels 1939–43*, Weidenfeld & Nicolson, 1970

Bolitho, Hector, *Combat Report: The Story of a Fighter Pilot*, Batsford, 1943

Booth, T. Michael, and Duncan Spencer, *Paratrooper: The Life of General James M. Gavin*, Casemate, 2013

Borghese, J. Valerio, *Sea Devils*, Andrew Melrose, 1953

Boris, Jean-Mathieu, *Combattant de la France Libre*, Tempus, 2012

Bradford White, Francelle, *Andrée's War: How One Young Woman Outwitted the Nazis*, Elliott & Thompson, 2014

Bradley, Omar N., and Clay Blair, *A General's Life*, Simon & Schuster, 1983

Brereton, Lewis H., *The Brereton Diaries*, William Morrow and Company, 1946

Brett-James, Antony, *Conversations With Montgomery*, William Kimber, 1984

Brown, Captain Eric 'Winkle', *Wings on My Sleeve*, Phoenix, 2007

Bullitt, Orville H. (ed.), *For the President, Personal and Secret: Correspondence between Franklin D. Roosevelt and William C. Bullitt*, André Deutsch, 1973

Burns, James MacGregor, *Roosevelt: The Soldier of Freedom, 1940–1945*, Weidenfeld & Nicolson, 1971

Campbell Begg, Dr Richard, and Dr Peter Liddle, *For Five Shillings a Day: Personal Histories of World War II*, HarperCollins, 2002

Cartwright-Hignett, Elizabeth (ed.), *Three Ladies of Siena: The Wartime Journals of the Chigi-Zondadari Family, 1943–1944*, Iford, 2011

Chambrun, René de, *I Saw France Fall*, Jarrolds, 1941

Chandler, Alfred D., Jr (ed.), *The Papers of Dwight David Eisenhower – The War Years*, Volume I, Johns Hopkins Press, 1970

Charlwood, Don, *No Moon Tonight*, Goodall, 1994

Cheall, Bill, *Fighting Through from Dunkirk to Hamburg: A Green Howard's Wartime Memoir*, Pen & Sword, 2011

Cheshire, Leonard, *Bomber Pilot*, Hutchinson, 1943

Churchill, Winston S., *The Second World War*, Volume I: *The Gathering Storm*, Cassell, 1948

—, *The Second World War*, Volume II: *Their Finest Hour*, Cassell, 1949

—, *The Second World War*, Volume III: *The Grand Alliance*, Cassell, 1950

— (ed. Charles Eade), *The War Speeches of the Rt Hon. Winston S. Churchill*, Volume 1, Cassell, 1951

Ciano, Count Galeazzo, *Diary, 1937–1943*, William Heinemann, 1947

Clark, Mark, *Calculated Risk*, Harper & Brothers, 1950

Clostermann, Pierre, *The Big Show: The Greatest Pilot's Story of World War II*, Cassell, 2005

Colville, John, *The Fringes of Power: Downing Street Diaries*, Volume 1, Sceptre, 1986

—, *The Fringes of Power: Downing Street Diaries*, Volume 2, Sceptre, 1987

Cooper, Johnny, *One of the Originals*, Pan Books, 1991

Cowles, Virginia, *The Phantom Major*, Companion Book Club, 1958

Cox, Rachel S., *Into the Dust: Five Young Americans Who Went First to Fight the Nazi Army*, Nap Caliber, 2012

Crook, David, *Spitfire Pilot*, Faber & Faber, 1942

Cunningham, Admiral of the Fleet Viscount, *A Sailor's Odyssey*, Hutchinson, 1951

Currie, Jack, *Lancaster Target*, Goodall, 1981

Dahl, Roald, *Going Solo*, Penguin Books, 1986

—, *Over to You*, Penguin Books, 2011

Davis, Richard G., *Carl A. Spaatz and the Air War in Europe*, Center for Air Force History, 1993

de Gaulle, General, *War Memoirs: The Call to Honour, 1940–1942*, Collins, 1955

—, *War Memoirs: Unity, 1942–1944*, Weidenfeld & Nicolson, 1956

Deane, Theresa M., and Joseph E. Schaps (eds.), *500 Days of Front Line Combat: The WWII Memoir of Ralph B. Schaps*, iUniverse Inc., 2003

Demarne, Cyril, *The London Blitz: A Fireman's Tale*, After the Battle, 1991

D'Este, Carlo, *Eisenhower: A Soldier's Life*, Henry Holt, 2002

Doe, Bob, *Bob Doe: Fighter Pilot*, CCB Associates, 1999

Doenitz, Karl, *Memoirs: Ten Years and Twenty Days*, Cassell, 2000

Doolittle, Gen. James H., *I Could Never be So Lucky Again*, Bantam Books, 1992

Dos, Margarete, and Kirsten Lieff, *Letters From Berlin*, Lyons Press, 2013

Drake, Billy, with Christopher Shores, *Billy Drake, Fighter Leader*, Grub Street, 2002

Dundas, Hugh, *Flying Start*, Penguin Books, 1990

Dutton, David, *Neville Chamberlain*, Hodder Education, 2001

Eisenhower, Dwight D., *Crusade in Europe*, William Heinemann, 1948

Embry, Basil, *Wingless Victory*, Morley Books, 1973

Engel, Major Gerhard, *At the Heart of the Reich: The Secret Diary of Hitler's Army Adjutant*, Greenhill, 2005

Fairbanks, Douglas, Jr, *A Hell of a War*, St. Martin's Press, 1993

Farrell, Nicholas, *Mussolini: A New Life*, Phoenix, 2004

Franks, Norman, *Buck McNair: Canadian Spitfire Ace*, Grub Street, 2001

Freidel, Frank, *Roosevelt: A Rendezvous with Destiny*, Little, Brown and Co., 1990

Frenay, Henri, *The Night Will End: Memoirs of the Resistance*, Abelard, 1976

Gafencu, Grigore, *The Last Days of Europe: A Diplomatic Journey in 1939*, Frederick Muller, 1947

Galland, Adolf, *The First and the Last*, Fontana, 1970

Gane Pushman, Muriel, *One Family's War*, Tempus, 2000

Gibson, Guy, *Enemy Coast Ahead*, Michael Joseph, 1946

—, *Enemy Coast Ahead Uncensored*, Crécy, 2014

Giese, Otto, and James E. Wise, Jr, *Shooting the War: The Memoir and Photographs of a U-Boat Officer in World War II*

Gilbert, Martin, *Finest Hour: Winston S. Churchill 1939–1941*, Minerva, 1983

Główczewski, Jerzy, *The Accidental Immigrant*, Xlibris, 2007

Gnecchi-Ruscone, Francesco, *When being Italian was Difficult*, Milan, 1999

Goodson, James, *Tumult in the Clouds*, Penguin Books, 2003

Görlitz, Walter (ed.), *The Memoirs of Field Marshal Wilhelm Keitel*, Cooper Square Press, 2000

Greene, Jack, and Alessandro Massignani, *The Black Prince and the Sea Devils: The Story of Valerio Borghese*, Da Capo, 2004

Gregg, Victor, with Rick Stroud, *Rifleman: A Front Line Life*, Bloomsbury, 2011

Grossjohann, Georg, *Five Years, Four Fronts*, Aberjona Press, 1999

Grundon, Imogen, *The Rash Adventurer*, Libri, 2007

Guderian, Heinz, *Panzer Leader*, Penguin Books, 2000

Guingand, Major-General Sir Francis de, *Operation Victory*, Hodder & Stoughton, 1960

Häberlen, Klaus, *A Luftwaffe Bomber Pilot Remembers: World War II from the Cockpit*, Schiffer, 2001

Hahn Beer, Edith, *The Nazi Officer's Wife*, Little, Brown and Co., 1999

Halder, Franz, *The Halder War Diary, 1939–1942*, Grenhill Books, 1988

Hartog, Kristen Den, and Tracy Kasaboski, *The Occupied Garden: A Family Memoir of War-Torn Holland*, St. Martin's Press, 2008

Hayes, Paul M., *Quisling*, David & Charles, 1971

Heaton, Colin D., and Anne-Marie Lewis, *The German Aces Speak: World War II through the Eyes of Four of the Luftwaffe's Most Important Commanders*, Zenith Press, 2011

—, *The German Aces Speak II: World War II through the Eyes of Four More of the Luftwaffe's Most Important Commanders*, Zenith Press, 2014

—, *The Star of Africa: The Story of Hans Marseille*, Zenith Press, 2012

Heiner, Albert P., *Henry J. Kaiser, American Empire Builder: An Insider's View*, P. Lang, 1989

Hélion, Jean, *They Shall Not Have Me*, Arcade, 2012

Henderson, Sir Nevile, *Failure of a Mission*, Hodder & Stoughton, 1940

Henrey, Mrs Robert, *A Farm in Normandy*, J. M. Dent & Sons, 1952

—, *London Under Fire 1940–45*, J. M. Dent & Sons, 1969

Herrmann, Hajo, *Eagle's Wings*, Airlife 1991

Hill, Alan, *Hedley Verity: A Portrait of a Cricketer*, Kingswood Press, 1986

Hinchliffe, Peter, *The Lent Papers: Helmut Lent*, Cerberus, 2003

Hodgson, Godfrey, *The Colonel: The Life and Wars of Henry Stimson, 1867–1950*, Alfred A. Knopf, 1990

Hodgson, Vere, *Few Eggs and No Oranges: The Diaries of Vere Hodgson, 1940–45*, Persephone, 1999

Horrocks, Lt.-Gen. Sir Brian, *A Full Life*, Collins, 1960

Humbert, Agnès, *Résistance: Memoirs of Occupied France*, Bloomsbury, 2009

Hurd, Anthony, *A Farmer in Whitehall: Britain's Farming Revolution 1939–1950*, Country Life, 1951

Irving, David, *Göring*, Macmillan, 1989

—, *The Rise and Fall of the Luftwaffe: The Life of Erhard Milch*, Weidenfeld & Nicolson, 1973

—, *The Trail of the Fox: The Life of Field Marshal Erwin Rommel*, Book Club Associates, 1977

Ismay, General Lord, *The Memoirs*, The Viking Press, 1960

Johnson, Boris, *The Churchill Factor: How One Man Made History*, Hodder & Stoughton, 2014

Johnson, Johnnie, *Wing Leader*, Penguin Books, 1959

Kennedy, Major-General Sir John, *The Business of War*, Hutchinson, 1957

Kennedy, Ludovic, *Sub-Lieutenant: A Personal Record of the War at Sea*, Batsford, 1941

Kershaw, Alex, *The Few: The American Knights of the Air Who Risked Everything to Fight in the Battle of Britain*, Da Capo, 2006

King, Ernest J., *Fleet Admiral King: A Naval Record*, W. W. Norton & Co., 1956

Kippenberger, Major-General Sir Howard, *Infantry Brigadier*, Oxford University Press, 1949

Knappe, Siegfried, with Ted Brusaw, *Soldat: Reflections of a German Soldier, 1936–1949*, Dell, 1992

Knocke, Heinz, *I Flew for the Führer*, Cassell, 2003

Knoller, Freddie, *Living with the Enemy: My Secret Life on the Run from the Nazis*, Metro, 2005

Kynoch, Joseph, *Norway 1940: The Forgotten Fiasco*, Airlife, 2002

La Mazière, Christian de, *Ashes of Honour*, Tattoo, 1976

Laidler, Graham, *The World of Pont*, Element Books, 1983

Laurier, Mathieu, *Il reste le drapeau noir et les copains*, Regain, 1953

Leahy, Admiral, *I Was There*, Victor Gollancz, 1950

Lee, Asher, *Goering: Air Leader*, Duckworth, 1972

Leutze, James (ed.), *The London Observer: The Journal of General Raymond E. Lee, 1940–1941*, Hutchinson, 1972

Liddell Hart, B. H. (ed.), *The Rommel Papers*, Collins, 1953

Lloyd, Air Marshal Sir Hugh, *Briefed to Attack*, Hodder & Stoughton, 1949

Lochner, Louis P. (ed.), *The Goebbels Diaries*, Hamish Hamilton, 1948

Lowenheim, Francis L., Harold D. Langley and Manfred Jonas, *Roosevelt and Churchill: Their Secret Wartime Correspondence*, Barrie & Jenkins, 1975

Luchaire, Corinne, *Ma drôle de vie*, Deterna, 1949

Luck, Hans von, *Panzer Commander*, Cassell, 2002

Lyttelton, Oliver, *The Memoirs of Lord Chandos*, The Bodley Head, 1962

MacGibbon, John, *Struan's War*, Ngaio Press, 2001

Macintyre, Captain Donald, *U-Boat Killer*, Rigel, 2004

Mack Smith, Denis, *Mussolini*, Paladin, 1983

Mahlke, Helmut, *Memoirs of a Stuka Pilot*, Frontline, 2013

Manstein, Field Marshal Erich von, *Lost Victories*, Zenith Press, 2004

Manville, Roger, and Heinrich Fraenkel, *Heinrich Himmler*, Greenhill, 2007

Martin, Albert, *Hellfire Tonight: The Diary of a Desert Rat*, Book Guild, 1996

McLaughlin, John J., *General Albert C. Wedemeyer: America's Unsung Strategist in World War II*, Casemate, 2012

Melinsky, Hugh, *Forming the Pathfinders: The Career of Air Vice-Marshal Sydney Bufton*, History Press, 2010

Mellenthin, F. W. von, *Panzer Battles*, Futura, 1977

Messenger, Charles, *Hitler's Gladiator: The Life and Wars of Panzer Army Commander Sepp Dietrich*, Skyhorse, 2011

Middleton, Drew, *The Sky Suspended*, Secker & Warburg, 1960

Miller, Lee G., *The Story of Ernie Pyle*, The Viking Press, 1950

Millgate, Helen D. (ed.), *Mr Brown's War: A Diary of the Second World War*, Sutton, 1998

Monsarrat, Nicholas, *Life is a Four-Letter Word*, Book One: *Breaking In*, Pan Books, 1966

—, *Life is a Four-Letter Word*, Book Two: *Breaking Out*, Pan Books, 1972

Montgomery, Field-Marshal the Viscount, *The Memoirs*, Collins, 1958

Morris, Richard, *Guy Gibson*, Penguin Books, 1995

Muggeridge, Malcolm (ed.), *Ciano's Diplomatic Papers*, Odhams Press, 1948

Murrow, Edward R., *This is London*, Cassell, 1941

Neil, Tom, *A Fighter in My Sights*, J&KH, 2001

—, *Onwards to Malta*, Corgi, 1994

Nicolson, Harold, *Diaries and Letters, 1939–1945*, Collins, 1967

Offenberg, Jean, *Lonely Warrior*, Granada, 1969

Ophüls, Marcel, *The Sorrow and the Pity: The Text from the Film*, Paladin, 1975

Orange, Vincent, *Dowding of Fighter Command*, Grub Street, 2008

—, *Park*, Grub Street, 2001

Overy, Richard, *Goering*, Phoenix, 2000

Parbery, Sergeant Alf, *Alf's War: With the Sixth Infantry Division*, Australian Military History Publications, 2005

Peyton, John, *Solly Zuckerman*, John Murray, 2001

Pickersgill, J. W., *The Mackenzie King Record*, Volume I: *1939–1944*, University of Toronto Press, 1960

Pocock, Tom, *Alan Moorehead*, Pimlico, 1990

Pogue, Forrest C., *George C. Marshall: Ordeal and Hope, 1939–1942*, MacGibbon & Kee, 1966

— (ed.), *George C. Marshall – Interviews and Reminiscences for Forrest Pogue*, Marshall Foundation, 1991

Pöppel, Martin, *Heaven and Hell: The War Diary of a German Paratrooper*, The History Press, 2011

Probert, Henry, *Bomber Harris: His Life and Times*, Greenhill, 2006

Pyle, Ernie, *Ernie Pyle in England*, Robert M. McBride & Co., 1941

Reynaud, Paul, *In the Thick of the Fight*, Cassell, 1955

Richey, Paul, *Fighter Pilot*, Batsford, 1941

Rieckhoff, Generalleutnant H. J., *Trumpf oder Bluff? 12 Jahre Deutsche Luftwaffe*, Inter Avia, 1945

Riols, Noreen, *The Secret Ministry of Ag. & Fish: My Life in Churchill's School for Spies*, Macmillan, 2013

Ripley, Tim, *Wehrmacht: The German Army in World War II, 1939–1945*, Reference Group Brown, 2003

Roberts, Andrew, *The Holy Fox: The Life of Lord Halifax*, Phoenix, 1991

Robertson, Terence, *The Golden Horseshoe*, Pan Books, 1957

Roll, David L., *The Hopkins Touch: Harry Hopkins and the Forging of the Alliance to Defeat Hitler*, Oxford University Press, 2013

Roosevelt, Franklin D., *The Public Papers and Addresses of Franklin D. Roosevelt*, Macmillan, 1939

Rudel, Hans-Ulrich, *Stuka Pilot*, Barbarossa Books, 2006

Rumpf, Hans, *The Bombing of Germany*, Holt, Rinehart, and Winston, 1961

Saward, Dudley, *Bomber Harris*, Sphere Books, 1985

Scheffel, Captain Charles, with Barry Basden, *Crack! and Thump: With a Combat Infantry Officer in World War II*, Camroc Press, 2007

Schlange-Schöningen, Hans, *The Morning After*, Victor Gollancz, 1948

Schmidt, Dr Paul, *Hitler's Interpreter*, William Heinemann, 1951

Schroeder, Liliane, *Journal d'Occupation: Paris 1940–1944*, François-Xavier de Guibert, 2000

Schroth, Raymond A., *The American Journey of Eric Sevareid*, Steerforth Press, 1995

Searby, John, *The Everlasting Arms: The War Memoirs of Air Commodore John Searby DSO, DFC*, William Kimber, 1988

Self, Robert, *Neville Chamberlain*, Ashgate, 2006

— (ed.), *The Neville Chamberlain Diary Letters*, Volume 4: *The Downing Street Years, 1934–1940*, Ashgate, 2005

Senger und Etterlin, General Frido von, *Neither Fear Nor Hope*, Presidio, 1989

Sereny, Gitta, *Albert Speer: His Battle with Truth*, Picador, 1996

Sevareid, Eric, *Not So Wild a Dream*, Atheneum, 1976

Sherwood, Robert E., *The White House Papers of Harry L. Hopkins: An Intimate History*, Volume I: *September 1939–January 1942*, Eyre & Spottiswoode, 1948

Shirer, William L., *Berlin Diary*, Hamish Hamilton, 1942

Slessor, Sir John, *The Central Blue*, Cassell, 1956

Soames, Mary, *A Daughter's Tale*, Doubleday, 2011

Sonsteby, Gunnar, *Report from No. 24*, Barricade Books, 1999

Spagnuolo, Mark M., *Mustang Ace: The Story of Don S. Gentile*, Cerberus, 1986

Spayd, P. A., *Bayerlein: From Afrikakorps to Panzer Lehr*, Schiffer, 2003

Spears, Major-General Sir Edward, *Assignment to Catastrophe*, The Reprint Society, 1954

—, *Fulfilment of a Mission: Syria and Lebanon, 1941–1944*, Leo Cooper, 1977

Speer, Albert, *Inside the Third Reich*, Phoenix, 1995

Sperber, A. M., *Murrow: His Life and Times*, Freundlich Books, 1986

Spooner, Tony, *Warburton's War*, Crécy, 1994

Squires, Mary, *An Army in the Fields*, Minerva Press, 2000

Stahl, Peter, *The Diving Eagle: A Ju88 Pilot's Diary*, William Kimber, 1984

Steinhilper, Ulrich, and Peter Osborne, *Spitfire on my Tail: A View from the Other Side*, Independent Books, 1989

Steinhoff, Johannes, *Messerschmitts Over Sicily*, Pen & Sword, 2004

—, Peter Pechel and Dennis Showalter, *Voices from the Third Reich: An Oral History*, Da Capo, 1994

Stimson, Henry L., *Prelude to Invasion: An Account Based upon Official Reports by Henry L. Stimson, Secretary of War*, Greenwood Press, 1974

—, and McGeorge Bundy, *On Active Service in Peace and War*, Harper & Brothers, 1948

Street, A. G., *Ditchampton Farm*, Eyre & Spottiswoode, 1946

—, *From Dusk till Dawn*, Oxford University Press, 1989

—, *Hitler's Whistle*, Eyre & Spottiswoode, 1943

—, *Round the Year on the Farm*, Oxford University Press, 1946

Street, Pamela, *My Father, A. G. Street*, Robert Hale, 1969

Suhren, Teddy, and Fritz Brustat-Naval, *Teddy Suhren – Ace of Aces*, Frontline, 2011

Taylor, A. J. P., *Beaverbrook*, Hamish Hamilton, 1972

Taylor, Fred (ed.), *The Goebbels Diaries 1939–1941*, Sphere Books, 1982

Tedder, Lord, Marshal of the Air Force, *With Prejudice*, Cassell, 1966

Tobin, James, *Ernie Pyle's War: America's Eyewitness to World War II*, University Press of Kansas, 1997

Topp, Erich, *The Odyssey of a U-Boat Commander: Recollections of Erich Topp*, Prager, 1992

Vann, Frank, *Willy Messerschmitt*, Patrick Stephens, 1993

Vansittart, The Rt Hon. Lord, *Lessons of My Life*, Hutchinson, 1942

Verity, Hugh, *We Landed by Moonlight*, Crécy, 2000

Warlimont, Walter, *Inside Hitler's Headquarters 1939–1945*, Presidio (n.d., but originally published 1962)

Warner, Oliver, *Cunningham of Hyndhope: Admiral of the Fleet*, John Murray, 1967

Weinronk, Jack 'Cobber', *The Vaulted Sky*, Merlin Books, 1993

Wendel, Else, *Hausfrau at War: A German Woman's Account of Life in Hitler's Reich*, Odhams Press, 1957

Werner, Herbert A., *Iron Coffins*, Cassell, 1999

West, Nigel (ed.), *The Guy Liddell Diaries*, Volume I: *1939–1942*, Routledge, 2009

—, *The Guy Liddell Diaries*, Volume II: *1942–1945*, Routledge, 2009

Williams, Charles, *The Last Great Frenchman: A Life of General de Gaulle*, John Wiley & Sons, 1993

Winn, Godfrey, *Godfrey Winn's Scrapbook of the War*, Hutchinson, 1942

Winterbotham, F. W., *The Ultra Spy*, Papermac, 1989

Winton, John, *Cunningham: The Greatest Admiral since Nelson*, John Murray, 1998

Woodhouse, C. M., *Something Ventured*, Granada 1992

Young, Desmond, *Rommel*, Collins, 1950

Young, Edward, *One of Our Submarines*, Wordsworth, 1997

Younghusband, Eileen, *One Woman's War*, Candy Jar Books, 2013

EQUIPMENT, WEAPONS AND TECHNICAL BOOKS

Barker, A. J., *British and American Infantry Weapons of World War 2*, Arms & Armour Press, 1969

Bidwell, Shelford, and Dominick Graham, *Fire-Power: British Army Weapons and Theories of War 1904–1945*, George Allen & Unwin, 1982

Bouchery, Jean, *The British Soldier*, Volume 1: *Uniforms, Insignia, Equipment*, Histoire & Collections, n.d.

—, *The British Soldier*, Volume 2: *Organisation, Armament, Tanks and Vehicles*, Histoire & Collections, n.d.

Brayley, Martin, *The British Army 1939–45 (1): North-West Europe*, Osprey, 2001

—, *British Web Equipment of the Two World Wars*, The Crowood Press, 2005

Bruce, Robert, *German Automatic Weapons of World War II*, The Crowood Press, 1996

Bull, Dr Stephen, *World War II Infantry Tactics*, Osprey, 2004

—, *World War II Street-Fighting Tactics*, Osprey, 2008

Chamberlain, Peter, and Chris Ellis, *Tanks of the World 1915–1945*, Cassell, 2002

Chesneau, Roger (ed.), *Conway's All the World's Fighting Ships 1922–1946*, Conway Maritime Press, 1980

Clark, Jeff, *Uniforms of the NSDAP*, Schiffer, 2007

Crociani, P., and P. P. Battistelli, *Italian Army Elite Units and Special Forces 1940–43*, Osprey, 2011

Dallies-Labourdette, Jean-Philippe, *S-Boote: German E-Boats in Action 1939–1945*, Histoire & Collections, n.d.

Davies, W. J. K., *German Army Handbook 1939–1945*, Military Book Society, 1973

Davis, Brian L., *German Combat Uniforms of World War II*, Volume II: Arms & Armour Press, 1985

Dibbs, John, and Tony Holmes, *Hurricane: A Fighter Legend*, Osprey, 1995

Dunning, Chris, *Courage Alone: The Italian Air Force 1940–1943*, Hikoki, 1998

Farrar-Hockley, Anthony, *Infantry Tactics 1939–1945*, Almark, 1976

Fleischer, Wolfgang, *The Illustrated Guide to German Panzers*, Schiffer, 2002

Forty, George, and Jack Livesey, *The Complete Guide to Tanks and Armoured Fighting Vehicles*, Southwater, 2012

Gander, Terry, and Peter Chamberlain, *Small Arms, Artillery and Special Weapons of the Third Reich*, Macdonald and Jane's, 1978

Gordon, David B., *Equipment of the WWII Tommy*, Pictorial Histories, 2004

—, *Uniforms of the WWII Tommy*, Pictorial Histories, 2005

—, *Weapons of the WWII Tommy*, Pictorial Histories, 2004

Grant, Neil, *The Bren Gun*, Osprey, 2013

Griehl, Manfred, and Joachim Dressel, *Luftwaffe Combat Aircraft: Development, Production, Operations, 1935–1945*, Schiffer, 1994

Gunston, Bill, *Fighting Aircraft of World War II*, Salamander, 1988

Hart, S., R. Hart and M. Hughes, *The German Soldier in World War II*, Spellmount, 2000

Hogg, Ian V. (Intro.), *The American Arsenal: The World War II Official Standard Ordnance Catalog of Small Arms, Tanks, Armored Cars, Artillery, Antiaircraft Guns, Ammunition, Grenades, Mines, etcetera*, Greenhill Books, 1996

—, *The Guns 1939–1945*, Macdonald, 1969

Jowett, Philip S., *The Italian Army 1940–45 (1): Europe 1940–43*, Osprey, 2000

—, *The Italian Army 1940–45 (2): Africa 1940–43*, Osprey, 2001

Kay, Antony L., and J. R. Smith, *German Aircraft of the Second World War*, Putnam, 2002

Konstam, Angus, *British Battlecruisers 1939–45*, Osprey, 2003

Lagarde, Jean de, *German Soldiers of World War II*, Histoire & Collections, n.d.

Lavery, Brian, *Churchill's Navy: The Ships, Men and Organisation 1939–1945*, Conway, 2006

Lee, Cyrus A., *Soldat*, Volume Two: *Equipping the German Army Foot Soldier in Europe 1943*, Pictorial Histories, 1988

Lepage, Jean-Denis G. G., *German Military Vehicles of World War II*, McFarland & Company, 2007

Lüdeke, Alexander, *Weapons of World War II*, Parragon, 2007
Mason, Chris, *Soldat*, Volume Eight: *Fallschirmjäger*, Pictorial Histories, 2000
McNab, Chris, *MG 34 and MG 42 Machine Guns*, Osprey, 2012
Mundt, Richard W., and Cyrus A. Lee, *Soldat*, Volume Six: *Equipping the Waffen-SS Panzer Divisions 1942-1945*, Pictorial Histories, 1997
Musgrave, Daniel D., *German Machineguns*, Greenhill Books, 1992
Myerscough, W., *Air Navigation Simply Explained*, Pitman & Sons, 1942
Saiz, Augustin, *Deutsche Soldaten*, Casemate, 2008
Stedman, Robert, *Kampfflieger: Bomber Crewman of the Luftwaffe 1939-45*, Osprey, 2005
Suermondt, Jan, *World War II Wehrmacht Vehicles*, The Crowood Press, 2003
Sumner, Ian, and François Vauvillier, *The French Army 1939-1945* (1), Osprey, 1998
Sutherland, Jonathan, *World War II Tanks and AFVs*, Airlife, 2002
Trye, Rex, *Mussolini's Soldiers*, Airlife, 1995
Vanderveen, Bart, *Historic Military Vehicles Directory*, After the Battle, 1989
Williamson, Gordon, *Gebirgsjäger*, Osprey, 2003
—, *German Mountain and Ski Troops 1939-45*, Osprey, 1996
—, *U-Boats vs Destroyer Escorts*, Osprey, 2007
Windrow, Richard, and Tim Hawkins, *The World War II GI: US Army Uniforms 1941-45*, The Crowood Press, 2003

GENERAL

Addison, Paul, and Angus Calder (eds.), *Time to Kill: The Soldier's Experience of War in the West, 1939-1945*, Pimlico, 1997
Addison, Paul, and Jeremy A. Crang (eds.), *The Burning Blue: A New History of the Battle of Britain*, Pimlico, 2000
Alexander, Martin S., *The Republic in Danger: General Maurice Gamelin and the Politics of French Defence, 1933-1940*, Cambridge University Press, 2002
Ansel, Walter, *Hitler Confronts England*, Duke University Press, 1960
Antill, Peter D., *Crete 1941*, Osprey, 2005
Asher, Michael, *The Regiment: The Real Story of the SAS*, Viking, 2007
Bailey, Roderick, *Forgotten Voices of the Secret War*, Ebury Press, 2008
Baldoli, Claudia, Andrew Knapp and Richard Overy (eds.), *Bombing, States and Peoples in Western Europe, 1940-1945*, Continuum, 2011
Barker, A. J., *Dunkirk: The Great Escape*, J. M. Dent & Sons, 1977
Barnett, Correlli, *The Audit of War: The Illusion and Reality of Britain as a Great Power*, Papermac, 1987
—, *Engage the Enemy More Closely*, Penguin, 1991
— (ed.), *Hitler's Generals*, Weidenfeld & Nicolson, 1989
Bartz, Karl, *Swastika in the Air: The Struggle and Defeat of the German Air Force 1939-1945*, William Kimber, 1956

Baumbach, Werner, *Broken Swastika*, George Mann, 1974

Baumer, Robert W., and Mark J. Reardon, *American Iliad: The 18th Infantry Regiment in World War II*, The Aberjona Press, 2004

Beevor, Antony, *Crete: The Battle and the Resistance*, Penguin Books, 1992

Bekker, Cajus, *The Luftwaffe War Diaries*, Corgi, 1969

Bell, P. M. H., *A Certain Eventuality: Britain and the Fall of France*, Saxon House, 1974

Bellamy, Chris, *Absolute War: Soviet Russia in the Second World War*, Pan Books, 2007

Biddle, Tami Davis, *Rhetoric and Reality in Air Warfare*, Princeton University Press, 2002

Bidwell, Shelford, *Gunners at War*, Arrow, 1972

Bishop, Patrick, *Bomber Boys: Fighting Back, 1940–1945*, Harper Press, 2007

—, *Fighter Boys: Saving Britain, 1940*, HarperCollins, 2003

Black, Jeremy, *The Age of Total War, 1860–1945*, Roman & Littlefield, 2010

—, *A Century of Conflict: War, 1914–2014*, Oxford University Press, 2015

—, *Rethinking World War Two: The Conflict and its Legacy*, Bloomsbury, 2015

—, *A Short History of Britain*, Bloomsbury Academic, 2015

—, *Why Wars Happen*, Reaktion Books, 1998

Blackbourn, David, *History of Germany, 1780–1918: The Long Nineteenth Century*, Blackwell, 2003

Blair, Clay, *Hitler's U-Boat War: The Hunters, 1939–1942*, Cassell, 2000

—, *Hitler's U-Boat War: The Hunted, 1942–1945*, Cassell, 2000

Boberach, Heinz (ed.), *Meldungen aus dem Reich: Auswahl aus den geheimen Lageberichten des Sicherheitsdienstes der SS 1939–1944*, Deutscher Taschenbuch Verlag, 1968

Bond, Brian, and Michael Taylor (eds.), *The Battle for France & Flanders Sixty Years On*, Pen & Sword, 2001

Bosworth, R. J. B., *Mussolini's Italy: Life under the Dictatorship*, Penguin Books, 2006

Bowman, Martin W., *USAAF Handbook 1939–1945*, Sutton, 2003

Brendon, Piers, *The Dark Valley: A Panorama of the 1930s*, Pimlico, 2001

Browning, Christopher R., *Ordinary Men: Reserve Police Battalion 101 and the Final Solution in Poland*, Penguin Books, 2001

Bryant, Arthur, and Edward Shanks, *The Battle of Britain/The Few*, Withy Grove Press, 1944

Buchheim, Lothar-Günther, *U-Boat War*, Collins, 1978

Budiansky, Stephen, *Battle of Wits*, Penguin Books, 2000

Bungay, Stephen, *The Most Dangerous Enemy*, Aurum, 2000

Burgwyn, H. James, *Mussolini Warlord: Failed Dreams of Empire 1940–1943*, Enigma Books, 2012

Burleigh, Michael, *Moral Combat: A History of World War II*, Harper Press, 2011

—, *The Third Reich: A New History*, Pan Books, 2001

Butler, Rupert, *Hitler's Death's Head Division*, Pen & Sword, 2004

Caddick-Adams, Peter, *Monty and Rommel: Parallel Lives*, Preface, 2011

—, *Snow and Steel*, Preface, 2014

Caine, Philip D., *American Pilots in the RAF: The WWII Eagle Squadrons*, Brassey's, 1998

Calder, Angus, *The Myth of the Blitz*, Pimlico, 1992

—, *The People's War: Britain 1939–1945*, Pimlico, 1992

Cardozier, V. R., *The Mobilization of the United States in World War II: How the Government, Military and Industry Prepared for War*, McFarland, 1995

Carrard, Philippe, *The French Who Fought for Hitler: Memories from the Outcasts*, Cambridge University Press, 2010

Carver, Field Marshal Sir Michael (ed.), *The War Lords*, Little, Brown and Co., 1976

Chant, Christopher, *Handbook of British Regiments*, Routledge, 1988

Churchill, Winston S., *The Story of the Malakand Field Force*, Lightning Source UK, 2009

Citino, Robert M., *Death of the Wehrmacht: The German Campaigns of 1942*, University Press of Kansas, 2007

—, *The German Way of War: From the Thirty Years' War to the Third Reich*, University Press of Kansas, 2005

—, *The Path to Blitzkrieg: Doctrine and Training in the German Army, 1920–1939*, Stackpole, 1999

—, *Quest for Decisive Victory: From Stalemate to Blitzkrieg in Europe, 1899–1940*, University Press of Kansas, 2002

—, *The Wehrmacht Retreats: Fighting a Lost War, 1943*, University Press of Kansas, 2012

Clark, Christopher, *Iron Kingdom: The Rise and Downfall of Prussia, 1600–1947*, Penguin Books, 2007

Clayton, Tim, and Phil Craig, *Finest Hour*, Hodder & Stoughton, 1999

Cloutier, Patrick, *Regio Esercito: The Italian Royal Army in Mussolini's Wars 1935–1943*, lulu.com, 2013

Cobb, Matthew, *The Resistance: The French Fight against the Nazis*, Pocket Books, 2009

Collier, Basil, *Hidden Weapons: Allied Secret or Undercover Services in World War II*, Pen & Sword, 2006

—, *Leader of the Few*, Jarrolds, 1957

Collier, Richard, *Eagle Day*, Cassell, 1999

—, *The Sands of Dunkirk*, Fontana, 1963

Collingham, Lizzie, *The Taste of War: World War II and the Battle for Food*, The Penguin Press, 2012

Cornwell, Peter D., *The Battle of France Then and Now*, After the Battle, 2007

Corum, James S., *The Luftwaffe: Creating the Operational Air War, 1918–1940*, University Press of Kansas, 1997

Creveld, Martin van, *Fighting Power: German and US Army Performance 1939–1945*, Greenwood Press, 1982

—, *Supplying War: Logistics from Wallenstein to Patton*, Cambridge University Press, 1977

Dallek, Robert, *Franklin D. Roosevelt and American Foreign Policy, 1932–1945*, Oxford University Press, 1995

Davidson, Basil, *Special Operations Europe*, Readers Union, 1980

Davis, Kenneth S., *The American Experience of War, 1939–1945*, Secker & Warburg, 1967

Deakin, F. W., *The Brutal Friendship: Mussolini, Hitler and the Fall of Italian Fascism*, Pelican Books, 1966

Deichmann, Paul, *Spearhead for Blitzkrieg: Luftwaffe Operations in Support of the Army, 1939–1945*, Greenhill, 1996

Deighton, Len, *Blitzkrieg*, Pimlico, 1993

—, *Blood, Tears and Folly: An Objective Look at World War II*, Pimlico, 1995

—, *Fighter: The True Story of the Battle of Britain*, Pimlico, 1996

Dennis, Peter, *Decision by Default: Peacetime Conscription and British Defence, 1919–39*, Routledge and Kegan Paul, 1972

Dietrich, Wolfgang, *Kampfgeschwader 'Edelweiss'*, Ian Allen, 1975

Dildy, Douglas C., *Denmark and Norway 1940*, Osprey, 2007

DiNardo, R. L., *Germany and the Axis Powers: From Coalition to Collapse*, University Press of Kansas, 2005

—, *Germany's Panzer Arm in WWII*, Stackpole, 2006

—, *Mechanized Juggernaut or Military Anachronism?*, Stackpole, 2008

Donnelly, Larry, *The Other Few*, Red Kite, 2004

Doubler, Michael D., *Closing with the Enemy: How GIs Fought the War in Europe, 1944–1945*, University Press of Kansas, 1994

Draper, Alfred, *Operation Fish: The Race to Save Europe's Wealth, 1939–1945*, Cassell, 1979

Duggan, Christopher, *Fascist Voices: An Intimate History of Mussolini's Italy*, Vintage, 2013

Earnshaw, James Douglas, *609 at War*, Vector, 2003

Eberle, Henrik, and Matthias Uhl (eds.), *The Hitler Book*, John Murray, 2006

Edgerton, David, *Britain's War Machine: Weapons, Resources and Experts in the Second World War*, Allen Lane, 2011

—, *England and the Aeroplane*, Macmillan, 1991

—, *Warfare State: Britain, 1920–1970*, Cambridge University Press, 2006

Ellis, John, *The Sharp End: The Fighting Man in World War II*, Pimlico, 1993

—, *The World War II Databook: The Essential Facts and Figures for All the Combatants*, Aurum, 1995

Elphick, Peter, *Liberty: The Ships That Won the War*, Chatham, 2001

Faber, David, *Munich: The 1938 Appeasement Crisis*, Pocket Books, 2008

Faldella, Emilio, *L'Italia e la seconda guerra mondiale*, Cappelli, 1967

Farquharson, J. E., *The Plough and the Swastika: The NSDAP and Agriculture in Germany, 1928–45*, Sage Publications, 1976

Fennell, Jonathan, *Combat and Morale in the North African Campaign*, Cambridge University Press, 2011

Fleming, Peter, *Operation Sea Lion*, Pan Books, 1957

Fletcher, David, *The Great Tank Scandal: British Armour in the Second World War*, Part I, HMSO, 1989

Flower, Desmond, and James Reeves (eds.), *The War 1939–1945: A Documentary History*, Da Capo, 1997

Foot, M. R. D., *Resistance: European Resistance to Nazism 1940–45*, Eyre Methuen, 1976

Forty, George, *The Battle of Crete*, Ian Allen, 2001

—, *British Army Handbook, 1939–1945*, Sutton, 1998

—, *US Army Handbook, 1939–1945*, Sutton, 1995

Fowler, Will, *Poland and Scandinavia, 1939–1940*, Ian Allen, 2001

Fraser, David, *And We Shall Shock Them: The British Army in the Second World War*, Cassell, 1999

Frieser, Karl-Heinz, *The Blitzkrieg Legend*, Naval Institute Press, 2005

Fullilove, Michael, *Rendezvous with Destiny: How Franklin D. Roosevelt and Five Extraordinary Men Took America into the War and into the World*, The Penguin Press, 2013

Gardiner, Juliet, *The Thirties: An Intimate History*, Harper Press, 2011

—, *Wartime: Britain 1939–1945*, Review, 2005

Gardner, W. J. R. (ed.), *The Evacuation from Dunkirk*, Frank Cass, 2000

Gelb, Norman, *Scramble: A Narrative History of the Battle of Britain*, Michael Joseph, 1986

Gildea, Robert, *Marianne in Chains: In Search of the German Occupation of France 1940–45*, Pan Books, 2003

Gilmour, David, *The Pursuit of Italy: A History of a Land, Its Regions and Their Peoples*, Penguin Books, 2012

Ginn, Peter, Ruth Goodman and Alex Langlands, *Wartime Farm*, Mitchell Beazley, 2012

Goerlitz, Walter, *History of the German General Staff*, Praeger, 1967

Goldhagen, Daniel Jonah, *Hitler's Willing Executioners*, Abacus, 1997

Graves, Charles, *The Home Guard of Great Britain*, Hutchinson, 1943

Grigg, P. J., *Prejudice and Judgment*, Alden Press, 1948

Grunberger, Richard, *A Social History of the Third Reich*, Phoenix, 2005

Guderian, Heinz (Foreword), *Blitzkrieg in Their Own Words: First-Hand Accounts from German Soldiers, 1939–1940*, Zenith Press, 2005

Guedalla, Philip, *Middle East 1940–1942: A Study in Air Power*, Hodder & Stoughton, 1944

Hadjipateras, Costas N., and Maria S. Fafalios, *Crete 1941 Eyewitnessed*, Efstathiadis Group, 1988

Hale, Oron J., *The Captive Press in the Third Reich*, Princeton University Press, 1964

Hall, David Ian, *The Strategy for Victory: The Development of British Tactical Air Power, 1919–1943*, Praeger Security International, 2008

Handel, Michael I. (ed.), *Intelligence and Military Operations*, Frank Cass, 1990

Hansell, Haywood S., Jr, *The Air Plan That Defeated Hitler*, Arno Press, 1980

Harries, Meirion and Susie, *Soldiers of the Sun: The Rise and Fall of the Imperial Japanese Army*, Random House, 1991

Harrison, Mark (ed.), *The Economics of World War II*, Cambridge University Press, 2000

Harrison Place, Timothy, *Military Training in the British Army, 1940–1944: From Dunkirk to D-Day*, Frank Cass, 2000

Hay, Ian, *The Army at War: The Battle of Flanders*, HMSO, 1941

Herman, Arthur, *Freedom's Forge: How American Business Produced Victory in World War II*, Random House, 2012

Hewitt, Nick, *Coastal Convoys, 1939–1945: The Indestructible Highway*, Pen & Sword, 2008

Holland, James, *The Battle of Britain*, Bantam Books, 2010

—, *Fortress Malta*, Orion, 2003

—, *Heroes*, HarperCollins, 2007

—, *Together We Stand – North Africa 1942–1943: Turning the Tide in the West*, Harper Collins, 2005

Holmes, Richard, *Soldiers: Army Lives and Loyalties from Redcoats to Dusty Warriors*, Harper Press, 2011

—, *The World at War*, Ebury Press, 2011

Horne, Alistair, *To Lose a Battle: France 1940*, Papermac, 1990

House, Jonathan M., *Combined Arms Warfare in the Twentieth Century*, University Press of Kansas, 2001

Howard, Michael, *The Mediterranean Strategy in the Second World War*, Greenhill Books, 1993

Howarth, Stephen, and Derek Law (eds.), *The Battle of the Atlantic 1939–1945: The 50th Anniversary International Naval Conference*, Greenhill, 1994

Hoyt, Edwin P., *The GI's War: American Soldiers in Europe During World War II*, Cooper Square Press, 2000

Hylton, Stuart, *Their Darkest Hour: The Hidden History of the Home Front, 1939–1945*, Sutton, 2003

Irons, Roy, *The Relentless Offensive: War and Bomber Command, 1939–1945*, Pen & Sword, 2009

Irving, David (ed.), *Breach of Security: The German Secret Intelligence File on Events Leading to the Second World War*, William Kimber, 1968

Jackson, Ashley, *The British Empire and the Second World War*, Hambledon Continuum, 2006

Jackson, W. G. F., *The North African Campaign, 1940–43*, Batsford, 1975

James, T. C. G., *The Battle of Britain*, Frank Cass, 2000

—, *The Growth of Fighter Command, 1936–1940*, Frank Cass, 2002

Jörgensen, Christer, *Rommel's Panzers*, Reference Group Brown, 2003

Joseph, Frank, *Mussolini's War*, Helion, 2010

Kallis, Aristotle A., *Nazi Propaganda and the Second World War*, Palgrave Macmillan, 2008

Kaplan, Philip, and Jack Currie, *Wolfpack: U-Boats at War 1939–1945*, Aurum, 1997

Keegan, John (ed.), *Churchill's Generals*, Abacus, 1991

Kemp, Anthony, *The SAS at War, 1941–1945*, Penguin Books, 2000

Kemp, Lt-Commander P. K., *Victory at Sea*, White Lion Publishers, 1957

Kersaudy, François, *Norway 1940*, Collins, 1990

Kershaw, Ian, *Fateful Choices: Ten Decisions that Changed the World, 1940–1941*, Allen Lane, 2007

—, *Hitler: 1936–1945, Nemesis*, Penguin Books, 2001

Kite, Ben, *Stout Hearts: The British and Canadians in Normandy 1944*, Helion, 2014

Klein, Maury, *A Call to Arms: Mobilizing America for World War II*, Bloomsbury, 2013

Knox, MacGregor, *Common Destiny: Dictatorship, Foreign Policy, and War in Fascist Italy and Nazi Germany*, Cambridge University Press, 2000

—, *Hitler's Italian Allies: Royal Armed Forces, Fascist Regime, and the War of 1940–1943*, Cambridge University Press, 2000

—, *Mussolini Unleashed, 1939–1941: Politics and Strategy in Fascist Italy's Last War*, Cambridge University Press, 1982

Kohn, Richard H., and Joseph P. Harahan, *Air Superiority in World War II and Korea*, Office of Air Force History, United States Air Force, 1983

Koht, Halvdan, *Norway Neutral and Invaded*, Hutchinson, 1941

Lampe, David, *The Last Ditch: Britain's Secret Resistance and the Nazi Invasion Plan*, Greenhill Books, 2007

Langer, William L., and S. Everett Gleason, *The Undeclared War 1940–1941*, Royal Institute of International Affairs, 1953

Langhorne, Richard (ed.), *Diplomacy and Intelligence during the Second World War: Essays in Honour of F. H. Hinsley*, Cambridge University Press, 1985

Lavery, Brian, *Hostilities Only: Training the Wartime Royal Navy*, Conway, 2004

—, *In Which They Served: The Royal Navy Officer Experience in the Second World War*, Conway, 2009

Lawrence, W. J., *No. 5 Bomber Group RAF*, Faber & Faber, 1951

Le Tissier, Tony, *The Third Reich Then and Now*, After the Battle, 2005

Lewin, Ronald, *The Life and Death of the Afrika Korps*, Pen & Sword, 2003

—, *Rommel as Military Commander*, Pen & Sword, 2004

—, *Ultra Goes to War: The Secret Story*, Penguin, 2001

Liddell Hart, B. H., *The Other Side of the Hill*, Cassell, 1951

Longmate, Norman, *The Real Dad's Army: The Story of the Home Guard*, Arrow, 1974

Lucas, James, *German Army Handbook, 1939–1945*, Sutton, 1998

Lukacs, John, *The Duel: Hitler vs. Churchill 10 May–31 July 1940*, Phoenix, 2000

Lund, Paul, and Harry Ludlam, *Trawlers Go to War*, New English Library, 1973

Lunde, Henrik O., *Hitler's Pre-Emptive War: The Battle for Norway, 1940*, Casemate, 2010

MacDonald, Callum, *The Lost Battle: Crete 1941*, Papermac, 1993

Mackenzie, William, *The Secret History of SOE: Special Operations Executive 1940–1945*, St Ermin's Press, 2000

Macksey, Major K. J., *Afrika Korps: Rommel's Desert Soldiers*, Ballantine, 1968

Macrae, Stuart, *Winston Churchill's Toyshop: The Inside Story of Military Intelligence (Research)*, Amberley, 2010

Mallman Showell, Jak P., *Hitler's Navy*, Seaforth Publishing, 2009

—, *Hitler's U-Boat Bases*, Sutton, 2007

Mason, Philip, *A Matter of Honour: An Account of the Indian Army, Its Officers & Men*, Book Club edition, 1974

Mass Observation, C. Madge and T. H. Harrison, *War Begins at Home*, Chatto & Windus, 1940

Mazower, Mark, *Hitler's Empire: Nazi Rule in Occupied Europe*, Allen Lane, 2008

McGaw Smyth, Howard, *Secrets of the Fascist Era*, Southern Illinois University Press, 1975

McGuirk, Dal, *Rommel's Army in Africa*, Stanley Paul, 1987

McKay, Sinclair, *The Secret Life of Bletchley Park*, Aurum, 2011

—, *The Secret Listeners*, Aurum, 2013

McKee, Alexander, *The Coal-Scuttle Brigade*, New English Library, 1957

McKinstry, Leo, *Hurricane: Victor of the Battle of Britain*, John Murray, 2010

—, *Operation Sealion: How Britain Crushed the German War Machine's Dreams of Invasion in 1940*, John Murray, 2014

—, *Spitfire: Portrait of a Legend*, John Murray, 2008

McLaine, Ian, *Ministry of Morale*, George Allen & Unwin, 1979

McNab, Chris (ed.), *German Paratroopers*, MBI, 2000

Meilinger, Colonel Phillip S., *The Paths of Heaven: The Evolution of Airpower Theory*, Air University Press, 1997

Messenger, Charles, *The Second World War in the West*, Cassell, 2001

Michel, Henri, *The Shadow War: Resistance in Europe 1939–45*, André Deutsch, 1972

Middlebrook, Martin, and Chris Everitt, *The Bomber Command War Diaries*, Penguin Books, 1990

Mierzejewski, Alfred C., *The Collapse of the German War Economy, 1944–1945: Allied Air Power and the German National Railway*, University of North Carolina Press, 1988

Milner, Marc, *The Battle of the Atlantic*, Tempus, 2005

Milward, Alan S., *War, Economy and Society, 1939–1945*, University of California Press, 1979

Mitcham, Samuel W., *Hitler's Legions: German Army Order of Battle, World War II*, Leo Cooper, 1985

Moorehead, Alan, *African Trilogy: Desert War, North Africa Campaign 1940–1943*, Cassell, 2000

Moorhouse, Roger, *The Devil's Alliance: Hitler's Pact with Stalin, 1939–1941*, The Bodley Head, 2014

Mortimer, Gavin, *The SAS in World War II: An Illustrated History*, Osprey, 2011

—, *Stirling's Men: The Inside History of the SAS in World War II*, Cassell, 2005

Morton, H. V., *Atlantic Meeting*, Methuen & Co., 1943

Murray, Williamson, *Luftwaffe: Strategy for Defeat 1933–45*, Grafton, 1988

Murray, Williamson, and Allan R. Millett, *A War to be Won: Fighting the Second World War*, Belknap Harvard, 2000

—, *Military Innovation in the Interwar Period*, Cambridge University Press, 1996

Neitzel, Sönke, and Harald Welzer, *Soldaten: On Fighting, Killing and Dying*, Simon & Schuster, 2012

Nielsen, Generalleutnant Andreas, USAF Historical Studies No. 173: *The German Air Force General Staff*, Arno Press, 1968

Noakes, Jeremy (ed.), *Nazism 1919–1945*, Volume 4: *The German Home Front in World War II*, University of Exeter Press, 1998

Noakes, J., and G. Pridham (eds.), *Nazism 1919–1945*, Volume 2: *State, Economy and Society 1933–1939*, University of Exeter Press, 1984

—, *Nazism 1919–1945*, Volume 3: *Foreign Policy, War and Racial Extermination*, University of Exeter Press, 1988

Oberkommando der Wehrmacht, *Fahrten und Flüge gegen England*, Zeitgeschichte-Verlag, Berlin, 1941

Overy, Richard, *The Bombing War: Europe 1939–1945*, Allen Lane, 2013

—, *The Road to War*, Vintage, 2009

— (ed.), *The New York Times Complete World War II 1939–1945*, Black Dog & Levanthal, 2013

Owen, James, *Commando: Winning World War II Behind Enemy Lines*, Abacus, 2012

Owen, Roderic, *The Desert Air Force*, Arrow, 1958

Owings, Alison, *Frauen: German Women Recall the Third Reich*, Penguin Books, 1995

Pallud, Jean-Paul, *Blitzkrieg in the West Then and Now*, After the Battle, 1991

— *The Desert War Then and Now*, After the Battle, 2012

Panagiotakis, George J., *The Battle of Crete*, Heraklion, 2000

Paxton, Robert O., *French Peasant Fascism*, Oxford University Press, 1997

Peitz, Bernd, *Afrikakorps: Rommel's Tropical Army in Original Color*, Schiffer, 2005

Petrow, Richard, *The Bitter Years*, Book Club edition, 1974

Porten, Edward P. von der, *The Germany Navy in World War II*, Arthur Baker, 1970

Price, Alfred, *The Hardest Day*, Book Club Associates, 1979

—, *Instruments of Darkness: The History of Electronic Warfare*, Macdonald and Jane's, 1978

Prysor, Glyn, *Citizen Sailors: The Royal Navy in the Second World War*, Viking, 2011

Ramsey, Winston G. (ed.), *The Battle of Britain: Then and Now Mk V*, After the Battle, 1980

—, *The Blitz Then and Now*, Volume 2, After the Battle, 1988

Reynolds, David, *The Creation of the Anglo-American Alliance, 1937–1941*, University of North Carolina Press, 1982

Richards, Denis, *RAF Bomber Command in the Second World War: The Hardest Victory*, Penguin Books, 2001

Ritchie, Sebastian, *Arnhem: Myth and Reality*, Robert Hale, 2011

—, *Industry and Air Power: The Expansion of British Aircraft Production, 1935–1941*, Routledge, 1997

Roberts, Andrew, *Eminent Churchillians*, Phoenix, 1995

—, *The Storm of War*, Harper Perennial, 2011

Rosenbaum, Ron, *Explaining Hitler: The Search for the Origins of His Evil*, Papermac, 1998

Roskill, Stephen, *The Navy at War, 1939–1945*, Wordsworth Editions, 1998

Saunders, Andy, *No 43 'Fighting Cocks' Squadron*, Osprey, 2003

Schell, Adolf von, *Battle Leadership*, Major Edwin F. Harding, 1933

Schramm, Percy E., *Kriegstagebuch des Oberkommandos der Wehrmacht 1939–1941*, Teilbänd I, II, Bernard & Graefe Verlag, 1982

Sebag-Montefiore, Hugh, *Dunkirk: Fight to the Last Man*, Penguin Books, 2007

Seydewitz, Max, *Civil Life in Wartime Germany: The Story of the Home Front*, The Viking Press, 1945

Seymour, Miranda, *Noble Endeavours: The Life of Two Countries, England and Germany, in Many Stories*, Simon & Schuster, 2014

Shores, Christopher, and Brian Cull, with Nicola Malizia, *Malta: The Hurricane Years, 1940–41*, Grub Street, 1987

—, *Malta: The Spitfire Year, 1942*, Grub Street, 1991

Shores, Christopher, and Hans Ring, *Fighters over the Desert*, Neville Spearman, 1969

Short, Brian, Charles Watkins and John Martin, *The Front Line of Freedom: British Farming in the Second World War*, British Agricultural History Society, 2006

Smart, Nicholas, *Biographical Dictionary of British Generals of the Second World War*, Pen & Sword, 2005

Spick, Mike, *Aces of the Reich: The Making of a Luftwaffe Fighter-Pilot*, Greenhill, 2006

—, *Allied Fighter Aces of World War II*, Greenhill, 1997

—, *Luftwaffe Fighter Aces*, Greenhill, 1996

Spitzy, Reinhard, *How We Squandered the Reich*, Michael Russell, 1997

Spooner, Tony, *Supreme Gallantry: Malta's Role in the Allied Victory 1939–1945*, John Murray, 1996

Stapledon, Sir George, *The Way of the Land*, Faber, 1943

Stephenson, Michael, *The Last Full Measure: How Soldiers Die in Battle*, Crown, 2012

Stevenson, David, *1914–1918: The History of the First World War*, Penguin Books, 2005

Stewart, Graham, *Burying Caesar: Churchill, Chamberlain and the Battle for the Tory Party*, Phoenix, 2000

Stewart, I. McD. G., *The Struggle for Crete: A Story of Lost Opportunity*, Oxford University Press, 1966

Suchenwirth, Richard, *Command and Leadership in the German Air Force*, USAF Historical Studies No. 174, Arno Press, 1969

—, *The Development of the German Air Force, 1919–1939*, University Press of the Pacific, 2005

—, *Historical Turning Points in the German Air Force War Effort*, University Press of the Pacific, 2004

Sweet, John Joseph Timothy, *Iron Arm: The Mechanization of Mussolini's Army, 1920–40*, Stackpole, 2007

Terraine, John, *The Right of the Line*, Hodder & Stoughton, 1985

Thacker, Toby, *Joseph Goebbels: Life and Death*, Palgrave Macmillan, 2008

Tooze, Adam, *The Wages of Destruction: The Making and Breaking of the Nazi Economy*, Penguin Books, 2007

Trevor-Roper, H. R. (ed.), *Hitler's War Directives 1939–1945*, Pan Books, 1966

Tuker, Sir Francis, *Approach to Battle*, Cassell, 1963

Urban, Mark, *The Tank War: The Men, the Machines, the Long Road to Victory 1939–45*, Little, Brown and Co., 2013

Vansittart, Lord, *Roots of the Trouble*, Hutchinson, 1940

Various, *World War II: Day by Day*, Dorling Kindersley, 2004

Vasco, John, *Messerschmitt Bf110 Bombsights over England*, Schiffer, 2002

Vella, Philip, *Malta: Blitzed But Not Beaten*, Progress Press Co., 1997

Vinen, Richard, *The Unfree French: Life under the Occupation*, Penguin Books, 2007

Ward, Sadie, *War in the Countryside, 1939–45*, Cameron Books, 1988

Warwicker, John, *Churchill's Underground Army*, Frontline Books, 2008

Weal, John, *Jagdgeschwader 2 'Richthofen'*, Osprey, 2000

—, *Jagdgeschwader 27 'Afrika'*, Osprey, 2003

—, *Jagdgeschwader 52: The Experten*, Osprey, 2004

—, *Jagdgeschwader 53 'Pik-As'*, Osprey, 2007

Weale, Adrian, *The SS: A New History*, Abacus, 2012

Wells, Mark K., *Courage and Air Warfare: The Allied Aircrew Experience in the Second World War*, Frank Cass, 1997

Werth, Alexander, *France 1940–1955*, Robert Hale, 1956

Wheal, Elizabeth-Anne, and Stephen Pope, *The Macmillan Dictionary of the Second World War*, Macmillan, 1989

Wheeler-Bennett, Sir John (ed.), *Action This Day: Working with Churchill*, Macmillan, 1968

White, Antonia, *BBC at War*, BBC, 1946

Whiting, Charles, *Hunters from the Sky: The German Parachute Corps, 1940–1945*, Cooper Square Press, 2001

Williams, Michael, *Steaming to Victory: How Britain's Railways Won the War*, Preface, 2013

Williamson, Gordon, *Waffen-SS Handbook, 1933–1945*, Sutton, 2003

Willmott, H. P., *The Great Crusade*, Pimlico, 1992

Winder, Simon, *Germania*, Picador, 2010

Wingate, John, *The Fighting Tenth*, Leo Cooper, 1991

Winterbotham, F. W., *The Ultra Secret*, Book Club edition, 1974

Wood, Derek, and Derek Dempster, *The Narrow Margin: The Battle of Britain and the Rise of Air Power, 1930–1949*, Pen & Sword, 2003

Woodman, Richard, *Malta Convoys*, John Murray, 2000

—, *The Real Cruel Sea: The Merchant Navy in the Battle of the Atlantic, 1939–1943*, John Murray, 2005

Wynn, Kenneth G., *Men of the Battle of Britain*, Gliddon Books, 1989

Wynter, Brigadier H. W., *Special Forces in the Desert War, 1940–1943*, Public Record Office War Histories, 2001

Ziegler, Frank H., *The Story of 609 Squadron: Under the White Rose*, Crécy, 1993

Ziegler, Philip, *London at War, 1939–1945*, Pimlico, 2002

Zweiniger-Bargielowska, Ina, *Austerity in Britain: Rationing, Controls, and Consumption, 1939–1955*, Oxford University Press, 2000

PAMPHLETS, JOURNALS, PERIODICALS AND MAGAZINES

Anon., 'German Army Transport', *Automobile Engineer*, October 1945

Denkhaus, Raymond A., 'Convoy PQ 17', *World War II Magazine*, February 1997

Felton, Monica, *Civilian Supplies in Wartime Britain*, Ministry of Information, 1945

Jarvis, Peter, *The Invasion of 1940*, Markham Memorial Lecture, Bletchley Park Reports, No. 18, March 2003

Peaty, John, 'Myth, Reality and Carlo D'Este', *War Studies Journal*, Vol. 1, no. 2, Spring 1996

Pether, John, *Funkers and Sparkers: Origins and Formation of the Y Service*, Bletchley Park Reports, No. 17, September 2000

Schell, Adolf von, 'Grundlagen der Motorisierung und ihre Entwicklung im Zweiten Weltkrieg', *Wehrwissenschaftliche Rundschau*, 13, 1963

Topp, Erich, 'In Memoriam Engelbert Endrass: Castor Mourns Pollux', in Theodore P. Savas (ed.), *Silent Hunters: German U-Boat Commanders of World War II*, Savas Publishing, 2013

Widder, Werner, '*Auftragstaktik* and *Innere Führung*: Trademarks of German Leadership', *Military Review*, September–October 2002

Zabecki, David, *Auftragstaktik*

—, *The Greatest General No-One Ever Heard Of*

FILM

The Battle of Britain, Harry Saltzman, 1969
Le Chagrin et le Pitié, Marcel Ophüls, 1969
Das Boot, Wolfgang Petersen, 1981
Die Deutsche Wochenschau, 1940–1941
Dunkirk, BBC, 2004
Finest Hour, BBC, 1999
Hitler's Search for the Holy Grail, Channel 4, 1999
London's War: The Beginning, London on Film, 2010
London's War: The Blitz, London on Film, 2010
Triumph of the Will, Leni Riefenstahl, 1935
The World at War, Jeremy Isaacs, 1973

ONLINE

Pearce, Richard 'Dick', *Recollections*, www.canadasnavalmemorial.ca
Interview with World War II Luftwaffe Eagle Johannes Steinhoff, www.historynet.com
White, Ian, 'A Short History of Air Intercept Radar and the British Night-Fighter, Part One, 1936–1945', www.600squadronassociation.com

Acknowledgements

Projects of this scale and ambition can never be achieved without a considerable amount of help, and I owe huge thanks to a number of people. First of all, I am very grateful to all the veterans who, over the past dozen years or so, have taken the trouble to talk to me at such length. I am also very grateful to all the staffs of the various museums and archives, although especial thanks go to Richard Hughes at the Imperial War Museum in London, to Doug McCabe at the University of Ohio, all the staff at the Deutsches Tagebucharchiv in Emmendingen and the Bundesarchiv-Militärarchiv in Freiburg, the staff at the United States Army Heritage Center at Carlisle Barracks, Pennsylvania, and Cathy Pugh of the Second World War Experience Centre in Yorkshire.

I have been fortunate enough to be able to pick the brains of a number of friends and colleagues, including Professor John Buckley and Professor David Zabecki. However, there are five people to whom I am particularly grateful and who have all become great friends, and who have freely given plenty of wise counsel and sage advice whenever they have been asked. The first is my good friend Sebastian Cox, Head of the Air Historical Branch at RAF Northolt. The second is another good friend Stephen Prince, Head of the Naval Historical Branch at Portsmouth. Professor Jeremy Black has also been a much-valued friend and academic mentor. Professor Rick Hillum is my technical guru and the best advisor I could hope for on any scientific matters. My greatest thanks, however, go to Dr Peter Caddick-Adams, whose perspectives, vast knowledge and friendship have been invaluable. Thank you.

A number of other people have helped with translations and research. In France, Elizabeth Gausseron and Alienor Youchtchenko; in Italy, James

Owen. My thanks, also, to David Walsh, a great friend who accompanied me to the various Italian archives. In Germany, Michelle Miles and Ingo Maerker have carried out an impressive amount of work and have become good friends as well as colleagues. Frances Bryon also helped with some key research, for which I am very grateful. Huge thanks are also due to Lalla Hitchings for transcribing so many of my interviews, but also to Tom and Mark Hitchings for their help with this too. My thanks to you all.

A number of other friends and colleagues have helped along the way: Oliver Barnham, David Christopherson, Peter Day, Rebecca Dobbs, Freya Eden-Ellis, Tobin Jones, Rob Owen, James Petrie, Richard Pocock, James Shopland, Guy Walters, Rowland White and Aaron Young. All have contributed in one way or another. And my thanks, also, to Colonel Simon Browne and Tim Lupprian for reading and checking the proofs.

I would also like to thank all those at Bantam Press and Grove Atlantic. To Larry Finlay, Mads Toy, Steve Mulcahey, Darcy Nicholson, Phil Lord, Vivien Thompson, Mark Handsley and all at Bantam – thank you so much. Particular thanks, however, go to Jamison Stoltz in New York, who has been a superb editor, and to Bill Scott-Kerr in London, who could not have been a better friend and supporter. To you both, huge thanks.

Thank you, also, to everyone at Conville and Walsh, but especially Patrick Walsh – a great agent and even better friend.

Finally, I would like to thank my family. Writing this book has been rather all-consuming at times, and they have had to put up with much. I am, I promise, eternally grateful. Rachel, Ned and Daisy – thank you.

Picture Acknowledgements

All photographs have been kindly supplied by the author except those listed below. Every effort has been made to trace copyright holders; those overlooked are invited to get in touch with the publishers.

Part Opener Pages:

Pages 6 and 7
War Begins: Imperial War Museum/HU 36171.

Pages 176 and 177
Germany Triumphant: Bundesarchiv, Bild 101III-Pleisser-005-20.

Pages 306 and 307
War in the Air and on the Sea: Imperial War Museum/CH 1512.

Pages 442 and 443
The Widening War: Imperial War Museum/A 5669.

Illustration Sections:

Section 1

Page 1
Hitler: Hugo Jaeger/Getty Images.

Pages 2 and 3
Captain Hedley Verity: Imperial War Museum/H 11730; The Royal Navy: Imperial War Museum/A 111.

Page 4
Helmut Lent: Bundesarchiv, Bild 101I-358-1908-09; Gudbrandsdal: Bundesarchiv, Bild 146-1984-105-13A; Me110: BundesArchiv, Bild 101I-399-0006-19; Cigarettes at Narvik: Imperial War Museum/HU 104673.

Pages 6 and 7
General Maurice Gamelin: Imperial War Museum/O 158; Belgian refugees: Imperial War Museum/F 4505; The BEF: Imperial War Museum/F 4689; Destroyed Ju52: GNU Free Documentation.

Page 8
The evacuation of Dunkirk: Imperial War Museum/ART LD 2277; French troops: Imperial War Museum/H 1688.

Section 2

Page 1
Mightier Yet: Onslows/Mary Evans Library; Churchill: Imperial War Museum/H 41846; Atlantic Convoy: Imperial War Museum, C 2647.

Pages 2 and 3
Teddy Suhren: Chatham Publishing; George Darley: Daniel Kirmatzis; Donald Macintyre: Imperial War Museum/A 16868; U-48: Imperial War Museum/HU 39625; Franklin D. Roosevelt: Library of Congress; Harry Hopkins: Library of Congress.

Pages 4 and 5
Adolf von Schell: Bundesarchiv, Bild 146-2006-0096; A. G. Street: Miranda Corben; Sheep: Museum of English Rural Life, University of Reading; Soldiers and a pig: Bundesarchiv, Bild 183-L24359; Radar Station: Imperial War Museum/ART LD 5735; 609 Squadron: Jim Earnshaw.

Pages 6 and 7
Mussolini: Culture Club/Getty Images; Italian Uniforms: US TME30-240; *Battle of Britain*, painting by Paul Nash: Imperial War Museum/ART LD 1550.

Page 8
Rolls-Royce engine construction: Imperial War Museum/D 12125; Ju88: Imperial War Museum/HU 73745.

Section 3

Page 1
Andrew Browne Cunningham: Imperial War Museum/A 9760; General Richard O'Connor: Imperial War Museum/E 1549; Italian POWs: Imperial War Museum/E 1579.

Pages 2 and 3
Indian troops: Imperial War Museum/E 2181; Hermann Balck: Bundesarchiv, Bild 146-1994-009-17; The Operations Room at Derby House: Imperial War Museum/A 4556; British Destroyer: Imperial War Museum/A 5667; Otto Kretschmer: Bundesarchiv, Bild 183-L22207; Erich Topp: Bundesarchiv, Bild 101ll-MW-3705-35.

Pages 4 and 5
The Bowles twins: Tim Bowles; Kit Inspection: Tim Bowles; Hajo Herrmann: Bundesarchiv, Bild 146-2005-0025; British forces on the retreat: Imperial War Museum/ART LD 3354; General John Kennedy: National Portrait Gallery/NPG x85677; Sherwood Rangers: Stanley Christopherson.

Pages 6 and 7
Liberty ships under construction, two images: Library of Congress; Oliver Lyttelton visits a British factory: Imperial War Museum/P 866; ID card of Andrée Griotteray: Francelle Bradford White; Freddie Knoller and family: Freddie Knoller; The Blitz: Imperial War Museum/HU 1129.

Page 8
General Bernard Freyberg VC: Imperial War Museum/E 3020E; German invasion of Crete: Imperial War Museum/A 4154; Evacuation of Crete: Imperial War museum/A 4200.

Appendices:

Pages 598 and 599
HMS *Ark Royal*: Ullstein Bild/Getty Images.

Page 599
Tanks and infantry in the Ardennes: Ullstein Bild/Getty Images.

Pages 600 and 601
Hampden bombers assembly workshop: Keystone-France/Getty Images.

Pages 602 and 603
Britain, arms factories: Popperfoto/Getty Images.

Page 604
Wartime cargo: Hulton Archive/Stringer/Getty Images.

Index

ABOUT THE AUTHOR

James Holland is a historian, writer and broadcaster. The author of the bestselling *Fortress Malta*, *Battle of Britain* and *Dam Busters*, he has also written nine works of historical fiction, five of which feature the heroic Jack Tanner, a soldier of the Second World War. He regularly appears on television and radio, and has written and presented a number of documentaries, most recently *Cold War, Hot Jets* and *Normandy 44* for the BBC. Co-founder and Programme Director of the Chalke Valley History Festival, he is also a Fellow of the Royal Historical Society.